CLEAN AIR AROUND THE WORLD

National and International Approaches to Air Pollution Control

Editor
Loveday Murley

British Library Cataloguing in Publication Data

Clean air around the world: national and international
approaches to air pollution control. – 2nd ed
I. Murley, Loveday II. International Union of Air
Pollution Prevention Associations
341.7623

ISBN 1-871688-01-9

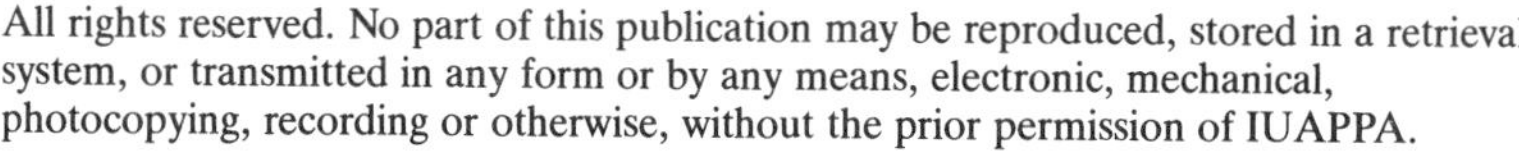

Text printed on recycled paper

Published in England by the
International Union of Air Pollution Prevention Associations
136 North Street, Brighton BN1 1RG

ABOUT IUAPPA

The International Union of Air Pollution Prevention Associations (IUAPPA) is a union of national professional and voluntary, non-profit making, non-political associations concerned with the maintenance of clean air. Founded in 1964 by seven national associations, IUAPPA now has 29 Members and Observers representing 31 countries (see appendix). It is funded by annual subscriptions from Members. Other, non-contributing, affiliates have the status of Observers.

IUAPPA's aim is to promote public education worldwide, in all matters relating to the value and importance of clean air and methods and consequences of air pollution control. This is achieved by convening World Congresses on air quality every three years; exchanging information about air pollution legislation and control techniques; encouraging use of uniform monitoring and measuring methods; liaising with other national and international scientific, technical and control organisations.

The International Board of IUAPPA is headed by the President, two Vice Presidents and Immediate Past President, and with one representative of each other member association. It meets as necessary, but at least once every three years, deciding IUAPPA affairs by resolution. An Executive Committee meets at least once a year to conduct the general affairs of IUAPPA.

The permanent secretariat of IUAPPA is at 136 North Street, Brighton BN1 1RG, United Kingdom. Telephone: (+44 273) 26313. Fax: (+44 273) 735802.

FOREWORD

When the International Union of Air Pollution Prevention Associations (IUAPPA) was founded in 1964, concern for the environment and of the need for effective legislation to control and prevent air pollution as a means of protecting it were not particularly high on anybody's agenda. Worsening air quality and other signs of environmental deprivation were seen as the price to be paid for industrial and economic development and a better standard of living. Now, however, although there is still some disagreement on the exact extent to which human activities are having a detrimental effect on the environment, it is agreed that we cannot afford to wait for more evidence. To delay taking action now may mean putting stress on the environment to the extent that it will be irreversibly damaged.

The action that needs to be taken is of course currently under discussion both nationally and internationally. But a key component of effective action is information. This is where I believe this book by members of IUAPPA can play a valuable role: one of the main objectives of IUAPPA is to promote public education worldwide in all matters relating to the importance of clean air and to the methods and consequences of air pollution control. In developing appropriate control strategies or legislation, or improving those that are already in place, it is helpful to draw on the experiences and practices of others.

The 27 countries covered in this book, representing countries at all stages of development, provide an excellent picture of the various approaches to air pollution control worldwide. The chapters on the international law of air pollution and on the policy of the European Communities demonstrate the role of the UN and EC in formulating policies to control air pollution — a role which can only become more vital as the world looks for international solutions to today's environmental problems.

I should therefore like to extend IUAPPA's grateful thanks to the authors of the various chapters, and to IUAPPA's secretariat — the UK National Society for Clean Air and Environmental Protection — in particular, NSCA's editor Loveday Murley. The support of all those involved in this edition of *Clean Air Around the World* has resulted in a book which will not only be a source of advice to those countries seeking to implement or improve air pollution control, but also a valuable reference book on the law and practice of clean air around the world.

Steve Hart
President
Canada, 9 July 1991

CONTENTS

GERMANY *(received February 1991)*

ISRAEL *(received October 1990)*

ITALY *(received September 1990)*

THE NETHERLANDS *(received October 1990)*

NEW ZEALAND *(received March 1991)*

NORWAY *(received October 1990)*

PAKISTAN *(received September 1990)*

PERU *(received March 1991)*

INTRODUCTION

There can be few people who now doubt that pollution of the environment is a fundamental problem for which urgent solutions need to be found. All too frequently television and newspaper reports show the environmental devastation now being experienced in entire regions of some countries; scientific studies too are gathering convincing evidence of environmental change, although the effects of such change are unclear. Even in the more advanced countries major issues of local environmental quality and transboundary pollution remain. The problems have largely been identified, but the development of an effective response has barely begun.

What is clear is that no response will be effective unless it has the support of governments worldwide — both from the developed economies and those still striving for economic development. This is where potential problems arise. It is hard to perceive how less fortunate countries can simultaneously improve their environmental quality and raise living standards to anything approaching those of the developed nations without massive consumption of resources and energy. Whilst the industrialized nations continue to be profligate in their use of the planet's riches, and fail to protect the earth's land, waters and atmosphere, the developing world can be forgiven for its suspicions about the noble concept of "sustainable development". Different countries have different aspirations and needs. The efforts of the United Nations Environment Programme and other international agencies, in providing a forum in which governments worldwide can come together, to develop an understanding of each other's priorities and to work towards effective agreements for tackling environmental problems must be supported.

However, the need for effective legislation at national level is also of crucial importance in tackling air pollution worldwide. Many countries already have legislation in place — even if some of it was enacted in the early part of this century. Many countries — not necessarily all in the developing or newly industrializing countries of the world — are only now realizing the need for, say, better controls on industrial processes or on vehicle emissions.

This second edition of IUAPPA's book, *Clean Air Around the World*, has been completely revised and restructured to enable easier comparison between countries and indeed more countries are covered — 27 against 14 in the first edition. It is worth pointing out that while the choice of countries was limited to those in which IUAPPA has a member, they do however represent a wide range of economic and industrial development and indeed relative wealth. As will be seen in the individual chapters, such diversity results in widely differing approaches to, and priorities for, legislation. Most contributors, however, also draw attention to the fact that many of today's pollution problems cannot be settled by countries acting on their own. The chapters which have been contributed on behalf of the UN and European Community are therefore of particular relevance in outlining their approaches to the control of air pollution and their effect on individual nations.

A final note on the preparation of this second edition of *Clean Air Around the World:* all the chapters were received between July 1990 and March 1991; all chapters were in English except those from Argentina, Brazil and Peru which have been translated into English. Following editing, all chapters were returned to their authors for verification: any queries on chapter content should be referred to the organization for the country concerned (see appendix at the back of the book). For ease of use, most chapters follow a standard format and this is reflected in the detailed contents list. The index at the back of the book has been limited to those topics not obviously covered by chapter sub-headings.

Loveday Murley
Editor
Brighton, 1 August 1991

ACKNOWLEDGEMENTS

With the exception of the first two, all chapters have been provided by the members of the International Union of Air Pollution Prevention Associations. For further information on individual chapters, please contact the relevant IUAPPA member. A full list of IUAPPA members and addresses is given at the back of this book. The Editor would like to extend her thanks to the following for their contributions to the book (authors/coordinators names in brackets).

UN Conference on Environment and Development: (Mr Peter H Sand, Principal Legal Officer).

European Commission: (Jean-Guy Bartaire, Industrial and Mining Engineer with CEC-DG XI/A/3).

Argentina: Asociación Argentina Contra la Contaminación Ambiental.

Australia: Clean Air Society of Australia and New Zealand (Mr Alan J Crapp).

Belgium: Koninklijke Vlaamse Chemische Vereniging (Dr R De Fré and Dr H J Peperstraete, Studiecentrum voor Kernenergie).

Brazil: Associacao Brasileira de Prevencao a Poluicao do Ar e Defesa do Meio Ambiente (Alfred Szwarc, Engineer MSc; Eduardo Antonio Licio, Engineer MSc; Roberto Godinho, Chemist MSc; the paper was supervised by ABPPOLAR President Dr. Randolpho Marques Lobato).

Canada: Air and Waste Management Association (Steve Hart).

Finland: Finnish Air Pollution Prevention Society (Ms Oili Rahnasto).

France: Association pour la Prevention de la Pollution Atmospherique (M Robert Leygonie, Président du CITEPA; Dr Michel Sommer, Président d'Honneur de l'APPA).

Germany: Kommission Reinhaltung der Luft im VDI und DIN (Dr Grefen, Dr. Werner, Mrs A Hesemann).

Israel: Israel Society for Ecology and Environmental Quality Sciences (Dr. Michael Graber, Head, Air Quality Division, Ministry of the Environment).

Italy: Comitato di Studio per l'Inquinamento Atmosferico/Associazione Termotecnica Italiana (Prof Ing Giuseppe Ferraiolo, President).

Japan: Japanese Union of Air Pollution Prevention Associations (Tatsuo Hiratini, Industrial Pollution Control Association of Japan).

Korea: Korea Air Pollution Research Association (Jingyun Na, Deogkil Rhee and Kangrae Cho, National Institute of Environmental Research).

Kuwait: Environment Protection Council (Ibrahim M Hadi, Secretary General).

Malaysia: Environmental Protection Society (Gurmit Singh KS, President),

Mexico: Centro de Ciencias de la Atmósfere (H Bravo A, R Torres J and R Sosa E).

The Netherlands: Vereniging Lucht (Ms Margot van Os-Hendrikse, Ministerie van Volkhuisvesting Ruimtelijke Ordening en Milieubeheer).

New Zealand: Clean Air Society of Australia and New Zealand (Alan J Crapp).

Norway: Norwegian Clean Air Association (Ms Eva Borge, Norwegian State Pollution Autthority).

Pakistan: Pollution Control Society of Sind (Mansoor Zaidi, President).

Peru: Asociación Peruana Contra La Contaminación Atmosférica (M A Vizcarra Andreu, President).

Saudi Arabia: Meteorology and Environmental Protection Administration (Abdulbar Al-Gain, President).

Singapore: The Environment Engineering Society of Singapore (Professor Chin, Dr. Ong Say Leong and Mr. Jospeh Hui).

South Africa: National Association for Clean Air (Mr Harold Egenes, Chairman, Natal Branch).

Taiwan: Environmental Protection Society of Taiwan (Dr Chuang).

United Kingdom: National Society for Clean Air and Environmental Protection (Ms Loveday Murley).

United States of America: Air and Waste Management Association (Joseph Padgett, Associate Director, US Environmental Protection Agency).

Yugoslavia: Yugoslav Union of Air Pollution Prevention Associations (Dr. Aleksandar Knezević).

INTERNATIONAL LAW OF AIR POLLUTION CONTROL

The law and practice of air pollution control is bound to raise transnational as well as national issues. One of the earliest illustrations of international legal aspects is the Trail Smelter case, which arose over damage caused to agricultural land in the United States by sulphur dioxide emitted from a zinc and lead smelter in Canada in the 1920s, and which was finally settled by arbitration in 1941[(1)].

While the weight of the Trail Smelter arbitration as evidence of international customary law remains controversial, it had an undeniable influence on subsequent developments, including principle 21 of the declaration adopted by the United Nations Conference on the Human Environment (Stockholm, June 1972):

> "States have, in accordance with the Charter of the United Nations and the principles of international law, the sovereign right to exploit their own resources pursuant to their own environmental policies, and the responsibility to ensure that activities within their jurisdiction or control do not cause damage to the environment of other States or of areas beyond the limits of national jurisdiction."

Besides bilateral legal arrangements on transboundary air pollution control (such as the United States agreements with Mexico in 1987 and with Canada in 1991[(2)], and the 1989 agreement between Finland and the USSR[(3)]), there is a growing volume of multilateral codifications in this field, ranging from binding treaty obligations to recommendatory "soft law" resolutions. The present survey will briefly summarize this ongoing process of international law-making at three levels: global atmospheric protection; regional air pollution abatement (with the exception of recent developments within the European Community, which has been addressed in a separate chapter[(4)]); and sectoral standard-setting for air pollution control.

I GLOBAL ATMOSPHERIC PROTECTION

Among the first global efforts to protect the atmospheric environment against harmful human interference were the 1963 Test Ban Treaty[(5)] and the 1977 Environmental Modification Convention (ENMOD)[(6)]. Further steps were the "provisions for cooperation between States in weather modification", endorsed by the Governing

Council of the United Nations Environment Programme (UNEP) in 1980[7], and the provisions concerning marine pollution from or through the atmosphere, in the 1982 Convention on the Law of the Sea[8].

The Vienna Convention for the Protection of the Ozone Layer[9], concluded under UNEP auspices in 1985, laid down general obligations to protect human health and the environment against man-made modifications of the stratospheric ozone layer, and established an institutional framework for intergovernmental cooperation. The related 1987 Montreal Protocol on Substances That Deplete the Ozone Layer[10] specified the regulatory measures to be taken and the substances (chlorofluorocarbons and halons) to be controlled for this purpose; following the 1989 Helsinki Declaration[11], the time-schedule for regulation was accelerated, the list of controlled substances expanded and the implementation mechanisms strengthened by the 1990 London amendments[12].

Pursuant to UN General Assembly Resolution 45/212 of 21 December 1990[13], a framework convention on climate change is currently being negotiated (with the focus on emissions of carbon dioxide and other "greenhouse gases") and is expected to be finalized at the UN Conference on Environment and Development, to be held in Rio de Janeiro (Brazil) in June 1992[14].

II REGIONAL AIR POLLUTION ABATEMENT

Following earlier regional efforts in Western Europe, notably by the Council of Europe[15] and the Organization for Economic Cooperation and Development (OECD)[16], a Convention on Long-range Transboundary Air Pollution was adopted in 1979 within the framework of the UN Economic Commission for Europe in Geneva[17]. In force since 1983, the Convention covers eastern and western Europe as well as North America, and its current membership includes 31 States and the European Community. It established common policy principles - with the focus on prevention rather than liability[18], and including a commitment to use "the best available technology that is economically feasible" for air pollution control - and permanent institutions for intergovernmental cooperation, through annual review meetings of an Executive Body and several subsidiary bodies. Moreover, it provided the legal framework for a number of joint programmes and specific agreements[19]:

1. On the basis of annual performance reports by Contracting Parties, a comprehensive review of national strategies and policies for air pollution abatement is undertaken every four years to ascertain the extent to which the objectives of the convention have

been met. The second of these major "audits" of compliance was carried out in 1990[20]; it provides country-by-country tables of the most recent emission statistics, data on applicable national standards, and an overview of regulatory and economic measures taken by each Party to comply with the treaty.

2. A protocol on the European Monitoring and Evaluation Programme (EMEP) was adopted in Geneva in 1984, ratified by 30 Parties, and entered into force in 1988[21]. The programme is financed by mandatory contributions and coordinated by international centres in Norway and the USSR, established in 1978 to calculate and verify air pollution flows on the basis of data from 96 monitoring stations across Europe[22]. Further optional programmes have been set up to monitor and assess air pollution effects on several main targets: forests (with annual surveys of forest damage carried out in 26 European countries); rivers and lakes; materials and monuments; and agricultural crops. A major effort is now underway to establish agreed critical loads of air pollution for sensitive ecosystems. After endorsement by the Executive Body, scientific results of these joint programmes are published regularly in the trilingual *Air Pollution Studies* series[23].

3. A sulphur protocol was adopted in Helsinki in 1985, ratified by 20 countries, and entered into force in 1987[24]. It commits governments to reduce their national emissions or transboundary fluxes of sulphur dioxide by at least 30 per cent between 1980 and 1993. As of 1990, 13 Parties had reached the 30 per cent target ahead of schedule, and 11 of these were planning to cut their emissions by at least 50 per cent until 1995[25]. EMEP data show an overall decrease of sulphur dioxide emissions in Europe by approximately 22 per cent from 1980 to 1990. A revision of the sulphur protocol, aiming at further reductions after the 1993 target year, is now being prepared.

4. A protocol on nitrogen oxides was adopted in Sofia in 1988, ratified by 18 countries, and entered into force in 1991[26]. It calls for a "freeze" of national nitrogen oxides emissions or transboundary fluxes by 1994 at 1987 levels (1978 for the United States), to be followed by reductions from 1996 onwards at a rate yet to be agreed. Twelve of the signatories went a step further and signed an additional declaration committing them to a 30 per cent reduction by 1998[27].

5. A further draft protocol on volatile organic compounds (VOCs) is under preparation, and is expected to be ready for signature at the ninth meeting of the Executive Body in November 1991. Next in line will probably be heavy metals and persistent organic pollutants.

Air pollution abatement has also been included in regional agreements for marine environment protection in the Baltic and the North Sea, the Mediterranean and the Southeast Pacific:

a) The 1974 Helsinki Convention on the Protection of the Marine Environment of the Baltic Sea Area[(28)] defines "land-based" pollution as including airborne discharges originating on land (article 2/2). Following the Baltic Sea Declaration adopted at a ministerial conference in Ronneby (Sweden) in September 1990, the Baltic Marine Environment Protection Commission (HELCOM) established a high-level task force to implement the target of a 50 per cent reduction of atmospheric emissions of specified toxic, persistent and bioaccumulative substances, heavy metals and nutrients.

b) While the 1974 Paris Convention on the Prevention of Marine Pollution from Land-based Sources[(29)], which applies to the Northeast Atlantic region, originally did not cover airborne pollution, an amendment protocol adopted in 1986[(30)] extended its scope to pollution inputs from the atmosphere. The third international conference on the protection of the North Sea, held at The Hague (The Netherlands) in March 1990, called for a 50 per cent reduction of industrial atmospheric emissions for 17 harmful substances (including heavy metals and persistent organic compounds), to be implemented through the Paris Commission (PARCOM) administering the convention.

c) Within the framework of the 1976 Barcelona Convention[(31)], the 1980 Athens Protocol for the Protection of the Mediterranean Sea against Pollution from Land-based Sources[(32)] applies to "pollution from land-based sources transported by the atmosphere" (article 4/1/b), and a special annex on atmospheric pollutants (with priority given to toxic heavy metals) is currently in preparation for adoption by the Conference of the Parties. Similarly, in the context of the 1981 Lima Convention[(33)], the 1983 Quito Protocol for the Protection of the Southeast Pacific against Pollution from Land-based Sources[(34)] includes pollution "through the atmosphere" (article II/c); so do the global (albeit non-mandatory) Montreal Guidelines for the Protection of the Marine Environment against Pollution from Land-based Sources, endorsed by the UNEP Governing Council in 1985[(35)].

III SECTORAL STANDARD-SETTING

International clean air standards exist in a number of sectors, either regulating specific pollution sources or prescribing and monitoring air quality levels. These standards may be global or regional in scope; while some are legally binding on States, others are indicative or recommendatory only.

For aircraft engine emissions, the Council of the International Civil Aviation Organization (ICAO) has since 1981 set world-wide uniform certification procedures, by technical annex 16 (II) of the 1944 Chicago Convention[36]. Under this system, ICAO member States mutually recognize certificates issued in conformity with common testing standards and emission levels for smoke and gaseous engine emissions including hydrocarbons, carbon monoxide and nitrogen oxides[37].

For emissions from motor vehicles, 21 European countries use as a basis for national licensing procedures the international regulations laid down in the annexes to a 1958 Geneva Agreement[38]. Under the uniform system so established, authorizations for marketing (including importation of vehicles or parts manufactured abroad) are based on type approval of vehicle models, which includes certification of compliance with agreed technical criteria determining hydrocarbons, carbon monoxide and nitrogen oxides pollutant emissions. These regulations are subject to regular amendment and updating, usually in response to subregional initiatives either by the European Community or by the "Stockholm Group" established in 1985[39]. In view of the fact that some of these regional standards are also followed on a voluntary basis by non-European countries[40], prospects for extending them with a view to global harmonization are currently under discussion.

For emissions from ships, the Marine Environment Protection Committee of the International Maritime Organization (IMO), at its 30th session in November 1990, established a working group on air pollution, which is to develop a new annex to the 1973/78 MARPOL Convention[41] with the focus on emission reductions for CFCs, halons, exhaust gases and volatile organic compounds. As regards air pollution from waste incineration at sea, the 13th consultative meeting of Contracting Parties to the 1972 London Dumping Convention[42] decided to terminate all marine incineration of liquid noxious wastes by the end of 1991, thereby accelerating and superseding related regional timetables, e.g. under the 1972 Oslo Convention[43].

As regards ambient air quality, reference is frequently made to the "environmental health criteria"[44] and "air quality guidelines for Europe"[45] developed under the auspices of the World Health Organization (WHO); though drafted by *ad hoc* expert groups without intergovernmental endorsement[46], they are now widely used as a yardstick for comparative evaluation of air quality[47]. By contrast, internationally binding obligations exist for air pollution prevention in the working environment, under the 1977 Occupational Hazards Convention[48] of the International Labour

Organization (ILO), and under similar ILO conventions dealing with benzene[49] and other chemicals[50]. Protection against radioactive air pollution, already addressed by an earlier ILO convention[51], is covered in the comprehensive "basic safety standards for radiation protection" recommended by the International Atomic Energy Agency (IAEA)[52] and in the mandatory regional standards adopted by the Council of the European Community under the 1957 EURATOM Treaty[53].

Uniform international standards for measurement of ambient air quality and of air pollutant emissions are regularly issued by the International Organization for Standardization (ISO)[54]. Further to the ongoing global harmonization of air pollution monitoring programmes through the World Meteorological Organization (WMO), UNEP initiated a project on "harmonization of environmental measurement" in 1989[55], aimed at enhancing the quality and compatibility of environmental information world-wide.

IV OUTLOOK

Legal instruments for air pollution control and prevention are a comparatively recent addition to the arsenal of international law. What is traditionally referred to as "international air law" still is predominantly understood today as the body of legal rules applicable to international aviation and air transport - not unsimilar to the historical evolution of the international law of marine and inland waters, which for centuries was synonymous with navigational rights. Yet, just as the contemporary law of the world's oceans and freshwater resources now has to cope with claims for a multitude of non-navigational uses[56], the future international "law of the air" will have to be resource-oriented rather than use-oriented[57], with precedence given to conservation of the resource as a whole over any single utilization.

The author, Mr Peter H Sand, is Principal Legal Officer, United Nations Conference on Environment and Development (UNCED), Geneva.

Views and opinions expressed are those of the author and do not necessarily reflect those of the UNCED secretariat.

REFERENCES

1. United Nations, *Reports of International Arbitral Awards*, vol. 3 (New York 1949), pp 1905-1982.

2. Agreement of cooperation between the United Mexican States and the United States of America regarding transboundary air pollution caused by copper smelters along their common border, of 29 January 1987; and Agreement between the Government of Canada and the Government of the United States of America on air quality, of 13 March 1991.

3. Action programme agreed between the Republic of Finland and the Union of Soviet Socialist Republics for the purpose of limiting and reducing the deposition and harmful effects of air pollutants emanating from areas near their common border, of 26 October 1989.

4. See Bartaire J G, "The Policy of the Commission of the European Communities in Respect of Atmospheric Pollution" (next chapter of this book).

5. Treaty banning nuclear weapon tests in the atmosphere, in outer space and under water, of 5 August 1983, text in *United Nations Treaty Series*, vol. 480 p 43.

6. Convention on the prohibition of military or any other hostile use of environmental modification techniques, of 18 May 1977, text in *United Nations Treaty Series*, vol. 1108 p 151. For background see Goldblat J, "The ENMOD Convention Review Conference", *Disarmament*, vol. 7 (1984), pp. 93-109; and Westing A H (ed), *Environmental Warfare: A Technical, Legal and Policy Appraisal* (Taylor & Francis: London 1984).

7. Decision 8/7(A) of 29 April 1980, text in UNEP *Environmental Law Guidelines and Principles No. 3.*

8. Articles 212 and 222, United Nations Convention on the Law of the Sea, of 10 December 1982, text in UN publication E.83.V.5 (New York 1983).

9. Of 22 March 1985, text in *International Legal Materials*, vol. 26 (1987), p 1529; for background see Benedick R E, *Ozone Diplomacy: New Directions in Safeguarding the Planet* (Harvard University Press: Cambridge/Mass. 1991).

10. Of 16 September 1987, text in *International Legal Materials*, vol. 26 (1987), p. 1550.

11. Adopted at the first meeting of the Parties to the Montreal Protocol, Helsinki, 2 May 1989; text in *International Legal Materials*, vol. 28 (1989), p. 1335.

12. Adopted at the second meeting of the Parties to the Montreal Protocol, London, 29 June 1990; text in *Environmental Policy and Law*, vol. 20 (1990), pp. 166-172.

13. "Protection of global climate for present and future generations of mankind"; see also the report of the first session of the Intergovernmental Negotiating Committee for a Framework Convention on Climate Change, Washington DC, February 1991, UN doc. A/AC.237/6 (1991).

14. One of the "major concerns" referred to the 1992 Conference by UN General Assembly Resolution 44/228 (of 22 December 1989) is "protection of the atmosphere by combating climate change, depletion of the ozone layer and transboundary air pollution."

15. See Adinolfi G, "First Steps Toward European Cooperation in Reducing Air Pollution: Activities of the Council of Europe", *Law and Contemporary Problems*, vol. 33 (1968), pp. 421-426; and Ercman S, "Activities of the Council of Europe and the European Economic Communities Related to Transboundary Air Pollution", in Flinterman C, et al (eds), *Transboundary Air Pollution: International Legal Aspects of the Cooperation of States* (Nijhoff: Dordrecht 1986), pp 131-140.

16. See Eliassen A, "The OECD Study of Long-range Transport of Air Pollutants: Long-range Transport Modelling", *Atmospheric Environment*, vol. 12 (1978), pp 479-487.

17. Of 13 November 1979, text in *International Legal Materials*, vol. 18 (1979), p 1442. See Chossudovsky E M, *"East-West" Diplomacy for Environment in the United Nations* (United Nations Institute for Training and Research: Geneva 1988); and Fraenkel A, "Convention on Long-range Transboundary Air Pollution", *Harvard International Law Journal*, vol. 30 (1989), pp 447-477.

18. A footnote to the official text specifies that "the present convention does not contain a rule on state liability as to damage."

19. See Sand P H, "Regional Approaches to Transboundary Air Pollution", in Helm J L (ed), *Energy: Production, Consumption, and Consequences* (National Academy Press: Washington DC 1990), pp 246-264.

20. United Nations Economic Commission for Europe, *National Strategies and Policies for Air Pollution Abatement: 1990 Update*, UN doc. ECE/EB.AIR/27 (1991).

21. Protocol on long-term financing of the cooperative programme for monitoring and evaluation of the long-range transmission of air pollutants in Europe (EMEP), of 28 September 1984; text in *International Legal Materials*, vol. 24 (1985), p 484.

22. See Dovland H, "Monitoring European Transboundary Air Pollution", *Environment*, vol. 29 No 10 (1987), pp 10-28.

23. United Nations Economic Commission for Europe, *Air Pollution Studies*, Nos. 1-7 (1984-1991).

24. Protocol on the reduction of sulphur emissions or their transboundary fluxes by at least 30 per cent, of 8 July 1985; text in *International Legal Materials*, vol. 27 (1988), p 707.

25. 1990 review (supra note 20), table 5.

26. Protocol concerning the control of emissions of nitrogen oxides or their transboundary fluxes, of 31 October 1988; text in *International Legal Materials*, vol. 28 (1989), p 214.

27. Sofia Declaration on the 30 per cent reduction of nitrogen oxide emissions, of 31 October 1988; text in *Environmental Policy and Law*, vol. 18 (1988), p 234.

28. Of 22 March 1974; text in *International Legal Materials*, vol. 13 (1974), p 546.

29. Of 4 June 1974, text in *International Legal Materials*, vol. 13 (1974), p 352.

30. Of 26 March 1986, text in *International Legal Materials*, vol. 27 (1986), p 625.

31. Convention for the protection of the Mediterranean Sea against pollution, of 16 February 1976; text in *International Legal Materials*, vol. 15 (1976), p 290.

32. Of 17 May 1980, text in *International Legal Materials*, vol. 19 (1980), p 869.

33. Convention for the protection of the marine environment and coastal areas of the Southeast Pacific, of 12 November 1981; text in *International Digest of Health Legislation*, vol. 33 (1982), p 96.

34. Of 22 July 1983; text in *International Digest of Health Legislation*, vol. 36 (1985), p 170.

35. Decision 13/18 (II) of 24 May 1985; text in Sand P H, *Marine Environment Law in the United Nations Environment Programmme* (Tycooly: London 1988), p 235.

36. Convention on international civil aviation, of 7 December 1944, text in *United Nations Treaty Series*, vol. 15 p 95. See Annex 16 (Environmental Protection), volume

II, adopted on 30 June 1981, with an amendment of 4 March 1988 (ICAO: Montreal 1988).

37. Pursuant to article 38 of the Chicago Convention, States may, however, notify the ICAO secretariat of national differences in standards. Ten member States availed themselves of this option as regards annex 16 (II).

38. United Nations Economic Commission for Europe, Agreement concerning the adoption of uniform conditions of approval and reciprocal recognition of approval for motor vehicles equipment and parts, of 20 March 1958, text in *United Nations Treaty Series*, vol. 335 p 211, as amended and supplemented by numerous technical regulations (for air pollutants in particular see Regulations No. 15, 24, 40, 47, 49 and 83).

39. In a joint Declaration on Air Pollution by Motor Vehicles signed in Stockholm on 5 July 1985, the environment ministers of eight countries (Austria, Canada, Denmark, Finland, Liechtenstein, Norway, Sweden and Switzerland) agreed to cooperate towards the introduction of national engine emission standards following 1983 US federal standards. The Stockholm Group has since continued to meet informally at the technical level, with the additional participation of Germany and The Netherlands.

40. e.g. Australia, New Zealand, Singapore; for a comparative survey see the Oil Companies' European Organization for Environmental and Health Protection, *Trends in Motor Vehicle Emission and Fuel Consumption Regulations: 1990 Update* (CONCAWE: Brussels 1991). Observers from Canada, Japan and the United States regularly participate in the UN/ECE Working Party on the Construction of Vehicles in charge of updating the regulations.

41. International convention for the prevention of pollution from ships, of 2 November 1973, as amended by the Protocol of 17 February 1978; texts in *International Legal Materials*, vol. 12 (1973) p 1319, and vol. 17 (1978), p 546.

42. Convention on the prevention of marine pollution by dumping of waste and other matter, of 29 December 1972, text in *United Nations Treaty Series*, vol. 1046, p 120.

43. Convention for the prevention of marine pollution by dumping from ships and aircraft, of 15 February 1972, text in *International Legal Materials*, vol. 11 (1972), p 263.

44. e.g. for nitrogen oxides, photochemical oxidants, sulphur oxides and suspended particulate matter, *WHO Environmental Health Criteria Documents* No. 4, 7 and 8 (World Health Organization: Geneva 1977-79).

45. *Air Quality Guidelines for Europe*, WHO Regional Publications: European Series No. 23 (Copenhagen 1987). Another set of criteria has been developed under the "indoor air quality programme" of the WHO Regional Office for Europe, covering organic pollutants, biological contaminants, combustion products and inorganic fibres.

46. On the range of informal WHO procedures in this field, see Shubber S, "The Role of WHO in Environmental Pollution Control", *Earth Law Journal*, vol. 2 (1976), pp 363-392.

47. e.g. see the UNEP/WHO report on *Assessment of Urban Air Quality* (Monitoring and Assessment Research Centre: London 1988) and the UNEP *Environmental Data Report 1989-90* (Blackwell: Oxford 1989), p 13; cf. French H, *Clearing the Air: A Global Agenda*, Worldwatch Paper No. 94 (Worldwatch Institute: Washington DC 1990), pp 9-16.

48. Convention concerning the protection of workers against occupational hazards in the working environment due to air pollution, noise and vibration, of 20 June 1977, text in *Command Paper* No. 7901 (1977).

49. Convention concerning protection against hazards of poisoning arising from benzene, of 23 June 1971, text in *United Nations Treaty Series*, vol. 885, p 45.

50. Convention No. 170 on safety in the use of chemicals at work, of 24 June 1990.

51. Convention concerning the protection of workers against ionizing radiations, of 22 June 1960, text in *United Nations Treaty Series*, vol. 431, p 41.

52. Text in IAEA *Safety Series* No. 9 (International Atomic Energy Agency: Vienna 1982, currently under revision). While the standards recommended pursuant to article 3 of the IAEA Statute of 26 October 1956 (*United Nations Treaty Series*, vol. 276, p 3) are not legally binding on States, compliance may be made a prerequisite for IAEA technical assistance; see Szasz P C, *The Law and Practice of the International Atomic Energy Agency* (IAEA Legal Series No.7: Vienna 1970), pp 684-693.

53. Articles 30-38 of the Treaty establishing the European Atomic Energy Community, of 25 March 1957, text in *United Nations Treaty Series*, vol. 298, p 167.

54. After preparation by ISO Technical Committee 146, draft standards are circulated to all national member authorities for voting by correspondence, and if 75 per cent of the votes cast are in favour, are published by the ISO Council as accepted international standards; see International Electrotechnical Commission & International Organization for Standardization, *Directives: Procedures for the Technical Work*, Part 1 (ISO: Geneva 1989), pp 14-23.

55. Following an initiative by the 1987 Economic Summit meeting in Venice; see UNEP/HEM, *A Survey of Environmental Monitoring and Information Management Programmes of International Organizations* (UNEP/HEM: Munich 1990).

56. e.g. current efforts of the UN International Law Commission to codify the law of non-navigational uses of international watercourses (sixth report, 1990).

57. See Sand P H, "Internationaler Umweltschutz und neue Rechtsfragen der Atmosphaerennutzung" (International environment protection and new legal problems relating to utilization of the atmosphere), *Zeitschrift fuer Luft- und Weltraumrecht* (German Journal of Air and Space Law), vol. 20 (1971), pp 109-133.

THE POLICY OF THE COMMISSION OF THE EUROPEAN COMMUNITIES IN RESPECT OF ATMOSPHERIC POLLUTION

1 INTRODUCTION

The European Economic Community (EEC) was established by the Treaty of Rome in 1957 by six countries: Belgium, France, West Germany, Italy, Luxembourg and The Netherlands. The main purpose was to provide a common market between those countries for their products, and the Treaty sets out the framework for this. The EEC now has twelve members: Denmark, Ireland and the United Kingdom joined in 1973, Greece in 1981 and Spain and Portugal in 1986.

The European Commission - responsible for the day to day administration of the Community - is split into various Directorates-General; that responsible for developing most environmental policy and drawing up legislative proposals in this area is DG XI, the Directorate General for the Environment and Nuclear Safety. The Council of Ministers - that is representatives from the appropriate ministry of Member States' governments - takes the final decision on the Commission's proposals. The European Parliament - which is directly elected by electors in each Member State - has rather limited powers: it cannot amend or reject decisions reached by the Council of Ministers, but can only ask the Council to reconsider.

Community legislation takes four forms:

a) *Regulations* are binding on all Member States in their entirety.

b) *Directives* are binding on Member States as to the result to be achieved, while leaving a degree of flexibility on how the measure will be implemented in national legislation.

c) *Decisions* are binding in their entirety and may be addressed to government, private enterprise or individuals.

d) *Recommendations* and *opinions* are not binding.

The 1957 Treaty of Rome contained nothing specific as regards the environment; however, in 1972 the heads of state and government launched a Community environment policy. This policy has made significant progress and received wide political and public support. A substantial body of law has been built up and principles and an approach aimed at protecting the environment established.

The situation changed with the *Single European Act* signed in 1986; this incorporates a Title VII on the environment and Articles 130R - 130T which, in particular, introduce the principles of preventive action on the environment, the "polluter pays", and incorporation of environment policy into the Community's other policies. In addition, Article 100A of the Treaty enables the Council to act on a qualified majority in certain specific instances relating to the environment.

In view of the task to be accomplished and to lay down guidelines for the work to be done up to 1992 the Commission sent to the Council its fourth programme of action on the environment (1987-92). (The first three programmes had covered 1973-76, 1977-81 and 1982-86.) It is that part of the fourth programme dealing with atmospheric pollution, and the political and scientific priorities emerging since the programme was drawn up, which will be expanded upon below. A fifth programme is to be drawn up shortly.

2 AIR QUALITY

So far the Council has adopted three Directives on air quality:

* Council Directive 80/779 of 15 July 1980 on air quality limit values and guide values for sulphur dioxide and suspended particulates, as amended by Council Directive 89/427 of 21 June 1989;
* Council Directive 82/884 of 3 December 1982 on a limit value for lead in air;
* Council Directive 85/203 of 7 March 1985 on air quality standards for nitrogen dioxide.

It is of crucial importance for the Community that these Directives are implemented by all Member States. However implementation raises a number of legal and technical problems.

2.1 Legal and Technical Implementation of the Air Quality Directives

The first stage is the transposition of Community law into national law. While this is happening, progress is somewhat slow.

It is clear that the new Member States, in particular, will have to make a special effort in the years ahead. The Commission has, in the past, detected a considerable number of omissions and discrepancies in national laws, and has been obliged to bring infringement actions against Member States to ensure national laws are made compatible with the requirements of Community laws.

In future the transposition of Community Directives into national law should receive more public attention since the Commission has decided to permit public access to its data base containing information on the national laws which officially implement Community law.

Apart from legal activity the other aspect of the practical implementation at national level of EEC Directives and of the true effectiveness of these as regards improving the quality of the environment also raises considerable problems.

In theory the Commission has the power to check whether Community acts and national laws based on them are in fact fully implemented in practical terms at local or regional level. This power derives from Article 55 of the Treaty and the articles of the various Directives which provide that Member States must report to the Commission on their implementation. However, the national reports are not always sent regularly and often do not provide sufficient detail to enable the Commission to assess accurately the implementation of laws in practice.

In order to solve those two problems - formal legal compliance and practical implementation - the Commission is stepping up its contacts with the national or regional administrations in the Member States; this will enable the Commission, as far as possible, to avoid having to bring infringement actions.

Together with the Member States and the Environment Institute in Ispra, Italy, the Commission has conducted a number of technical activities, and is continuing to do so to improve technical implementation of Directives. These include:

- the quality assurance programmes carried out under Directive 80/779 (sulphur dioxide and suspended particulates) enabling the quality and mutual comparability of the pollution measures carried out by Member States to be assured in network stations and national reference laboratories;
- studies on the design of networks intended to measure air pollution by sulphur dioxide, black smoke and nitrogen dioxide. (Studies funded by the Commission and carried out by various European laboratories and experts);
- assessment of network compliance with air quality Directives (Paris Network);
- the holding of seminars or symposia in order to exchange know

how between air pollution specialists (International Meeting held in Lyon in November 1988).

2.2 Present and Proposed Actions Regarding Air Quality

As part of its present and future activities regarding air quality the Commission (DG XI) is working on the following items:

- the preparation in 1990-91 of a quality assurance programme on the implementation of Directive 85/203 (nitrogen dioxide);
- evaluation, in 1990, of the compliance of the Madrid air pollution measuring network with the air quality Directives;
- a green paper on the urban environment, available in 1990, to enable the Commission to improve the urban environment in the broad sense of the term and more particularly air pollution;
- development of a data base on air quality in Europe which, in the long term, could constitute a basic tool enabling Member States to assess more accurately the state of air quality in Europe and thus to adapt the air quality Directives to the reality.
- drawing-up of an air quality Directive for tropospheric ozone, which will lay down the quality aims for that pollutant. This is a new approach put forward by the Commission and - in direct contrast to the preceding air quality Directives which lay down limit values that must be met without fail by a certain date - the quality aims may be exceeded. When this is noted the Member State concerned must draw up air quality improvement programmes.

This new approach has been adopted for ozone owing to the complexity of the physical/chemical phenomena causing pollution of this type and which involve a reduction of the emissions of photochemical precursors (nitrogen oxides and volatile organic compounds), ozone being a secondary pollutant.

While it was preparing the air quality Directive on ozone, DG XI set up a Committee on the Reduction of Photochemical Pollution; among its tasks are:

- to define, together with the Commission, the practical stages of a Community strategy for the reduction of photochemical pollution;
- to assist the Commission and its contractors in implementing the stages defined by the Committee;

This Committee will, in particular, have to:

- define the most immediate targets for the reduction of precursor emissions at national and international levels;
- help coordinate national activities aimed at reducing precursor levels;

- exchange information on the technologies used to reduce emissions and the costs generated.

In effect this Committee will be the body which defines the broad outline of activities aimed at reducing photochemical pollution, while the more technical work will be performed within specialist working parties such as those on:

* Southern Europe;
* VOC measuring techniques;
* the reduction of emissions of precursors from stationary sources (cf. section 3);
* the reduction of emissions of precursors from mobile sources (cf. section 4).

3 REDUCING POLLUTANT EMISSIONS FROM STATIONARY SOURCES

Four Directives on industrial emissions have so far been adopted by the Council, together with a Directive (87/217) applying to industrial and other types of emission. These are:

* Council Directive 84/360 of 28 June 1984 on the combating of atmospheric pollution from industrial plants;
* Council Directive 87/217 of 19 March 1987 on the prevention and reduction of pollution of the environment by asbestos;
* Council Directive 88/609 of 24 November 1988 on the limitation of emissions of certain pollutants into the air from large combustion plants;
* Council Directive 89/369 of 8 June 1989 on the prevention of air pollution from new municipal waste incineration plants;
* Council Directive 89/429 of 21 June 1989 on the prevention of air pollution from existing municipal waste incineration plants.

The latter two Directives lay down limit values for the emission of certain pollutants such as dust, heavy metals, sulphur dioxide, hydrogen chloride and hydrogen fluoride.

It should again be pointed out that Directive 87/217/EEC lays down measures for the prevention and reduction of environmental pollution by asbestos to protect both human health and the environment. It covers asbestos emissions to atmosphere, water-borne effluent and solid asbestos waste. A number of limit values have been laid down and sampling and analysis methods are described in the annex. The Directive also applies to asbestos factories and to the working of products containing asbestos, the demolition of buildings, structures and installations containing asbestos and to the removal, from the above, of asbestos or materials containing asbestos which cause the release of asbestos fibres or dust into the environment (Article 7). Member States had to adopt the legal and administrative provisions and regulations needed to comply with the Directive by at the latest 31 December 1988 and in the case of plants built or authorized before 31 December 1988, by 30 June 1991.

Apart from the first three Directives mentioned above implementation of these Community instruments is of less immediate importance except as regards air quality since they are quite recent. On the other hand extensive work is in progress on setting out in detail, defining and implementing Directives 84/360 and 88/609, relating to emissions from industrial plant and from large combustion plant, respectively.

3.1 Work in Progress on Directive 84/360

Directive 84/360 lays down the measures and procedures that are intended to avoid or reduce atmospheric pollution from industrial plants within the Community. It contains, in particular, the following provisions:

a) Member States shall take the necessary measures to ensure that the operation of the plants in the categories listed in Annex I require prior authorization by the competent authorities.

b) Authorization is also required in the case of substantial alteration of all plants in the categories listed in Annex I or which as a result of modification will fall within those categories.

Without prejudice to national and Community requirements having an aim other than that of this Directive, authorization may only be given when the competent authority has ensured that:

- all measures appropriate to the prevention of atmospheric pollution, including the use of the best possible technology, have been taken, provided that measures of that type do not involve excessive cost;
- operation of the installation does not cause significant atmospheric pollution, above all via the emission of the substances listed in Annex II to the Directive;
- none of the emission limit values applying shall be exceeded;
- all of the air quality limit values applying shall be taken into account.

Member States shall monitor developments concerning the best technology available and the environmental situation.

In addition Article 7 of the Directive provides that subject to the provisions regarding commercial secrecy, Member States shall exchange information among themselves and with the Commission regarding their experience and knowledge of measures for the prevention and reduction of air pollution, as well as technical processes and equipment and air quality and emission limit values.

Directive 84/360 does not lay down detailed technical standards for the plants falling within its scope, nor does it lay down emission limit values for the various pollutants referred to. General procedures and criteria for the prevention of atmospheric pollution from all industrial plant are specified. However, Article 8 provides that:

- The Council acting unanimously on a proposal from the Commission, shall if necessary fix emission limit values based on the best available technology not entailing excessive costs, and taking into account the nature, quantities and harmfulness of the emissions concerned.
- The Council, acting unanimously on a proposal from the Commission, shall stipulate suitable measurement and assessment techniques and methods.

In view of these articles the Council has enacted technical and emission standards for large combustion plant (Directive 88/609/EEC) and for municipal waste incinerators (Directives 89/369/EEC and 89/425/EEC).

Where it considers it to be necessary, the Commission reserves the right to introduce proposals for Directives aimed at other major stationary industrial sources, more particularly as part of the provisions of Article 8 referred to above.

Of the conditions laid down in Directive 84/360 as regards the authorization of industrial plant, the use of best technology available which does not give rise to excessive costs is of very special importance. However, implementation of that provision requires a major effort in defining the technologies which should be referred to under the various conditions which may arise throughout the Community. The - very general - definition provided by the Directive on this subject, which must apply to a large number of heterogeneous sectors and to an even greater number of processes requires that a procedure be set up for the identification and monitoring of the technologies at issue.

The Commission has conducted a survey of the measures taken by Member States to implement Articles 12 and 7; (Article 12 requests Member States to follow developments as regards the best available technology and the environmental situation). The main conclusion which should be drawn from the analysis is that effective and harmonized implementation at Community level of the provisions governing the use of the best available technologies encounters major difficulties. The Commission has therefore felt that the exchange of information provided for in Article 7 of the Directive should be organized and structured with a view to preparing technical memoranda on the best technologies available, the conditions for their use, emission levels and other major aspects of the implementation of the Directive.

The structure of these technical memoranda may be summarized as follows:

- definition of the category of industrial plant covered;
- description of the industrial processes available;
- study of the measures available for reducing pollution;
- study of the multi-environment aspects;
- identification of the best technology or technologies available for reducing pollution and the levels of emission of the various pollutants of each technology identified. These levels are to be expressed in the form of limit values for the emission to atmosphere of the various pollutants. Those levels will provide a criterion for the choice of technology and the authorization procedure for the industrial plants at issue;
- study of the methods of supervising pollutant emissions;
- study of procedures for the storage of raw materials or products;
- study of the measures needed in order to minimize emissions during plant start up.

Technical working parties have been set up comprising representatives of the Commission, the Member States and the parts of industry concerned; these will draft the technical memoranda and submit them for approval by a coordinating committee covering the same bodies. In addition the coordinating committee is responsible for defining the preference to be given to the various activities involved in drafting the technical memoranda and in particular determining the industrial sectors receiving priority.

The following technical memoranda have already been produced and approved and were available at the end of 1990 in the form of EUR publications:

* production of sulphuric acid
* production of nitric acid
* production of ammonia
* production and storage of benzene
* incineration of toxic or dangerous waste
* production of cement.

Technical memoranda covering the following were expected to be produced during 1990-91:

* refining industry
* coke ovens
* ore sintering, oxygen steelworks
* electric-arc steelworks
* foundries.

The Commission planned in 1990 to send the Council those technical memoranda already approved in the form of a communication. In 1990 the Commission also started to examine the structure of the technical memoranda and the areas of industrial emissions that will need priority in future.

It is suggested that Directive 84/360 could be amended in such a way as to change the committee for the coordination of the definition of the best available technologies into a regulatory committee to ease and speed up implementation of the Directive.

3.2 Present and Proposed Actions

Work is in hand on the following:

- Preparation of a Directive on the prevention of atmospheric pollution from dangerous waste incinerators, expected to be sent to the Council by the end of 1990.

- Analysis of the technical and legal implementation of Directive 88/609/EEC in Member States and definition of any harmonization to be conducted together with the Member States. This Directive which covers combustion plants with an output of more that 50 MWth incorporates two basic provisions:

  a) an overall reduction in emissions of sulphur dioxide and nitrogen oxides imposed upon each Member State;

  b) limit values for the emission of sulphur dioxide, nitrogen oxides and dust from new or modified plants.

  The Directive contains a number of technical and legal obligations applying to Member States and the Commission, the first of which concerns the transposition into national law of the Directive before 30 June 1990. Member States were required to send to the Commission by 31 December 1990 at the latest their detailed programmes for the reduction of emissions.

- Further work on reducing VOC emissions from stationary sources as part of the fight against photochemical pollution as described in section 1. During 1990 preparatory work will be done on future Directives which will limit VOC emissions from printing, metal degreasing, vehicle painting and the private use of paints. The dry cleaning, wood and metal-surface treatment sectors will be dealt with during a second phase (1991).

At the end of 1990 and from 1991 onwards preparatory work will be done on possible Directives covering gas turbines, combustion plant delivering less that 50 MWth, and solid-fuel combustion plant developing between 50 and 100 MWth.

4 REDUCTION OF POLLUTANT EMISSIONS FROM MOBILE SOURCES

A large number of activities have already been carried out on mobile sources and these are still in progress.

4.1 Brief Background History and Current Situation

- In the "Luxembourg Compromise" in June 1985 the Council defined the broad outline for a timetable and the level of emission standards for cars having both a large engine capacity (more than 2000 cm^3) and a medium engine capacity (1400 - 2000 cm^3). By late 1986, early 1987, these broad outlines were still in abeyance - i.e. they had not been ratified by a formal legal act, or in other words as a Directive adopted by the Council.

- The entry into force of the *Single European Act* on 1 July 1987 enabled the Luxembourg Agreement to be finalized and given legal force, within certain limits, thanks to the new Article 100A of the *Single Act.* On 7 July 1987 the Commission sent the Council a new proposal for a Directive replacing its initial proposal of 6 June 1984. (It should be remembered that this 1984 proposal in effect finally imposed the American standards from 1995.)

- The main features of the Commission's second proposal of 1987 were (a) that their legal basis is Article 100A and (b) that its structure follows the philosophy of the Luxembourg Agreement of June 1985 as regards deadlines, engine capacity categories, the severity of the standards and other technical details.

- On 21 July 1987 the Council reached a political agreement in principle by means of a qualified majority on a proposal from the Commission. That agreement took practical form on 7 September 1987 in the form of a joint Council proposal sent to Parliament; it was given a favourable reception and approved on 18 November 1987.

- On 3 December 1987 the Council was finally able officially to adopt by a qualified majority the Directive laying down air pollution standards for the exhaust gases of petrol-engined vehicles weighing up to 3.5 tonnes (Directive 88/76/EEC). This Directive lays down separate standards for the three engine capacity categories and different deadlines for implementation, depending on whether they cover new types or models of car or simply new cars. The standards to be met govern the mass of carbon monoxide, the combined mass of hydrocarbons and nitrogen oxides, and the mass of nitrogen oxides. In addition the Directive lays down different standards for the type approval of vehicles, carried out on a typical vehicle, and for the checking of conformity of production models on production lines (Tables 1 and 2). The standards for cylinder capacity of less than 1400 cm^3 are at an early stage.

Table 1: Standards for the Approval of a Vehicle Model or Type (Directive 88/78/EEC, 3 December 1987)

	Date of introduction of new emission standards		*Emission standards to be complied with (in grammes per test)*		
Vehicle category (engine capacity)	*New models of car*	*New cars*	*Mass of carbon monoxide*	*Combined mass of hydrocarbons and nitrogen oxide*	*Mass of nitrogen oxide*
More than 2000 cm^3	1.10.88	1.10.89	25	6.5	3.5
Between 1400 and 2000 cm^3	1.10.91	1.10.93	30	8	–
Direct injection (turbo) (diesel engines)	1.10.94	1.10.96			
less than 1400 cm^3	1.10.90	1.10.91	45	15	6

Table 2: Component Type Approval or Series Production Approval Standards (Directive 88/76/EEC, 3 December 1987)

	Date of introduction of new emission standards		*Emission standards to be complied with (in grammes per test)*		
Vehicle category (engine capacity)	*New models of car*	*New cars*	*Mass of carbon monoxide*	*Combined mass of hydrocarbons and nitrogen oxide*	*Mass of nitrogen oxide*
More than 2000 cm^3	1.10.88	1.10.89	30	8.1	4.4
Between 1400 and 2000 cm^3	1.10.91	1.10.93	36	10	–
Direct injection (turbo) (diesel engines)	1.10.94	1.10.96			
less than 1400 cm^3	1.10.90	1.10.91	54	19	7.5

In the Directive itself the Council undertakes to act before the end of 1987 on the final, more stringent standards to be applied to small cars from 1992, in the case of new models, and 1993 in the case of new cars. The Directive also incorporates the following provisions:

- the standards adopted for petrol-engined cars also apply in principle to diesel-engined cars, with certain adjustments;
- engines of the vehicles covered by the Directive will have to be able to operate on unleaded petrol;
- the test method underlying the calculation of the limit values will be revised in order to include, more specifically, non-urban trips;
- Member States may, if they so wish, implement the new limit values set out in the Directive in advance.

Council Directive 88/77/EEC of 3 December 1987 introduces for the first time into the Community emission standards for gaseous pollutants that are to be complied with by new types of diesel engines from 1 July 1988 and for new heavy vehicles from 1 October 1990 (Table 3). Article 6 of the Directive states that, by the end of 1988 at the latest, the Council will examine a new Commission proposal intended (a) to lay down more stringent limit values and (b) to establish limit values for particulate emissions from heavy vehicles.

Table 3: Emission Standards for Gaseous Pollutants from Diesel Lorries and Buses (1st Stage) (Directive 88/77/EEC, 3 December 1987)

Date of introduction of standards		*Type approval standards*			*Conformity of production standards*		
New types of heavy vehicle (new engines) (>3.5 t)	*New heavy vehicles (>3.5 t)*	*Mass of carbon monoxide, CO, g/kWh*	*Mass of hydro carbons, HC, g/kWh*	*Mass of nitrogen oxide NO_x g/kWh*	*Mass of carbon monoxide CO g/kWh*	*Mass of hydro carbons HC, h/kWh*	*Mass of nitrogen oxide NO_x g/kWh*
1.7.88	1.10.90	11.2	2.4	14.4	12.8	2.6	15.8

Council Directive 88/436/EEC of 16 June 1988 lays down particulate emission standards for diesel cars. The limit values for a second stage (Article 4 of the Directive) was to have been adopted by the Council on a proposal from the Commission by, at the latest, the end of 1989. In addition vehicles having an engine capacity of more than 2000 cm^3 must meet the limit values for gaseous pollutants from petrol-engined cars for the category of cylinder capacities lying between 1400 and 2000 cm^3. Diesel-engined cars fitted with direct injection and having a cylinder capacity lying between 1400 and 2000 cm^3 will have longer in which to comply with the standards laid down for exhaust gases (1 October 1994 and 1 October 1996).

Table 4: Standards for Particulate Emissions from Diesel Cars (1st Stage) (Directive 88/436/EEC, 16 June 1988)

Engine capacity	*Date of introduction of new standards*		*Mass of diesel particulates*	
	New car models	*New cars*	*Type approval standards*	*Series-production approval standards*
All cylinder capacities	1.10.89	1.10.90	1.1 (gr/test)	1.4 (gr/test)

Finally, owing both to its justification and content, Council Directive 89/458/EEC on air pollution by motor vehicles may be considered to be a true environmental Directive in respect of air pollution by motor vehicles. The environmental aims are indeed clearly expressed in the Directive which deals not only with the choice of standards and of the timetable but also, importantly, with acceptance of tax incentives and the commitment by the Council to limit future emissions of carbon dioxide from motor vehicles.

The standards contained in Directive 89/458/EEC are a second stage for small cars and will require the use of regulated three-way catalytic converters, thereby expressing the Council's wish to see the principle of the best available technology without excessive costs also being applied to the control of air pollution from mobile sources. In addition the Directive contains the following provisions:

- Article 5 stipulates that, before the end of 1990, the Council will align cars having an engine capacity between 1400 and 2000 cm^3 with the standards and dates laid down in the earlier Directive on small cars. This replaces the initial Directive 88/76/EEC. In addition the new emission values will have to be based on the new European test procedure which will incorporate driving conditions outside built up areas;
- Article 2 stipulates that Member States shall apply the standards laid down to new types of vehicle from 1 July 1992 and to all new vehicles from 31 December 1992.

On 17 July 1989, the Commission adopted Directive 89/491/EEC which is essentially technical annexes to the various motor vehicle Directives adopted since 1970.

4.2 Current and Proposed Action on Air Pollution by Motor Vehicles

The activities, either planned or in progress, derive from the Directives already adopted and described above.

1st Stage: Alignment of the Standards for Large and Medium Cars with those applying to Small Cars

Substantial technical and legal activity is in progress to adapt the anti-pollution standards applying to large and medium cars to the new philosophy of Directive 89/458/EEC as quickly as possible. Indeed, it would be quite paradoxical and illogical to lay down less stringent standards for large and medium cars than those applying to smaller engines as is, legally speaking, currently the case.

The Commission's proposals as regards the standards at present before the Council are, for the first time, based on the new European reference test method which should soon become the only method applying within the Community. (At the moment the industry still has the choice between the European limit values and test procedure or the 1983 US limit values and test procedure FTP-75.) The Council adopted the regulations at the end of 1990.

In addition, the Directive proposes restrictions on hydrocarbon emissions via evaporation. This has become necessary mainly to fight photochemical pollution. Emissions will be reduced by the fitting of a canister or filter to vehicles enabling evaporative emissions to be reduced considerably.

2nd Stage: New Regulation on Gaseous Pollutants and Particulates applying to Heavy Vehicles (Diesel Engines fitted to Lorries and Motor Buses) (Amendment of Directive 88/77/EEC)

According to the timetable provided in the above Directive, the Council should have made its views known on the new limit values by the end of 1989. This of course has now been postponed. A Commission proposal was sent to the Council on 7-8 June 1990, but was neither discussed nor adopted. It consists of two stages.

The dates of implementation of the first stage coincide with the introduction of stringent European standards for cars, i.e. 1 July 1992 for the approval of new types and 1 January 1993 for the first placing in service of all new vehicles. The proposed emission standards are as follows:

- for the approval of new types of diesel engine: 4.5 g/kWh for carbon monoxide, 1.1 g/kWh for hydrocarbons, 8 g/kWh for nitrogen oxides and 0.63 g/kWh for particulates and engines developing less than 85 kW or 0.36 g/kWh for particulates and engines developing more than 85 kW.
- for all new diesel engines: 4.9 g/kWh for carbon monoxide, 1.23 g/kW for hydrocarbons, 9 g/kWh for nitrogen oxides and 0.7 g/kWh for particulates and engines developing less than 85 kW or 0.4 g/kWh for particulates and engines developing more than 85 kW.

The second stage is based on the Commission's conviction that it is now necessary to lay down longer term aims in order to enable the industry to develop and prepare the series production of new technologies which are likely drastically to reduce pollutant emissions by diesel engines. For this purpose the Commission proposed 4 g/kWh for carbon monoxide, 1.1 g/kWh for hydrocarbons, 7 g/kWh for nitrogen oxides and 0.3 or 0.15 g/kWh for particulates. These values would apply to new types from October 1996 and to all new diesel engines from October 1997. The test procedure for these two stages will be as described in Directive 88/77.

It should also be borne in mind with regard to gaseous pollutants from diesel cars that difficulties could result from the decision to apply the standards for exhaust gases from petrol-engine cars to diesel cars (Directive 88/436/EEC).

5 QUALITY OF PRODUCTS WHICH CAUSE AIR POLLUTION

Actions in this area basically cover liquid and solid fuels and chlorofluorocarbons.

5.1 Solid and Liquid Fuels

Several regulations have already been adopted including:

* Council Directive 75/176 of 24 November 1975 on the approximation of the laws of the Member States relating to the sulphur content of certain liquid fuels;
* Council Directive 87/219 of 30 March 1987 which revises and supplements Directive 75/176.

In addition Directives 86/210 (20 March 1985), 85/581 (20 December 1985), and 87/416 (21 July 1987) have resulted in the lead content of petrol being reduced to a maximum of 0.15 g/l, the introduction of unleaded petrol and the benzene content of petrol being limited to 5 per cent by volume maximum.

5.2 Chlorofluorocarbons and Other Substances that Deplete the Stratospheric Ozone Layer

The following regulatory instruments which have already been adopted are of relevance:

* Council Decision 80/372 of 26 March 1980 concerning chlorofluorocarbons (CFCs) in the environment;
* Council Decision 82/795 of 15 November 1982 on the consolidation of precautionary measures concerning in the environment;
* Council Regulation 3322/88 of 14 October 1982 on the conclusion of the Vienna Convention on the protection of the

ozone layer and the Montreal Protocol on Substances that Deplete the Ozone Layer;

* Commission Decision 89/419 of 30 June 1989 allocating import quotas for CFCs for the period 1 July 1989 to 30 June 1990;
* Council Resolution of 30 May 1978 on CFCs in the environment;
* Commission Recommendation of 13 April 1988 on the limitation of use of CFCs by the aerosol industry (no CFCs in aerosol sprays by the end of 1990);
* Council Resolution of 14 October 1988 on the limitation of use of CFCs halons (cessation of use of halons in extinguishers by the year 2000);
* Community Regulation on Substances that Deplete the Ozone Layer. This was approved by the Council at the end of 1990 and radically amends Council Regulation 3322/88. CFCs will cease to be used by 1997, i.e. three years before the date jointly adopted at world level; the Commission has ensured that the revision of the Montreal Protocol, agreed in June 1990, will be as effective as possible.

5.3 Present and Proposed Work on Product Quality

The following initiatives are in hand:

- In 1990 the Commission was expected to send the Council a draft Directive limiting the maximum sulphur content of heating oil and diesel fuel to a maximum of 0.2 per cent. The Commission will shortly review the value for DERV.
- Preparatory work on a possible restriction of the benzene content of liquid fuels to be carried out in late 1990 and early 1991.
- In addition, changes in the quality of diesel fuels in Europe are due to be studied by the Commission in the years ahead.
- Work is continuing on a scheme for the ecological labelling of products, to be set up following establishment of the European Environmental Agency.

6 THE GREENHOUSE EFFECT AND CARBON DIOXIDE

The greenhouse effect and the increase in the amount of carbon dioxide in the atmosphere have in recent years become politically sensitive subjects within the Commission and have triggered a number of activities.

On 21 June 1989 the Council adopted a Resolution entitled "Greenhouse Effect and the Community". This declared that the

Community should devote increasing attention to the risk of possible climatic changes associated with the greenhouse effect. It gave a favourable reception to the Commission launching a work programme on the assessment of the political options open for tackling the risks associated with the greenhouse effect. The Commission was to have submitted a progress report, together with practical proposals to the Council in mid-1990; a final report on the results of the work programme, together with conclusions is expected by the end of 1991. Adoption of the resolution of 21 June 1989 gives effect to the Commission's activities on the greenhouse effect in 1990 and 1991. It should be noted in this connection that:

a) A research programme called EPOCH has been launched covering, in particular, the study of historical climates and climatic changes; the study of climatic phenomena and models; and a study of the effects and risks linked with the climate and its changes.

b) A working party on the problems involved in the greenhouse effect and the changes to the environment was set up in January 1990.

c) The Commission decided to participate actively in international activities (IPCC - World Climate Conference).

d) The THERMIE programmes on the promotion of energy technology in Europe and SAVE, a programme of special action aimed at high energy efficiency, have been launched.

e) At the request of the Council thought is being given to possible pollutant and energy taxes by the Commission; the principle of a tax on carbon dioxide emissions is beginning to take shape.

In addition the Commission sent the Council on 14 March 1990 a communication defining its political aims as regards the greenhouse effect. This communication enables the concepts detailed in the communication of 21 June 1989 to be expressed in further, close detail. It stresses in particular the urgent need to obtain a clear commitment from the industrialized countries to stabilize their carbon dioxide emissions up to the year 2000, to reduce them by 2010, and to stop deforestation by 2000.

7 ENERGY AND THE ENVIRONMENT

It is difficult to speak of the greenhouse effect and of carbon dioxide without tackling the major problem of energy in the environment. To this end the Commission, and more particularly DGs XVII (Energy) and XI (Environment), sent a communication to the Council on energy and the environment on 13 February 1990.

If based on a business as usual scenario, this communication shows that air pollution by sulphur dioxide and nitrogen oxides resulting from the use of fossil fuels will diminish significantly during the period 1980-2010 while carbon dioxide emissions will increase. Completion of the internal market within the Community may speed up pollution because of the spurt in economic growth and the rise in demand for energy if that effect is not offset by appropriate control and savings.

The Commission is proposing four major forms of action to tackle the energy aspects linked with the environment:

a) The THERMIE programme (see section 6);

b) The SAVE programme (see section 6);

c) The setting up of a committee of national experts whose brief would be to assist the Commission in analyzing tax schedules (see section 6);

d) Preparation of codes of conduct together with the Community energy industry. Those codes of conduct would be intended to establish the manner in which the energy industries will react to environmental problems.

Finally the Commission suggests that Member States and the energy industries within the Community should pursue energy strategies favouring the environment along the following lines:

- use of best technologies available which do not give rise to excessive costs;
- assessments of the environmental impact and risks deriving from the energy sector;
- ensuring that energy costs reflect as far as possible all environmental costs;
- taking account of the high level of environmental protection and the specific ecological conditions applying to the Member States and in particular the outlying regions;
- setting out a legal framework offering flexible, stable conditions providing industry with a secure basis for action;
- improving the institutional links and the cooperation between the administration that are responsible for energy and the environment;
- scientific research;
- acquisition and expansion of statistical information in this area.

The Council was expected to reach a decision on this Commission communication in the near future.

8 FUTURE DEVELOPMENTS

The establishment of the European Environmental Agency is awaited eagerly by DG XI since this will enable it to have technical support and information for its regulatory activities. The CORINE (Coordination of Information on the Environment in Europe) project developed by DG XI is a good example of an effective technical structure that is essential for DG XI and which the Agency can take over to advantage. It should be remembered in this connection that CORINAIR, the CORINE unit dealing with air, constitutes the first genuine European inventory of dust, sulphur dioxide, nitrogen oxides and hydrocarbon emissions from stationary and mobile sources within the Community. It could in future be supplemented by a European data bank on air quality.

A move towards an integrated approach (water, air, soil) has been reaffirmed by DG XI in the work carried out by the various units and Directorates. Finally, it should be borne in mind that DG XI is closely monitoring the activities carried out by the Environment Institute in Ispra on indoor air. Indoor pollution caused by mineral fibres, radon, combustion products, formaldehyde and tobacco smoking form part of the current activities, plus a more general approach towards "sick buildings". European ventilation standards are being studied, as are indoor pollution problems caused by bacteria.

9 BIBLIOGRAPHY

Corcelle, G. *Clean Cars in Europe: There is Light at the End of the Tunnel.*

Resolution of the Council on the Continuation and Implementation of a European Community Policy and Action Programme on the Environment (1987-92) (The Fourth Action Programme). Adopted 19 October 1987. OJ No. C328, 7 December 1987.

Bartaire, J-G. *The EEC Policy on Indoor Pollution.* EUR doc. June 1989.

Bartaire, J-G, Zierock, K-H. *The EEC Policy on Photochemical Oxidants.* Atmospheric Pollution. November 1989.

Acknowledgements

The author, Jean-Guy Bartaire, is an Industrial and Mining Engineer with CEC-DG XI/A/3. He would like to thank Mr P Stief-Tauch, A3 Head of Unit within DG XI and Mr P Hecq, Mr M Wold, Mr B Delogu, Mr G Strongylis and Mr P Perera within DG XI for their invaluable help in drawing up this paper, and Mrs K Lievens for the original typing, organization and page-setting of the document.

ARGENTINA

1 INTRODUCTION

1.1 Topography, Climate, Population

The Republic of Argentina has a total surface area of 2 791 810 sq. km, a population of nearly 33 million and a population density of 11.8 per sq. km. It is located in the southernmost part of America, between 22 degrees and 56 degrees latitude south and between 54 degrees and 72 degrees longitude west. Its boundaries are to the north, Bolivia, Paraguay and Brazil; to the west, Chile; to the south, the South Pole; and to the east, Brazil, Uruguay and the Atlantic Ocean. The country is flanked to the west by the Andes, one of the most vast mountain ranges on the planet, and to the east by the Atlantic Ocean, with more than 4500 km of coastline.

Argentina is made up of an immense plain and thick forests. In some areas the soil is arid and in others extremely fertile; there is a wide range of climates, from tropical heat to areas where the temperature is below zero degrees. This gives rise to great variations in the countryside.

Argentina is a Federal Republic. The federal system means that the political organization corresponds to a single State with other smaller states called provinces. The provinces are consolidated in a Federal State, keeping their autonomous governments. In the same way, municipalities exist within each province and answer to the provincial government. The Federal Government is made up of the Executive Power (performed by the President of the Nation); the Legislative Power or Congress, (made up of two Chambers, one of Representatives and the other of Senators from the Provinces and from the Capital); and the Judicial Power (made up of the Supreme Court of Justice, the Courts of Appeal and the Courts of First Instance). The provinces have their own Constitutions and local institutions and are governed by them, electing their Governors, Legislators and other officials.

There are 23 provinces in the Republic of Argentina, its capital being the city of Buenos Aires which is a national dependency. More than 3 million people live in the city and when its neighbouring suburbs are included, the Metropolitan Area, covering 7700 sq. km, has a population greater than 14 million inhabitants. This means that practically 42 per cent of the total population of the country is concentrated into 0.28 per cent of national territory. Within this region there are approximately one million motor vehicles.

There are 72 ports in the country (61 of these are fluvial) which makes continual loading and unloading of merchandise possible. Considerable manufacturing activity has been developed in the towns neighbouring the city of Buenos Aires, because of the proximity to the Port of Buenos Aires. This means there is a risk of air pollution, although except for the winter period, there is a fairly high capacity for cleaning the atmosphere in the region.

The importance of agriculture to the national economy is paramount, this sector covering internal needs as well as providing an export market. According to recent information, the country plans for more than 250 million hectares of land to be used for agriculture and cattle farming, of which approximately two-thirds will be made up of pasture land. Principal crops are wheat, maize, linseed, oats, fodder, soya, sunflower, peanuts and sugar cane. The cultivation of fodder is very important for the arable areas as well as for cattle production. Argentine cattle raising is centred on two types of operation: firstly, breeding and secondly, winter pasture or fattening. It is estimated that there are approximately 50 million cattle, 40 million sheep, 40 million chickens and 4 million pigs.

Within the country, there are important mineral stocks, solid and liquid fuels and a less important amount of industrial activity.

1.2 Specific National Problems

Currently, one of the main problems of the country is the economy. On the one hand its industrial activity is declining, on the other, its debt, particularly its foreign debt, is on the increase.

2 DEVELOPMENT OF AIR POLLUTION CONTROLS AND LEGISLATION

It should be made clear that Argentina lacks a National Law to regulate all sources of environmental pollution in an organized manner, although for some time it has been working to solve the difficulties involved in such a project. Unlike other countries, the National Constitution lacks standards directed towards the regulation of natural resources and, more understandably lacks references to the environment. There are no specific standards on the administration of resources or on the power of government. There are, however, national and provincial laws, byelaws, decrees, rules and resolutions in Argentina which contain standard regulations for various matters related to the correct management and improvement of the environment.

In accordance with Article 104 of the National Constitution, the provinces maintain all powers not delegated to them by the Federal Government. This limits national legislation on the environment: the provinces are, therefore, responsible for adopting the legislation necessary to preserve the environment within their regions.

The adoption of some national laws on the environment has, however, been justified on the basis of other stipulations in the National Constitution. This situation does however mean that plans for national legislation on the environment have been delayed, and it may be necessary to amend the National Constitution in order to adapt it to current circumstances.

Nevertheless, despite administrative power belonging to the provinces under the constitutional system and without excluding the possibility of adopting a National Law on the subject, there are still procedures which can adequately overcome the constitutional difficulty.

2.1 National Laws

In April 1973, Law 20,284 was passed; its purpose is to preserve the air, avoid atmospheric pollution and protect the corresponding section of the biosphere. It is a law of consent, federal jurisdiction being limited to requesting the provinces to adhere to the law.

Having regard to federalism, the law maintains local application of its provisions, in turn entrusting structures and the execution of a federal programme related to the causes, aims, methods of prevention and control of atmospheric pollution, to the national health authority.

Within the Statement of Aims, it declares that the right to health is part of the birthright of the various human communities; it notes that air, water and soil are elements which make up the ecological environment in which man develops, and that all actions which lead to preserving them in the best possible condition are directed towards the societies which are served by them.

The notes to Law 20,284 describe atmospheric pollution as "the presence in the atmosphere of any physical, chemical or biological agent, or conditions pertaining to the same, in places, forms and concentrations which are or may be harmful to the health, safety or wellbeing of the population, or which may be prejudicial to animal or plant life, or which prevent the use and enjoyment of the properties and places of recreation". Sources of pollution are seen as being "motor vehicles, machinery, equipment, installations or temporary or permanent incinerators, fixed or mobile, whatever their field of application or use may be, which give off substances which produce or can produce atmospheric pollution". The emission of "any pollutant which passes into the atmosphere as a consequence of physical, chemical or biological processes".

Law 20,284 and its three annexes is applicable to all sources capable of producing atmospheric pollution located within federal jurisdiction and in those provinces adhering to the Law. Authority to apply the Law is given to the national and provincial health authorities and that of the municipality of the City of Buenos Aires in its respective jurisdictions. Under this Law, an Official Register of Sources of Pollution has been created which is the responsibility of the national health authority; it will also be empowered "to monitor air quality standards and concentrations of pollutants corresponding to the Plan to Prevent Critical Atmospheric Pollution Situations".

Article 7 of the Law empowers the local health authority to fix maximum emission levels for the various types of fixed sources for each area; Article 8 establishes the same levels for mobile sources. Manufacturers of mobile sources are also required to carry out tests to certify that their units comply with the law.

Chapter III of Law 20,284 requires the local health authority to establish a Plan to Prevent Critical Atmospheric Pollution Situations, based on three levels of concentration of pollutants in the air. These will be determined as states of alert, alarm and emergency. Table 1 details the maximum concentrations for each level. An Interjurisdictional Committee is to be established to determine this legal standard, which may be requested by any of the authorities

Table 1: Maximum Permissible Pollutant Concentrations

Pollutant	*Maximum limit permissible*	*Alert*	*Alarm*	*Emergency*
Carbon Monoxide	10ppm (8hrs) 50ppm (1h)	15ppm (8hrs) 100ppm (1hr)	30ppm (8hrs) 120ppm (1hr)	50ppm (8hrs) 150ppm (1hr)
Nitrogen Oxides	0.45ppm (1hr)	0.6ppm (1hr) 0.15ppm (24hrs)	1.2ppm (1hr) 0.3ppm (24hrs)	0.4ppm (24hrs)
Sulphur Dioxide	0.3ppm (70 $\mu g/m^3$) (monthly average)	1ppm (1hr) 0.3ppm (8hrs)	5ppm (1hr)	10ppm (1hr)
Ozone and Oxidants	0.10ppm (1hr) expressed as 0_3	0.15ppm (1hr)	0.25ppm (1hr)	0.4ppm (1hr)
Particles in suspension	150 $\mu g/m^3$ monthly average			
Sedimental particles	1.0 mg/(cm2 30 days) 10 ton/(km2 30 days)			
(ppm expressed in volume/volume)				

involved in problems of atmospheric pollution or by the national health authority. The Committee will function within the jurisdiction of the National Executive Power.

Chapter VI establishes the following sanctions: fines; temporary or permanent closure of polluting sources; temporary or permanent disqualification of licenses in the case of air, land, sea or river transport. Chapter VII (Procedure in the Federal Capital) lays down that the Municipal Court of Default is responsible for the judging of infringements.

2.2 Provincial Laws

Article 430 of the *Rural Code of the Province of Buenos Aires*, in referring to the climate, establishes that changes to the climate achieved by seeding clouds or other systems directed towards causing artificial rain, avoiding hail and other atmospheric phenomena, should be authorized by the competent organization, even in cases where experiments of a scientific nature are being carried out. Article 431 establishes that damages and interests produced by the official agency involved with third parties must be insured by the same.

Law 7,229/66 regulated by Decree 7,488/72 is currently in force in the Province of Buenos Aires. Article 1 refers to its field of application, in relation to industrial establishments situated or to be situated within the Province. In order to be granted permission to operate, they must comply with the regulations regarding location, construction, installation and equipment as laid down by the Law, with the aim of maintaining the safety, health and hygiene of staff and nearby populations, as well as their material assets. Article 2 defines an industrial establishment as being directed towards the obtaining, transformation, conservation and preparation of natural products, raw materials and all types of articles required by society, through the use of industrial methods.

In accordance with Article 3, health and safety are the responsibility of the Ministry of Social Welfare in the Province. An industrial establishment is considered to comply with safety regulations when certificates of establishment and operation have been issued. Article 5 establishes the requirements for a certificate of establishment, incorporating a body to monitor the impact on the environment, including reporting on its operations on the safety, health and hygiene of neighbouring populations as well as all the material assets.

Article 6 establishes environmental categories for establishments in an area. Within the first category are those considered to be innocuous, given that their operation does not constitute any risk or damage to the safety, health and hygiene of nearby populations, nor do they cause damage to material goods. The second category includes those which are considered to be a nuisance because they can cause discomfort to the safety, health and hygiene of nearby populations or damage to material goods. The third category refers to establishments considered dangerous as their operation constitutes a risk to the safety, health and hygiene of nearby populations. Article 7 refers to the regulations which establish the standards to which the siting of industries (included in Decree 7,488/72) are adjusted.

The environmental requirements of the certificate of operation are laid down in Article 9 as follows:

a) environmental characteristics of establishments must meet the conditions of safety, health and hygiene laid down in the corresponding regulations.

b) installations and equipment in establishments must meet the safety regulations and other precautions established in the regulations.

c) installations dealing in the elimination of liquid and gaseous effluents, as well as the composition of emissions must meet the conditions of safety, health and hygiene included in the regulations.

d) staff in the establishments must comply with adequate safety and protection measures and with the necessary health certificates.

e) health protection measures for staff, and the prevention of illnesses which could affect them as a result of their work and the conditions worked in, must be implemented by a medical service working within the establishment.

f) all standards established by regulations which are laid down for the safety, health and hygiene of staff and of neighbouring populations, as well as of material assets, must be complied with.

Article 10 requires industrial establishments in the province to inform the Ministry of Social Welfare of any extension, alteration or change to the buildings, environment and installations, by means of its specific dependencies so that it can proceed to approve and grant the corresponding certificate of operation.

Article 14 delegates duties to the town councils to help the municipal authorities, enabling them to issue standards which complement the established requirements.

Article 15 confirms the Ministry of Social Welfare as being the overseeing body and establishes fines in cases of non-fulfilment, which reflect the infringement and the seriousness of its consequences.

Article 16 lays down the temporary or definitive closure of the offending establishment as a sanction. Article 17 establishes a system of municipal delegation in order to apply the present law.

2.3 Municipal activity

Another example of the Argentine federal system is Municipal Bye-Law 390-25 of 31 May 1983 in the City of Buenos Aires which approves the *Environmental Pollution Prevention Code.* The first section of the Code deals with general, basic points, and the field of application. The second part is concerned with pollutants originating from mobile sources and the third section refers to solid residues. The fourth section includes liquid effluents. The fifth deals with noise pollution and the sixth is concerned with ionizing radiation.

3 FUTURE DEVELOPMENTS

As a result of the reduction in the ozone layer in the southern region of South America, in June 1990 the Natural Resources and Conservation of the Human Environment Committee of the House of Representatives of the Legislative Power of the Nation, asked the National Executive Power for information regarding various aspects of the problem. The views of a number of government departments will be taken into account; these include: the Ministries of Foreign Affairs and of Health and Social Welfare, the National Committee of Environmental Policy, the National Atomic Energy Committee, the National Meteorological Service and other organizations competent on this matter. The following work will be carried out:

a) information gathered to bring Argentina up-to-date with regard to monitoring the content of the ozone stratosphere over its territories;

b) dimensions of the "hole in the ozone layer";

c) research into the incidence of ultraviolet radiation on the health of the population;

d) recommendations to be produced by the health authorities for protecting the population from an excess of ultraviolet radiation;

e) activities and strategies to be implemented to monitor the effect of ultraviolet radiation on ecosystems;

f) the international stance to be taken by Argentina on this matter.

4 BIBLIOGRAPHY

Arnolds, A (1988). *Geografía Politica y Económica de la República Argentina* (Political and Economic Geography of the Republic of Argentina), 4th Edition. Kapelusz Edition. Buenos Aires.

Law Decree No. 7.229/66 - Official Journal of 15th November 1966. Buenos Aires.

Decree No. 7 488/72. Province of Buenos Aires. Ministry of Health.

Law no. 20,284. Buenos Aires, 16th April 1973. Official Journal No. 22658.

Municipal Bye-Law No. 390-25. Municipality of the City of Buenos Aires.

Código de Prevención de la Contaminación Ambiental del 31 de mayo de 1983 (Environmental Pollution Prevention Code).

Pigretti, E A and Bellorio D L (1980). *La Legislación sobre Protección de la Naturaleza* (Legislation regarding Protection of Nature). Journal of the University of Buenos Aires. Vol.III.

Terrera G A (1979). *Geopolitica Argentina, Población, Fronteras, Comunidades, Antropologias* (Argentine Geopolitics, Population, Borders, Communities, Anthropology). Plus Ultra Edition. Buenos Aires.

AUSTRALIA

1 INTRODUCTION

1.1 Topography, Climate, Population

Australia, which is situated in the Southern Hemisphere, is a federation of six sovereign states - New South Wales, Victoria, South Australia, Queensland and Tasmania - and some additional territories, such as the Northern Territory and Australian Capital Territory. It has a total land area of about 7 682 300 sq. km and a population of 17 million. Australia's climate ranges from sub-temperate to tropical with 50 per cent of the country having less than 300 mm of rain per year.

Australia has very large reserves of coal and moderate reserves of natural gas and low sulphur crude oil. Although Australia imports approximately 35 per cent of its crude oil requirements, it is a major net exporter of fossil and nuclear fuel. Because of the availability of low cost coal in most industrialized and high population areas, electricity is relatively cheap and is commonly used as a clean form of domestic and commercial heating and air conditioning.

1.2 Specific National Problems

Statistically and geographically, one might expect air pollution not to be a problem in Australia since on average there are only two people per sq. km and the country is entirely surrounded by oceans and seas. In fact, about 70 per cent of Australia's inhabitants live in urban areas, mainly around the southeastern coastal region. State capital cities - Sydney, Brisbane, Perth, Adelaide and Melbourne - have already demonstrated their ability to produce ozone and other photo-oxidants as a result of the relatively high concentrations of man-made pollutants over those cities. All these cities - each with populations of over 750 000 - have an incidence of air pollution from man-made sources requiring control. Fortunately they are all remote from one another and significant air pollution does not cross State boundaries. Also the prevailing winds often carry pollutants well out to sea, but almost never over international boundaries.

Australia also has a very high per capita rate of motor vehicle ownership. So, despite a very low average population density, air pollution values can reach relatively high levels by international standards, particularly in the largest cities and in cities based around ferrous or non-ferrous smelting industries.

Because Australia is a major producer and exporter of primary products both agricultural and mineral, even quite remote localities can be subject to high levels of air pollution in the vicinity of mining and trans-shipment operations.

Australia's two largest cities, Sydney and Melbourne, exceed 0.12 ppm ozone one hour average on several days a year and other cities have the potential to produce this level without some control.

2 DEVELOPMENT OF AIR POLLUTION CONTROLS AND LEGISLATION

2.1 Clean Air Philosophy

Australian States have borrowed to varying degrees from the two basic philosophies of air pollution control: best practicable means (BPM) as has been used in the United Kingdom and air quality standards as used in the USA. BPM was and still is, but to a lesser extent, the more commonly used. However air quality standards (AQS) are gaining greater support as the extent and reliability of ambient monitoring networks is improving and the concentration of industry produces cumulative effects on ambient levels of pollutants in certain areas.

The division of administrative responsibility between State and local government, by the use of a schedule of industries or activities having greater potential to cause air pollution, is universal among the States. However, there is some variation from State to State in the make-up of the industries and activities listed in their schedule. Licensing of scheduled premises or activities is also universal as a means of administering and controlling operations of these industries.

Considerable importance is placed on air pollution levels from new sources. New or re-built industrial plant are required, in all States, to adopt BPM as a minimum standard and, depending on the sensitivity of the locality and existing ambient air pollution levels, best available control technology can be required regardless of the legislated emission limits for existing operations. Some States have more stringent limits for new plant compared with plant which has been in operation for some years. Even so, this does not mean that lower efficiency control equipment may be used if it can be shown that higher efficiency controls are practicable or justified.

In those States where air quality standards have not been adopted, authorities compare existing ambient air quality standards adopted elsewhere - e.g. by the World Health Organization or US Environmental Protection Agency - to assess the level of control required to avoid unacceptable levels of air quality and to determine policies for future controls.

Air quality and air pollution potential are factors which are generally taken into account in land use planning. However, there are many other factors to be considered and sometimes planning decisions are made which are far from ideal for air quality and cost effective control of industrial air pollution, e.g. the building of medium density housing adjacent to long-established major chemical complexes.

Most States now have some overall system of environmental impact assessment for proposed major developments prior to the granting of development approval. Air pollution control authorities generally have the opportunity to make submissions on environmental impact statements for consideration in the final assessment. Where separate air pollution approval is required subsequent to the planning approval, air pollution control authorities are expected to indicate their likely approval or refusal during the planning assessment stage. There is a trend towards greater integration of planning and pollution approval procedures.

Policies for air pollution control based on economic factors do vary somewhat from State to State. However, there are some fundamental precepts that are common:

- the principle of the polluter pays applies throughout Australia. There are no government subsidies to help polluting industries install control equipment, which is normally expected to meet best practicable means criteria.
- greater emphasis on minimizing air pollution is placed on new or highly modified plant and equipment during design and construction rather than on existing plant that is meeting emission limits appropriate to its age. Old plant that is used as standby or at part capacity is often allowed to continue in this mode even though it might not always meet appropriate emission limits.

  Table 1 sets out emission limits recommended by the National Health and Medical Research Council and the Australian and New Zealand Environment Council for new plant. The limits represent capabilities for plant fitted with the cost effective controls that are broadly considered as economically acceptable. They are frequently adopted by State control agencies as conditions of approval for new plant, despite the fact that they are generally more stringent than the regulation limits for the particular process or plant.

- Fees are charged by State control authorities, where licenses are issued under air pollution control legislation. Scales of license fees vary significantly from State to State but within each are graduated to take account of the potential of the plant to cause air pollution.

2.2 Early Controls

Prior to the 1960s, control of air pollution was highly fragmented, with the main responsibility falling on local, municipal and shire councils. Standards of control varied widely and relatively few councils committed adequate resources to the problem to have significant impact. Action to control air pollution was taken under Local Government Ordinances or in some cases under state statutes dealing with public health, noxious trades or similar. Common Law, although basically unsuited to resolving issues of air pollution, was sometimes used.

During the 1960s, following various serious air pollution episodes in Europe and the USA, State governments individually enacted clean air legislation, generally assuming overall responsibility for control policy and ambient monitoring and direct control of the more serious sources of air pollution through a system of licensing. Control of domestic, commercial and light industrial air pollution incidents remained the responsibility of local government in most cases.

All States have substantially upgraded their legislation for control of air pollution at least once since original enactment. In some cases this has included emission limits for new motor vehicles.

2.3 Legislation and Instruments

The various States and Territories are responsible for the control of air pollution from stationary sources. However, the Federal Government has, since 1976, set design rules governing all new motor vehicles intended for sale in Australia to ensure uniform minimum control standards throughout the nation. In 1989, the Federal Government formally took over responsibility from the States for setting motor vehicle emission standards although the States are currently still responsible for their enforcement. A brief explanation of each State's air pollution control legislation follows.

2.3.1 New South Wales

Under the NSW *Clean Air Act 1961*, the Minister for the Environment has power to issue regulations. In practise this power is administered through the State Pollution Control Commission which was established in 1971 to deal with five major areas of concern - air, water, noise, solid waste and environmentally hazardous chemicals.

All premises are subject to the Act, but those on which certain operations are carried out, or where more than 300 kg of combustible material can be consumed hourly are subject to licensing, stricter regulations, and other controls and monitoring. As these are listed in a schedule to the Act the term "scheduled premises" or "scheduled equipment" is used to describe such stationary sources. Emissions from mobile industrial plant and equipment are also subject to the Act (Part IV B) and regulations. Standards of concentration and rates of emission for major industries and/or pollutants are shown in Table 2.

Since 1974, further restrictions on the sulphur content of fuel (to 0.5, 1.0 or 2.5 per cent) have applied based on the maximum capacity of all oil-burning equipment on the premises. Plants with control equipment for reducing sulphur-compound emissions may use fuel oil with more than the maximum permitted sulphur content.

There are no statutory regulations for sulphur dioxide emissions, except for sulphuric acid plants. Sulphur dioxide is controlled by requiring all occupiers of scheduled premises to obtain approval for stack heights before building them. Bosanquet-Sutton or other suitable procedures are used to determine heights needed to ensure ground level concentrations do not exceed about 16-20 pphm sulphur dioxide. Practically speaking, these procedures require all oil burning plant with stacks less than 21 m to use fuel with not more than 0.5 per cent sulphur.

The *Environmental Offences and Penalties Act 1989*, which was updated in late 1990, provides for three levels of penalties:

- *Tier 1:* where environmental harm is caused due to wilful acts or negligence, fines of up to Aus. $1 million for corporations and up to $250 000 and/or seven year gaol for individuals may be imposed.
- *Tier 2:* for strict liability offences, such as in the *Clean Air Act*, maximum penalties are $125 000 for a corporation and $60 000 for an individual.
- *Tier 3:* infringement notices (on the spot fines) for minor offences, with fines in the range $150 - $160 for littering, failure to comply with a license condition, noisy vehicle exhausts, etc.

In mid 1991, an Environment Protection Authority was established; it will assume the responsibilities of the previous control agency, as well as take on wider environmental responsibilities, with a strong emphasis on waste minimization.

2.3.2 Victoria

When the *Environment Protection Review Act* was passed in May 1984, it represented a major change in pollution control and environmental legislation in the State. Amendments contained in that legislation represented a comprehensive review of the original Act, based on 13 years of legislative experience. Much of the philosophy and principle of the original Act was retained with the 1984 Act providing a framework for long term environmental management while protecting beneficial land use.

The 1984 Act introduced a works approval system and an extended abatement notice system with scheduling of industries for works approval and licensing. Occupiers of scheduled premises must obtain approval before installing or modifying plant (when such modifications are likely to change waste discharges). The emission standards which apply for stationary sources are shown in Table 3.

The Environment Protection Authority is thus involved in the planning stage and can specify the incorporation of appropriate pollution control equipment. Routine applications take about six weeks but more complex applications may warrant the maximum time limit of six months for consideration. If a license already exists, and proposed works will not adversely affect the environment, the EPA may exempt the operator from the requirement for a works approval; this saves time and safeguards against unnecessary works approvals. Specific exemptions also apply for routine maintenance.

Unscheduled premises are controlled by regulation and an expanded pollution abatement notice system.

A special minor works' pollution abatement notice has been developed for situations requiring urgent action where compliance costs do not exceed $45 000.

State Environment Protection Policy (air environment) is an integral part of pollution control work. Strong emphasis is given to pollution prevention and high priority is given to involving the public in policy formulation and setting environmental quality objectives. The public can thus decide what beneficial uses need to be protected and at what cost. Declared policies play a key role in works approvals, as consistency with policy objectives and protection of identified beneficial uses must be maintained. There is some flexibility, however, as policy objectives can be deviated from if local environments need higher levels of protection or where industry can achieve a higher standard of pollution control using available technology.

Social and economic factors are considered when formulating policy now and do not outweigh environmental considerations. The main aim continues to be protection of the environment.

2.3.3 South Australia

The *Clean Air Regulations* of 1969 and 1978 made under the *Health*

Act 1935 have been replaced by *Clean Air Regulations* made under the *Clean Air Act 1984.* This Act is administered by the Department of Environment and Planning and provides for the licensing of prescribed activities and the charging of fees. Occupiers of prescribed activities must seek approval to conduct building work and may not make specified changes to the activity without ministerial approval.

All occupiers of premises are required to maintain equipment and conduct their activities so as not to cause air pollution. They must also conform to prescribed emission standards (Table 4).

Officers authorized under the Act have the power to instruct a person in charge - or apparently in charge - of an activity which in the officer's opinion is injurious to health or causing serious nuisance to take action specified by the officer, which may include closing down the activity.

Odours are again subject to the opinions of an authorized officer. Where a complaint has been made of excessive odour and the officer detects the odour and deems it to be excessive, the occupier of the premises is guilty of an offence.

The *Planning Act* contains two schedules of particular relevance to industrial activities: schedule 8 lists similar activities to those scheduled under the *Clean Air Act.* These industries, when proposing to locate anywhere in South Australia, must submit their proposals to the local authority who must then obtain approval from the Minister for Environment and Planning. If the Minister considers the proposal unsuitable from an air pollution viewpoint, he may refuse it. There is no appeal against this decision.

Schedule 8 refers to industries having less pollution potential. These industries must apply to the local authority which must again submit the application to the Minister. However, in this case the Minister will only advise the local authority on whether it should approve the submission and suggest conditions of approval.

2.3.4 Western Australia

Clean Air Regulations were promulgated in 1967 under the *Clean Air Act 1964.* The same concept of scheduled premises is applied as in the other States. These include such industries as:

> abrasive blasting works; cement works; fibreglass works; ferrous and non-ferrous metal plants where smelting, casting or coating operations are carried out; grinding and milling works; oil refineries; metal smelters; scrap metal recovery plants; sewage or waste water treatment plants; stock holding paddocks; any premises with boilers.

In 1981, the *Clean Air Act* was amended giving the Minister power to revoke licenses and to impose conditions at any time. The *Clean Air Regulations* were also amended, the main changes being that dark smoke is now defined as that being greater than Ringelmann 1 and the introduction of "Determination of Air Impurities in Gases Discharged to the Atmosphere". Maximum penalties under the Act are $50 000 for corporations and $25 000 for individuals. Table 5 shows the emission standards in the *Clean Air Act.*

In June 1985 responsibility for the *Clean Air Act* was transferred from the Minister of Health to the Minister for the Environment, and the Clean Air Section became a branch of the Department of Conservation and Environment.

Sulphur dioxide control is regulated by control of chimney height calculated in accordance with the UK *Memorandum on Chimney Heights* (Third Edition). The regulation applies to all fuel burning equipment capable of emitting 1.5 kg of sulphur dioxide in one hour. For large industrial premises, a predictive modelling technique for determining ground level concentrations of sulphur dioxide is used. In some designated areas, control is established by environmental protection policies.

There is a trend towards specific requirements by license conditions, rather than general compliance with regulatory limits.

2.3.5 Queensland

Clean air regulations first came into operation in 1968 under the authority of the *Clean Air Act 1963* and were comprehensively reviewed in 1982. Legislation is administered by the Department of Environmental Heritage. Like most other Australian States the legislation provides for licensing of scheduled premises and limitation of pollutant discharges. The schedule includes:

> ceramic works; cement works; glass works; hot-mix plant; concrete works; crushing or grinding works; bauxite or alumina works; sugar mills; primary smelting works; coke works; gas works; galvanized works; chemical works; oil refineries; petroleum products storage; tanneries; rendering works; electric power stations; premises on which more that 300 kg/h of combustible material is burnt or on which more than 30 tonnes/year of metal is melted.

Sulphur dioxide control is achieved by regulating chimney height to the requirements of the Air Pollution Council; there is no prescribed method. The sulphur content of fuel oil is limited to a maximum of 3 per cent by weight throughout the State. Table 6 shows the current major standards for concentration of air impurities.

Emission tests on particulate matter are based on or adjusted to a flue gas carbon dioxide content of 12 per cent boilers and incinerators.

2.3.6 Tasmania

Atmospheric pollution prevention regulations made under the *Environmental Protection Act 1973* apply to both fixed and mobile sources of air pollution.

Scheduled premises are licensed and include all fuel burning installations, chemical plant, cement works, hot-mix plants, crushing and grinding works and primary metallurgical works. In-service motor vehicles are required to meet gaseous and smoke limits.

If fuel oil containing more than 1 per cent sulphur is used, the height of the chimney must be approved by the Director of Environmental Control. Chimney heights and emission limits are generally determined in accordance with the Victorian EPA's *Plume Calculation Procedure*(publication 98/1980) and the US *Guidelines for Air Quality Maintenance Planning and Analysis*, Vol. 10.

Standards (Table 7) for pollutant concentrations at the point of emission can be exceeded when an operator can demonstrate that specified air quality criteria shall be achieved and that the methods adopted for emission control are the best practicable means in current use. The emission of air pollutants not covered in the regulations relating to source emissions (e.g. sulphur dioxide) must meet the specified air quality criteria.

2.3.7 Australian Capital Territory

Air pollution is controlled under the *Air Pollution Act 1984* and *Air Pollution Regulations 1984, No. 24.* The Act seeks to control air pollution from domestic and industrial premises by limiting the burning of combustible material in the open, limiting the emission of specified pollutants (Table 8) and requiring practicable measures to control fugitive emissions. The Authority may require plant to be installed, altered or replaced if the emission standards are exceeded.

2.4 Mobile Sources

The design of vehicles to meet air pollution standards is controlled under the Australian Design Rule System administered by the Federal Department of Transport. Australian Design Rules are agreed by the Australian Transport Advisory Council and attain legislative standing by being included in the Road Traffic Acts of the various States. Australian Design Rules (ADR) for pollution are prepared by a joint advisory committee of the Australian Transport Advisory Council and the Australian and New Zealand Environment Council.

Since 1986, all new motor cars in Australia have to run on 91-93 RON petrol and meet 0.93 g/km for hydrocarbons, 9.3 g/km for carbon monoxide and 1.93 g/km for oxides of nitrogen.

Motor vehicle emissions legislation is also contained in the NSW *Clean Air Act* (see section 2.3.1) and the Victorian *Environment Protection Act* (see section 2.3.2). Although basically similar to the ADRs there are significant differences in the States' legislation. Both NSW and Victoria require every vehicle to comply with the emissions standards and allow no stabilization distance to be accrued by the engine before testing. Vehicles to be tested are taken from manufacturers' agents.

The NSW legislation provides for prohibition of registration and for the recall of vehicles where the proportion failing, or likely to fail the emission test exceeds that prescribed. NSW also requires that all petrol engined vehicles be designed to use unleaded petrol and not just passenger cars and derivatives.

From 1 January 1988, all forward controlled passenger vehicles below 2.7 tonne gross vehicle mass were required to meet ADR-37 in NSW. Inservice smoke control is implemented in NSW, Victoria and Tasmania. All these States limit visible smoke from motor vehicles to a continuous period not exceeding 10 seconds.

2.5 Domestic and Miscellaneous Sources

Legislation in all States applies to all premises to some degree. Domestic and minor sources are generally controlled to a less stringent standard than for those premises covered by licensing. Normally, regulations covering such premises are limited to the more common pollutants like smoke, particulate matter, soot, etc. and frequently single household residences are exempted from controls such as open burning of garden and kitchen refuse, which are applicable to smaller industrial and commercial premises.

Emission of solid particles is set by regulation in the various States to a level in the range of 0.4 to 0.5 g/m^3 for non-scheduled premises and smoke to either Ringelmann shade 1 or 2. Enforcement of legislation is generally by the local, municipal or shire authority.

There is a growing trend in the more heavily populated cities in Australia for increasing restriction on the burning of domestic and garden refuse by individual households. Refuse burning is either prohibited or restricted to a few hours per day in several cities.

Most States prohibited open burning of refuse on industrial and commercial premises in large urban areas during the 1970s. Agricultural open burning is normally permitted as is open burning for bush fire hazard reduction and fire fighting training.

Because home heating is frequently fuelled by gas, electricity or low sulphur liquid fuel, the significance of home heating as a regional air pollution problem is limited to relatively few areas where topographical and meteorological factors combine with widespread use of wood or bituminous coal. Otherwise, air pollution is normally limited to local nuisance problems caused by poorly maintained or badly operated heaters.

2.6 Ozone Layer Protection

The Federal Government enacted the *Ozone Protection Act 1989* to give effect to the 1987 Montreal Protocol. As well as legislating for a 50 per cent reduction (1986 base) in designated ozone depleting substance by 1998, it calls for a progressive reduction in export of CFCs and halons by 5 per cent per year and restricts certain end-uses such as do-it-yourself automotive air conditioning refrigerant replacement, some aerosol propellant and polystyrene foam blowing applications.

All States have introduced legislation to partly or wholly implement the provisions of the Australian and New Zealand Environment Council Strategy for Ozone Control. This sets a target of 95 per cent reduction of designated substances by 1995 and an effective total phase out by 1998.

2.7 Nuisance

Some States have introduced legislation specifically to tackle the major nuisance problem of odour. The level of odour at which an offense is committed varies from State to State. A system of odour units is used in one State, based on theoretical dispersion to the boundary of the premises or beyond to set a maximum "in stack" odour concentration on the license for that industry. Other States rely on an "Authorized Officer" to detect odours outside the boundaries of the premises at a level that is either offensive or detectable, depending on the State.

There is also a growing trend for authorized officers to be permitted to issue a notice requiring a polluter to stop the process or operation which is causing a serious nuisance or health hazard.

3 IMPLEMENTATION AND ENFORCEMENT

3.1 National Enforcement

The Federal Government is responsible for controlling pollution from mobile sources and may also have removed any former powers exercised by the States. At national level, the Department of the Arts,

Sport, the Environment, Tourism and Territories has the following areas of interest:

- policy, rather than day to day operations, in regulatory control;
- cooperation and work with States and Territories for a nationally uniform approach to environmental management;
- in the specific area of air quality, endeavour to achieve national coordination mainly through the Australian and New Zealand Environment Council (ANZEC) and its technical committees;
- provide secretariat services for the ANZEC and its technical committees;
- implement, in collaboration with State authorities, a National Air Monitoring Programme which includes the operation of a national Air Quality Data Centre. The Data Centre collates, archives and analyses data so that uniform and comparable data and statistics are readily available to guide the development of Government policies and for use by research institutes and the private sector;
- provide advice to the Commonwealth in international activities directed towards safeguarding and improving the global air environment, on issues such as the greenhouse effect and protection of stratospheric ozone.

The Federal Government also increasingly plays a coordinating role with regard to other forms of pollution through intergovernmental groups such as the National Health & Medical Research Council (NH&MRC), the ANZEC and the Australian Transport Advisory Council (ATAC). They issue guidelines such as recommended emission concentrations from new plant for a variety of common air impurities, recommended ambient air quality goals, uniform methods of measuring air impurities and design rules for emission controls on new motor vehicles sold in Australia. State authorities are encouraged to take these national figures into account when setting their own legislated emission limits on air quality standards.

3.2 State Enforcement

Each State operates its own control authority from the respective capital city and, because distances are often great between major industrial and population centres, most States operate regional offices. States carry out all licensing activities for air pollution from stationary sources and are responsible for enforcement of statutes on all such licensed premises.

Control of non-licensed (non-scheduled) sources is normally through the health departments of local councils.

Implementation and enforcement is achieved by one or more of the following means, according to the judgement and experience of the responsible authority:

- negotiate with the operator of the plant to improve the standard of equipment or the level of maintenance and operation to achieve the desired performance;
- attach conditions to the license issued under the *Clean Air Act*, if the operation is scheduled;
- issue a notice to install, alter or repair equipment to obtain necessary level of control;
- prosecute for failure to comply with a regulation or requirement of the Act.

Manpower levels for control of air pollution in the State authorities is in the range 10 - 15 per million of population. In those States with motor vehicle emission control facilities, the manpower levels are increased by 2 - 3 per million of population. These numbers cover the control, enforcement, monitoring and management functions.

3.3 Monitoring

Each State control authority monitors air quality within its jurisdiction. Air monitoring effectively commenced in the 1960s and early 1970s as a result of the passing of clean air legislation in the various States. Over the years, it has expanded to include a wide range of pollutants. There are now indications of a reduction in input to monitoring as air quality has progressively improved to levels acceptable to most recognized standards, except in a few areas where specific pollutants are still a problem.

There is also a growing trend to require ambient air quality monitoring to be carried out by the major polluters in an area, rather than by the State control authorities. At present, this only extends to such plants as major electricity power stations, large aluminium, copper, lead and zinc smelters, open cut mines, and steelworks. The number and range of industries being required to undertake air quality monitoring is expanding.

Standards Australia has published standard methods for measuring the major air pollutants and adherence to standard methods is considered important to validate comparisons against air quality goals or standards that have been adopted by various authorities.

Each State publishes its own annual report of air quality monitoring which summarizes and analyses air quality trends.

Table 9 sets out air quality goals currently recommended by the National Health and Medical Research Council. Victoria has adopted Air Quality Objectives and Tasmania has also published Ambient Air Quality Criteria. The State of Victoria's Environment Protection Policy also contains comprehensive schedules of Indicators and Design Ground Level concentrations.

4 FUTURE DEVELOPMENTS

As with most industrialized nations of the world, all governments in Australia are coming under increasing electoral pressure to become "greener".

Legislation aimed at protection of the ozone layer has now been passed in all States and Federally. Likewise the National Government legislated in 1989 to take over all motor vehicle emission standard setting. Until then only the two most populous States had brought in such legislation. The National Government also adopted a goal of 20 per cent reduction in greenhouse gases by the year 2000 and is examining the economic implications of such a reduction. A programme to plant one billion trees was announced in 1989.

Through the Australian Environment Council, a forum of Federal and State Environment Ministers, there is a strong move for greater consistency of environmental standards and for a progressive tightening of these standards. Also, when any State develops a new control guideline for an industry or process, all States are encouraged (following consultation) to adopt it, and thus produce an accepted national guideline.

The National Government has recently put forward for discussion a proposal for a Federal environmental protection agency; it is suggested that it would formally take over from the States all setting of emission standards and air quality criteria. This degree of centralizing power is unlikely to proceeed in the short term; greater cooperation within the framework of the Environment Council is preferred.

5 BIBLIOGRAPHY

Most air pollution control, research and policy development in Australia is carried out by or on behalf of the individual State agencies. Accordingly most literature deals with issues within a particular State or region of a State. There are very few publications that provide an integral perspective of air pollution activity in all Australia. Some, listed below, represent multiple papers sufficient to derive an impression of most (if not all) States.

Australian Environment Council & National Health and Medical Research Council (1986). *National Guidelines for Control of Emission of Air Pollutants from New Stationary Sources: Recommended Methods for Monitoring Air Pollutants in the Environment. 1985.* Australian Government Publishing Service, Canberra.

Australian Environment Council. *Report No. 22, Air Emission Inventories (1985) for the Australian Capital Cities.* Compiled by V. Farrington. Australian Government Publishing Service, Canberra.

CASANZ (1990). International Clean Air Conference: Proceedings Auckland, NZ, March 1990. (Ed. Philippa Gibson).

CASANZ (1990). *Air Pollution Measurement - A Practical Guide to Sampling and Analysis.* 4th Edition.

CASANZ (1990). *Air Pollution Control Manual.* 2nd Edition.

Gilpin A (1980). *Environment Policy in Australia.* University of Queensland Press - CH 8 Air Pollution.

Table 1: National Guidelines For Control of Emission on Air Pollutants From New Stationary Sources: Schedule of Pollutants

Pollutant	*Standard applicable to*	*Standard*	*Notes*
Dark smoke (a)	Stationary fuel-burning sources		
	1. Fired by solid fuel	Ringelmann 1	
	2. Fired by any other fuel	Ringelmann 1	
	Shipping	Ringelmann 1	
Opacity (a) (excluding effect of water vapour)	All sources except the following:	20%	
	Portland cement plants		
	– clinker cooler	10%	
	— other	20%	
	Nitric acid plants	10%	
	Iron and steel plants		
	— basic oxygen process furnaces	10%	
	— dust handling equipment	10%	
	— other	20%	
	Primary aluminium reduction plants		
	— prebake	10%	
	— other	20%	
	Lime manufacturing plants		
	— rotary lime kilns	10%	
	— other	20%	
	Petroleum refinery FCCU		
	— other	30%	
	Kraft pulp mills		
	— recovery furnaces	35%	
	— other	20%	
Solid particles	Boilers other than power stations burning solid fuels	0.25 g/cu.m	12%CO2 reference level
	Power station boiler Incinerators	0.08 g/cu.m	12%CO2 reference level
	— less than 300 kg/hr	0.5 g/cu.m	12%CO2 reference level
	equal to or greater than 300 kg/hr	0.25 g/cu.m	12%CO2 reference level
	Furnaces for the heating of metals	0.1 g/cu.m	Except where standards in Schedule of hazardous pollutants apply

Pollutant	Standard applicable to	Standard	Notes
	Any other trade, industry process industrial plant or fuelburning equipment	0.25 g/cu.m	
Soot	Any boiler or furnace burning liquid or gaseous fuels	Bacharach Shade 3	Other than for lighting or soot blowing
Sulphuric acid mist and sulphur trioxide	Any trade, industry or process other than sulphuric acid plants and fuelburning equipment	0.1 g/cu.m expressed as SO_3	
	Fuelburning equipment	0.2 g/cu.m expressed as SO_3	
	Sulphuric acid plants or plants producing sulphur trioxide	0.075 kg/t of 100% acid or equivalent	
Sulphur dioxide	Any trade, industry or process manufacturing sulphuric acid	2.0 kg/t of 100% acid	
Acid gases		0.4 g/cu.m	Acid gases and mists readily soluble in water and expressed as hydrochloric acid
Nitric acid or Oxides of Nitrogen	Nitric Acid Plants	2.0 g/cu.m	Expressed as NO_2
	Steam Boilers		Nitrogen oxides calculated as NO_2 at a 7% oxygen reference level (b)
	● For liquid and solid fuels		
	— general industrial	0.5 g/cu.m	
	— for electricity generation where rated electrical output is as follows:		
	less than 30 MW	0.5 g/cu.m	
	greater than 30 MW	0.8 g/cu.m	
	● For gaseous fuels	0.35 g/cu.m	
	Gas Turbines		Nitrogen oxides calculated as NO_2 at a 15% oxygen reference level (b).
	● For gaseous fuels		
	— rated electrical output as follows:		
	less than 10 MW	0.09 g/cu.m	
	greater than 10 MW	0.07 g/cu.m	
	For other fuels		
	— rated electrical output as follows:		
	less than 10 MW	0.09 g/cu.m	
	greater than 10 MW	0.15 g/cu.m	

Pollutant	*Standard applicable to*	*Standard*	*Notes*
Fluoride compounds	Any process or industrial plant used for the manufacture of aluminium from alumina	0.02 g/cu.m expressed as hydrofluoric acid	
		1.0 kg F or F compounds expressed as F per tonne of aluminium produced	Limit refers to total emissions from new primary aluminium smelting facilities
	Any other trade, industry or process	0.05 g/cu.m expressed as hydrofluoric acid	
Chlorine and Chlorine compounds other than Hydrochloric Acid	Any trade, industry or process	0.2 g/cu.m expressed as chlorine	
Carbon monoxide	Any trade, industry or process other than cement manufacture, brick manufacture and stationary industrial diesels	1.0 g/cu.m	Processes exempt should be fitted with stacks in order to achieve adequate dispersion
Hydrogen sulphide	Any trade, industry or process	5.0 mg/cu.m	
Total of antimony, arsenic, cadmium, lead, mercury and vanadium and their respective compounds	Any trade, industry or process	10.0 mg/cu.m	Addition of each metal or compound expressed as the metal in each case
Cadmium and its compounds	Any trade, industry or process	3.0 mg/cu.m expressed as cadmium	
Mercury and its compounds	Any trade, industry or process	3.0 mg/cu.m expressed as mercury	

(a) The more stringent (level) of Dark Smoke or Opacity to apply, dependent on measurements available

(b) The corrected nitrogen oxide emission concentration is calculated as follows:

Corrected NOx concentration = Measured NOx concentration X

$$\frac{[21\%\ \text{volume, minus Reference Oxygen Concentration (\% volume)}]}{[21\%\ \text{volume, minus Measured Oxygen Concentration (\% volume)}]}$$

Pollutant	Standard applicable to	Standard	Notes
SCHEDULE OF HAZARDOUS POLLUTANTS*			
Nickel and its compounds, except nickel carbonyl	Any trade, industry or process	20.0 mg/cu.m expressed as nickel	
Nickel carbonyl	Any trade, industry or process	0.5 mg/cu.m expressed as nickel	Tentative standard only
Beryllium and its compounds	Extraction plants, ceramic plants, foundries, etc.	10.0 g over 24 hr period	Limit refers to total emissions from all points in a facility
Mercury and its compounds	Mineral ore processing and mercury cell chlor-alkali plants	2300 g over 24 hr period	Limit refers to total emissions from all points in a facility
	Waste-water-sludge incinerators	3200 g over 24 hr period	Limit refers to total emissions from all points in a facility
Vinyl chloride monomer	Ethylene dichloride purification	20.0 mg/cu.m	
	Oxychlorination	0.1 g/kg 100% ethylene dichloride product	Limit refers to total emissions from all points in a facility
	Vinyl chloride formation and purification	20.0 mg/cu.m	
	Polyvinyl chloride polymerisation plants	20.0 mg/cu.m	
Asbestos	An emission standard for asbestos fibres is at present exceedingly difficult to define. To assist in the design of equipment for the control of asbestos emissions, the following is recommended: All emissions shall be passed through a fabric filter collection device complying with section 61.154 of the United States Federal Register 48 (135):p, 32132, July 13, 1983, or equivalent before they escape to or are vented to the outside air. There shall be no visible emissions. Best available control technology shall be used to minimise fugitive emissions. There shall be no visible fugitive emissions.		

*These pollutants will be kept under review. Further standards will be declared when appropriate.

Table 2: New South Wales — Clean Air Regulations (Stationary Sources)
(Applicable to all scheduled premises and scheduled equipment and to non-scheduled premises where noted.)

Pollutant	*Standard applicable to*	*Standard*	*Notes*
Smoke	Fuel burning equipment (except kilns used for the firing of bricks, tiles, pipes, pottery or refractories) or industrial plant where the fuel being used is coal or in connection with which fire is being used to burn coal	R2	Applies to Group A and also applies to non-scheduled premises
		R3	For lighting up any boiler or incinerator for a period of 20 min/24 hr. Applies to Group A and also applies to non-scheduled premises
		R3	For soot blowing of boiler for a period of 10 min/8 hr when burning 1 t of fuel/hr or 20 min/8 hr when burning 1 t fuel/hr and 5 t fuel/hr or 30 min/8 hr when burning > 5 t fuel/hr
			Applies to Group A
		R3	For soot blowing of boiler on non-scheduled premises for a period 10 min/8 hr
	All other fuel burning equipment (except kilns used for firing of bricks, tiles, pipes, pottery, or refractories) or industrial plant where fuel being used is other than coal or in connection with which matter other than coal is burnt	R1	Applies to Group A and also applies to all fuel burning equipment and industrial plant on non-scheduled premises where the fuel is other than coal
	All fuel burning equipment or industrial plant	R1	Applies to Group B
		R3	Applies to Group B where fuel used is coal, for soot blowing or lighting up, for a period of 10 min/8 hr

Pollutant	*Standard applicable to*	*Standard*	*Notes*
	Kilns used for firing of bricks, tiles, pipes, pottery or refractories except kilns used for firing dark-red and dark-brown face bricks formed by dry-press brick machines	R2	Darker than R2 but always R3 for not more than 10 min/hr
	Kilns used for firing dark-red and dark-brown face bricks formed by dry-press brick machines	R3	
Soot	Any boiler or furnace consuming oil or gas	Bacharach 3	Also applies to non-scheduled premises
Particulate Matter	Any trade, industry, process, industrial plant or fuel burning equipment excluding boilers and incinerators	0.4 g/cu.m	Applies to Group A, except for installations where plant is used for heating of metals (other than cold-blast foundry cupolas) Also applies to non-scheduled premises
		0.25 g/cu.m	Applies to Group B, except for installations where plant is used for the heating of metals or metal ores (other than cold-blast foundry cupolas)
	Boilers or incinerators emitting solid particles	0.4 g/cu.m	Adjusted to a basis of 12% CO2. Applies to Group A and also applies to non-scheduled premises
		0.25 g/cu.m	Adjusted to a basis of 12% CO2 Applies to Group B
	Plant used for heating metals	0.25 g/cu.m	Other than cold-blast foundry cupolas

Pollutant	*Standard applicable to*	*Standard*	*Notes*
Sulfuric acid mist or Sulfur trioxide	Any trade, industry or process emitting sulfuric acid mist or sulphur trioxide	0.2 g/cu.m as SO3	Applies to Group A
		0.1 g/cu.m as SO3	Applies to Group B which also includes fuel burning equipment and industrial plant emitting sulfuric acid mist or sulfur trioxide
Oxides of Nitrogen	Any trade, industry or process emitting oxides of nitrogen	2.5 g/cu.m as nitrogen dioxide (NO2)	New installations to tighter limits by licence condition (typically 0.5 to 1.0 g/cu.m)
Sulfur Dioxide	Any trade, industry or process manufacturing sulfur acid		
	(a) from elemental sulfur emitting sulfur dioxide	5.6 g/cu.m	Applies to Group A
		2.8 g/cu.m	Applies to Group B
	(b) using as the source of sulfur other than elemental sulfur	7.2 g/cu.m	
Fluorine, Hydrofluoric acid, Inorganic Fluorine Compounds	(i) Any trade, industry or process unless manufacturing aluminium from alumina	0.1 g/cu.m as hydrofluoric acid (HF)	Applies to Group A
		0.05 g/cu.m as HF	Applies to Group B
	(ii) Any trade, industry or process manufacturing from alumina		
	(a) Entire premises	0.04 g/cu.m as HF	Applies to Group A
		0.02 g/cu.m as HF	To installations for which application for approval made after January 1972 and before 1 July 1979
	(b) From individual sources	0.02 g/cu.m as HF	To installations for which application for approval made after 1 July 1979
	1. Roof ventilators of a potroom group	0.8 kg fluoride per tonne of aluminium produced	

Pollutant	Standard applicable to	Standard	Notes
	2. The control system serving a potroom group	0.15 kg fluoride per tonne of aluminium produced	
	3. Anode bake plant of a primary aluminium smelter	0.05 kg of fluoride per tonne of aluminium equivalent produced	
Chlorine	Any trade, industry or process emitting chlorine gas	0.2 g/cu.m as chlorine	
Hydrogen Sulfide	Any trade, industry or process emitting hydrogen sulfide gas	5 mg/cu.m	
Total of Lead, Arsenic, Antimony, Cadmium, Mercury or any compound thereof	Any trade, industry or process	20 mg/cu.m total expressed as their elements	
Total of Lead, Arsenic Antimony, Cadmium, Mercury and Vanadium and any of their compounds	Any trade, industry or process	10 mg/cu.m for all elements and compounds of these elements with maximum of 3 mg/cu.m each for mercury + compounds and cadmium + compounds	Applies to Group B
		Cd and its compounds alone 3 mg/cu.m as Cd alone	Will apply for new plants
		Hg and its compounds alone 3 mgm	Will apply for new plants
Hydrogen chloride	Any trade, industry or process emitting acids or acid gases excepting the industry manufacturing glazed terra cotta roofing tiles	0.4 gm/cu.m as HC1	

Pollutant	*Standard applicable to*	*Standard*	*Notes*
Organic Vapours	Storage of prescribed organic liquids* stored in large stationary tanks and:		Limits for both incineration (a), and recovery (b) applies to all installations in Sydney, Newcastle and Wollongong areas
	(a) if vapours emitted from the tank are incinerated	1.5 gm/cu.m of unburnt organic vapours	adjusted to a basis of 12% 002
	(b) if vapours emitted from the tank are recovered	110 mg for each litre of organic liquid passing into the tank	during any period of 4 hours
	Transfer of prescribed organic liquids* into delivery tanks capacity exceeding 12kL at a rate exceeding 30 ML per year		Limits for both incineration (a), and recovery (b) applies to all installations in the Sydney area adjusted to a basis of 12% 002
	(a) if vapours emitted from the tank are incinerated	1.5 gm/cu.m of unburnt organic vapours	
	(b) if vapours resulting from loading operations are recovered	110 mg for each litre of organic liquid passing out of the plant	during any period of 4 hours

Group A covers all installations on scheduled premises, for which an application for approval under Section 16 of the Clean Air Act were made before 1 January 1972.

Group B covers all installations on scheduled premises, for which an application for approval pursuant to Section 16 of the Clean Air Act is made on or after 1 January 1972.

*Prescribed organic liquids include crude oil, crude petroleum, petrol, gasoline (or other liquids suitable for spark ignition engines but not tractor vaporising oil) and any liquid containing more than 50% by volume of heptene, toluene, trichlorethylene, xylene, or any mixture of these.

Table 3: Victoria — Schedule G Emission Limits for Stationary Sources

Pollutant	*Standard applicable to*	*Standard (a) (b)*		*Notes*
1. Visible emissions	All stationary sources except 1. Smoke from fires set for the reduction of a fire hazard or for instruction in the methods of fighting fire or forestry operations. 2. Normal agricultural operations.	Ringelmann 1 (BS 2742C, 1957); or of such opacity as to obscure an observer's view to the same degree as emissions corresponding with Ringlemann I, above.		1. Ringlemann 2 acceptable for periods aggregating not more than 3 minutes in any 60 min. period. 2. Does not apply to emission of water vapour.
2. Combustion particulates	Solid fuel fired units All other units	0.3 g/cu.m 0.25 g/cu.m		Gas volume calculated 12 per cent CO2
3. Particulate matter	All stationary sources except fuel fired units for steam or electricity generation and incinerators and glass manufacturing furnaces	Process Weight Rate kg/min	Max Emission Rate g/min	
		0-3	17.5	Process weight is the weight of all materials introduced into any specific process which may discharge contaminants into the atmosphere: solid fuels charged shall be considered as part of the process weight, but liquid and gaseous fuels and air shall not
		3.0-10	17.5 plus 2.5 per kg/min, process weight in excess of 3.	
		10-100	35 plus 1.0 per kg/min. process weight in excess of 10.	
		over 100	125 plus 0.2 per kg/min. process weight in excess of 100.	
4. Total particulate	All stationary sources	0.5 g/cu.m		
5. Sulfur Dioxide	Sulfuric acid plants	5.6 g/cu.m		
6. Sulfuric acid mist and Sulfur trioxide	All stationary sources	0.2 g/cu.m as SO3		

Pollutant	*Standard applicable to*	*Standard (a) (b)*	*Notes*
7. Hydrogen sulfide	All stationary sources	7.5 mg/cu.m	
8. Nitric acid and Oxides of Nitrogen	Nitric acid plants	3.0 g/cu.m of nitric acid plus nitrogen oxides, calculated as NO2	
9. Oxides of Nitrogen	Fuel burning units (other than internal combustion engines and glass manufacturing plants) having a maximum heat input rate greater than 150 000 MJ/h gross.	1.0 g/cu.m	Nitrogen calculated as a 7 per cent oxygen reference level (c). Emission limit = Cm(20.9 — %02 reference) / 20.9 — %02 measured
10. Lead and its compounds	All stationary sources	10 mg/cu.m expressed as lead	
11. Fluoride compounds	Any new sources manufacturing aluminium from alumina	0.02 g/cu.m expressed as HF	
	All other stationary sources	0.05 g/cu.m expressed as HF	
12. Chlorine and Chlorine compounds	All stationary sources	0.2 g/cu.m expressed as chlorine	
13. Total of Antimony Arsenic, Cadmium, Lead and Mercury		10 mg/cu.m (Addition of each metal or compound expressed as the metal in each case).	
14. Antimony and its compounds		10 mg/cu.m expressed as antimony	
15. Arsenic and its compounds		10 mg/cu.m expressed as arsenic	
16. Cadmium		3 mg/cu.m expressed as cadmium	
17. Nickel and its compounds except Nickel Carbonyl		20 mg/cu.m expressed as nickel	
18. Nickel Carbonyl		0.5 mg/cu.m expressed as nickel	

(a) Gas volumes are expressed dry at 0°C at an absolute pressure of one atmosphere (101.325 kPa).
(b) Dilution of wastes to meet emission limits shall not be permitted except where noted.
(c) Cm is the measured concentration of oxides of nitrogen in grams per cubic metre.
Oxygen concentrations are expressed on a volumetric basis.

Schedule H Emission Limits for New Stationary Sources in Air Quality Regions

Pollutant	*Standard applicable to*	*Standard (a) (b)*	*Notes*
1. Visible emissions	All stationary sources except 1. Smoke from fires set for the reduction of a fire hazard or for instruction in the methods of fighting fire or forestry operations. 2. Normal agricultural operations.	Ringelmann 1 (BS 2742C, 1957); or of such opacity as to obscure an observer's view to the same degree as emissions corresponding with Ringlemann I, above.	1. Ringlemann 2 acceptable for periods aggregating not more than 3 minutes in any 60 min. period. 2. Does not apply to emission of water vapour.
2. Combustion particulates	(a) All stationary sources except as described hereunder. (b) Incinerators with design burning rates of 300 kg per hour or less	0.25 g/cu.m 0.5 g/cu.m	Gas volume calculated 12 per cent CO_2
3. Particulate matter	All stationary sources except fuel fired units for steam or electricity generation, incinerators and glass manufacturing furnaces	Process Weight Rate kg/min — Max Emission Rate g/min 0.3 — 14 3.0-10 — 14 plus 2.0 per kg/min, process weight in excess of 3. 10-100 — 28 plus 0.8 per kg/min. process weight in excess of 10. over 100 — 100 plus 0.18 per kg/min. process weight in excess of 100.	Process weight is the weight of all materials introduced into any specific process which may discharge contaminants into the atmosphere: solid fuels charged shall be considered as part of the process weight, but liquid and gaseous fuels and air shall not
4. Total particulate matter	All stationary sources except as provided in 2b	0.25 g/cu.m	
5. Sulfur Dioxide	Sulfuric acid plants	2.0 k/g tonne of 100% acid	
6. Sulfuric acid mist and Sulfur trioxide	(a) All stationary sources (b) Sulfuric acid plants	0.2 g/cu.m as SO_3 0.075 kg/tonne of 100% acid expressed as H_2SO_4	

Pollutant	*Standard applicable to*	*Standard (a) (b)*	*Notes*
7. Hydrogen sulfide	All stationary sources	5.0 mg/cu.m	Any source discharging H2S at a rate of less than 2 g/h may dilute to meet the provisions of Section 7.
8. Nitric acid and Oxides of Nitrogen	Nitric acid plants	2.0 g/cu.m of nitric acid plus nitrogen oxides, calculated as NO2	
9. Oxides of Nitrogen	Fuel burning units (other than internal combustion engines and glass manufacturing plants) having a maximum heat input rate greater than 150 000 MJ/h gross except as described hereunder:	(a) 0.35 g/cu.m for gaseous fuels (b) 0.5 g/cu.m or liquid or solid fuels	Nitrogen oxides calculated as NO2 at a 7% oxygen reference level (c). Emission limit = Cm(20.9 — %02 reference) 20.9 — %02 measured
	Power station boilers for electricity generation of rated output equal to or greater than 250 MW	0.7 g/cu.m for solid fuels	This limit may be relaxed to 0.78 g/cu.m in individual cases where it can be shown that 0.7 g/cu.m is too restrictive in relation to such matters as the type of fuel being burned, existing emission control technology and factors of health and safety.
	Gas turbines for electricity generation — Rated output equal to or greater than 30 MW	(a) 0.07 g/cu.m for gaseous fuels (b) 0.15 g/cu.m for other	Nitrogen oxides calculated as NO2 at a 15 per cent oxygen reference level (c).
	— Rated output less than 30 MW	0.09 g/cu.m for gaseous fuels	
10. Carbon Monoxide	All stationary sources except internal combustion engines and cold blast cupolas	2.5 g/cu.m	
11. Lead and its compounds	All stationary sources	10 mg/cu.m expressed as lead	
12. Fluorine compounds	Any plant manufacturing aluminium from alumina	0.02 g/cu.m expressed as HF	
	All other sources	0.05 g/cu.m expressed as HF	
13. Chlorine and Chlorine compounds	All stationary sources	0.2 g/cu.m expressed as chlorine	

Pollutant	*Standard applicable to*	*Standard (a) (b)*	*Notes*
14. Total of Antimony, Arsenic, Cadmium, Lead and Mercury		10 mg/cu.m (Addition of each metal or compound expressed as the metal in each case)	
15. Antimony and its compounds		10 mg/cu.m expressed as antimony	
16. Arsenic and its compounds		10 mg/cu.m expressed as arsenic	
17. Cadmium		3 mg/cu.m expressed as cadmium	
18. Nickel and its compounds except Nickel Carbonyl		20 mg/cu.m expressed as nickel	
19. Nickel Carbonyl		0.5 mg/cu.m expressed as nickel	

(a) Gas volumes are expressed dry at 0°C at an absolute pressure of one atmosphere (101.325 kPa)
(b) Dilution of wastes to meet emission limits shall not be permitted except where noted.
(c) Cm is the measured concentration of oxides of nitrogen in grams per cubic metre.
Oxygen concentrations are expressed on a volumetric basis.

Table 4: South Australia

Pollutant	*Standard applicable to*	*Standard*	*Notes*
Smoke	All fuel burning equipment or industrial plant	R1	Where fuel used is coal or wood or forms part of a vessel
			R3 for up to 10 mins. in 8 hours when lighting up and soot blowing.
Particulate matter	All stationary sources except	0.25 g/cu.m	Adjusted to 12% CO2 for incinerators and boilers
	plants for metal heating other than cold blast foundary cupolas	0.10 g/cu.m	
	Incinerators	0.45 g/cu.m	
Sulfuric acid mist and Sulfuric trioxide	Any industry, operation or process fuel burning equipment or plant emitting H2SO4 mist or SO3 except:	0.2 g/cu.m as SO3	
	manufacture of H2SO4	3.0 g/cu.m as SO3	Effluent gas not to contain persistent mist
Nitric acid, Oxides of Nitrogen	Any industry operation or process except:	0.5 g/cu.m as NO2	Effluent gas shall be colourless
	manufacture HN0 or H2SO4	2.0 g/cu.m as N02	
Fluorine, Hydrofluoric acid, Inorganic Fluorine Compounds	Any trade, plant or industry except: Manufacture of Al from Al203 (Primary Smelter)	0.05 g/cu.m as HF .02 g/cu.m as HF	
Chlorine	Any industry operation or process	0.20 g/cu.m as Cl2	
Hydrogen sulfide	Any industry operation or process	5 mg/cu.m	
Total of Lead, Arsenic, Antimony, Cadium, Mercury or any compound thereof	Any industry operation or process	0.01 g/cu.m total expressed as the element	Addition of each metal or compound expressed as the metal in each case Cd or Hg alone max is 3 mg/cu.m
Carbon monoxide	Any industry operation or process	1 g/cu.m	

Note: Emission limits apply to plants commissioned after July 1984
For plants commissioned before 1984 emission limits contained in the Clean Air Regulation 1969 and 1972 under the Health Act 1935 or as issued as a requirement under those regulations apply

Table 5: Western Australia

Pollutant	*Standard applicable to*	*Standard*	*Notes*
Smoke	All industrial premises	R1	Maximum 4 mins. in the hour
	Lighting up, each chimney	R1	Maximum 20 mins. in the aggregate in any period of 24 hours

Note: In general the Minister for the Environment uses the National guidelines for control of emission of air pollutants from new stationary sources, when setting standard for new plant in WA.

Table 6: Queensland

Pollutant	*Standard applicable to*	*Standard*	*Notes*
Smoke	All industrial plant or fuel burning equipment except ceramic kilns and vessels	R2	Aggregate emission of 16 minutes/ 8 hours
		R3	Continuous emission for up to 2 minutes/30 minutes
	Ceramic furnaces		
	— not reducing	R2	Aggregate of 5 minutes/hour
	—reducing	R3	Aggregate of 4 hours/24 hours
	Vessels		
	— propelling machinery	R2	Aggregate of 10 minutes/hour
	— non propelling machinery	R2	Aggregate of 5 minutes/hour

Pollutant	*Standard applicable to*	*Standard*	*Notes*
Particulate matter	Any trade, industry or process except:	0.45 g/cu.m	
	Sugar mill boilers installed prior to 1 June, 1972	0.8 g/cu.m	
	Heating of metals other than cold blast cupolas	0.1 g/cu.m	
Sulfuric acid mist or Sulfur trioxide	Any trade, industry or process except combustion processes and H2SO4 manufacture	0.2 g/cu.m as SO3	
Nitric acid Oxides of Nitrogen	Any trade, industry or process except HNO3 manufacture	2.5 g/cu.m equivalent of nitrogen dioxide	
Fluorine, Hydrofluoric acid, Inorganic Fluorine	Any trade except manufacture of aluminium from alumina	0.1 g/cu.m as HF	
Chlorine	Any trade	0.2 g/cu.m	
Hydrogen sulfide	Any trade	5 ppm v/v	
Lead, Arsenic, Antimony, Cadium, Mercury or any of their compounds	Any trade	0.02 g/cu.m total as element	

Table 7: Tasmania: Emission Standards

Pollutant	*Standard applicable to*	*Standard*	*Notes*
Smoke	All stationary fuel burning equipment		
	(1) in operation before 1/1/75	R2	
	except during lighting up,	R3	Max. 20 mins. in 24 hrs.
	or soot blowing	R5	In an 8 hr period once for max. 10 mins with fuel cons. 1t/h; 20 mins with fuel cons. 1t-5t/h; 30 mins with fuel cons. 5t/h
	(2) Commencing after 1/1/75	R1	
	except during lighting up or soot blowing	R3	Once for max. 10 mins in 8 hrs.
Soot	All stationary fuel burning equipment	Bacharach 3	
Particulate Matter	All stationary fuel burning equipment		
	(1) In operation before 1/1/75	0.46 g/cu.m	adjusted to 12% CO2
	(2) commencing after 1/1/75	0.25 g/cu.m	adjusted to 12% CO2
	Metal heating except cold blast foundry cupolas	0.25 g/cu.m	operating before 1/1/75
		0.1 g/cu.m	commencing after 1/1/75
	Other installations	0.46 g/cu.m	operating before 1/1/75
		0.25 g/cu.m	commencing after 1/1/75

Pollutant	*Standard applicable to*	*Standard*	*Notes*
Sulphuric acid mist of Sulphur trioxide	H2S04 manufacture other than from elemental S	9.2 g/cu.m as S03	
	H2S04 manufacture from elemental S	7.0 g/cu.m as S03	operating before 1/1/75
		3.0 g/cu.m as S03	commencing after 1/1/75
	all other plants	0.23 g/cu.m as S02	operating before 1/1/75
		0.1 g/cu.m as S03	operating after 1/1/75
Nitric acid, Oxides of Nitrogen	HN03 or H2S04 manufacture	4.6 g/cu.m as N02	operating before 1/1/75
		1.0 g/cu.m as N02	commencing after 1/1/75
	other installations	2.5 g/cu.m as N02	operating before 1/1/75
		1.0 g/cu.m as N02	commencing after 1/1/75
Chlorine	Any installation	0.23 g/cu.m	operating before 1/1/75
		0.2 g/cu.m	commencing after 1/1/75
Fluorine, Hydrofluoric acid, Inorganic Fluorine	Aluminium refineries	0.04 g/cu.m as HF	operating before 1/1/75
		0.02 g/cu.m as HF	commencing after 1/1/75
	Other installations	0.115 g/cu.m as HF	operating before 1/1/75
		0.05 g/cu.m as HF	commencing after 1/1/75
Hydrogen sulphide	All installations	7.5 mg/cu.m	operating before 1/1/75
		0.05 g/cu.m as HF	commencing after 1/1/75
Hydrogen chloride	Installations other than for the manufacture of glazed terra cotta tiles	0.4 g/cu.m	

Pollutant	*Standard applicable to*	*Standard (a) (b)*	*Notes*
Lead Arsenic, Antimony, Cadmium, Mercury and Compounds	Any installation		
	(1) operating before 1/1/75	0.023 g/cu.m	total as elements
	(2) commencing after 1/1/75	0.01 g/cu.m 0.003 g/cu.m	total as elements total as Cd

Table 8: Australian Capital Territory
All concentrations apply after 19/11/84 unless otherwise noted.

Pollutant	*Standard application to*	*Standard*	*Notes*
Smoke	All stationary fuel burning equipment emitting dark smoke	R1	
	except during lighting up	R3	Max. 20 mins. in 24 hrs.
	Soot blowing	R5	Max. 10 mins. in 8 hrs.
	emitting white smoke	20% obscuration	
Soot	Oil or gas fired plant	Bacharach 3	
	except during lighting up	Bacharach 5	Max. 20 mins. in 24 hrs.
	Soot blowing	Bacharach 10	Max. 5 mins. in 8 hrs.

Pollutant	*Standard applicable to*	*Standard*	*Notes*
Particulate Matter	Boilers burning solid fuel incinerators	0.25 g/cu.m	Adjusted to 12% C02
	a. less than 300 kg/hr	0.5 g/cu.m	Adjusted to 12% C02
	b. more than 300 kg/hr	0.25 g/cu.m	Adjusted to 12% C02
	Furnaces for heating metal other than cold blast foundry cupolas	0.1 g/cu.m	
	Any other plant or equipment other than Boilers and Incinerators	0.25 g/cu.m	
Sulphuric acid mist and Sulphur trioxide	Any process	0.1 g/cu.m as sulphur trioxide	
Nitric acid	Any process manufacturing nitric acid	2.0 g/cu.m as nitrogen dioxide	
	Any process manufacturing sulphuric acid	1.0 g/cu.m as nitrogen dioxide	
	Any process other than — a. a process manufacturing nitric acid or sulphuric acid; or b. a gas fired power station	0.5 g/cu.m as nitrogen dioxide	
Oxides of Nitrogen	Any process manufacturing nitric acid	2.0 g/cu.m as nitrogen dioxide	
	Any process manufacturing sulphuric acid	1.0 g/cu.m as nitrogen dioxide	
	Any process other than — a. a process manufacturing nitric acid or sulphuric acid; or b. a gas fired power station	0.5 g/cu.m as nitrogen dioxide	
	Gas fired power station	0.35 g/cu.m as nitrogen dioxide	
Carbon monoxide	Any process	1.0 g/cu.m as carbon monoxide	

Pollutant	Standard applicable to	Standard	Notes
Fluorine and its compounds	Any process manufacturing aluminium from alumina	0.02 g/cu.m as hydrofluoric acid	
	Any other process	0.05 g/cu.m as hydrofluoric acid	
Chlorine and its compounds	Any process	0.2 g/cu.m as chlorine	
Hydrogen sulphide	Any process	5 mg/cu.m as hydrogen sulphide	
Cadmium and its compounds	Any process	3 mg/cu.m as cadmium	
Mercury and its compounds	Any process	3 mg/cu.m as mercury	
Antimony, Arsenic, Cadmium, Lead and Mercury and their compounds	Any process	10 mg/cu.m	Total expressed as individual elements
Acids and acid gases	Any process other than a process manufacturing glazed terra cotta roofing tiles	0.4 g/cu.m as hydrogen chloride	Except for Clinical Waste incinerators which must have scrubbers and meet 0.2 g/cu.m

Table 9: National Ambient Air Quality Objectives
Air Quality Goals Recommended by the National Health and Medical Research Council — Australia

Pollutant	*Goals for maximum permissible levels of pollutants in ambient air** *ug/cu.m*	*ppm*	*Measurement criteria*	*Notes*
Lead	1.5	—	Three months average maximum	—
Photochemical Oxidants (as ozone)	240	0.12	hourly average not to be exceeded more than once a year	A public warning to be given if ozone levels are expected to exceed 500 ug/cu.m (0.25 ppm)
Sulphur Dioxide (S02)	60	0.02	Annual mean	Short term goal in preparation S02 and
Total Suspended Particulates (TSP)	90	—	Annual mean	TSP goals to be read in conjunction
Nitrogen Dioxide (N02)	320	0.16	One-hour level not be to exceeded more than once a month	0.16 ppm replaces 0.17 ppm to conform with the method of measurement
	mg/cu.m	ppm		
Carbon Monoxide (CO)	10.0	9	Eight hour average not to be exceeded more than once a year	This period of measurement is not to be confused with that for Threshold Limit Values

Expressed at 0°C and 101.3 kPa and determined by methods recommended in the AEC/NHMRC document 'Recommended Methods of Monitoring Air Environment' (1985).

BELGIUM

1 INTRODUCTION

1.1 Topography, Climate, Population

Belgium is situated in Western Europe between France and Germany. In the north it shares a border with The Netherlands and it has a 60 km North Sea coast. The population is 9.93 million and the area 30 500 sq. km. The northern Dutch speaking region, called Flanders, has the highest population density and is rather flat, with good farming land in the west and sandy plateaux in the east. The largest industrial areas of Flanders are located around the harbours of Antwerpen and Gent. The chemical industry, metallurgy and refineries are relatively important.

The Belgian capital, Brussels, with a population of one million, has a central position in the fertile undulating plains of middle Belgium. It is the major administrative and business centre, surrounded by mainly lighter industries in the suburban zones.

The southern French speaking part of Belgium, called Wallony, has its industry and population concentrated in the Meuse and Sambre valleys with the cities of Liege and Charleroi. By the 19th century heavy industries like steel works and coal mining had brought prosperity to this region, but the mineral resources have lost significance and since the second half of this century have declined. South of the Sambre-Meuse Valley extends High Belgium with the densely forested Ardennes.

Belgium has a moderate sea climate with cool summers and mild winters. The annual average temperature is 10 degrees C and the annual precipitation 700-1000 mm. The dominant Atlantic southwesterly winds generally give a good dispersion of air pollution, but continental easterly winds with low speed and unfavourable dispersion conditions have caused winter smog or summer ozone episodes during the last few years.

Since 1974 Belgium has been transformed from a unitary state to a federation with three autonomous regions: Flanders, Wallony and Brussels. In environmental matters, especially, the regions have taken over most of the responsibilities of the national government. Only international relations, general standards - such as car emissions or sulphur content of fuels - and radioactivity remain within national jurisdiction.

1.2 Specific National Problems

Belgium has a relatively high density of sulphur dioxide emission sources. While actual total emissions have decreased to about 60 per cent of 1980 levels, since 1985 the pace of reduction has slowed down. Nationwide the annual average concentrations in the air are well below the limit values, but in some cities and industrial areas, days with high concentrations have still occurred in the last few years more frequently than the quality standard allows. The target values set by the World Health Organization for sulphur dioxide are not yet obtained everywhere.

In relation to acid deposition it is obvious that substantial emission reductions are still necessary. The actual Belgian sulphur and nitrogen acidifying emissions account for 8840 equivalents/ha/year, while 2400 eq/ha/y would be tolerable for the least susceptible soils in the long term.

Nitrogen oxides emissions have decreased little since 1980, and were increasing again in 1988-89, due to the ever growing automobile traffic, which accounts for more than half of these emissions. The air quality limit value for nitrogen oxides is not exceeded anywhere, but the target values of 50 $\mu g/m^3$ (median of hourly values) and 135 $\mu g/m^3$ (98 percentile) are not obtained in a few areas. In 1989 and 1990 alarming nitrogen dioxide levels have been reported in traffic tunnels in Brussels. It is doubtful if the growing traffic intensity will be counterbalanced by the expected improvement of exhaust gas quality in the coming years.

Heavy metals in the environment are an old problem at several sites in Belgium where non-ferrous metallurgical plants are located. The pollution from airborne heavy metals however has been greatly reduced. There is an air quality standard of 2 $\mu g/m^3$ annual average for lead, which is now observed everywhere. A remarkable decrease of lead concentrations in city air was obtained by cutting lead concentrations in petrol. The WHO target values for cadmium, lead, arsenic and nickel are still largely exceeded in the vicinity of some metallurgical plants.

Summertime ozone measurements above the hourly "alarm level" of 200 $\mu g/m^3$ in recent years have drawn attention to the fact that hydrocarbon and nitrogen oxides emissions are to be reduced by an estimated 50 per cent. However there is no elaborate strategy for avoiding ozone pollution episodes in the future.

Odour nuisance problems account for the largest number of

complaints about air quality in Belgium, but nevertheless an air quality standard for odour nuisance is not available. Agricultural activities, especially intensive cattle farming, and specific chemical industries are the most frequent cause of complaints.

In the political sphere the absence of a single Ministry for the Environment is a decelerating factor in the approach to environmental problems. At the moment nine national ministers have authority over miscellaneous environmental matters. The most important role is reserved for the State Secretary of the Environment who is under the Minister of Public Health. The creation of three federal administrations, each with their department for the environment, and the transfer of powers to these federal departments, has resulted in a complicated structure, where problems of cooperation remain to be solved.

2 DEVELOPMENT OF AIR POLLUTION CONTROLS AND LEGISLATION

2.1 Principles and Philosophy of Clean Air Legislation

The original principle of air pollution control legislation, as described in the Regental Decree of 11.02.1946, was to reduce nuisance and health risks to the neighbourhood from dangerous, unhealthy and polluting activities, by making such activities subject to prior licensing. This source oriented approach is still in use, with the special conditions attached to the license as the main tool to control air pollution from industrial activities.

The air quality standards approach was introduced by the *Air Pollution Prevention Act 1964*, but an effective Royal Decree on air quality standards for sulphur dioxide and particles did not appear before 1983.

From 1971, fuel quality standards, emission limits and a chimney height formula for combustion sources were introduced as a way of improving air quality, especially in the five metropolitan areas, where special protection zones were established.

In 1979, with the signing of the Geneva Convention, Belgium started to participate in internationally concerted actions to reduce emissions of sulphur dioxide and nitrogen oxides.

At present the European Community Directives on air quality are the basis of Belgian air quality legislation. The development of the federal system has enabled divergencies of environmental standards in the regions, but the national and European standards will have to be implemented as minimum standards.

In general, clean air legislation can be described as realistic, effective and verifiable. The realism implies that the standards are not the most progressive in Europe, but the objectives are feasible with reasonable efforts from the industry. For all pollutants that have legally imposed limit values, monitoring networks are in operation to verify compliance over the entire territory.

2.2 Development of Air Pollution Control Legislation

One of the first documented catastrophes of industrial air pollution occurred in 1930, when the Meuse Valley between Huy and Liege remained covered with a smog of sulphur dioxide and particulates during the first five days of December. Sixty-three people died and several hundred suffered severe respiratory troubles. It was later estimated that sulphur dioxide concentrations as high as 100 000 µg/m^3 may have occurred. The then existing legislation - a Napoleonic decree of 1810, regulating nuisance from certain industrial activities - had clearly not anticipated large scale air pollution. Recommendations to start air quality monitoring and control further industrial expansion did not however result in any legislative action until 1946.

In 1946 the *General Regulation of Labour Protection* came into force, as a completion of the 1810 Decree. Although intended primarily to safeguard health and safety in the workplace, the Regulation remained for more than twenty years the most important set of prescriptions for industrial environmental hygiene, including air pollution, noise, water pollution, radiation and waste.

For emissions from lead and zinc metallurgical plants maximum sulphur content and minimum stack heights are given. The Regulation also contains the classification lists of activities and processes which are subject to authorization. The activities with the highest potential environmental impact, designated as Class I, need a license issued by the provincial government, while Class II can be authorized by the municipalities.

For Class I activities with potential air pollution effects, it is now general practice that emission standards are included in the special conditions attached to the license.

The Act of 28 December 1964 concerning the *Prevention of Air Pollution* is the first legislation specifically aimed at improving air quality. However this Act is a so called "framework" law, which means that itself, it contains no executable clauses, but offers a framework for further regulation by Execution Decrees, mostly Royal Decrees. One important exception to this principle is the power given to the Crown to take all necessary safety measures in the event of serious air pollution. Responsibility for the various matters related to air pollution is divided between several ministerial departments. The Act further contains instructions on the organization of controls and sanctions, and entitles the Minister of Public Health to coordinate all actions to prevent air pollution, specifically air quality monitoring, investigation of health effects, preventive measures and public information.

2.3 Air Quality Legislation

Legally imposed air quality standards in Belgium are limited to sulphur dioxide and suspended particles, lead, and nitrogen dioxide.

2.3.1 Sulphur Dioxide and Suspended Particles

The Royal Decree of 16 March 1983 defines limit values and guide or target values for sulphur dioxide and suspended particles. The limit values which are not to be exceeded from 1 April 1983 are given in Table 1. If still higher values occur after this date, plans are to be submitted which ensure compliance not later than April 1993. The guide values are given in Table 2.

The Regions are entitled to indicate zones where standards are based on guide values and special protection zones where lower standards than the guide values apply. In practice the Regions have not yet designated such zones.

Table 1: Air Quality Standards For Sulphur Dioxide And Suspended Particles

Sulphur Dioxide		
Period	*Maximum allowable value of SO2 µg/m3*	*Related value for suspended particles µg/m3*
	Median of daily values:	Median of daily values:
Year	80	>40
	120	<=40
Winter (Oct-Mar)	130	>60
	180	<=60
Year	98 percentile of daily values:	98 percentile of daily values:
	250(*)	>150
	350(*)	<=150

Suspended Particles, in µg/m3, measured as black smoke	
Period	*Maximum allowable value*
Year	80 Median of daily values
	250(*) 98 percentile daily values
Winter (Oct-Mar)	130 Median of daily values

(*) values not to be exceeded during more than 3 consecutive days

Table 2: Guide Values For Sulphur Dioxide And Suspended Particles

SO2 in µg/m3	
Period	*Guide value*
Year	40 to 60 (arithmetic mean of daily values)
24 hour	100 to 150 (daily average value)
Suspended Particles, in µg/m3, measured as black smoke	
Period	*Guide value*
Year	40 to 60 (arithmetic mean of daily values)
24 hour	100 to 150 (daily average value)

2.3.2 Lead

The Royal Decree of 3 August 1984 imposes an air quality standard for lead of 2 µg/m^3 as an annual average. The standard was applicable from 1 December 1987, and in case of violations plans had to be submitted to obtain this value not later than 1 December 1989. This Decree implements European Directive 82/884/EEC. Before this Decree a special regulation existed for the municipality of Hoboken where a higher level of lead pollution existed which was gradually reduced in order to attain the 2 µg/m^3 limit.

2.3.3 Nitrogen Dioxide

The Royal Decree of 1 July 1987 contains the air quality standard for nitrogen dioxide. The 98 percentile of the hourly values during one year must not exceed 200 µg/m^3. The guide value for the 98 percentile is 135 µg/m^3 and for the 50 percentile 50 µg/m^3.

2.3.4 Other Pollutants

Although there are no legal air quality standards for air pollutants other than the four cited above, quality objectives are sometimes defined with reference to international or foreign guidelines for specific problems. Some examples of these are:

- the Institute of Hygiene and Epidemiology heavy metals quality objectives as defined in the reports of the heavy metals network and based on WHO guidelines;
- the 240 µg/m^3 hourly ozone concentration as the mutual warning level defined by the Benelux Directive M/78/16;
- the 5 ppb organic sulphur concentration limit as a practical limit for odour nuisance in the region of Tessenderlo.

2.3.5 Chlorofluorocarbons

The Royal Decree of 3 March 1982 demands that manufacturers of aerosol cans reduce their consumption of F-11 and F-12 by at least 30 per cent relative to the 1976 production levels. More recent law projects and covenants aim at a complete ban on the use of CFCs by Belgian industry before 1995.

2.4 Industrial Air Pollution

The 1964 *Air Pollution Act* has until now been completed by only four execution decrees which limit the emissions from industrial sources: two Royal Decrees treat combustion sources, one asbestos emissions and one the sulphur content of liquid fuels.

The Royal Decree of 8 August 1975 is applicable for industrial combustion sources, but for new units above 50 MW it has now been superseded by that of 18 August 1986 (see below). The Decree does not apply to chemical processes or plants where flue gases are used for drying or product treatment. Deviations are allowed for greenhouse heating by a Ministerial Decree of 1976.

Maximum emission concentrations are given for dust in case of coal firing and for sulphur dioxide with liquid fuels. The limits depend on the size of the units and there are different rules for electricity and other types of combustion furnaces. More severe limits apply in the special protection zones and in case of unfavourable atmospheric conditions. The maximum sulphur content of fuels is limited proportionally to the emission limits, and the seller must specify the sulphur content of fuels on the invoice.

A formula is given to calculate minimum chimney height, based on maximum ambient concentrations of 0.200 mg/m^3 sulphur dioxide, or 0.100 mg/m^3 in the special protection zones. Oil fired power stations larger than 200 MW and oil refineries are required to monitor ambient air and to take the necessary precautions if the maximum 24 hour average concentration of 500 μg/m^3 is likely to be exceeded. The administration may impose more stringent conditions in the licenses of individual plants.

The allowable emission concentrations given in this Decree - ranging from 5 to 0.85 g/m^3 for sulphur dioxide and from 500 to 150 mg/m^3 for dust - can now be considered as much too permissive, but they still apply to the majority of Belgian industrial furnaces. The implementation of the European Directive 88/609/EEC relating to large combustion plant in 1990 demanded a collective emission reduction plan for these existing furnaces, which may eventually replace most of the clauses of the 1975 decree.

The Royal Decree of 18 August 1986 is applicable to large new furnaces with thermal power exceeding 50 MW, fired with solid, liquid or gaseous fuels. Maximum allowable emission concentrations of dust, sulphur dioxide and nitrogen oxides are given as a function of capacity and fuel type. Lower limits apply for new units to be licensed after 1995. The Decree also specifies measures in case of defective gas cleaning equipment, the maximum chimney height, the interpretation of continuous measurements, and the ambient air monitoring for units larger than 200 MW. This Decree is based on the European Directive 88/609/EEC but deviates from it in the emission limits for some categories and in the timing of emission reductions.

The Royal Decree of 29 December 1988 on the prevention of air pollution by asbestos imposes a maximum allowable emission concentration of 0.1 mg/m^3 of asbestos fibres for industrial plants treating more than 100 kg/year of crude asbestos.

The Royal Decree of 18 November 1988 limits the sulphur content of heavy liquid fuels. It complements the two Decrees concerning combustion sources mentioned above, since it will automatically apply to existing and small (< 50 MW) furnaces. Medium and heavy fuel oils are allowed to have a maximum sulphur content of one per cent. Very heavy fuel oils are subdivided into three categories: A, B and C, with a maximum sulphur content of 1, 2 and 3 per cent respectively.

2.5 Space Heating

The technical approval of new combustion equipment, emission standards, and the operation and maintenance of combustion units in use are now regulated by the Royal Decree of 6 January 1978. Soot emissions, temperature and dilution of the flue gas are regulated. A yearly inspection by a qualified technician and yearly chimney sweeping are imposed for liquid and solid fuels.

In 1971 special protection zones were established around the densely populated metropolitan areas of Antwerpen, Brussels, Charleroi, Gent and Liege. In these areas the following fuels are prohibited: peat, lignite, non smokeless pressed coal, liquid and solid fuels with sulphur content higher than one per cent. Moreover, it is forbidden to burn waste in the open air in these zones.

The Royal Decree of 19 October 1988 gives specifications for domestic heating oils and limits their sulphur content to 0.2 per cent by weight, starting from 1 January 1989. The inspection of the properties of fuels is carried out by the Department of Economic Affairs. Concerning the sulphur content, officials of the Service of Nuisances and of the Institute for Hygiene and Epidemiology (both belonging to the Department of Public Health and the Environment) are entitled to carry out inspections.

2.6 Mobile Sources

The technical performances of cars, including exhaust gas quality, are prescribed by the Royal Decree of 15 March 1968, which includes the *General Regulation on Technical Requirements for Vehicles.* There is a double control system:

- *type approval*: for new models to be introduced on the Belgian market, a prototype has to be submitted for authorization. The tests are done by the Royal Military School. For opacity of diesel exhaust, Article 39 specifies the maximum absorption coefficient of 0.975 m^{-1} during the test, or eventually a reference absorption coefficient to be established during the type approval test.
- *technical inspection (Article 23)*: cars in use must be inspected every year once they are four years old in regional stations, where mainly safety related tests are carried out. Gasoline cars have to undergo a carbon monoxide emission test with idling engine and must comply with the 4.5 volume per cent limit, as imposed by the Royal Decree of 8 November 1971. Diesel exhaust quality is not measured during these inspections.

The *Framework Law* of 21 June 1985 enables the definition of more advanced technical regulations for type approval of cars by the Ministry of Traffic. In practice this was achieved by the Royal Decree of 30 December 1988 which implemented the numerous European Directives on motor vehicle exhaust. The emission limits given in these guidelines will therefore in time replace the older Belgian legislation.

The maximum lead content of gasoline was lowered from 0.4 g/1 to 0.15 g/1 by the Royal Decree of 12 September 1986. At the same time unleaded gasoline, containing no more than 0.013 g/1, was to be made generally available through the distribution network and the benzene content was limited to 5 per cent by volume.

For diesel fuel, the Royal Decree of 19 October 1988 sets a maximum allowable sulphur content of 0.2 per cent by weight.

2.7 Relation with Planning Controls

Although Belgium is a densely populated country where industrial areas are in many cases adjacent to urban zones, the first law on planning and land use was not issued until 1962. The actual locations of industrial and residential areas are therefore not always the best and can only be corrected to a limited extent. The Regional Governments have now taken over responsibility for planning on their territories and further development has to be strictly in accordance with the regional plans. Licenses are now granted for industrial projects only if the location is consistent with the industrial plan for the area. Recently the two major regions, Wallony and Flanders, have implemented the European Directive on Environmental Impact Assessment. In the impact statements submitted under this legislation, the air pollution impact of a project is generally predicted by mathematical modelling of existing and future situations.

3 IMPLEMENTATION AND ENFORCEMENT

3.1 National Enforcement

The division of environmental responsibility between nine or ten national Departments has already been mentioned as a specific problem of Belgian environmental policy. Therefore in 1972 a Ministerial Committee of the Environment was established in which all responsible ministers have a seat.

Since the Regions are now in control of the administrations which enforce environmental legislation, the national State Secretary of the Environment further coordinates the national policy by a monthly meeting with the regional ministers in the Interministerial Conference on the Environment.

In the continuing process of transfer of powers from the national to the regional governments, it is not yet clear whether the federal system will leave adequate powers to the national authority, e.g. in cases where Belgium as a whole has to comply with European Directives or international agreements. The State Secretary of the Environment stressed the need for such powers on several occasions in 1990.

An approach that has been used a few times as a substitute for enforcement by the national department is that of "Covenants" between government and industry. In these voluntary agreements industry commits itself, e.g. to reduce the use of CFCs or mercury in batteries.

In relation to air pollution, specific tasks of the national departments include:

- the national Department of Public Health and the Environment is entitled to set general and sectoral quality standards in cases where no EC standards exist. The Department is further responsible for the national monitoring networks operated by the Institute for Hygiene and Epidemiology (IHE), and it keeps the national emissions inventory through the Service of Environmental Nuisance. For the implementation of European Directives like those concerning air quality standards, and other international agreements, the national Department of the Environment is liable to ensure compliance of the Belgian nation as a whole.

Protection from radiation is also a national issue which has received renewed attention since the Chernobyl accident in 1986. A radioactivity measuring network is now being set up.

- compliance with emission standards by new vehicles with the technical prescriptions and the technical inspection of vehicles in use is controlled by the Department of Transport.
- protection of the population from disasters is organized by the Department of the Interior, which controls the Service of Civil Protection.
- quality of fuels for heating and transport, in general, but including sulphur, lead and benzene content, is controlled by the Department of Economic Affairs. The Institute for Hygiene and Epidemiology is equally authorised to supervise fuel quality in relation to air pollution.

Violations of air pollution legislation can be established by judiciary officers and police. Like the officials of the regional administrations they have the right to enter industrial premises where illegal air pollution is suspected at any time, to take samples, and close down plants temporarily. In practice, but with a few notorious exceptions, justice has until now played only a minor role in air pollution law enforcement. The fact that industrial licenses are confidential and may vary from case to case, combined with the difficulty of collecting substantial evidence, are some of the reasons why legal actions related to air pollution are rare. Furthermore the fines and sanctions specified in the law are generally considered to be very mild.

The enforcement of air quality standards poses a special problem, since eventual violation of these standards is not necessarily caused by the exceeding of emission limits. In the case of imminent high sulphur dioxide episodes, the industry is asked to switch to low sulphur fuels and, in the case of persistent air pollution, to prepare for eventual shutdown of certain operations. By the Act of 1964 such requests can be enforced if necessary. However, at the moment detailed action plans for the authorities to cope with these situations are not yet available.

3.2 Regional Enforcement

The *Special Law* of 8 August 1980 delegates to the regions the responsibility and the power for the protection of the environment, with an obligation to respect the general and sectorial standards established by the national government. European (EEC) standards are to be implemented by the regions with priority over the national standards. The regions have Executives to translate these responsibilities into regional legislation, and have established administrations to ensure enforcement. As an example, the two large regions have established their own legislation on waste, which contains emission limits for incinerators in Flanders. In the smaller Brussels Region there has been some delay in setting up the institutions needed for environmental planning and the Region was therefore late in implementing some of the European Directives.

The *Special Law* of 8 August 1980 also assigns responsibility for policing dangerous, unhealthy and polluting activities. Consequently the regions now control the regulation of industrial air pollution sources, from the issuing of licenses to the inspection. The regional administrations have unfortunately inherited from the former national institutions the shortage of staff thus making it more difficult for them to carry out sufficient and adequate inspections. Most inspections therefore result from complaints and do not take place regularly.

Both the large regions now apply the European Environmental Impact Directive and from this principle a more systematic approach to air pollution control can be expected. The Flemish administration has announced its intention to apply the German TA Luft standards in future licenses for those sectors where no regulations are available.

The Provinces have a mainly administrative and advisory task in the issuing of licenses for Class I industrial activities. They have limited authority to make police regulations to ensure public health and safety, and some operate environmental services or laboratories. The Province governor has a coordinating role in the event of disasters.

The Municipalities have the authority to give Class II licenses, and have directives on the environmental conditions to be imposed. They also have the possibility to regulate environmental matters which were not regulated by higher ranking authorities. Additionally they can impose special conditions for enterprises that rent or buy their land. An example of this is the city of Antwerp, where the environmental service (CLW) has played a pioneering role in the prevention of air pollution.

The municipal police commissioner, being a judiciary officer, can establish violations of environmental legislation. In the last decade more and smaller towns have started environmental services, which are expected to acquire environmental police authority in the future.

3.3 Monitoring Agencies

Most of the monitoring of ambient air quality is carried out by the Air Section of the Institute for Hygiene and Epidemiology. The Air Section operates the national monitoring networks on behalf of the Service of Environmental Nuisance and publishes the results every year. It also runs the regional monitoring networks and coordinates measurements and research of other institutes in the field of air pollution. The most important monitoring networks in Belgium are the following:

- The sulphur dioxide-black smoke network has been in operation from 1968 and comprises 100 stations, including 11 in Luxembourg. The stations are concentrated in the five large urban zones and the industrial areas. Sulphur dioxide and particles (as black smoke) are measured with the acidimetric and nefelometric methods recommended by the OECD, as 24 hour averages.
- The automatic network for air pollution monitoring has 72 stations and came into operation in 1972. The network is mainly concentrated on urban and industrial areas, where the risk of exceedances is highest. The intention to cover the territory with a regular grid of stations has only been partially realized (11 stations). All stations have at least a continuous sulphur dioxide measurement, and sometimes additional instruments to monitor particulate matter, nitrogen oxides, non methane hydrocarbons and ozone. Meteorological data are collected by 21 stations. The data from all stations are transmitted by wire to five regional data reduction and validation centers, and from there to the central data terminal at the IHE in Brussels, where a direct overview of the air quality in the country is available.
- The heavy metals network now consists of 60 stations where each day a filter is loaded with suspended particles and subsequently analyzed by X-ray fluorescence. The number of heavy metals analyzed depends on the site, the most important being lead, cadmium, zinc, chromium, vanadium and copper.

The monitoring networks described above must be kept in operation to comply with the air quality legislation for sulphur dioxide, black smoke, nitrogen oxides and lead. Other networks are:

- The rain network with ten wet deposition collectors spread over the country, where acid deposition parameters are measured.
- The deposition network for heavy metals with some 60 deposition gauges, mostly in the vicinity of metallurgical industries.
- Local automatic networks with a limited number of stations are temporarily in use in regions with elevated local emissions, e.g. in

Vilvoorde and Engis. Furthermore some industries and power stations, or private organizations assigned by them are active in air quality monitoring according to legal obligations.

Mobile and airborne measurements are occasionally carried out by the IHE in order to determine fluxes and transport of air pollution. For the monitoring of air pollution from traffic, fixed stations and a mobile laboratory are in operation.

Emission monitoring in Belgium is not carried out by public organizations, but generally by private companies, some universities and scientific and technological institutions. An official homologation is required for a laboratory to perform analyses in relation to air pollution, without distinction between emission and air quality measurements. A separate homologation issued by the Ministry of Labour is needed to measure air quality at work stations. A quality control programme for these laboratories is not in operation.

3.4 Role of Private Interest Groups

In the process of legislation private persons or interest groups have no official role to play since they are represented by the elected parliament which is the legislator. Nevertheless the influence of economic, social and environmental groups on legislation is very marked, since it begins with the preparation of law projects. Representatives of the groups concerned normally have a seat on commissions where proposals are prepared or are otherwise invited to comment on law proposals before voting by the national and regional parliaments.

The effects of lobbying by private interest groups are difficult to assess, but it is common knowledge that, for example, delays in legislation and implementation occur through such actions. Influential groups are considered to be national and regional associations of industrialists, electricity boards and agricultural organizations. Environmental groups have become well organized only in the last decade. Their presence in working groups and commissions is now generally accepted, but the right to start court actions was denied to them by the famous Eickendael judgement stating that legal action could only be undertaken by a legal person defending a direct and personal interest. Obviously environmental pollution is more frequently a matter of collective interests and the present coalition has plans to regulate this issue. Law suits by groups may thus become an instrument of air pollution law enforcement in the future.

In relation to some air pollution problems industry has committed itself to voluntary actions, e.g. the reduction of CFC use, the limitation of mercury content of batteries and cooperating in preparing an emission inventory of the Flemish region. These initiatives have so far compensated for the lack of legislation, but perhaps in the long run the avoidance of more adequate regulatory measures will be more beneficial to industry than to environmental policy.

4 EFFECTIVENESS OF CONTROLS

4.1 Air Quality Improvement

In the last decade a remarkable reduction in air pollution by sulphur dioxide has been measured. In Brussels the IHE has measured yearly averages of nearly 180 $\mu g/m^3$ in 1968 and of 30 $\mu g/m^3$ in 1988. The decrease is attributed mainly to the construction of higher chimneys in the seventies, energy savings, the lower sulphur content of fuels and a shift in fuel use for electricity generation. From 1985 on, a stabilization of the levels in ambient air was observed. The yearly average concentrations are below the air quality standards of 120 $\mu g/m^3$, but violations of the short term quality standard - the 98 percentile of 250 $\mu g/m^3$ in places with high dust levels or unavailable dust data - may still occur in industrial areas adjacent to large urban zones. The WHO guidelines of 50 $\mu g/m^3$ as the yearly average and 125 $\mu g/m^3$ as the maximum daily value have not yet been obtained.

The concentrations of black smoke or suspended particles are now well below the legal quality standards and even below the WHO guidelines (50 and 125 $\mu g/m^3$ as median and 98 percentile of daily values respectively). Since 1985 black smoke levels have stabilized, probably due to an increased use of coal and diesel vehicles.

Nitrogen dioxide levels in ambient air have not shown the same rate of decrease as other pollutants. The quality standard is not exceeded anywhere, but the same is not true for the guide values, especially the 135 $\mu g/m^3$ limit for the 98 percentile of hourly values, and the WHO guideline of 190 $\mu g/m^3$ as hourly maximum. Problems from local high industrial emissions have been largely solved, but emissions from mobile sources are still growing. The air concentrations of lead have decreased below the 2 $\mu g/m^3$ quality standard everywhere. Measurements by the IHE have demonstrated that the progressive lowering of the lead content of gasoline has had an almost proportional effect on the air quality in cities. Other heavy metals in the air, and the deposition of heavy metals are not subjected to the legal quality standards. However, where national or regional standards are not available it has become common practice to refer to international or reputable foreign standards such as the WHO Air Quality Guidelines for Europe or the German TA Luft 1986. If these limits were to be applied to heavy metals, non-compliance would still be noted for cadmium, lead, arsenic and nickel in the vicinity of nonferrous metallurgical plants.

4.2 Emission Reductions

The Belgian emissions inventory is kept by the Service of Environmental Nuisance of the Department of Public Health, where estimations of yearly emissions are made with the help of data collected by the regions. The official data are available only after a delay of a few years.

For sulphur dioxide, from 1980 to 1987 a 50 per cent emission reduction from 840 kton to 420 kton was achieved. Most of this reduction was obtained by the growth of nuclear power from 25 per cent in 1978 to 66 per cent in 1988, combined with the almost complete elimination of oil firing in power stations. In 1987, 79 per cent of sulphur dioxide emissions originated from industry (including power and refineries), 17 per cent from space heating and 4 per cent from mobile sources.

The emission reductions achieved for nitrogen oxides, from 330 to 300 kton between 1980 and 1987 are not significant, due to the increasing emissions from vehicles. The share of road traffic in the 1987 nitrogen oxides emissions was 53 per cent, while industry accounted for 37 per cent and space heating for 10 per cent.

In contrast with the high contribution to emissions, the use of catalysts for exhaust gas cleaning on cars is practically limited to spark ignition engines over 2200 cc, to which a legal obligation applies. The fiscal inducement to introduce catalysts on smaller cars has remained unsuccessful.

In relation to acid deposition, ammonia emissions from agricultural activities are known to be at least of the same importance as nitrogen oxides. However a steady increase from 117 kton in 1980 to 123 kton in 1987 was observed. No legal limitations on ammonia emissions have been established as yet.

4.3 International Agreements

In 1982 Belgium ratified the 1979 *Geneva Convention on Transboundary Transport of Air Pollution.* More detailed emission reduction plans were made in the two following Protocols:

- The Helsinki Protocol of 1985, where a 30 per cent decrease on the 1980 sulphur dioxide emissions was agreed by 1993.
- The Sofia Protocol of 1988, where a freezing of nitrogen oxides emissions to the 1987 level was agreed by the year 1994. Belgium belongs to the 12 West European countries that have agreed an additional 30 per cent reduction before 1998.

As already indicated, EEC Directives play an important role in Belgian air quality legislation and in the planning of emission reductions. For large furnaces the following reductions are planned in line with Directive 88/609/EEC on air pollution from large combustion plant (50 MW or more):

	1980	*1993*	*1998*	*2003*
SO2	100%	–40%	–60%	–70%
NOx	100%	–20%	–40%	

In 1988 the 1985 Vienna Convention on the protection of the ozone layer was implemented, and completed by the Montreal Protocol in 1987(and the Review of 1990). Relative to the 1986 production of CFCs, a 20 per cent reduction by 1996 and a 50 per cent reduction by 1999 was agreed. Belgium has accepted the stricter cuts formulated at the 1990 Review of the Protocol which will result in the complete elimination of CFCs by the year 2000.

The gradual elimination of CFCs by Belgian industry (aerosol cans, refrigeration and foamed plastics) before 1995 will be regulated by voluntary covenants containing agreements for reductions beyond the legal requirements. For aerosol cans an interim decree was issued in 1989. The 1989 use of CFCs in aerosol cans was estimated to be 800 tons, compared to 8000 tons in 1976.

5 FUTURE DEVELOPMENTS

The implementation of European Directives by the national and regional governments will determine much of the legislative work in the near future. To meet the sulphur dioxide and nitrogen oxides emission reduction schemes without the further expansion of nuclear energy, will require the imposition of new emission limits for existing large furnaces. For emissions from small combustion units and mobile sources a product law is in preparation, which will set general standards for fuel and car exhaust gas.

In relation to the problem of acid deposition, the quality objectives for soils require reductions of the order of 75 per cent of the 1987 level for all acidifying emissions, to be realized in the first decade of the next century.

The reduction of carbon dioxide emissions will receive more attention in the coming years. Although stabilization of emissions can be achieved by a reduction in electricity generation, this will be compensated for by an increase from mobile sources. Further reduction plans for these and other sectors are in preparation and will be submitted to the EEC in 1991.

6 REFERENCES

L'environnenment en Belgique. Présent et Avenir. Etat de l'Environnement, Miet Smet, Secretaire d'Etat de l'Environnement, 1990.

Mina Plan 2000. *Analyse en Voorstellen voor een Vernieuwd Vlaams Milieu- en Natuurbeleid*, Theo Kelchtermans, 1989.

Juridisch Milieucompendium, Rubriek C: *Luchtverontreiniging.* Editor: Stichting Leefmilieu, Antwerpen, 1988.

Milieugids, 5th edition 1990, Kluwer - Stichting Leefmilieu.

Luchtverontreiniging, 20 jaar meetervaring in België, J. Kretzschmar, 1990.

BRAZIL

1 INTRODUCTION

1.1 Topography, Climate, Population

Brazil lies in the east-centre region of South America. Its coastline is about 9000 km long and with an area of 8 511 965 sq. km, it is the largest country in Latin America and fifth largest in the world; Brazil is only slightly smaller than the Soviet Union, the United States, Canada, and the People's Republic of China.

The Federal Republic of Brazil is divided into 26 states and a federal district, where the country's capital, Brasilia, is located. The 1980 census revealed that at the time the country had a population of 121 million. Although there are no details from any more recent census, current estimates indicate a population of about 145 million. The population is concentrated in the coastal zone, especially in the south eastern region where Brazil's two biggest metropolitan areas are situated - Rio de Janeiro with about 11 million inhabitants, and São Paulo with almost 17 million.

As well as continuing to be a world supplier of raw materials and agricultural products, Brazil makes high technology products such as aircraft and industrial automation systems. It also builds ships, rockets, satellites and computers.

With a population of 32 million, the state of São Paulo is, without a doubt, the hub of the Brazilian economy. The state capital - the City of São Paulo, population 11 million - is responsible for 50 per cent of Brazil's industrial production. Over the years it has been transformed into the chief commercial and industrial centre of Latin America. In addition to São Paulo State, the States of Minas Gerais, Rio de Janeiro, Rio Grande do Sul and Parana also enjoy great economic importance.

1.2 Specific National Problems

For a country of continental proportions, Brazil shows a supremely varied distribution of its population which is concentrated for the most part in large metropolitan areas along the coast. As in other developing countries, the evidence of an accelerated process of urbanization without planning can be seen in these areas. This, associated with a high population density, results in numerous social problems, such as lack of housing, basic sanitation, urban infrastructure and environmental pollution.

With such problems, it would be understandable if Brazil were to give less priority to pollution control than to its urgent social problems - nutrition, health, education, crime rate, etc. However, in some regions of Brazil atmospheric pollution is so serious and its effects on the population and environment so harmful that pollution control has been given a certain priority in these regions.

There are currently several metropolitan areas with atmospheric pollution problems similar to those observed in other regions of the world recognized as polluted. Outstanding among them - being those with the greatest problems - are the metropolitan areas of São Paulo (SP), Rio de Janeiro (RJ) and Belo Horizonte (MG, i.e. the State of Minas Gerais). This is due not only to the magnitude of the pollution and the variety of sources of emission, but also because of their large populations, which amount to 33 million people (about 23 per cent of the total Brazilian population). Other metropolitan areas, such as Porto Alegre (RS), Recife (PE), Salvador (BA) and Vitoria (ES), also face the challenge of combating pollution, although the situation is less critical.

1.3 Major Sources of Atmospheric Pollution

As a consequence of the size of the country and the variety of land use and population density, air pollution in Brazil is marked by regional characteristics and is closely related to socio-economic activities and local culture. Air pollution in Brazil may be characterized as being caused by burning in rural areas and the bush (such as the Amazonian forest), by industrial sources in urban areas or industrial zones, and by transport systems and small industrial and commercial plants (principally in the large cities).

1.3.1 Burning

Every year thousands of hectares of forest are burned in the northern and north-centre regions of Brazil as a rapid means of clearing large forest areas for agriculture and grazing. This results in significant quantities of carbon monoxide, carbon dioxide, nitrogen oxides, hydrocarbons and particles being released into the atmosphere. This has a deleterious effect on the quality of local and regional air and on that of the planet as a whole.

It is estimated that, due to deforestation by burning[(1)], Brazil is responsible for about 5 per cent of the world's carbon emissions. The burning process is used seasonally with less far reaching impacts in the sugar regions, located principally in the north east and south east of Brazil, as part of the process of harvesting sugar cane. This not only pollutes the air locally, but also that of vast urban areas adjacent to the sugar plantations, causing serious inconvenience due to soot and smoke.

1.3.2 Industrial Zones

Brazil has a well developed industrial centre in its south eastern region and several industrial zones spread throughout the south and north east of the country. Within these, the principal sources of pollution are the petrochemical, steel making and coal mining zones of the south; the petrochemical, steel making, alcohol production and light and heavy industrial zones of the south east; the petrochemical, alcohol production and chlorochemical zones of the north east; and in each area, the associated processing industries.

The most highly developed industrial complex in the country is centred on the State of São Paulo and involves installations ranging from basic industries to firms manufacturing state of the art products. The Cubatão petrochemical zone, on the coast of São Paulo State, is the largest in Latin America and gained notoriety in the 1970s because of the magnitude of its pollution output. Considerable resources were devoted to identifying the problem and to the corrective action which followed.

Working from the available data, it is possible to show that, with the exception of certain centres of pollution located principally in the industrial zones, Brazil's greatest air pollution problems are concentrated in the metropolitan areas of São Paulo and Rio de Janeiro. The municipality of Cubatão in São Paulo State is a typical case of a centre of pollution caused by the presence of an industrial zone.

In Brazil, industrial activity bears a large responsibility for the environmental degradation which can be seen, not only because of the quantity of pollutants emitted but also their variety and toxicity.

1.3.3 Large Cities

As is the case in the majority of developing countries, environmental conditions in Brazil's great metropolitan centres are still quite precarious. Rapid population growth, lack of urban infrastructure and unplanned industrialization have led to the development of large conurbations having every kind of social and environmental problem.

Emissions from motor vehicles and industry, poor environmental conservation in the cities and marginal commercial activities and services, generate levels of pollution which, as a general rule, exceed the standards for air quality.

The air pollution problems in the São Paulo and Rio de Janeiro metropolitan areas are similar, and are basically caused by the density of motor vehicle traffic. Thus, the legally established standards of air quality for particles in suspension, carbon monoxide, ozone and nitrogen dioxide are regularly violated.

1.4 Fuel Characteristics

The characteristics of the different fuels are one of the principal factors influencing the emission of atmospheric pollutants. In Brazil, according to information in the 1988 analysis of energy report(2), the principal fuels in terms of final energy consumption were diesel oil (13.5 per cent), sugar cane bagasse (7.9 per cent), wood (12.0 per cent), fuel oil (6.4 per cent), petrol (3.6 per cent) and ethyl alcohol (3.9 per cent). The greatest energy consumption, fortunately, is of a "clean" type - electricity (39.4 per cent) generated by hydroelectric power stations.

Fuels derived from crude oil, as a general rule, have a high sulphur content, as in the case of fuel oil type A in which it can reach 5.5 per cent by weight, or in that of diesel oil or petrol in which it can reach 1.3 per cent and 0.25 per cent by weight respectively.

The presence of such levels of sulphur results in a high emission of sulphur oxides, besides favouring the formation of particles. It is estimated that in the São Paulo metropolitan area alone the emission of sulphur oxides was 107 000 metric tons in 1989(3).

Due to the heavy demand for diesel oil, the refinement of which involves the consumption of about 35 per cent of a barrel of crude, the quality of this fuel is becoming lower; the result is an increased tendency towards the formation of particles during the combustion process.

The addition of 22 per cent anhydrous ethanol to petrol is a positive step since besides reducing the fuel's sulphur content, it favours a reduction in the emission of significant pollutants, such as carbon monoxide, hydrocarbons, particles and sulphur oxides. The use of hydrous ethanol as a fuel reveals highly interesting environmental characteristics due to its low pollution potential.

The use of ethanol, both as an additive in petrol and alone as a vehicle fuel, has contributed to reducing the increase in the emission of several pollutants, particularly carbon monoxide(4). The production of ethanol from sugar cane still allows the use of bagasse as an alternative fuel for boilers. However, when they are operated without the necessary controls, they become significant sources of pollution.

Wood, like other solid fuels, has a tendency to emit a large quantity of particles and other pollutants when burned inefficiently, as is commonly the case in Brazil. An energy source derived from wood is charcoal which in 1988 accounted for 3.8 per cent of the country's total energy consumption[(2)]. It is used principally in the steel making sector, and the process by which it is obtained is obsolete, involving partial burning resulting in the release of volatile substances into the atmosphere. The intensive use of wood and charcoal, besides generating a considerable quantity of pollutants, especially in the case of wood, also contributes to the destruction of the natural forests since some of the wood used comes from these forests.

Finally, Brazilian coal which in 1988 represented 4.4 per cent of the country's total energy consumption[(2)]. It is of low quality, having a high ash content (40 per cent) and sulphur (3 per cent); consequently stringent pollution control systems are needed. Air pollution due to the use of coal as a fuel is largely restricted to the coal mining regions in the south of Brazil.

2 DEVELOPMENT OF AIR POLLUTION CONTROLS AND LEGISLATION

Brazil is a federal republic, and is made up of states which have the independent right to lay down requirements for environmental control. In addition, there is a general framework for control drawn up by the federal government which is valid in those regions with no legislation of their own.

The National Environmental Policy of Brazil is laid down in Law No. 6938 of 31 August 1981 and in Decree No. 88351 of 1 July 1983. The National Environmental System (SISNAMA), which was created by this legislation, is made up of organizations and bodies at the different levels of public administration; these are responsible for the protection and improvement of the quality of the environment; the National Environment Council (CONAMA) sets standards and maintains the SISNAMA. The central organization for technical and administrative support is the Brazilian Institute for the Environment and Renewable Natural Resources (IBAMA) which comes under the Special Environmental Secretariat.

The legislation also established, among other things, the licensing system for potentially polluting activities and the requirement for environmental impact assessment of certain undertakings. CONAMA is empowered to make resolutions relating to the environment.

The basis of air pollution control and prevention in Brazil is laid down in CONAMA Resolution No. 05/89 of 15 June 1989, which created the National Programme for Air Quality Control (PRONAR).

The basic strategy of the PRONAR is the limitation of emissions, according to source type and priority of pollutant, by means of establishing maximum emission limits. These limits are set by CONAMA resolutions. One resolution - CONAMA Resolution No. 08/90 of 6 December 1990 - establishes standards of emission for particles and sulphur dioxide from stationary sources of combustion.

Table 1: Maximum Emission Limits for Stationary Sources of Combustion – CONAMA Resolution No. 08 of 06.12.1990

	Source Strength < 70MW			*Source Strength > 70 MW*		
Area	*Particles Total*	*Sulphur Dioxide*	*Smoke*	*Particles Total*	*Sulphur Dioxide*	*Smoke*
Class 1 (Protected areas)	Zero[a]	Zero[a]	Zero[a]	Zero[a]	Zero[a]	Zero[a]
(Conservation areas[b])	120g/ Mkcal	2000g/ Mkcal	Ring- elmann 1	Zero[a]	Zero[a]	Zero[a]
Class 2 or Class 3	350g/ Mkcal (Oil) 1500g/ Mkcal (Coal)	5000g/ Mkcal	Ring- elmann 1	120g/ Mkcal (Oil) 800g/ Mkcal (Coal)	2000g/ Mkcal	Ring- elmann 1

[a]=installation of the source of pollution prohibited.
[b]=oil consumption limited to a maximum of 3000 metric tons/year.

With regard to mobile sources, CONAMA Resolution No. 18/86 of 6 May 1986 (together with other complementary resolutions) instituted the Programme of Motor Vehicle Air Pollution Control (PROCONVE). This laid down emission limits to be attained in stages specified in a schedule. The goal of PROCONVE is to reach the control levels at present in force in the USA for light duty vehicles, and in western Europe for diesel vehicles, in 1997 and 1995 respectively.

The standards for air quality (primary and secondary) were established by CONAMA Resolution No. 03/90 of 28 June 1990 for total suspended particles (TSP), particles which can be inhaled, smoke, sulphur dioxide, carbon monoxide, ozone, and nitrogen dioxide. The criteria for acute air pollution episodes were also specified in this resolution. The national standards for air quality and the criteria for acute episodes are shown in Tables 2 and 3.

The adoption of a policy aimed at the prevention of significant deterioration in air quality, the creation of a national air quality network, the management of the licensing of air pollution sources, the drawing up of a national inventory of emissions and the execution of a development programme in the field of air pollution are specified as strategies within PRONAR.

Table 2: National Standards for Air Quality – CONAMA Resolution No. 03 of 28.06.1990

Pollutant	*Averaging Time*	*Primary Standard (ug/m³)*	*Sec'ry Standard (ug/m³)*	*Measuring System*
Sulphur dioxide	24 hour† AAM*	365 80	100 40	Pararosaniline
Total particles in suspension	24 hour† AGM**	240 80	150 60	High volume sampler
Breatheable particles <10µm	24 hour† AAM*	150 50	150 50	Inertial separation /Filtration
Smoke	24 hour† AAM*	150 60	100 40	Reflectance
Carbon monoxide	1 hour† 8 hour†	40,000 (35 ppm) 10,000 (9 ppm)	40,000 (35 ppm) 10,000 (9 ppm)	Non-dispersive infrared
Ozone	1 hour†	160	160	Chemiluminescence
Nitrogen dioxide	1 hour† AAM*	320 100	190 100	Chemiluminescence

†=Should not be exceeded more than once per year.
**=Annual geometric mean.
*=Annual arithmetic mean.

Table 3: Criteria for Acute Air Pollution Episodes — CONAMA Resolution No. 03 of 28.06.1990

Parameter	*Levels*		
	Caution	*Alert*	*Emergency*
Sulphur dioxide (ug/m³) — 24 hr	800	1,600	2,100
Total suspended particles (TSP) (ug/m³) — 24 hr	375	625	875
SO_2 × TSP (ug/m³) — 24 hr	65,000	261,000	393,000
Inhalable particles (ug/m³) — 24 hr	250	420	500
Smoke (ug/m³) — 24 hr	250	420	500
Carbon monoxide (ppm) — 8 hr	15	30	40
Ozone (ug/m³) — 1 hr	400	800	1,000
Nitrogen dioxide (ug/m³) — 1 hr	1,130	2,260	3,000

It is important to point out that although all the principles of PRONAR are established by CONAMA Resolutions, it has been very difficult to actually put the intended system into operation. Since the approval of PRONAR, only two complementary resolutions have been produced - one setting standards of air quality and one setting standards of emission for stationary combustion sources.

2.1 Stationary Sources

For the control of emissions from stationary sources the requirements vary, basically according to state development policy, extent of existing pollution and/or the polluting potential of the source. In the more developed regions, it is common to use emission standards based on reasonable control technology. Higher levels of control are enforced on potentially highly polluting sources and/or in areas where the standards of air quality are violated. Apart from this, in some regions, such as the São Paulo metropolitan area and Cubatão, specific control programmes were established, and have benefitted from some financing through the World Bank. Unfortunately, there are no figures available at national level to allow a more in-depth examination of the matter.

Table 4: Emission Limits for Light Duty Vehicles Fitted with an Otto Cycle Engine – CONAMA Resolutions No. 18 of 06.05.1986 and No. 03 of 15.06.89

<table>
<tr><th rowspan="2">Type of Emission</th><th rowspan="2">Effective From</th><th rowspan="2">Vehicle Types</th><th colspan="5">Emission Limits (g/km)</th></tr>
<tr><th>CO</th><th>HC</th><th>NO_x</th><th>Ald[1]</th><th>CO at idle</th></tr>
<tr><td rowspan="6">EXHAUST</td><td>1.6.88</td><td>New models</td><td rowspan="4">24.0</td><td rowspan="4">2.1</td><td rowspan="4">2.0</td><td rowspan="3"></td><td rowspan="4">3.0</td></tr>
<tr><td>1.1.89</td><td>50% of production</td></tr>
<tr><td>1.1.90</td><td>100% of production cars and car derivatives</td></tr>
<tr><td>1.1.92</td><td>Light commercials not car derived</td><td>0.15</td></tr>
<tr><td>1.1.92</td><td>Cars and car derivatives</td><td>12.0</td><td>1.2</td><td>1.4</td><td>0.15</td><td>2.5</td></tr>
<tr><td>1.1.97</td><td>100% of light duty vehicles</td><td>2.0</td><td>0.3</td><td>0.6</td><td>0.03</td><td>0.5</td></tr>
<tr><td>Evaporative[2]</td><td>1.1.90</td><td>100% of light duty vehicles</td><td></td><td>6.0</td><td></td><td></td><td></td></tr>
<tr><td>Crank-case</td><td>1.1.88</td><td>100% of light duty vehicles</td><td colspan="5">Emission must be zero under any condition of engine operation</td></tr>
<tr><td colspan="8">Notes:
(1) Ald = Aldehydes, i.e. the sum of acetaldehyde and formaldehyde.
(2) Evaporative emission is expressed in g/test.</td></tr>
</table>

2.2 Mobile Sources

As far as mobile sources are concerned, the established control strategy, the principal tool of which was the PROCONVE, was the adoption at national level of emission limits for new motor vehicles, as shown in Tables 4 and 5, based on existing international experience.

Table 5: Emission Limits for Heavy Duty Vehicles – CONAMA Resolutions No. 18 of 06.05.1986, No. 04 of 15.06.88 and No. 10 of 14.09.89

<table>
<tr><th rowspan="3">Type of Emission</th><th rowspan="3">Effective From</th><th rowspan="3">Vehicle Types</th><th colspan="4">Emission Limits</th></tr>
<tr><th>k*</th><th colspan="3">g/kWh</th></tr>
<tr><th>Smoke</th><th>CO</th><th>HC</th><th>NO_x</th></tr>
<tr><td rowspan="4">EXHAUST</td><td>1.10.87</td><td>Urban diesel bus</td><td rowspan="4">2.5</td><td rowspan="2"></td><td rowspan="2"></td><td rowspan="2"></td></tr>
<tr><td>1.1.89</td><td rowspan="3">All diesel vehicles</td></tr>
<tr><td>1.1.93</td><td rowspan="2">11.2</td><td rowspan="2">2.8</td><td>18.0</td></tr>
<tr><td>1.1.95</td><td>14.4</td></tr>
<tr><td rowspan="4">Crank-case</td><td>1.1.88</td><td>Urban diesel bus</td><td rowspan="3" colspan="4">Emission zero under any condition of engine operation</td></tr>
<tr><td>1.1.89</td><td>Otto cycle engines</td></tr>
<tr><td>1.7.89</td><td>Diesel engines natural aspirat'n</td></tr>
<tr><td>1.1.93</td><td>Diesel engines turbocharged</td><td colspan="4">Emission zero or included in HC emission of exhaust</td></tr>
<tr><td>Evapor-ative</td><td>To be Proposed</td><td>Otto cycle engines</td><td colspan="4">To be proposed</td></tr>
</table>

(*) $k = \frac{c}{\sqrt{G}}$ c = carbon concentration (g/m^3)
G = nominal air flow (l/s)

For diesel vehicles in use, there are federal and state requirements for the control of black smoke emissions based on the Ringelmann scale Grade No. 2 has been adopted for urban areas.

Research is currently being conducted to determine the viability of setting up regional inspection and maintenance programmes (I/M), both for heavy duty vehicles, basically diesel driven, and for light duty vehicles which have been developed for use with hydrous ethanol or gasohol (78 per cent petrol + 22 per cent anhydrous ethanol). The establishment of such a system, which would make the granting of the vehicle's annual license dependent on passing an emission test, is justified by the large number of vehicles being run in bad condition.

In the 8.051 sq. km of the São Paulo metropolitan area (which includes the state capital and 36 adjacent municipalities, there are about 2.5 million vehicles on the road every day. Research indicates that approximately 75 per cent of vehicles are running with badly adjusted engines(5). This not only results in greater pollutant emissions but also to a rise in fuel consumption.

Natural gas use has been growing, particularly in the regions of São Paulo and Rio de Janeiro. This clean fuel has, so far, mainly been used as an industrial fuel. In 1991, the municipalities of the cities of São Paulo and Rio de Janeiro have required full conversion of the present diesel driven urban bus fleet to natural gas over a period of eight (RJ) to ten (SP) years in order to cut down the smoke emissions.

3 IMPLEMENTATION AND ENFORCEMENT

3.1 Monitoring

Brazil currently has no systematic air quality assessment programme. The first step in this direction is provided for in PRONAR (CONAMA Resolution No. 05/89) which proposes the creation of a basic sampling network on a national level.

At the present time, there are only a few independent sampling networks which have been set up by some of the states. These are: São Paulo, Rio de Janeiro, Rio Grande do Sul, Parana, Minas Gerais, Espirito Santo, Bahia, Ceará and Pernambuco. There are big differences between the state systems. The methodology in use ranges from stationary methods (rate of sulphation, rate of settled dust) in less developed states to automatic methods in São Paulo and Rio de Janeiro.

In general the air quality assessment programmes leave quite a lot to be desired since they are frequently subject to interruptions due to limited resources. In the majority of cases, the sequences of data contain flaws making them considerably less meaningful. In a great majority of cases the information is not made available to the general population, as it is only published in papers circulated within administrative organizations.

The exception - principally in regard to publication - is the air quality assessment programme of the State of São Paulo. Measurements have been routinely carried out for more than a decade; the information is released daily to the press and compiled annually in a widely distributed report(3).

3.2 Research and Education

The Companhia de Tecnologia Ambiental do Estado de São Paulo -

CETESB, is an official organization with more than 2000 researchers and technicians, and is the largest and most important in Latin America. It has an ongoing programme of educational campaigns against the pollution of water, air and soil and against noise throughout the state. For the guidance of the population of the state capital itself and of Greater São Paulo, it has installed dozens of electronic panels to indicate the level of air pollution. The panels have been erected at the principal city intersections where 2.5 million vehicles pass daily. The periodic adjustment of vehicle engines is also promoted by CETESB.

In 1988, CETESB's Environmental Education Management promoted a voluntary ban on the whole of São Paulo city centre, simulating a State of Alert against air pollution generated by motor vehicles. The State of Alert, proclaimed on a certain day, was to prepare the population for the possible occurrence of a State of Emergency. The ban was a success and received the support of members of the Civil Defense and public services, such as transport. Once the State of Alert had been proclaimed nearly 200 000 vehicles spontaneously stopped running for a day in the city centre. The 10 per cent who did not respond to the ban were fined a symbolic amount.

The Brazilian Association for the Prevention of Air Pollution and Defence of the Environment (ABPPOLAR) was founded in 1966 and is recognized as of value to the community under Law No. 1909/78. During this time, ABPPOLAR and its President, Randolpho Marques Lobato, have contributed decisively to the creation, growth and development of CETESB and other federal, state and municipal bodies which operate throughout Brazil to defend the environment against pollution and to promote alternative forms of energy.

It is however a matter of urgency in national terms to set up a minimum air quality assessment programme which takes regional differences into account. It should take into account the need for methodological standardization, training and resources so as to support a network which functions uniformly and without interruption, and which provides mutually compatible data which can be systematically published.

4 EFFECTS OF POLLUTION

The effects of atmospheric pollution are abundantly documented in international literature. In Brazil, especially in the last ten years, there has been an increase in the number of scientific investigations carried out to determine the nature of these effects, particularly on health.

The investigations have been conducted principally in the São Paulo metropolitan area and in the municipality of Cubatão; the evidence indicates a relationship between the high levels of observed pollution and a rise in morbidity mainly related to cardio-respiratory diseases.

A point worth recording is that susceptibility to the effects of air pollution is normally greater in populations which show nutritional deficiencies. In Brazil - as in the majority of developing countries - a large part of the population is undernourished, and this gives the level of Brazil's air pollution an even more worrying character.

The only record which exists in Brazil of death directly attributed to atmospheric pollution concerns an accidental discharge in 1962 which occurred in Bauru in the heartland of São Paulo State and which caused one death. On this occasion, there was a heavy emission of powder generated in the process of castor oil extraction, and which in addition caused several allergic reactions among the population. The lack of further records of incidents related to air pollution does not imply the absence of other possible cases of harm to the exposed population.

With respect to effects on the environment, much scientific interest was shown in the effects on the natural vegetation around Cubatão from industrial pollution. The vegetation suffered serious damage over the years, especially as a result of the presence of fluorides in the atmosphere. At the present time, a slow recovery can be observed in the vegetation coverage as a result of action to control pollutant emissions and a programme of artificial sowing.

It is also thought that those trees which grow in the metropolitan area of São Paulo show low resistance to disease - premature death, weak and decaying branches and trunks - because of the continuous effect of pollutants.

Research on the assessment of air quality and the effects of pollution has been growing as a result of the various legal requirements which demand environmental impact assessment studies and also due to social pressures for pollution control.

5 CONCLUSION

Brazil is currently facing the challenge of development and of attaining a quality of life similar to that in the countries of the first world. Contrary to what was hoped, the search for rapid progress has brought with it a perceptible decline in environmental quality which, in the final analysis, represents a retrograde step in the search for a better quality of life.

In this context, air quality, though not critical in national terms, shows worrying levels of pollution which demand a high priority for their control in several regions of Brazil. Today, the causes of pollution, its effects and the technological alternatives for its control are known. Sufficient resources, however, remain unavailable to put into effect even those control operations which are compatible with reality in a developing country such as Brazil.

REFERENCES

1. Goldenberg J. How to Stop Global Warming. *Technology Review.* Vol. 93, No. 8. p. 25-31, Cambridge, MA, 1990.

2. *Anuário Estatistico do Brasil.* IBGE - Instituto Brasileiro de Geografia e Estatística, Rio de Janeiro, RJ, 1990.

3. *Relatório de Qualidade do Ar na Região Metropolitana de São Paulo e en Cubatão -* 1989. CETESB - Companhia de Tecnologia de Saneamento Ambiental, São Paulo, SP, 1990.

4. Murgel E M. *Avaliacão dos Principais Efeitos do Proálcool sobre a Emissão de Poluentes por Veiculos Automotores.* Confederacao Nacional da Industria, Rio de Janeiro, RJ, 1990.

5. *Postos de Diagnóstico da Poluicão - Resumo dos Resultados Otidos - 1990.* CETESB - Companhia de Tecnologia de Saneamento Ambiental, São Paulo, SP, 1990.

Figure 1: Principal Sources of Atmospheric Pollution

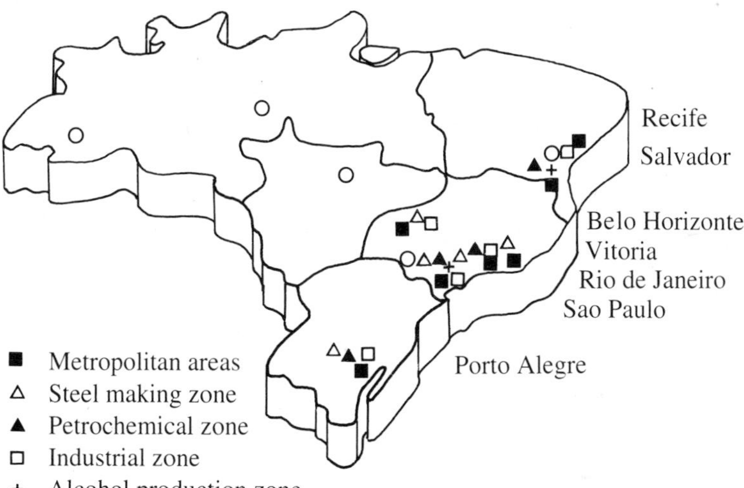

CANADA

1 INTRODUCTION

1.1 Topography, Climate, Population

Canada with an area of almost 10 million sq. km is the largest country in the Western Hemisphere, and the second largest in the world. Politically, the country is divided into ten provinces and two territories, with extensive borders and a varied land mass. It stretches from the rugged eastern coastline of Newfoundland, rising from the Atlantic Ocean, to the flat fertile lowland areas of the prairie provinces, and on to the lofty mountain peaks of British Columbia on the Pacific coast. This diverse geographical character creates a varied cross section of climatic conditions for the country's population which now exceeds 26 million.

Canada is a federal state which was founded on the *Constitution Act of 1867*, and now has its foundation in the *Constitution Act of 1982*, which includes its Charter of Rights and Freedoms. A central government - the federal government - has legislative jurisdiction primarily over matters of national concern such as defence, foreign policy and monetary matters, and over other matters not assigned to the provinces. The ten provincial governments are assigned specific areas of legislative jurisdiction. Environmental protection is a shared jurisdiction between the federal and provincial governments which necessitates a close cooperative approach to the management of environmental issues.

1.2 Specific National Problems

Air quality in terms of impacts of the common air pollutants on the health of most Canadians, particularly in major urban centres, is being well managed and will continue to be. The situation in Canada with respect to major air pollution issues is described below.

1.2.1 Long Range Transport of Air Pollution/Acid Rain

In eastern Canada, most of the acid rain problem is the result of sulphur dioxide emitted from eastern Canadian smelters and power plants, and from power plants in the north-central United States and carried northeast by prevailing winds. Emissions of nitrogen oxides, although a contributing factor, are not considered the major source of acidification in eastern Canada, when compared with sulphur dioxide.

Much of eastern Canada and parts of western and northern Canada are sensitive, by their geology, to acidic attack. These regions are naturally deficient in alkaline minerals which serve to neutralize acidic pollutants. In eastern Canada this sensitivity, combined with chronic acidic attack, has led to widespread acidification of lakes, harmful effects on fish and other aquatic life, damage to soils and forests, and other undesirable effects.

A research program begun early in 1970 led to the establishment, in 1982, of a target loading of 20 kilograms per hectare per year of wet sulphate deposition in eastern Canada to protect moderately sensitive aquatic ecosystems. Monitoring has shown that this target is being exceeded in much of eastern Canada.

Under a series of federal-provincial agreements, the provinces have focussed on those smelter and power plant sources where the largest reductions in sulphur dioxide emissions can be efficiently achieved. The objective is to achieve a total reduction, by 1994, of approximately 50 per cent from the 1980 base year total of some 4600 kilotonnes of sulphur dioxide emissions. Present indications are that the objective will be met.

The federal government has, as part of the overall program, supported research and development of sulphur dioxide emission reduction technologies such as new combustion techniques and flue gas desulphurization.

Internationally, Canada is a signatory to the United Nations Economic Commission for Europe (ECE) Convention on Long Range Transboundary Air Pollution (1979), and the companion protocol on Sulphur Dioxide (1985) which requires a 30 per cent reduction in sulphur dioxide emissions from 1980 levels by 1993. Long standing discussions are continuing with the United States towards the objective of a bilateral accord on acid rain.

1.2.2 Depletion of the Ozone layer

Science tells us that chemicals known as chlorofluorocarbons (CFCs) and halons, widely used throughout the developed world, are causing depletion of the stratospheric ozone layer which protects the earth's surface from harmful rays of the sun. Science also tells us that continued ozone depletion could lead to increases in skin cancer, damage to the human immune system, reduced crop yields and organic disruption in the upper ocean layers.

Protecting the ozone layer from further damage is a global problem in need of a global solution. Again and again in the past decade, international cooperation has begun to play a major role in attempts to resolve global environmental protection issues. In this case international efforts begun in 1977, under the auspices of the United Nations Environment Program, have produced a concerted program which is exerting a significant influence on the domestic control program of participating nations. Canada is an active participant in this successful endeavour to forge a multilateral solution to the ozone problem, and is committed to seeing it through to completion.

As a signatory to the Vienna Convention for the Protection of the Ozone Layer, which entered into force in September 1988, Canada is also a Party to the Montreal Protocol, which entered into force on 1 January 1989. The Protocol provides for the 59 participating countries, which together represent over 80 per cent of consumption in the chemical pollutants to be controlled, to achieve specific cutbacks in the consumption of the chemicals concerned. At a meeting in June 1990 in London, the Parties to the Protocol agreed to a revised and expanded Montreal Protocol which calls for the phase-out of the use of all ozone depleting substances by the year 2000, with scheduled intermediate reductions. Canada ratified the amended Protocol immediately following the London meeting, and is moving forward with a regulatory program which will meet and, in some cases, exceed our obligations under the Protocol.

1.2.3 Ground-Level Ozone/Urban Smog

Ground-level ozone, a major component of urban smog, is recognized as one of the more serious air quality problems in Canada today. More than half of all Canadians are at times exposed in summer to ozone levels that are known to have adverse effects on health. Ozone is also known to cause significant damage to agricultural crops and other forms of vegetation in parts of Canada.

High concentrations of ground-level ozone are caused by the interaction of nitrogen oxides and photochemically active volatile organic compounds (VOCs) reacting in the atmosphere in the presence of sunlight. Recognizing the seriousness of the ground-level ozone problems, the Canadian Council of Ministers of the Environment decided, in October 1988, to develop a a management plan for the control of nitrogen oxides and volatile organic compounds.

The initial plan, which is nearing completion, will cover Phase I of a multi-phase control program aimed at resolving ground-level ozone problems in Canada by the year 2005. It contains specific initiatives for emission reductions of nitrogen oxides and volatile organic compounds emission reductions as well as study initiatives to provide information for preparing the Phase II plan in 1994 and, if necessary, Phase III in 1997.

The Phase I emission reductions initiatives are to be put in place from 1991 to 1994 and will affect mobile and stationary sources such as automobiles, power plants and refineries. Overall, the measures in the Phase I plan will establish a strong national prevention plan and a comprehensive set of remedial actions in the primary ozone problem areas.

The program is a shared responsibility of the federal, provincial and municipal governments. It will result in significant costs to government and industry, and is dependent to some degree on public adaptation and response to the need for lifestyle changes to improve and conserve the quality of the environment.

1.2.4 Global Warming

The composition of the earth's atmosphere is threatened by major global change. Human activities, such as air pollution, deforestation, the burning of fossil fuels and agricultural practices are now starting to alter the balance of gases in our atmosphere. There is widespread concern that this may cause changes in world climate. Average global temperatures may rise. Rainfall patterns may shift. The effects on our society could be immense. Canada, being a country of climatic extremes, would be among the most significantly affected areas in the world.

Concern centres on what is often described as the greenhouse effect. Major contributors to the greenhouse effect are carbon dioxide, CFCs, methane, nitrous oxide and ozone.

Environment Canada research programs are keeping track of the rising levels of the most important greenhouse gases in the atmosphere. Studies are being carried out on how these gases could change our climate and the potential impact on Canadian society. The Canadian Climate Program is coordinating the related research efforts of government, industry and universities across the country. As the issue is a global concern, Canada is also participating in international efforts to further understanding and action on this complex problem.

It is significant to note the inter-relationships between global warming and other major issues such as depletion of the ozone layer and urban smog. Fortunately, progress made on one issue is often beneficial to others, which points to the need to avoid dealing with these issues in isolation.

2 DEVELOPMENT OF AIR POLLUTION CONTROLS AND LEGISLATION

2.1 Basic Principles

The period since the publication of the first edition of *Clean Air Around The World* has seen a major change in Canada's approach to protection of the environment, with the enactment of the Canadian *Environmental Protection Act* (CEPA) which entered into force 28 June 1988. This legislation gives the federal government the power to protect both human health and the environment from the risks associated with the use of chemicals and from exposure to toxic substances. The Act is the result of an extensive public consultation process which began in 1982. It combines several previously existing environmental acts, including the *Clean Air Act,* to create a comprehensive approach to environmental protection in Canada. Environment Canada and Health and Welfare Canada share responsibility for CEPA.

The Act defines substances very broadly as any distinguishable kind of animate or inanimate, organic or inorganic matter, and includes chemicals, products of biotechnology and mixtures, including emissions and effluents. A substance is considered toxic if it has the potential to cause harm to the environment or to human life when it is dispensed into the environment, or when it causes another substance to become harmful to the environment or to human life.

2.2 Clean Air Philosophy

The establishment and development of Canada's air pollution control program involved the use of a closed circle concept with the following elements:

- an inventory of pollutants and sources;
- a set of national air quality objectives with desirable, acceptable and tolerable ranges (see Table 1);

Table 1: Three Tiered System of Air Quality Objectives

High Pollutant Levels		maximum tolerable limit
	Tolerable Range of Air Quality	
		maximum acceptable limit
	Acceptable Range of Air Quality	
		maximum desirable limit
	Desirable Range of Air Quality	
Low Pollutant Levels		

- pollution controls which are based on containment at source, using the best practicable technology, or on air resource management;
- a monitoring system to gather data which could be evaluated to show whether the air quality objectives were being met.

The emphasis was on urban air quality, and the program has been successful in achieving and maintaining air quality levels in the acceptable and desirable ranges in urban centres across Canada (see section 4, Table 5), with the exception of ozone.

However, the emergence in the late 1970s of the long-range transport of air pollution and in particular the acid rain issue has caused Canada, like many other countries, to rethink its approach to, and strategies for, the management of air pollution. Increased knowledge of the long-term effects of low concentrations of air pollutants, as exemplified by acid aerosols and ozone, has shown that we must avoid assumptions about the assimilative capacities of air and ecosystems generally. Other fundamental aspects of air pollution, as well as other forms of pollution, have been brought into focus. For example, the transboundary flow of air pollution is now a major issue in many parts of the world. The realization that specific pollution problems, be they air, water or waste, cannot be effectively managed in isolation from other related pollution problems but must be dealt with as well.

The global nature of air pollution issues, such as the depletion of the ozone layer and global warming, mandates that international solutions be found. Therefore, while Canada will continue to guard against deterioration in its urban air quality, the emphasis is now on management of air pollution on an issue basis.

2.3 The Economics of Environmental Protection

Consistent with the principles of fairness and avoidance of undue economic burden, Canada requires that all regulatory proposals be accompanied by a regulatory impact statement indicating the social and economic benefits and costs of compliance. The regulatory process also provides for thorough consultation with industry and other interested parties at several decision points, affording an opportunity for discussion of the benefits and costs of the regulation. Overall, Canada strongly subscribes to the concept of environmentally sustainable development.

2.4 Legislation and Instruments

The Canadian *Environmental Protection Act* (CEPA) has been described in section 2.1. It is a multi-media type of legislation which is well suited to today's complex environmental issues involving more than a single medium or ecosystem. A number of instruments, originally developed under the authority of the *Clean Air Act*, have been incorporated in CEPA as follows:

- National Air Quality Objectives - Table 2;
- National Emission Guidelines - Table 3;
- National Emission Standards for the control of lead from secondary lead smelters; emissions from asbestos mining, milling and manufacturing, mercury from chloro-alkali plants and vinyl chloride from the manufacture of vinyl and polyvinyl chlorides;
- Lead in gasoline regulations under CEPA require the complete phase-out of lead in gasoline as of December 1990.

Motor vehicle emission standards are prescribed under the *Motor Vehicle Safety Act.* The standards are:

	Grams per mile				
	HC	CO	NO_x	Evaporative	Particulate (Diesel)
Passenger Cars	.41	3.4	1.0	2.0	.20
Light Duty Trucks	.80	10.0	1.2	2.0	.26
	Grams per brake horse power hour				
Heavy Duty Trucks–Diesel	1.3	15.5	6.0		.60
Heavy Duty Trucks–Gas (<14,000 lbs)	1.1	14.4	6.0	3.0 (per test)	
Heavy Duty Trucks–Gas (>14,000 lbs)	1.9	37.1	6.0	4.0 (per test)	

Because of the shared jurisdiction aspects of pollution control in Canada, the Canadian *Environmental Protection Act* (CEPA) allows the recognition of provincial requirements as equivalent to regulations promulgated under CEPA. Where such equivalency exists, the federal government may enter into agreements with the province concerned to ensure enforcement of the provincial requirements. For example, the National Emission Standards previously referred to (see Table 2) are mandatory regulations which limit emissions of the toxic pollutants specified in each standard. Federal regulations are applicable to these emissions because protection of human health, a federal jurisdiction, is the basis for them. Their enforcement is a federal responsibility, but in practice, administrative arrangements have been made in certain provinces under which those provinces administer the federal regulations.

Table 2: National Air Quality Objectives*

Air contaminant	*Maximum desirable level*	*Maximum acceptable level*	*Maximum tolerable level*
Sulphur dioxide			
Annual arithmetic mean	30 mg/m³ (0.01 ppm)	60 mg/m³ (0.02 ppm)	
Average concentration over a 24-h period	150 mg/m³ (0.06 ppm)	300 mg/m³ (0.11 ppm)	800 mg/m³ (0.31 ppm)
Average concentration over a 1-h period	450 mg/m³ (0.17 ppm)	900 mg/m³ (0.34 ppm)	
Suspended particulate matter			
Annual geometric mean	60 mg/m³	70 mg/m³	
Average concentration over a 24-h period		120 mg/m³	400 mg/m³
Carbon monoxide			
Average concentration over a 8-h period	6 mg/m³ (5 ppm)	15 mg/m³ (13 ppm)	20 mg/m³ (17 ppm)
Average concentration over a 1-h period	15 mg/m³ (13 ppm)	35 mg/m³ (31 ppm)	
Oxidants (ozone)			
Annual arithmetic mean		30 mg/m³ (0.015 ppm)	
Average concentration over a 1-h period	100 mg/m³ (0.05 ppm)	160 mg/m³ (0.08 ppm)	300 mg/m³ (0.15 ppm)
Nitrogen dioxide			
Annual arithmetic mean	60 mg/m³ (0.03 ppm)	100 mg/m³ (0.05 ppm)	
Average concentration over a 24-h period		200 mg/m³ (0.11 ppm)	300 mg/m³ (0.16 ppm)
Average concentration		400 mg/m³ (0.21 ppm)	1000 mg/m³ (0.53 ppm)
Hydrogen fluoride†			
Average concentration over a 70 day period		0.20 mg/m³ (0.2 ppb)	
Average concentration over a 30 day period		0.35 mg/m³ (0.4 ppb)	
Average concentration over a 7 day period	0.20 mg/m³ (0.2 ppb)	0.55 mg/m³ (0.7 ppb)	
Average concentration over a 24-h period	0.040 mg/m³ (0.5 ppb)	0.85 mg/m³ (3.6 ppb)	
Hydrogen sulphide†			
Average concentration over a 24-h period		5.0 mg/m³ (3.6 ppb)	
Average concentration over a 1-h period	1.0 mg/m³ (0.7 ppb)	15.0 mg/m³ (10.8 ppb)	

* Conditions of 25°C and 101.325 kPa are used as the basis for conversion from mg/m³ to ppm and ppb
† Proposed

The National Emission Guidelines, shown under Table 3, are not mandatory, but were developed by the federal government in consultation with the provincial environmental agencies in order to establish a national base for control of emissions from the industries concerned. Many of the provinces have adopted the guideline emission limits as regulations in their jurisdictions. An example is the wood pulping industry National Emissions Guidelines for new stationary sources.

Table 3: National Emission Guidelines

a) Cement Industry National Emission Guidelines
b) Asphalt Paving Industry National Emission Guidelines
c) Metallurgical Coke Manufacturing Industry National Emission Guidelines
d) Arctic Mining Industry Emission Guidelines
e) Packaged Incinerators National Emission Guidelines for New Stationary Sources
f) Thermal Power Generation Emissions — National Guidelines for New Stationary Sources
A number of provinces have introduced regulations under their air pollution legislation which are based upon these national guidelines.

The provincial agencies use a variety of approaches to control industrial emissions to the atmosphere, including emissions tests, approval permits, etc. Smoke controls are generally not used in Canada. Emissions from domestic woodburners have been resolved through the development of combustion efficiency requirements for the burners.

3 IMPLEMENTATION AND ENFORCEMENT

3.1 Enforcement

Traditionally, the federal government shares jurisdiction with the provinces and territories in many aspects of environmental protection, including air pollution, because of the constitutional division of powers between the two levels of government. Agreements are being developed to identify the roles of the two levels of government in administering the Canadian *Environmental Protection Act* (CEPA) to ensure that they work together efficiently to protect the environment. Of major importance in this area is the Federal Provincial Advisory Committee to CEPA. In addition, the Canadian Council of Ministers of the Environment continues to be a forum for the federal and provincial ministers to become well informed and to cooperate in the management of environmental issues. Also involved is the Federal-Provincial Advisory Committee on Air Quality, formerly known as the Federal Provincial Committee on Air Pollution, which for seventeen years has been the vehicle to achieve consensus on air pollution problems and their resolution.

Consistent with the federal government policy of consultation with all interested parties on environmental issues is the establishment of the Canadian Environmental Advisory Council. This body, representing a broad cross-section of Canadians who are knowledgeable and concerned about the environment, operates in a confidential advisory capacity to the Federal Minister of the Environment.

3.2 Measurement Methods and Networks

A knowledge of the nature and extent of air pollution across Canada is fundamental to the sound planning of pollution abatement programmes. The federal and provincial governments fulfil this need jointly by sharing responsibility for operating the National Air Pollution Surveillance (NAPS) Network. As of December 1987, the network consists of approximately 400 monitors operating around the clock at 135 stations in 59 cities generating ambient air quality data.

Monitoring stations are located in most Canadian cities with populations over 100 000, measuring sulphur dioxide, nitrogen dioxide, carbon monoxide, particulates and ozone. Particulate samples are analyzed for various contaminants such as sulphates, nitrates and lead. The data collected is used to determine trends in ambient air quality and to develop or modify air pollution control programs. If air pollution is observed to increase, surveillance activities also increase. Most NAPS stations are operated by provincial or municipal authorities. The network is expanding its capability and capacity to monitor other pollutants, in particular organic compounds and heavy metals that are health and environmental concerns.

Canada also operates the Canadian Air and Precipitation Monitoring Network consisting of 18 sites coordinated with 8 sites for measuring air pollutants.

The following standard reference methods have been developed for the measurement of pollutant emissions at source, for the measurement of pollutants in ambient air, and for testing fuels:

a) Standard Reference - Methods for Pollutants in Ambient Air:

- Ambient Testing for Hydrogen Sulphide (Gas Chromatographic Method);
- Measurement of Suspended Particulates in the Atmosphere (High Volume Method);
- Measurement of Nitrogen Dioxide in the Atmosphere (Chemiluminescence Method);
- Determination of Lead in Airborne Particulates (Atomic Absorption Spectrophotometry);
- Measurement of Carbon Monoxide in the Atmosphere (Non-dispersive Infra-red Spectrometry);

- Measurement of Ozone in the Atmosphere (Chemiluminescence Method) (revised 1981);
- Measurement of Sulphur Dioxide in the Atmosphere (West-Gaeke Method).

b) Standard Reference Methods for the Measurement of Source:

- Emissions from Asbestos Mining and Milling;
- Method S-3 Sampling of Drill Baghouse Exhaust Emissions;
- Measurement of Opacity of Emissions from Stationary Sources;
- Emissions from Mercury Cell Chlor-Alkali Plants;
- Particulate Emissions from Stationary Sources;
- Emissions from Vinyl Chloride and Polyvinyl Chloride Manufacturing;
- Sulphur Dioxide Emissions from Stationary Sources;
- Nitrogen Oxide Emissions from Stationary Sources;
- Particulates and Lead Emissions from Secondary Lead Smelters;
- Arsenic Emissions from Gold Roasting.

c) Standard Reference Methods for Testing Fuels:

- Determination of Lead in Automotive Gasoline (Atomic Absorption) (Revised 1981);
- Determination of Phosphorous in Automotive Gasoline (Spectrophotometric Method) (Revised 1980).

3.3 Role of Private Interest Groups

The private sector and public interest groups have traditionally been directly involved in the development of Canada's air pollution control program. The National Emission Guidelines and Standards listed in Tables 2 and 3 were, for the most part, developed using a Task Force approach led by the federal government with participation by the provinces, industry and public interest environmental groups. At this time, federal government regulatory policy requires that all new regulatory proposals be subjected to public consultation. As a consequence, private and public interest stakeholders are involved in consultation with the federal government during development of new regulations, and again when the regulatory proposal is announced in the *Canada Gazette* with a ninety day period for submission of comments.

4 EFFECTIVENESS OF CONTROLS

Significant declines in the annual average levels of sulphur dioxide, nitrogen dioxide, carbon monoxide, suspended particulate and lead in urban areas have been achieved since 1974 (see Table 4). No general trend in ozone levels is apparent however, and this is a reflection of the complexity of the problem as discussed previously in section 1.2.3 on Ground-level Ozone/Urban Smog.

Table 4: A Summary of Seven Pollutants Measured by NAPS Network

Pollutant	*1987 average concentrations*	*Percent decline 1978-1987*	*Percent decline 1974-1987*
Sulphur dioxide	5 ppb	50	61
Nitrogen dioxide	21 ppb	27	29
Carbon monoxide	1 ppm	33	58
Ozone	16 ppb	no change	NA
Total suspended particulate	48 $\mu g/m^3$	22	40
Particulate lead	0.1 $\mu g/m^3$	76	85
Coefficient of haze	2.28 COH	no change	26

NA – not available for 1974

Air quality index values for many Canadian cities show a definite trend towards good air quality overall. Compliance by industry with national emissions standards is generally very high, and substantial reductions are seen in the total amounts of pollutants like mercury and vinyl chloride emitted to the environment since the introduction of regulations.

Collectively, the air pollution control programs of federal, provincial and municipal authorities have led to some significant decreases in emissions of pollutants, and to progressively better air quality. Rising energy costs and a growing awareness of the seriousness of air pollution as a public concern have been effective catalysts in the progress that has been made. Emissions regulations, the introduction of pollution abatement equipment, improvements in industrial processes and the use of cleaner fuels are the means by which most of this progress has been achieved. This progress is shown in Table 5 which indicates attainment of the Acceptable Level of the National Ambient Air Quality Objectives in 1987 compared to 1974.

Table 5: Attainment of the Acceptable (NAAQO) Level in 1974 and 1987

Pollutant	*Annual objective*		*1-hour objective*		*8-hour objective*		*24-hour objective*	
	1974	*1987*	*1974*	*1987*	*1974*	*1987*	*1974*	*1987*
Sulphur dioxide	82	100	87	93	—	—	85	97
*Nitrogen dioxide	96	100	86	100	—	—	84	100
Carbon monoxide	—	—	97	100	71	94	—	—
*Ozone	50	43	18	45	—	—	—	—
Total Suspended	51	98	—	—	—	—	N/A	N/A

— no objective
* for NO_2 and O_3 the attainment rate is compared to 1977 and 1979 respectively

The major air pollution issues - long range transport of air pollution/acid rain, ozone layer depletion, urban smog and global warming - will require long-term monitoring to evaluate the impacts of control programs. In the near term progress will be evaluated on the basis of achieved emission reductions, or reductions in consumption of the chemicals concerned.

5 FUTURE DEVELOPMENTS

The control of industrial air pollution, and other primary sources such as automobiles, will continue to be addressed in Canada in order to sustain acceptable air quality and to prevent degradation of that quality, particularly in the urban environment.

The advent of long term global environmental issues such as deterioration of the ozone layer, acid rain and global warming have, however, brought about some significant changes in the way the air pollution prevention program is developed and managed. The issue management approach has evolved, and greater emphasis is being placed on Canada's role and responsibilities in an international context; this is resulting in strong support for and participation in the United Nations Environment Program, other similar organizations, and through bilateral cooperation with the United States. In addition, the recognition of the inter-relationships between various forms of pollution has and will continue to require the adoption of policies and programs which avoid addressing any one environmental problem in isolation.

FINLAND

1 INTRODUCTION

1.1 Topography, Climate, Population

Finland is situated between the 60th and 70th latitudes with one quarter of the country being north of the Arctic Circle. Finland is bound on the west and south by the Baltic Sea, with a coastline of about 1000 km, and over 20 000 islands. With a total area of 338 145 sq. km, Finland is the fifth largest country in Europe. The level of the land is rising to such an extent that the country's area grows by 7 sq. km annually. Most of the country is lowland. The bedrock is mostly part of the broad pre-Cambrian zone and contains a wide range of minerals but usually in small amounts.

The climate is relatively mild compared to that of many other areas on the same latitudes, largely because the Gulf Stream has a warming effect. The growing season, however, is short: 175-188 days on the south coast and about 130 days around the Arctic Circle. The ground remains covered with snow for about three months of the year in the south and as many as seven months in the north.

Finland has a population of about 4.94 million. The country is rather sparsely populated with 14.5 inhabitants per sq. km, with the south and south-west being the most densely populated areas. Lapland is the most sparsely populated with some districts having only two to three inhabitants per sq. km. The concentration of the population in the south western and southern parts of Finland is the result of the considerable rural emigration and urbanization that started in the mid-1950s. Today about 40 per cent of the population inhabits rural areas, while 60 per cent live in towns and urban districts. The larger cities and in particular the Helsinki area have grown most rapidly. Five cities have a population of more than 100 000: Helsinki (492 000), Tampere (171 000), Espoo (168 000), Turku (160 000) and Vantaa (151 000).

1.2 Specific National Problems

Since Finland is a sparsely populated country located at the northern edge of Europe and away from major industrial areas, its air quality is generally quite good. However, overall pollution loads have increased over the years and, in the recent past, levels have been reached that are in excess of proposed critical loads for sensitive environmental systems. In addition, local air pollution problems have existed and continue to exist.

The major cause of air pollution is the use of fossil fuels in stationary and mobile sources. At national level, acidification of freshwater and soil is a serious threat to water quality and forest growth. This may ultimately have significant negative implications for fisheries, recreation activities, and the wood and wood products industry, upon which the country's overall income is heavily dependant.

The major local air pollution problem today is exhaust emissions from road traffic. In addition to the effects of exhausts, air quality is threatened by dust raised from the roads. The problems caused by malodorous gases are still very serious in many regions near pulp mills.

2 DEVELOPMENT OF AIR POLLUTION CONTROLS AND LEGISLATION

In Finland the effects of air pollution were first observed in the immediate surroundings of industrial establishments from 1910-1929. Finland has, however, been spared from air pollution catastrophes.

Malodorous gases, especially from chemical pulp mills, have always been a particlular air pollution problem in Finland. Attention was first drawn to it when the work of an ad hoc Sulphate Pulp Committee led to an enactment, in 1920, of legislation entitled "*An Act on Particular Neighbourhood Relations*". The *Neighbourhood Act* made feasible a substantially broader participation than was normally the case. The Act gives a right of appeal to all those who own land or apartments in the vicinity of an industrial activity, or who may be otherwise affected by the activity. Grounds for an appeal extend to causes like air pollution and noise pollution.

Until 1982, air pollution issues were covered mainly by the *Neighbourhood Act* and the *Public Health Act.* Before 1982, practical air pollution control was carried out mainly on a voluntary basis. In October 1982, the *Air Pollution Control Act* was passed, together with an explanatory Decree concerning its implementation.

The objectives of the *Air Pollution Control Act* are

a) to prevent pollution of the atmosphere in order to protect human health;

b) to protect flora, fauna and the environment in general;

c) to prevent economic losses and decline in the quality of life as a consequence of deteriorating air quality.

The *Air Pollution Control Act* sets out several preventative measures, including general recommendations and regulations which may be issued by the Government concerning:

- ambient air quality guidelines or maximum concentration levels;
- fuel and product specifications;
- maximum emission levels.

While the *Air Pollution Control Act* itself does not provide for an authorization procedure, it does provide for a notification procedure under which the Provincial Office, after a hearing and negotiation process, makes a decision on notification. This decision may include emission limits and monitoring requirements.

Some legal instruments applying to domestic heating and miscellaneous sources are published in the *Public Health Act* and in the *Neighbourhood Act*. The health authorities consider the situation taking into account possible health effects when granting the license for location or when giving a statement to the physical planning authorities. For example, the Neighbourhood Act regulates the location of odour or dirty dust causing activities.

The administrative apparatus for environmental protection was strengthened considerably in 1983 with the establishment of the Ministry of the Environment. In the Ministry there is a special division for air pollution control and noise abatement. The administrative apparatus was strengthened even more with the establishment of environmental protection divisions in the Provincial Offices in 1983 and local environment protection boards in all municipalities over 3000 inhabitants of which there are about 350, in 1986.

3 IMPLEMENTATION AND ENFORCEMENT

3.1 National Enforcement

Finland has no single, comprehensive environmental law and consequently, no uniform national enforcement procedures. Environmental legislation is composed of a number of individual acts of secondary regulations or instructions, each of which refer to only one specific sector of environmental protection.

The two principal means by which the objectives of the *Air Pollution Control Act* can be achieved are regulations and guidelines issued by the Government in Finland and the notification procedure for facilities causing air pollution and the associated decisions.

Decisions made by the Government may be used to govern air pollution control on a nationwide basis. Fifteen such decisions have been made so far. Decisions, especially those on the composition of fuel and on emission limits, have proved effective in advancing air pollution control. New global problems in air pollution control, especially the depletion of the ozone layer, have resulted in a need to increase the authority of the Government. Thus in 1989 the *Air Pollution Control Act* was reinforced to tackle this problem.

The Government has issued the following regulations and guidelines:

3.1.1 Air Quality

Table 1: Air Quality Guidelines (as of 1 September 1984)

Substance	*Concentration*	*Time*	*Calculated determinations*
Sulphur dioxide	40 μg/m³	1 a	arithmetic mean value
	200 μg/m³	1 d	98% of values < 200 μg/m³ (period 1 year)
	500 μg/m³	1 h	99% of values < 500 μg/m³ (period 30 days)
Total suspended particulates	60 μg/m³	1 a	arithmetic mean value
	150 μg/m³	1 d	98% of values < 150 μg/m³ (period 1 year)
Nitrogen dioxide	150 μg/m³	1 d	98% of values < 150 μg/m³ (period 1 year)
	300 μg/m³	1 h	99% of values < 300 μg/m³ (period 30 days)
Carbon monoxide	10 mg³	8 h	arithmetic mean value
	30 mg³	1 h	arithmetic mean value

At the same time as issuing air quality guidelines the Government defined the long term goals of air quality policy as follows:

- To protect conifers in wide forest and agricultural areas or nature conservation areas, annual sulphur dioxide levels outside towns and bigger villages should not be more than 25 μg/m³;
- To avoid acidification effects the total sulphur deposition should be under 0.5 g S/m².

3.1.2 Emissions

- *Guidelines for particulate emissions from energy production (1987)* vary from 25 mg/MJ (50 MWth) to 200 mg/MJ (1 MWth) when using peat or other domestic fuels; from 25 mg/MJ (50 MWth) to 150 mg/MJ (1 MWth) when using coal; and from 40 mg/MJ (50 MWth) to 90 mg/MJ (1 MWth) when using fuel oil.

- *Regulation of sulphur dioxide emissions from coal fired power plants and boilers (1987, 1990)*: emissions from new power plants within the range 50-150 MWth must not exceed 230 mg/MJ. Emissions from new plants over 150 MWth must not exceed 140 mg/MJ. Emissions from existing plant bigger than 200 MWth must not exceed 230 mg/MJ after 1 January 1994.

- *General regulations on the limitation of sulphur compound emissions from sulphate pulp mills (1987)*: emissions from new mills may at most be 4.0 kg SO_2/ton pulp produced. Emissions from existing mills must not exceed 6.0 kg SO_2/ton pulp produced after 1 January 1998.

- *General regulations on the limitation of sulphur compound emissions from oil refineries (1987)*: emissions from oil refineries must not, in the main refinery, exceed 8 per cent and in the small and old plant exceed 12 per cent of the total sulphur input into the refinery after 1 January 1992).

- *General regulations on the limitation of sulphur dioxide emissions from power plants using heavy fuel oil (1987):* emissions from power plants must not exceed 500 mg/MJ in densely inhabited areas in southern Finland and 1350 mg/MJ in other parts of the country after 1 January 1991.

- *Regulations on the limitation of sulphur compound emissions from sulphuric acid plants (1987)*: emissions from new plant using gas with a sulphur dioxide content of over 7 per cent must not exceed 4-5 kg/ton produced sulphuric acid calculated as a hundred per cent sulphuric acid and emissions from corresponding old plant must not exceed 5.5-7.0 kg/ton produced after 1 January 1993. Emissions from plant using gas with a sulphur dioxide content of less than 7 per cent must not exceed 15 kg/ton sulphuric acid produced, calculated as a hundred per cent sulphuric acid.

3.1.3 Composition of Products

- *Regulation on the sulphur content of light fuel oil and diesel oil (1987)*: the sulphur content of light fuel oil and diesel oil must not exceed 0.2 per cent in weight.

- *Regulation on the sulphur content of coal (1987)*: the coal imported to the country for plant other than those provided with desulphurization equipment must not contain more than 1.2 per cent sulphur after 1 March 1988 and and after 1 January 1994, more than 1.0 per cent.

- *Regulation on the limitation of the burning of oil wastes (1987)*: The burning of waste oils is prohibited in smaller boilers.

- *Regulation on the lead and benzene content in motor petrol (1988)*: The production and import of leaded petrol (octane value <95) is prohibited as of 1 September 1989.

3.1.4 Reduction in Use and Import of Products

- *The prohibition of the import of CFCs and halons from countries not parties to the Montreal Protocol (1989)*: self explanatory.

- *The prohibition of use of CFCs in all plants where CFCs have not been used (1989)*: the regulation prohibits the use of CFCs in all units where they had not been used prior to the regulation entering into force.

The Ministry of the Environment is responsible for the legislation and regulation of air pollution sources. Exceptions are nuclear power plants, which come under the jurisdiction of the Ministry of Trade and Industry and regulations concerning radiation protection and supervision of the safety of nuclear power plants, for which the Centre for Radiation and Nuclear Safety within the Ministry of Social Affairs and Health is responsible.

3.2 Regional and Local Enforcement

Administratively Finland is divided into twelve provinces and 461 municipalities of which 94 are towns. The twelve Provincial Offices, which are in formal terms totally independent of the Cabinet and Ministers, have supreme executive authority in regional administration and are responsible for the enforcement of environmental pollution regulations.

Under special acts, the Provincial Offices make decisions on permits and notifications and issue statements to other authorities. The environmental protection tasks of the Provincial Offices, which have increased considerably as a result of development of legislation, are comprehensive, and demand wide-ranging and thorough expertise. The handling of tasks is particularly hampered by the shortage of personnel. Over the past five years, more staff have been taken on for technical duties covering waste management and air pollution control, but the resources are still not sufficient.

The explanatory Decree relating to the *Air Pollution Control Act* provides for a notification procedure but leaves the enforcement of compliance to the Provincial Offices. The purpose of the notification procedure is to give the supervisory provincial authority an opportunity to review the details of industrial activities and, as necessary, to impose appropriate operating conditions.

Industries listed in the explanatory Decree (Table 2) are obliged to notify the Provincial Office of their activities. About 1500 establishments are required to submit notifications, in addition to the 100-200 establishments which are either new or change the nature of their operations.

Table 2: Establishments Required Under the Air Pollution Control Act to Submit Notifications

- Chemical pulp mills;
- Iron and steel works, sintering works or factories manufacturing ferrous alloys;
- Cement factories, lime works and factories manufacturing asbestos products or mineral-based fibres;
- Hazardous wastes treatment facilities;
- Waste incinerators or any plants at which at least one ton per hour or 5000 tonnes per year of wastes are burned;
- Plants manufacturing artificial fibres or their raw materials;
- Power stations burning oil, coal, wood, peat or any other combustible substance, or boiler units with a maximum output in excess of 5MW or at which the annual amount of energy in the fuel used exceeds 54 TJ;
- Non-ferrous metal refineries and calcination plants;
- Plants producing inorganic industrial chemicals such as acids, alkalis, chlorine, pigments, or titanium dioxide;
- Fertilizer factories;
- Oil refineries;
- Plants manufacturing basic organic chemicals;
- Ferrous metal foundries with annual outputs of at least 500 tonnes or any other foundry or smelting unit with an annual output exceeding 200 tonnes;
- Fodder protein or bone meal factories;
- Factories manufacturing synthetic rubber or raw materials for the plastic industry;
- Stationary stone crushing plants or asphalt units as well as those which are transportable and operate at a specific location for a period of more than a year;
- Battery factories;
- Particle board or plywood mills;
- Plant using materials containing evaporative solvents, when the amount which is bound to or remains in the product is subtracted, at least 50 tonnes annually, or the corresponding maximum consumption of which is at least 100 kg an hour;
- Factories using more than 1000 kg per year of chlorofluorocarbons.

Official processing of notifications involves the assessment of air pollution control at industrial premises, obtaining all necessary submissions of statements, and considering the views of concerned parties. Notifications have to be published for comment in at least one local newspaper, and private citizens are included among the parties having the right to submit comments. In many instances nature conservation bodies or residents' organizations, condominia managements and cooperative housing bodies, as well as public meetings, have been responsible for drawing attention to nuisances, deleterious effects on the environment or human health and have called for reductions in emissions.

On the basis of a notification the Provincial Office makes a decision, which usually includes binding regulations necessary to prevent air pollution. These can be limits on emissions, other protective measures relating to emissions and monitoring emissions and their impact on air quality.

The establishments concerned and the municipal authorities responsible for air pollution can appeal against a decision taken by the Provincial Office at the end of a notification. Private citizens, by contrast, do not have this right.

3.3 Air Quality Monitoring

Air quality in Finland is monitored both at the municipal level and by background stations. The Meteorological Institute is responsible for measurements at background stations. Responsibility for monitoring air quality at the municipal level is divided among the municipal authorities and industry.

Since 1971, deposition has been monitored on a nationwide basis by the National Board of Waters and the Environment at forty background stations.

Air quality is monitored either by direct or indirect methods. Direct methods include air quality measurements and surveys of the dispersion of pollutants in the air. When using indirect methods the air quality is assessed in terms of emissions or their effects.

In the municipalities monitoring of air quality is divided into three stages according to extent and content: preliminary survey, comprehensive survey and continuous monitoring. As at October 1990 preliminary or comprehensive surveys had been carried out and continuous monitoring is performed in 40 municipalities. (There are 461 municipalities in Finland.) Measurement is the most common method of air quality monitoring. The pollutants most commonly measured in ambient air quality are sulphur dioxide and particles (TSP). Measurements of nitrogen dioxide and ozone have been started in larger cities.

With the reduction in sulphur emissions and the increasing use of district heating, sulphur dioxide concentrations have been reduced significantly in many urban areas. On the other hand, concentrations of pollutants mainly caused by traffic, such as nitrogen oxides, carbon monoxide and particles are still high, especially in urban areas. The level of the recommended values for total suspended particles has been exceeded in some urban areas, including the Helsinki region.

4 EFFECTIVENESS OF CONTROLS

While more knowledge on air pollution is continuously gained, this also leads to new problems being detected. Substances formerly considered safe are found to have deleterious effects at concentrations previously thought harmless. Much information has been obtained in recent years on the effects of atmospheric pollution on forests and waterways. Studies of these and research on human health and wellbeing are also of importance for the future. This also sets challenges for air quality monitoring and research work carried out by the local authorities.

The *Air Pollution Control Act* has been in force since October 1982. Decisions, especially those on the composition of fuel and on emission limits, made by the Government and implemented in the notification procedure by the Provincial Offices have proved effective in advancing air pollution control. Through the notification procedure the Provincial Offices deal with air pollution questions related to individual facilities.

The most serious global air pollution problems are climate change and the depletion of the ozone layer. These global problems have resulted in a need to increase the authority of Government in prohibiting, for example, substances harmful to the ozone layer. In 1989 a Bill for an alteration of the *Air Pollution Control Act* in accordance with this was passed by the Parliament.

The Government has started a new study project on global air pollution. Scientific as well as socio-economic aspects of possible climate change will be studied. Without a major structural change in energy generation, carbon dioxide emissions will be much higher in the near future.

5 FUTURE DEVELOPMENTS

Over the last few years, the main emphasis has been on limiting emissions of sulphur compounds and nitrogen oxides. Since 1980, sulphur emissions have been reduced by about 60 per cent. This is mainly due to structural changes such as the introduction of nuclear power, switching from heavy fuel oil to hard coal, and development of processes in the pulp and paper industry and chemical industries. The positive reductions in sulphur dioxide emissions seen in Table 3 have also been influenced by the *Air Pollution Control Act* and decisions taken according to it.

Table 3: Sulphur Emissions (1000 t as $S0_2$)

Year	*Emissions*
1980	584
1985	371
1986	323
1987	324
1988	305
1989	242

Nitrogen oxide emissions have been increasing and are still on the rise in Finland, as shown by Table 4.

Table 4: Nitrogen Oxide Emissions (1000 t as $N0_2$)

Year	*Emissions*
1980	264
1985	251
1987	270
1988	276

The national acidification project studied the effects of emissions from fuel use and other sources on Finnish nature for five years. The results of the project, which were published in August 1990 indicate that the internationally proposed critical levels of nitrogen and sulphur deposition are being exceeded over almost the whole country and the most sensitive bio-indicators have reacted. Unless a reduction in emissions is achieved, the risk of damage to forests from air pollution will definitely increase over time.

The Government has adopted an action plan for reducing sulphur emissions by 80 per cent of the 1980 level by the year 2000. The enforcement of this programme will require tightening the regulations on sulphur emissions issued by the Government in 1987.

An ad hoc Commission on nitrogen oxides appointed to draft a programme to reduce the nitrogen oxide emissions nationwide by 30 per cent compared with 1980 levels completed its work in April 1990. It has made the following proposals:

- Emission guidelines for new and existing boilers and power plants: the guidelines for existing plants only apply to plants over 100 MWth. Combustion modification is the main means of achieving reduction in emissions. Large coal fired plants may have to resort to the catalytic treatment of flue gases.
- Exhaust emission regulations for heavy duty vehicles will be tightened: the limit values which it is proposed to issue by 1995 at the latest, mean that nitrogen dioxide emissions will correspond to the US regulations of 1994 for lorries. Permitted emissions will be reduced by 60 per cent compared with the present.
- Exhaust emission regulations for delivery vehicles will be tightened in 1992 (new models) and in 1993 (all new vehicles): the regulation means the enforcement of US exhaust regulations for light duty trucks; in gasoline-engine cars catalysing equipment will be mandatory.
- On diesel engines in farm and forestry tractors the regulations (ECE R-49) now applicable to present diesel engines for vehicles will be applied as of 1994.
- Regulations on exhaust emissions from gasoline-engine cars will be tightened at the technically possible rate. The present regulation on exhaust limit values for passenger cars corresponds to the US regulation of 1983. In gasoline-engine cars catalyst equipment is mandatory.

The Nitrogen Oxides Commission estimated that by adopting the above mentioned measures it will be possible to reduce nitrogen oxides emissions by 15 per cent compared with 1980 levels but the target of 30 per cent reduction will not be achieved. This will require further measures.

Worldwide environmental problems include climate change and the depletion of the ozone layer. International cooperation is important to solve these.

The Montreal Protocol on Substances that Deplete the Ozone Layer was signed in September 1987. At the second meeting in June 1990 in London the parties of the Montreal Protocol decided on adjustments and the amendments of the Protocol which will prohibit the use of CFCs by the year 2000. Finland has, however, set an earlier target for the reduction in CFC use and aims to stop all use of CFCs by 1998. The Government has decided to phase out CFC compounds by the end of 1994.

Finland has participated in the preliminary preparations of the international convention on climate change and has also recently started domestic preparations for participation in international negotiations on the global convention.

Finland has no single, comprehensive environmental law. Instead, environmental legislation is composed of a number of individual acts. As a consequence, permission and notification procedures lack uniformity and do not provide full coverage in all instances where protection is required. Furthermore, permission may take a variety of forms for a given installation, according to different environmental effects, and may still require to be addressed to several authorities. Similarly, enforcement procedures are varied as are formal provisions for environmental offences.

In view of this an ad hoc Committee on Permission and Notification Procedures, which completed its work in spring 1990, proposed that permission and notification procedures should be coordinated. The Finnish Government subsequently introduced a bill in the Parliament for an *Environmental Permits Procedure Act.* This was passed in January 1991 and it is proposed that the Act should enter into force in 1992.

Currently several permits covering a single plant - such as the *Air Pollution Control Notification, the Waste Management Plan,* and permits under the *Public Health Act* and the *Neighbourhood Act* are required. Under the new procedure these will be combined into a single permit. This will harmonize the processing of permit applications as all permits for a plant (except those concerning waste water discharges) will be obtained from one public authority The reform will also facilitate a concentrated assessment of the overall effects of the plant on the environment.

6 BIBLIOGRAPHY

Ministry of the Environment, Environmental Protection Department (1990). *Air Quality Management in Finland* (Finnish and English). 15:1989.

Ministry of the Environment (1986). *Report of Sulphur Compound Commission* (Finnish, summary in Swedish and English). Commission Report 1986:33.

Ministry of the Environment (1990). *Report of Nitrogen Oxides Commission* (Finnish, summary in Swedish and English). Commission Report 1990:11.

Ministry of the Environment (1989). *Report of Committee on Permission and Notification Procedures* (Finnish, Swedish summary). Committee Report 1989:52.

Ministry of the Environment (1984). *General Guidelines on the Notification Procedure for Air Pollution Control* (No. 4638/401/84).

Ministry of the Environment (1986). *General Guidelines on Measuring Air Quality and Comparing Results with Guidelines* (No. 4638/401/86).

Ministry of the Environment (1987). *General Guidelines on the Air Pollution Control Tasks of Provincial Offices and Municipalities* (No. 1954/401/87).

Ministry of the Environment (1989). *General Guidelines on the Monitoring of Emissions* (No. 681/401/89).

Ministry of the Environment (1989). *General Guidelines on the Enforcement and Monitoring of the Government Decision on the sulphur content of coal* (No. 358/401/89).

(General guidelines in Finnish and in Swedish)

Ministry of the Environment and the Ministry of Agriculture and Forestry (1990). *Acidification in Finland*; Report of the Finnish Acidification Programme (Finnish, Swedish and English). Series A 89:1990.

FRANCE

1 INTRODUCTION

1.1 Topography, Climate, Population

France has a surface area of 551 000 sq. km, and is the largest country in Europe after the USSR. It is situated in the middle of the north temperate zone (between latitudes 42 and 51 degrees).

It enjoys an Atlantic climate on the large western half, a somewhat continental climate in the east and north-east (especially the Vosges mountains, Alsace plain and Jura mountains) and a Mediterranean climate in the south-east.

Two important mountain ranges limit the country: the Pyrenees and Alps, with altitudes exceeding 3000 metres and 4000 metres respectively; here the climates are typical of a mountainous region. The three other mountainous zones are the Massif Central (maximum altitude 1886 metres), the Vosges and Jura in the Eastern part of the country. The Massif Central with its Cévennes range abruptly separates the Atlantic and Mediterranean climates.

In general, the mountainous and plain areas in France are fairly equally distributed (two-thirds of the country has an altitude lower than 250 metres).

The oceanic climate is characterized by sizeable precipitations, except in the summer. The Mediterranean climate is particularly dry and hot in summer with frequent forest fires. For some years, however, severe drought has not been unknown even in north-west areas which are generally considered wet.

The relation between climate and atmospheric pollution is of course complex, but may be summarized as follows:

- in the western side of the country, the prevailing westerly winds favour the dispersion of pollutants;
- in the south-east, there are periods of strong or very strong north and north westerly winds (the famous Mistral and also the Tramontane).

Sometimes, rather long anticyclonic periods, with little or no wind may result in high pollution levels, chiefly in winter (mainly sulphur dioxide and nitrogen oxides), and also in summer (ozone peaks). These high pollution levels correspond to temperature inversions which are frequent in valleys (the areas of Alsace, Lyon and Grenoble). In winter, strong peaks of sulphur dioxide are observed in Alsace when the winds blow from the north east.

France has the largest forested area in the European Community (27 per cent of the territory in 1980). Although there is dieback in some forests (especially Vosges and Jura), the phenomenon is not as severe as in Germany.

Metropolitan France has 56,5 million inhabitants (against 40 million in 1950), which corresponds to an average density of about 100 inhabitants per sq. km. Thus France appears relatively underpopulated. However, it is important to note that since 1945 there has been a significant population shift from rural to urban areas: what we call the "rural exodus".

Agricultural productivity has increased tremendously, the traditional almost self-sufficient family farm having been replaced, chiefly on the plains, by highly productive agriculture, using large amounts of fertiliser and mechanical instruments. Moreover, large-scale production of cattle, pigs and poultry - chiefly in the west (Brittany) - has resulted in serious environmental problems (odours, ammonia emissions, nitrate pollution of rivers and underground water).

As a result of these developments, many towns have increased in size. There are now 37 towns with more than 100 000 inhabitants (as compared with 25 in 1851); 75 per cent of people now live in towns or work in urban activities. A recent development is that many people leave town centres, moving to cottages in suburbs or nearby villages and commute by car, thus creating daily traffic jams and pollution. In addition, there is a serious risk of the countryside becoming unmanaged, all the more so as European policy for abating agricultural overproduction could result in an extension of fallow lands.

1.2 Industry

France has a long industrial tradition. During the past 30 years, there has however been extensive modernization, largely due to the decline of coal mining and of heavy industries centred on collieries.

Heavy industry is now concentrated on three main centres: Lower Seine, Lyon-Grenoble and Fos-Berre. Seven other, less important areas are the North of France (which has diversified following the decline of collieries), Nantes (lower Loire), Strasbourg, Paris area, Lorraine, Dunkirk and Toulouse. Whereas industry in the three main areas is centred on petroleum and petrochemicals and fertilizers, it is more diversified in the other seven areas which include most aspects of modern industry, such as car manufacture, plastics, electronics, computers and aeronautics. The aluminium industry is centred mainly in the Pyrenees and Alps.

Needless to say, the main atmospheric pollution problems are in the three areas of heavy industry, aggravated by automobile pollution.

1.3 Energy

Energy production and utilization are key points in evaluating atmospheric pollution. France has rather modest domestic fossil energy sources. Petroleum production reached 3,7 Mt in 1989 (south-west of France and east of Paris). The large sulphurous gas field in Lacq (near the Pyrenees), and its satellites, are declining. In 1988, it produced 2 150 000 metric tons.

Coal extraction has also considerably declined: 14,5 Mt in 1988 versus 22,5 Mt in 1978, of which 9 Mt in Lorraine and 3 Mt of highly sulphurous coal extracted at the Gardanne collieries near Marseilles.

The energy picture of France has undergone a tremendous change during the last 10 years, as illustrated by Table 1.

Table 1: Primary Energy Consumption (M tonnes of oil equivalent)

	1973	*1980*	*1989*
Coal	28,1	31,2	19,6
Petroleum	128,5	119,4	89,4
Gas	13,6	21,1	24,4
Primary electricity*	13,3	30,0	69,9
Other energies (non fossil)	2,0	3,0	4,2
	185,5	204,7	206,5 †

* – Hydraulic + Nuclear
† – 12,9 have been used in non energetic uses

Now, 75 per cent of electricity is of nuclear origin, which is the highest percentage in the world. Total nuclear power is 52,5 MWe (1 January 1989), second to the USA (98 MWe).

Another interesting development is the progress of district heating, based on coal and, in some places like Paris, on urban waste incineration. Cogeneration, which is said to be a key procedure for saving energy, is still very limited (an example is urban waste incineration in the Paris area).

2 DEVELOPMENT OF AIR POLLUTION CONTROLS AND LEGISLATION

2.1 Principles of Atmospheric Pollution Control

There are eight principles which may be said to form the basis of any consideration of air pollution control in France:

- *Rarely indisputable scientific bases:* in spite of innumerable biological studies on the effects of pollutants on human health (and also on the general environment) scientists are reluctant to say below which level pollution is harmless. In this instance, the policy is to resort to any proven means with acceptable cost liable to lower pollution. A preventive approach must be preferred to a curative one, with clean technologies strongly encouraged by public authorities.

- *Polluter pays principle:* the emitter of pollutants must pay for abating them but its operating costs and selling prices will of course reflect the corresponding cost. This approach encourages innovation in favour of more efficient and/or less costly processes. Of course, when the origin of an environmental damage is proven, the party responsible has to pay for it, in addition to a possible fine.

- *Public authorities must determine objectives:* objectives might include emission limits which industry can then decide how to meet. The objectives should take into account technical possibilities which implies open co-operation between industry and public authorities.

- *One cannot stop progress:* public authorities must encourage research on more efficient and/or less costly procedures for preventing, limiting and monitoring emissions. As a result, "eco-industries" are becoming a growing segment of the national industry.

- *The "autosurveillance" principle or automonitoring:* this principle arises in a Circular dated 28 March 1988. Emitters must monitor their emissions and inform authorities, who have the possibility of checking by reference to certified laboratories or experts.

- *Integrated conservation of the environment:* it is not acceptable to contaminate water or ground with waste from atmospheric pollution control (and the reverse). The *Act on Environmentally Registered Installations* (19 July 1976) is the key regulation for activities of all kinds which create environmental problems. This Act, which is of relevance to atmospheric and other emissions, is summarized in section 2.2.1.

- *Reasonable decentralization of environmental action:*

decentralization is based on the belief that environmental issues are often better solved at local level, where people know exactly what the problem is. Nevertheless national acts, decrees, orders and circulars are necessary to define policy, and to ensure reasonable consistency throughout the regions.

Often the national texts are circulars or instructions which are not compulsory, but give guidance to local authorities when they establish prefectoral orders. Generally the instruction contains detailed propositions and figures, in particular emission limits and the local orders only need to be adapted to local situations.

- *France wants to be a good citizen of the EEC:* France does its best to apply European regulations by translating Directives and other texts into the French legal system and reporting to the EEC as required.

2.2 Legislation

Legislation covering the control of air pollution from industrial sources can be found in two major Acts: the Act of 19 July 1976 on *Installations Registered for Environmental Conservation,* and the *Basic Act of 1961.*

For the purposes of this paper, Acts are the legal texts (lois) voted on by Parliament. Decrees are prepared and signed by ministers. Orders (arrêtés) are legal texts signed by ministers or local political authorities (préfets, mayors).

2.2.1 Installations Registered for Environment Conservation, Act of 19 July 1976

This Act applies to atmospheric and other forms of pollution. As such, it is of central importance to French legislation and thus is summarized in some detail.

General Features

The Act dates back to a Decree of 15 October 1810, and was developed into comprehensive legislation by the Act of 19 December 1917, updated and completed by the 19 July 1976 Act, now in force. The Act covers about 500 000 private or public installations of all kinds which present any kind of environmental risk: manufactures and factories, workshops, buildings, warehouses and depots, large animal breeding facilities etc. All transportation facilities (cars, boats, trains, etc), nuclear plant and all facilities depending on national defence are excluded, as there are specific regulations covering them.

An official register of activities attached to the 1976 Act is continuously revised and updated by governmental decrees.

The 1976 Act is very comprehensive in that it regulates all environmental hazards for air and water and also concerns noise and waste. Accidental as well as persistent pollution are considered, and the Act also pays attention to workers' health and safety, and to fire protection.

The registered activities presenting the greatest risks for the environment require an authorization from the Préfet. The less hazardous ones have to be declared before being started. Generally, the register specifies plant capacities above which an authorization is required and size intervals for declaration. Very small plants are outside the scope of the Act.

All the official procedures are described in detail in the Decree of 21 September 1977. As already said, although the Act and Decree were issued by the Central Government, implementation is essentially local.

Activities requiring Authorizations

Industry represents the bulk of these activities. When a company, i.e. the applicant wants to erect a new installation or substantially modify an existing one, it must first provide the following documents:

a) A detailed report describing the purpose, nature, location of the proposed activity, raw materials, intermediate and finished products involved, nuisance generated, etc, and how it is planned to eliminate or reduce these nuisances to acceptable levels.

b) A study of the impact on the environment (the legal basis for this impact study is the 10 July 1976 Act on nature protection, which imposes impact studies for many kinds of large projects, such as new motorways, canals, pipelines, etc).

c) A study on accidental type risks and their reduction.

These reports are carefully reviewed by the local Registered Installation Inspectors who discuss them with the applicant. After that, the Préfet issues an order nominating an enquiry commissioner and setting a date for the public enquiry.

The whole document is accessible to people in town halls for one month, after advertisement in the local media. At the same time, the project is submitted to local administrative services (hygiene, safety etc.) and to town councils. All these procedures are consultative, and comments are invited on the applications. The commissioner then compiles all the comments for the inspectors who write an order project after further discussion with the applicant. It is finally published as an "arrêté préfectoral", which states in detail how the plant is to be erected, operated and monitored so as to reduce pollution and all environmental risks to the minimum possible.

In general, the orders contain limit values for emissions, provisions for monitoring effluents and sometimes the neighbourhood (quality of atmosphere, watercourse and underground waters). Safe waste disposal is also considered.

Other features worth mentioning are:

- Confidential information is released only to inspectors in a special mail.
- Complementary orders may be issued by the Préfet if installations are substantially modified or extended; if there are neighbourhood complaints or an accident, or in general if new facts justify it.
- During the life of the project, the inspectors have free access to the plant and are entitled to receive all information on plant operations and emissions. The applicant must of course declare any significant accidents.
- In the case of especially hazardous operations or products, an elaborate risk study has to be submitted to local authorities in line with the Seveso European Directive (82/501/EEC).
- If the operations are to be discontinued for a long time, local authorities must be informed. If a plant is to be dismantled, the cleared site has to remain environmentally acceptable.
- If a non-registered installation creates serious environmental problems, the Préfet may issue an appropriate order.
- In rare cases when a very large plant would affect the environment of several départements or a foreign country, the procedure may be referred to the ministry in charge of environment.
- Time limits are specified for the whole procedure.
- Regulations to be applied by certain types of industry may be fixed at ministry level, either by an order or, more often, by a circular translated locally into orders by inspectors, and signed by the Préfet.

Activities Requiring a Declaration

Industrial, commercial, agricultural and miscellaneous activities which may represent only a limited hazard to the environment must be declared under the Act, before being started.

The declaration is submitted to the Préfet before completion of the project, with a report similar to the one above, but generally much simpler. The Préfet replies by sending the applicant a copy of conditions appropriate to installations of the type.

Other Provisions of the Act and Decree

- Special inspectors and ad hoc local administrative bodies handle the procedure for agricultural projects and the food industry.
- A series of penalties is specified by the Act for offenders.
- Annual fees have to be paid by all registered installations.
- Provisions specify under what conditions and delays decisions may be brought to the administrative court by the applicant or by any third party.

A third party who acquires or leases land or a building in the vicinity of a registered installation after the publication of an order cannot challenge this order in the courts.

(NB: English translations of the *Registered Installation Act* and decree, and also of the register, are available at APPA, 58 rue du Rocher, 75008 Paris.)

2.2.2 The Basic Act 1961

The most important Act in current French legislation on atmospheric pollution is the 1961 Act (Act of 2 August 1961 on air pollution and odour abatement). This Act is an enabling law and implementation is carried out through decrees, orders and instructions. It enables the relevant authorities to regulate all emitters (large or small, stationary or mobile, residential or industrial, etc) to protect the environment, to require formal approval for new facilities, to impose inspections, to penalise contraventions.

As a result of this Act, a series of three legal texts have been issued:

- Limitation on burning certain fuels either locally (Special Protection Zones) or temporarily (Alarm Zones).
- Control and limitation of emissions by combustion from certain types of installation.
- Environmentally oriented product specifications.

The cornerstone of combustion regulation is however the Ministerial Order of 20 June 1975 on the equipment and operation of thermal power plants with a view to abating pollution and saving energy. The main provisions are as follows:

a) It is applicable to all installations above 75 thermies/hour 86 kW, excepting gas turbines, diesel engines, process furnaces, flares, incinerators.

b) Equipment for monitoring combustion and pollution emissions, must be installed appropriate for the size of plant.

c) Calculation of minimum stack height as regards sulphur dioxide dispersion, using tables and a formula, the parameters of which are percentage S in fuel, flue gas output (with minimum velocities specified), average sulphur dioxide concentrations at ground level, etc. (The calculation procedure had already been presented in a ministerial instruction of 24 November 1970. A similar formula for particulates was published on 13 August 1971).

d) Maximum particulate emissions as specified by the Smoke Index and specifications by weight, approximately:

- 150 mg/thermie for new plants (1 thermie = 4.1855 MJ)
- 250 mg/thermie for existing plants with higher figures acceptable during limited number of hours per year.

A series of regulations was issued at the time of the first energy crisis (1973-1974); these generally consolidate provisions for energy conservation and pollution abatement.

The Decree of 15 May 1974 authorizes the appropriate ministries to regulate by order combustion, space heating and incineration plants (equipment specifications and approvals, plant operation and emission monitoring, consultation of authorities on new projects, official inspections, etc, and penalties for offenders).

The order of 5 July 1977 and circular letter of 16 June 1978 require periodic visits and detailed audits of combustion plants by certified experts, the objective being both energy conservation and environmental protection. These texts specify in detail the various pieces of equipment and points to be checked at the plant, especially conformity with environmental regulations. Experts may recommend improvements. (Articles set out the procedure for experts to be officially certified.) The data collected by the experts on inspected plants are forwarded to the Regional Divisions for Industry and Research (DRIRs).

2.2.3 Regulation concerning Fuel Products

Gasolines: As of 1 August 1989, the maximum lead content of gasoline was legally lowered to 0,25 g/1 (order of 9 June 1989). Sales of unleaded gasoline are still growing.

Heating Oil and Diesel Fuel: An order of 28 March 1980 limits sulphur content at 0,3 per cent maximum, effective 1 September 1980.

Heavy Fuel Oil: Three grades of HFO are specified as regards maximum sulphur content:

Percentage S max =

- Regular grade 4.0

- BTS grade 2.0 (Basse Teneur en Soufre - Low Sulphur Content).
- TBTS grade 1.0 (Très Basse Teneur en Soufre - Very Low Sulphur Content).

BTS and TBTS grades are used in special protection and alarm zones (see sections 3.6 and 3.7) and in some industrial processes where too much sulphur is undesirable.

Specifications of gasoline (lead content) and middle distillates are in line with relevant EEC Directives.

2.2.4 Air Quality Standards (EEC Directives)

France is bound by the Air Quality Directives issued by the European Community:

- Sulphur dioxide and suspended particulates - 15 July 1980, 80/779/EEC;
- Nitrogen dioxide - 7 March 1985, 85/205/EEC;
- Lead - 3 December 1982, 82/884/EEC.

These Directives require that monitoring networks (see section 3.3) be set up to check compliance with them.

2.2.5 Taxes on Pollutants

Updating legal texts, dated 9 June 1985, a Decree and an order of 13 May 1990 extend pollution taxes to sulphur derivatives, nitrogen oxides, hydrochloric acid, VOCs and particulates. For the time being, the taxes are levied only on the first three pollutants at the rate of 150 F/t expressed in sulphur dioxide, nitrogen dioxide and hydrogen chloride. All combustion plants consuming at least 20 MW energy are liable to the tax, as well as any other installations (of combustion, of incineration, chemical or other), emitting annually more than 150 tonnes of one or more of the above pollutants.

A managing committee including civil servants and industrialists is in charge of allocating the money collected to Rand D type projects, to new installations (under strict conditions), to developments in emission measuring instruments, to monitoring networks and even promotional actions in favour of pollution control. The money collected should amount to 185 MF/year. Only industrial plants paying the tax benefit from aid for their projects. The overall system is administered by the Agence pour la Qualité de l'Air. (Rand D type projects are those relating to the development of new or improved processes for abating pollutants.)

2.2.6 The Order of 27 June 1990

This order implements the EC Directive on large combustion plants

(88/609/EEC). The Directive imposes two sets of obligations on Member States:

a) Reduction of overall sulphur dioxide and nitrogen oxide emissions of existing large combustion plants (50 MW or more) by imposed percentages, taking 1980 as the reference date. For France, the figures are:

	1993 %	*1998* %	*2003* %
Sulphur dioxide	40	60	70
Nitrogen oxides	20	40	—

Due to the progress made in nuclear energy, gas, and energy conservation, the 1993 and 1998 goals have already been reached.

b) Emission limit values for new installations, concerning sulphur dioxide, nitrogen oxides, particulates, and dispositions for monitoring these emissions.

The French order integrally transcribes item b) above and has added a regulation concerning the calculation of stack height. The formula is a modernization of the one contained in instructions of 24 November 1970 (for sulphur dioxide) and 13 August 1971 (see above). The new regulation prescribes calculations based on sulphur dioxide, nitrogen oxides, particulates. The highest of the three figures obtained must be retained. Above 100 MW, the use of computer modelling is compulsory (it is optional below this).

2.2.7 Regulations on Volatile Organic Compounds

In 1985, public authorities became conscious that tropospheric ozone was a growing problem and that an abatement policy for VOCs was necessary. An objective of 30 per cent VOC reduction between 1985 and 2000 was established, and a series of regulations enacted to meet this objective:

- Convention between paint manufacturers and government for the development of low solvent and solvent-free paints and varnishes, and the commercial promotion of the new products (19 February 1986).
- Order and circular of 4 September 1986 on reduction of hydrocarbon emissions by petroleum product storage. This applies to existing tanks with a capacity of at least 2500 m^3, and to new tanks of at least 1500 m^3.
- Circular of 9 September 1986 on printing plants in the declaration range of registered installations.

- Circular of 11 June 1987 on solvent emission reduction in car assembly line painting (maximum 10,5 kg per vehicle as of 1 January 1991 at the latest).
- Circular and technical instruction of 5 April 1988 on graphic reproduction workshops.
- Circular of 25 August 1988 on coilcoating plants. This circular limits emission of hydrocarbons and metals (lead, chromium, zinc, cadmium) and also regulates water pollution, waste elimination, noise.

2.2.8 Regulation on Mobile Sources

France generally follows the EEC Directives on automobile emissions, in particular Directives 88/76/EEC and 88/77/EEC of 3 December 1987, on passenger cars and heavy duty vehicles. These Directives have been superseded by Directives 89/458/EEC of 19 July 1989. Consequently, all new passenger cars will require 3-way catalytic converters after 1 January 1993.

2.2.9 Urban Waste Incineration

France has enacted a circular (9 June 1986) regulating the gaseous, particulate and heavy metal emissions of new urban waste incinerators.

It also contains provisions for water pollution prevention and waste disposal. Subsequently, two European Directives have been issued dated 8 June 1989 (new plants) and 21 June 1989 (existing plants). These are currently being transcribed into a French order, and will include provisions on water pollution and waste disposal.

2.2.10 Miscellaneous Regulations

A number of other regulations are in force at national level, and all refer to the Act on Registered Installations. Some are derived from European Directives which will have an increasing influence on French legislation. The following are some official texts (circular: C, to be locally transcribed into prefectoral orders if the need arises) and some ministerial orders (0):

Register Number	*Activity*	*Dates*
22	Manufacture of nitric acid	C 31.07.74
32	Steel manufacture	C 08.03.73
125	Manufacture of lime, plaster	C 04.12.75
146	Manufacture of cement	C 25.08.81

167 c	Treatment of incineration of industrial wastes from registered installations	C 21.03.83
183 bis	Asphalt coating of road materials	C 14.01.74
235	Petroleum refineries	O 04.09.67 O 12.09.73
284	Metal and alloy foundries	C 08.03.73
292 bis	Agglomeration of iron ore	C 24.07.72

2.2.11 Prevention of Major Risks

The ministry in charge of environmental affairs also has responsibility for major technological and natural risks; these were formerly the responsibility of a specific State secretariat. This activity involves accidental pollution of water, air and ground, etc, man-made or natural.

Risk assessment is now a section of environmental impact studies required by the *Act on Registered Installations.* A circular of 28 December 1983 defines how risk assessment studies shall be made:

- Description of the installation and its environment.
- Identification of scenarios describing possible accidents to the plant, either internal or external, and whatever the cause.
- Evaluation of effects on workers and on the environment.
- Justification of preventive measures.
- Description and operating procedures for intervention personnel and equipment.

An external expert may be called on for the study. Operational plans to be put in action in the event of an accident must be established by the plant involving the Préfet for important accidents.

This is in line with the Directive of 24 June 1982 - the Seveso Directive. As a result of this Directive, about 300 hazardous installations have been subject to risk assessment studies, often detailed and exhaustive, and many improvements have subsequently been made to equipment and procedures.

Following the Seveso Directive, information and leaflets have been distributed to the neighbourhood, advising them on what to do in the event of an alert.

The regulation concerning the distance between hazardous installations and private or public buildings is being revised and strengthened.

3 IMPLEMENTATION AND ENFORCEMENT

3.1 Central Organization

Environmental affairs are now the responsibility of a delegate ministry reporting directly to the Prime Minister.

The French Ministry of Environment was created in 1971 and has broad objectives covering air and water protection, noise abatement, waste elimination and recycling, the protection of nature and wildlife, fishing and hunting, and the quality of life in general. Recently, it was given responsibility for accidental risks - both naturally occurring or resulting from human activities.

Air pollution problems within their regulatory and related aspects are handled by the "Direction de l'Eau, de la Prévention des Pollutions et des Risques", and within this division, by the Sous-Direction Pollution de l'Air.

There is a division in charge of promoting and financing scientific research. It cooperates with CNRS (Centre National de la Recherche Scientifique), universities and various institutions and often liaises with foreign organizations.

Another major governmental institution is the "Agence pour la Qualité de l'Air" (Air Quality Agency) whose functions are:

- To assist the development of new technologies for preventing or abating pollution, for monitoring pollutants at emission or in the atmosphere.
- To assist with the first industrial application of a new technology.
- To participate in financing new investments in the field of air quality monitoring (see below, Networks).

These activities are achieved by partially subsidising the corresponding expenditure on public funds. The AQA allocates subsidies or loans, taken from public funds, to selected projects presented by industrialists, laboratories or by monitoring associations.

The AQA also administers the collection and utilisation of funds raised through a tax on pollutants (see section 2.2.5). A further function of the AQA is to provide public information through publications, films and videotapes, lectures, and answering individual questions, etc.

3.2 Regional and Local Governmental Bodies

The local orders implementing environmental policy are enacted by the "Préfet" (Prefect) in each "département" (district). The Préfet is the government delegate and is appointed not elected. There are about one hundred départements in France but all the basic investigations, inquiries and writing of the orders are carried out by DRIR (Directions Régionales de l'Industrie et de la Recherche - Regional Divisions for Industry and Research) - now DRIRE to include environment - under the direction of the Ministry of Environment. There are 24 DRIRs (including La Réunion and Caribbean Islands). In these divisions, the "inspection des installations classées" (Registered Installation Inspection), has a central role which goes beyond the management of registered installations. (These points will also be developed in the following section). The inspections address all environmental aspects: air, water, wastes, noise, risks, etc.

Currently, the Ministry has little proper manpower outside central offices and works through local personnel hired from other ministries, a situation which may change as a consequence of the "Plan National pour l'Environnement" (National Environmental Plan) which is described in section 5.

3.3 Monitoring Networks

Air quality has been monitored in a number of urban and industrial areas for several decades. About 20 pollutants are measured at 1940 stations installed in 1420 sites as follows:

Pollutant	*Approximate number of stations*
Sulphur dioxide	770
Nitrogen oxides	100
Particulates and black smoke	250
Carbon monoxide	60
Lead	50

Twenty-two of the thirty-four urban areas of more than 200 000 inhabitants have a network.

The trend is now to measure non-methane hydrocarbons and micropollutants such as heavy metals. Several regions have mobile laboratories for monitoring campaigns. Some stations are "multi-functional", i.e. they continuously measure several substances.

In current continuous monitoring, the sampling time is 15 minutes; the figures are automatically sent by telephone (or sometimes by radio) to a central computer which displays pollutant concentrations on maps, memorizes the data and makes calculations required by operators.

3.4 Main Networks

Nearly all monitoring sites are organized into networks operated by non profit associations, mainly of two types:

- During the 1960s and early 1970s, the Association pour la Prévention de la Pollution Atmosphérique (APPA), through its regional committees, created a number of networks with participation from local public authorities, industries and various other participants. A dozen towns have networks of this type.
- Starting in 1973, governmental action was aimed at creating enlarged associations comprising the Regional Divisions for Industry and Research (DRIRs), local industries, local communities, various environmental associations including APPA in a number cases. They are managed by DRIR.

These associations, of which there are now twenty-three, consolidated and extended existing networks chiefly in large towns and industrial areas. They provide a useful means of cooperation between members of associations.

Other networks are aimed at specific industries, for instance hydrofluoric acid around aluminium plants.

Governmental services, in particular the Agence pour la Qualité de l'Air (AQA), largely participate in capital expenditure. Operating and maintenance costs are financed by association members.

Some networks, which resulted from the combining of two or more previous sub-networks needed rationalization which resulted in eliminating redundant stations and displacing some others.

In Bordeaux, continuous measurements of carbon monoxide in carefully selected streets are fed into a computer which houses the data for regulating the traffic so as to minimize traffic jams (GERTRUDE system - Gestion Electronique et Régulation du Trafic Routier Urbain Défiant les Embouteillages).

The associations periodically publish figures and maps, giving mean and peak levels of pollution on a monthly and annual basis. Some have published public relations brochures, often of excellent quality. Some networks have a telephone number and/or a MINITEL connection which everybody can consult.

3.5 Other Networks

France operates three EMEP (European Monitoring and Evaluation Programme) stations and three BAPMON (Background Air Pollution Monitoring Network) stations which belong to Meteo France.

In order to investigate the various factors involved in forest decline, the French Government has set up the DEFORPA research programme (Dépérissement des Forêts attribué à la Pollution Atmosphérique). For this, a new network of twelve monitoring stations which are remote from local emitters, sample air, aerosols, precipitations and measure sulphur dioxide, nitrogen oxides, hydrocarbons, ozone and sulphates, on a daily basis. The main station, at the Donon pass in the Vosges, collects samples at three levels above ground level, on a specially built tower. It has been partially financed by the European Community. The whole system is named MERA. Several MERA stations will soon be used as EMEP stations.

3.6 Special Protection Zones (SPZ)

In urban/industrial areas where mean atmospheric concentrations tend to be too high (sulphur dioxide and particulates, an order limits the use of fuels to those with low levels of sulphur. Emissions of dust may also be limited.

A decree of 15 May 1974 specifies the general basis for creating SPZs, of which there are presently six:

- Paris intra muros (1978)
- Paris adjacent districts (1978)
- Lille and nine adjacent municipalities (1974)
- Lyon and Villeurbanne (1974)
- Marseilles (1981) (in winter only)
- Strasbourg (1990).

These orders are signed by ministries.

In the Lille SPZ, fuels up to 2,0 per cent sulphur are authorized. The limit is 1,0 per cent maximum in other zones.

Other provisions of orders refer to limitation of smoke and particulates in stack gases, to stack height, to monitoring and recording operating data, to periodic inspections by experts, etc, varying from one SPZ to another.

3.7 Alarm Zones

In urban industrial areas where severe pollution peaks are observed, the Préfet may enact an order setting up an alarm zone. When meteorological conditions are such that peak pollution levels appear or are likely to appear, major fuel consumers are obliged to switch to low sulphur fuels (less than 1 per cent in general). Some industrial operations have also to be discontinued or slowed down, or not to be started up.

The procedure is economically attractive since it limits the use of expensive high quality fuels. The map below gives the location of networks, of special protection zones and of alarm zones.

Distribution of Atmospheric Pollution Surveillance Networks

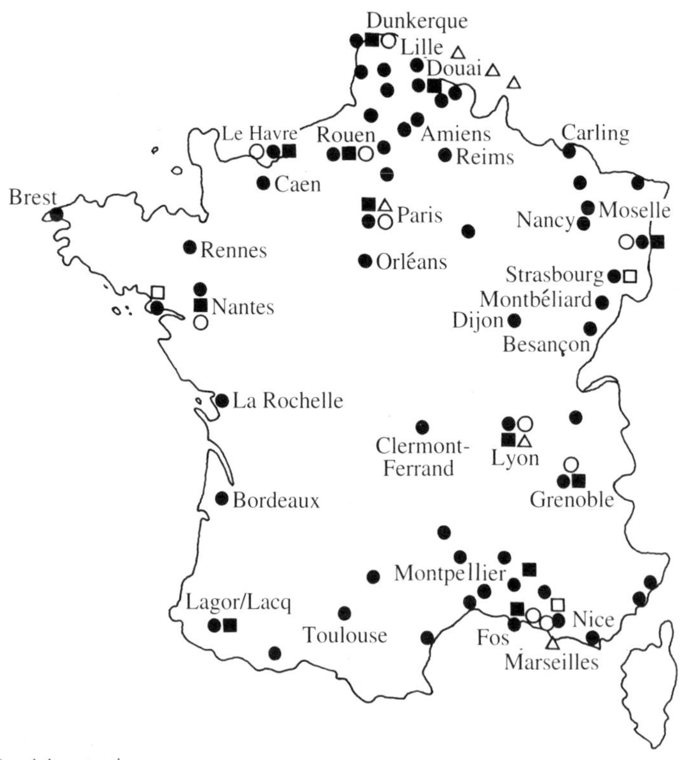

Key

△ Special protection zone
■ Alarm zone
□ Projected alarm zone
● Projected and/or Monitoring networks
○ Network with SO_2 alarm

4 EFFECTIVENESS OF CONTROLS

4.1 Figures and Statistics on Atmospheric Pollution

4.1.1 Emissions

a) Sulphur Dioxide in 1000's tonnes/year

	1980	*1989*
Residential and tertiary sectors including district heating	423	186
Industry + agriculture	1 053	279
Power plants	1 224	374
Energy conversion*	210	113
Industrial processes	302	184
Transportation	127	135
Total	3 339	1 271
* – Essentially oil refineries		

The steep decline in emissions is due to the development of nuclear electricity, to the progress of natural gas, and to a strong policy of energy conservation. Indeed, the total figure for 1989 is 5 per cent higher than 1988 because of the drought and trouble at nuclear plants, mainly shortage of cooling water, resulting in more coal burned in power plants.

b) Nitrogen Oxides (expressed as nitrogen dioxide in 1000's tonnes)

	1980	*1989*
Residential and tertiary including district heating	95	77
Industry + agriculture	221	97
Power plants	321	121
Energy conversion*	27	16
Industrial processes	138	106
Transportation	1 033	1 342
Total	1 835	1 759

Automobile emissions represent 76 per cent of 1989 emissions, against 56 per cent in 1980.

Two developments are of relevance: the fast development of automobile traffic and the significant decline of stationary source emissions for the same reasons as for sulphur dioxide.

c) Particulates (in 1000's tonnes)

	1980	*1989*
Residential and tertiary including district heating	25	14
Industry + agriculture	39	20
Power plants	91	35
Energy conversion*	13	9
Industrial processes	205	132
Transportation	54	81
Total	427	291

The decrease related to combustion has roughly the same causes as that of sulphur dioxide. Particulate filters partly explain the decline in process emissions, while the progress of diesel engines is responsible for the increase in the case of transportation.

4.1.2 Atmospheric Pollution in Nine French Towns

The graphs for nine large towns show a general decline in average sulphur dioxide concentrations from 1976 to 1988. This is clearly explained by the decrease in emissions.

The relatively high figures for Strasbourg are partly explained by sulphur dioxide brought from outside by easterly winds in winter.

The increase in nitrogen oxides mean concentrations are general in 1989. On the other hand, lead content of air is continuously declining due to lowering of lead concentrations in gasoline.

Atmospheric Pollution in Nine French Towns

Mean annual SO_2 concentrations

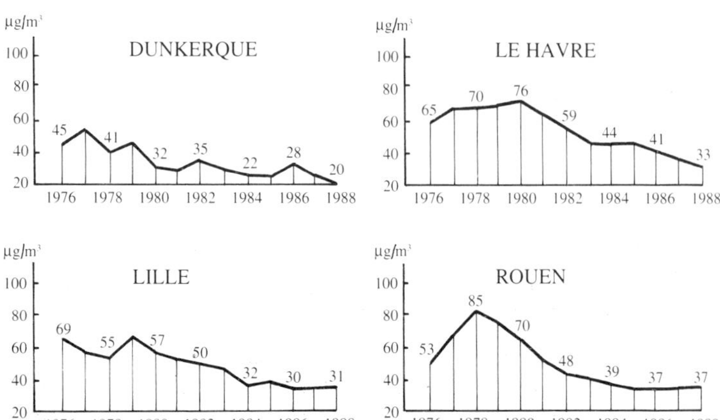

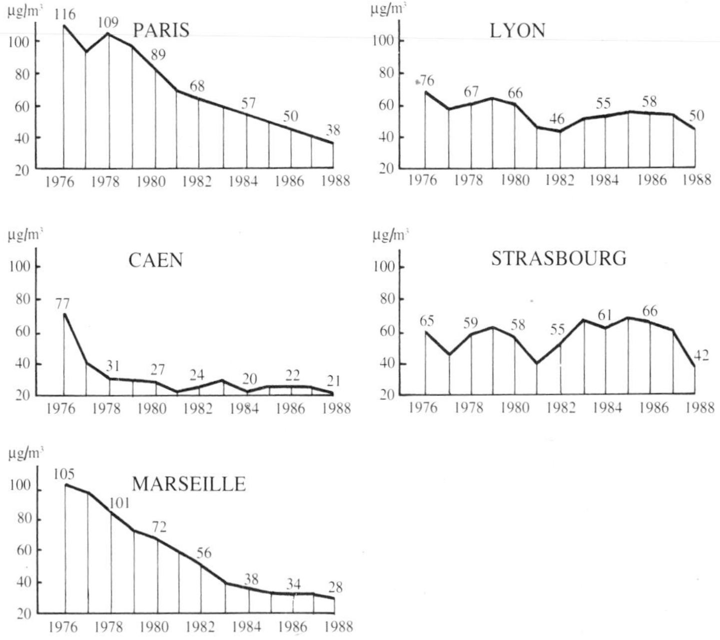

Sources: *Secretariat d'Etat Charge de l'Environnement. Direction de l'Eau de la Prevention des Pollutions et des risques. Sous-Direction de la Pollution de l'Air. Service de l'Environnement Industriel.*

Monitoring stations are located in places considered as the most representative of pollution levels. The locations are thus specific to each town, and comparisons between towns therefore have little significance.

5 FUTURE DEVELOPMENTS

5.1 A New Environmental Policy in France

The ministry in charge of environmental affairs has issued a draft for a "Plan National pour l'Environnement" (PNE) which proposes a radical strengthening of environmental policy in all areas. The report states that France is late in dealing with a number of points compared with the most advanced countries in the field of the environment.

Sectoral objectives for atmospheric pollution are as follows:

- Further decrease in sulphur dioxide emissions by 25 to 30 per cent before 2000;
- Abate nitrogen oxide emissions;

- Actively promote stabilization of European carbon dioxide emissions (taking 1990 as reference) or setting a quota per inhabitant, etc.

Administrative structures will be drastically revamped at ministry level and environmental services will be created at regional level. The environmental budget will be tripled in five years, and the total staff will reach 3000 workers. Local authorities will be given more responsibilities in the regions, departements and municipalities.

A French Environment Institute will be established, which will operate as an observatory and a data bank, connected with he European Environmental Institute; it will supply scientific and technical data necessary for efficient legislation and discussion at EEC level.

Overall expenditure on the environment will reach F.Fr. 115 billion in 1995 (30 billion more than now) and F.Fr. 155 billion in the year 2000. Money will be collected through an extension of the polluter pays principle (involving consumers, who will pay higher prices for a better environmental quality), and by a number of new and increased taxes, in particular an extension of the existing tax on pollutants (see above). Taxes will also be put on wastes.

A labelling system for the so called "ecoproduits" (products which do not hurt the environment) will be instituted in liaison with the EEC.

The basic philosophy underlying the PNE is that environmental affairs are not only the concern of specialized circles, but of all human activities; therefore each ministry, each actor in the economy, each citizen must correctly handle the environmental side of his activity.

The most important long range project is that related to the greenhouse effect. France works closely with the EEC on this topic. An inter-ministerial committee on the greenhouse effect has been appointed. A research programme named ECLAT (Etude des Climat et de l'Atmosphere) has been started, aimed at studying the possible impact of climate change on ecosystems and on the French economy, the programme will aim to develop possible policies and cooperate with international initiatives such as the IGBP (International Geosphere-Biosphere Programme), WCRP (World Climate Research Programme), and IPCC (Intergovernmental Panel on Climate Change).

France has just proposed a programme for preventing the greenhouse effect, featuring a high, dissuasive tax on fossil carbon, applicable to EEC and OECD countries, growing year after year, but compensated by decreases in other taxes so as to maintain the overall levy on the economy.

6 BIBLIOGRAPHY

APPA, *Pollution Atmosphérique,* quarterly scientific and review journal. Available APPA, 58 rue du Rocher, 75008 Paris.

Etudes Documentaires du CITEPA (Centre Interprofessionnel Technique d'Etudes de la Pollution Atmosphérique). Available 3 rue Henri Heine, 75016 Paris.

Secrétariat d'Etat à l'Environnement (NN 1989), *La Prévention des Pollution et Risques des Activites Economiques,* Service de l'Environnement Industriel. Available 14 bd du General Leclerc, 92524 Neuilly sur Seine Cedex.

Secrétariat d'Etat à l'Environnement, Etat de l'Environnement (Edition 1989), Données statistiques commentées. Available, as above.

Secrétariat à l'Environnement, *Plan National pour l'Environnement* (Brice Lalonde), Revue Actualité Environnement Supplément No. 122 (Septembre 1990). Available, as above.

GERMANY

1 INTRODUCTION

October 3, 1990 is a date of major importance in the history of Germany. Following a separation of more than 40 years as a result of the Second World War, the five states which had been constituted as the territory of the former German Democratic Republic (GDR) declared their accession to the Federal Republic of Germany (FRG). Politically and historically, it is therefore no longer necessary to distinguish between East and West Germany. It will of course take several years and much effort to overcome the consequences of the separate development of the GDR and FRG, not least in the areas of economy, ecology and human relations.

1.1 Topography, Climate, Population

The total area of the unified Germany is 441 000 sq. km. The population is 79 million, giving an average density of 179 persons per sq. km, with the former FRG being the more densely populated area. Germany shares borders with a number of countries, and its northern border is on the North Sea. The North German lowlands are characterized by agriculture with several industrialized centres in big cities. From the centre to the south, there are hills with large forested areas. The whole of Germany has a moderate climate, typical of Central Europe with a maritime influence prevailing in the north and west; the east and south are mainly influenced by a continental climate.

The former FRG has a mainly industrial economy, with heavy industry mainly centred on the Rhine, Elbe and Ruhr Rivers: main industries include coal mining, iron and steel production, manufacture of steel and metal products, chemicals and textiles. The former GDR was one of the main producers worldwide of lignite; other industries of importance included iron and steel, chemicals and petrochemicals, shipbuilding and transport equipment.

1.2 Specific National Problems

The specific problems of a modern industrial nation such as Germany determine the outlines of clean air strategy and policy both at the present time and in the future. The problems of the old FRG are thus secondary to the pressing environmental problems in the former GDR. These specific and severe problems are dealt with below.

The former GDR was the country, and is now the territory, within the FRG with the highest level of air pollution in Europe. After the oil crisis in 1973 and the resultant replacement of oil, coal and gas by lignite there was an enormous increase in sulphur dioxide emissions. The highest air pollution levels today are measured in the industrial centres of Halle and Leipzig. The unification has also brought about a new start in legislation, as well as in responsibility for management, implementation and enforcement of environmental pollution control.

The environment in the former GDR has been particularly damaged because of the structure of its energy source which is unique in the world. Seventy-three per cent of the GDR's primary energy consumption is supplied by the extraction of 320 mill. t of raw lignite (sulphur content 0.6 to 3 per cent). Oil and natural gas amount to only 12 and 10 per cent respectively. As a result, there has been a constant increase in sulphur dioxide and dust emissions in the former GDR. Because of the "replacement strategies" for coke and gas, the emitter groups "households and residential areas" have also contributed to this. While in international treaties the GDR was until recently still working on the basis of sulphur dioxide emissions of 4.0 mill. t (from 1978), a peak of 5.6 mill. t. was reached in 1987. In addition to this, there was a dust emission of 2.3 mill. t.

Because of wrong decisions in energy and structural policy and a growing discrepancy between ecology and economy, no improvements in the air hygiene situation had been achieved in the last decade.

So the former GDR was far and away the leader among European countries with regard to sulphur dioxide and dust emission per inhabitant at 316 kg or 125 kg per year (for comparison: 120 kg in Poland and 17 kg in the old Federal Republic for sulphur dioxide). The emission density for sulphur dioxide is 49 t/km^2 and for dust 19 t/km^2 per year. These emission data also resulted in an unacceptably high emission load for 36.6 per cent of the population for sulphur dioxide and 26.3 per cent for dust.

The former GDR held first place for primary energy consumption per inhabitant in Europe and worldwide comes behind the USA and Canada in third place. The country consumed 40 per cent more energy per head of population than the old Federal Republic of Germany.

As clean air and energy consumption are closely related, special programmes are necessary for energy supply as well as shutting down, modernization and new construction of works.

In the former GDR, smog episodes in the towns were largely caused by decentralized fireplaces, domestic heating and small industries. Centralization of heat supply, rational energy application and optimum availability of low-emission energy sources are, therefore, an essential requirement for prophylactic health protection. The new energy policy also includes as its main requirement a reduction in energy demand.

Among the measures planned are the reduction of lignite production from the present level of 320 mill. t to 180 to 200 mill. t, the increase in coal and coke imports from 5.7 mill. t to 10.6 mill. t as well as increasing natural gas imports from 8 to 18 bill. m^3 per year. In addition, thermal insulation programmes for buildings, energy saving household appliances and waste heat recovery must form part of a new energy saving policy.

The use of gas and district heating will result in the reduction of coal-heated dwellings in the former GDR from the current 65 per cent to 45 per cent. Very simple technical requirements for temperature control in dwellings and public buildings are, however, to be created in order to counteract the waste of energy in housing.

The lignite power stations in the former GDR will continue to be operated to safeguard energy supplies. The use of the most modern technology is then all the more necessary to reduce emissions to the required level. The new German environmental situation is an acid test for the elimination of the ecological imbalance in Europe and could not only provide examples for economic projects for clean air in the former GDR but in the whole of Europe - in the East and West. The time factor plays a decisive part in this, both for ecological and economic reasons. Rapid success is necessary in order to show potential and weaker cooperation partners throughout Europe that joint efforts can pay off both economically and ecologically. The protection of our forests is an excellent example of this and at the same time a worthwhile objective.

2 DEVELOPMENT OF AIR POLLUTION CONTROLS AND LEGISLATION

2.1 Clean Air Philosophy

The Federal Government's environmental programme of 1971 was based on three fundamental principles:

- causative
- precautionary
- cooperation.

Clean air regulations, acts and measures can be undertaken as follows within the framework of these fundamental principles:

- Facility related measures (e.g. measures for plant requiring official authorization and plant not subject to official authorization);
- Area related measures (e.g. clean air plans, Smog Ordinance, detection of immissions* in polluted areas);
- Product related measures;
- General supplementary and supporting measures.

The *causative* principle is generally considered to be the fundamental concept of environmental policy. As a cost assessment principle, it is primarily of an economic nature. Its original definition was based on the known theoretical economic concept of supplementary social costs. All costs are accordingly basically ascribed to the products or services which incur the respective costs.

The principle embraces the method for the inclusion and charging of costs incurred by measures relating to environmental policies. The inclusion and charging of these costs is subject to the principle of relativity. Its usefulness and applicability must be demonstrated for each case within the framework of efficacious and efficient control procedures.

The *precautionary* principle is also of fundamental importance in environmental policy. Responsibility for precaution is imposed on the operators of plant requiring official approval under the *Federal Immission Control Act*, Section 5, No. 2; Section 5, No. 1 contains risk prevention measures. The obligation to take risk prevention measures normally implies the observance of immission values according to TA Luft (TI Air) (see sections 2.2 and 2.3.1). Section 5, No. 2 calls for precautions to be taken against projected risks.

The precautionary principle is also subject to technological progress with regard to the application of the guaranteed principle of relativity under constitutional law, despite the single reference in FICA, Section 5, No. 2. The correct level of preventive technology

---

*"Immission" is a German term for which there is no simple English equivalent. In Germany, immissions ("Immissionen") are legally defined as "air pollutants, noise, vibration, light, heat, radiation and associated environmental factors affecting human beings, animals, plants or other objects", that is the transfer of contaminants from the atmosphere to a receptor. "Immissions" (pronounced "eyemissions") are to be distinguished from emissions ("Emissionen"), which are defined as "air pollutants, noise, vibration, heat, light, radiation and associated phenomena originating from an installation".

promoted in this respect is achieved after weighing up the potential use and degree of protection obtained by the measure to be taken for the property to be protected.

Under the *cooperation* principle the Federal Government pursues the early participation of social groups in the decision making process and in the formulation of informed opinion in respect of environmental policies.

2.2 Basic Laws and Regulations

The basic law for air pollution and noise abatement in the unified Federal Republic of Germany is the *Federal Imission Control Act* (FICA). This law came into force on 1 April 1974 and forms the legal basis for almost all immission control measures. The law requires all industrial plants to be built and operated in such as way that they do not cause any effects which are dangerous or harmful to the environment. Plant operators must employ "state of the art" precautions to prevent harmful environmental effects.

The *Technical Instruction on Air Pollution Control* (TA Luft) forms the most important administrative regulation to implement the *Federal Immission Control Act.* It plays a central and decisive part in the enforcement of FICA by the 16 German States (five more after unification with the former GDR) and constitutes an established instrument of the licensing and supervising authorities.

Besides the statutory regulations for immission control in Germany (laws, ordinances etc), technical standards, e.g. guidelines of VDI (Association of German Engineers) and standards of DIN (German Institute of Standardization), serve as a decision making aid for specialists in this field, in the preparatory stages of legislation as well as in the elaboration of regulations and directives.

According to FICA, operators of plants requiring to be licensed have to appoint an Immission Control Officer, whose functions are:

- to develop processes and products which are harmless to the environment;
- to check the environmental compatibility of new processes and products;
- to check on the observance of statutory and official environmental protection requirements within the company and make proposals to eliminate faults;
- to explain to employees of the company the requirements of the immission control law.

The Immission Control Officer is obliged to submit an annual report to the operator, in particular covering measures taken and planned to fulfil the above functions. Section 56 of FICA also stipulates that the Immission Control Officer should advise the employer on investment decisions which could be important with regard to immission control.

2.3 Legislation and Instruments

Germany has a highly diversified, effective range of legal standards for air quality control. In accordance with the German tradition of legislation, there is a tendency to systemize, complete, specify and update these instruments by means of continual revision. A hierarchical system of statutory regulations has arisen at Federal level and in the 11 "old" states of the Federal Republic since the 1960s; these aim at extensive air quality control as one aspect of conservation and at the same time full enforcement of the system. Air quality control is subject to complementary legislation under regulations for the Federal states; Federal law however takes precedence and the laws of the states can only be implemented in areas where no statutory Federal regulations exist or where the Federal Republic has empowered the states to implement their own regulations. As stipulated in the unification treaty, the five eastern states are to adopt Federal environmental legislation, but with different deadlines.

The basis for all state regulations for air quality control is the *Federal Immission Control Act* (full title: *Act for Protection from Harmful Environmental Effects of Air Pollution, Noise, Vibration and Similar Occurrences*; official abbreviation BImSchG (FICA) of 1974, last amended in 1990). A number of other acts, e.g. for land use planning, energy supply, waste management etc. have an indirect effect on air quality control. A series of important statutory Federal ordinances and State ordinances for the implementation of the FICA are based on this Act, for example:

* First Ordinance for Implementation of the FICA (Ordinance of Furnaces; 1st BImSchV (FICO) of 1974, last amended 1988;
* Second Ordinance (on Emission Control of Volatile Halogenated Hydrocarbons; 2nd FICO) of 1974, last amended 1986;
* Third Ordinance (on Sulphur Content in Light Fuel Oil and Diesel Fuel) of 1975;
* Fourth Ordinance (on Facilities Subject to Licensing) of 1975, last amended in 1985;
* Fifth and Sixth Ordinances (on Immission Control Officers) of 1978;
* Eleventh Ordinance (on Emission Inventory Declaration) of 1978;

* Twelfth Ordinance (on Hazardous Incidents) of 1988;
* Seventeenth Ordinance (on Waste Incineration Plants) of 1990.

The *General Administration Regulations* for the FICA and for the implementation of the ordinances do not have the status of acts, but together with circulars from the respective Federal Minister they directly oblige the supervisory and licensing authorities to ensure uniform implementation of statutory regulations in all the States of Germany. They are enacted in agreement with the State governments.

The best known and most important set of regulations are the *First General Administrative Regulation* for the FICA (Technical Instructions on Air Quality Control - TI Air - TA Luft) last amended in 1983 and 1986. The circular of 24 July 1985 on "The suitability of electronic systems for the evaluation of continuous measurements of emissions" serves as an example of detailed ministerial regulations.

2.3.1 Industrial Processes

Emissions from specific types of plant are defined by the above-mentioned ordinances. The 13th FICO (Thirteenth Ordinance) of 1983 applies to "the installation, nature and operation of furnaces with a heat capacity of 50 MW and above...". It contains restrictions in respect of the emission of dust, carbon monoxide, nitrogen oxides, sulphur oxides and inorganic gaseous halogen compounds. Emissions of halogenated hydrocarbons from equipment used for surface treatment (e.g. removal of grease), for dry cleaning of textiles and also from extraction plant are controlled by the 2nd FICO. The Seventh Ordinance aims to reduce the emission of sawdust from relevant plant.

TI Air applies to all other stationary plant and new installations subject to authorization which are listed in the 4th FICO. The instructions contained therein must be observed for authorization procedures, subsequent regulations, the measurement of emissions from a plant and for immissions in the area affected. Limits for concentrations of immission have been established in respect of suspended dust, deposited dust and constituents of dust (lead, cadmium and titanium) and also for gaseous compounds (chlorine, hydrogen chloride, hydrogen fluoride, carbon monoxide, sulphur dioxide and nitrogen dioxide). Detailed regulations for the removal of waste gases and the calculation of the height of stacks are given in Section 2.4 of TI Air.

Section 2.3 gives the limits for emissions for a series of carcinogenic substances. Section 3.1 contains a set of technical regulations for the reduction of emissions and specific limits for the emission of total dust, constituents of dust (20 metals and metalloids), inorganic gaseous matter (4 categories): arsine, cyanogen chloride, phosgene, phosphene, bromine compounds, chlorine, hydrogen cyanide, fluorine compounds, hydrogen sulphide, chlorine compounds, sulphur oxides and nitrogen oxides, together with 150 named organic compounds. Regulations for the prevention of pollution due to strong smelling substances were also enacted for the first time in 1986.

Section 3.2 of TI Air is devoted primarily to the continuous measurement of emissions which can be classified according to the mass flow of emissions. A series of technical precautions to be taken in specific types of plant and limits which deviate from restrictions in respect of the emission of specific substances have been listed in Section 3.3 to allow for the special characteristics of specific plant.

Section 4, which includes regulations on the retrofitting of existing ("old") plant is of very great importance and also has significant economic implications for trade and industry. These regulations are new, compared with the TI Air edition of 1974. They specify the periods within which old plant must be brought within the emission levels required for new plant. The deadlines for old plant to be brought up to the higher standard vary with the extent to which they fall below the emission level of new plant, i.e. forthwith, 1989, 1991 or 1994.

As well as the FICA, a series of other Federal Acts are also important to air quality control in trade and industry, for example *Waste Act, Used Oil Act, Chemicals Act, Energy Savings Act, Disposal of Animal Corpses Act* and finally the *Criminal Code.*

2.3.2 Mobile Sources

As well as Directives from the European Community, of which Germany is a member, a number of national acts and ordinances for the reduction of emissions from vehicles are of importance:

- *The Lead in Petrol Reduction Act of 1971*, last amended in 1987, gradually led to a reduction in the lead content of petrol;
- The 3rd FICO (Third Ordinance under the FICA) of 1976 gradually led to a reduction in the sulphur content of diesel fuel to 0.3 per cent by weight in 1979;
- On the basis of various amendments to the Ordinance on Road Traffic Licensing, all licensed vehicles with spark ignition engines must undergo an exhaust gas test every 12 months, in order to ensure the minimising of emissions of pollutants according to the latest technological developments;

- Motor vehicles emitting low levels of pollutants and suitable modified motor vehicles are defined under the same ordinance. These are fully or partially exempted from tax for a transitional period, to promote the purchase of cars which emit low levels of pollutants or are equipped with three way catalytic converters. For this reason lead-free fuels are being temporarily taxed at a lower rate than fuels containing lead;
- Private traffic may be banned in certain areas under the Smog Ordinances for the States.

2.3.3 Domestic

Statutory regulations for smaller furnaces and other government measures are aimed at:

- the use of fuels which are low in sulphur, for example low sulphur fuel oil (Third Ordinance under the FICA) and increased use of natural gas;
- the lowest possible level of emissions during the operation of furnaces with regular monitoring and measurement of waste gas (First Ordinance under the FICA, *Chimney Sweep Act*);
- energy saving during the operation of furnaces and thermal insulation in heated buildings *(Energy Saving Act of 1976*);
- use of district heating.

2.3.4 Miscellaneous Sources

The *Trading Regulations* date back hundreds of years, and earlier versions contained important elements of the current *Immission Control Act.* They specify that, in the event of violation of the *Immission Control Act*, authorization for the practice of a trade may be refused, may be granted subject to conditions or can be withdrawn again. Finally, the Place of Work Ordinance, which contains strict regulations for the protection of the atmosphere at the place of work and prevention of noise, is also based on this Act.

2.3.5 Nuisance Provisions

Industrial and police regulations for the prevention of pollution due to odours have been implemented since time immemorial, in some cases by means of reserve provisions. Objective methods of measurement for the evaluation of odours from emission (olfactometry) were introduced for the first time in the TI Air of 1986. VDI and DIN (see also section 2.2) are currently involved in the standardization of methods for odour assessment. Suitable national regulations can be based on these and are awaited.

A comprehensive system of statutory regulations for noise abatement similar to that for air pollution also exists. It is based on the FICA and is expressed in ordinances under it, e.g. Lawn Mower Noise Ordinance (Eighth Ordinance in a TI Noise from 1986 similar to TI Air) and in many acts, ordinances and administrative regulations. The regulations include the measurement and reduction of emissions and passive precautions as well as factors to be taken into consideration in town planning.

3 IMPLEMENTATION AND ENFORCEMENT

3.1 Fundamental Legal Principles

Basic (constitutional) law in the Federal Republic ensures that "competing" laws enacted by the States are always subordinate to Federal Laws. Clean Air laws for example, enacted by the States can only be implemented if there is no Federal law governing the same area of immission control.

This means that the Federal Republic is the supreme authority for legislative law in this sector. The State of the Federal Republic therefore mainly implement Federal acts, as shown by the example of the *Federal Immission Control Act.* Even if statutory regulations are implemented by the various authorities of the respective States of the Federal Republic, "standardization of regulations" is nevertheless guaranteed by Federal law.

3.2 Implementation of Regulations

Air quality control in Germany, and the effectiveness of the controls, are explained below, taking the Federal State of North Rhine Westphalia (NRW) as an example.

Air pollution is primarily a problem associated with heavily populated and industrial areas and is closely related to economic trends. It is not difficult to deduce that such environmental problems are most serious in NRW where the Ruhr is to be found, for this is the most industrialized and densely populated State of Germany. With 17 million inhabitants contained within 34 000 sq. km, the population density is nearly three times as high in NRW as in the Federal Republic generally and even seven times as high in the Ruhr. NRW is essentially characterized by the Ruhr, which represents the largest single industrial area in Europe. Eighty per cent of German coal is obtained from the Ruhr and more than 70 per cent of German steel is produced in this area. Fifty per cent of electrical energy and 42 per cent of all chemical products come from NRW.

The state factory inspectorates are responsible for industrial operations and plant and the mining authorities are responsible for mining plant. The factory inspectorates have the right to carry out inspections at any time during operational periods. The owners and operators of plants and owners of property on which plant is operated must grant access to members of the factory inspectorates and allow them to carry out tests, including the determination of emissions and immissions and submit the necessary records for the fulfilment of their duties.

3.2.1 Monitoring

In addition to the emission of industrial pollutants, emissions from domestic fuel and traffic also play an important role. The highest concentrations of pollutants in the air are accordingly to be found in the Ruhr area - and also in the strip of the Rhineland between Duisburg and Bonn. Concentrations of pollutants have been quite considerably reduced in NRW in the last 25 years, for example:

- by 80 per cent for sulphur dioxide (0.15 mg/m^3 in 1966 to 0.03 mg/m^3 in 1988);
- by 67 per cent for the deposition of dust (312 000 tonnes per annum for 1963/64 to 102 000 tonnes per annum for 1988).

The question of the order of magnitude of air pollutants is of particular interest and can only be answered with the aid of an emission inventory, i.e. a list of all anthropogenic sources of air polluting matter in a particular area.

The various emissions categories - industry, domestic, factories and traffic - are differentiated in the emission inventory. Emission data for domestic fuel, small factories and traffic (especially road traffic) are ascertained for areas in grid or block form and also for rail systems (main lines).

Quantities of fuel which are consumed in an area or on a rail system in a given unit of time are evaluated, in order to determine the corresponding amounts of respective pollutants emitted with the aid of specific emission factors (= estimated experimental values). The emission data for the industrial category must be ascertained because of the many air polluting substances and the diversity of sources for each industrial plant. The emission inventory for NRW is kept by the State Institute for Air Pollution Control and Noise Abatement in Essen.

As well as the configuration or sources which may be taken directly from the emission inventory, local meteorological parameters are also necessary as input, in order to obtain a spatial, time-related statement of the immission situation to be expected from the emission situation.

3.2.2 Control of Immissions

According to the FICA, the States of the Federal Republic in the so-called pollution zones must continually determine the nature and extent of certain air pollutants in the atmosphere which may have harmful environmental effects. They must investigate the circumstances of their origin and proliferation: continuous immission measurements for relevant pollutants must be carried out in polluted areas and at the same time meteorological conditions and proliferation parameters must be established. The sulphur dioxide, carbon monoxide, nitrogen dioxide, ozone and suspended dust contents must be continuously measured as indicators of the air pollution level by the 76 TEMES monitoring stations (TEMES: telemetric actual time multicomponent detection system) operated by the State Institute of NRW. The measured data is transmitted directly via telephone lines to the State Institute computer centre. The fully automatic air monitoring system permits a regular review of the current situation with regard to the quality of air in the Rhine-Ruhr Area.

Immission measurements can be supplemented by immission data as required, which is obtained by conversion of values from the emission inventory.

3.2.3 Detection and Notification of a Smog Situation

The risk of a build up of harmful pollutants in the air reaching concentrations which would endanger health must always be considered during long periods of atmospheric stability. In such situations it is therefore essential to determine the level of disturbance due to the exchange of air masses from the meteorological service and also to measure the immission load at regular intervals.

The State Ministry for the Environment is informed if a static weather situation which will persist for a significant period of time is reported by the German Weather Service and a continuous increase in the concentration of immissions is established from values transmitted by various TEMES monitoring stations. There is then permanent contact between the Ministry for the Environment, the State Institute of NRW and the German Weather Service. The Ministry must then decide if any smog alert should be given.

3.2.4 Patrols and Measuring and Testing Services for State Factory Inspectorates

Motorized patrols equipped with automatic telephones are used in 14 of the 22 state factory inspectorates in NRW. They operate on a shift system giving 24 hour coverage. The patrols deal with serious complaints from the population in respect of damage and pollution due to contamination of the air and also ensure that factory and industrial plant comply with immission control regulations. If a situation cannot be clarified by inspection, inquiries, checking of records, taking of random samples or random measurements, the patrols alert the inspectorate's measuring and testing services, who will carry out extensive tests and measurements to identify any plant emitting pollutants in contravention of the regulations.

Measuring and testing services are established at all the regional factory inspectorates. As a special team, they have the task of taking specific measurements for the control of immissions, which are necessary due to complaints by neighbours or are in the interests of an objective, official usable evaluation of emissions.

Measurements are taken directly from the sources of emissions, to check the observance of given emission limits and technological progress.

3.2.5 Measuring Service

The measuring and testing service can call upon the expertise of the State Institute of NRW in the case of particularly difficult industrial measurements. This type of measuring service also deals with the development and testing of techniques for the measurement of emissions during operation of plant and is active in an advisory capacity in the installation of continuous recording instruments.

3.2.6 Emergency Service

The expert advice of the factory inspectorate is available for the investigation of cases of damage and risk, whereas the task group formed by the State Institute of NRW can be consulted in cases of damage due to air pollution. The heads of operations are instructed directly by the factory inspectorates. Action for the support of the factory inspectorates takes priority over all other activities.

The emergency service has a mobile laboratory equipped with highly sensitive analytical instruments for measuring and determining pollutants in the air and their concentrations including odorous immissions.

The emergency service does not however have any executive powers. It is solely active in an expert advisory capacity. Decisions relating to the implementation of clean air measures can therefore only be made by the factory inspectorates.

3.2.7 Conversion of Results of Measurements and Determinations

The state factory inspectorates are responsible for supervising the implementation of the FICA and the respective statutory ordinances in NRW in accordance with regulations in a jurisdiction ordinance. Supervision also involves the determination of pollutants emitted during inspections, by means of measurements and examination of the results. If results of measurements indicate values above specified emission limits, the supervisory authority will decree that measures are taken which guarantee the observance of the permissible emissions level during the operation of the plant. If the operator is not willing voluntarily to implement measures for limiting or reducing emissions, the supervisory authority will implement the measures by means of an administrative act, normally a decree. It can also issue formal warnings and institute legal proceedings.

3.2.8 Research in NRW Relating to Air Quality Control

Pollutants in the air have an adverse effect on humans and the environment. Certain air pollutants can damage plants, destroy materials, endanger animals and impair health. The State Government of NRW has placed the main emphasis of research on the detailed investigation of the effects on health of air pollutants and the associated causes of air pollutants and damage to forests.

The "Team for the Effects of Immissions on Man" is particularly concerned with the relationship between air pollution and pseudo-croup (disease, whose symptoms - laryngitis, difficulty in breathing, coughing - simulate croup). Other main research topics are the problems of the risk of cancer due to air pollutants and effects on groups at risk. The team is to carry out thorough investigations on all these aspects.

The new form of damage to forests, which occurred in NRW for the first time in 1982 and has increased to a worrying extent, required further scientific evaluation of possible causes, in addition to rigorous implementation of the "Action programme for the prevention of the death of forests". A research programme "Air pollution and damage to forests" was established in the State of NRW.

3.2.9 Advisory Bodies

Research advisory bodies have been created to fulfil and carry out the objectives and tasks mentioned above. They include doctors, toxicologists, chemists and biologists; their main responsibilities are:

- advising the State Government on matters of research in the areas mentioned;
- coordination of research and development projects;
- setting up and continuation of research requirements;
- identification of gaps in research and research requirements;

- conversion of research results;
- encouragement of new solutions and recommendations with reference to concrete research and development proposals.

4 FUTURE DEVELOPMENTS

In view of the fact that air quality control has to an increasing extent become an international problem and that general aspects of conservation (air, soil, water, waste) must be implemented, in order to achieve permanent solutions, the following main topics and longer term objectives may be considered to be applicable:

a) Increased national and international efforts for the protection of the atmosphere:

   - Ban on chlorofluorocarbons (CFCs);
   - Intensification of relevant activities at international level and at the same time suitable national measures;
   - Intensification of research on the effects of carbon dioxide immissions and the possibilities of reducing these immissions on a national scale and worldwide;
   - Cooperation with third world countries - at both national and EEC levels, to prevent the clearing of tropical rain forests.

b) Further reduction of emissions from motor vehicles:

   - National ban on three-star petrol containing lead additives on the basis of a suitable EEC guideline.
   - Reduction of emissions of particles from vehicles using diesel fuel;
   - Imposing more rigorous limits for gaseous pollutants and reducing permissible amounts of particles emitted on the basis of the Federal Government's concept in respect of farm, military, commercial and public vehicles; checking of taxation requirements for heavy goods vehicles emitting low levels of pollutants;
   - Retention of fuel fumes by means of an improved filling system.

c) Rigorous pursuance and continuation of measures to control damage to forests (e.g. further reduction of pollutants emitted from furnaces and vehicles, forestry measures, intensification of research and development work).

d) Overcoming problems of deposition of waste and disused loads.

e) Retrofitting of old plant (Old Plant Renovation Programme).

5 BIBLIOGRAPHY

Feldhaus G (ed). *Bundesimmissionsschutzrecht.* Wiesbaden: Deutscher Fachschriften-Verlag Braun & Co KG. (Looseleaf collection, in German)

Davids P, Lange M. *Die TA Luft '86, Technischer Kommentar.* Düsseldorf: VDI-Verlag 1986. (In German)

Verein Deutscher Ingenieure. VDI-Handbuch Reinhaltung der Luft, Vol. 1 - Vol. 6. Berlin: Beuth Verlag. (Collection of guidelines; drafts in German; final versions bilingual German/English since 1982)

Handbuch des Umweltschutzes. Weinheim: Verlag Moderne Industrie. (Looseleaf collection, in German)

Umweltbundesamt: *Daten zur Umwelt 1988/89.* Berlin. Erich-Schmidt-Verlag 1989. (In German)

ISRAEL

1 INTRODUCTION

1.1 Topography, Climate, Population

Israel is situated along the south-easterly corner of the Mediterranean Sea. It is, from north to south, about 420 km long, and on average only 50 km wide. In spite of its small area, which extends to somewhat more than 20 000 sq. km, desert, tropical and alpine environments are found in close proximity. Whereas the northern part of Israel has a Mediterranean climate, the southern half can be classified as a desert. This variety results from the country's topographical structure and its location at a world "cross-roads" of climatic and botanic regions.

There are three main climatic regions: the Mediterranean climate covers the densely populated coastal area along the Mediterranean Sea and the mountain area adjacent to it in the east, i.e, the Galilee, Carmel, Samaria and Judea regions (see map). The dry desert and steppe climates, with precipitation below 250 mm per annum and falling to as low as 20 mm per annum in Eilat (on the Red Sea), cover the sparsely inhabited Negev, Judean Desert and Jordan Valley in the south and the east[(1)].

The outstanding features of the Mediterranean climate are windy, mild, rainy winters and relatively calm, hot, dry summers. The cool season extends from October to May, with most of the rain falling in the three months from November to February. The warm season lasts from June to September. The transitional seasons of spring and autumn are periods of "indecision", where the change from winter to summer and back again take place in a number of false starts.

The population of Israel is characterized by an outstanding rate of growth. Over the last 42 years, its population has increased from 870 000 in 1948 to 4 520 000 in 1989. Much of this increase was brought about by large scale immigration, mainly from Europe, Asia and Africa. However, by 1973 already 50 per cent of the population was born in Israel itself[(40)].

The rapid rise in population is reflected in the density of settlements. The overall density of the country rose from 43 persons per sq. km in 1948 to 210 in 1989. The distribution of settlements over the country, however, is very uneven. About 60 per cent of the

Air Quality Monitoring Network

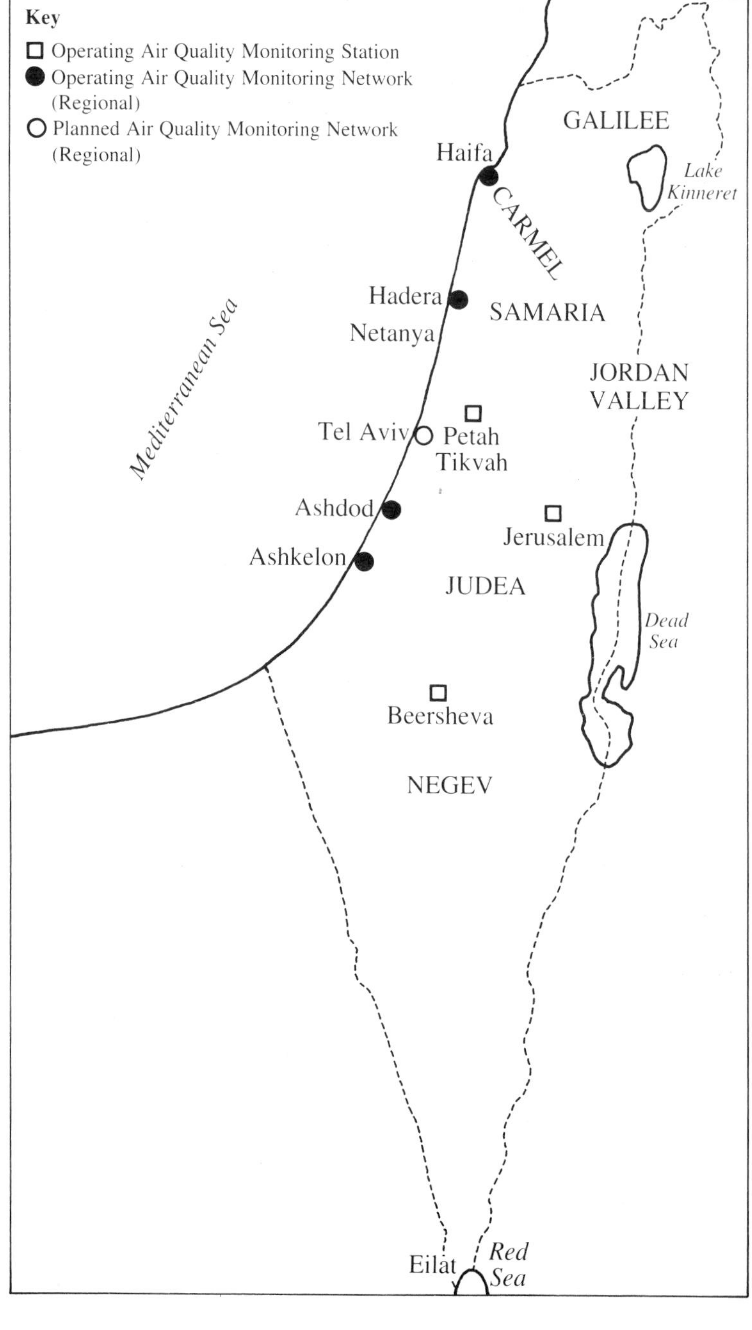

country much of it in the south, is sparsely settled with an average density of only 24.3 per sq. km[40]. The growth of manufacturing, industry and services, as well as vehicular traffic, has largely been concentrated in urban centres around Tel Aviv and Haifa, along the Mediterranean coast. Thus, Israel has a very high rate of urbanization, with 79 per cent of its population living in towns of over 10 000 inhabitants and 52 per cent living in towns of over 50 000. At the present time, the coastal plain, where most of the population is already concentrated, remains the major focus of development.

1.2 Specific National Problems

As has been pointed out by Neumann in 1971 in the first conference on the environment held in Israel[66], natural conditions for pollution dispersion in the atmosphere of the coastal plain are not favourable. The extremely high amount of solar radiation available in this part of the world, results in photochemical air pollution similar to that occurring in Los Angeles, California, and is only to be expected[88]. A trend of increasing ozone concentration is indeed evident (see section 3.2).

However, the most problematic pollutant, as shown by air quality monitoring carried out in Israel since 1970, is sulphur dioxide. Relatively high concentrations are routinely recorded in the Ashdod area and the Haifa Bay. One reason for this is the high sulphur content of the heavy fuel oil in use in Israel: the countrywide average at present is 2.7 wt per cent down from 3.5 wt per cent five years ago. The Haifa Bay, which has the most intense industrial atmospheric activity in the country, and difficult atmospheric dispersion conditions caused by the influence of the Mediterranean Sea and the complex topography of the Mt. Carmel, make it probably the most polluted area in the country. The Ashdod area comes a close second (see section 3.2).

The number of vehicles also cause air pollution problems, mainly in the densely populated urban centres of Tel Aviv, Jerusalem and Haifa. Black soot emitted from diesel powered vehicles is the reason for a major portion of complaints from the public, and is also a cause of visible soiling of stone buildings in the centre of big towns. It should be noted that in Israel - which lacks a developed railway system - diesel powered buses, trucks and taxis account for a very high proportion of the vehicular fleet - about 17 per cent - and over 15 per cent of the buses are of an old and smoky model built before 1973[40].

Also, although the degree of motorization at present is not high (in 1989 there were 216 cars for every 1000 persons), the rate of increase is very rapid and for the period 1987-1989 showed an average increase of 5.4 per cent per annum. Should this trend continue, as is expected[72], the degree of motorization in Israel will approach the levels found in European countries today. Thus air quality in Israel, especially in the coastal area, can expect to deteriorate to the level of that in other cities of the world with similar climates (e.g. Athens, Los Angeles or New Mexico).

2 DEVELOPMENT OF AIR POLLUTION CONTROLS AND LEGISLATION

Israel lacks the comprehensive and modern law necessary for rational and efficient management of its air resources. In addition to the *Abatement of Nuisances Law 1961* which deals exclusively with air pollution, noise and odours, there are various statutes and regulations which deal with some aspects of air pollution control. Together they provide an important foundation for air quality management in Israel.

Legislation applicable to air pollution prevention is summarized below.

2.1 The Abatement of Nuisances Law 1961

The first legislative instrument in Israel for controlling air pollution, the *Abatement of Nuisances Law*, was enacted in 1961. The Ministers of the Interior and Health were given joint responsibility and authority to carry out its provisions[47, 48], but in May 1982, the Knesset (the Israel Parliament) confirmed the Government decision to transfer sole responsibility and authority for it to the Minister of the Interior, and in December 1988 responsibility was transferred to the newly created Ministry of the Environment. It should be emphasized that contravention is a criminal offence and is also grounds for civil proceedings.

Section 4 of the law deals in a broad fashion with the prevention of air pollution, stating that a person shall not cause any considerable or reasonable pollution of the air, from any source whatsoever, if it disturbs or is likely to disturb a person in its vicinity, or a passer-by. In a similar manner Section 3 covers the more specific nuisances of odours. Under Section 5 the Minister of the Environment is given authority to promulgate regulations defining what is considerable or unreasonable odour or pollution of the air. Israeli ambient air quality standards have been defined in a regulation promulgated in 1971 (see section 3.2).

Pursuant to Section 8, the Minister of the Environment has the authority to address specific polluters with individual decrees which give guidance as to the steps they should take to prevent the air pollution nuisances which they create. Such decrees have become the backbone for controlling industrial air pollution throughout the country and so far, about 20 have been issued (see section 3.1).

In Section 6 local authorities are authorized to enact bye-laws with special provisions related to the law. Indeed, the Municipality of Petah Tikva, near Tel Aviv, was the first local authority in Israel to enact, in 1988, a bye-law on air pollution prevention. Under Section 9, any permit issued to licensed businesses under the *Trades and Industries Ordinance*, or any other permit required for the operation of and undertaking, shall be deemed to be conditional upon compliance with the provisions of this law.

Since enactment of the law, seven regulations have been promulgated:

* *The Regulation on Air Pollution from Premises 1962* prohibits the emission of black smoke into the air in the public domain or in the domain of others. Black smoke is defined as an emission into the air with a visual density equal or greater than shade No. 2 on the Ringelmann chart. Denser emissions are allowed if they last for less than six consecutive minutes in any one hour. Excluded from these provisions are sea-going vessels.
* *The Regulation on Air Pollution from Vehicles 1963* prohibits the emission of black smoke from motor vehicles the visual density of which exceeds 60 units on the scale of a Hartridge Smoke Meter.
* *The Regulation on Hartridge Test for Vehicles 1963* specifies the exact conditions to be adopted for measuring black smoke emissions from vehicles on a Chassis Dynamometer.
* *The Regulation on Air Quality 1971* defines unreasonable air pollution as concentration in the air above a specified level for sulphur dioxide, hydrogen sulphide, oxidants, carbon monoxide, nitrogen oxides, total particulate matter, lead particles and soiling index (see section 3.2).
* *The Regulation on Emission of Particulate Matter into the Air 1972* defines the permissible emission rate of particulate matter from a plant (in kg per hour), as a function of the quantity of raw material supplied to the production process (also in kg per hour). It requires plants emitting particulate matter into the air to carry out stack sampling at least once a year. No other regulations on emission standards have been promulgated in Israel, although some limits on emissions have been imposed on certain pollution sources as provisions of individual decrees.
* *The Regulation on Air Pollution from Heavy Fuel Oil Burners used for Household Heating 1972* prohibits the use of heavy fuel oil in households for central space heating systems. It does not apply to

users of heavy fuel oil traditionally located in residential areas, such as hospitals or large hotels.

* *The Regulation on Prevention of Unreasonable Air Pollution and Odours from Solid Waste Disposal Sites 1990* entered into force in August 1990. It obliges operators of solid waste disposal sites (i.e. landfills) to maintain and operate such facilities in a manner that shall prevent emissions of air pollution, smoke and odours. Operators of landfills (in most cases, local authorities), are required to prevent open burning of municipal waste and to extinguish any fire on the site should it occur.

It should be noted that in view of the fact that the *Abatement of Nuisances Law* was enacted almost 30 years ago, it is remarkably advanced and progressive. However, other than the transfer of authority from the Ministers of the Interior and Health to the Minister of the Environment today, no changes or revisions have been introduced.

The Abatement of Nuisances Law does not recognize some of the more modern approaches to air resources management such as: air quality monitoring, determination of emission standards (both for stationary or mobile sources), creation of protected areas where significant deterioration of air quality is prohibited, or utilization of the environmental impact assessment process[(35)]. Specifically, it does not delegate any authority to nominate inspectors, or handle new types of problems such as protecting the stratospheric ozone layer or prevention of manmade climatic change.

2.2 The Planning and Building Law 1965

This is a comprehensive statute, with enabling regulations, which regulates and monitors all the land-use allocation and the planning stages of construction. It covers, by issuing building permits a wide range - from the largest construction projects on the national level, such as siting of electric power plants, to the construction of a small stack for residential space-heaters, on the local level[(47)].

The Regulation of Environmental Impact Statements 1982 states that planning agencies (i.e. the National Planning Council of the Regional and Local Planning Committees) shall not review certain new construction projects and shall not issue building permits unless Environmental Impact Statements (EIS) have been prepared and submitted for approval together with the construction plans. So far, more than 140 EISs have been prepared (see section 3.1).

2.3 The Tel Aviv Power Plant Law 1967

This law authorizes the Government to approve the plan to build a 450 MW power plant ("Reading D", to the north of Tel Aviv), dispensing with the need for any license, confirmation or exemption necessary for such a construction project under the Planning and Building Law[47]. However, the Government is empowered to make regulations as to the performance, use and operation of the power plant, and even to subjugate it to the provisions of the *Planning and Building Law.* It has been pointed out by Laster (1973) that this law must be seen as an attempt to by-pass the new *Planning and Building Law,* with its modernistic approach to planning.

The Regulation of this Law on the Tel Aviv Power Plant 1968 is, however, of special interest in that it set up the framework for the first air quality monitoring network to be operated in Israel[21]. It also provided the framework for the alert system operated in the Tel Aviv area to determine and respond to dangerous air pollution levels resulting from the emissions of the "Reading D" power plant[11].

2.4 The Licensing of Business Law 1968

This law empowers the Minister of the Interior to designate those types of business which must obtain a license for their operation. Control over the operation of the business is granted to the local authority of the area in which it is located, under the supervision of the appropriate national authority (e.g. the Ministry of Health for a food related business).

The head of the local authority may impose, as part of the business license, special provisions as he sees fit to prevent the business from causing nuisances (air pollution or other) in its vicinity.

The requirement in the *Abatement of Nuisances Law* that all businesses subject to the *Licensing and Business Law* should operate according to its provisions, means in effect that the license of a business which does not meet the limitations set in the *Abatement of Nuisances Law* can be revoked or suspended until such time as the business complies with it.

2.5 The Traffic Ordinance, New Version (1961)

Section 25 of this ordinance authorizes traffic magistrates to deal with offenses as defined by the *Abatement of Nuisances Law* or its related regulations. A number of the many regulations under this ordinance, relate to the control of emissions from motor vehicles:

- Regulations Nos. 155 and 316 prohibit the emission of smoke beyond the normal amount for the vehicle of that type.
- Regulation No. 273a requires the measurement of smoke emissions from diesel powered vehicles at its mandatory annual registration and inspection. The measurement must be performed according to the provisions set in the *Regulation on Hartridge Test for Vehicles 1963 of the Abatement of Nuisances Law.*

- Regulation No. 282 prohibits the registration or issue of a license to any motor vehicle unless the Motor Vehicle Authority in the Ministry of Transport has inspected a prototype of it.
- Regulation No. 282a refers to Regulation No. 15.03 of the UN Economic Commission for Europe (ECE) in Geneva or to Directive No. 78/665 of the European Economic Community (EEC) in Brussels regarding emissions form gasoline-powered vehicles, and to ECE Regulation No. 24 or EEC Directive No. 72/306 regarding diesel-powered vehicles. Certification of prototypes by the Motor Vehicle Authority involves the inspection of the vehicle and of the documents provided with it. The Motor Vehicle Authority may exempt any type of motor vehicle from some or all of the provisions detailed in this Regulation.
- Regulation No. 282c defines a gasoline-powered vehicle and allows it to be registered only if, beginning with model year 1985, it conforms with the provision of ECE Regulation No. 15.03 or with the provision of the EEC Directive No. 78/665.
- Regulation 282d requires that diesel-powered vehicles, beginning with model year 1977, conform to the provisions of the ECE Regulations or EEC Directives.
- Regulation 282e requires any motor vehicle owner to submit, on the demand of the Director of the Division of Motor Vehicles in the Ministry of Transport, a written document from a certified laboratory as proof that the motor vehicle indeed satisfies the requirements of Regulations Nos. 282c and 282d.
- Regulation No. 318a requires the measurement of pollution emitted from gasoline-powered vehicles at its mandatory annual registration and inspection. The measurements are to be performed for specified pollutants by methods also specified by the Director of the Division of Motor Vehicles, and notified officially by him. For carbon monoxide emissions from the exhaust system, a maximum of 4.5 vol per cent is allowed.

2.6 Petah Tikva (Prevention of Air Pollution) Bye-law 1988

Severe air pollution problems in the town of Petah Tikva, 10 km east of Tel Aviv, prompted the Unit for Environmental Protection of the Municipality of Petah Tikva to initiate the enactment of a bye-law designed to help the municipality deal with local industries causing air pollution. As such it constitutes an important breakthrough in the implementation of the *Abatement of Nuisances Law* by local authorities. It grants the municipality of Petah Tikva new and innovative tools with which to handle air pollution and odours from industrial plant within its jurisdiction. The major elements of the Law are:

- Establishment of pollutant levels to be emitted into the air locally from industrial plant as a result of fuel combustion or production processes (emission standards). Standards have been set for sulphur dioxide (400 mg m^{-3}, assuming a maximum fuel oil sulphur content of about 1 wt per cent); nitrogen oxides (500 mg m^{-3}); total and respirable particulate matter (150 and 75 mg m^{-3}, respectively); black and opaque smoke (Ringelmann shade No. 2 and 20 per cent opacity, respectively).
- Owners must adopt all necessary means to prevent unreasonable air pollution, including improving the maintenance of boilers and fuel combustion processes and improving production processes and efficiency of pollution prevention equipment. Plant owners are required to submit to the mayor plans for the prevention of air pollution from their plants.
- The bye-law distinguishes between large industrial plant, (defined as consuming more than 1000 tons of fuel oil per annum) and small plant. It imposes on plant owners various obligations such as:
    * a requirement for all large plant to install continuous monitoring devices for measuring emissions of particulate matter (opacimeters). Only those small plant decided upon specifically by the mayor are required to install stack monitoring devices;
    * a prohibition on burning coal in small plant and restriction on coal burning in large plant;
    * an obligation to take all necessary steps to prevent odours and fugitive dust nuisances in the vicinity of the plant.

3 IMPLEMENTATION AND ENFORCEMENT

3.1 National Enforcement

The policy of the Ministry of the Environment has always been that "an ounce of prevention is worth a pound of cure" i.e. it is preferable to prevent, in the sense of avoiding in advance, air pollution nuisances through rational physical planning processes, based on reliable data obtained from assessments of environmental impact, rather than control emissions after they have been formed, or rectifying a bad environmental situation that has developed over the years.

The *Planning and Building Law*, through its *Regulation on Environmental Impact Statements* (see section 2.2), is one of the main tools for preserving air quality in the country, by controlling emissions of air pollution from new sources planned to be built.

Preparation of an Environmental Impact Statement (EIS) is mandatory for any of the following types of projects, if in the opinion of the planning agency it will have a significant impact on its environment (and air quality): electric power plants; airports; hazardous waste disposal sites; mines and quarries; and industrial plant located outside areas assigned for industrial activities where the siting, scope of activity or production process is likely to cause a significant impact on the environment beyond the local neighbourhood. In addition, any member of the planning agency reviewing the project construction may require at any stage of the review the preparation of an EIS by the project proponent, to be submitted to the planning agency.

The Minister of the Interior has appointed the Director General of the Ministry of the Environment as the "Environmental Advisor" to the National Planning Council for the purpose of this Regulation. This appointment establishes a central authority which provides the project proponents with statutory guidelines as to how to prepare the environmental assessment and submit the EIS.

Since the promulgation of this Regulation in 1962, more than 140 EISs of major construction projects have been submitted, reviewed and approved by the planning authorities, many of which have a significant impact on the air quality in Israel. The list includes: the coal-fired electric power plants in Hadera (1400 MW)[15] and Ashkelon (1100 MW), the new 1100 MW power plant in Hadera[34], the crude oil refineries in Haifa and Ashdod, the Portland cement plants in Haifa, Bet Shemesh and Ramle, chemical, petrochemical, metallurgical, food textiles, electronics and other industries.

Since 1977 control and enforcement of air pollution laws throughout Israel has been carried out mainly by the environmental protection units of the local authorities. Now, more than 50 per cent of the population live within the jurisdiction of local authorities where environmental protection units exist. The establishment of more environmental protection units in the local authorities, as well as establishing regional offices for the Ministry of Environment in order to achieve better coverage and physical presence in the country, is a high priority within the Ministry.

In the absence of emission standards, one of the most important legal instruments in Israel for achieving air pollution control of stationary sources is the use of individual decrees, issued by the Minister of the Environment under the authority given to him by the *Abatement of Nuisances Law* (see section 2.1). In all of these the authority controlling and enforcing their provisions is the head of the environmental protection unit responsible for the area in which the pollution source is located. Approximately 20 such decrees have been issued, amongst them: the older electric power plants in Haifa (the "Haifa" Power Plant), in Ashdod (the "Eshkol" Power Plant), and in Tel Aviv (the "Reading D" Power Plant), the crude oil refineries in Haifa and Ashdod, the Portland cement plants in Haifa, Bet Shemesh and Ramle, the phosphate loading terminal in the Ashdod port, several chemical and petrochemical plants located mainly in the Haifa Bay, two asphalt plants in Be'er Sheva and near Jerusalem, a food production factory in Bnei Brak and a lead battery factory in the Galilee.

Steps to prevent environmental nuisances such as air pollution can also be enforced by the local authority introducing special environmental limits into the business license that they issue under the *Licensing of Business Law.* Those limits are often based on the emission standards included in the US EPA regulations for the Standards of Performance for New Stationary Sources[(91)], or on the emission standards issued by the Federal Government of Germany[(90)]. Enforcement of these provisions by the local authority is usually carried out by personnel from the departments of health or environmental protection.

Enforcement of the provisions of the *Traffic Ordinance* and its regulations has until now been the responsibility of the Ministry of Transport. However, because of the limited resources available to the Ministry, enforcement of the existing regulations regarding prevention of air pollution from motor vehicles is not effective.

3.2 Ambient Air Quality Standards and Monitoring

Israeli ambient air quality standards, promulgated in 1971, covered five pollutants which are mainly the product of fuel combustion: sulphur dioxide, nitrogen oxides, carbon monoxide, lead particles and Soiling Index (SI), as well as oxidants, hydrogen sulphide and Total Suspended Particulates. These air quality standards incorporated a frequency parameter which allowed an excess of the level of pollution specified in the standard for about one per cent of the time of the year (see Table 1).

Since 1982, these ambient standards have been under review by an interdisciplinary committee of experts[(89)]. The Committee has prepared proposals for modified standards, with the appropriate criteria documents (in Hebrew) for sulphur dioxide, ozone, carbon monoxide, and particulate matter (including: TSP, respirable particulates (PM_{10}), dust fall, lead, and sulphates).

A revised version of the *Regulation on Air Quality* was signed by the Minister of the Environment but has not yet entered into force (Table 1). This also includes additional ambient air quality standards proposed by the Ministry of Health, based on the 1987 World Health

Organization Air Quality Guidelines. These standards include chemical substances such as dichloroethane, dichloromethane, toluene, tetrachloroethylene, styrene, formaldehyde and the metals vanadium and cadmium. The question of how to approach the problem of carcinogenic compounds in the regulation of air quality is still open, since for these substances WHO cites no threshold values for their adverse health effects. It should be noted that the statistical terminology (i.e. the allowance to exceed the specified level for one per cent of the time) was omitted from the new version of the Regulation.

Table 1: Israeli Ambient Air Quality Standards for the Major Pollutants, mg m^{-3}

Pollutant	*Averaging time*	*Regulation on air quality, 1971*		*Revised air quality regulation, 1989*	*Measurement method*
		(1) (2)	*(1) (3)*		*(4)*
SO_2	0.5 h 24 h 1 yr	0.780 0.260 —	1.560 0.390 0.060	0.780 0.280 0.060	Flame Photometric, or UV Fluorescence
H_2S	0.5 h 24 h	0.15 0.05	0.30 0.07	0.045 0.015	Flame Photometric
0_3	0.5 h 8 h 24 h	0.4 (5) 0.2 (5) —	0.8 (5) 0.35 (5) —	0.230 (6) 0.065 (6)	Chemiluminescence, or UV Absorption
CO	0.5 h 8 h	35 11	70 19	60 11	NDIR, Gas Filter CO Corr. Analyzer
NO_x, as NO_2	0.5 h 24 h	0.940 0.560	1.880 0.840	0.940 0.560	Chemiluminescence
Total Particulate Matter	3 h 24 h 1 yr	— 0.200 —	— 0.300 0.075	0.300 0.200 0.075	High Volume Sampler, or Beta Gauge
Respirable Partic. Mat.	24 h 1 yr	— —	— —	0.150 0.060	High Volume Sampler
Lead Particles	24 h 30 d 1 yr	0.005 — —	0.0075 — —	0.0050 0.0015 0.0005	Atomic Absorption Analysis of Hi-Vol Samples
Settling Dust	30 d	—	—	20 ton km^{-2}	ASTM D1739-70, 1979
Soiling Index	0.5 h 2.0 h	2 CoH/10^3 1.ft 1 CoH/10^3 1.ft		— —	AISI Tape Sampler

Comments:
(1) Concentrations were originally given in units of parts per million (ppm)
(2) Not to be exceeded more than 1% of the time of the year
(3) Maximum permissible concentration
(4) Measurement methods prescribed by the USEPA in Regulations on National Primary and Secondary Ambient Air Quality Standards (40CFR50), or equivalent, are requested.
(5) Applies to oxidants measured by the KI method.
(6) Will be replaced by a 4-6 hour standard.

Routine monitoring of air pollutants started in Israel in 1969 with the operation by the Ministry of Health and the Israel Electric Corporation of 10 individual monitoring stations spread over the Tel Aviv area around the "Reading D" power plant[11]. In 1976, following the initiative and efforts of the Environmental Protection Service (then, in the Ministry of the Interior), modern monitoring stations began to operate under the Environmental Protection Units of the local authorities of Haifa, Jerusalem, Tel Aviv, Ashdod and Be'er Sheva[41, 30].

In 1979, the first automatic real-time air pollution monitoring network was established in the Hadera area (see map), around the new 1400 MW coal-fired power plant. It includes 12 monitoring stations and a computerized control centre, located in the office of the Environmental Protection Unit of the Association of Towns - Hadera Area[56].

In 1986, the second network, which includes five stations, began monitoring the air quality of the Ashdod area, around the local electric power plant and oil refinery. The third network, with seven monitoring stations, began operating in 1989 in Ashkelon. Data from the fourth network in the Haifa area, with eight monitoring stations, begun to flow to its control centre in October 1990. In all of these, special attention is given to the monitoring of sulphur dioxide. Other pollutants monitored include nitrogen oxides, carbon monoxide, ozone, total suspended particulates and in some cases, hydrocarbons. Meteorological parameters such as wind speed and barometric pressure are also continuously measured at network stations.

As can be seen in Table 2, and as was pointed out in section 1.2, sulphur dioxide pollution is a severe problem, especially in the Haifa and Ashdod areas. High concentrations occur in Haifa usually at night or early morning, especially in spring and autumn[31]. It has been claimed that with the introduction of intermittent control systems (in which low sulphur fuel (1 wt per cent S) is used at certain atmospheric conditions) in the oil refineries in Haifa and Ashdod and in the electric power plants in Haifa, Ashdod and Tel Aviv[45], a trend of reduction in levels can be observed[5].

The extremely high amounts of solar radiation in the Middle East[83], resulting in photochemical air pollution similar to that occurring in Los Angeles, California was only to be expected[88]. Indeed, ozone levels shown in Table 3 are quite high and a trend of increase in its concentration is evident[86, 53].

Dust levels are naturally high in Israel, especially under conditions of dust storms. However, a significant portion of the dust can be attributed to human activities (see section 1.1). Particulate matter

Table 2: Concentrations of SO_2 and NO_x in the Atmosphere in Israel, 1985-1989 (microgram per cubic meter) (ICBS, 1990)[(1)]

Year	*Annual Average*	*Maximum Daily Average*	*Maximum 1/2 hour Average*	*Uptime of Monitor (%)*	*Annual Average*	*Maximum Daily Average*	*Maximum 1/2 hour Average*	*Uptime of Monitor (%)*
	SULPHUR DIOXIDE				NITROGEN OXIDES			
			Commercial Urban Center					
			Jerusalem (Russian Compound)					
1985	—	(16)	(81)	(24)	37	87	415	75
1986	11	24	63	88	20	86	371	86
1987	10	50	259	85	42	143	520	86
1988	10	39	226	80	34	159	443	82
1989	18	52	228	39	71	352	1064	73
			Tel Aviv (Municipality)					
1985	—	—	—	(0)	44	207	477	85
1986	—	—	—	(0)	37	153	477	50
1987	(21)	(86)	(338)	(25)	—	(66)	—	(20)
1988	21	109	504	67	—	—	—	(0)
1989	—	—	—	(0)	—	—	—	(0)
			Petah Tikva (Central Bus Depot)					
1985	34	162	1200	42	53	202	475	77
1986	(17)	(68)	(226)	(28)	38	182	400	66
1987	(21)	(86)	(338)	(25)	69	154	393	42
1988	36	104	385	46	49	192	391	80
1989	—	—	—	0	—	—	—	(0)
			Industrial Urban Center					
			Haifa (Talpiyot Market)					
1985	(96)	(173)	(681)	(19)	—	—	—	(0)
1986	85	197	1271	97	—	—	—	(0)
1987	42	286	2552	99	—	—	—	(0)
1988	56	182	967	85	—	—	—	(0)
1989	47	338	1949	81	—	—	—	(0)
			Industrial Suburb					
			Ashdod (Yavne Region)					
1985	—	—	—	(0)	—	—	—	(0)
1986	—	(144)	(1696)	(23)	—	(68	(384)	(22)
1987	27	246	2251	96	26	130	465	97
1988	18	213	907	92	23	90	547	98
1989	22	133	1539	85	95	369	1635	86
			Hadera (Bet Eli'ezer)					
1985	8	39	236	63	10	25	336	51
1986	8	52	304	53	11	43	277	53
1987	—	—	424	88	—	—	208	84
1988	—	—	374	95	—	—	221	92
1989	—	—	346	98	—	60	448	98
			Residential Suburb					
			Netanya (North)					
1985	8	23	160	64	21	54	246	67
1986	8	26	361	63	18	50	171	41
1987	—	—	125	88	—	—	215	83
1988	—	—	104	91	—	—	280	87
1989	—	18	208	92	—	124	526	92

Table 2: (cont)

Year	*Annual Average*	*Maximum Daily Average*	*Maximum 1/2 hour Average*	*Uptime of Monitor (%)*	*Annual Average*	*Maximum Daily Average*	*Maximum 1/2 hour Average*	*Uptime of Monitor (%)*
			Kibbutz HaMa'apil					
1985	5	21	320	63	15	37	241	55
1986	5	20	178	49	12	36	354	47
1987	—	—	254	88	—	—	116	89
1988	—	—	239	93	—	—	171	92
1989	—	36	367	87	—	49	223	87
			Be'er Sheva (University)					
1985	—	—	—	(0)	—	—	—	(0)
1986	5	26	191	47	—	—	—	(0)
1987	9	17	197	69	96	133	397	82
1988	—	—	—	0	—	—	—	(0)
1989	—	—	—	0	—	—	—	(0)

Comment: (1) Data of monitoring stations with uptime of less than 35% may not be representative and is given in brackets.

Table 3: Concentrations of O_3 and Total Particulate Matter (TPS) in the Atmosphere in Israel, 1985-1989 (microgram per cubic meter) (ICBS, 1990)[(1)]

Year	*Annual Average*	*Maximum Daily Average*	*Maximum 1/2 hour Average*	*Uptime of Monitor (%)*	*Annual Average*	*Maximum Daily Average*	*Uptime of Monitor (%)*
			OZONE			TPS	
			Commercial Urban Center				
			Jerusalem (Russian Compound)				
1985	—	—	245	79	48	286	70
1986	84	143	265	76	35	128	49
1987	80	143	312	68	45	155	74
1988	68	119	200	93	38	101	76
1989	65	110	232	65	—	—	(0)
			Tel Aviv (Municipality)				
1985	39	91	163	79	—	—	(0)
1986	36	75	151	57	—	—	(0)
1987	—	(61)	(129)	(20)	—	—	(0)
1988	—	—	436	44	—	—	(0)
1989	—	—	—	(0)	—	—	(0)
			Petah Tikva (Central Bus Depot)				
1985	59	120	357	46	202	475	77
1986	44	86	230	39	182	400	66
1987	37	73	337	43	154	393	42
1988	—	—	358	64	192	391	80
1989	—	—	—	(0)	—	—	(0)

pollution in the form of black soot emitted from power plants and soiling by smoke from diesel-powered vehicles constitute severe problems. Only sporadic data regarding measurements of these pollutants exist and are not presented here.

Table 3: (cont)

Year	*Annual Average*	*Maximum Daily Average*	*Maximum 1/2 hour Average*	*Uptime of Monitor (%)*	*Annual Average*	*Maximum Daily Average*	*Uptime of Monitor (%)*
	OZONE				TPS		
			Industrial Suburb				
			Ashdod (Yavne Region)				
1985	–	–	–	(0)	–	–	(0)
1986	15	–	(257)	(21)	–	–	(0)
1987	–	–	378	87	–	–	(0)
1988	–	–	290	83	–	–	(0)
1989	44	90	314	92	–	–	(0)
			Hadera (Bet Eli'ezer)				
1985	–	–	732	46	57	202	60
1986	–	–	–	(0)	54	147	51
1987	–	–	–	(0)	100	308	97
1988	–	–	–	(0)	117	408	40
1989	–	–	–	(0)	–	–	(0)
			Residential Suburb				
			Netanya (North)				
1985	–	–	–	(0)	29	248	57
1986	–	–	–	(0)	21	84	64
1987	–	–	–	(0)	–	–	(0)
1988	–	–	–	(0)	–	–	(0)
1989	–	–	–	(0)	–	–	(0)
			Kibbutz HaMa'apil				
1985	–	–	–	(0)	34	1177	55
1986	–	–	–	(0)	–	(90)	(26)
1987	–	–	–	(0)	–	–	(0)
1988	–	–	–	(0)	–	–	(0)
1989	–	–	–	(0)	–	–	(0)
			Be'er Sheva (University)				
1985	–	–	–	(0)	(126)	(2119)	(27)
1986	–	(153)	(230)	(27)	119	998	57
1987	67	184	332	69	116	599	53
1988	–	–	–	0	–	–	(0)
1989	–	–	–	0	–	–	(0)

Comment: (1) Data of monitoring stations with uptime of less than 35% may not be representative and is given in brackets.

The data from the monitoring networks regarding nitrogen oxides (see Table 2) and carbon monoxide (not presented here), do not show high concentrations. However, Luria et al[58] have shown recently that high levels of these pollutants exist in the congested urban centre of Jerusalem.

3.3 Energy Requirements and Air Pollutant Emission Inventory

As nuclear energy and hydroelectric energy sources are not available to Israel the country relies on fossil fuels for most of its energy requirements. It should be noted that although Israel is the world leader per capita in the use of solar panels for domestic use (mainly residential and commercial) water heating, solar energy consists of only 3.2 per cent of its total energy requirement[40], and the rest (96.8 per cent) comes from fossil fuels.

An air pollutant emission inventory of air pollutants originating from fossil fuel combustion is presented in Table 4, according to fuel type. Natural gas and liquified petroleum gas (LPG) are used in Israel in small quantities: natural gas for industry (0.3 per cent of the total national energy requirement), and LPG mainly for domestic heating such as space and water heating and cooking (1.5 per cent of the energy total national energy requirement). Use of gasoline constitutes about 13 per cent of the total national energy requirement, and kerosene about 7 per cent, most of which is supplied as jet fuel and a small portion for domestic space heating and cooking. Distillate fuel oil (equivalent to ASTM fuel oil No. 2) is used (about 11 per cent of the total energy requitement) by diesel powered vehicles and other stationary diesel motors, by electric gas turbines and for domestic space and water heating.

Relatively small amounts of light residual oil (equivalent to ASTM fuel oil grades No. 4 and 5) are used mostly for steam generation in small to medium sized boilers, especially when the plant is located near residential areas.

Heavy fuel oil (equivalent to ASTM fuel oil grade No. 6), constituting about 32 per cent of the total energy requirements of Israel, is used mainly for electricity generation (22 per cent of the energy requirement), and by heavy industries such as oil refineries, in cement kilns, and in large industrial steam boilers.

Most of the coal in Israel is used for electricity generation (96 per cent); the rest goes to cement production and steam generation. Coal supplies 21 per cent of the total energy requirement of the country.

The emission inventory of combustion derived pollutants presented in Table 4 was calculated using emission factors published by the US Environmental Protection Agency[91], and adapted to the specific conditions existing in Israel[33]. The following can be seen:

- In spite of the 30 per cent increase in the total national energy requirement that occurred from 1980 to 1989, total sulphur dioxide emissions in that period were reduced by 5 per cent. This is a result of the partial shift in electricity generation from high sulphur residual oil (3.5 wt per cent S, and more) used in 1980 to a relatively low sulphur coal (about 1 wt per cent S), and the reduction of the countrywide average sulphur content of the heavy residual oil to 2.7 wt per cent S.
- Carbon monoxide emissions have increased dramatically, as can be expected from the increase in the number of motor vehicles. It

Table 4: Emissions of Air Pollutants from Fuel Burning in Israel, by Type of Fuel, 1980 (thousands of tons) and some Economic Growth Indicators (ICBS, 1990)

Fuel Type / Year	*1980*	*1984*	*1985*	*1986*	*1987*	*1988*	*1989*
Average population (in millions)	3.88	4.16	4.23	4.30	4.37	4.44	4.56
Gross national product ($\times 10^9$\$/1986)	24.6	27.2	28.3	29.4	30.9	31.4	32.7
Energy requirements ($\times 10^3$ T.O.E.)	7889	8591	8478	8773	9667	10148	10631
Number of motor vehicles ($\times 10^3$)	539	760	776	819	882	953	984
SO_2 total (1)	267.1	238.7	213.2	222.7	245.8	240.5	253.8
Thereof:							
Gasoline	3.0	3.8	3.7	4.1	4.5	5.0	5.3
Kerosene	0.3	0.2	0.2	0.2	0.2	0.2	0.2
Distillate fuel oil	7.6	7.1	6.9	7.2	7.6	7.7	8.2
Light residual oil	10.8	11.0	11.2	11.0	11.6	10.2	10.2
Heavy residual oil	245.4	176.4	147.2	151.8	172.3	168.5	175.0
Bituminous coal	0	40.2	44.0	48.4	49.6	48.9	54.9
CO total (1)	283.8	362.4	370.7	382.3	420.5	449.9	498.9
Thereof:							
Gasoline	261.0	335.0	342.5	353.2	386.1	412.9	459.2
Distillate fuel oil	20.4	25.1	25.7	26.4	31.5	33.8	36.4
Light residual oil	0.1	0.1	0.1	0.1	0.1	0.1	0.1
Heavy residual oil	2.2	1.5	1.4	1.5	1.7	2.0	2.0
Bituminous coal	0	0.8	0.9	1.0	1.0	1.0	1.1
No_x total	74.0	104.1	106.1	111.4	123.5	131.4	142.9
Thereof:							
LPG	0.2	0.2	0.2	0.2	0.3	0.3	0.3
Gasoline	16.6	21.3	21.8	22.5	24.5	26.3	29.2
Kerosene	0.2	0.2	0.1	0.1	0.2	0.1	0.2
Distillate fuel oil	27.1	32.7	33.4	34.4	40.9	44.0	47.4
Light residual oil	0.5	0.5	0.5	0.5	0.5	0.5	0.5
Heavy residual oil	29.4	21.1	19.3	19.9	22.5	26.1	27.0
Bituminous coal	0	28.1	30.8	33.8	34.6	34.1	38.3
Hydrocarbons total	34.4	44.1	45.1	46.5	50.9	54.4	60.5
Co_2 total (2)	5491	7424	7337	7626	8359	8765	9424
STP total (1)	23.9	20.6	18.9	19.5	22.3	24.8	24.2
Thereof:							
Gasoline	0.4	0.5	0.5	0.5	0.6	0.6	0.7
Distillate fuel oil	4.6	5.2	5.5	5.7	7.0	7.5	8.2
Light residual oil	0.1	0.1	0.1	0.1	0.1	0.1	0.1
Heavy residual oil	18.8	13.8	11.6	12.0	13.2	13.2	13.6
Bituminous coal	0	1.0	1.1	1.2	1.4	1.4	1.6
Lead particles							
Gasoline	0.43	0.55	0.54	0.60	0.66	0.51	0.28

Comments:
(1) Small quantities for LPG, Kerosene or distillate fuel oil not presented.
(2) Quantities also include emissions of CO_2 from klinker production in cement kilns.

should be noted that it is planned to introduce cars equipped with catalytic converters in Israel only in Model Year 1992 (i.e. August 1991).

- Hydrocarbon emissions have also increased with the large increase in the quantity of gasoline used by cars. However, due to the fact that gasoline specifications in Israel dictate a rather low vapour pressure (RVP of 8.5 psig), losses of gasoline into the air from evaporation are reduced and emissions are not large.
- Lead particle emissions into the air have been significantly reduced with the adoption by the Ministry of Energy in 1989 of the European Economic Community Directive (87/416/EEC, 21 July 1987) which specifies a maximum allowable lead content in gasoline (0.15 gram lead compound per litre). With the gradual introduction of unleaded gasoline, beginning in 1991, a further reduction in lead emissions is expected.
- Most of the total suspended particulates (TSP) emissions originate from the combustion of heavy residual oil. The heavy residual oil used in Israel is very rich in asphaltenes and sulphur, resulting in emissions of large quantities of black soot, flyash and sulphate particles[(87)]. Diesel oil specifications in Israel allow a high sulphur content of 0.4 wt per cent, which also contributes to increased TSP emissions from diesel powered vehicles and stationary diesel motors. However, TSP emissions have not increased much from 1980 to 1989, mainly because of the introduction of coal-fired power plants, in which particulate matter emissions are controlled by high efficiency electrostatic precipitators.

Carbon dioxide and nitrogen oxides emissions have increased significantly from 1980 to 1989 in line with the increase in the demand for fossil fuel energy in that period.

3.4 Role of Private Interest Groups

Israel cannot boast of a wide or deep involvement of its citizens in environmental issues. However the first private environmental interest group in Israel "MALRAZ" (the Public Council for the Prevention of Noise and Air Pollution) was established in 1961, following enactment of the *Abatement of Nuisances Law* (see section 2.1). MALRAZ is a non-profit voluntary organization which aims to arouse community concern on specific local noise and air pollution nuisance problems. Since MALRAZ sees the major cause of environmental problems in Israel as the lax enforcement of existing laws, it has tried to encourage the Government and local authorities to enforce them more vigorously.

In the late 1960s, MALRAZ was at the centre of litigation against the Government and the Israel Electric Corporation regarding the decision to build the 450 MW "Reading D" power plant in the northern part of Tel Aviv[71, 47]. MALRAZ also spearheaded the action against the air pollution caused by the "Nesher" Portland cement plant in Haifa. As a direct result of an appeal by MALRAZ to the Supreme Court of Justice on the Regulations on Air Quality and on Particulate Matter Emissions were finally promulgated[48].

3.5 Research on Air Quality

Extensive research is being carried out in Israel on various aspects of air quality, dispersion of pollutants, long range transport of pollution, effects of pollution on humans and vegetation etc. A detailed list is given in the reference section at the end of this chapter.

4 FUTURE DEVELOPMENTS

To improve air quality in Israel, a comprehensive air pollution action programme was launched in 1987. Most of the issues included in the original programme can still serve as the basis for future developments. The following is a synopsis of this 10-point programme.

- The definition of ambient air quality standards in the *Regulation on Air Quality 1972* has to be revised so that they are understood as national goals for air quality that should be achieved. The existing air quality standards included in the Regulation should be revised, as well as expanded to include, in addition to the combustion-generated pollutants, a list of standards for chemical substances and hazardous air pollutants;
- Performance and emission standards suitable to the conditions in Israel should be promulgated. This will eliminate the need in the future to rely on personal decrees for enforcement. First on the list of priorities for setting performance standards should be large power plant steam boilers, medium sized industrial steam boilers, cement kilns, toxic- and municipal-waste standards for sulphur dioxide, nitrogen oxides and particulate matter emitted from all sizes of stationary fuel combustion installations, and for carbon monoxide, smoke, nitrogen dioxide and hydrocarbons emitted from mobile sources;
- Tighter standards for fuel quality based on environmental considerations should be promulgated. It is especially important to reduce the sulphur content in heavy residual oil (from the present 2.7 wt per cent S) and in diesel oil (from the present 0.4 wt per cent S). It should be noted that the target for reducing the lead content in gasoline to 0.15 g/l set in 1987 has already been met;

- The use of oxygenated fuels as alternatives to gasoline for motor vehicles should be encouraged;
- A regulation for combatting fires in garbage dumps has already been achieved (see section 2.1);
- A large number of very old and smoky buses are still in active service, mainly in the centres of big cities. These should be taken out of service at a faster rate than at present;
- The use of CFCs and halons in Israel should be reduced now and subsequently abolished, as required by the Montreal Protocol of 1987 (revised 1990). As all the CFCs in use in the country are imported (in 1986, 3700 tons), a ban on imports of CFCs and CFC-containing products should be imposed;
- More air quality monitoring systems should be established in areas not yet covered, such as the Tel Aviv area, the Galilee and the Negev;
- Administrative measures should be taken to strengthen enforcement of air pollution laws and regulations, especially the imposition of heavy fines on offenders;
- Research on air pollution control and air quality monitoring should be expanded and more funds provided for that purpose.

New issues which have arisen since 1987 and were not included in the original action programme, are:

- Providing a strong legal basis for air pollution enforcement procedures through a revised *Abatement of Nuisances Law*. Specifically, the inspection authorities in the environmental protection units should be provided with high quality and accessible stack- and exhaust-sampling services and a broad and efficient system for controlling motor vehicle emissions should be established;
- Israeli environmental standards should be matched with international requirements such as those set by provisions of global conventions and protocols and by the guidelines and Directives issued by the European Economic Community;
- Modern and energy efficient public transportation systems should be established in order to replace both private and public motor vehicles (especially in the Tel Aviv area);
- The use of electricity, and other types of energy, as alternatives to gasoline and diesel fuel for motor vehicles, should be encouraged;
- Beginning 1 January 1993, all new motor vehicles introduced in Israel should be equipped with catalytic converters. Also, low-

volatility unleaded gasoline should be introduced and its use in motor cars encouraged as quickly as possible;

- An air quality monitoring system should be developed, based on the principle of remote sensing;
- A country-wide air pollution dispersion model should be developed to enable the impact on air quality of large national projects to be evaluated (e.g. electric power plants);
- Emissions into the atmosphere of greenhouse gases such as carbon dioxide should be reduced and energy conservation in the domestic and industrial sectors strongly encouraged. Measures should be taken to reduce emissions of the other greenhouse gases, especially methane and CFCs.

5 BIBLIOGRAPHY

Hanna S R, Briggs G A, and Hosker R P, (1982). *Handbook on Atmospheric Diffusion.* USDoE Document No. DOE/TIC-11223, US Dept. Energy, Washington DC, US.

Seinfeld J H, (1986). *Atmospheric Chemistry and Physics of Air Pollution.* J Wiley, New York, NY, US.

Stern A C (Ed), (1986). *Air Pollution*, 3rd Ed, Vols. 1-5 and Vols. 6-8 (Supplements, 1986). Academic Press, Orlando, FA, US.

US EPA, (1985). *Compilation of Air Pollutants Emission Factors*, 4th Ed. US EPA Document No. AP-42, US Government Printing Office, Washington DC, US.

WHO, (1987). *Air Quality Guidelines for Europe.* WHO Regional Publications - European Series No. 78, World Health Organization (WHO), Copenhagen, Denmark.

Periodicals

Annual Reports on the State of the Environment in Israel, Ministry of the Environment, Jerusalem, since 1973 (Hebrew).

Environmental Science and Technology (ES&T), The American Chemical Society, Washington DC, US.

Ha'Bioshera (The Biosphere), monthly Magazine of the Ministry of the Environment, Jerusalem, since 1970 (Hebrew).

Israel Environmental Bulletin, quarterly Bulletin of the Ministry of the Environment, Jerusalem, since 1974.

Journal of the Air and Waste Management Association (formerly Journal of the Air Pollution Control Association, JAPCA), Pittsburgh, PA, US.

REFERENCES

1. Amiran D (Ed), (1985). *Atlas of Israel*, 3rd Edition. Survey of Israel and MacMillan Publication Co, Tel Aviv, London.

2. Alpert P, Cohen A, Neumann J & Doron E. (1982). A Model Simulation of the Summer Circulation from the Eastern Mediterranean Past Lake Kinneret in the Jordan Valley. Month. Weath. Rev, Vol. 110(8): pp. 994-1006.

3. Asculai E, Doron E & Terliuc B, (1984). Mesoscale Flow Over Complex Terrain - A Field Study in the Lake Kinneret Area. Bound. Layer Meteor, Vol. 30: pp. 313-331.

4. Azmon E & Offer Z Y, (1989). Atmospheric Mineralogy and Chemistry of Dust Storms in the Negev Desert, Israel. *Environmental Quality and Ecosystem Stability*, Vol. 4/A: pp. 143-150. ISEEQS Publ, Jerusalem.

5. Balmor Y & Gutman A, (1989). Atmospheric SO2 Trends in Israel. *Environmental Quality and Ecosystem Stability*, Vol. 4/A: pp. 67-72. ISEEQS Publ, Jerusalem.

6. Bitan A, (1977). The Influence of the Special Shape of the Dead Sea and its Environment on the Local Wind System. Arch. Meteor. Geoph. Biolk, Ser. B, Vol. 24: pp. 283-301.

7. Dayan U, (1986). Climatology of Back Trajectories from Israel Based on Synoptic Analysis. Jour. of Appl. Meteorol, Vol. 25: pp. 591-595.

8. Dayan U, Shenhav & Graber M, (1988). The Spatial and Temporal Behaviour of the Mixed Layer in Israel. Jour. of Appl. Meteor, Vol. 27(12): pp. 1388-1394.

9. Dayan U & Koch J, (1989). Assessment of the Critical Conditions for Dispersion and Transport of Plumes from Tall Stacks in the Haifa Area. *Environmental Quality and Ecosystem Stability*, Vol. 4/A: pp. 27-36. ISEEQS Publ, Jerusalem.

10. Dayan U, Balmor Y & Gutman, (1989). Wind Structure of the Shallow Atmospheric Layer in a Coastal vs. Arid Site in Israel. *Environmental Quality and Ecosystem Stability*, Vol. 4/A: pp. 103-112. ISEEQS Publ, Jerusalem.

11. Donagi A, Naveh M, Manes A, Rindsberger M, Gat Y & Friedland A, (1973). A Dual-Purpose Air Pollution Alert and Implementation System for the Greater Tel Aviv Areas. *Pollution Engineering and Scientific Solutions* (Barrekette E S Ed): pp. 671-679. Plenum Publ. Co, New York.

12. Donagi A, Ganor A, Shenhar & Cember H, (1979). Some Metallic Trace Elements in the Atmospheric Aerosols of the Tel Aviv Urban Area. Jour. of the Air Pollut. Contr. Assoc, Vol. 29(1): pp. 53-54.

13. Doron E, (1979). Objective Analysis of Mesoscale Flow Fields in Israel and Trajectory Calculations. Isr. Jour. of Earth-Sci, vol. 28: pp. 33-41.

14. Doron E & Kinrot A, (1989). Numerical Simulation of Worst SO2 Pollution Episodes in the Haifa Bay and Mount Carmel Area. *Environmental Quality and Ecosystem Stability*, Vol. 4/A: pp. 45-55. ISEEQS Publ, Jerusalem.

15. Etzion R, Graber M, Cohen Y & Brovender S, (1986). An Historic Center and a New Power Plant - Can They Coexist in a Neighbouring Environment? The Application of the Israeli Environmental Impact Statement System, Prepared for the Priority Action Plan (PAP), Regional Activity Centre, UNEP, Split, Yugoslavia: 70pp. The Environmental Protection Service, Ministry of the Interior, Jerusalem.

16. Foner H A, Lahav Y, Zohar & Goldberger Z, (1989). A Study of Vanadium and Nickel Contamination in the Ashdod Area - Preliminary Results. *Environmental Quality and Ecosystem Stability*, Vol, 4/A: pp. 133-142. ISEEQS Publ, Jerusalem.

17. Foner H A, (1990). The Distribution of Petrol-Derived Lead in Israel. Sci. of the Total Envir, vol. 93: pp. 43-50.

18. Gale J & Easton J, (1975). Rapid Deterioration of the Pine Forests in the Abu-Ghosh Gulch - Possible Involvement of Air Pollution form Motor Vehicles (Fishelson L Ed). Proc. of the 6th Scien. Conf. of the Isr. Ecological Soc: pp. 64-72.

19. Ganor E, Beck Y R E & Donagi A, (1978). Ozone Concentrations and Meteorological Conditions in Tel Aviv - 1975. Atmos. Envir, Vol. 12: pp. 1081-1085.

20. Ganor E & Mamane Y, (1982). Transport of Saharan Dust across the Eastern Mediterranean. Atmos. Envir, Vol. 16(3): pp. 581-587.

21. Ganor E, (1985). Environmental Quality and Air Pollution. *Atlas of Israel*, 3rd Edition, Sheet 39 (Amiran D Ed). Survey of Israel & MacMillan Publ. Co, Tel Aviv & London.

22. Ganor E, Altshuller S, Foner H A, Brenner S & Gabbay J, (1988). Vanadium and Nickel in Dustfall as Indicators of Power Plant Pollution. Water, Air & Soil Poll, Vol. 42: pp. 241-252.

23. Ganor E & Foner H F (1989). Composition of some Urban Atmospheric Aerosols in Israel. *Environmental Quality and Ecosystem Stability*, Vol. 4/A: pp. 121-131. ISEEQS Publ, Jerusalem.

24. Garty J & Hagemeyer J, (1988). Heavy Metals in the Lichen "Ramalina Duriaei" Transplanted at Biomonitoring Stations in the Region of a Coal-Fired Power Plant in Israel after 3 Years of Operation. Water, Air & Soil Poll, Vol. 38: pp. 311-323.

25. Gat J R & Rindsberger M, (1985). The Isotopic Signature of Precipitation Originating in the Mediterranean Sea Area: A Possible Monitor of Climate Modification? Isr. Jour. of Earth-Sci, Vol. 34: pp. 80-85.

26. Gat Y & Friedland A C, (1975). Sulfur Dioxide Concentration Measurements in Haifa. Proc. of the 6th Scien. Conf. of the Isr. Ecological Soc. (Fishelson L Ed): pp. 73-82.

27. Gat Y & Balmor Y & Kovacs S, (1983). An Intermittent Control System for Sulfur Dioxide Utilizing Fuel Switching at Eshkol Power Plant. *Developments in Ecology and Environmental Quality*, Vol. 2: pp. 105-113. Balaban ISS, Philadelphia, PA.

28. Goren A I & Goldsmith J R, (1986). Epidemiology of Childhood Respiratory Disease in Israel. Europ. Jour. of Epidemiology. Vol. 2 (2): pp. 139-150.

29. Goren A I, Brenner S & Hellmann S, (1988). Cross-Sectional Health Study in Polluted and Non-polluted Agricultural Settlements in Israel. Environ. Res, Vol. 46: pp. 107-119.

30. Graber M, (1980). Data Processing and Analysis of the Israeli National Air Quality Monitoring Network. CODATA Bulletin, ?23?39, December, 1980: pp. 6-14.

31. Graber M, Dayan U & Laznow J, (1984). Development of a Dispersion Model for Power Plant Siting Applications in Coastal Israel. Conference Volume, 4th Joint Conference on Applications of Air Pollution Meteorology, 16-19 Oct, 1984: pp. 268-269. Amer, Meteor, Soc, Boston, MA.

32. Graber M, (1988). Air Pollution Assessment of Chemical Plants in Israel. Presented at the International Conference on Environmental Impact Analysis for Developing Countries, New-Delhi, 28 Nov - 2 Dec 1988. (also in Isr. Environ. Bull, (1989) Vol. 12 (1): pp. 16-24).

33. Graber M, (1988). National Air Pollutant Emission Inventory from Fuel Combustion in Israel for the Years 1980, 1984-1987. *Ha'Biosphera*, Vol. 17(12): pp. 5-13.

34. Graber M, Dayan U, Doron E, Luria M, Mahrer Y & Shenav R, (1989). Carrying Capacity of Pollutants in the Atmosphere in Relation to the New Electric

Power Plant Planned in Northern Israel. *Environmental Quality and Ecosystem Stability*, Vol. 4/A: pp. 15-25. ISEEQS Publ, Jerusalem.

35. Graber M, (1989). Tools for Ambient Air Quality Management, Training Series on Environmental Technologies Promotion No. 1, August 1989. Document UNIDO/IPCT.88(SPEC). Prepared for The United Nations Industrial Development Organization (UNIDO), Vienna.

36. Gutman M, Hocherman I & Stotter A, (1981). Some Aspects of Vehicle Pollution Estimation in Israel. *Developments in Arid Zone Ecology and Environmental Quality*: pp. 399-405. Balaban ISS, Philadelphia, PA.

37. Halevy G & Steinberger E H, (1974). Inland Penetration of the Summer Inversion from the Mediterranean Coast in Israel. Isr. Jour. of Earth-Sci, Vol. 23: pp. 47-54.

38. Hirsch Y, Peleg M & Luria M, (1981). Characterization of Suspended Dust Particles in the Jerusalem Air. Envir. Sci. & Tech, Vol. 15(12): pp. 1456-1460.

39. Huss A & Feliks Y, (1981). A Mesometeorological Numerical Model of the Sea and Land Breezes Involving Sea-Atmospheric Interaction. Contrib. Atmosph. Physics, Vol. 54(2): pp. 238-257.

40. ICBS, (1990). *Statistical Abstracts of Israel - 1990*, No. 41. Israel Central Bureau of Statistics (Hebrew and English), Jerusalem.

41. Jones K H, (1976). National Plan for Air Quality Assessment and Monitoring in the Major Urban and Industrial Centres of Israel - Haifa, Tel Aviv, Jerusalem, Be'er Sheva and Ashdod: pp. 24-61. *Air Quality in Israel Selected Topics*, Environmental Protection Service, Ministry of the Interior, Jerusalem.

42. Joseph J, Manes A & Ashbel D, (1973). Desert Aerosols Transported by Khamsinic Depressions and their Climatic Effects. Jour. of Climate & Appl, Meteor, Vol. 12: pp. 792-797.

43. Katsnelson J, (1970). Frequency of Duststorms at Be'er Sheva. Isr. Jour. of Earth-Sci, Vol. 19: pp. 69-76.

44. Kolton-Shapira R, Lakritz T, & Luria M, (1984). Rainwater pH in the Vicinity of Hadera Power Plant, Israel During the Winter Season of 1981/82. Atmos. Envir, Vol. 18(6): pp. 1245-1248.

45. Kovacs S P & Balmor Y, (1987). Operation of Intermittent control Systems for Sulfur Dioxide. *VGB Kraftwerkstechnik*, Vol. 67(6): pp. 600-605 (in German; see also internal IEC publication ECD-86-10).

46. Kushelevski A, Shani G & Hacoun A H, (1983). Effect of Meteorological Conditions on Total Suspended Particulate (TSP) Levels and elemental Concentration of Aerosols in a Semi-Arid Zone (Be'er Sheva, Israel). Tellus, 35B: pp. 481-505.

47. Laster R E, (1973). Reading D - Planning and Building of Building and then Planning? Isr. Law Rev, (Vol. 8(4): pp. 481-505.

48. Laster R E, (1973a). *Portland Cement Plant "Nesher Ltd" (Haifa) - A Case study.* Publication No. 73-01, Environmental Protection Service, Ministry of Interior, Jerusalem (Hebrew).

49. Laster R E & Rotenberg R, (1985) *Air Quality. Compendium of Environmental Laws and Regulations in Israel*, 2nd Revision. Environmental Protection Service, Ministry of the Interior, Jerusalem (Hebrew).

50. Lerman Sh & Kopfstein M, (1988). The Effects of Fly Ash on Citrus Fruit - Characterization of Injury Symptoms and Assessment of Crop Loss (Poster Session Summaries). Environ. Pollution, Vol. 53(1-4): pp. 443-444.

51. Levin Z & Lindberg J D, (1979). Size Distribution, Chemical Composition, and Optical Prosperities of Urban and Desert Aerosols in Israel. Jour. of Geophys. Res, Vol. 84(C11): pp. 6941-6950.

52. Levin Z, Price C & Ganor E, (1990). The Contribution of Sulphate and Desert Aerosols to Acidification of Clouds and Rain in Israel, Atmos. Environ, Vol. 24: pp. 1143-1151.

53. Lifshitz B, Peleg M & Luria M, (1988). The Influence of Medium-Range Transport on O3 Levels at a Rural Site in Israel, Jour. Atmos. Chem, Vol. 7: pp. 19-33.

54. Luria M, Almog H & Peleg M, (1984). Transport and Transformation of Air Pollutants from Israel's Coastal Area, Atmos. Envir, Vol. 18(10): pp. 2215-2221.

55. Luria M, Vinig Z, & Peleg M, (1984a). The Contribution of City Buses to Urban Air Pollution in Jerusalem, Israel. Jour. of the Air Pollut. Contr. Assoc, Vol. 34: pp. 828-831.

56. Luria M, Glaser E & Lakretz Y, (1985). Establishment and Initial Operation of an Air Monitoring Network in the Vicinity of a 1400 MW Coal-fired Power Plant, Hadera, Israel. Isr. Environ, Bull, Vol. 9(3): pp. 16-24.

57. Luria M, Liftshitz B & Peleg M, (1989). Particulate Sulfate Levels at a Rural Site in Israel. Jour. Atmos. Chem, Vol. 8: pp. 241-250.

58. Luria M, Weisinger R & Peleg M, (1990). Air Pollution Levels at the Centre of City Roads. Atmos. Envir, 24B: pp. 93-99.

59. Mahrer Y & Pielke R A, (1977), The Effect of Topography on Sea and Land Breezes in a Two-Dimensional Numerical Model, Monthly Weather Rev, Vol. 105: pp. 1151-1162.

60. Mahrer I, (1985). A Numerical Study of the Effects of Sea Surface Temperature on the Sea and Land Breeze Circulation. Isr. Jour. of Earth-Sci, Vol. 34: pp. 91-95.

61. Mamane Y, Ganor E & Donagi A E, (1981). Aerosol Composition of Urban and Desert Origin in the Eastern Mediterranean. Individual Particle Analysis, Water Air Soil Poll, Vol. 14: pp. 23-43.

62. Mamane Y, Ganor E & Donagi A E, (1980). Analysis of Air Quality Data During a Day of Relatively Low Emissions. Jour. Air Polut. Contr. Assoc, Vol. 31(6): pp. 678-679.

63. Mamane Y, (1987). Chemistry of Precipitation in Israel. Sci. of the Total Env, Vol.61: pp. 1-13.

64. Nativ R, Zangvil A, Issar A & Karniele A, (1985). The Occurrance of Sulfate-Rich Rains in the Negev Desert - Israel. *Tellus*, Vol. 37(13): pp. 166-172.

65. Naveh Z, Steinberger E H, Chaim S & Ratman A, (1980). Photochemical Air Pollutants - A Threat to Mediterranean Coniferous Forests and Upland Ecosystems. Envir. Conser, Vol. & (4): pp. 301-309.

66. Neumann J, (1971). Some Meteorological Aspects of Air Pollution in Israel. Man in an Antagonistic Environment, Proceedings of the Conference, 29-30 March 1971, The National Research and Development Council and The Israel National Academy of Sciences, Jerusalem. (Hebrew)

67. Neumann J & Mahrer Y, (1971). A Theoretical Study of the Land and Sea Breeze Circulation. Jour. Atmos. Sci, Vol. 28: pp. 532-542.

68. Neumann J, (1977). On the Rotation Rate of the Direction of Sea and Land Breezes. Jour. of Atmos. Sci, Vol. 28: pp. 1913-1917.

69. Peleg M, Burla E, Cohen I & Luria M, (1989). Deterioration of Jerusalem Limestone from Air Pollutants - Field Observation and Laboratory Simulation. Envir. Monitor. & Assess, Vol. 12: pp. 191-201.

70. Navrot J & Amiel A J, (1974). Metallic Contaminants in Dust Storms Deposited in the Rehovot Area. Isr. Jour. Earth-Sci, Vol. 23: pp. 9-11.

71. Peranio A, (1971). The Tall Stacks - Technical and Social Aspects. Proceedings of the 2nd International Clean Air Congress. Academic Press, New York.

72. Pruginin A & Glass Y, (1990). *Environmental Quality in Israel, Beyond the Year 2000 - Trends and Possible Scenarios.* Ministry of the Environment, Jerusalem.

73. Rindsberger M, (1976). Air Pollution Potential in Greater Tel Aviv Area. Isr. Jour. of Earth-Sci, Vol. 25: pp. 127-132.

74. Rindsberger M, Magaritz M, Carmi I & Gilad D, (1983). The Relation Between Air Mass Trajectories and the Water Isotope Composition of the Mediterranean Sea Area. Geophys. Res. Letters, Vol. 10(1): pp. 43-46.

75. Schiller G, (1977). Interrelations Between Site Factors and Performance of Allepo Pine in the Sha'ar Hagay Forest. La'Ya'aran, Vol. 27(1-4): pp. 13-23. (Hebrew, English abstract)

76. Segal M, Mahrer Y & Pielke R A, (1982). Evaluation of Onshore Pollutant Recirculation Over the Mediterranean Coastal Area of Central Israel. Isr. Jour. Earth-Sci, Vol. 31: pp. 39-46.

77. Segal M, Mahrer Y, Pielke R A & Kessler R C, (1985). Model Evaluation of the Summer Daytime Induced Flow Over Southern Israel. Isr. Jour. Earth-Sci, Vol. 34: pp. 39-46.

78. Sharf G, Peleg M, Livnat M & Luria M, (1989). Instrumented Aircraft Measurements of Plume Rise from Large Point Sources. *Environmental Quality and Ecosystem Stability,* Vol 4/A: pp. 37-44. ISEEQS Publ, Jerusalem.

79. Shechter M & Zeidner M, (1990). Psychological Responses Towards Air Pollution - Some Personality And Demographic Correlates. Jour. Environ. Psychology, Vol. 48.

80. Shechter M, & Kim M, (1991). Valuation of Pollution Abatement Benefits: Direct and Indirect Measurements. To be published in Jour. Urban Economics.

81. Skibin D & Hod A, (1979). Subjective Analysis of Mesoscale Flow Patterns in Northern Israel. Jour. of Appl. Meteor, Vol. 18: pp. 329-338.

82. Soudine A, (1989). Air Pollution of the Mediterranean Sea. *Environmental Quality and Ecosystem Stability,* Vol. 4/Suppl. ISEEQS Publ, Jerusalem (Abstract).

83. Stanhill G, (1970). Measurements of Global Solar Radiation in Israel. Isr. Jour. of Earth-Sci, Vol. 19: pp. 91-96.

84. Steinberger E H, (1974). A Study of the Influence of Meteorological Parameters of Oxidant Concentrations in Jerusalem. Isr. Jour. of Earth-Sci, Vol. 23: pp. 19-22.

85. Steinberger E H & Balmor Y, (1975). Sulphur Dioxide in the Atmosphere in Jerusalem and the Role of Meteorology on Pollutant Concentrations in Subtropical Regions. Atmos. Envir, Vol. 9: pp. 409-416.

86. Steinberger E H, (1982). Trends in Ozone Concentrations in Jerusalem. Sci. of the Total Env, Vol. 23: pp. 93-105.

87. Taback H, Hersh S & Graber M, (1983). Fallout from Heavy Oil Combustion in Israel - Cause and Cure. *Developments in Ecology and Environmental Quality,* Vol. 2: pp. 115-125. Balaban ISS, Philadelphia, PA.

88. Tadmor J & Manes A, (1973). Photochemical Smog Potential of Urban Areas in Israel. Isr. Jour. Earth-Sci, Vol. 22: pp. 93-105.

89. Tadmor J, Graber M, Amir S, Goldsmith J, Lerman S & Shechter M, (1986). A New (Revised) Israeli Ambient Air Quality Standard Proposed for Sulfur Dioxide.

Environmental Quality and Ecosystem Stability Vol. 3: pp. 611-617. Bar-Ilan Univ. Press, Ramat-Gan.

90. TA Luft, (1986). Technische Anleitung zur Reinhaltung der Luft (TA Luft), Teil 3.3. Besondere Regelungen fuer bestimmte Anlagenarten, Federal Ministry of the Environment, Berlin.

91. US EPA Regulations: National Primary and Secondary Ambient Air Quality Standards and Appendices A-K. US Code of Federal Register Title 40, Part 50 (40 CFR 50); Ambient Air Monitoring Reference and Equivalent Methods. US Code of Federal Register Title 40, Part 53 (40 CFR 53); Ambient Air Quality Surveillance Regulations. US Code of Federal Register Title 40, Part 58 (40 CFR 58); Standards of Performance for New Stationary Sources, Subparts A-TTT and Appendix A (Reference Methods). US Code of Federal Register Title 40, Part 60 (40 CFR 60), US EPA, Washington, DC, US.

92. Yaalon D H & Ganor E, (1968). Chemical Composition of Dew and Fallout in Jerusalem, *Israel. Nature*, Vol. 217(5134): pp. 1139-1140.

ITALY

1 INTRODUCTION

1.1 Topography, Climate, Population

Italy is a large peninsula which projects from the mass of central Europe far to the south in the Mediterranean sea where the island of Sicily may be considered as a continuation of the continental promontory.

The portion of the Mediterranean, commonly termed the Tyrrhenian sea, forms its limit on the west and south and the Adriatic on the east.

Where Italy joins the main continent of Europe to the north, it is separated from the adjacent regions by the barrier of the Alps which sweep round in a vast semicircle from the head of the Adriatic to the French border. Italy's northern land frontier is in fact formed by the Alps which divide it from France, Switzerland, Austria and Yugoslavia.

The configuration and internal geography of Italy is determined almost entirely by the great chain of the Apennines. One result of the way in which the Apennines traverse Italy from the Mediterranean to the Adriatic is the marked division between northern Italy, including the region north of the Apennines and extending thence to the foot of the Alps, and the central and southern parts of the peninsula.

Sardinia is the second largest island in the Mediterranean and lies only 12 km from the French island of Corsica.

The geographical position of Italy makes it one of the hottest countries in Europe. The effect of its southern latitude is, however, tempered by its peninsular character and by the great range of the Alps with their snows and glaciers to the north.

There are thus irregular variations of climate and huge differences between northern and southern Italy. Rainfall is heaviest in the Alps and lightest in the lowlands and the prevailing westerly winds bring rain to the west of the mountains while the east remains comparatively dry.

Italy is 301 224 sq. km in area while the population, according to the most recent census, is 57 200 000, giving a density per sq. km of 190. Italy is politically subdivided into 20 regions and included in its territory are also the Repubblica of San Marino and the Citta del Vaticano.

1.2 Specific National Problems

Better and more efficient coordination on environmental issues among central authorities and regions, and between the regions themselves, needs to be established. Some Italian regions are still facing problems in setting up an effective organization to deal with the new responsibilities transferred to them by Law No. 616/1977. This transferred certain powers from Central Government to the Regions.

The Local Health Units (USL) have an effective organization in the field of health and hygiene but have yet to establish an equally effective air pollution control organization. The Local Health Units, which have responsibilities for both the internal and external aspects of environmental conservation, are often not competent enough in the diverse fields of their duties. Also political pressures may sometimes interfere in the interpretation and implementation of legislation, and the attitude of some regional authorities also gives rise to concern. Some of them also enact local laws which impose measures which are more severe than national legislation.

As a result of the Seveso accident in 1976, interest in and concern about air pollution problems grew rapidly and activist groups pursued environmental issues in a highly emotive way. Also as a direct result of the Seveso accident and other international incidents, the European Commission issued a Directive on major hazards from certain industrial activities and related risk assessment (82/501/EEC).

The authorities are, at the present time, giving increasing attention to accidental releases of pollutants and are requiring industries to carry out proper risk analysis studies on potentially dangerous processes. The first example of risk analysis studies limited to fire accidents, as required by the Cabinet Decree (DM) of 2 August 1984 where the noxious or hazardous consequences of pollutant releases are considered, represents a preliminary application of the Seveso Directive. Risk analysis has been enforced upon many industries after the promulgation of the Decree of the President of the Republic (DPR) 175/88 which applies the Seveso Directive to Italy.

The application of the Environmental Impact Assessment (EIA) Directive (85/337/EEC) is likely to give rise to problems for the authorities and other interested parties both because of the complexity of its requirements and because of the public audit.

2 DEVELOPMENT OF AIR POLLUTION CONTROLS AND LEGISLATION

2.1 Development of Air Pollution Controls

There were no effective air pollution controls in Italy until 1966, when the first *Air Pollution Law*, No. 615, was issued by the Public Health Department. Before 1966 certain articles of the Penal Code were used to take legal action against polluters, for example the old *Health Law Consolidation Act* (1934); this is still in force for specific cases, such as the unhealthy industrial activities classification procedure.

The Air Pollution Law, No. 615, was subsequently supplemented by the technical regulation for domestic heating emissions (1970), industrial emissions (1971) and diesel engine vehicles' emissions (1971). As a result of Law No. 616, issued in 1977, most aspects of governmental concern have now been transferred to the regions, provinces and municipalities.

The National Health Service Law (23 December 1978), No. 833, setting up the Local Health Units (USL) which are also responsible for environmental controls, was issued in 1978.

More recently, various EEC Directives have been implemented in Italy, including those relating to the sulphur content of certain liquid fuels (1982); lead content of petrol (1982); the air quality standards (AQS) for sulphur dioxide and suspended particulate matter (SPM) (1983), together with other standards such as those for nitrogen dioxide, ozone, carbon monoxide, lead and fluorine.

Although all the most recent laws have been enacted, some of them have not yet been fully implemented. Recently, the Department for the Environment was set up (Law No. 349 of 8 July 1986); it is responsible for the coordination of those environmental issues which were previously handled by various government departments. Environmental legislation is currently under revision in this Department which is liaising with the Public Health Department and other Departments such as the Industry and Trade Department and the Civil Protection Department.

In setting criteria for air pollution control, Italian legislators have adopted some basic principles according to which the *Air Pollution Law*, and related technical regulations, have been prepared. The major features can be summarized as follows:

- Promulgation of a general law covering dispositions for domestic heating, industries and automotive emissions control.
- Creation of two control zones, "A" and "B", as a function of population and geographical position of towns.

- Limitation of sulphur content relative to viscosity in liquid fuels; the sulphur percentage allowed in solid fuels will vary according to zones and heating plants' thermal capacity.
- Exemption for gaseous fuels, petroleum distillates and for some types of coal depending upon their content of sulphur and volatile matters.
- Preparation of specific technical regulation for emissions from both stationary and mobile sources.
- Setting of ground level concentration limits for discharges from domestic heating plants.
- Definition of ground level concentration limits for some pollutants emitted by industrial plants as a sole industry contribution.
- General dispositions including the air pollution control responsibilities among central, regional, provincial and municipal authorities.
- Final dispositions on administrative goals to be accomplished by both government and local authorities.

Subsequently the legislators felt it necessary, in order to rationalize air pollution control and health protection, to adopt air quality standards (AQS) for the most significant pollutants. These measures were also undertaken in connection with the implementation of the related EEC Directive in several European countries. As a consequence of the adoption of the air quality standard a draft for a new air pollution law has been prepared by the relevant government authorities.

2.2 Industrial Processes

The major legal instruments applying to industrial processes are the *Air Pollution Law* of 13 July 1966, No. 615, and the following:

- Technical Regulation for industrial emissions covered in the Decree of the President of the Republic (DPR)* of 15 April 1971, No. 322;
- The provision of the Decree of the President of the Cabinet (DPCM)* of 23 March 1983;
- DPR No. 203, of 24 May 1988 concerning air quality standards for seven pollutants; and
- Various articles of the Penal Code (especially Article 674).

In addition Article 216 of the *Health Law Consolidation Act* of 27 July 1934, No. 1265, and the related list of unhealthy industrial activities classification, as shown in the Cabinet Decree (DM)* of 12 February 1971, are also applied.

The most significant features of the above-mentioned legal instruments can be summarized as follows:

- According to Article 20 of Law No. 615, all industrial plants, in addition to observing obligations deriving from Article 216 of Law No. 1265, of 27 July 1934, must have installations and devices for the abatement of air pollutants to the lowest technically feasible levels, i.e. adopt the "best practicable means" available.
- During the formulation of urban development plans the site of industrial districts, as distinct from residential areas, must be taken into due consideration as required by Article 21.
- According to Article 3 of the Technical Regulation (DPR, No. 322 of 15 April 1971) all sections of an industrial factory which can contribute to air pollution must have an abatement plant. This must be designed and constructed at the same time as the industrial plant to which it is connected.
- For any on-going condition of the industrial plant the associated pollution control devices must operate so that the emission limits, established by the authorities on approval of the project, are observed.
- Local authorities are responsible for the control of ground level concentration of air pollutants emitted from industrial sources.
- Prior to the enforcement of the air quality standards (DPCM of 28 March 1983) the ground level concentration limits for eleven substances were established as peak (30 or 120 minutes) and average (8 or 24 hours) concentration and considered as the sole contribution from industrial plants (Article 8 of DPR No. 322, of 15 April 1971).
- For the protection of the population's health, maximum acceptable concentration levels, and related maximum exposure values (AQS), of seven air pollutants, have been fixed in the DPCM of 28 March 1983 as mentioned in above.
- The ground level concentration limits for chlorine, hydrochloric acid, sulphides, organic substances (hydrocarbons) and silicon dioxide, listed in Article 8, DPR No. 322, of 15 April 1971, are still in force since the corresponding air quality standards have not yet been established.

---

*All the different types of decree are of equal importance and are issued by the national government.

- As far as the Penal Code is concerned, Article 674 has often been used as the basis for action against nuisance and for emissions of gases, vapours and smoke when these cause problems for the population.
- Article 216 of the *Health Law Consolidation Act*, approved by Royal Decree of 27 July 1934, No. 1265, established that industries having unhealthy or dangerous processes must be classified according to their risk potential. In the first class are included those industries which because of their dangerous processes, should be located far from houses, in the countryside. The industries listed in the second class are those that require special precautions for their neighbours' safety.
- The control of air pollutants emitted by industry is accomplished by measuring the ground level concentration as peak or average values (chlorine, hydrochloric acid, hydrocarbons, silicon dioxide) or adopting the percentile values required by the air quality standards for sulphur dioxide, nitrogen dioxide, ozone, carbon monoxide, lead, fluorine, suspended particulate matter).
- Where meteorological conditions favour the dispersion of pollutants in the atmosphere, the authorities can consider a chimney of convenient height as an adequate abatement device.
- A standard calculation formula for the stack height has, however, not been adopted in Italy. The chimney height calculation is different in the various regions which creates problems for comparison of results.
- As far as fuel oil standards are concerned, the same characteristics and limitations (sulphur and viscosity) for the domestic heating sector are applied to space heating plant inside industrial premises.
- Local authorities can, however, impose emission limits on industrial space heating plant for combustion pollutants in addition to the corresponding AQS concentration limit.
- Recently some new allowances for the emission limits of air pollutants established by local authorities have been granted to industries; this procedure is likely to be extended to other Italian regions.
- Under this new approach, industrial plant, operating under standard conditions, are allowed to exceed the emission limits, for given pollutants, for a specified period of time, quoted as a maximum total period in any year.

A new decree concerning guidelines for the reduction of air pollutants and for the determination of the lowest emission limits was issued on 12 July 1990. The major features of this decree concern the emission values and the emissions pertinent to specific types of industrial plants, such as large combustion units and crude oil refineries, petroleum and geothermal fluid extraction plants. In addition sampling, analysis, emissions evaluation methods and the abatement techniques are also considered.

2.3 Domestic Heating

The major legal instruments applying to domestic heating are *Air Pollution Law* No. 615, 13 July 1966, and the related Technical Regulation issued as DPR No. 1391, 22 December 1970.

The most important features of these instruments can be summarized as follows:

- Under Article 8 of the Law, only thermal plants located in control zones "A" and "B" of the national territory with a thermal capacity higher than 30 000 Kcal/h are subject to the domestic heating regulation.
- As far as fuel limitations are concerned, Article 12 of the Law allows gaseous fuels (methane) and petroleum distillates (kerosene and gas oil) with a sulphur content no higher than 0.3 per cent weight to be freely used.
- In addition, metallurgical coke with volatile matter and sulphur content up to 2 per cent and 1.0 per cent weight respectively, and anthracite with volatile matter and sulphur content up to 13 per cent and 2 per cent weight respectively can be freely used.
- Article 13 of the Law permits petroleum distillates with a sulphur content no higher than 0.5 per cent weight to be used in areas other than those classified as control zones "A" and "B".
- The fuel oil limitations described in Article 13 of the Law are based on two types of fuels having a viscosity lower than 5 degrees E and sulphur content 3.0 per cent weight maximum and viscosity higher than 5 degrees with sulphur content of 4.0 per cent weight maximum.
- The first mentioned fuel can be freely used in thermal plants located in the control zone "A", in industrial plant in zone "B" and also for those (non industrial) plant in the same zone with thermal capacity higher than 500 000 Kcal/h.
- The second mentioned fuel can be used, if authorized by the local authorities, for industrial plant in any zone and thermal capacity and also for domestic plant with a thermal capacity higher than 1 million Kcal/h provided that the combustion efficiency is continuously monitored.

- Article 1.1 of the Technical Regulation (DPR No. 1391, 22 December 1970) covering domestic emissions, states that it applies only to thermal plants not included in any industrial production cycle.
- The Technical Regulation also applies to miscellaneous uses such as production of hot water for domestic use, production of heat for catering, dish washing, laundry, medical decontamination and sterilization, combustion in ovens for bread production, furnaces of artisan enterprises and for incineration of waste material.
- In the case of miscellaneous heat uses the Technical Regulation does not apply when the heat production is mainly for industrial applications.
- As far as emission limits from combustion units are concerned, Article 13 of the Technical Regulation states that sulphur dioxide emissions, at the stack, should not exceed a value of 0.2 per cent by volume, that is 2000 parts per million (ppm). The suspended particulate matter (SPM) at the chimney should not exceed the value of 250 mg per cubic metre plus a certain percentage increment evaluated as a function of the plant capacity and stack height.
- Carbon dioxide emissions from thermal plants operating with liquid fuels should be in the range of 10-13 per cent by volume as an index of good combustion efficiency of the plant itself.
- The solid and liquid fuels used in domestic heating plant must comply with the specific chemical and physical characteristics established by Article 14 of the Technical Regulation concerning district heating.

2.4 Mobile Sources

As far as emissions from mobile sources are concerned, a Law together with Technical Regulations was established in 1971 by the Transport and Civil Aviation Department.

Under this Law, No. 437, 3 June 1971, Otto internal combustion engine cars are subject to the homologation tests specified in the technical attachments.

For new cars, exhaust gases are analyzed for emissions of carbon monoxide and unburnt hydrocarbons. In addition the evaluation of carbon monoxide at idle and that one regarding the blowby are also performed. For used cars, only the measurement of carbon monoxide at idle is required.

As far as diesel engine cars and trucks are concerned, the Public Health Department issued the Technical Regulation for Law No. 615,

13 July 1966, contained in the DPR No. 323, 22 February 1971. The major analysis carried out on both new and used cars/trucks homologation concern the smoke opacity of the exhaust gases.

The smoke emission limits established for new vehicles are 45 per cent for urban buses and 50 per cent for other cars while for in-service vehicles the limits are 65 per cent and 70 per cent respectively, all expressed in terms of smoke opacity where the zero value corresponds to complete transparency.

Fuel quality standards for both gasoline and diesel oil are established by the National Committee for Automobile Unification (CUNA).

2.5 Miscellaneous Sources

Interest in and concern about indoor pollution problems is growing rapidly in Italy and is attracting increasing attention from both government authorities and environmental groups.

As far as the emission of odours is concerned, there is still the problem of establishing a legal limit for the different types of pollutants while the development of abatement techniques is in progress. The problems are worsened by the low odour thresholds of smell which are often below the sensitivity of the measuring instrument.

According to the World Health Organization (WHO), asbestos emissions in both indoor and outdoor environments should be progressively reduced to the zero value.

The EEC Directives concerning waste and toxic and dangerous wastes have been implemented through DPR No. 915, 10 September 1982. The law requires processes for waste disposal to be carried out in such a way as not to create environmental and air pollution problems.

The only significant provision concerning nuisance is contained in Article 674 of the Penal Code as described earlier. Nuisance problems are often encountered as a result of the emission of particulate matter from large combustion plants for domestic heating, or from power stations, the larger particle sizes being quickly deposited in close proximity to the plant.

Air pollution effects on humans, animals, plant life and buildings have been ascertained by means of several studies and research carried out in Italy. As far as effects on humans are concerned, scientists today recognize the need to carry out further epidemiological studies to investigate and better understand the cause/effect relationship for various pollutants. Clear effects of air pollution on buildings, historical monuments, works of art, etc, and on vegetation have been demonstrated in several towns (Florence, Milan, Rome and Venice) and in the countryside on pine forests, vegetable and fruit cultivation, and so on.

In Italy, at the moment, there is no law which enables an injured party to sue for compensation for any pollution related health damages.

3 IMPLEMENTATION AND ENFORCEMENT

3.1 National Enforcement

Only those Articles of *Air Pollution Law* No. 615, 13 July 1966 which did not require any technical regulations to be implemented were enforced in 1966. The law was, however, fully implemented from 1970 onwards by the introduction of a number of Technical Regulations: DPR No. 1391, 22 December 1970 applies to the domestic heating sector; DPR No. 322, 15 April 1971 applies to industrial emissions; and DPR No 323, 22 February 1971 applies to diesel engined vehicles.

Two complementary laws, still relevant to the administration of air pollution control, are DPR No. 616, 24 July 1977, regarding the transfer of power to the regions, and Law No. 833, 23 December 1978 on the setting up of the National Health Service; these were issued in 1977 and 1978 respectively.

More recently, in 1983, *Air Pollution Law* No. 615 was integrated with the DPCM of 28 March 1983 and DPR No. 203, 24 May 1988 which contains provisions for the application of the air quality standard relative to some air pollutants. The full implementation of this Decree should occur within ten years of its enforcement date, that is by 1993.

The Law No. 183, 16 April 1987 concerning the implementation of EEC Directives in Italian legislation was enforced in 1987.

The DPCM of 28 March 1983, containing provisions for the application of the AQS was revised and updated according to DPR No. 203, 24 May 1988.

The Regulations for environmental impact assessment studies, as far as compatibility is concerned, have been enforced through DPCM No. 377, 10 August 1988 and subsequently through the DPCM of 27 December 1988.

More recently the Act for direction and coordination for regions regarding the AQS (DPR No. 203, 24 May 1988) was enforced by the DPCM of 21 July 1989.

3.2 Local/Regional Enforcement

As previously mentioned, most aspects of government with regard to the environment have been assigned to the regions, provinces and municipalities under Law No. 616 issued in 1977. Several regions have enacted laws and regulations which are more restrictive than national legislation. The interpretation and application of national laws at regional level does, however, give rise to concern, particularly in connection with political pressures.

3.3 Monitoring

3.3.1 Agencies/Networks

The evaluation of the performance of air quality controls is now feasible since many networks for air pollution measurements have been set up throughout Italy during the last twenty years.

Most of the networks are equipped for monitoring major pollutants, such as sulphur oxides, nitrogen oxides and suspended particulates; some also monitor other substances, such as lead, carbon monoxide, fluorine.

In some instances industries have combined to establish air pollution monitoring networks, like the ENEL power stations network and the CIPA Syracuse Consortium, or they cooperate with local authorities (Leghorn Consortium and Porto Marghera Consortium) and supply them with information on air quality with regard to specific pollutants in the monitored areas.

In addition, the former Provincial Laboratories for Hygiene and Prophylaxis, (now incorporated in the Local Health Units (USL) by Law No. 833), and the hygiene offices of some municipalities have established their own networks for air pollution measurement and supply all the data to a central office of the Public Health Department.

3.3.2 Air Quality Standards

Two major environmental quality standards implemented in 1983 as acceptable levels for the protection of human health are those for sulphur dioxide and nitrogen dioxide. The air quality standard concentration limits, related exposure averaging time and guide values, together with the guide value for suspended particulates, are as follows:

- Sulphur Dioxide
- Median of daily average concentration for one year - 80 µg/cm (April-March)
- 98° percentile of the daily average concentration for one year: 250 µg/cm (April-March)

- Median of daily average concentration for winter (October - March): 130 μg/cm
- Arithmetic mean of daily average concentrations for one year: 40 - 60 μg/cm (April - March)
- Average value for 24 hours: 100 - 150 μg/cm (each day).

● Nitrogen Dioxide

- 98° percentile of the mean of one hour average concentration for one year: 200 μg/cm
- 50° percentile of the hourly average concentrations for one year: 50 μg/cm

  98° percentile of the hourly average concentrations for one year: 135 μg/cm.

● Suspended Particulate Matter

- Arithmetic mean of the daily average concentrations for one year: 40 - 60 μg/cm black smoke equivalent.
- Average value for 24 hours: 100 - 150 μg/cm black smoke equivalent.

3.3.3 Monitoring Procedures

The major features of the measurement methods, networks, reporting techniques, and record keeping with regard to the monitoring of air pollutants can be briefly summarized as follows:

- The analytical methods described in the technical regulations are "reference" procedures which have been selected from among the available techniques for their reliability as far as specificity and replication are concerned.
- The sampling devices, which are standard equipment for samples drawing all air pollutants, and their assembly line, are also described.
- While the "reference" procedures are obviously based on manual analytical methods, some guidelines for the selection and adoption of automatic equipment for sampling and analysis of air pollutants are also provided in the technical regulation.
- The reference procedure for the determination of sulphur dioxide in the air is based upon the pararosaniline "spectrophotometric" method.
- The reference method for the determination of nitrogen dioxide in the atmosphere is based on the chemiluminescence reaction of nitrogen dioxide and ozone in a gaseous phase.

- The reference procedure for the determination of the black smoke index is based upon the collection of the dust on a filter and the black spot is measured with a reflectometer.
- The reference method for the determination of lead compound in the atmosphere is based upon the collection of the dust on a filter which is then mineralised with nitric acid and the lead content is evaluated by means of the atomic absorption "spectrophotometric" technique.
- The reference procedure for the determination for carbon monoxide in the air is based upon the "non-dispersive" infra-red "spectrophotometric" technique. The infra-red radiations are absorbed by the carbon monoxide with the changes in intensity being directly proportional to the pollutant concentration.
- The reference method for the determination of ozone in the atmosphere is based upon the chemiluminescence reaction of ozone with ethylene in a gaseous phase. The intensity of the light emitted is directly proportional to the ozone concentration.
- The reference method for the determination of hydrocarbons (methane excluded) in the air is based upon the hydrogen flame ionization procedure. The intensity of the ionic current produced is approximately proportional to the number of carbon atoms contained in the sample.
- The reference method for the evaluation of fluorine in the atmosphere is based upon bubbling of the gaseous stream containing the fluorine compounds into an absorbent alkaline-buffered solution. The fluorine ion concentration is then determined by means of a potentiometer using an electrode which is specific for the ions.
- As far as networks are concerned they are generally equipped with the most sophisticated devices such as computerized data obtained via a telephone cable from the peripheral sampling and analysis stations.
- Data print out and in/out teletypewriter to establish a dialogue between operator and computer are also available in the operating centre of the network.
- In the control room there is also a synoptic panel with several light-emitting diodes to give the alarm when the ground level concentration of a certain pollutant exceeds the legal limit or when the sampling and analysis station is out of use.
- The operating centre of a network is sometimes connected with terminals located in the offices of the public authorities for the immediate transmission of the air pollution data.

- Adequate meteorological stations for the measurement of the most significant environmental parameters are an integral part of the network.
- Reporting techniques and record keeping are of a standard adopted by large and well organized networks.
- Air pollution data obtained by the Hygiene and Prophylaxis Laboratories are tabulated in a special form and then delivered to the central office of the Public Health Department which carries out computer analysis.
- The data analyzed by the Public Health Department are then delivered to a central office of the EEC which coordinates the European programme for monitoring air pollutants.
- The impacts of controls in terms of improvements in air quality have been, generally, well defined and positive.
- For the most polluted areas, for example, Milan, the operation of a convenient network for the measurement of the most important air pollutants gave excellent results.

It is worth noting that the setting up, many years ago, of the monitoring network, allowed the authorities to consider and apply effective measures for the substantial reduction of ground level concentration sulphur dioxide and suspended particulate matter. The need for a good monitoring network operating on a continuous basis is becoming increasingly important given that air pollution data must be statistically processed in order to compare them with the air quality standards of statistical type such as those established for sulphur dioxide. Furthermore, for the implementation by 1993 of the air quality standards listed in the DPCM of 28 March 1983 and DPR No. 203, 24 May 1988, the authorities need to have a clear picture of the air pollution situation for any given area under their control and this task can be accomplished only with a good network.

3.4 Role of Private Interest Groups

Private groups play an important role in supplying authorities with scientific and technical information on environmental matters obtained from both national and international sources. They also advise national and local authorities on technical aspects, thus ensuring a sound basis for the implementation and enforcement of legislation.

A typical example of the scientific and technical cooperation with authorities is represented by the setting up of an ad hoc committee, within the Public Health Department, to study the preparation and application of air quality standards.

The national industries federation (Confindustria) operates with a group of specialists from industries to give advice and assistance to central and local authorities.

4 EFFECTIVENESS OF CONTROLS

4.1 Transport

The adoption of the EEC Directive concerning the disposal of used lubricating oils (75/439 EEC), the reduction of sulphur content in gas oil (75/716 EEC) and of the lead content in petrol (78/611 EEC) have substantially reduced the emissions of these pollutants.

4.2 Energy Policy and Economic Basis

Italy is very dependent on foreign supplies of crude oil and coal to meet national energy requirements (about 60 per cent crude oil and 10 per cent coal). A national Energy Plan (PEN) to promote use of the available sources of energy supply was set up some years ago, and is periodically revised. Energy management and conservation programmes have been developed in Italy by public and private enterprises since the 1970s. These have resulted in an appreciable reduction in the concentration of air pollutants from stationary combustion sources together with appreciable energy savings.

The strategy for the most economic use of fuel requires low grade, high sulphur heavy fuel oils to be burned only in those industrial plant and power stations which have efficient pollution control equipment. The higher quality fuels and distillates are mainly reserved for district heating where the efficient abatement of air pollutants is technically and economically not feasible.

As far as industry is concerned, DPR 203/88 specifies that all industrial plant must adopt the best available technology to abate air pollutants to the lowest possible level, at a reasonable cost. Thus the general principle, that the technical requirements for pollution control must be economically feasible, has been introduced into Italian law.

4.3 Ozone Depletion and Global Warming

As far as ozone depletion and global warming are concerned both the authorities and private institutions recognize the need to face the important issues connected with these problems in cooperation with international private and public organizations.

5 FUTURE DEVELOPMENTS

At the present time no significant legislative developments are expected in the near future apart from the implementation of existing laws.

6 SELECTIVE BIBLIOGRAPHY

CONCAWE, *The Calculation of Atmospheric Dispersion.* A CONCAWE Publication (1966). CONCAWE The Hague 1986.

CONCAWE, Pubblicazioni varie del CONCAWE su tematiche relative all'inquinanmento atmosferico.

Documento CEE - Proposta di Direttiva della CEE per gli Standard di Qualità dell'aria relativi all'anidride solforosa ed alle polveri.

Larsen, R I, (1971). *A Mathematical Model for Relating Air Quality Measurements to Air Quality Standards.* US Environmental Protection Agency.

Larsen, R I, (1977). An air quality data analysis system for interrelating effects-standards and needed source reductions - Part 4: A three parameter averaging time model. *Journal of the Air Pollution Control Association* Vol. 27, No 5.

Stern, A C, (1986). *Air Pollution* (3rd Edition). Academic Press, New York.

REFERENCES

National Legislation

RD n. 1265, 24.07.1934 - Testo unico delle Leggi Sanitarie.

LEGGE n. 615, 13.07.1966 - Provvedimenti contro l'inquinamento atmosferico.

DPR n. 1288, 24.10.1967 - Regolamento esecuzione Legge n. 615 - Riscaldamento.

DPR n. 1391, 22.12.1970 - Regolamento esecuzione Legge n. 615 - Riscaldamento.

DPR n. 322, 15.04.1971 - Regolamento esecuzione Legge n. 615 -Industrie.

DPR n. 323, 22.02.1971 - Regolamento esecuzione Legge n. 615 - Veicoli Diesel.

LEGGE n. 437, 03.06.1971 - Inquinamento atmosferico da autoveicoli.

DM, 05.10.1974 - Norme relative alla omologazione parziale CEE dei tipi de veicolo a motore per quanto riguarda l'inquinamento prodotto dai motori diesel di propulsione.

DM, 07.03.1975 - Norme relative alla omologazione parziale CEE dei tipi di veicolo a motore per quanto riguarda le emissioni dei motori ad accensione comandata.

DM, 23.12.1976 - Elenco delle industrie insalubri di cui all'art 216 del testo unico delle leggi sanitarie.

DM, 29.03.1977 - Rettifica del DM 23.12.1976, riguardante l'elenco delle industrie insalubri di cui all'art. 216 del testo unico delle leggi sanitaire.

DPR n. 616, 24.07.1977 - Decreto delegato di attuazione Art.1 Legge n. 382, 22.7.1975.

DDL n. 1044, 15.12.1977 - Smaltimento rifiuti solidi.

LEGGE n. 383, 23.12.1978 - Istituzione del Servizio Sanitario Nazionale.

DDL n. 954, 12.06.1980 - Disposizioni per smaltimento rifiuti solidi.

DDL n. 1903, 16.08.1980 - Delega al Governo ad emanare norme per la attuazione della Direttiva CEE.

DPCM, 28.03.1983 - Limiti massime de accettabilità delle concentrazioni e di esposizione relativi a inquinanti dell'aria nell'ambiente esterno.

LEGGE n. 349, 08.07.1986 - Istituzione del Ministero dell'ambiente e norme in materia de danno ambientale.

LEGGE n. 183, 16.04.1987 - Coordinamento delle politiche comunitarie riguardanti l'appartenenza del l'Italia alle Comunita europee e adeguamento dell'ordinamneto interno agli atti normativi comunitari.

DPR n. 203, 24.05.1988 - Attuazione delle direttive CEE numeri 80/779, 82/884, 84/360 e 85/203 contenenti norme in materia di qualità dell'aria, relativamente a specifici agenti inquinanti, e di inquinamento prodotto dagli impianti industriali ai sensi dell'articolo 15 della Legge n. 183, 16.04.1987.

DPCM n. 377, 10.08.1988 - Regolamentazione delle pronunce di compatibilità ambientale de cui all'articolo 6 della Legge n. 349, 08.07.1986, recante l'istituzione del Ministero dell'ambiente e norme in materia de danno ambientale.

DPCM, 27.12.1988 - Norme techniche per la redazione degli studi di impatto ambientale e la formulazione del giudizio di compatibilità di cui all'articolo 6 della Legge n. 349, 08.07.1986, adottate ai sensi dell'articolo 3 del DPCM n. 377, 10.08.1988.

DPCM, 21.07.1989 - Atto di indirizzo e coordinamento alle refioni ai sensi dell'articolo 9 della Legge n. 349, 08.07.1986, per l'attuazione e la interpretazione del DPR n. 203, 24.05.1988, recante norme in materia de qualità dell'aria relativamente a specifici agenti inquinanti e di inquinamento prodotto da impianti industriali.

JAPAN

1 INTRODUCTION

A decade before the UN Conference on the Human Environment in Stockholm had called the world's attention to the idea of "Only One Earth" or "Spaceship Earth", Buckminster Fuller had already predicted that the continuing dependence on existing technologies based on the burning of fossil fuels and the use of natural resources would inevitably draw the human race towards serious global environmental disarray before long. In his "Operating Manual for the Spaceship Earth", he also discussed how the earth as an element of the universe would need to counteract the side effects of its economic activities on which our standards of living depend by making fundamental changes to this way of doing things.

Since then, local pollution problems, such as those affecting air and water courses have grown to global magnitude. The world is now having to face the fact that emissions resulting from human activities are substantially increasing atmospheric concentrations of greenhouse gases, and are causing acid precipitation leading to forest depletion and other impacts worldwide.

The conflict between economic growth and the needs of the environment should be reviewed not by individual countries alone, but by coalitions of neighbouring countries and the world as a whole. The economic activities of one country do not limit the resulting environmental problems to within its territorial boundary but may have a climatic impact on neighbouring countries as well, often with disproportionate harm, as evidenced by the acid precipitation on those areas of the world which are free of industrial activities.

1.1 Topography, Climate, Population

It is well recognized that population growth, resource availability, geological and climatic conditions, as well as national development plans, are inextricably linked together; therefore, any grand design to reconcile the needs of the environment with economic growth requires an understanding of the interaction between all the factors involved.

Japan is shaped like a crescent extending to 3000 km and consists of four main islands lying off the east coast of Asia. Japan has a land area of 378 000 sq. km, slightly larger than that of Malaysia. It has an average annual temperature of 15 degrees C, and relatively high precipitation for a country in the temperate zone.

There are a number of volcanic ranges running through the country which is relatively mountainous with 67 per cent covered with forest; there are a number of short and fast flowing rivers, many lakes of limited size; Japan is also subject to frequent earthquakes.

The Pacific seaboard, where the weather is mild, is densely populated. The country has a population of about 120 million (1984 census), currently ranking seventh in the world. However, the forecast drop in the birthrate in the 1990s is likely to present a serious problem in terms of the labourforce and the spread of the age structure in the future.

1.2 Specific National Problems

1.2.1 Socio-economic and Topographical Conditions

One of the salient socio-economic features in Japan is that spatial concentration of both production and consumption sites are limited to coastal and urban areas unique to the country's mountainous topography. Only one quarter of the total area of 378 000 sq. km is estimated to be relatively flat. Thus since the Second World War most industrial complexes have been sited on coastal flat lands; this also has the advantage of making access to raw material imports from abroad or product shipments easier. The siting of factories in near-urban areas also made it easier to get labour, and helped industrialists to get the products into consumer markets. A large and increasing number of industrial complexes were thus placed along the Pacific coastline of the archipelago as the country's economy grew.

Under the circumstances, the idea of balancing economic growth with the carefully designed land plan separating industrial zones from non-industrial areas was virtually neglected; this later led to the many incidents in major urban area like Tokyo, Osaka and Nagoya. Even today when emissions from industrial stationary sources are significantly less, urban/household pollution requires continuing abatement efforts with respect to domestic effluent, motor vehicle emissions, construction and municipal waste disposal, traffic noise and other nuisances. Onshore location of industrial establishments, on the other hand, has made enterprises very sensitive to maintaining the water quality of nearby closed seas and bays.

The second noteworthy factor is the environmental impact caused by the comparatively faster economic growth that the country has achieved during the past twenty years with expansion mostly based on heavy and petrochemical industries. The proportion of heavy and chemical industries - i.e. the total of steel, non-ferrous metal, machinery, chemical, oil, and coal industries compared to all other manufacturing stood at about 36 per cent in 1955 but rose to about 50 per cent in 1965 and 60 per cent in 1975. This very evident tendency towards heavy industries has resulted in increasing loads on the environment.

Environmental disruption was further aggravated by the delay in public investment in urban infrastructures. During the rapid economic growth and move by industrial activities to urban areas, Japan should have speeded up the building of the necessary infrastructures so that the environmental impact could be abated. However, such public spending could not keep up with the rate of industrialization in the private sector.

A significant portion of the household sewerage system in urban areas, including Tokyo, still remains unsupported by public spending. However, municipalities across the country with large populations are now striving to improve this city infrastructure. One argument put forward to explain the delayed spending on public infrastructures is that "the country had no choice but to prioritize industry growth in order to rebuild the viable and competitive economy emerging out of postwar chaos". However this does not excuse the status quo with the historical environmental incidents dealt with in the next section. And indeed those socio-economic factors with adverse effects were found to be of secondary importance and did not present major stumbling blocks for the corrective actions taken jointly by both industry and the administration in the late 1970s and early 1980s.

2 DEVELOPMENT OF AIR POLLUTION CONTROLS AND LEGISLATION

2.1 Early Controls

Environmental policies in the 1970s were dominated by the need to respond to major incidents:

- *Minamata disease:* One of the most tragic incidents that the country faced in the history of industrial pollution was "Minamata disease" - a nervous disease caused by the residents ingesting organic mercury concentrated in the shellfish and fish in Minamata Bay in Kyushu Island in the mid-1950s. The residents along the Agano river in Niigata Prefecture were affected by similar incidents in 1964. Both cases were said to have been caused by methyl mercury compounds in the waste water discharged by chemical plants.

- *Yokkaichi asthma:* The residents of Yokkaichi city suffered this asthma-like disease from 1961 to 1967 and the incident is said to have been caused by air pollutants (mainly sulphur dioxide in the flue gases emitted from the petrochemical complex).

Both these incidents had a great effect on the Japanese, and resulted in legal actions and disputes. However, 1970 is said to be a turning point when the Government shifted its long held attitude and gave more priority to environmental conservation and people's welfare. In the new climate, a special declaration of economic growth triggered by the oil crisis required industry to change its energy/ resources-intensive structure: every possible effort was made to streamline production units so that the use of energy could be reduced to the minimum. Simultaneously, the national economy started to detach its traditional GNP growth/increased energy consumption relationship and gradually shifted from the high priority given to its growth to environmental issues. Figure 1 and Table 1 show the historical change in energy demand and GNP, and primary energy consumption by GNP respectively.

While many regulatory standards were put into force in rapid succession in the early 1970s, some of them lacked supporting scientific evidence to justify them or sufficient insight into the technology itself to make compliance possible. A typical example was the case of nitrogen dioxide control which was initially enacted in May 1973 and then revised in July 1978 (see section 2.2) as it is an important landmark in the evolution of Japanese environmental policies during the 1970s/1980s. During the same period (1974) the *Pollution-Related Health Damage Compensation Law* was enacted. This law, unlike those in other countries based on judiciary compensation, is unique in providing quick relief to victims on the basis of the polluter's civil rights responsibilities.

The environmental improvements made in the late 1970s and changes in socio-economic conditions called for a new set of policies to be developed in the 1980s. Urban and household pollution in which the victims are often found to be the polluters became prominent and in the longer perspective there was a stronger need for Japan to build alternative energy options to lessen its dependence on imports of oil.

The principle ideas to be included were:

- reinforcement of preventive environmental impact assessment;
- formulation of a set of environmental policies consistent with the development and utilization of petroleum-alternative energy sources;
- abatement of pollution caused by progressive urbanization;
- preservation of the quality of life and nature.

The government also stressed the need to correct its former "symptomatic ex post facto" pollution control policy primarily based on regulatory emission standards for polluters. The implication was the need to shift the traditional end-of-the-pipe measures to the predictive/preventive measures that comprise a wider spectrum of control options. The EIA approach (started in 1976) is certainly one such effort and has been practised in line with the policy changes.

Table 2 summarizes the *Basic Law* and Figure 2 shows the system chart of relevant laws.

2.2 Air Quality Standards

Environmental quality standards in Japan are explicitly defined in the *Basic Law for Environmental Pollution Control.* They define the pollutant levels aimed at protecting the health and living environment of inhabitants from ambient pollutants and are the administrative target of control. The goal of the standards is, however, the level which is "desirable to be maintained", and exceeding the level does not necessarily imply immediate harm to health. If the excess continues, however, it may cause chronic health effects. Accordingly the target is thought of as an indirect one that does not address the direct control of emission sources.

The environmental quality standards in Japan, for sulphur dioxide were set in 1969, for carbon monoxide in 1970, for suspended particulate matter in 1972 and for photochemical oxidants and nitrogen dioxide in 1973. The sulphur dioxide standards were revised in 1973, and that for nitrogen dioxide in 1978.

It is worth noting that the figure set in 1973 that the daily average of hourly concentration of nitrogen dioxide should be lower than 0.02 ppm was the most stringent in the world, and immediately aroused scepticism about its rationality and was also the subject of much debate. Nevertheless, industry strived to comply with the standard by tightening controls on stationary sources. The emission standards for mobile sources had been progressively strengthened and were eventually reduced to one-tenth of the previous level. However, the environmental concentration level of nitrogen dioxide did not decline contrary to expectation and remained almost the same as before.

The standard was met at only 10 per cent of all environmental air monitoring stations across the country. The scientific verification of such nitrogen dioxide levels on human health was also not attained and scepticism increased. Under the circumstances, the Industrial Structure Council being an advisory organ to MITI reported that "what is most urgently required at present is to review the nitrogen dioxide standards for its revision to a more rational one". A year later, the Environment Agency submitted the agenda of "judgement criteria for health hazards of nitrogen dioxide" to the Air Quality Subcommittee of the Central Council for Control of Environmental Pollution. They responded, in turn in 1978 and the standard was revised in the same year so that the daily average of hourly nitrogen dioxide concentrations should be lower or within the range of 0.04 to 0.06 ppm.

Table 3 shows the national environmental air quality standards.

To formulate the standards, a special study committee called the "Central Council for Environmental Control" was established and reported to the Director General of the Environmental Agency. The members of the council were chosen and appointed by the Prime Minister based on their expertise and experience.

Together with this central council, there are prefectural and municipal level councils called "Local Councils for Control of Environmental Pollution" and "Municipal Councils for Control of Environmental Pollution" respectively. These act as advisory bodies for the local governor, investigating and examining the local conditions coming from topographical, climatic and other regional specifics.

2.3 Air Pollution Control Law

In December 1968, the *Air Pollution Control Law* was enacted to replace the old "Smoke and Soot Regulation Law". The schematic diagram of the law is shown in Figure 3 and an outline of specific controls in Figure 4. There are a variety of regulatory standards for the substances under control such as general emission standards, special emission standards, total emission volume control standards, fuel use standards, standards relevant to equipment structure, its operation, and management, the maximum permissible limit, security standard and add-on (more stringent) prefectural standards. All these standards were set to meet the environmental quality standards.

The general emission standard is used in two ways: firstly as a control mechanism - if pollution is due to excessive concentration of industrial plant, the reduction of total emission volume of the impacted area is considered as a determinant to achieve regulatory compliance with atmospheric control standards; secondly, however, when the number of emission sources is limited, mere dilution can be an option to lower the pollutant to an acceptable level. Thus in the *Air Pollution Control Law*, sulphur dioxide and dust are subject to the first control mechanism because they are locally concentrated in most cases. Emission standards for hazardous substances (cadmium and its compounds, chlorine and hydrogen chloride, fluorine, hydrogen fluoride and silicon fluoride, lead and its compounds, nitrogen oxides), however, are formulated using the second method because sources are normally intermittent.

The special emission standard is applied mainly for expediting regulatory compliance addressing the affected area (by sulphur oxides and dust). Newly built processes are subject to a more stringent emission standard than existing ones.

The add-on prefectural standard supplements the general emission standard set by the central government which is not always effective enough to achieve the required atmospheric air quality for human health protection and the living environment. Thus local government can set the standard under the provision of the ordinance. Pollutants subject to add-on standards, however, exclude sulphur oxides since the general standard already accounts for local specifics (The parameter K-value applied in control formula varies from one region to another. The equation giving emission standards is $q = K \times 10^{-3} \times He^2$, where q is the hourly volume of sulphur oxides, Nm^3, He is the effective height of the stack.) The basic approach, reduction of sulphur in fuel oil, is uniformly applied nationwide.

Sometimes, the abatement effort of pollutants, for example, sulphur oxides, cannot ensure final compliance even by the combined implementation of the special emission standard and add-on local standards because both address the ground concentration of pollutants and not their total volume. Thus a total emission volume control standard is applied to certain areas (specified by central government). This total volume reduction approach is the most powerful means to be applied to the affected areas where pollution sources are densely sited.

3 EFFECTIVENESS OF CONTROLS

Table 4 summarizes a series of implemented options for desulphurization and denitrification in Japan. In order to reduce oxides of sulphur emissions, the progressive introduction of LNG as clean energy, desulphurization of heavy fuel oil and flue gas treatment of desulphurization units are all used. The screening of imported fuels and raw materials low in sulphur is another effective approach. It is also worth noting that the conversion of industrial processes to reduce energy consumption and emissions is actively proceeding. The converter that has replaced and totally eliminated open hearth furnaces, for example, has made it possible for steel plants to recover the unburnt off-gas virtually sulphur free from the furnace; continuous casting of steel slabs eliminated reheating and use of excess fuel.

Figures 5 and 6 show the historical change of denitrification and desulphurization units installed both in terms of number and flue gas capacity. Table 5 shows the amount of investments made in various industries in Japan. Table 6, charting the historical change of sulphur content in heavy fuel oil supplied by domestic refineries, shows that the national average dropped to 1.09 per cent as of 1987. Figure 7 shows how the percentage of nitrogen oxides emissions from diesel-powered vehicles has historically changed.

Some extracted data about atmospheric concentrations of pollutants are shown in Figure 8 (annual average sulphur dioxide concentration at 15 monitoring stations); Figure 9 (annual average carbon monoxide concentration at 15 automobile exhaust monitoring stations in continuous operation); and Figure 10 (annually average concentration of suspended particulate matter continuously measured at 40 monitoring stations.

It can be said that both nationwide and locally, atmospheric pollutant levels have steadily reduced except for nitrogen oxides. In 1988, the Environmental Agency announced the result of a survey on nitrogen oxides conducted in 1987 in districts where total volume emission control is utilized. The reported result is outlined in Figure 11 in terms of measured annual mean and 98 per cent of the daily averages of monitoring stations; this shows that the reduction has not been even. The Agency also concluded that the situation was most probably due to a high frequency of meteorological conditions which make the dispersion of air difficult especially in winter, reflecting a background of active business activities and resulting vehicular traffic.

Countermeasures envisaged to enable more stringent control of nitrogen oxides are proper air ratio control in boiler burners, proper temperature setting of household air conditioners, screening of fuels less likely to cause emissions, restriction of high emission cargo trucks and better enforcement of all current controls.

With regard to the effect of lead on human health, there have been no reported incidents since the use of leaded gasoline was completely phased out in the mid 1970s.

4 FUTURE DEVELOPMENTS

With a view to combating global environmental problems, a recent proposal from the Ministry of International Trade and Industry is interesting and conceptually suggests a series of R&D projects to push forward the technology frontiers. The concept is named as "the New Earth 21" and comprises such elements as carbon dioxide fixation and re-utilization; development of advanced substitutes for CFCs, environmentally benign materials like biodegradable plastics, advanced environmentally benign manufacturing processes based on biological rather than energy intensive chemical reactions and new energy developments to replace fossil fuel burning. The action plan needs further development but is shown in Table 7. The necessary research work will be centred around the Institute of Industrial Technology for the Global Environment, recently founded with a budget in 1990 of some seven billion yens.

However, it is unlikely that such technological innovation alone, if realized, can solve current environmental problems. The time has come for the world to appreciate Buckminster Fuller's idea, that the world can prove even today that it can realize the highest ever standards of living using only proven technologies and already exploited resources, so long as it is honest enough to deploy the technologies only for the welfare of mankind while avoiding all loss and inefficiency inherent in excess market competition, bureaucracy, uneven resource sharing, and regional interests which lead to conflicts. To attain that objective, the role of an organization like UNEP must be fully recognized.

5 SELECTIVE BIBLIOGRAPHY

Ando J, (1989). Global *Environmental Changes by Greenhouse Effects and Countermeasures.* Honda Foundation Report No. 60.

Buckminster Fuller R, (1963). *Operating Manual for Spaceship Earth.*

Environment Agency, (1988, 1989). *Japan Environment Summary,* Vol. 16, No. 10, Vol. 17, No. 2.

Hiratani T, (1990). *Environmental Control Regulations in Japan.* IPCAJ, Japan.

IPCAJ, (1983). *Environmental Protection in Industrial Sector in Japan.* IPCAJ, Japan.

MITI, (1990). *The Global Environmental Challenge: Japanese Initiative for Technological Breakthrough.* MITI, Japan.

Asahi Shinbun (newspaper), (1988). Kankyo Gyousei (Environmental Administration). M. Hasimoto, Japan.

Table 1: Change of Unit Energy Consumption by GNP in Japan

FY	*1960*	*1965*	*1970*	*1973*	*1975*	*1980*	*1985*	*1987*
Unit energy consumption by GNP (*kl*/ hundred million Y)	186.4 <83>	200.4 <89>	221.0 <98>	224.5 <100>	206.3 <92>	176.4 <79>	140.1 <66>	143.8 <64>
Improvement ratio (annual mean)		1.46%	1.98%	0.53%	-4.14%	-3.08%	-3.31%	-0.72%

< >: Relative figures when the year 1973 is 100
Sources: National economic accounting (GNP: the year 1980)
General Energy Statistics

Table 2: Summary of National Environment Control Laws in Japan

Basic Law for Environmental Pollution Control (1967)

Air pollution	Air pollution control law (1968) Electric power industry law (1964) Gas industry law (1954) Road transport and motor vehicle law (1951) (Permissible limits of motor vehicle exhaust gas) Road traffic law (1960) (For ex. CO emission control) Mine safety law (1949)
Water pollution	Water pollution control law (1970) Electric power industry law Mine safety law, etc. Law relating to the prevention of marine pollution and maritime disaster (1970) (Ordinance against violations such as discharge of oil from ships, etc.) Port regulation law (1948) Sewerage law (1958) Law concerning special measures for conservation of the Seto inland sea (1973) Law concerning special measures for prevention of lake water quality (1984)
Soil pollution	Agricultural land soil pollution prevention law (1970) Agricultural chemicals regulation law (1948)
Noise pollution	Noise regulation law (1968) Mine safety law
Vibration pollution	Vibration Regulation law (1976) Mine safety law
Offensive odour	Offensive odour control law (1971)
Waste management	Waste disposal and public cleaning law (1970) Law relating to prevention of marine pollution and maritime disaster (1970) (Ordinance against violation waste discharge from ships, etc.)
Land subsidence	Industrial water law (1956) Law concerning the regulation of pumping-up underground-water for use in buildings (1962)

Indirect environmental improvement
Factory location law (1959)
Industrial relocation promotion law (1972)

- ☆ Law for the punishment of crimes relating to the environmental pollution which adversely affect the health of persons (1970)
- ☆ Pollution-related health damage compensation law (1973)
- ☆ Law concerning the improvement of pollution prevention system in specific factories (1975)

Table 3: Ambient Air Quality Standard

Substance	*Condition*		*Method of measurement*	*Remarks*
	Content	*Standard value*		
SO_2	One hour value	Under 0.1 ppm	Electric conductivity method	
	Daily average of one hour value	Under 0.04 ppm		
CO	8-hour average of one hour value	Under 20 ppm	Absorption photometry using Saltzman reagent (Saltzman's co-efficient being 0.84)	
	Daily average of one hour value	Under 10 ppm		
Suspended particulate matter	One hour value	Under 0.20 mg/m^3	Weight and concentration method by filter collection, or light-scattering method by which values having a linear relationship with the former method	Suspended particulate matter means the particulate matter suspended in air whose diameter is under 10 um.
	Daily average of one hour value	Under 0.10 mg/m^3		
NO_2	Daily average of one hour value	Within the range between 0.04-0.06 ppm or below	Absorption photometry using neutral potassium iodine solution, or coulometric method	
Photo-chemical oxidant	One hour value	Under 0.06 ppm	Light absorption using neutral potassium iodine solution, or coulometric method	Photochemical oxidants are oxidizing substances such as ozone and peroxiacetyl nitrate produced by photo-chemical reactions (only those capable of isolating iodine from neutral potassium iodide, excluding nitrogen dioxide).

Table 4: Control Measure for SOx and NOx Pollutants

I Sulphur Oxides

1. Emission Control

(i) K value control: Control standards have been made progressively more stringent from implementation (Dec. 1968) to the 8th revision.

	1st stage	8th revision
K value	20.4-29.2	3.0-17.5 from the first in

(ii) Emission volume control: Number of areas subject to control has also increased up to the present 24 districts since 1974.

2. Pollutant Source Control

(i) Import of low sulphur fuel oil: Types of fuel low in sulphur content like LNG were imported and increased in the share of primary energy as shown below.

FY 1973	FY 1988
1.5% (6.3 million kl)	abt. 10% (abt. 45 million kl)

Import of crude oil low in sulphur content was promoted as shown as below.

FY 1973 1.93% FY 1988 1.08%

(ii) Desulphurization of heavy fuel oil: Number of desulphurization units has been increased and operated since 1967.

– Direct desulphurization: Hydrosulphurization of reduced crude brings the S content down to 0.1-1.0% (desulphurization = 70%)

– Indirect desulphurization: Reduced crude is treated by vacuum distillator and obtained vacuum gas oil is subject to Hydrosulphurization. (desulphurization = 40%). *Hydrosulphurization is a treatment to remove the oil sulphur through combined effects of catalyst and high temperature-high pressure hydrogen gas stream.

– Capacities of desulphurization units is equivalent to about 30% of imported oil. Indirect 12 units (66,000 kl/d), Direct 29 units (138,000 kl/d).

(iii) Flue gas desulphurization (dry and wet): 1962-1973 Large scale national industrial development project; 1970- Commercial units were commissioned. As for wet type, either lime or quick lime is commonly in use. Thus water consumption gets larger and effluent requires treatment.

II Nitrogen Oxides

1. Emission Control

(i) Emission control standards:

Gas firing boiler	60-150ppm*
Liquid fuel firing boiler	130-180ppm*
Solid fuel firing boiler	200-500ppm*
Metal heating furnace	100-180ppm*

*Value varies by the size of facility and date of its installation.

(ii) Emission volume control: Total emission control is set for designated areas : 3 areas

2. Pollutant Source Control

(i) NOx abatement

– NOx concentration in combustion gas (ppm)

	Gas N = 0%	Oil N = 0.1-0.5%	Coal N = 1-3%
Without CM	200-300	300-500	500-1,000
With CM	50-100	80-200	200- 400

CM = Combustion modification

– Principles and methods of NOx Abatement

Type of NOx	Principles of reduction	Method of reduction	Type
Fuel NOx (from N in fuel)	Use of low-N Fuel	N removal from fuel	Fuel modification
	Low oxygen combustion	Change of fuel	Fuel modification
Thermal NOx (from N_2 in air)	Low flame temperature	Change of combustion condition	Combustion modification
	Short retention time at high temperature	Change of combustion facility	Combustion modification

Table 4: continued

(ii) Flue gas denitrification
— Approximate numbers and capacities of NOx removal plants in Japan (1985)

Process	*Number*	*Capacity (1,000 Nm³/h)*
Selective catalytic reduction	200	110,000
Selective noncatalytic reduction	40	3,000
Others (including simultaneous removal)	15	800
Total	255	113,800

Table 5: Amount of Equipment Investment for Pollution Control (Industries under the jurisdiction of MITI) (unit : hundred million ¥)

Industries *FY*	*1975-1984*	*1985-1987*	*1965-1987*
All industries	49,549	8,934	81,034
Electric power	20,890	6,290	31,243
Iron and steel	9,646	615	14,925
Petroleum	4,117	266	7,566
Chemical (excl. petrochemical)	3,488	285	6,347
Machinery	2,460	649	4,643
Pulp/paper	1,497	394	3,191
Petrochemical	1,602	75	2,814
Mining (excl. coal)	1,417	37	2,549
Non-ferrous	709	46	1,628
Cement	787	38	1,285
Textile	497	74	1,059
Ceramics (excl. cement)	285	33	640
City gas	293	53	584
Coal	277	52	388
Miscellaneous goods	87	16	226
Building materials	117	10	214

(source: Association of industries and environment)

Table 6: Changes of Sulphur Content in Heavy Fuel Oil (Domestic Demands) Shipped from Domestic Refineries

FY	*A Type*			*B Type*			*C Type*			*Total Amount*		
	1	*2*	*3*	*1*	*2*	*3*	*1*	*2*	*3*	*1*	*2*	*3*
70	10,281	0.8465	0.87	12,338	0.9118	2.07	83,169	0.9342	2.05	105,789	0.9230	1.93
75	19,251	0.8448	0.70	10,079	0.9080	1.83	85,432	0.9235	1.52	114,762	0.9089	1.42
80	21,261	0.8509	0.63	5,007	0.9110	1.85	75,744	0.9264	1.48	102,011	0.9100	1.33
85	19,519	0.8622	0.52	2,030	0.9208	1.53	44,236	0.9354	1.38	65,785	0.9132	1.13
86	19,620	0.8610	0.49	1,742	0.9174	1.54	41,903	0.9348	1.36	63,264	0.9114	1.10
87	21,336	0.8610	0.50	1,745	0.9184	1.58	40,358	0.9369	1.38	63,440	0.9109	1.09

1 Shipment (unit : thousand kl)
2 Mean specific gravity (15/4°C)
3 Mean sulphur content (unit : %)

(source: Petroleum Association of Japan)

Table 7: "The New Earth 21": Action Program for the 21st Century

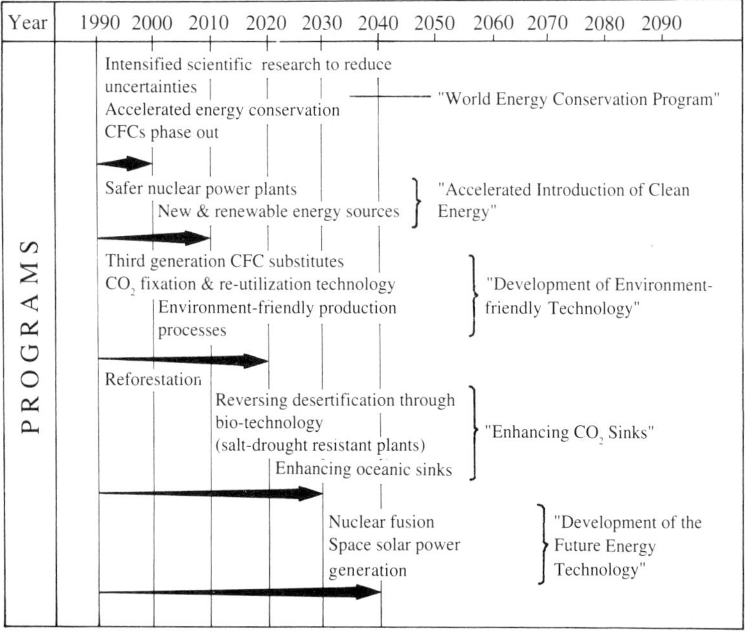

Figure 1: Change of Energy Demand and GNP

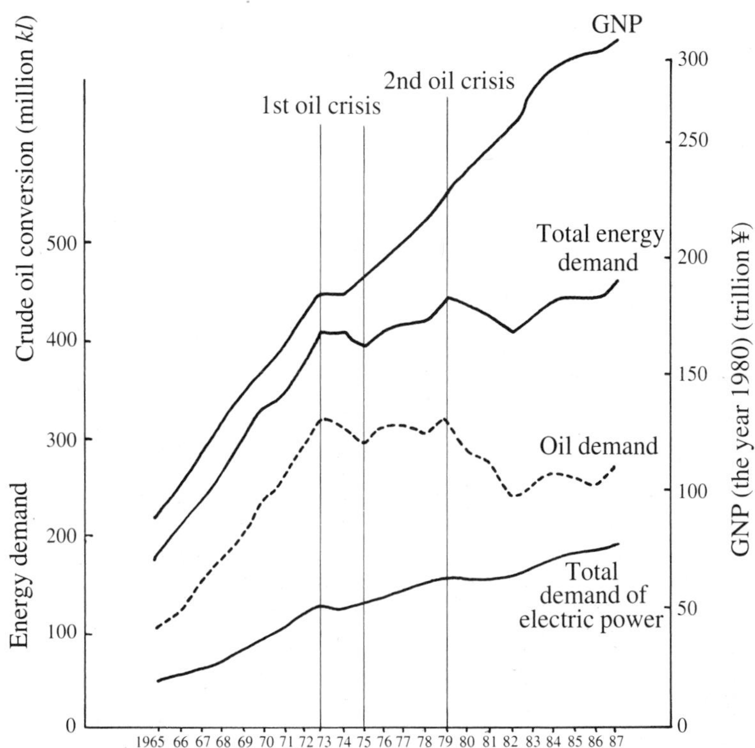

Source: The Energy Conservation Center, Japan

Figure 2: System Chart of Laws Concerning Environmental Pollution Control in Japan

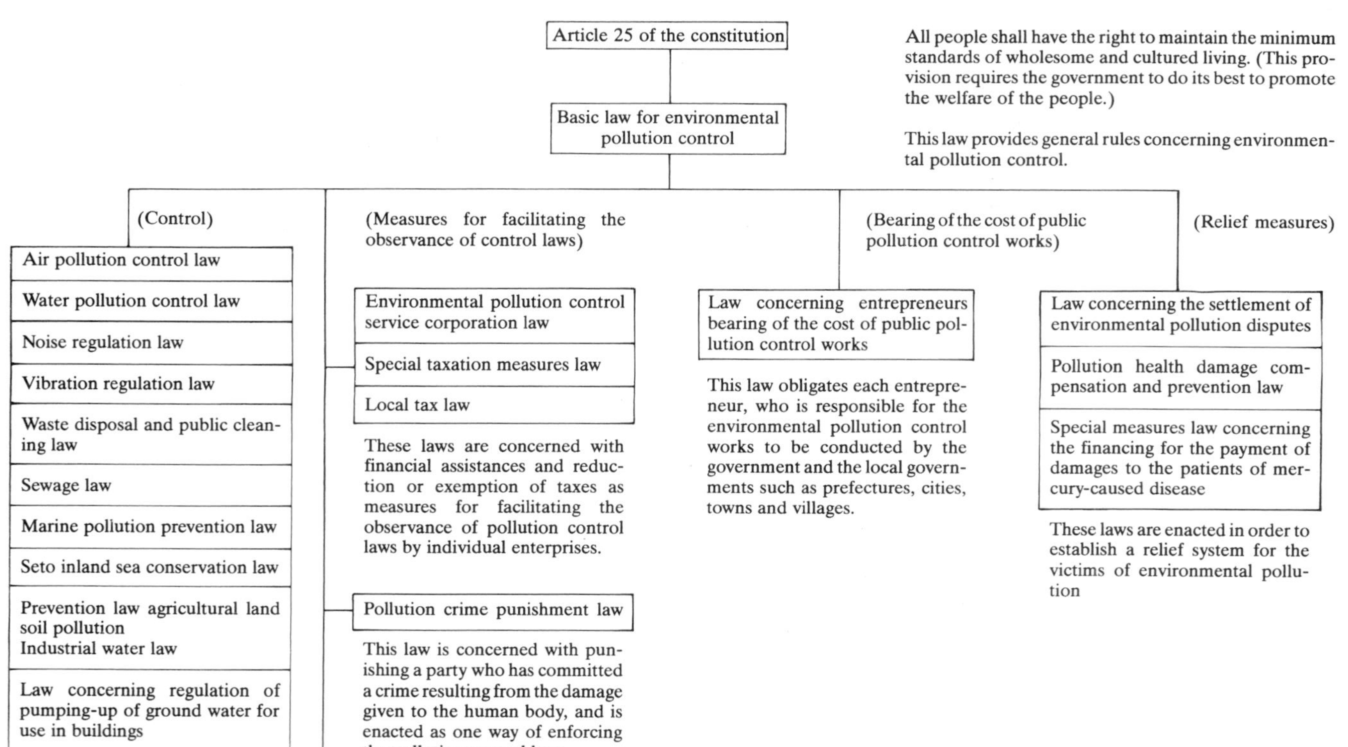

Offensive odor control law

Law concerning examination and manufacture of chemical substances

These laws are concerned with the establishment of the standards to prevention of environmental pollution, and require environmental pollution sources to be reported.

Law for the establishment of organization for pollution control in specified factories

This law is enacted to obligate each factory to establish an organization for pollution control

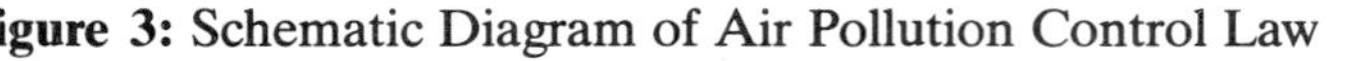

Figure 3: Schematic Diagram of Air Pollution Control Law

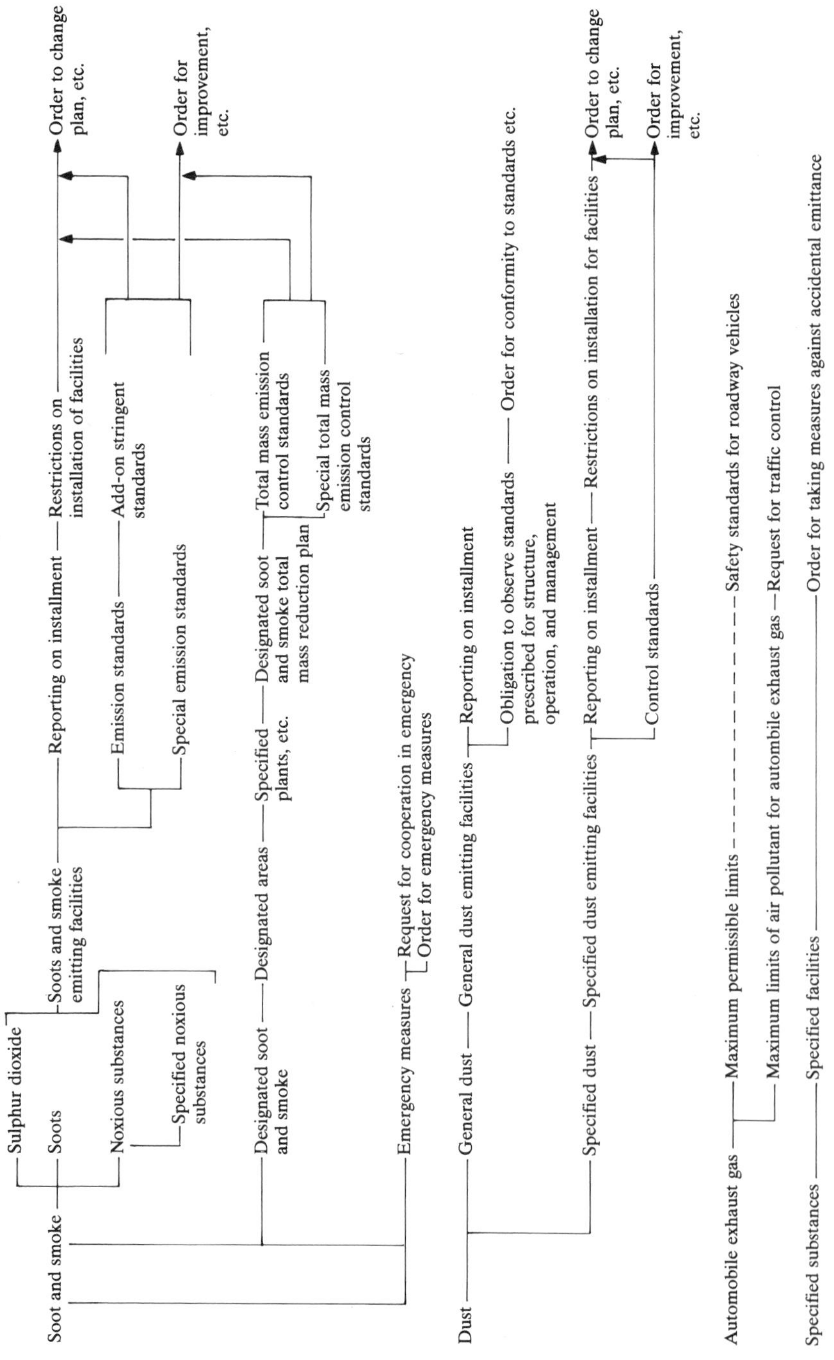

Figure 4: Air pollution Control Law

- (1) Soot and smoke
  - Sulphur oxide
    - "K value control"
      K value is a specified value to be applied to calculate the sulphur oxides volume by knowing the stack height.
      Applicable K values are set for respective areas. K value: 3.0-17.5 (16 rank)
    - Fuel use regulation
      - Area designation
      - Season designation
      - Sulfur content in fuel (0.5-1.2%)
    - Total emission control
      Applied to specified factories in respective regions. (24 regions)
  - Soots (emission dust)
    - Regulation value differs depending on the type and size of facility within the range of 0.03-0.50 g/Nm³
  - Noxious substances
    - Cadmium and its compounds — 1.0 mg/Nm³ *
    - Lead and its compounds — 10-30 mg/Nm³ *
    - Fluorine and its compounds — 10-30 mg/Nm³ *
    - Hydrogen chlorine — 80-700 mg/Nm³ *
    - Chlorine — 30 mg/Nm³ *

      *: Value varies by the type of facility
    - Nitrogen oxides
      - Gas firing boiler — 60-150 ppm *
      - Liquid fuel firing boiler — 130-180 ppm *
      - Solid fuel firing boiler — 200-550 ppm *
      - Metal heating furnace — 100-180 ppm *
      - Total emission control is set for designed areas: 3 areas

      *: Value varies by the size of facility and date of its installation

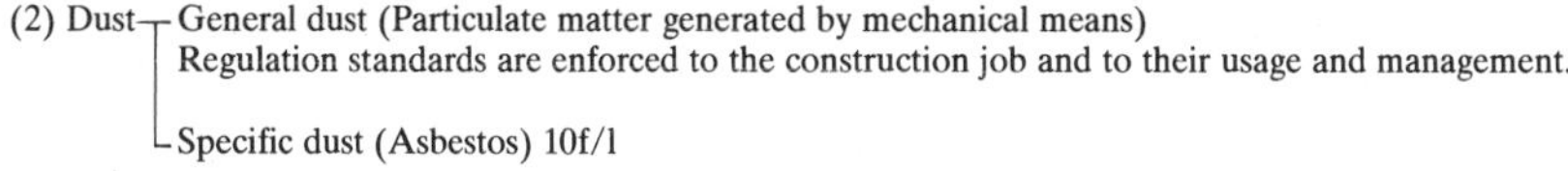

- (2) Dust
  - General dust (Particulate matter generated by mechanical means)
    Regulation standards are enforced to the construction job and to their usage and management.
  - Specific dust (Asbestos) 10f/l

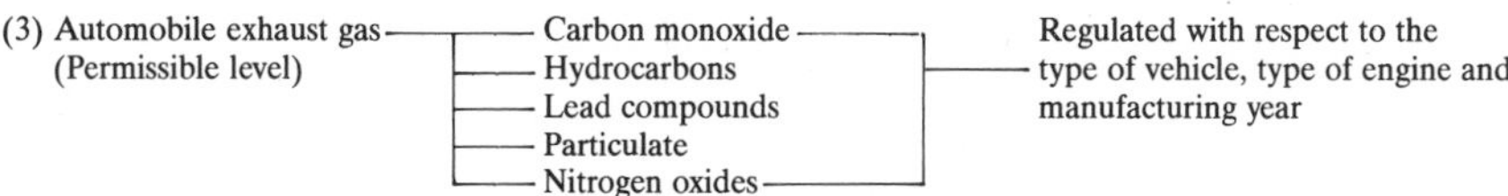

- (3) Automobile exhaust gas (Permissible level)
  - Carbon monoxide
  - Hydrocarbons
  - Lead compounds
  - Particulate
  - Nitrogen oxides

  → Regulated with respect to the type of vehicle, type of engine and manufacturing year

(4) Specified substances
Chemical substances of 28 kinds are designated such as ammonia, hydrogen cyanide, formaldehyde, acrolein, etc.

Figure 5: Annual Trend and State of Establishment of Flue Gas Denitrification Units

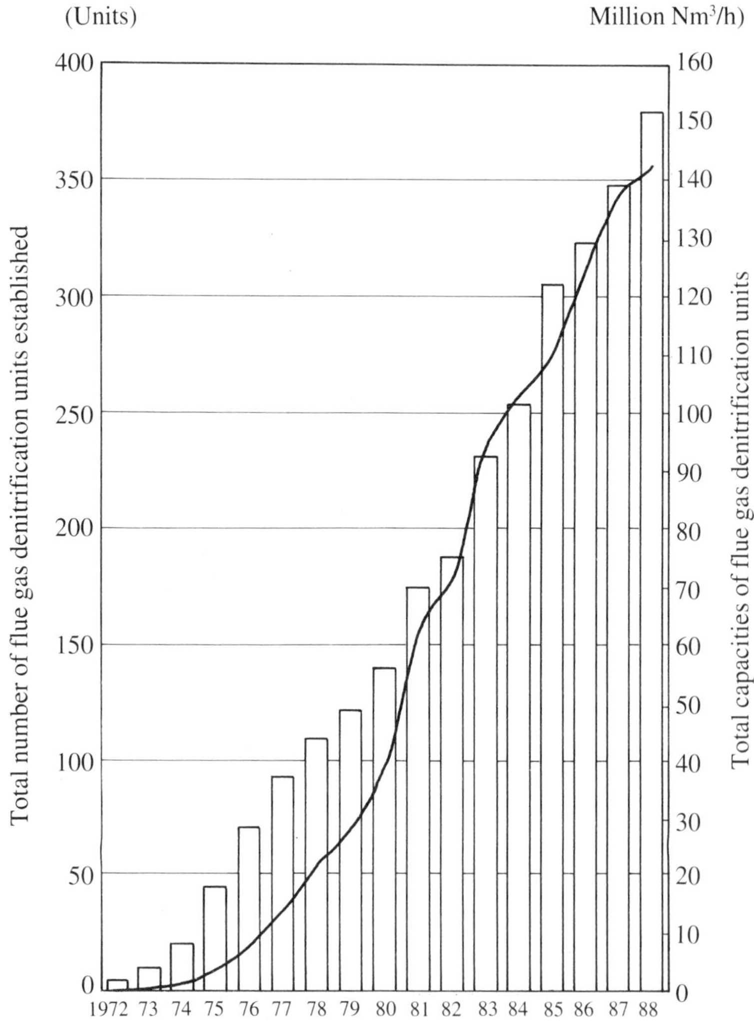

Notes 1. Figures for 1984 and after are based on the projects performed for preparation of the data reported about the facilities that emit flue gas.

2. Figures are as of January and each year until 1982, the one after 1983 are as of 31 March of each year.

Figure 6: Change in the Number and Total Capacities of Flue Gas Desulfurization Units

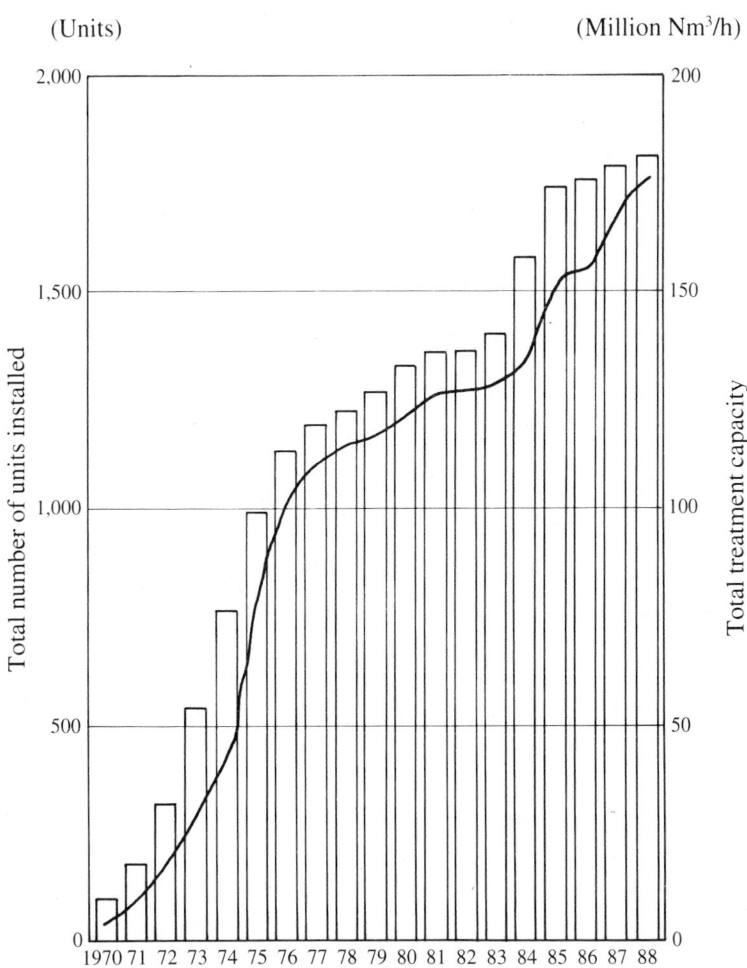

Note: Figures are as of 1 January for each year until 1983, and the ones after 1983 are as of 31 March of each year.

Figure 7: Effects of Regulation on Automobile Exhaust (Average values of NO_x emissions)

Trucks and buses

Indirect injection type (gross vehicle weight of 1.7-ton or less)

100%	Prior to September 1974 (no effective regulation)
80%	September 1974 (1974 regulation)
68%	August 1977 (1977 regulation)
60%	April 1979 (1979 regulation)
52%	October 1982 (1982 regulation)
36%	December 1988 (1988 regulation)

Indirect injection type (gross vehicle weight of more than 1.7 ton)

100%	Prior to September 1974 (no effective regulation)
80%	September 1974 (1974 regulation)
68%	August 1977 (1977 regulation)
60%	April 1979 (1979 regulation)
52%	October 1982 (1982 regulation)
47%	

(Vehicles with gross vehicle weight of more than 1.7 ton and not exceeding 2.5 ton, December 1988 (1988 regulation)) (Vehicles with gross vehicle weight of more than 2.5 ton, October 1989 (1988 regulation))

Direct injection type (gross vehicle weight of more than 1.7-ton and not exceeding 2.5-ton)

100%	Prior to September 1974 (no effective regulation)
80%	September 1974 (1974 regulation)
68%	August 1977 (1977 regulation)
56%	April 1979 (1979 regulation)
49%	August 1983 (1983 regulation)
40%	December 1988 (1988 regulation)

Direct injection type (gross vehicle weight of more than 2.5-ton)

100%	Prior to September 1974 (no effective regulation)
80%	September 1974 (1974 regulation)
68%	August 1977 (1977 regulation)
56%	April 1979 (1979 regulation)
49%	August 1983 (1983 regulation)
42%	

(Vehicles with gross vehicle weight of 3.5-ton or less, December 1988 (1988 regulation)) (Vehicles with gross vehicle weight exceeding 3.5-ton, October 1989 (1989 regulation)) (Large-sized tractors and crane trucks, October 1990 (1990 regulation))

Passenger cars

100%	Prior to September 1974 (no effective regulation)
80%	September 1974 (1974 regulation)
68%	August 1977 (1977 regulation)
60%	April 1979 (1979 regulation)
52%	January 1982 (1982 regulation)
37%	(for vehicles exceeding 1.25-ton in EIW)
29%	(for vehicles below 1.25-ton in EIW)
26%	(for vehicles exceeding 1.25-ton in EIW)
21%	(for vehicles below 1.25-ton in EIW)

(Phase-1 targets) Vehicles with manual transmission
October, 1986 (1986 regulation) (Phase-2 targets) October, 1987 (1987 regulation)

Figure 8: Changes in Annual Average Concentration of SO_2 (Average of 15 Air Pollution Monitoring Stations)

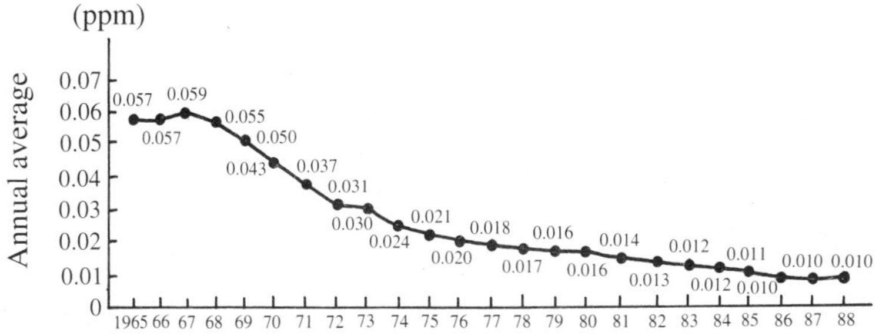

Figure 9: Changes in Annual Average Concentration of CO (Average of 15 Automobile Exhaust Monitoring Stations in Continuous Operation)

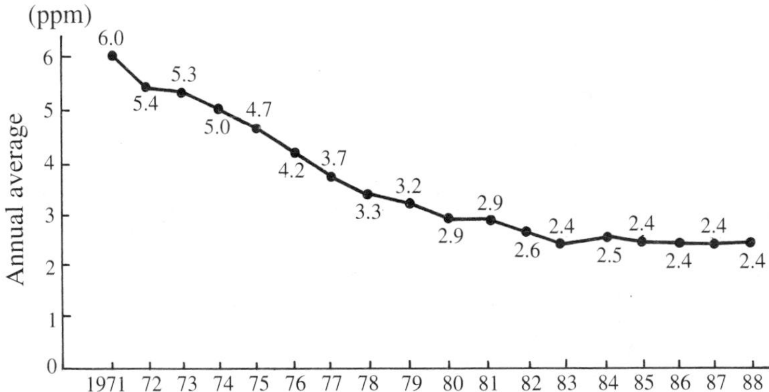

Figure 10: Annual Changes in Arithmetical Average of the Annual Average Value of Suspended Particulates Measured Continually at 40 Monitoring Stations (Air Pollution Monitoring Stations)

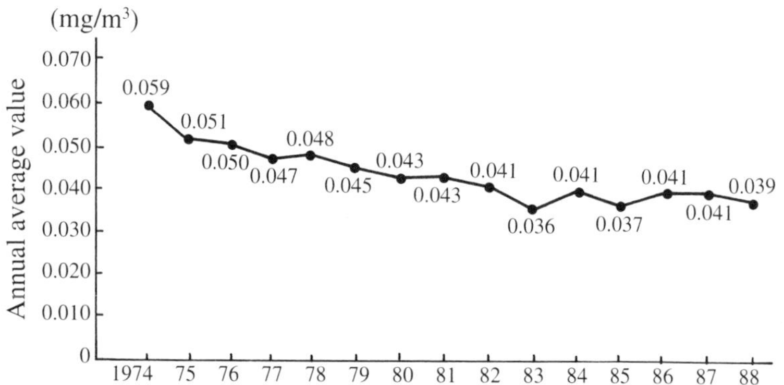

Figure 11: Change of NO_2 Concentration at Volume Controlled Areas by Year

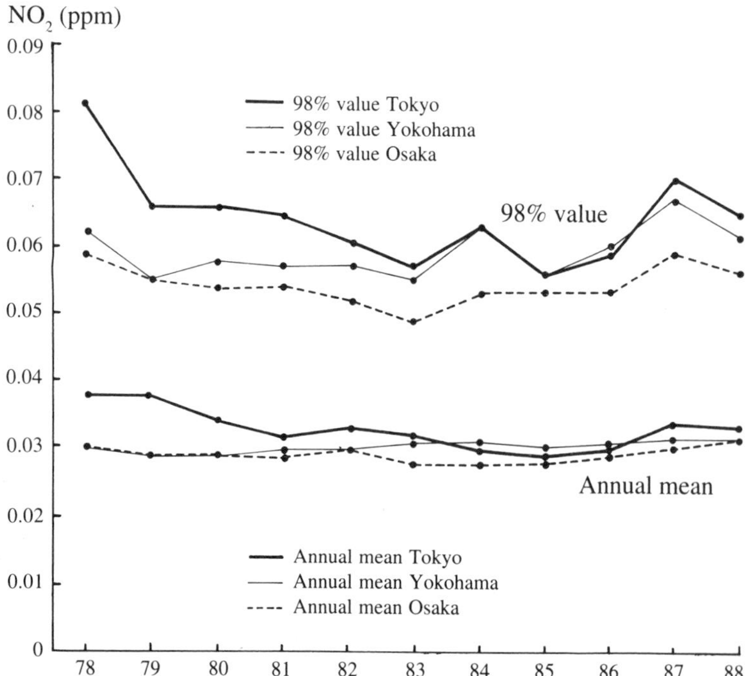

KOREA

1 INTRODUCTION

1.1 Topography, Climate, Population

The Korean peninsula juts out from the north east Asian continent in a southerly direction. It is separated from Manchuria and Siberia by the Amrok and Tuman Rivers, respectively, and surrounded by the Yellow Sea and the East Sea (Sea of Japan). The peninsula with its 3579 associated islands clustered mostly off the south western coast lies latitudinally between 124 degrees E - 131 degrees E, the northern temperate zone of the eastern hemisphere.

The total area of the Korean peninsula is 220 100 sq. km. North Korea is 122 370 sq. km, while the Republic of Korea (Korea) is 99 223 sq. km. The Korean peninsula is approximately 1000 km. in total north-south length and 216 km at its narrowest point.

Korea is mountainous and three-quarters of the area is unsuitable for agriculture. Generally, mountains in northern and eastern areas are higher than those in southern and western areas, with the eastern part of the mountains steep, while the west is a gently rolling area. Most of the mountains are geologically ancient.

Rivers flowing into the East Sea are short and fast, while those running into the Yellow Sea and the South Sea are relatively long and slow due to topographical characteristics.

Korea has relatively mild weather with a clear distinction between the four seasons, influenced by both continental and marine climates. The hottest months are July and August, and the coldest are December and January. Except for the far north, which is affected by the Siberian continental polar air mass, the winter is milder with cold and warm weather alternating with three cold days and four warm days as a general rule. The rainy season begins in late June and ends in early August, and about 60 per cent of the annual total precipitation is concentrated in that period. The annual amount of precipitation varies from 500 mm in the north to 1400 mm in the south coast area. The wind prevalence is westerly and the annual average of the surface wind speed is around 3 metres per second.

The current population of Korea is 42.8 million, which is approximately double that of North Korea. The number includes about 30 000 aliens who are mainly Chinese. The population density in Korea is 432 persons per sq. km and the annual population growth rate is 0.97 per cent.

The capital city of Korea is Seoul, which has been the nation's capital since the 14th century. With a population of about 10 million, Seoul is one of the ten largest cities in the world.

Seoul was devastated during the Korean War but has been rebuilt into a modern metropolis which serves as the nation's political, economic, social and cultural centre, with many modern conveniences and facilities such as high-rise buildings, first-rate hotels, subways, and other transportation systems.

1.2 Specific National Problems

Air pollution problems in Korea mainly arise in large cities and industrial complexes. Industry has developed very rapidly since the first 5-year Economic Development Plan was initiated in 1962. In conjunction with the rapid economic development, the population of large cities has increased with an enormous inflow from rural areas, leading to an acceleration of air pollution problems in urban areas.

Although the annual population growth rate in 1990 was 0.97 per cent (2.84 per cent in 1960), the nation's population density is about the fourth highest in the world, being just below that of Bahrain, Bangladesh and Taiwan. In particular, 15 million people - equivalent to one third of the total population of South Korea - live in the greater Seoul metropolitan area, and this overpopulation accelerates air pollution in the area.

In addition, the number of automobiles in Korea amounted to 3.3 million at the end of 1990 (of which 1.2 million are concentrated in Seoul), from 300 000 in 1960, with a very rapid increase recently. Automobile exhaust gas has become one of the major air pollution sources in Korea. The automobile industry and the related industries have also given rise to various environmental problems.

The Ministry of Environment of Korea operates 62 air pollution monitoring stations located in 28 large cities to monitor the concentration of sulphur dioxide, total suspended particulates, nitrogen dioxide, carbon monoxide, ozone and hydrocarbons in the ambient air. The sulphur dioxide concentration in Seoul and Incheon, and the total suspended particulate concentration in Seoul, Pusan, Incheon and the industrial city of Ulsan do not meet relevant air quality standards.

In the case of Seoul, the sulphur dioxide concentration in air has frequently exceeded the air quality standard (0.005 ppm) in winter months since 1980, though this trend is gradually decreasing. On some winter days, however, levels have been known to rise by twice the air quality standard in some heavily populated residential areas which use coal briquettes for heating. Visibility is often poor due to automobile emissions and suspended particulate matter. Occurrences of photochemical smog which have developed due to the chemical reactions by solar radiation among air pollutants emitted from automobiles are at a warning level in summer.

2 DEVELOPMENT OF AIR POLLUTION CONTROLS AND LEGISLATION

2.1 Philosophy

As environmental conservation is essential for human health, the ultimate object is to preserve natural resources and to maintain sustainable development in order to benefit people of both present and future generations. Environmental conservation targets should therefore be seen as a priority by both Government and citizens before any activities are considered. This basic concept will not only maintain continuous national development but will also sustain clean air.

2.2 Evolution of Environmental Controls

For the last three decades, Korea has achieved a rapid and remarkable economic growth coupled with the industrialization, urbanization and population increase, which have led to serious environmental degradation, e.g. air, water and solid waste pollution, and deterioration of natural resources.

The development of environmental protection controls in Korea can be divided into three phases: commencement of pollution control activities in the 1960s, industrial pollution control in the 1970s, and comprehensive environmental protection in the 1980s.

2.2.1 Commencement of Pollution Control Activities

Unemployment and poverty were the most serious problems confronting Korea in the 1960s. The first 5-Year Development Plan was initiated in 1962, and from then, all national resources and efforts were concentrated on economic development.

The *Public Nuisance Prevention Law* (PNPL) was enacted in 1963 and enforced by the Environmental Sanitation Division in the Ministry of Health and Social Affairs. However, there was no serious pollution at that time and pollution control activities were meagre and limited.

2.2.2 Industrial Pollution Control

As a consequence of all national resources being directed towards economic growth and industrialization, Korea's environment began to deteriorate. Many heavy and chemical industrial complexes were constructed during the 1970s, and as a result environmental problems arose.

To cope with the increasing pollution, particularly in the large cities and industrial complexes, the *Environmental Preservation Law* (EPL), together with the *Marine Pollution Control Law,* were promulgated in 1977 and a law dealing with the disposal of waste plastics enacted in 1979.

Although the basic foundation for pollution control was laid in the 1970s, national priority was still given to economic development, taking no account of environmental protection. Consequently, environmental pollution accelerated and became one of the serious issues facing Korea in the late 1970s.

2.2.3 Comprehensive Environmental Protection

With the success of national economic policies at the beginning of the 1980s and improved national living standards, the need for environmental protection and better quality of life became evident. A new article proclaiming people's environmental rights was added to the National Constitution, and together with the establishment of the Environment Administration in 1980, subsequent laws were strengthened to enforce environmental regulations which had been neglected.

The basis of the Korean Government's environmental policy was "to secure the balance and harmony between economic development and environmental conservation". Under this national policy, various environmental programmes and projects were undertaken. The Environment Administration developed and implemented policies for the improvement of air quality in urban areas. In 1986, the organizational structure of environmental administration was significantly improved, with the establishment of six Regional Environment Offices (REOs) and the semi-governmental agencies such as the Korea Resources Recycling Corporation and Korea Environment Management Corporation.

Based on this organizational foundation many energetic environmental programmes were implemented resulting in production of low pollution cars, use of unleaded gasoline, and construction of desulphurization plants by major oil refinery companies. This enabled Korea to maintain fair environmental quality in air, water and sea during the 24th Olympiad held in Seoul in 1988.

The Environment Administration, the head of which was at vice-ministerial level under the Ministry of Health and Social Affairs, was not however able to play a leading role in formulating and implementing national environmental policies among other development oriented ministries. Recognizing this situation, the Korean Government upgraded the Environment Administration to the Ministry of Environment in January 1990.

The Ministry of Environment (MOE) is responsible for policy formulation, programme development and implementation of environmental protection activities in Korea. MOE has two offices, four bureaux, twenty-one divisions, thirteen officers in charge at its headquarters, six Regional Environment Offices (REOs) and a technical arm - the National Institute of Environmental Research. The total number of staff is 1216.

2.3 Air Quality Control Law

As noted in the previous section, the *Public Nuisance Prevention Law* was promulgated in 1963 and revised in 1971. However, the revised law could not successfully cope with the increasing environmental problems occurring as a result of the rapid economic development.

Concern about environmental pollution increased as the standard of living improved and people became aware that prevention of pollution should not be neglected in Korea. The major concern about environmental protection changed from the prevention of public nuisances to broader environmental conservation.

These considerations resulted in the comprehensive *Environmental Preservation Law* (EPL) of 1977, replacing the previous PNPL. The EPL was amended in 1979, and authority for implementation transferred from the Minister of Health and Social Affairs to the Administrator of the Environment Administration. In 1981, the EPL was strengthened through the introduction of a pollution charge system, and the promotion of an environmental pollution prevention fund.

This law was amended again in 1986 to strengthen emission standards for air pollutants. It was, however, generally agreed that the EPL covered too wide a range of environmental administration and that it was no longer an adequate response to the rapidly changing and increasingly complex economic and social conditions. The Government therefore decided to improve the legal system of environmental administration, and enacted six new laws replacing the former EPL.

Thus the present structure of environmental laws in Korea consists of three layers: at the top is Article 35 of the Constitution; the *Basic Law for National Environmental Policy* covers basic environmental policy matters; sectoral laws then follow to deal with specific aspects of the environment. These laws include the *Environment Dispute Settlement Law, Air Quality Control Law, Water Quality Control Law, Noise and Vibration Control Law, Hazardous Chemical Substances Management Law, Solid Waste Management Law, Marine Pollution Prevention Law,* and the *Law for Resources Recycling.*

The major articles relating to air quality management in the *Basic Law for National Environmental Policy* (BLNEP) establish ambient air quality standards, responsibilities of government, industry and citizens, special countermeasures for significantly deteriorating areas, environment pollution control in affected areas, and environmental impact assessment (EIA) for various development projects (e.g. urban, industrial estate and energy developments, port and road construction, water resources development, and so on).

The *Air Quality Control Law* (AQCL) includes continuous monitoring of air quality; authorization procedure for air pollutants emission facilities; establishment of emissions standards; use of low sulphur fuel and prohibition of solid-fuel use; inspection and improvement orders for automobiles; and establishment of special emissions standards in the special countermeasure areas. Current ambient air quality standards are shown in Table 1.

Table 1: Ambient Air Quality Standards

Pollutants	*Ambient standards*
SO_2	Annual Average: below 0.05ppm 24-Hour Average: below 0.15ppm (shall not exceed more than 3 times a year)
CO	Monthly Average: below 8ppm 8-Hour Average: below 20ppm (shall not exceed more than 3 times a year)
NO_2	Annual Average: below 0.05ppm 1-Hour Average: below 0.15ppm (shall not exceed more than 3 times a year)
Total Suspended Particulates (TSP)	Annual Average: below 150 $\mu g/m^3$ 24-Hour Average: below 300$\mu g/m^3$ (shall not exceed more than 3 times a year)
Oxidants (as 0_3)	Annual Average: below 0.02ppm 1-Hour Average: below 0.1ppm (shall not exceed more than 3 times a year)
Hydrocarbon (HC)	Annual Average: below 3ppm 1-Hour Average: below 10ppm (shall not exceed more than 3 times a year)

3 IMPLEMENTATION AND ENFORCEMENT

3.1 National Enforcement

3.1.1 Stationary Sources

Under the provisions of the AQCL, any person who intends to establish pollution discharge facilities should obtain permission from the Administrator of the relevant Regional Environment Office or the Governor/Mayor of the relevant provinces and cities by submitting detailed documents including pollution control facilities. Following construction of the facility, it should be operated in a manner consistent with good air pollution control practises so that no air pollutant is discharged at a level in excess of the permissible emission standards shown in Table 2 (see end of this chapter).

If the Administrator or Governor/Mayor finds that the facility discharges air pollutants in excess of the permissible emission standards, he may issue the following orders: order of improvement, suspension of operation, relocation of the facility, or cancellation of permission as the final sanction.

Since 1983, the Government has prosecuted and also imposed financial penalties on those industries which discharge pollution exceeding permissible limits as a means of discouraging and preventing illegal discharges. The amount of the penalty is decided on the basis of the pollution discharged beyond the control limit, period of discharge and the pollutants. The air pollutants resulting in pollution charges include sulphur dioxide, particulate matter, and offensive odours.

3.1.2 Motor Vehicle Emission Controls

New Vehicles: Since 1980, emission standards for new motor vehicles have been as shown in Table 3 and strict controls over exhaust emissions implemented for gasoline and LPG vehicles. As shown in Table 3, 10 mode test procedures were adopted for passenger cars and light-duty trucks from 1980 to June 1987, and thereafter CVS-75 test procedures, which are similar to FTP-75 of the United States. With the adoption of the CVS-75 test procedures, controls over evaporative hydrocarbons were initiated from 1987.

The life of new motor vehicles is set at 80 000 km or 5 years in the standards. After 1990, the performance of exhaust control devices will be guaranteed during the vehicle's life by performance warranty or recall programmes. The quality of parts related to exhaust control systems has been improved through type-approval tests for prototype cars, audit tests and surveillance tests for mass production cars. These standards are applied to imported cars as well as domestic cars.

Table 3: Emission Standards for New Vehicles

A. Gasoline and LPG Vehicle

Type of Vehicle	*Model Year*	*Test Procedure*	*CO* (g/km)	*NOx* (g/km)	*HC* Exhaust (g/km)	*HC* Evaporative (g/test)
Small Car[1]	1987. 7. 1.	CVS – 75	8.0	1.5	2.1	4.0
	2000. 1. 1.	CVS – 75	2.11	0.62	0.25	2.0
Passenger Car	1987. 7. 1.	CVS – 75	2.11	0.62	0.25	2.0
	2000. 1. 1.	CVS – 75	2.11	0.25	0.16	2.0
Light – Duty Vehicle	1987. 7. 1.	CVS – 75	6.21	1.43	0.50	2.0
	2000. 1. 1.	CVS – 75[2]	2.11	0.62	0.25	2.0
		CVS – 75[3]	6.21	1.43	0.5	2.0
Heavy – Duty Vehicle	1991. 2. 1.	G-13Mode(g/KWH)	33.5	11.4	1.3	–
	2000. 1. 1.	G-13Mode(g/KWH)	33.5	5.5	1.3	–

B. Diesel Vehicle

Type of Vehicle	*Model Year*	*Test Procedure*	*CO*	*NOx*	*HC*	*Part.*	*Smoke*
Passenger Car	1988. 1. 1.	6mode(ppm)	980	850/450[4]	670	–	50%
	1993. 1. 1.	CVS – 75(g/km)	2.11	1.25	0.25	0.25	–
	1996. 1. 1.	CVS – 75(g/km)	2.11	0.62	0.25	0.12	–
	2000. 1. 1.	CVS – 75(g/km)	2.11	0.62	0.25	0.05	–
Light – Duty	1988. 1. 1.	6mode (ppm)	980	850/450	670	–	50%
	1993. 1. 1.	6mode (ppm)	980	750/350	670	–	40%
	1996. 1. 1.	CVS – 75(g/km)	6.21	1.43	0.5	0.31	–
	2000. 1. 1.	CVS – 75(g/km)[2]	2.11	0.62	0.25	0.05	–
		CVS – 75(g/km)[3]	6.21	1.43	0.5	0.16	–
Heavy – Duty	1988. 1. 1.	6mode (ppm)	980	850/450	670	–	50%
	1993. 1. 1.	6mode (ppm)	980	750/350	670	–	40%
	1996. 1. 1.	D-13mode(g/ KWH)	4.9	11.0	1.2	0.9	40%
	2000. 1. 1.	D-13mode(g/KWH)	4.9	6.0	1.2	0.25[5] (0.1)	25%

Note:
1 Less than 800cc of displacement
2 Loaded weight 1.5 ton or less of truck and passenger car capable of seating 15 persons or less
3 Light duty truck except (2)
4 Direct Injection/Indirect Injection
5 ( ) City bus

Inspection and Maintenance Programmes: Exhaust emission standards for in-use vehicles, shown in Table 4, are applied through periodic and roadside inspections. Safety performance and exhaust emissions for in-use motor vehicles are tested in a periodic inspection, once every six months to two years depending on the type of motor vehicle.

To encourage maintenance of emission conditions of motor vehicles, random roadside inspections are carried out as well as periodic inspections, either by full-time inspection teams of the REO or by inspection teams temporarily organized with the cooperation of city or provincial administrative and prosecuting authorities. Motor vehicles that exceed the standards are subject to a maintenance order, with or without penalty. The driver of the offending vehicle is fined up to a maximum of K. Wons 2 million. In the case of company-owned vehicles, both the owner and the driver of the vehicle are subject to a fine up to a maximum of K. Wons 4 million in total.

Fuel quality: Three types of gasoline are currently available in Korea - leaded regular gasoline (octane number 86 RON/79 MON), unleaded premium gasoline (octane number 95 RON/87 MON), and unleaded regular gasoline (octane number 91 RON/83 MON). The lead content of leaded and unleaded gasoline is currently limited to 0.32 g/l (TEL 0.3 ml/l) and 0.013 g/l respectively. Diesel fuel with cetane number over 45 and sulphur content below 0.4 per cent by weight is currently supplied in Korea.

Table 4: Emission Standards for In-use Cars

Type of Vehicle	*Pollutants*	*CO*	*HC*	*Smoke*	*Remark*
Gasoline & LPG Cars	1979-1984.6	4.5%	—	—	
	1984.7-1987.7	4.5%	1200ppm	—	
	As of July 1987.8	4.5%	1200ppm	—	Old model car
		1.2%	220ppm	—	New model gasoline car
		1.2%	400ppm	—	New model LPG car
Diesel Cars	1979-1990 As of Jan. 1991	—	—	50% 40%	
Test Method. CO/HC: Idling (NDIR) Smoke: Free acceleration (opacity)					

3.1.3 Monitoring Agencies

There are six Regional Environment Offices (REOs), under the Ministry of the Environment (MOE), responsible for continuous ambient air quality monitoring using the telemetering system and for environmental control of their respective regions. These are Seoul, Pusan, Kwanjoo, Daegu, Daejon and Wonjoo.

The REOs implement measures to protect their regional environment in line with the relevant rules, regulations, and orders of the MOE. Pusan REO has installed a stack monitoring network in the Ulsan Industrial Complex.

3.1.4 Nationwide Ambient Air Monitoring Network

The MOE's air pollution monitoring programme is designed to evaluate general air quality conditions and to provide the basis for the study of long term air pollution trends; to guide the development of control strategies; to analyze compliance with ambient air quality standards; and to support the development and implementation of atmospheric dispersion modelling for future air quality impact studies.

As of December 1990, there are 62 (Seoul REO 24; Pusan REO 8; Kwangjoo REO 7; Daejeon REO 4; Wonjoo REO 4) monitoring stations providing information on ambient concentrations of six pollutants: suspended particulate matter, sulphur dioxide, nitrogen dioxide, ozone, and hydrocarbons. Meteorological elements such as wind speed, wind direction and temperature are also measured. In addition, the MOE has three mobile monitoring vans for special studies and the Seoul City Government operates another ten monitoring stations in the city. The network also includes sites for monitoring acid deposition.

3.1.5 Stack Monitoring Network

A stack monitoring network is used as part of an overall programme to improve air quality as a special countermeasure where the air quality is currently unacceptable. In 1989, it was operated for the first time at industrial sites emitting major air pollutants in the Ulsan Industrial Complex, under the Pusan REO. The network has been operated regularly since 1990. The monitoring network yields data in particulate matter. Sulphur dioxide, nitrogen dioxide, hydrogen chloride, hydrogen fluoride, ammonia and ozone. At present, a total of 58 stacks from 31 industries are monitored. The number of stacks monitored will gradually increase, and in 1991, the programme is to be applied to the Yo-Cheon Industrial Complex, which is under the administration of the Kwangjoo REO.

3.1.6 Telemetering System

One of the key components for an effective air quality data base is the timely acquisition of information. A telemetered, real-time air quality data acquisition system can enhance overall data reliability. This can be obtained basically from the identification and prompt resolution of sampling and analysis instrument problems. Another purpose of this system is programme development and implementation of emergency air pollution control measures during episodes when air pollutant concentrations build up to unusually high levels due to stagnant meteorological conditions. To this end, Korea has developed a programme for a telemetered air monitoring network linking major metropolitan areas.

As an initial stage of the project undertaken in 1989, the on-line telemetering system was installed and operated between two districts - greater Seoul metropolitan area and Ulsan industrial area - and was later expanded to connect all the sampling sites across the nation by investing a total of K. Wons 1.6 billion. Nationwide information on air pollution can be immediately obtained. Data signals from all monitors are now sent to a computer at each local control system, and then transferred to a main frame computer at the Central Environmental Control System (CECS) in the MOE. Personnel in the CECS collect the data and make a master file. A data base management system has been developed to manage nationwide air pollution effectively and also to develop statistical models for estimating emissions of various pollutants.

Of the twenty monitors located in Seoul, ten operated by Seoul City Government do not have on-line telemetering systems, and these data are recorded manually every 10 days. By mid-1991 the monitors will be equipped with on-line telemetering systems. The data produced will also be transferred to the CECS.

3.2 Local/Regional Enforcement

There are 15 administrative districts (local autonomy entities) in Korea: 1 special city, 5 supervisory cities, and 9 provinces. Under the *Basic Law for National Environmental Policy* and the *Air Quality Control Law*, each district is authorized by the MOE and then carries out air protection tasks. In particular, each district is encouraged to introduce air pollution related bills, to establish administrative plans, and to enforce the existing laws. In addition, since some local areas are classified as "special countermeasure areas" according to the BLNEP, when they have or may have pollution levels exceeding air quality standards, the district of that area carries out a special all-out plan devised by the MOE. To do that, air pollutants emitted from industrial companies in a special countermeasure area can be controlled on the basis of total amounts of pollutants emitted according to the AQCL.

3.3 Role of Private Interest Groups

In addition to government agencies in the environmental field, some public interest groups have been established by Government investment. These include the Environment Management Corporation (EMC), Korea Resources Recovery and Reutilization Corporation (KRRRC), and the Korea Environmental Preservation Association (KEPA). The EMC has five branches and was founded to carry out air pollution control business and to handle environmental pollution control funds. For air pollution business, it collects and incinerates toxic hazardous wastes generated by industry. The KRRC has a main office and eight branches. They recover resources from wastes, for example synthetic resin wastes, and re-use them to protect the natural environment. The KEPA also has a main office and eleven branches in Korea. They conduct field investigation studies, technological development, education campaigns, personnel education, measurement and analysis for small industries, and environmental impact assessment.

Since environmental issues are of increasing concern to society, about twenty purely private groups from concerned industries have been organized to resolve environmental problems occurring in local areas and in workplaces. While their activities are not extensive, they perform public campaigns for environmental preservation and measurement of specific pollutants near and inside industrial complexes. In addition, more than twenty private groups including KEMF (Korea Environmental Manager Federation) and KEPI (Korea Environmental Protection Institute) are active in contributing to the solution of environmental problems by attending public hearings and commenting on government environmental policies.

4 EFFECTIVENESS OF CONTROLS

The most serious air pollutants in Korea are sulphur dioxide and total suspended particulates. These two pollutants arise from the combustion of fuel to generate energy for commercial production and for domestic use. It is in this context that major policies/programmes for air pollution control are related to, and dependent on, the energy sector - for example the substitution of "dirty fuel" by "clean fuel" is a key component in preserving the air environment. Emission limits on nitrogen oxides and other pollutants are also inevitable due to the rapid increase in the number of automobiles.

4.1 Control of Sulphur Dioxide

Sulphur dioxide is one of the most serious air contaminants in large cities in Korea. To combat sulphur dioxide pollution, the government has since 1981 supplied low sulphur oil to large cities and industrial facilities.

Major oil refineries in Korea are now constructing desulphurization facilities to supply low sulphur oil at the request of the Ministry of the Environment. By 1993, when the construction of desulphurization facilities is complete, the MOE is planning to reduce the permissible sulphur content in oil. For example, the sulphur limit in B-C oil will be reduced from 1.6 per cent to 1.0 per cent, and light oil from 0.4 per cent to 0.2 per cent.

It is expected that in the 1990s the low sulphur oil supply in Korea will be equivalent to that of the developed countries. Accordingly sulphur dioxide pollution will be sharply reduced.

Supply of clean fuels such as liquified natural gas (LNG) as a cleaner energy substitute for coal and oil has also been expanded starting in large cities. Since September 1988 the MOE has designated 14 large cities and towns as LNG-using areas. In these cities and towns LNG should be used for heating facilities with capacities of more than 2 tons per day in business and public buildings. By the next century, LNG will be used as the heating fuel all over the country. In parallel with the expansion of LNG use, emphasis will be placed on the development and application of clean coal technology.

4.2 Control of Total Suspended Particulates

In large cities in Korea, the TSP standard in ambient air which is 150 $\mu g/m^3$ on a long-term basis is often exceeded. This is due to TSP from the rapidly increasing number of motor vehicles, construction practises and industry emissions (see Table 5). Major programmes for TSP removal are as follows:

- Replace coal and B-C oil with cleaner fuels;
- Relocate those industries producing high emissions of particulate matter;
- Strengthen regulation of fugitive dust from industries and construction sites;
- Increase number of street cleaning equipment including vacuum sweeping vehicles;
- Install stack monitors in primary sources.

4.3 Motor Vehicle Emission Control

Vehicle emission gas has become a major air pollution source in Korea. Consequently the control of vehicle emissions has become a very important part of air quality policy and programmes.

To meet the new emission standards, several new models of gasoline and LPG passenger cars were required to be equipped with catalytic converters and to use unleaded fuel from July 1987, and from January 1988, the requirement was extended to all passenger cars. Korea has thus become the fourth country in the world to make regulations to use low emission vehicles and unleaded gasoline.

Diesel engine vehicles, in particular buses and trucks, emit greater amounts of pollutants. In Korea, the proportion of diesel vehicles is much higher than in other developed countries. Government policy is to decrease their number, and to introduce technologies for low emission engines.

Table 5: Trends in Yearly Concentrations of SO_2 and TSP at Major Cities[1]

Cities	*1984*		*1985*		*1986*		*1987*		*1988*		*1989*	
	SO_2[2]	*TSP*[3]	*SO_2*	*TSP*	*SO_2*	*TSP*	*SO_2*	*TSP*	*SO_2*	*TSP*	*SO_2*	*TSP*
Seoul	66	210	56	216	54	183	56	175	62	179	56	149
Pusan	50	228	47	184	42	194	39	197	44	214	47	178
Daegu	40	224	39	190	43	140	55	146	52	155	48	128
Kwangjoo	26	132	20	159	20	133	14	105	19	100	21	116
Daejeon	30	—	33	—	27	—	26	175	34	178	35	119
Incheon	56	161	52	194	53	153	56	163	56	162	65	152
Ulsan	24	177	30	159	32	172	27	190	28	238	29	165

1 Source: Ministry of Environment, Korea
2 Sulphur dioxide in ppb
3 Total suspended particulates in $\mu g/m^3$

5 FUTURE DEVELOPMENTS

The increase in energy use is inevitable due to the population increase and accelerated industrialization. As this is directly related to air pollution problems, the following form future fuel policy.

5.1 More Stringent Emission Standards

The economic penalty system for violations of emission standards is an environmental strategy to encourage emission generators to keep to the regulations by imposing an economic penalty according to the degree of violation. This system was applied to sulphur dioxide, hydrogen fluoride, particulate matter and odour until 1990; and has been extended to ammonia, hydrogen sulphide, carbon disulphide, hydrogen chloride, and chlorine from 1991. It will be further extended to all air pollutants in the future. The Ministry of the Environment will also be gradually strengthening emission standards for industrial processes as pollution control technologies are developed. The MOE is, therefore, considering the introduction of a notification plan for important air pollutants. Under the plan the government would publish, several years in advance, timetables detailing the stages by which air pollutant emission standards will be strengthened.

5.2 Total Emission Amount Control

Although it has not been implemented in spite of its existence in the law, the total emission amount control, as the most stringent regulatory tool, will be applied particularly in the special strategy area where environmental standards have not been met. This plan implies that the government sets total permissible amounts of emission regardless of the emission standards in the area where significant health effects are expected or in the special countermeasure area, and forces the emission generators to meet this goal.

5.3 Constraints and Policy issues

There are many problems and issues faced by Korea in protecting her environment. Major constraints are a shortage of resources for establishing environmental facilities, a lack of skilled manpower and technology, and a lack of coordination among government agencies. Major pending issues of current controversy are summarized below.

First, Korea is still one of the developing countries and needs economic growth and development. Thus, the national priority is given to the economy and it is not easy to allocate funds for environmental sector programmes in the national budget. A recent analysis showed that Korea is spending 0.15 per cent of Gross National Product (GNP) on the environmental sector, which is one half to one seventh of the environmental budgets (as ratio to GNP) in the developed countries (i.e. Japan, 0.34 per cent; USA 0.57 per cent; Great Britain, 0.74 per cent; and Switzerland, 1.03 per cent).

Second, the development of clean technologies, i.e. low and non-waste technologies, is important for both environmental and energy sectors because they help the reduction of pollution generated by conventional industrial processes, the improvement of process efficiency, and energy conservation and the optimisation of the use of raw materials and resources. Introduction of clean technologies is slow in Korea because of limited investment in research and development in this field and lack of capital to change industrial processes. One of the challenges which Korea faces in the 1990s is to encourage clean technology development which will be of benefit to the economy and environment.

Third, the environmental problems of today are not simply a matter restricted to one country but extend across borders to the entire earth. Major environmental issues of global concern are global warming by greenhouse gases such as carbon dioxide, nitrous oxides and methane; depletion of stratospheric ozone layer by chlorofluorocarbons (CFCs); acid rain; desertification; threats to natural ecosystems and so on. These problems cannot be solved by one ministry, one country, or any single United Nations organization. In the 1990s, therefore, all people, governments, and international organizations should cooperate in protecting the "only one earth" for the survival and prosperity of mankind.

6 REFERENCES AND SELECTIVE BIBLIOGRAPHY

Environment Administration, ROK, (1982). *Environment Conservation in Korea*, pp 229.

Environment Administration, ROK, (1984). *Environmental Protection*, pp 57.

Ministry of Environment, ROK, (1990). *Environment Protection in Korea*, pp 33.

Ministry of Environment, ROK, (1990). *Basic Law for National Environmental Policy* (Draft).

Ministry of Environment, ROK, (1990). *Air Quality Control Law* (Draft).

Table 2: Emission Standards in Korea

A. Gaseous matters

Pollutants	*Subject Facilities*	*Permissible Discharge Standards*[1]		
		Pre-Dec 31'94	*From Jan 1'95 to Dec 31'98*	*Post-Jan 1'99*
Ammonia	a. Chemical fertilizer production	150	100	50
	b. Cosmetics and dyes production	100	70	70
	c. Other facilities	200	200	100
Carbon monoxide	a. Power plant or boilers			
	a.1 Liquid fuel burning	350(4)[2]	350(4)[2]	350(4)[2]
	a.2 Solid fuel burning	400(6)	400(6)	400(6)
	b. Incineration of refuse or incinerators	600(12)	600(12)	600(12)
	c. Cement kilns	600(12)	600(12)	600(12)
	d. Other facilities	700	700	700
Hydrogen chloride	a. Hydrochloric acid production	25	15	6
	b. Phosphoric acid production	5	2	0.6
	c. Chemical fertilizer production	15	10	10
	d. Metal surface etching; acid treatment facilities	10	5	2
	e. Incineration of refuse or incinerators	80(12)	60(12)	50(12)
	f. Glass melting furnaces or smelters	5	2	0.6
	g. Other facilities	10	6	6
Chlorine	1. Incineration of refuse or incinerators	80(12)	60(12)	60(12)
	b. Other facilities	10	10	10
Sulphur oxides (as SO_2)	a. Boiler			
	a.1 Liquid fuel burning			
	a.1.1 Low sulphur oil using area	850(4)	540(4)	540(4)
	a.1.2 Other areas	1950(4)	1950(4)	540(4)
	a.2 Solid fuel (including mixed fuel) burning			
	a.2.1 Restricted solid fuel burning areas	500(6)	250(6)	250(6)
	a.2.2 Other areas			
	a.2.2.1 Domestic coal burning	1,200(6)	700(6)	500(6)
	a.2.2.2 Other solid fuel burning	700(6)	500(6)	250(6)
	b. Power plant			
	b.1 Liquid fuel burning			
	b.1.1 < 500 MW	1,200(4)	1,200(4)	270(4)
	b.1.2 ≧ 500 MW	1,200(4)	540(4)	270(4)
	b.2 Solid fuel (including mixed fuel) burning			
	b.2.1 Domestic coal burning			
	b.2.1.1 Pusan and Kangwon-do area	1,650(6)	1,650(6)	270(6)
	b.2.1.2 Other areas	1,200(6)	1,200(6)	270(6)
	b.2.2 Other solid fuel burning	700(6)	500(6)	270(6)
	c. Metallurgical processes; roasting, blast, and cupola furnace	650	650	650
	d. Sulphuric acid plants			
	d.1 Sulphur burning	500(8)	200(8)	100(8)
	d.2 Other plants	500(8)	200(8)	200(8)
	e. Fertilizer production; mixing, reaction, refining and enriching facilities	350(4)	350(4)	350(4)
	f. Petroleum refineries; heating, sulphur recovery, and refuse gas burning	800(4)	500(4)	300(4)
	g. Coke Production	300(12)	150(7)	150(7)
	h. Incineration of refuse or incinerators	300(12)	300(12)	300(12)
	i. Other facilities	800	500	500

Table 2: Continued

Pollutants	*Subject Facilities*	*Permissible Discharge Standards*[1]		
		Pre-Dec 31'94	*From Jan 1'95 to Dec 31'98*	*Post-Jan 1'99*
Nitrogen oxides (as NO_2)	a. Liquid fuel burning b. Solid fuel burning c. Gas burning for power plant c.1 Internal combustion engine c.2 Other power plants d. Other facilities	250(4) 350(6) 1,200(13) 400 200	250(4) 350(6) 950(13) 400 200	250(4) 350(6) 950(13) 400 200
Carbon disulfide	a. Viscose rayon process b. Other facilities	100 30	100 30	80 30
Formaldehyde	All facilities	20	20	20
Hydrogen sulfide	a. Petroleum refineries; heating, sulphur recovery, and refuse gas burning b. Pulp mills c. Other facilities	10 10 15	6 5 15	6 5 15
Fluorine and its compounds (as F)	a. Crockery, pottery, and clay industry; melting, smelting furnaces or kilns b. Other facilities	10(16) 5	10(16) 3	5(16) 3
Hydrogen cyanide	All facilities	10	10	10
Bromine and its compounds (as Br)	All facilities	5	5	5
Benzene and its compounds (as C_6H_6)	All facilities	50	50	50
Phenol and its compounds (as C_6H_5OH	All facilities	10	10	10
Mercury and its compounds (as Hg)	All facilities	*5	*5	*5
Arsenic and its compounds (as As)	All facilities	3	3	3

B. Particulate matters

Pollutants	*Subject Facilities*	*Permissible Discharge Standards in mg/Sm³*		
		Pre-Dec 31'94	*From Jan 1'95 to Dec 31'98*	*Post-Jan 1'99*
Particulate matters	a. Power plant or boilers			
	a.1 Liquid fuel burning			
	a.1.1 Flue gases, ≧ 200,000 m³/hr	100(4)[2]	60(4)[2]	40(4)[2]
	a.1.2 Flue gases, 30,000-200,000 m³/hr	150(4)	100(4)	50(4)
	a.1.3 Flue gases, 6,000-30,000 m³/hr	200(4)	150(4)	100(4)
	a.1.4 Flue gases, < 6,000 m³/hr	300(4)	200(4)	150(4)
	a.2 Solid fuel (including mixed fuel) burning			
	a.2.1 Flue gases, ≧30,000 m³/hr	250(6)	100(6)	50(6)
	a.2.2 Flue gases, 6,000-30,000 m³/hr	250(6)	150(6)	50(6)
	a.2.3 Flue gases, < 6,000 m³/hr	300(6)	200(6)	150(6)
	b. Incineration of refuse or incinerators			
	b.1 Flue gases, ≧40,000 m³/hr	100(12)	80(12)	80(12)
	b.2 Flue gases, < 40,000 m³/hr	200(12)	100(12)	100(12)
	c. Metallurgical processes			
	c.1 Arc or induction furnace	30	20	10
	c.2 Blast, cupola, and roasting furnace	70	50	50
	c.3 Sintering furnace	200	70	50
	c.4 Heating furnace	100(11)	100(11)	70(11)
	d. Fertilizer or phosphoric acid and its compounds production; kilns, drying facilities	70(10)	70(10)	50(10)
	e. Petrochemistry production; heating facilities	70(4)	50(4)	50(4)
	f. Coke production	100(7)	100(7)	100(7)
	g. Asphalt concrete plants	100(10)	100(10)	100(10)
	h. Petroleum refineries			
	h.1 Catalyst regenerators	100(6)	100(6)	70(6)
	h.2 Sulphur recovery	100(6)	50(6)	50(6)
	h.3 Heating facilities	70(4)	50(4)	50(4)
	i. Glass production			
	i.1 Continuous tank furnace	100(13)	70(13)	50(13)
	i.2 Other facilities	100	70	50
	j. Crockery, pottery, and clay industry; melting, smelting furnaces, kilns or cooling facilities	100(16)	100(16)	70(16)
	k. Cement, lime and plaster production			
	k.1 Kilns and drying facilities	200(13)	100(13)	50(13)
	k.2 Cooling facilities	100	50	50
	l. Asbestos production			
	l.1 Spinning	30	30	30
	1.2 Other facilities	100	100	100
	m. All other facilities	120	120	120
Cadmium and its compounds (as Cd)	All facilities	1.0	1.0	1.0
Lead and its compounds (as Pb)	a. Metallurgical processes; melting, smelting, blast, and refining facilities	20	20	10
	b. Other facilities	10	10	5
Chromium and its compounds (as Cr)	All facilities	1.0	1.0	1.0
Copper and its compounds (as Cu)	a. Copper smelter	20	20	20
	b. Other facilities	10	10	10

Table 2: Continued

Pollutants	*Subject Facilities*	*Permissible Discharge Standards in mg/Sm³*		
		Pre-Dec 31'94	*From Jan 1'95 to Dec 31'98*	*Post-Jan 1'99*
Nickel and its compounds (as Ni)	All facilities	20	20	20
Zinc and its compounds (as Zn)	a. Metal smelter, electric furnaces, and incineration of refuse	30	30	30
	b. Other facilities	10	10	10
Fugitive dust	All facilities	1.5	1.0	0.5
Smoke	All facilities	Less than 2 degrees on Ringlemann's smoke density chart	Less than 2 degrees on Ringlemann's smoke density chart	Less than 2 degrees on Ringlemann's smoke density chart

Note:

1 Concentrations in ppm, unless marked as * or identified as mg/Sm^3

2 Value in ( ) is standard 0_2 percentage, which is the excess supplied 0_2 over the demanded theoretial 0_2 for perfect combustion of fuels.

3 Concentrations in mg/Sm^3, if marked as *.

KUWAIT

This chapter was received by IUAPPA on 18 July 1990

1 INTRODUCTION

1.1 Topography, Climate, Population

Kuwait is a small country - 18 000 sq. km - situated at the north eastern corner of the Arabian Peninsular. It is bound by Iraq from the north and west, from the south by Saudi Arabia and by the Arabian Gulf from the east. Kuwait has almost featureless topography: generally the terrain is flat with a mild west to east slope and there are low hills broken by occasional shallow depressions.

The climate in Kuwait is of the desert type, characterized by extremely hot dry summers with an average daily temperature of 45 degrees Celsius in July and mild to cool winters with an average temperature of 12 degrees Celsius in January. Large differences are also seen between the day and night. The prevailing winds are the northerly and north westerly (56 per cent) followed by the south south east (20 per cent). The annual rainfall varies from 8-33 cm and occurs during winter and fall. The established ground based thermal inversion of the desert type 200 m high is recorded for over 95 per cent of nights.

According to the 1985 census, Kuwait's population was just under two million, an increase of 528 per cent over the 1961 census. The rise is mostly attributed to immigration, with nationals representing a minority of the population.

The economy is based on the export of oil, with the revenues being used to build the infrastructure of the State. Petrochemicals and oil refining is the major type of industry. Power plants are used to provide the steam for the multiflash units that produce distilled water which is the principle source of fresh water used for drinking and/or municipality purposes.

The population enjoys a high level of affluence with high per capita income. This is reflected in the car ownership and the rate of electricity consumption. The growth rate in the number of cars is estimated to be four per cent annually. The growth in industry is around seven per cent and the increase in electricity consumption is around ten per cent annually. These figures were used in estimating the emission load in the pollution inventory for the next five year environment protection plan.

1.2 Urban Development

Kuwait is a recent State: the urban area was developed according to

Figure 1: Distribution of the radial and ring roads together with the residential and industrial areas in Kuwait

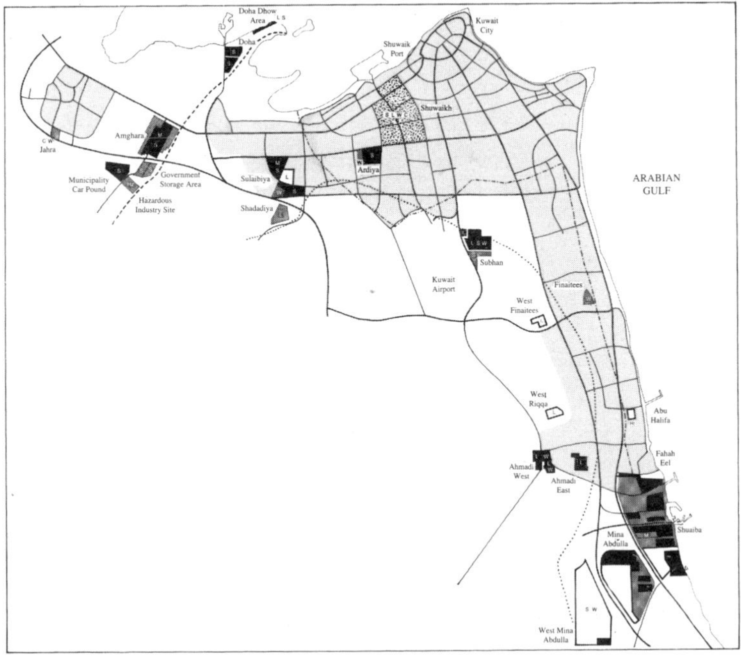

Key

- Existing Industrial Sites
- Sites Proposed for Development 1985-1995
- Sites Proposed for Development 1995-2005
- Shuwaikh Industrial Area
- Metropolitan Area
- ----- Proposed Route of Railway
- .... Oil Rights Boundary (KOC)
- -·-·-· Government Property Line

Designation:

- M Major Manufacturing Industry
- L Light Manufacturing Industry
- W Workshops, Servicing and Small Manufacturing Industry
- S Storage, Warehousing and Transport Industry
- Ht Hi-Technology Industry
- Hz Hazardous Industry
- C Commercial Uses

an ambitious Master Plan prepared in 1961. This has been revised several times and was undergoing further revision in 1990. Urban development is based on the old Kuwait Town, the developed area extending along the Gulf. Only 5.7 per cent of the country is developed, with the remainder being barren desert. A number of radial and circular ring roads separate a number of detached low density neighbourhoods. No industrial development is allowed in residential areas.

Several industrial areas were allocated for light industries and for commodity wholesales (Fig. 1). Heavy industries, mostly oil refining and petrochemicals, are situated in a special area (Shauaiba) 50 km to the south. Air quality and air pollution potential are generally considered in land-use planning. Some environmental impact assessments were carried out prior to the approval of the areas and type of activity to be allowed.

Certain rules are applied for land distribution inside industrial areas, mostly to prevent air pollutants generated by one industry from affecting others within the area or residential areas downwind. Food and non polluting industries are situated to the north west with the metallurgical industries to the south east. A buffer zone has been established around the industrial areas, the width is between 100-750 m according to the activity and the wind direction with the wider dimension to the south east.

So far as the heavy industrial area allocated for petrochemicals is concerned, the most polluting industries have been situated in the centre and the light, less polluting ones, on the boundary. A buffer zone 1500 m is left north west to 6400 m to the south east. The size of the buffer zone was determined according to the height of the stacks, the exit velocity and temperature of the flue gas and other factors influencing the dispersion of air contaminants.

This arrangement is agreed and adopted by the Municipality which owns the land and no residential development is allowed in these areas. Similar buffer zones are left around the highways and the flyovers though the width is mostly determined by the noise requirement rather than the exhaust of motor cars.

Residential areas have been developed around a neighbourhood centre, and through traffic is not encouraged. Domestic activities do not however contribute significantly to the pollution load. Electricity is highly subsidised and is used for domestic air conditioning which is extensively used in summer for cooling. Cooking is mostly by gas but it is more of an indoor problem. The incineration of domestic waste was discontinued some years ago and sanitary filling is used instead.

1.3 Specific National Problems

1.3.1 Dust

Dust is a serious problem, with one or another form of dust reported in the atmosphere for almost 13 per cent of the time, increasing to 25 per cent between April and August. Dust storms and rising sand occur with fresh winds. Dust in suspension is the most common type, followed by the dust haze.

Kuwait is in the centre of the dustfall area in the Middle East. The mean monthly weight of the settled dust in 1989 was 146.7 tons per sq. km. Much higher values are reported in the summer months, the maximum (762.9 tons per sq. km) having been reported in June 1990. The high silica content together with the high alumina dust point to the soil origin of the dust.

The overall geometric mean of the suspended particulates in some representative areas of Kuwait during 1989 was 355.5 $\mu g\ m^{-3}$, with a much higher mean reported for the desert areas (1143 $\mu g\ m^{-3}$) and the summer months: May (589), June (2673) and July (832 $\mu g\ m^{-3}$). Similar to the settled dust, the principal source is the soil. The aluminium and the iron content of the dust is quite high.

The very arid environment, the high evaporation rates, the long dry summer and the fresh winds are the major factors causing generation of dust. Several contributing factors include overgrazing, off-road vehicles, quarrying for sand and gravel, use of plants for fire by nomads, together with other anthropogenic activities. The control of dust originating from soil is not easy and combatting desertification is a long process that needs an integrated approach in the region.

1.3.2 Methane/Non-Methane Hydrocarbons

The other air pollution problem is the high level of methane and non-methane hydrocarbons. The arithmetic annual mean for methane is 1.735 ppm and for non-methane 0.621 ppm. The contribution of activities relating to the exploration, drilling, refining and export of oil is being investigated. Seepage of oil from the ground and the significantly high levels of hydrocarbons found when digging any water well in the vicinity of the oil fields have been frequently reported. Control of hydrocarbons from such an extensive non-point source is a challenge which is very difficult to handle.

1.3.3 Solar UV

Another problem is the intense solar UV particularly in the summer months. The maximum is seen in June at 1130 in the morning. The level of UVA is also quite high. The deterioration of the ozone layer expected in the next years will cause a further rise in UV. The protective capability of the dark skins of the population may be over estimated and the threat of skin cancer is as high as that for Caucasians.

The role of the intense UV and the high reactive non-methane hydrocarbons on the generation of oxidants is well documented. Currently, the frequency of non-attainment of ozone levels is low probably due to the relatively low level of nitrogen oxides. However with the industrial, agricultural and power plant developments this may change. Pollution by oxidants is a problem that would be anticipated.

1.3.4 Acid Deposition

The high level of sulphur in Kuwait crude is another problem. This is the type available directly for local consumption. The desulphurization process is rather expensive. The problem of acid rain is not immediately felt owing to the arid climate and the virtual absence of fresh water lakes, the poor vegetation and limited agricultural development. Indeed, it took a lot of persuasion from the environment protection authorities to get the approval of the Ministry of Oil to provide 1 per cent sulphur fuel to fire power plants.

1.3.5 Enforcement

Only limited numbers of professionals have been available for investigating environmental impacts and monitoring the level of pollution. There is a lack of practical experience among the officers involved in pollution control and the need for specialized training is apparent. At present training facilities are insufficient and not well organized. The University of Kuwait and the Technological Institute have been approached to establish a programme for graduation of technicians and professionals. The Environment Protection Council has also invested heavily in in-service training.

2 DEVELOPMENT OF AIR POLLUTION CONTROLS AND LEGISLATION

2.1 Philosophy

To a varying degree both the UK "Best Practicable Means" (BPM) approach and "Air Quality Standards" (AQS) favoured by the US are used in Kuwait. The BPM approach is mainly used for licensing of premises or activities as a means of administering and controlling operations of these industries. The AQS is gaining greater support as the extent and reliability of ambient monitoring networks improves.

Some undesirable features in both approaches are recognized, such as the scientific uncertainties surrounding the assimilative capacity of the air, and the fact that best practicable technology does not in itself ensure uniform air quality. Air quality standards are used as a management tool for planning, organizing and gauging the effectiveness of air pollution control programmes. The bubble concept is being considered for the Shuaiba petrochemical industrial area.

2.2 Air Quality Standards

The air quality standards for the primary air pollutants were proposed for Kuwait in 1975, and were originally based on the protection of public health with the WHO figures being adopted as a starting point. The Environment Protection Council established a working group representing the oil sector, power plants, industry, health and environment protection: this group was entrusted with the revision of the AQS proposed in 1975.

The working group reviewed the literature, studied the results of the monitoring stations, the geographic distribution of the sources, the level of technical expertise and the regulations followed by the other Gulf Cooperation Council (GCC) countries, as well as the industrialized and developing countries. The working group felt that the Shuaiba industrial area was a special case and that attainment of standards for sulphur oxides and hydrogen sulphides would be very difficult.

The AQS, together with the standard methods for determination, are summarized in Table 1. Three levels, namely the annual, 24 hours, and 1 hour values are proposed. All the primary pollutants together with lead are included, as well as ammonia and chlorine gas. For hydrocarbons, one-tenth of the threshold limit values was taken as the standard for the individual compounds. The total, however, should not exceed a pre-set value (to be determined later) and the provisional value of 0.24 ppm was suggested.

Certain other pollutants were investigated and it was decided to postpone taking any decisions until further information was available. For the petrochemical industrial area the annual AQS for sulphur dioxide is almost double that for residential areas; the 24 hour level is almost triple and the hourly values slightly less than double the ambient levels. The level for hydrogen sulphide is based on health criteria and not as a nuisance gas causing odours.

The proposed AQS have been approved by the EPC. They were circulated among the relevant authorities for comment and the necessary amendments introduced. Although not yet legally binding, they are, for all practical purposes, already accepted and are being enforced.

Table 1: Ambient Air Quality Standards Approved by the Environment Protection Council

Pollutant	*Concentration (ppm)* Annual	*24 hrs*	*1 hr*	*Method*
Sulphur dioxide	0.03	0.06*	0.17**	Pararosaniline
Particulate matter	90 μg/m³	350 μg/m³*	—	Size selective high-volume gravimetric
Hydrogen sulphide	—	0.006	—	Gas Chromatography
Nitrogen dioxide	—	0.05	—	Chemiluminescence
Ozone	—	—	0.08	Chemiluminescence
Carbon monoxide	10(8 hrs)	8	35	Non-Dispersive Infra-Red
Ammonia	0.14	—	0.8	
Chlorine	—	0.01	0.03 (30 min)	Gas Chromatography UV Spectrophotometry Mass Spectrometry
Hydrocarbons (non-methane)	1/10 TLV for each Hydrocarbon (non-CH4)			Flame Ionization Detector
Lead	—	2.0 μg/m³	—	Atomic Absorption

Notes: * Maximum 24 hrs average concentration should not be exceeded more than once per year.

** Average of the hourly means for the 24 hrs value shall not be exceeded more than twice at any location during any 30 day period.

*** Maximum one hour average concentration not to be exceeded more than twice per year.

Table 2: Emission Rates Resulting from Various Operations by the Ministry of Oil in the Extraction and Refining of Oil in Kuwait

Pollutant	*Maximum Rate of Emission*
Sulphur Dioxide	— 1.5 pounds per million BTU as thermal energy during one hour period, for emissions resulting from fuel burning equipment. — 6.5 pounds of residual sulphur dioxide gas per ton of 100 per cent sulphuric acid production for the emissions resulting from the sulphuric acid producing plants. — 0.5 pounds per ton of sulphuric acid production for the emissions of residual acid gas, and 0.2 pounds per ton of sulphuric acid productions for the emissions of sulphur trioxide. — Emission resulting from sulphur recovery units shall not exceed 0.16 pounds of sulphur dioxide per pound of sulphur processed in the units of sulphur recovery from natural gas and 0.08 pounds of sulphur dioxide resulting from sources other than those of sulphur recovery from natural gases.
Nitrogen Oxide (Calculated as Nitrogen Dioxide from fuel burning equipment)	— 0.2 pounds per million BTU per each hour as thermal energy resulting from gas burning. — 0.3 pounds per million BTU per each hour as thermal energy resulting from burning other kinds of liquid fuel.

2.3 Emission Standards

Emission standards were being prepared in 1990. The Ministry of Oil has emission standards for petroleum operations, covering drilling, extraction, refining and export. The operator conducts a preliminary survey of the potential environmental impacts from the exploratory or production wells including the offshore operations and is asked to prepare an emergency contingency plan. A report has to be submitted to the authorities stating the location of all points of emission of any contaminant to the atmosphere, expected average daily emission rates, levels, concentrations and quantities of contaminants at each point of emission, expected average quality of ambient air at ground level, the methods proposed for monitoring the contaminants, and expected temperature of discharge. The maximum rates of emission resulting from various operations are shown in Table 2.

2.4 Polluter Pays Principle

The polluter pays principle is generally accepted in Kuwait. The polluters themselves must take the necessary technical or other means for emission reductions. However it should be borne in mind that the major sources of air pollution are the petroleum-petrochemical industry and power plants, which are both owned, run and financed by the State Government. Any legal suits against them therefore are unlikely to succeed.

2.5 Economic Controls

Economic considerations are fundamental to the control of air pollution, with economic impact analysis recognized as an important tool for air pollution control. The Environment Protection Council (EPC) has introduced this concept for dealing with the regulatory measures included in the environment protection plan.

Economic analyses are carried out for the control of pollutants associated with the use of motor vehicles, reducing and eliminating lead from gasoline, reducing sulphur dioxide emissions, control of nitrogen dioxide and particulates, and assessing the damage caused to the environment by off-road vehicles and quarrying in the desert areas. The cost benefit of the various measures in terms of social, health benefits are also considered.

2.6 Environment Protection Act 1980

The *Environment Protection Act* is an enabling law, the enforcement of which is through decrees, orders, instructions and codes of practice. This law also established the Environment Protection Council, which is chaired by the Minister of Public Health, with membership including all the government organizations dealing with industrial or urban development, as well as educational, research and public health authorities.

The Council has wide-ranging responsibilities which include general policy for the protection of the environment, suggesting work plans, and coordinating the activities of the different departments. The Council studies pollution problems, suggests control measures and participates in setting research policies. It also prepares bills, regulations and orders and supervises their enforcement, studies regional and international agreements and conventions, and advises on their ratification.

Enforcement is mostly through the licensing system. Greater emphasis is placed on minimizing air pollution from new or substantially modified plant and equipment during design and construction rather than on existing plant which is meeting emission limits appropriate to its age. Old plant is often allowed to continue in this mode even though it might not always meet appropriate emission limits. Approval is required for stack heights before building to ensure that ground level concentrations do not exceed ambient standards.

For violations by existing firms, the Environment Protection Council can order the suspension of work or ban the use of any tool, machine or material, either partially or totally, if it threatens the environment. The initial suspension is for one week and may be extended for another week if necessary. The EPC has the right to authorize its Chairman to issue an order in case of emergencies for a period of three days, after which the case must be presented to the Council.

Violations by government establishments or companies in which the government has a share of more than 50 per cent, are considered by a special committee comprising the Chairman of the EPC and the Ministers of Oil, Commerce and Industry, and Electricity and Water. This committee decides what measures are to be taken.

The *Environment Protection Act* also provided for the establishment of the Environment Protection Department to assist the Council in carrying out its tasks and in following up the enforcement of its decisions and orders. The Department carries out the necessary monitoring, inspection of pollution sources and prepares legal suits against the violators. Fines for breaches of the Act are quite substantial, although no daily penalties are included.

The Chairman of the EPC nominates the Environment Protection Inspectors required by this law; they are given the responsibility of enforcing its provisions and reporting any violations. The inspectors have the right to enter any violating institutions, make legal suits, take samples, and conduct studies and measurements to specify the extent of environmental pollution, identify the sources of pollution and ensure the application of regulations and conditions regarding environmental protection.

Generally enforcement is exercised through the Environment Protection Department, Ministry of Public Health. The Department also has responsibility for the working environment. Factory inspection is provided for and measures taken to ensure that the threshold limit values (TLVs) are being complied with. The integration of the protection of the working and general environment in a single body has proved to be quite cost effective as regards trained manpower. Moreover, no conflicts of the type that can arise from taking certain measures to clean the working environment at the expense of the outdoor air quality have been encountered.

3 IMPLEMENTATION AND ENFORCEMENT

Responsibility for the implementation and enforcement of pollution legislation has largely been dealt with in the previous section.

3.1 Monitoring

Three fixed stations are used for monitoring the primary pollutants and weather variables, with solar UV and infra-red monitored at one of them. Two similar stations are being commissioned, and there are several mobile laboratories. A fully equipped mobile laboratory is used for monitoring the level of pollution along highways and in the vicinity of parking lots. A number of others are used to investigate the level of hydrogen sulphide near sewage treatment plants, gathering centres and refineries. Another is used to monitor the level of methane in the vicinity of old waste sites. A sonic radar is fixed on a truck and is used to investigate the presence and height of the thermal inversion layer.

High volume samplers are fixed at roof level at four sites, and the findings reported to the UN Environment Programme's Global Environment Monitoring System (GEMS). The size distribution is measured using the Anderson head. The samples are analyzed to determine the level of heavy metals and certain elements are also measured and the relative distribution used for finger printing. Monthly dust fall is collected from nine sites. The soluble, non-soluble, combustible and ash fractions are determined for different samples.

The Shuaiba Area Authority which runs its own monitoring system has seven ground based stations for monitoring the level of principal pollutants together with ammonia. Meteorological variables are measured at two sites. All the stations are connected to a central mainframe computer which calibrates the equipment and stores the data. A number of dustfall and high volume samplers are distributed throughout the industrial area. The continuous monitoring of the emission through the stacks was not provided for in the past but the necessary legislation is being discussed as an item in the decree setting emission standards.

3.2 Administration

The Council has established a number of sub-committees to deal specifically with legal affairs, planning and research, environmental impact assessment, and public education. An environment protection policy was prepared by the Council and circulated among all the concerned organizations. Comments were solicited and the policy revised and amended accordingly. The policy was adopted by the Cabinet of Ministers and thus acquired the required legal status.

Public education is considered complementary to the development and enforcement of legislation. The Environment Protection Society, an NGO, was established in 1974 to help promote the interest of the public in the environment. A large number of citizens of differing backgrounds are active members of the society and more than 50 government and non-government institutions are also registered members. The Society publishes a monthly journal and a booklet discussing the major local and international environmental problems. Education of school-children is also a major activity of the Society.

Several ministerial orders and decrees have been promulgated, including an order providing for environment impact statements. The order sets out the procedures for submission of statements and the projects covered; these include any industrial projects likely to consume 300 kg of fuel per hour or likely to emit 100 tons of pollutants per year without using any control measures. Incinerators, highways, airports, asphalt batching plants and other dusty projects are also subject to the legislation.

This order can be seen as legalizing the existing practice. Since every project should seek a license, and the license is a pre-requisite to obtaining the land and the building permit, enforcing the order is unlikely to cause any problems. While best practical technology is the basis, assimilative capacity of the site and the existing background level for the specific pollution is also taken into consideration.

3.3 Management of Air Pollution

The Environment Protection Council has prepared a five year plan (1991-1996) for the protection of the environment. The plan is based on the environment protection policy adopted by the Council of Ministers in 1988. The major items relevant to air pollution control include updating the inventory for emission loads from the major sources. The inventory is used to highlight the major sources and for setting priorities. The emission load of the primary pollutants for the major sources is summarized in Table 3. The estimates are based on the size of the activities and the emission factors ascribed to each.

Table 3: The Emission of the Primary Pollutants (Tons/Year) Estimated from the Major Sources in Kuwait, 1990

Pollutant		*Traffic*	*Industrial*	*Power plants*	*Oil drilling & refining*	*Total*
Particulates	T/Y	3410	72354	5750	30	81544
(10 mic)	%	4.2	88.7	7.1	0.0	100
Sulphur	T/Y	916	43666	328143	92773	465498
Dioxide	%	0.2	9.4	70.5	19.9	100
Nitrogen	T/Y	34000	24773	77842	1337	137952
Dioxide	%	24.6	18.0	56.4	1.0	100
Hydrocarbons	T/Y	63057	16708	694	55	80514
(N M)	%	77.4	20.5	0.8	0.1	100
Carbon	T/Y	408026	16621	3845	334	428826
Monoxide	%	95.1	3.9	0.9	0.1	100
Lead	T/Y	1083				
	%	100				

Particulates are limited to those 10 microns or less (P10) and those resulting from traffic exclude particulates generated from the road surface or movement on non-paved roads. Sulphur dioxide emissions arise mainly from the use of high sulphur crude by power plants, although this situation will improve substantially with the use of fuel with a one per cent sulphur content. The other major source of sulphur dioxide is the practice of flaring off sour gas in the oil fields.

Emissions of nitrogen oxide result mainly from power plants and reported levels are based on the existing situation, where no flue gas treatment or other control method is used. The emission load for traffic is based on the existing Gulf Cooperation Council (GCC) standard used in Kuwait and the other Gulf countries and use of leaded gasoline. Estimates for hydrocarbons are rather crude and do not include the geogenic sources. Revision of the estimates using a reconciliation technique is being done at the moment.

Carbon monoxide and lead result from traffic movements, with industrial sources making a minimal contribution. The gasoline on sale in Kuwait contains 0.4 gm of lead per litre. The Environment Protection Plan (EPP) contains a special chapter on the control of emissions from traffic. The principal items include changing the present GCC specification which is a version of the UN Economic

Commission for Europe Regulation, ECE R15, to a stricter specification similar to the Japanese (10 mode cycle) or the US FTP (1975). This is currently being negotiated with the other GCC members.

Also under the Environment Protection Plan, leaded gasoline is to be phased out by 1998, and a centralized inspection and maintenance programme to be established. Inspections will be carried out annually as part of the licensing of the vehicle. Road checks have also been initiated. The fourth item in the Programme is the synchronization of traffic movements by linking the traffic lights to avoid any traffic jams. The Programme will be run by the Traffic Department, Ministry of the Interior. The Environment Protection Department will continue monitoring for exhaust gases in residential areas, along highways and in the vicinity of parking lots. The effectiveness of the programme will be evaluated and the necessary changes introduced.

Control of pollution from power plants is being discussed among the relevant organizations. Controls were mainly based on the use of high (200 m) stacks, but since the introduction of one per cent sulphur fuel for power plants, the situation is expected to improve. The use of natural gas is also being considered. Flue gas desulphurization as an additional measure is being investigated and the cost effectiveness of the process looked into.

Control of nitrogen oxides is based on the control of the flue gas in power plants. Selective catalytic reduction is the most likely candidate, which has to be retrofitted into existing plant. Abatement of nitrogen oxides emissions by combustion modification is likely to be followed for new plant. The other item will be the use of the three-way catalytic converters in gasoline powered vehicles, the predominant type in Kuwait.

The control of particulates is more difficult owing to the major contribution of non-point sources resulting from dust storms and off-road vehicles. An ambitious programme for paving ground parking lots and pavements along the roads in the city and the highways has been launched. The effect is being evaluated.

The use of tertiary treated effluent for irrigation of the shrubs and trees along the highways and the buffer zones around the industrial areas is expected to improve the situation at least inside the city. Combatting desertification is an extensive programme of international dimensions and goes beyond the scope of air pollution control.

The control of hydrocarbons is similar to that of dust. The contribution of non-point sources, particularly seepages from the oil fields is causing concern, although the magnitude of the problem has not yet been determined and the quantity is not yet known. Control is rather difficult and several experts have been called to look at the problem. Hydrocarbons resulting from traffic movements are expected to gradually diminish in the next decade and the strategies for achieving this have already been approved. Regulations for control of industrial sources is being drafted.

3.4 International

Internationally, Kuwait participated in many of the meetings which discussed the problem of ozone depletion and the resulting Protocol to protect the ozone layer. Kuwait took an active role in persuading the GCC countries to ratify the Protocol as a group. The high UV level in Kuwait and the other countries of the region is an impetus.

With global warming, the situation is probably more critical. Environment protection agencies are aware of the grave consequences. The long shore line and the flat terrain of Kuwait is cause for concern. The economic consequences will probably be more substantial. The freeze in oil consumption will influence sales of the petroleum which is the major source of income for Kuwait and other OPEC countries. The continuing practice of flaring off sour gas is likely to be given attention by the Environment Protection Council.

4 FUTURE DEVELOPMENTS

Kuwait is cooperating with the GCC countries and with the Arab League in the control and management of certain problems of common concern. Desertification is singled out as a regional problem of social, economic and environmental dimensions. It is also an important item in the control of climatic changes at the global level.

Kuwait is, however, a developing country and knows its limitations as regards technical and manpower resources. Kuwait has benefitted from the experience of other countries and aims to share its vision and experience with other countries for the common benefit of this and future generations.

5 REFERENCES

El Desouky M et al, (1987a). *Level of Hydrocarbons in the Urban Areas, Kuwait.* Environment Protection Department, Ministry of Public Health, Kuwait.

El Desouky M et al, (1987b). *Level of Nitrous Oxides in the Urban Areas, Kuwait.* Environment Protection Department, Ministry of Public Health, Kuwait.

El Desouky M and Abd Al-Wahhab S, (1985). *Ground Based Thermal Inversion in Kuwait.* Environment Protection Department, Ministry of Public Health, Kuwait.

Environment Protection Council, (1981). *Buffer Zone and the Stationary Sources of Pollution* (Arabic Report). Environment Protection Council, Kuwait.

Environment Protection Council, (1989). *The 5-Year Plan for the Protection of the Environment.* Environment Protection Council, Kuwait.

Environment Protection Department, (1990). *Annual Report, 1989.* Environment Protection Department, Ministry of Public Health, Kuwait.

Kollias N and Baqer A, (1990). *Solar Middle Ultraviolet Radiation in Kuwait.* Report submitted to the Environment Protection Council, Kuwait.

Meteorology Department, (1989). *Annual Report, Meteorology Department.* Directorate General of Civil Aviation, Kuwait.

M P, (1988). *Statistical Abstract, 1988.* Ministry of Planning, Kuwait.

6 POSTSCRIPT

The above chapter was prepared in June 1990. About one month later, the Iraqis invaded Kuwait in one of the worst political and humanitarian disasters ever recorded in the recent history. For seven months, Kuwait was occupied and its economic activities paralysed. With regard to air quality all monitoring was suspended and many of the facilities looted, including all the mobile laboratories, the particle samplers and most of the sophisticated analytical equipment.

Before pulling their troops out of Kuwait, the Iraqis set fire to over 900 oil wells distributed among eight oil fields to the north and south of the urban area. Over 600 wells were ignited, causing probably the worst manmade air pollution incident in recent history. The wells that failed to ignite caused the discharge of large quantities of crude oil and large pools of oil are seen around the wells. There are currently no accurate estimations of the quantity of burning oil or of the exact number of wells on fire.

The best estimate is that 6 million barrels are burnt every day. This will cause the release into the atmosphere of 40 000 tons of soot, 60 000 tons of sulphur dioxide and large amounts of nitrogen oxides, daily. The air quality monitoring system was designed to look after the pollution coming from the power plants, traffic and industry. The problem of the oil well fires was not anticipated or accounted for and the siting of the monitoring stations was for most of the time out of the wake of the plume.

The heat islands created by the extensive well fires is changing the surface wind regime beyond anticipation and the US NOAA was kind enough to install 15 weather stations around the urban area and the oil fields. The data will be fed into the Health Alert System. The public will be informed of any alarming increase in the level of pollutants and the hospitals advised to make the necessary arrangements. At the time being with the rise of the plume thousands of feet, the hot summer, and the fresh winds ventilating the plume, the level of pollution is not likely to be a great concern to the health of the people. The situation may however change after a large proportion of the burning wells are extinguished and with a more stagnant climate in early fall. The Health Alert System should be in place before next September and all the efforts are being concentrated in this direction.

Two of the air quality monitoring stations have been working since April and May. Despite the existing limitations about the siting of the stations, some information is still being collected. Very high frequencies of methane and non-methane hydrocarbons are seen at the two stations with some figures reaching 20 ppm. Some carbon monoxide recordings are up to 30 ppm, though the mean carbon monoxide is quite low owing to the very low traffic density. Sulphur dioxide is within the permissible values and ozone is quite low. Seven PM10 monitors have been installed, and plans to commission two other air quality monitoring stations are being accelerated. Norway has offered to help by providing the two monitors along with the communication system that will be the basis of the Health Alert System that is being developed.

MALAYSIA

1 INTRODUCTION

1.1 Topography, Climate, Population

Malaysia lies in South East Asia; it is 329 749 sq. km in area and has a population of approximately 18 million. The average daily temperature ranges from 21 - 32 degrees C; there are two monsoon seasons - the northwest and southwest - and rainfall averages about 3000 mm a year.

Oil fired power plants have provided the main source of electrical energy generation in Malaysia. In the early 1970s more than 90 per cent of the national energy supply was generated by oil. Since that time, the level has decreased to approximately 75 per cent as a result of a National Energy Policy (which is almost exclusively concerned with electricity generation), aimed at substituting oil with natural gas.

Despite the fact that Malaysia has its own sources of low sulphur oil, it exports that oil to Japan and imports cheaper oil with high levels of sulphur. The Government prefers not to lose the income from exporting the higher grade oil. As a consequence the oil burned in power plants is more polluting than it need be. Another disturbing development has been the increasing use of imported coal in electricity generation and cement manufacturing in the 1980s.

1.2 Specific National Problems

There are three principal sources of air pollution in Malaysia: motor vehicles, industry and open burning.

Motor vehicles are the greatest contributors to the problem and account for approximately 50 per cent of total estimated pollution. The number of vehicles on the roads in Malaysia continues to increase steadily and, as a result, there has been a corresponding rise in the level of lead and black smoke in the air.

As Malaysia continues to pursue a policy of rapid industrialization, it is beginning to feel the consequences of increasing numbers of power stations, boilers, furnaces and incinerators, not to mention the more traditional industrial air pollution sources from wood mills and concrete plants.

The open burning of construction material, garbage, residual vegetation (at urban and agricultural land clearings) has proved to be a great source of air pollution. In 1989, the Department of Environment (DOE) examined 29 out of 102 waste disposal sites and all were practising open burning in one form or another.

These three sources of air pollution have caused extended periods of haze in 1982 and again in 1990. Worst affected by the problem has been the Klang Valley. However, this phenomenon has been observed in many other parts of the country as well. The levels of lead, dust fallout and particulates are extremely high, especially where there is heavy vehicular traffic and in industrial areas.

Acid precipitation or acid rain is not yet a major problem but acid levels have been on the rise since monitoring started in the mid 1980s. A 1990 study conducted in Peninsular Malaysia found the levels to be highest in Kuala Lumpur, Selangor, Johor and Kedah. Motor vehicles are the major contributors with power stations, open burning and industry as other contributors.

Much of the air pollution in Malaysia may be traced to its rapid rate of industrialization. The Government has an active policy to encourage the development of industrial plants. Many international corporations have taken up the invitation, secure in the knowledge that Malaysia is slack in enforcing its environmental laws.

It must be stressed that the country still lacks a comprehensive air monitoring system and even the data published by the DOE, although improving in quality, is still fragmentary and cannot be the basis of realistic assessment of national problems.

2 DEVELOPMENT OF AIR POLLUTION CONTROLS AND LEGISLATION

2.1 Clean Air Philosophy

There is no clear cut philosophy, which is not surprising since the country does not even have a national environmental policy. The philosophy can only be implied through reading various Government documents, such as the Department of Environment's annual report and the development plans. While there seems to be some desire to cut back the visible pollutants like black smoke, there is little commitment to monitor comprehensively air quality nationwide or to resolve the recurrent haze that regularly envelopes the country's most developed area, the Klang Valley (in which the capital Kuala Lumpur is located).

Even legislative concern seems to be with emission levels rather than ambient air quality. The working environment itself is only controlled in factories and that too for only a few air pollutants, such as lead and asbestos.

2.2 Development of Controls

Although Malaysia is a federation of 13 states and 2 federal territories, and land/natural resource usages are state matters, air quality control has been very much a Federal responsibility. This is partly due to the fact that motorized transport, industries and energy generation have been centrally controlled. In addition, local authorities have been negligent in controlling even instances of open burning within their areas of jurisdiction.

Specific action to control the most blatant air pollution only began in 1977 and 1978 as shown by the sequence of legislation listed below:

* *Road and Traffic Ordinance 1958: Motor Vehicles (Control of Smoke and Gas Emission) Rules 1977*;
* *Environmental Quality Act 1974: Environmental Quality (Clean Air) Regulations 1978*;
* *Environmental Quality (Control of Lead Concentrations in Motor Gasoline) Regulations 1985*;
* *Environmental Quality (Control of Emissions from Diesel Engines) Regulations 1986.*

2.3 Industrial Processes

All industrial processes, except for palm oil and raw natural rubber, are regulated under the *Environmental Quality (Clean Air) Regulations 1978.* These Regulations cover industrial facilities, the burning of waste, black smoke, air impurities, and construction. Industrial facilities may not be located adjacent to residential areas. The Regulations require that any erection, installation, re-siting, or alteration of fuel burning equipment be granted prior approval from the Director General of the DOE. The burning of industrial waste must be done in incinerators, where possible. A license for open burning may be granted if it is proven that there are no other feasible alternatives or if it does not cause air pollution.

The Regulations set the limit for dark smoke at No. 1 on the Ringelmann Chart for new facilities and at No. 2 for existing facilities. The Regulations on air impurities set emission standards for several pollutants, including metal particulates, gases, concrete, asphalt, asbestos, and silica. However, factories established prior to the pollution control regulations are allowed to continue operations even if their emissions do not comply with the standards.

Firms may apply for a contravention license if it is judged that they cannot conform to the Regulations. For example, factories are permitted to openly burn vulcanized rubber until an appropriate technology may be found to burn their waste more safely. This is just one of many contraventions. Betwen 1984 and 1989 applications to discharge waste into the atmosphere increased by 450 per cent. For all these Regulations the onus is on the industry to monitor its emissions, and to make that information available to the DOE when required. On the whole, there is but rudimentary control of smoke emissions from industrial sites. The Malaysian Government seems to be more concerned with industrial expansion than air pollution.

2.4 Mobile Sources

The greatest source of air pollution in Malaysia is from mobile sources. As the number of vehicles on the roads has increased, so too has their contribution to air pollution. The levels of lead, particulates and dust fallout are extremely high in areas of heavy traffic.

Emission of black smoke is controlled under the *Motor Vehicles (Control of Smoke and Gas Emission) Rules 1977.* The rules are enforced by the DOE in cooperation with the traffic police and the Road Transport Department - a fact which causes some confusion between the various parties involved. The DOE has 10 "Pajeros" to act as mobile test stations. It tests vehicles with a Hartridge Smokemeter to ensure that the limit of 50 Hartridge Smoke Units (HSU) is met. Recently there has been an increasing rate of non-compliance. In 1989, 18 - 20 per cent of vehicles tested exceeded the black smoke limit.

Lead is controlled by the *Environmental Quality (Control of Lead Concentrations in Motor Gasoline) Regulations 1985.* On 1 January 1990, the regulated standard of lead in gasoline was reduced from 0.4 g/l to 0.15 g/l. On 1 July 1990, unleaded gasoline was selectively introduced, making Malaysia one of the few countries in SE Asia to do so. The recommended Malaysian Guideline for lead is 1.5 $\mu g/m^3$ averaged over a three month period. Of the 16 stations measuring lead in 1989, four did not comply with the limit.

Diesel vehicles are governed by the *Environmental Quality (Control of Emissions from Diesel Engines) Regulations 1986.* Emission limits are set at 50 HSU. The Government is making an effort to promote the use of Liquefied Petroleum Gas and Compressed Natural Gas by requiring that all new public service vehicles operate on either one of these fuels. A total ban on diesel-run public service vehicles is planned by 1 January 1997.

Total suspended particulates (TSP) are measured in micrograms per cubic meter over a period of 24 hours. There are six stations measuring TSP throughout Malaysia. In 1989 five of the six stations recorded mean concentrations above the Recommended Malaysian Annual Guideline of 90 $\mu g/m^3$; however, they generally complied with the Daily Guideline of 260 $\mu g/m^3$ over the mean of a 24 hour measurement.

3 IMPLEMENTATION AND ENFORCEMENT

3.1 National Enforcement

Generally, the Department of Environment suffers from a shortage of funds and manpower. This means that it is difficult to effectively monitor and enforce air pollution standards. As a result, the Department has been forced to prioritize its work. Recently, with the increased concern over haze, the DOE has been clamping down on open burning and black smoke emissions from vehicles.

Under Section 22 (1) of the *Environmental Quality Act 1974*, contravention licenses are permitted. This allows for exemptions from the various regulations and guidelines. Ninety per cent of such licenses issued in 1989 were for open burning - a practice which contributes to Malaysia's haze problem. Such licenses are allowed if there is no other practicable waste disposal method, or if it is proven that burning will not unduly pollute the air. In 1989, there was an 84 per cent increase in the number of applications for contravention licenses over the previous year.

Enforcement of Malaysia's air pollution control legislation is scant. In 1989, 22 cases were prosecuted with only 23 per cent of these cases being under the *Environmental Quality (Clean Air) Regulations 1978*. The majority of offenses related to the open burning of waste. Moreover, the fines are too negligible to encourage future compliance on the part of the polluter.

3.2 Monitoring

The Department of the Environment has an Air Quality Monitoring Programme which measures TSP, atmospheric lead, and dust fallout at 224 monitoring stations; 32 stations measure TSP, while 192 measure dust fallout. High Volume Samplers and Deposit Gauges are used.

The highest levels of TSP are generally found in industrial areas with heavy traffic, where the Recommended Malaysian Annual Guideline is regularly exceeded. In 1989, the highest concentration at 150 $\mu g/m^3$ from 47 daily observations was measured in an industrial area near Kuala Lumpur. In residential and rural areas TSP is less of a problem.

The Recommended Malaysian Guideline for dust fallout is 133 $\mu g/m^3$ per day (based on the annual mean of monthly values). Several questions have been raised concerning this value:

- how was the limit set?
- how reliable are the measurements, given the fact that they are only periodic?
- why has no standard been set for inhaled dust which is more indicative of the effects on human health?

Atmospheric lead follows a similar pattern, with industrial areas and areas with heavy traffic having the highest measurements. The Government has attempted to crack down on vehicles which contravene the lead and diesel emission standards; however the DOE lacks a comprehensive inspection and maintenance programme, thus limiting its effectiveness.

Emissions of carbon monoxide, nitrates, sulphates and hydrocarbons are estimated based on emission factors of production rates, materials, quantity, type of fuel, and control equipment used. There is currently no formal or definitive means of monitoring these pollutants.

In 1988, the DOE commissioned a study to develop criteria and standards for air quality and to develop a quality assurance programme for air quality monitoring. It was designed to cover such things as TSP, particulates smaller than 10 μm, dustfall, lead sulphur dioxide, carbon dioxide, carbon monoxide, ozone and nitrogen. The proposals are contained in Table 1.

A National Acid Rain Monitoring Network, comprising three departments under the Ministry of Science, Technology and Environment, has been using 17 monitoring sites since 1967. Acidity is measured with the help of automatic precipitation collectors, high volume air samplers and photometers.

4 EFFECTIVENESS OF CONTROLS

Generally the *Environmental Quality Act* is poorly enforced. It has many loopholes and is too lenient on polluters; fines are not sufficient to be a deterrent.

As far as other clean air legislation is concerned, there is often an overlap between the laws and the Departments concerned with their enforcement. On the whole, the Government's response to the problem of air pollution has been on an ad hoc basis. The Department of Environment lacks a long term air pollution control programme. This is in part due to its shortage of funds and manpower, which makes it difficult to inspect and ensure compliance with regulations.

Such air quality standards that do exist deal only with emission standards. There is a pressing need for the setting and enforcement of ambient air quality standards in order to ensure that human health is protected.

Table 1: Malaysia: Recommended Air Quality Guidelines (at 25° Celsius and 101.13 kPa)

Pollutant and method	*Averaging time*	*Malaysian guidelines* *ppm*	*µg/m3*
Ozone	1 hour	0.10	200
AS 2524	8 hours	0.06	120
Carbon monoxide	1 hour	30	35†
AS 2695	8 hours	9	10†
Nitrogen dioxide	1 hour	0.17	320
AS 2447			
Sulphur Dioxide	10 minutes	0.19	500
AS 2523	1 hour	0.13	350
	24 hours	0.04	105
Particles TSP	24 hours		260
AS 2724.3	1 year		90
PM10	24 hours		150
AS 2724.6	1 year		50
Lead AS 2800	3 month		1.5
Dustfall AS 2724.1	1 year	133*	

*Key: †=mg/m3 *=mg/m2/day*

MEXICO

1 INTRODUCTION

This chapter concentrates on ozone and sulphur dioxide concentrations in the Metropolitan Area of Mexico City (MACM); as will be seen, levels of these pollutants are particularly high leading to serious problems in Mexico City. The total population (1985 census) of the Republic of Mexico is 74 981 000, of which almost 29 per cent (15 656 000) live in the Metropolitan Zone of Mexico City.

The Metropolitan Area of Mexico City lies on the south-eastern part of the Mexico basin at an altitude of 2240 m above sea level. The basin is surrounded by mountains, with a pattern of winds blowing from the north west and the north east (Figure 1). The geographical situation of the basin, its meteorological characteristics, and the emission of air pollutants combine to make it a great natural reservoir in which complex photochemical reactions produce oxidant chemical compounds. The presence of ozone as an atmospheric pollutant in Mexico City was noticed as long ago as 1958 (Bravo et al, 1958).

2 THE PROBLEM

Uncontrolled automobile exhaust emissions are important sources of air pollution. The polluting emissions of almost 2.5 million vehicles in the Mexico City Metropolitan Zone (MCMZ) are estimated to be approximately 11 000 tons a day, composed of particles (0.3 per cent), carbon monoxide (89.25 per cent), oxides of sulphur (0.3 per cent), oxides of nitrogen (0.9 per cent), and hydrocarbons (9.15 per cent).

Despite the fact that nitrogen oxides and hydrocarbons constitute little more than 10 per cent of these emissions, their importance in the generation of photochemical air pollution makes them potentially the most serious problem for air quality in the MCMZ at the present time. Ozone is produced when sunlight triggers chemical nitrogen oxides. Levels are highest during the day, usually after heavy morning traffic has released large amounts of the precursor pollutants. As a result of wind transport of the mass pollutants containing ozone precursors emitted in the northern and central parts of the City, the maximum concentrations appear downwind of the emission zones, towards the southern part of the urban area. Figure 2 illustrates this situation with a schematic representation of the maximum hourly values measured at the monitoring stations of the Centro de Ciencias de la Atmósfera and the Urban Development and Ecology (SEDUE, 1987).

On the other hand, the use of heavy bunker oil and diesel oil with a relatively high sulphur content (3.5 per cent weight) in most of the industrial plants, including two power plants, is responsible for the main sulphur dioxide emissions and consequently the higher levels of sulphur dioxide on the North of the MCMZ, where the industrial zone is located.

During the fall of 1986, Petróleos Mexicanos reduced the amount of fuel oil used in different industrial activities such as the petroleum refinery of Azcapotzalco and two power plants of the Comision Federal de Electricidad, all of them located in the north of the MCMZ. Using natural gas instead, PEMEX stated that this would diminish the sulphur dioxide concentrations observed in Mexico City in previous years (SEDUE, 1989a). However, two facts emerge from this action. First, governmental data show no decrease in consumption of fuel oil, but instead a constant upwards trend for MCMZ (SEDUE, 1989b). Secondly, natural gas combustion boilers without modification in the furnace design could result in an increase in the nitrogen oxides emissions. There is evidence that nitrogen oxide emissions from the power plants are contributing to the ozone problem (Torres, 1991).

The hypothesis presented here is that the reduction on fuel oil was offset by its equivalent head capacity for natural gas with other industrial plants in the same area; a statistical trend analysis of sulphur dioxide data will show how the air pollution control strategy by PEMEX worked.

The major air pollution problem in Mexico City is the presence of high levels of ozone showing a spatial southward increase in the urban area, governed by the local advection transport of air parcels by the prevalent diurnal wind and by the photochemical mechanisms (Bravo et al, 1989). Sulphur dioxide levels are important too, showing a spatial southward decrease due to the influence of local sources and wind diffusion. Even though, sulphur dioxide levels in the southern area are relatively low.

3 RESEARCH AND MONITORING

Measurements of precursors, ozone and sulphur dioxide have been made since 1980 at the Centro de Ciencias de la Atmósfera (University station), located on the southern area of Mexico City where the maximum ozone concentrations of the whole Metropolitan Zone are currently recorded. Lead content analysis in total suspended particles are routinely made by the Under Secretary of Ecology (SEDUE).

The ozone data at the University station show that the ozone levels before September 1986 exceeded the air quality standard for ozone of 0.11 ppm (maximum hourly average) on just a few days since 1980 (Bravo and Torres, 1985). The ozone situation has worsened since September 1986, coinciding with the introduction by Petróleos Mexicanos of a new formulation in the regular gasoline (NOVA-PLUS), looking for a reduction of the high lead concentrations previously observed in the suspended particles (PEMEX, 1986; SEDUE, 1986: IMP, 1987).

Figure 3 shows the monthly averages of maximum ozone concentrations and the number of days per month with ozone events in which the Mexican air quality standard for ozone was exceeded since 1984 at the University station.

According to technicians of PEMEX, the regular gasoline before the NOVA-PLUS, was formulated of refinery strength run gasoline of low octane, so high quantities of tetraethyl lead were required to be added in order to raise the octane number of the new gasoline.

The NOVA-PLUS gasoline was formulated with refinery reformatted gasolines with high levels of olefins, alkyl and aromatic blends and with a low content of tetraethyl lead, resulting in a high octane gasoline.

The reduction in the lead content worked as expected. However, the side effect of the use of the new gasoline in a fleet without catalytic converters was a significant increase in ozone formation. The nitrogen oxides increased because of the new high temperature in the combustion of the NOVA-PLUS gasoline, and the balance in the reactive organic gases emitted by the mobile sources changed to a rich percentage of very reactive organic compounds.

Figure 4 shows the tetraethyl lead content and the gasoline consumed in the Metropolitan Area of Mexico City over the period 1980-1987 (PEMEX, 1988). Figure 5 shows the lead content in total suspended particles reported by SEDUE (SEDUE, 1986).

The ozone effects in the ecosystems of the Mexico Basin are notorious. The phytopathological damage due to ozone is already present in the woods and vegetation of the southern zone of Mexico City, such as Xochimilco, Ajusco and Desierto de los Leones (de Bauer et al, 1985). Further effects are to be expected not only on vegetation, but also on the health of Mexico City's inhabitants as they are exposed to ozone levels considerably in excess of those of previous years.

The sulphur dioxide air pollution problem is different. The annual mean distribution of sulphur dioxide concentrations (December 1987 through November 1988) on the MCMZ is shown in Figure 6, following a three dimensional representation. Concentrations are highest near the industrial area of Xalostoc and the industrial corridor of Tlalnepantla-Naucalpan-Azcapotzaco showing a southward decrease. According to Figure 6, most of the urban area exceeds a sulphur dioxide concentration value of 30 ppb, which corresponds to the annual US primary air quality standard. The small peak at Iztapalapa is attributed to a small industrial complex located there.

The same southward decrease pattern is found throughout the different seasons of the year, but the concentration gradient becomes steeper during the winter months when values are higher, leading to a markedly decreased north-south gradient. Figure 7 shows the December 1987 mean distribution of sulphur dioxide on the MACM.

The one year mean sulphur dioxide concentration data are plotted in Figure 8 as a semilog function of distance, from imaginary east-west power station sites connecting line from the northern area towards the south of the MACM. The best fitted line in Figure 8 is described by the equation:

$$x = 4.28\ e^{(-0.0107\ x)}$$

where, x = S02 concentration (ppb); x = distance (km).

The one winter month concentration data are plotted in Figure 9 following the same procedure as Figure 6. The best fitted line in Figure 9 is described by the equation:

$$x = 4.51\ e^{(-0.0509\ x)}$$

The trend shown in the last four figures confirms the industrial area as the principal area source of sulphur dioxide present in the MCMZ.

The diurnal sulphur dioxide spatial distribution in the MACM is shown in Figure 10. The diagrams were constructed using mean three/four hour periods (0300-0600; 0900-1200; 1500-1800; and 2100-2400) for December 1987 data.

As can be seen from graph 0300-0600, the influence of some nocturnal activity in the industrial zone shows an apparent sulphur dioxide accumulation near Naucalpan and Tlalnepantla. The period 0900-1200 shows an increase in sulphur dioxide from the industrial areas towards the south of the City. That for 1500-1800 shows that sulphur dioxide moves on MCMZ in an apparent eastward displacement. This displacement has been partially explained by Jauregui (1988) as a meteorological effect produced by surface air flow and a heat-island gradient present in the urban area. Furthermore, the mixing height inversion is well developed at this time, so sulphur dioxide concentrations are low even compared with the 0300-0600 sulphur dioxide spatial distribution. From 2100-2400 an apparent sulphur dioxide accumulation near La Villa and the downtown area towards the East can be seen, and there is also a slight displacement of remaining sulphur dioxide concentrations from the south to the central part of the City.

4 ANNUAL VARIATION OF OZONE AND SULPHUR DIOXIDE

The number of exceedences of the ozone air quality standard by month of the year during the period 1987-1989 at the University station is shown in Figure 11. As can be seen from this graph, there is an apparently greater number of occurrences of exceedences by the end of each year, but it is inconclusive to establish definitive monthly patterns.

Monthly average concentrations of sulphur dioxide at all monitoring stations show a marked annual cycle with the maximum usually in winter and the minimum in the summer months. Typical curves are illustrated in Figure 12 for two representative stations: Tlalnepantla (industrial area) and the University station (semi-urban downwind area). Table 1 shows the quarterly average sulphur dioxide concentrations for the monitoring stations during 1987-1988.

Table 1: Quarterly Average Sulphur Dioxide Concentrations (ppb) for Monitoring Stations at the MZMC, 1987-88

Monitoring Station	*Winter*	*Spring* *Sulphur dioxide*	*Summer*	*Autumn*
Airport	40.3	34.3	35.0	40.6
Azcapotzalco	69.0	39.6	33.3	41.6
Iztapalapa	49.3	53.3	37.3	63.3
La Presa	41.0	32.3	20.0	37.6
La Villa	57.0	53.0	38.6	54.6
Merced	44.3	42.3	52.3	67.3
Pedregal	50.3	34.6	23.6	25.0
San Agustin	36.3	29.3	30.0	77.0
Tacuba	63.6	53.3	61.6	67.6
Tlalnepantla	65.3	51.0	54.3	60.6
Univ. Station	31.6	22.6	17.3	25.0
Vallejo	69.6	47.3	29.0	35.0
Xalostoc	80.0	83.66	56.0	67.6

5 WEEKLY AND DIURNAL VARIATION OF OZONE AND SULPHUR DIOXIDE

Figure 13 shows the quarterly trend of the average of the hourly maximums of ozone concentrations during 1987-1989 for weekdays,

Saturdays and Sundays at the University station. The ozone levels during the workdays are very close to those of the weekend levels, in spite of the occurrence of a significant reduction of traffic during the weekends. The hypothesis presented is that an excess of precursors from the workdays still remains during the weekends, sustaining the photochemical process.

The sulphur dioxide concentration data for December 1987 was analyzed to determine if weekend concentrations differed from weekdays. Weekday mean and weekend means are shown in Figure 14 for two representative stations: Tlalnepantla and the University station. This shows that concentrations on normal working days are significantly higher than those of other non-working days. Thus can be seen the influence of industrial activity on the daily average, since on Saturday, Sunday and the other non-working days an important percentage of industry ceases operation resulting in a reduction of some sulphur dioxide emissions.

However, the University station data do not show any significant difference, due to the absence of important sulphur dioxide around it, although there is stronger evidence that sulphur dioxide in the air mass transported to the south is being chemically converted to sulphate aerosols (Bravo et al, 1089; Hoggan et al, 1989).

The diurnal pattern of the exceedences to the ozone air quality standard, recorded at the University station for the period 1987-1989, is shown in Figure 15. As can be seen in the graph, the higher number of exceedences occurs after noon, although it is notorious the upward tendencies through the years.

The diurnal cycle of the sulphur dioxide concentration is also well marked. Although the amplitude is greater at the industrial zone, stations show a morning peak and afternoon or evening minimum. The morning sulphur dioxide peak shifts between 0900 to 1300 hrs local time depending on the position of the urban area. Figures 16 and 17 show mean hourly sulphur dioxide concentrations at Tlalnepantla and the University station for weekdays and weekends respectively during December 1989.

6 OZONE AND SULPHUR DIOXIDE TREND

The University station is located in the downwind zone of the MCMZ so the ozone data collected here are representative of the problem in the City. Figure 15 clearly shows the growing problem.

On the other hand, according to US EPA site exposure criteria for sulphur dioxide monitoring stations, the characteristics of the site location of the University station are appropriate for assessing annual or quarterly ground level urban sulphur dioxide patterns (EPA,

1977). Figure 18 shows the 95 per cent confidence intervals for quarterly data (Dec-Jan-Feb 1986 through 1989) according to a procedure by Pollack and Hunt (1985). These confidence intervals are used to compare periods; if the confidence intervals for any two periods do not overlap, then the composite averages of the two periods are significantly different.

From Figure 18 it is clear that sulphur dioxide concentrations are growing with time; the confidence intervals do not overlap so the trend is completely positive.

7 CONCLUSIONS

From the above discussion it is clear that very reactive organic compounds and nitrogen oxides in excess are emitted by cars without control emissions as a consequence of using reformatted gasolines rich in olefinic and alkyl-aromatic compounds. The direct effect of the presence of these precursors in the atmosphere of the MACM is the formation of high levels of ozone.

On the other hand, sulphur dioxide emissions are almost exclusively point-source orientated. Peak sulphur dioxide concentrations occur when the wind blows from point sources adjacent to receptor sites. From this it seems that sulphur dioxide concentrations originating from point sources are more sensitive to wind direction than wind speed.

The ozone and the sulphur dioxide air pollution problems in the MCMZ are growing with time and they are the result of the application of wrong air pollution control strategies. There is a great necessity in Mexico for professionals with a background knowledge in the air pollution control engineering field.

8 BIBLIOGRAPHY

Bravo H A, Pérez M and Siliceo M I (1958). *Muestreo y análisis de gases en la atmósfera.* Draft report. Dirección de Higiene Industrial, SSA Mexico, DF.

Bravo H A and Torres R J (1958). “Ozone monitoring and night concentration events at the campus of the University of Mexico”. Paper 85-59. B4, 78th Annual Meeting of Air Pollution Control Association. Detroit, Mi, June 16-21.

Bravo H A, Perrin F G, Sosa R E and Torres R J (1989a). “Gasoline’s lead reduction in Mexico: Its effects on the air quality”. SAE Technical Paper Series Number 890583. Society of American Engineers International Congress and Exposition. Detroit, Mi, February 27-March 3.

Bravo H A, Camacho R C, Saavedra M I, Sosa E R and Torres R J (1989b). "Concentrations of nitrates and sulfates in total suspended and respirable particles as result of air pollution control strategies in Mexico City". Paper 89-15.5, 82nd Air Pollution Control and Hazardous Waste Management Annual Meeting, Anaheim, Ca, June 25-30.

de Bauer M L and Tejada T (1985). "Ozone causes needle injury and tree decline in Pinus Hartweggi at high altitudes in the mountains around Mexico City". J Air Poll. Contr. Assoc. 35 (8): 838.

EPA (1977). *Optimum site exposure criteria for sulphur dioxide monitoring* EPA-450/3-77-013, US Environmental Protection Agency Research Triangle Park, NC.

Hoggan M, Hsu M, Kahn M and Call T (1989). "Weekday/weekend differences in diurnal variation in carbon monoxide, nitrogen dioxide, sulphur dioxide, and ozone implications for control strategies". Paper 89-125.5 82nd Air Pollution Control and hazardous Waste Management Annual Meeting, Anaheim, Ca, June 25-30.

TMP (1987). *Comportamiento de las nuevas gasolinas PLUS de Petróleos Mexicanos.* Report. Instituto Mexicano del Petróleo. México. January.

Jauregui E O (1988). Local wind and air pollution interaction in the Mexico Basin. *Atmósfera,* 1 (3): 131-140.

PEMEX (1986). Aspectos generales del plomo y su comportamiento en el medio ambiente. Report number GPTA-E-003 Petróleos Mexicanos. México. Diciembre.

PEMEX (1981). Memorias de labores. Petróleos Mexicanos. México.

Pollack A and Hunt W (1985). "Analysis of trends and variability in extreme and annual average sulphur dioxide concentrations". Presented at the Air Pollution Control Association & American Society for Quality Control Specialty Conference on Quality Assurance in Air Pollution Measurement. Boulder, Co.

SEDUE (1986). Informe sobre el medio ambiente en México. Report. Secretaría de Desarrollo Urbano y Ecología. México DF.

SEDUE (1986a). Consulta para el programa nacional de conservación ecológica y de protección al ambiente 1988-1994: Lineamientos. Report. Secretaría de Desarrollo Urbano y Ecología/ Conade. México, DF.

SEDUE (1989b). Programa integal de lucha contra la contaminación atmosférica. Report. Secretaría de Desarrollo Urbano y Ecología. México. DF.

Torres R J (1991). Construcción y aplicación de trayectorias de retroceso de parcelas de aire al estudio de la contaminación atmosférica por ozono en la zona Metropolitana de la Ciudad de México. MS Thesis. Facultad de Ingeniería, Universidad Nacional Autónoma de México.

Figure 1: Schematic representation of the Air Mass Transport by Diurnal Wind Action in Mexico City Metropolitan Zone

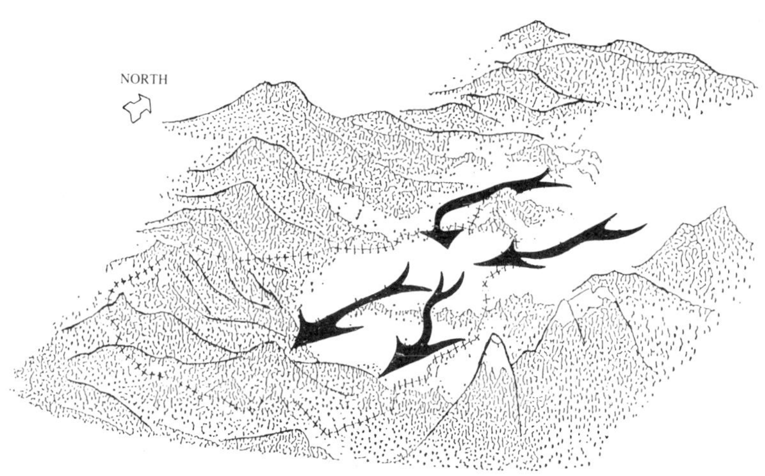

Figure 2: Schematic representation of ozone isopleths in ppm on the Mexico City Metropolitan Zone (29 November 1986)

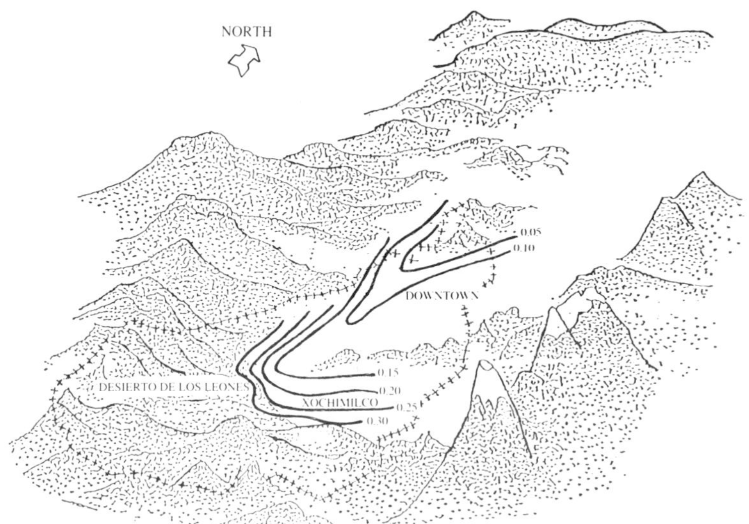

Figure 3: Maximum monthly average concentration of ozone, days and hours above standard at the University of Mexico monitoring station from 1984 through 1989

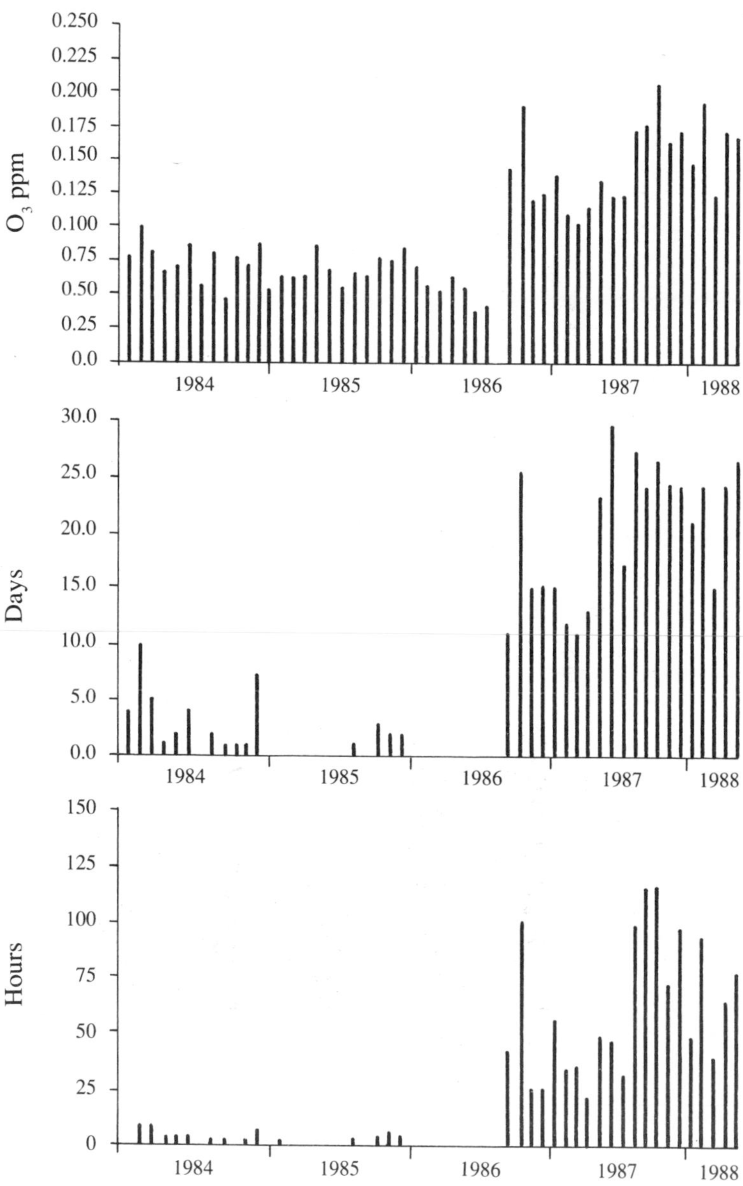

Figure 4: Tetraethyl lead content in Mexican gasolines

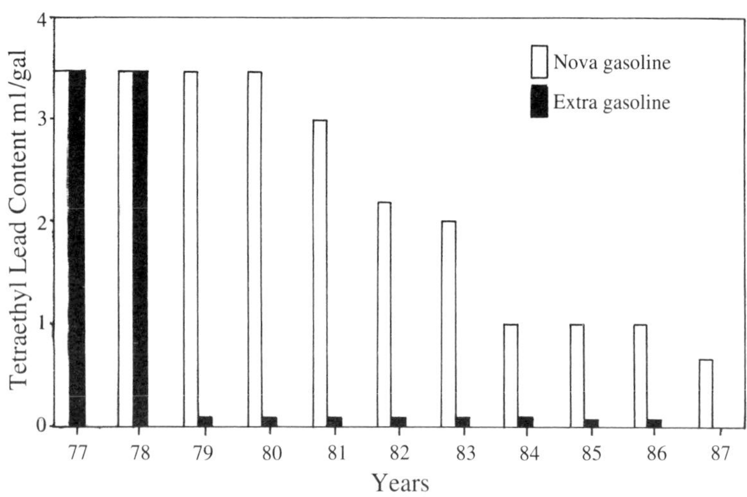

Figure 5: Lead in TSP for Museo and La Villa sites in a quarterly schedule (November - December - January)

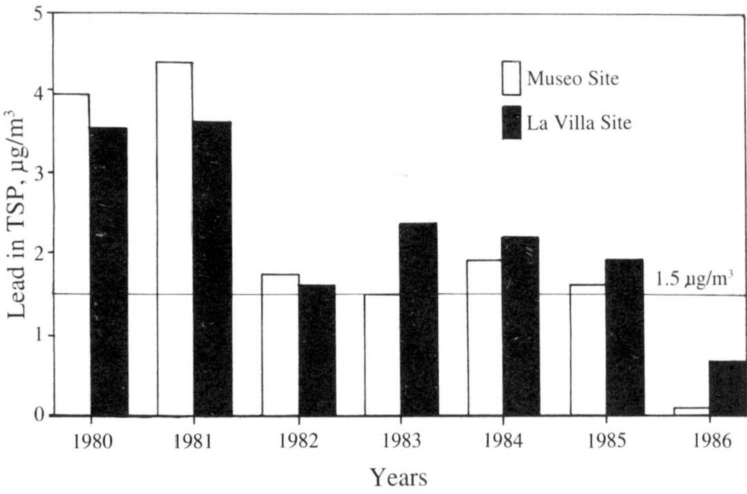

Figure 6: Three dimensional plot of one year average sulfur dioxide concentrations at the Metropolitan Zone of Mexico City for a grid of 20 x 20 km

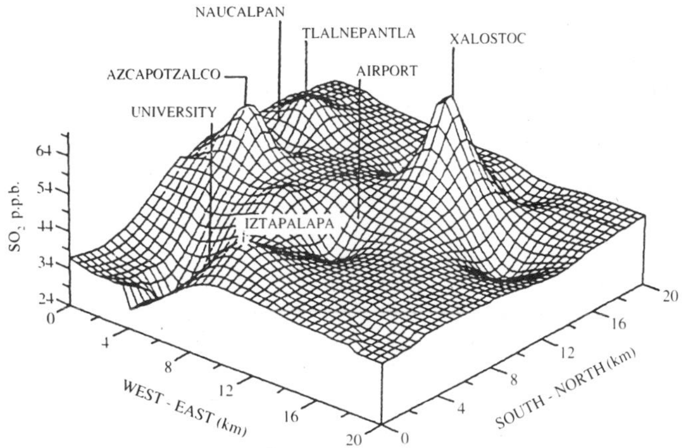

Figure 7: Three dimensional plot of one month average sulfur dioxide concentrations at the Metropolitan Zone of Mexico City for a grid of 20 x 20 km (December 1987)

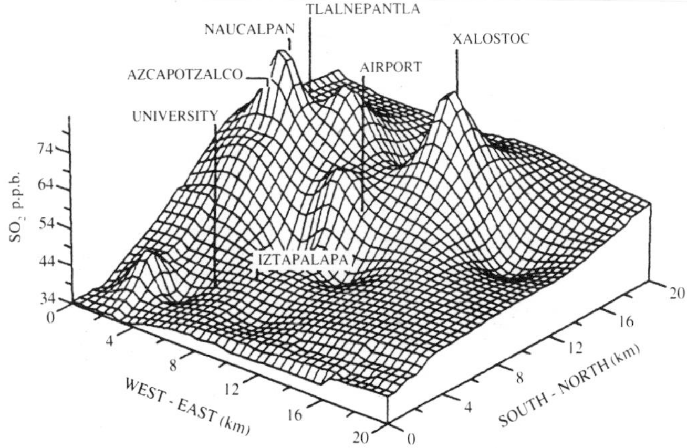

Figure 8: Change of mean annual sulphur dioxide concentration with distance from the North of the Metropolitan Zone of Mexico City (1987-1988)

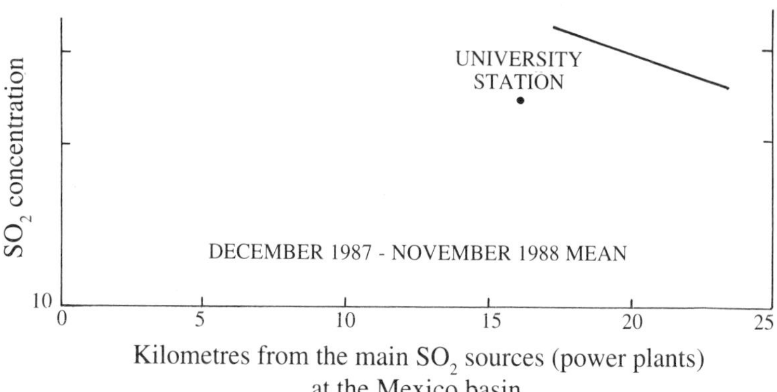

Figure 9: Change of mean monthly sulphur dioxide concentration with distance from the North of the Metropolitan Zone of Mexico City (December 1987)

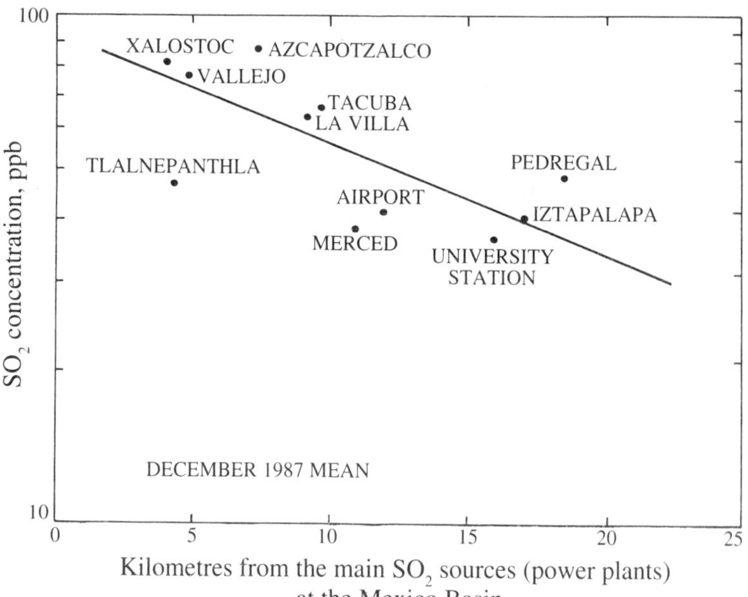

Figure 10: Spatial 3 hour monthly periods during December 1987

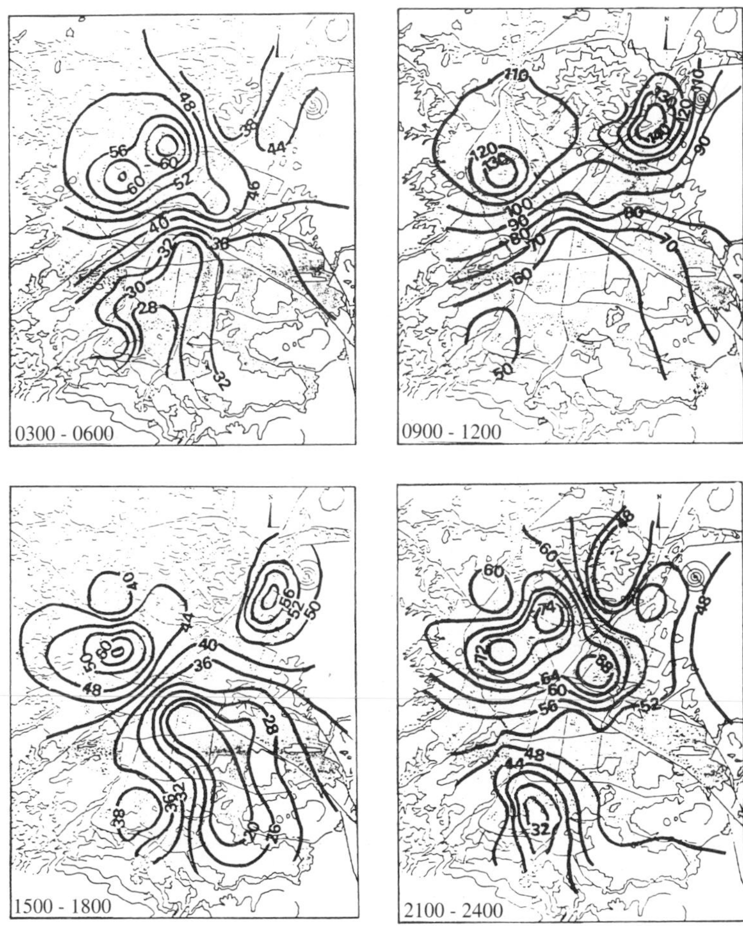

Figure 11: Number of exceedences per month to the Mexican air quality standard for ozone recorded at the University of Mexico monitoring station (1987-1989)

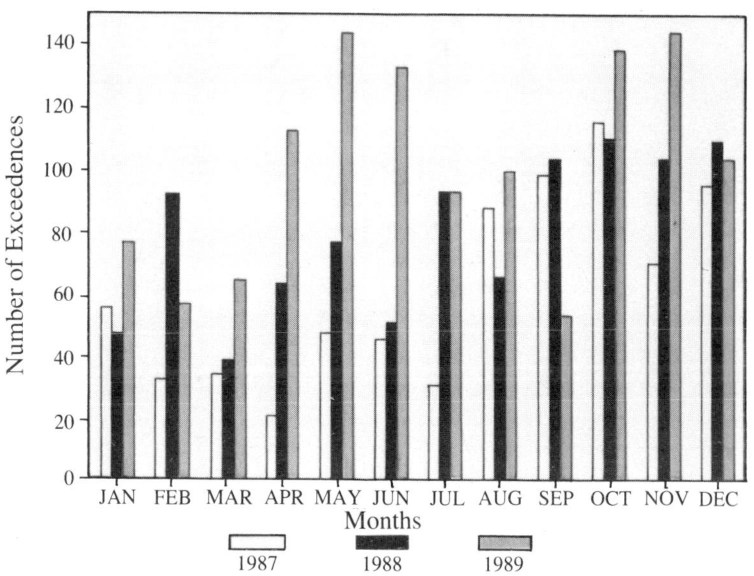

Figure 12: Annual cycle of sulphur dioxide concentration at Tlalnepantla and University of Mexico monitoring stations from monthly means (1987-1988)

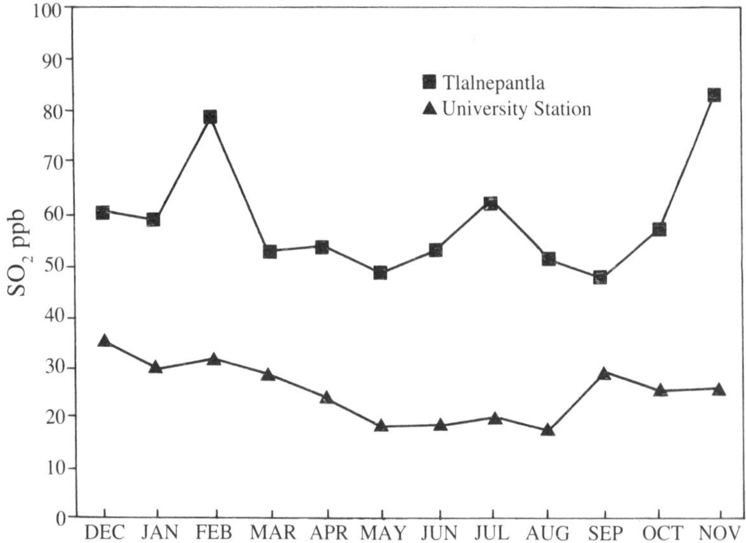

Figure 13: Quarterly average of ozone hourly maximum concentrations for weekdays, Saturdays and Sundays at the University of Mexico monitoring station during 1987-1989)

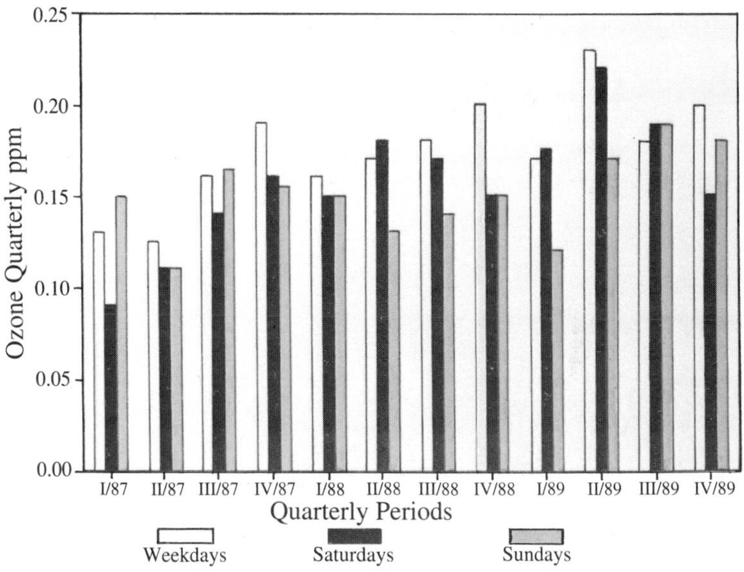

Figure 14: Weekday and weekend average sulphur dioxide concentrations at Tlalnepantla and University of Mexico monitoring stations during December 1987

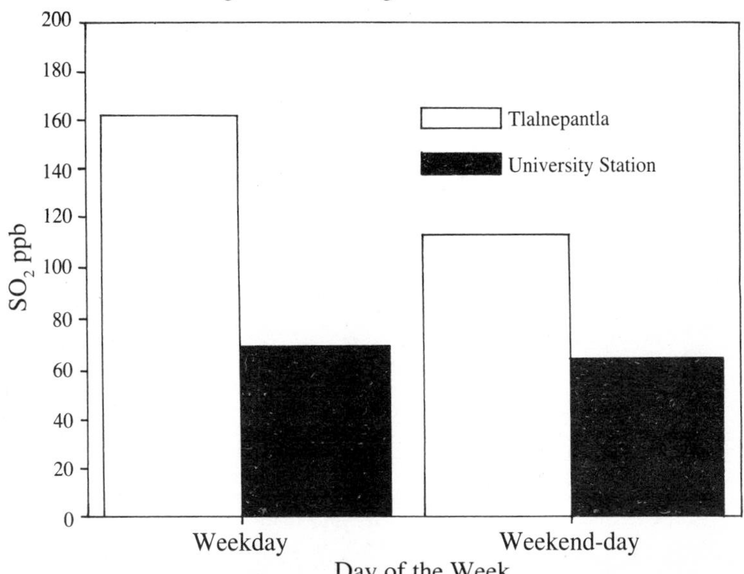

Figure 15: Number of exceedences per hour of the year to the Mexican air quality standard for ozone recorded at the University station during 1987 through 1989

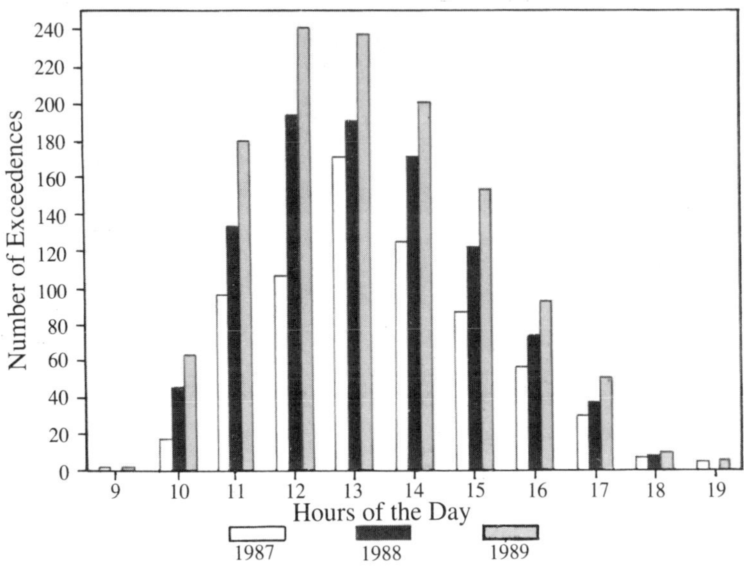

Figure 16: Weekday mean hourly SO_2 concentrations at Tlalnepantla and University of Mexico monitoring stations during December 1987

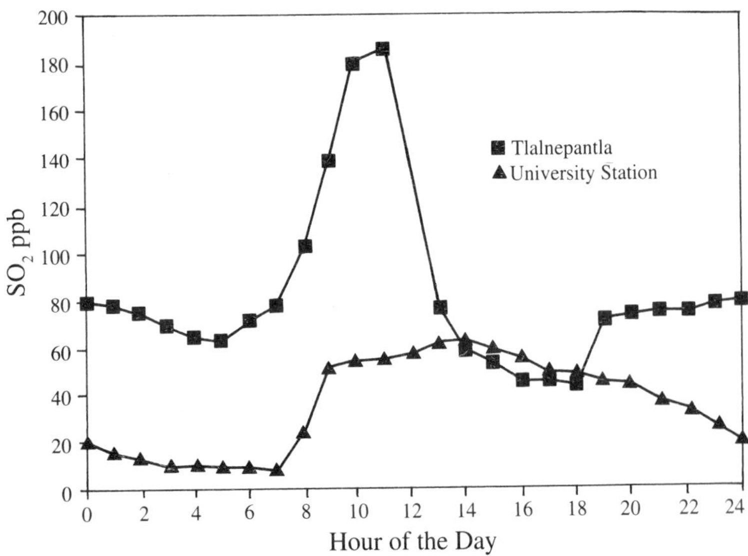

Figure 17: Weekend mean hourly SO_2 concentrations at Tlalnepantla and University of Mexico monitoring stations during December 1987

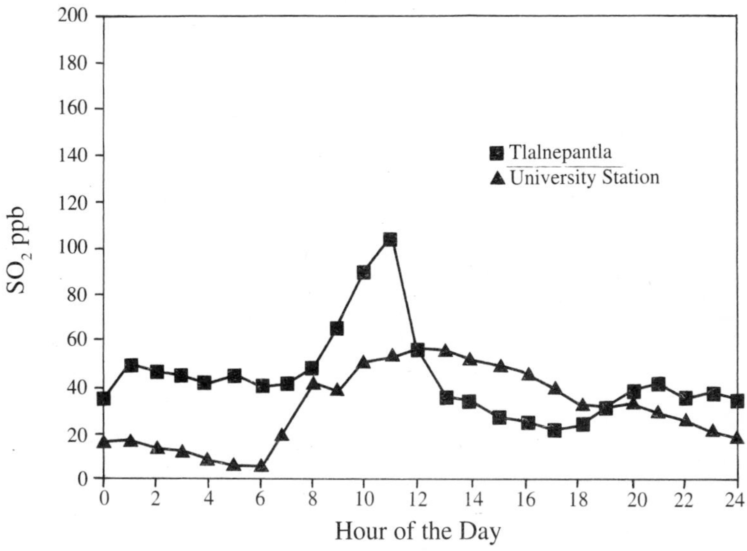

Figure 18: Sulphur dioxide air quality trend in the 95% confidence interval about quarterly mean at the University of Mexico monitoring station (December - January - February, 1986 through 1989)

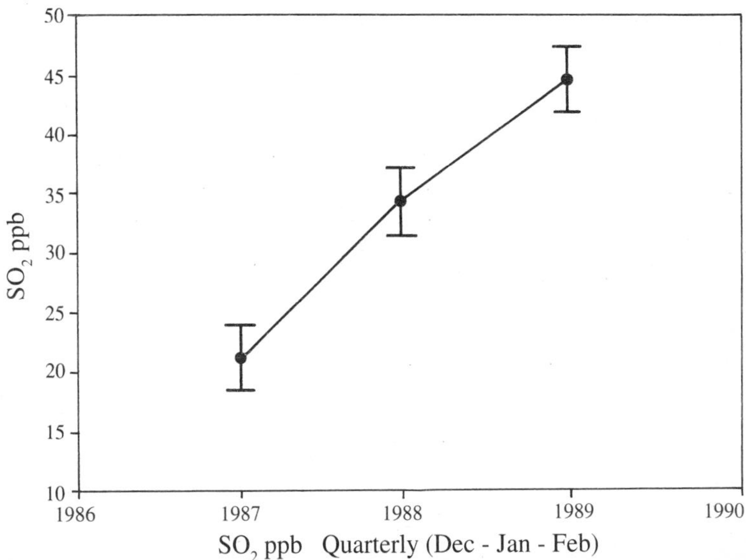

THE NETHERLANDS

1 INTRODUCTION

1.1 Topography, Climate, Population

The Netherlands, one of the EEC countries, is situated on the North Sea. It lies on the delta of three major European rivers, the Rhine, the Meuse and the Scheldt. The special feature of The Netherlands is that more than half of its land mass is no higher than one metre above sea-level. About 27 per cent of this land mass lies below sea level. It is from this fact that the country's name is derived: the low lands or Netherlands.

The Netherlands has a temperate maritime climate with an average temperature in January of 2 degrees Centigrade and an average temperature in July of 17 degrees Centigrade.

In 1989 the population of The Netherlands was nearly 15 million; that is 436 inhabitants per sq. km, making it one of the most densely populated countries in the world. In addition there are almost 6 million automobiles. Energy consumption is high and there is a great deal of industry and livestock: in 1989 there were nearly 5 million beef and dairy cattle, 14 million pigs and 90 million chickens (figures from The Netherlands Central Bureau of Statistics).

Compared to other countries The Netherlands has few natural areas. In most cases the terrestrial systems (such as forests and heathlands) are very sensitive to environmental influences. Very great value is attached to those natural areas which do exist. Partly as a consequence a great deal of attention is paid to the environment in The Netherlands.

Due to the circumstances described above, such as its geography and high population density, The Netherlands was confronted with environmental problems at a very early stage. Air pollution is one of those problems.

1.2 Recent Developments

A great deal has happened in the environmental area during the past few years in The Netherlands, and the topic of environment, including air pollution, has been given a high spot on the political agenda. The accompanying developments have also been of great importance for policy pertaining to air pollution.

The *National Environmental Policy Plan* (NEPP) was published in May 1989. This document contains the medium- to long-term strategy for environmental policy, including a firm action programme for 1990-1994. To emphasize the need for rigorous action to protect the environment, the plan is sub-titled "To Choose or to Lose". Some of the financial aspects proved such a problem to Parliament that the government was brought down.

The NEPP is aimed at "sustainable development". This strategy is based largely on the recommendations of the World Commission for Environment and Development, chaired by Norwegian Prime Minister Mrs Gro Harlem Brundtland, which published the report *Our Common Future* in 1987. The Commission defined "sustainable development" as "development that meets the needs of the present generation without compromising the ability of future generations to meet their own needs".

A great deal of scientific data were needed to elaborate this basic principle. The National Institute of Public Health and Environmental Protection was therefore commissioned to carry out an integrated environmental survey for the long term (1985-2010), which was published under the name "Concern for Tomorrow". Environmental problems were reviewed. Potential developments up to the year 2010 were examined, as were the effects of existing environmental policy. Five scale levels were distinguished: local (the living and working environment), regional (the landscape), fluvial (river basins and coastal waters), continental (atmospheric and marine currents) and global (higher layers of the atmosphere). Each level has its "own" problems, but all are interrelated.

This was the first time that such a complete scientific overview of the environment in The Netherlands had been produced, and it shocked the nation. The conclusion was that the Dutch environment is in poor condition and that long-term objectives and frames of reference are needed for the environment. A very drastic reduction in emissions of numerous substances is needed (in the order of 70-90 per cent). The NEPP is intended as a response to these facts.

How will the NEPP turn this disastrous development around? To begin with, the following well-known premises will be adhered to in initiating and assessing new developments:

- the stand still principle;
- abatement at source: remove causes rather than ameliorate effects;

these source-oriented measures are determined on the basis of effect-oriented norms;

- polluter pays principle;
- application of best practical means in abating pollution (preventing unnecessary pollution);
- carefully controlled waste disposal;
- internalization: motivating people to good environmental behaviour.

The core of the new approach which must lay the basis for sustainable development is:

- closing substance cycles (including product life-cycle management): the chain from raw material via production process to product and waste must contain as few "leaks" as possible which cause energy and raw material losses and environmental pollution;
- conserving energy, together with improving the efficiency and utilization of renewable energy sources (solar, wind and water power);
- promoting the quality of production processes and products.

In addition to controlling detrimental environmental effects as such, another goal enunciated in the NEPP is to reduce the chances of negative effects occurring (risks). The standards being established to that end will take into account the health of people, environmental functions and nature values.

For each scale level, the NEPP states the most important objectives to be realized by the year 2000 for the purpose of sustainable development. In the shorter term, for the years 1990-1994, it states concrete actions necessary to attain these objectives.

Environmental policy is divided into a number of themes:

- Climate change
- Acidification
- Eutrophication
- Dispersion of environmentally hazardous substances
- Disposal of waste
- Nuisance (such as noise and odour)
- Dehydration
- Squandering.

Most of the themes are not confined to a single environmental compartment. An integrated approach is needed.

In order to streamline implementation of the NEPP as much as possible, the approach of source-oriented policy is primarily group-related, directed at "target groups". This term refers to clusters of pollution sources and groups which play an important social role in achieving environmental targets. Objectives have been formulated for each target group, each of which has been closely consulted on the development and implementation of policy. The following target groups have been distinguished:

- Agriculture
- Traffic and transport
- Industry, chemical industry and other industrial sectors
- Energy sector
- Refineries
- Building trade
- Consumers and retail trade
- Waste collection and disposal services.

The Government policy statement drawn up by the new Government in November 1989, stated that environmental policy had to be made more stringent in a number of areas to achieve the sustainable development objectives of the NEPP as rapidly as possible. It listed the points on which intensification of environmental policy was required:

- reducing carbon dioxide emissions;
- stepping up policy on acidification;
- stepping up policy for the conservation and development of nature;
- managing entire waste chains, also viewed in relation to product policy;
- cleaning up soil and underwater soil;
- energy conservation policy.

The intensification on these points does not entail any strategic reversal relative to the *National Environmental Policy Plan*, but it does mean an accelerated introduction of measures so that the long-term objectives needed for sustainable development are likely to be achieved earlier. The NEPP-Plus, which was issued in June 1990, indicates which aspects of policy are being highlighted and the additional measures this will require in relation to the NEPP.

The NEPP-Plus together with the NEPP provide the main features of the environmental policy to be pursued during the 1990s - the strategy, the objectives and the measures to be taken in the period 1990-1994 in order to bring sustainable development within reach in The Netherlands.

1.3 Specific National Problems

1.3.1 Climate Change

Man-made emissions of gases such as carbon dioxide, methane, chlorofluorocarbons and nitrous oxide, which have the ability to absorb the heat of the sun, give rise to what is called the greenhouse effect. As the concentration of these gases increases in the atmosphere, the potential to absorb solar heat increases. As a consequence it is likely that there will be intensified global warming. Such warming may result in sea level rise, climatic extremes like storm surges, cyclones and typhoons, and a movement of agricultural zones. Sea level rise would put all low-lying countries, including The Netherlands, at risk. Cyclones will increase the need for emergency relief worldwide. As agricultural zones and ecosystems will not be able to adapt as quickly to the movement of climatic zones, there will be severe negative impacts on our ecosystems and possibly on food production. Furthermore, change in local weather patterns will force people to change their lifestyles and habits.

For all these reasons and for reasons of intergenerational and international equity - and of course to give direction to the basic principle of sustainable development - The Netherlands has put climate change high on the national political agenda.

Climate policy in The Netherlands has been developed through the combined efforts of several ministries and is supported and reinforced by the National Research Programme sponsored by seven Ministries. Through this integrated approach, national greenhouse gas emission targets have been established. According to these targets The Netherlands has to reduce its greenhouse gas emissions by two per cent of projected growth every year and should, therefore, stabilize at 1989-90 levels by 1994-1995 and should decrease by three to five per cent by the year 2000 (Table 1).

Table 1

Target: Stabilisation of CO_2 emissions in 1994-1995 · Reduction of CO_2 emissions by 3-5% in 2000 (with respect to 1989/1990 emission levels)	
1. Energy sector:	75% of the target
2. Transport sector:	15% of the target
3. Waste sector:	10% of the target

In order to achieve this the Government is aiming to double the expected energy efficiency increase of one per cent to more than two per cent annually through improvements in building codes, insulation, cogeneration, and shifts to renewable energy sources such as wind power and solar energy. The transport sector will stabilize carbon dioxide emissions by the year 1994-1995 at 1989 levels through a three track approach of attacking pollution:

- at the source, e.g. to limit air pollution per car;
- by reducing car use; and
- through stricter enforcement of restrictive measures in urban areas such as parking restrictions, etc.

The waste sector will ensure that by the year 2000 55 per cent of the projected waste will be re-used and 10 per cent will be prevented. The forestry sector will plant 25 000 hectares by the year 2000. Through a judicious combination of subsidies and taxes, public information campaigns and consumer education, consumers and industries will be invited to change their own behaviour and become more "green". At an international level we are actively cooperating in the process of building up research and policy on the issue of climate change in various fora such as the Intergovernmental Panel on Climate Change established by UNEP and WMO.

1.3.2 Acidification

The natural environment of The Netherlands is being harmed by acidification on a large scale. Only half of Dutch forests remain vital (partly due to acidification); most of the heathland has been invaded by grass and the majority of the fens have undergone damage from acidification or eutrophication. In addition, forest ecosystems in a number of places are becoming saturated with nitrogen, with as a consequence eutrophication of surface and groundwater, impoverishment of forest soils and a sharp increase in nitrate concentrations in groundwater. The aluminium concentration in groundwater is also rising to such an extent that the harmful effects on humans and plants may increase.

In this context, the NEPP states as an objective that environmental quality must be improved so that important ecosystems can continue to exist without drastic measures. The environmental quality aimed for is a prerequisite for recovery of vital forests in Europe.

The Dutch policy for the abatement of acidifying air pollutants is set out in "The Netherlands Acidification Abatement Plan" (NAAP). The goal is to reduce the effects of air pollution to a negligible level in the long term. (During the 1980s acid deposition in The Netherlands varied between 5800 acid equivalents per ha per year in 1980 and 4500 equivalents in 1988.) In order to achieve the levels at which all detrimental effects are prevented, drastic measures are needed in The Netherlands and Europe. These levels cannot be met until some time in the next century. They will therefore be adhered to as target values. A less far-reaching goal - namely, prevention of the most serious damage - is being aimed for as the objective to be achieved in the foreseeable future (2010). A schedule has been set out, with interim objectives for 1994 and 2000:

Table 2: Objectives of Acidification Policy

	1994	*2000*	*Long term (2010)*	*Target value*
Acid deposition [eq H^+/ha/y]	4000	2400	1400[1]	400
ozone [$\mu g(O_3)/m^3$]				
*max. 1 [h] average	—	240[2]	240	120
*8 [h] average	—	160[3]	160	
*growing season average	—	100	100	50

[1]based on current knowledge; the uncertainty margin is 30-40%.
[2]maximum number of exceedances per year: 2.
[3]maximum number of exceedances per year: 5.

In order to achieve the 2010 objectives, emissions of ammonia, nitrogen oxides, sulphur dioxide and volatile organic compounds, must be reduced by 80-90 per cent relative to 1980 in The Netherlands as well as abroad. Partly based on expectations regarding reductions in emissions of various compounds in other countries, the following reductions are needed in The Netherlands to reach the objectives for 1994 and 2000:

Table 3: Emission Reductions

	1994 NEPP	*2000 NEPP*	*2000 NEPP+*
NH_3	30%	70%	70%
NO_X	20%	50%	55%
SO_2	60%	80%	85%
VOC	30%	60%	60%

The NAAP describes the measures to be taken to achieve these reductions.

The measures for abating VOC and ammonia emissions are elaborated further in the reports "Project Hydrocarbons 2000", and "Plan of Approach: Limiting Agricultural Ammonia Emissions". Recently (June 1990) measures were slightly intensified resulting in an acceleration by two to three years of the Dutch efforts to reach the "2000" target load of 2400 (eq.H^+/ha/y).

VOC emission abatement is aimed mainly at preventing emissions by lowering the VOC content of products and/or switching to low-emission (production) techniques. Measures have been agreed upon by government and industry on a sector-by-sector basis. VOC sources that could not be eliminated by emission prevention will have to implement add-on control technology. See also section 2.8.

Measures for reducing agricultural ammonia emissions include:

- attuning the N-content of feedstuffs to animal needs;
- stimulating minerals accounting; registration system per farm;
- emission standards and zoning for animal housing; emission standards for manure treatment/processing plants;
- covering manure storage;
- optimization of (moment of) manure application and mandatory use of low-emission spreading techniques.

Details relating to measures to abate emissions of nitrogen oxides and sulphur dioxide are given in sections 2.3, 2.4, 2.5 and 4.2.

1.3.3 Dispersion of Environmentally Dangerous Compounds

One of the NEPP objectives aimed at sustainable development is the reduction to an acceptable or, if possible, to a negligible level of the risks posed to humans and the environment by individual or groups of substances.

Through dispersion, large parts of the environment in The Netherlands are subject to temporary (e.g. smog episodes) or prolonged exposure to concentrations of substances that are damaging (toxic, carcinogenic) to organisms and can disrupt ecosystems. Periods of sharply increased air pollution (smog) can occur due to meteorological conditions. Under unfavourable circumstances, photochemical air pollution in the summer can lead to ozone concentrations in The Netherlands as high as 400 $\mu g/m^3$ as an hourly average. During unfavourable weather conditions in the winter, sulphur dioxide, aerosols and nitrogen oxides concentrations of respectively 500, 400 and 200 $\mu g/m^3$ are measured. The high concentrations are caused to a significant extent by air pollution transported from other parts of Europe.

The Netherlands has a response system - which is still provisional - for both summer and winter smog; the system proceeds from three progressively more serious smog phases and defines the measures which must be taken in each.

The approach to environmentally dangerous substances in the Netherlands is characterized by systematic establishment of priorities based on an integral risk assessment, i.e. taking into account multi-media distribution and risk evaluation for each of the environmental compartments.

A framework for risk management has been developed in which the various kinds of environmental risks have been dealt with, as much as possible, in a similar way. An upper limit for the risks is indicated above which the risk of effects on humans and the environment is considered unacceptable, and a lower limit below which the risk is considered negligible (Table 4).

Table 4: Framework for Risk Management in Dutch Environmental Policy

		Individual cancer risk per substance (mortality, man)	*Individual risk per substance (effects with threshold levels, man)*	*Collective risk per substance (function of ecosystem)*
unnacceptable risk				
	max. acceptable level	10^{-6}/year	"no-effect-concentration" (taking into account sensitive groups)	concentration at which 95% of the species in an ecosystem are protected
risk reduction desirable				
	negligible level (target value)	10^{-8}/year	1% of upper limit	1% of upper limit
negligible risks				

The substances posing the highest risks to man and/or the environment are designated "priority substances "(ca. 50 substances, see Table 5).

Levels of several air pollutants currently exceed the upper limit (e.g. ozone, PACs, fluorides, cadmium, particulate matter).

Environmental standards are usually developed for the priority substances on the basis of all relevant information, collected in a so-called "basis document" (emission sources, dispersion, monitoring methods, effects, abatement techniques, control costs) and all environmental compartments (air, water and soil) and their interrelationships are considered. In the basis document "no-effect levels" will be indicated for human as well as ecosystem exposure, about which the National Health Council will provide an advisory report. This "no-effect-level" is related to the upper limit of risk. The lower limit of risk is related to the so-called "target value". In principle, standards are set in the range between the target value and the maximum acceptable level; they are the result of trade-offs among the risk that detrimental effects for humans and the environment will occur, social and economic aspects and technical possibilities (see section 2.7).

In addition to the list of priority substances there is also a list of "black substances", that have the potential to cause serious effects for humans and the environment. This list is intended for use by provincial and municipal authorities in making permitting decisions. For substances appearing on this list maximum reduction is required, in principle regardless of costs.

Table 5: Priority Substances

1. *Metals and metalloids* Arsenic Cadmium Chromium (VI) Copper Mercury Lead Zinc 2. *Organic compounds* a. Non-halogenated mineral oil and (gaseous) hydrocarbons Acroleine Acrylonitrile Benzene Ethylene Phenol(s) Phthalates Methanal (formaldehyde) Methylbenzene (toluene) Methyloxirane (propylene oxide) Oxirane (ethylene oxide) Polycyclic aromatic hydrocarbons Styrene b. Halogenated aromatics Chloroanilines Chlorobenzenes Chlorophenols Dioxins PCBs and PCTs	c. Other halogenated compounds Chlorofluorocarbons 1, 2-dichloroethane Dichloromethane Hexachlorocyclohexane Methylbromide Tetrachloroethylene Tetrachloromethane 1, 1, 1-trichloroethane Trichloroethylene Trichloromethane Vinylchloride 3. *Other substances* Asbestos Fluorides Carbon monoxide Ozone Particulates (coarse and fine) Hydrogen sulphide 4. *Acidifying and fertilizing substances* Ammonia Phosphates Nitrate Nitrogen oxides Sulphur dioxide

1.3.4 Disruption, Odour

Policies relating to "disruption" involve reaching and maintaining good environmental quality with respect to aspects such as noise and odour. The objective presented in the NEPP in this connection is that environmental quality at the local and regional level must be such in 2010 that only negligible health risks are run in the direct ambient environment and no serious nuisance is experienced; no one has to restrict himself excessively in residential choice, behaviour or activities.

Approximately 20 per cent of the Dutch population experiences nuisance from odour, nine per cent of which is caused by industrial sources, seven per cent by traffic and four per cent by agriculture. The NEPP sets as a goal a reduction in the percentage of the population experiencing nuisance to 12 per cent in 2000 and 7.5 per cent in 2010. This goal must be attained through reducing emissions and zoning new residential construction.

Use is being made of an odour concentration standard for industry and standardized measures have been elaborated for a number of industrial sectors. Distance guidelines apply to agriculture and emissions of odour arising from the application of manure to the land for fertilization purposes will be limited through working the manure under the surface or injecting it. There are no measures available for limiting odour caused by traffic; attempts will be made to regulate traffic streams optimally and to include odour emissions in the introduction of new "low-emission" engines.

Instruments such as zoning are also being utilized in The Netherlands to ensure that a good living environment can be attained over the longer term.

2 DEVELOPMENT OF AIR POLLUTION CONTROLS AND LEGISLATION

2.1 Principles and Philosophy

The principles and philosophy underlying air pollution control policies are essentially those based on "sustainable development" which were described in section 1.2 on the NEPP and NEPP-Plus.

2.2 Legislation on Air Pollution and Other Instruments

There are two laws relating to air pollution in force in The Netherlands: the *Nuisance Act*, dating from 1875 (revised 1952 and 1981) and the *Air Pollution Act*, dating from 1970 (revised 1986). The *General Environmental Provisions Act*, which is currently still largely a procedural law, is also increasingly important.

In order to promote integral environmental policy, existing comparable regulations in the various sectoral acts are, where possible, being brought into line in the *General Environmental Provisions Act 1979*. Procedures for permitting, advisory procedures and financial provisions, for example, have already been codified in the Act. The regulation on environmental impact assessment is also an important part of this Act.

The *Nuisance Act* is directed at protecting the areas surrounding installations from danger, damage or nuisance. The installations covered by the Act are defined by *General Administrative Order*. Local authority permits are required for the operation of these installations. Central government can set general rules for categories of installations, and has done so in a number of cases. Only a small percentage of total air pollutant emissions (about 10-15 per cent) are regulated by the *Nuisance Act*. It relates primarily to small installations.

The *Air Pollution Act* is aimed at preventing and controlling air pollution. The Act covers not only stationary sources of pollution, but also other sources ("apparatus" such as spray cans, cars and motorcycles, as well as polluting activities). Rules on ambient air quality, fuel quality, products and installations can be set by *General Administrative Order* based on the Act.

No installation belonging to a category specified on the basis of the Act may be set up or operated without a permit issued by the provincial authority. Where emission standards have been formulated, permits must be subject to compliance with these standards. So far, emission standards have been set for combustion plants and nitric acid plants.

Further details of measures based on the *Air Pollution Act* are given in sections 2.3 - 2.7.

The *General Environmental Provisions Act* provides several financial instruments which may be used for the implementation of environmental policy. Central government can impose levies and can also offer financial aid. There are two types of levies:

- *Revenue-raising levies:* these serve to finance (some of) the Government's expenditure on environmental policy. Levies have been imposed on fuels.
- *Regulatory levies:* the main purpose of these levies is to influence consumer conduct. There is a regulatory levy on leaded petrol.

The Netherlands adheres to the principle that "the polluter pays". However where investments to limit or reduce pollution lead to excessive costs for the polluter, the central government may compensate these costs under certain circumstances. There is also a fund from which non-attributable damage caused by air pollution can be compensated under certain circumstances.

2.3 Mobile Sources

2.3.1 Cars, Trucks

As far as mobile sources are concerned, emission standards are in agreement with the relevant Directives of the European Communities and regulations of the UN Economic Commission for Europe (ECE).

Table 6: Emission Standards for Cars (g/ECE Test Cycle)

	New			
Cylinder vol.	*Entry into force*	*CO*	*$HC+NO_X$*	*NO_X*
> 2000 cm^3	1-10-1988/1989	25	6.5	3.5
1400-2000 cm^3	1-10-1991/1993	30	8	
< 1400 cm^3	a. 1-10-1990/1991	45	15	6
	b. 1-6-1992	19	5	(new types)
	31-12-1992	19	5	(all new registrations)

In addition to these internationally agreed standards, there are also legal emission standards in The Netherlands for cars in use (4.5 per cent vol CO (idling)). A modification is being prepared.

The standards contained in the first phase of an EEC emission reduction programme for trucks have been introduced by means of *General Administrative Order.*

2.3.2 Fiscal Measures to Stimulate the Sale of "Clean Cars" and Unleaded Gasoline

To stimulate sales of "clean cars", the once-off (purchase) tax on new cars complying with US-standards is reduced by Dfl. 1700,- and that on new cars complying with the new EEC standards (see Table 6) by Dfl. 850,-. These measures are very successful. By July 1990 the share in total sales of new cars complying with US-standards was about 75 per cent. This tax programme will remain in force until late 1992, when the new EEC standards enter into force.

To stimulate the availability and sales of unleaded gasoline, The Netherlands has fiscal measures set up in such a way that unleaded gasoline enjoys a price advantage at the pump. As a result, unleaded gasoline's share in total sales was about 50 per cent by July 1990.

2.4 Fuel Quality Standards

The 1974 *General Administrative Order* on the sulphur content of fuels regulates the sulphur content of all fuels on a nationwide basis. Since 1974 quality standards have been tightened on a step-by-step basis.

Table 7: Fuel Quality Standards

Fuel oil		*Solid fuel*		*Gasoline*
gasoil	0.2% S	hard coals	1.2% S	0.15 g Pb/1
light	0.7% S	lignite	1.2% S	5% vol
medium/heavy	1.0% S			benzene

Unleaded super gasoline is available on a voluntary basis. Regular gasoline is unleaded.

2.5 Emission Standards: Industrial Plant

All industrial plants causing air pollution are required to have a permit, either under the *Air Pollution Act* for the large ones or under the *Nuisance Act* for the small ones. A permit sets limits on permissible emissions for individual plants.

Emission standards for combustion installations have been established on a nationwide base for new and existing plants. The relevant *General Administrative Order* under the *Air Pollution Act* for the large industries entered into force in 1987. A similar *General Administrative Order* under the *Nuisance Act* for the smaller industries entered into force in August 1990.

Standards for sulphur dioxide and nitrogen oxides are given for both new and existing plants, and are differentiated for coal, oil and gaseous fuels (see Table 8). Existing plants are plants for which a permit was granted before 29 May 1987. Other plants are considered as new.

Table 8: Emission Standards for Combustion Installations

	SO_2 (mg/m^3)	NO_X (mg/m^3)	*Particulates* (mg/m^3)
New > 300 MW_{th}			
Coal	400[1]	650/400[2]	50-(20)[3]
Oil	400[1]	450/300[2]	—
Gas:			
refinery gas	35	350/200[2]	—
natural gas	—	350/200[2]	—
oxygas	35	350/200[2]	20
blast furnace gas	200	350/200[2]	20
coke oven gas	800	350/200[2]	20
New < 300 MW_{th}			
Coal	700	650/500[2]	50-(20)[3]
Oil	1700	450/300[2]	—
Gas	idem	300 MW_{th}	—
Existing ≥ 300 MW_{th}			
Coal	400[1]	1000-(800)[3]	—
Oil	400[1]	700-(450)[3]	—
Gas	idem new ≥	500-(350)[3]	idem new
Existing < 300 MW_{th}			
Coal, max. S-content	1.2%	—	—
Oil	1700	700-450	—
Gas	idem new	500-350	idem new

[1]At least 85% desulphurization.
[2]Installations for which permit was granted after 01-08-88.
[3]Permitting authority may set more stringent standards but not below the value in brackets (standards in force as of 01-01-89).

There are special nitrogen oxides standards for gas turbines and stationary engines. Special sulphur dioxide standards have been set for refinery complexes as a whole. Refineries have to comply with a standard of 2500 mg SO_2/m^3 for combustion emission standards. From 1 January 1991 and 1 January 1996 respectively, the standard is being decreased to 2000 and 1500 mg SO_2/m^3 (including process emissions).

As announced in "The Netherlands Acidification Abatement Plan" (NAAP), emission standards, especially for nitrogen oxides, will be tightened in the near future. Table 9 shows the intended emission standard in general for combustion installations. To implement these standards a draft *General Administrative Order* was published for comment in 1990.

Table 9: NO_X Emission Standards in mg/m³, announced in the NAAP

Permits granted:	*before 29-05-87*	*after 01-01-92*	*after 01-01-94*
solid fuel	650	200	100
liquid fuel	400[1]/200	150	110
gaseous fuel	150	100	60

[1]Only for heavy fuel oil

The standards for power plants will be slightly different, due to an agreement between the Government, the permitting authorities and the representatives of the Dutch Electricity Generating Board (SEP). That agreement laid down the overall reduction of sulphur dioxide and nitrogen oxides emissions that power plants must reach in the year 2000. Furthermore, there are emission standards for nitrogen oxides from nitric acid plants. The relevant *General Administrative Order* entered into force in 1987.

The permitting authorities may set requirements which are more stringent than the national emission standards in a number of cases.

2.6 CFC Pollution Control and Legislation

Since the 1970s The Netherlands has been promoting national and international action to protect the ozone layer. Within the UNEP framework, it was a member of the Coordinating Committee on the Ozone Layer since its establishment in 1977. It played an active role in the preparation of the Vienna Convention on the Protection of the Ozone layer and subsequently the *Montreal Protocol on Substances that Deplete the Ozone Layer.* Recently, during the second meeting of parties to the Montreal Protocol in June 1990, The Netherlands was nominated as a member of the Executive Committee in charge of the interim Financial Mechanism established to assist developing countries in implementing measures to pro-tect the ozone layer.

As a member of the EEC, The Netherlands has to harmonize its national policies with EEC policies. As a result, it has been actively promoting CFC policies within the EEC. This, for example, contributed to a Decision of the Council of Ministers to reduce the consumption of fully halogenated CFCs and halons in the EC by at least 85 per cent in 1995 and to terminate consumption not later than 1998. A proposed modification to EEC Regulations was agreed in 1990 and this will also have an impact on policy in The Netherlands.

In the meantime, The Netherlands formulated its own CFC Action Programme in June 1990. This states that it will terminate the consumption and emission of fully halogenated CFCs in 1995 or as rapidly as possible thereafter. This plan has been developed through the cooperative efforts of the CFC industry and the Government and is being implemented through a voluntary reduction scheme.

In addition, subject to the approval of the European Commission, a *General Administrative Order* is expected to be passed in 1991 requiring, *inter alia*, that all refrigerators and fire-fighting equipment be installed and maintained only by people trained to work in accordance with the existing rules on CFCs. This will also enable the Dutch Government to achieve its goal of 100 per cent recycling of used CFCs. CFCs will not be allowed for use in newly built commercial refrigeration equipment after 1992 and in insulation materials as of 1 January 1994. There will be a ban on the production of all CFCs, and products containing CFCs, as of 31 December 1997 or earlier if the European Community decides upon that. However, it is expected that the production and use of newly produced CFCs will have stopped long before then.

2.7 Ambient Air Quality Standards

Air quality standards for sulphur dioxide, suspended particulates, carbon monoxide, lead and nitrogen dioxide have been legally set (see

Table 10: Legal Air Quality Standards (Limit† Values and Guide† Values (μg/m³))

	Limit value	*Guide value*	*P = percentile*
Sulphur dioxide	75	30	50-P/24-h
	200	80	95-P/24-h
	250	100	98-P/24-h
	500		24-h
	830		h
Particulates	30		50-P/24-h
(black smoke)	75		95-P/24-h
	90		98-P/24-h
	150		24-h
Carbon monoxide*	6,000		98-P/8-h
	40,000		99.99-P/h
Nitrogen dioxide*	135	80	98-P/h
	175		99.5-P/h
		25	50-P/h
Lead	2		98-P/24-h
	0.5		year
Benzene*	10	1	year

*Temporarily less stringent standards for street canyons.
†Limit values are to be reached and/or maintained in the short run (within a few years). Guide values indicate air quality levels that are striven for in a longer time frame, but they should be maintained if already reached.

Table 10); the ambient air quality standard for benzene is expected to be in force early in 1991.

2.8 Agreements and Covenants

The preceding sections have already discussed the fact that air pollution policy in The Netherlands is implemented not only through statutory regulations, but also through means such as voluntary agreements between the Government and industry. These can be laid down in the form of covenants, a special kind of written agreement.

The joint "commitment package" drawn up for the control of VOCs (the "Hydrocarbons 2000 project") has already been mentioned. This control strategy covers a range of agreements on the measures to be taken, their date of introduction and the method of implementation. It is intended to realise a percentage reduction agreed in advance (in this case, 50-60 per cent of the 1981 emission levels by the year 2000). These firm agreements are laid down in a joint control and implementation plan drawn up by central government, industry, provincial and local authorities and other concerned parties.

A covenant which has not been mentioned yet is that on asbestos-free friction materials. In anticipation of a complete prohibition on asbestos-containing friction materials, car manufacturers and importers (of new passenger cars and light vans) have agreed to supply only vehicles with asbestos-free friction material (starting on 1 July 1989). This agreement covers about 90 per cent of the market.

A very recent form of agreement is the project started in 1990 entitled "Dutch Emission Guidelines". The purpose of this project is to put together emission guidelines to be used in permits under the *Nuisance* and *Air Pollution Acts.* In principle guidelines are being developed for all categories of firms. The project is a collaborative effort of private industry, the environmental inspectorates, municipalities, provinces and the national government.

3 IMPLEMENTATION AND ENFORCEMENT

3.1 National Enforcement

The Government policy statement of November 1989 states that environmental policy is one of the main pillars of its policy. This has consequences for the trade-offs made in all kinds of different policy fields, and also for the cooperation within the national Government. Both the NEPP and the NEPP-Plus were issued by the Minister for Housing, Physical Planning and Environment in cooperation with his colleagues for Transport and Public Works, Agriculture, Nature Management and Fisheries, and Economic Affairs.

Three different levels of government are involved in air pollution policy in The Netherlands: the national government, the provinces and the municipalities.

The national government devotes itself primarily to national regulations and to setting environmental objectives and quality standards, such as ambient air quality standards.

Implementation, however, rests largely with the provinces and municipalities. They are responsible for the air quality within their territories. The granting of permits is one of their tasks. Provincial authorities are empowered to grant permits under the *Air Pollution Act.* Municipal authorities are empowered to grant permits under the *Nuisance Act.*

The national government can supervise the way in which provinces and municipalities perform their tasks via the regional environmental inspectorates. A special branch of the inspectorate - the Environmental Legislation Enforcement Division - is charged with:

- taking care of enforcement of those laws for which the Minister for Housing, Physical Planning and Environment bears special responsibility;
- supporting lower governments in their enforcement tasks;
- carrying out investigative tasks on behalf of the Public Prosecutor.

3.2 Local/Regional Enforcement

As already mentioned above, the granting of permits is one of the tasks with which provinces and municipalities have been charged.

Provinces and local authorities are responsible for air quality within their territory. In that context they have independent regulatory powers and they draft policy plans. They also carry out measurements. The aim of these measurements is often:

- to supervise compliance with permit requirements;
- to supervise compliance with national emission standards and national or provincial ambient air quality standards;
- to investigate the scope of specific local air pollution problems.

The Royal Commissioner in a province has special authority in cases where dangerous air pollution threatens as a result of either an incident (malfunction of an installation) or special meteorological conditions. He can order the installation, apparatus or activity causing the threat to be closed, not used or ceased, respectively. In special meteorological conditions (smog), he may take measures which include the total prohibition of traffic and the complete or partial termination of industrial activities. (See also section 1.3.3).

The municipalities play an important role in carrying out the air quality decrees. They have been charged with controlling air quality on streets and maintaining the limit values. The national government helps the municipalities to carry out these tasks. This has been done via the transfer of information by means of manuals, workshops, etc, the provision of aids such as the CAR-model (Calculation of Air Pollution from Road Traffic), creation of the possibility for making environmental traffic maps and setting up financial support programmes.

Provinces and, through them, municipalities are required to report to the national government annually on whether the legal ambient air quality standards have been exceeded. If this is the case, then they are also obliged to report what measures are planned for reducing violations in the future.

3.3 Monitoring Agencies

The Netherlands has had an extensive national air quality monitoring network since 1976, which was modernized in 1986. The aim of this network, which contains approximately 100 monitoring sites, is to gain insight into air quality in The Netherlands in general, survey the transport of air pollutants, determine trends in order to evaluate the success of air pollution abatement policy and supervise compliance with air quality standards.

Most measurements are carried out automatically and concentrations of various pollutants determined continuously. The most important substances are: sulphur dioxide, nitrogen oxides, ozone, carbon monoxide, suspended particulates, lead and fluorides. In addition, several other substances are determined in short term programmes.

Transport and fluxes are monitored with remote sensing equipment and also calculated from monitoring network data and emission inventories. The deposition of various substances is also calculated from data supplied by the national air quality monitoring network.

The network has been integrated with monitoring networks for rain water and groundwater at a number of monitoring stations. In addition to quantitative measurements of components, biological effects on plants and lichens are also monitored. Integrated monitoring (air, groundwater, soil, trees) in forests also takes place, in order to determine the relationships between air pollution, (acid) deposition and effects on trees and the soil.

The air quality monitoring network has already been linked to a number of other countries in western and eastern Europe and additional links are being prepared.

3.4 Role of Private Interest Groups

Private interest groups play a role in the target group policy in the framework of sustainable development (see section 1.2 on target groups).

Also noteworthy in connection with private interest groups is the Central Council for Environmental Protection. This group advises the Government in the area of environmental policy. The Council is composed of representatives of various groups and organizations in society, each of which has its own interest in environmental policy: employee and employer organizations, the Agricultural Board, environmental organizations, the public utilities, women's groups, consumer organizations and so forth. The Council provides unsolicited as well as solicited advice. The solicited advice generally concerns proposed bills or general administrative orders, but the Council may also decide on its own initiative to offer advice on proposed policies contained in memoranda or plans which touch on issues which it considers important for environmental policy.

4 EFFECTIVENESS OF CONTROLS

4.1 Monitoring Results

Monitoring data provide a gauge of the effectiveness of air pollution control policies.

Data for the year 1989 from the National Institute of Public Health and Environmental Protection (which is responsible for national measurements, see section 3.3) indicate the following with respect to the substances for which national standards have been set: the one hour average limit value for sulphur dioxide (830 $\mu g/m^3$) was exceeded once at one monitoring station. The declining trend in sulphur dioxide concentrations which started in 1979 continued in 1989. Except for by busy traffic arteries, no violations of the limit values were measured for nitrogen oxides, carbon monoxide or black smoke. Nor were any violations of the limit value for lead measured. Measures taken by the national Government, such as the introduction of lead-free gasoline and the lowering of the lead content in premium gasoline, have resulted in a drastic decline in the concentrations of lead in the air.

4.2 Integration of Environmental Policy Relating to Air Pollution with Other Areas

It is becoming increasingly clear in The Netherlands that policies to control air pollution can only be effective if they are related to other policies, e.g. those relating to transport, energy and international initiatives. Of course, this applies to environmental policies in general and not only to those policies aimed at controlling air pollution. It was for this reason that the Government's decision on the Traffic and Transport Structure Scheme was issued simultaneously with the NEPP-Plus. The Structure Scheme chose a sustainable society as a measuring stick for traffic and transport policies. It elaborated objectives and measures for drastically reducing the traffic sector's contribution to air pollution and its energy consumption.

Objectives and measures which are significant for air pollution policy include:

- emissions of nitrogen dioxide and hydrocarbons from car traffic will be 75 per cent lower in 2010 than they were in 1986. In 1995 they will be 20 per cent lower;
- emissions of carbon dioxide will be at least 10 per cent lower in 2010 than in 1986; in 1995 they will be at their 1989/1990 level;
- a drop in the projected growth of automobility from 70 per cent to 35 per cent between 1986 and 2010;
- increasing excise duties and introducing a rush hour surcharge and tolls in order to discourage car use;
- public transport and facilities for cycling will be improved;
- strict parking standards (number of parking places per 100 employees) for firms which have good access to public transportation;
- firms with more than 50 employees are being asked to draw up a Transport Management Plan;
- freight transport by rail and water is being promoted.

The Memorandum on Energy Conservation of the Ministry of Economic Affairs was also issued at the same time as the NEPP-Plus. That Memorandum announced that energy conservation budgets are to be doubled. The Memorandum contains a start toward action programmes for conserving energy in the various industrial sectors, agriculture, the service sectors, households and the transport and traffic sectors through improving energy efficiency.

The NEPP-Plus determined that carbon dioxide is a pollutant as defined in the *Air Pollution Act.* This makes it possible to require the application of energy conservation techniques in environmental permits.

The Netherlands can make a substantial effort to limit the burden on the environment. However, the Dutch situation is such that much of the pollution originates from other countries, while much of the pollution it produces is dispersed to neighbouring countries.

Furthermore, The Netherlands is part of an international community in which factors such as international competition and constraints to trade etc. play an important role. This makes it essential that environmental measures be taken on an international scale. The Netherlands attaches a great deal of importance to this and plays an active role in international action and cooperation.

The Netherlands' position as a member of the EC is of major influence on the policy options concerning environmental issues. In a number of cases for example EC regulations do not allow for more stringent national measures.

The Netherlands is actively involved in different fora on the issue of climate change. It participates in the Intergovernmental Panel on Climate Change, established by UNEP and WMO. At a regional level it is cooperating with the EEC and the OECD to achieve some kind of common policy. In addition, The Netherlands participates in sectoral bodies such as the Tropical Forestry Action Plan and the International Energy Agency, among other reasons in order to achieve our climate objectives. It is also very much involved with the discussions within the World Bank on a global environmental facility.

The involvement of The Netherlands is at the level of joint research and monitoring, at the level of coordination and policy development and at the level of financing activities of the international community.

Furthermore The Netherlands is strongly involved in UN-ECE activities concerning acidification abatement. It is a party to the Convention on Long Range Transboundary Air Pollution and to the sulphur dioxide and nitrogen oxides Protocols under it. The Netherlands is playing an active role in the development of an ECE strategy for acidification abatement. In that respect the role of the Coordinating Centre West on Effects, established in The Netherlands should be mentioned.

5 FUTURE DEVELOPMENTS

Significant changes in the legislation relating to air pollution control may be expected during the coming years. The NEPP-Plus announced that a further expansion of the *General Environmental Provisions Act* is thought to be necessary. This Act is currently primarily a procedural law, but during the coming years it will be amended and expanded into a general framework act for environmental policy. Its name will be changed to the *Environmental Protection Act.* The purpose will be to protect all parts of the environment integrally and efficiently. The sectoral legislation will be amended where necessary. This will obviously have repercussions for the *Air Pollution Act.*

The NEPP-Plus has shifted somewhat the emphasis in the choice of policy instruments to be used in environmental protection. It has been announced that there will be more attention for regulation as a basis for the execution of policy; implementation and enforcement elements will be strengthened. There will also be increased attention for the development and application of economic incentives such as, for example, subsidies, deposit-return systems and regulatory charges.

The application of economic incentives rests on the expectation that in certain cases it will be more effective to make certain products or substances more or less expensive, than to try to regulate their production or use. A recent example is the Subsidy Programme for Cleaner Trucks and Buses which came into effect in August 1990. By keeping ahead of the European regulations The Netherlands is better able to meet the objectives of the NEPP, despite the strong growth in freight traffic.

6 REFERENCES AND SELECTIVE BIBLIOGRAPHY

National Environmental Policy Plan (NEPP), Second Chamber, session 1988-1989, 21 137, nos. 1-2.

World Commission on Environment and Development (Brundtland Commission), *Our Common Future.* UNEP, 1987.

National Institute of Public Health and Environmental Protection, Samson H D. Tjeenk Willink, *Concern for Tomorrow.* Alphen aan den Rijn, 1988.

The Netherlands *National Environmental Policy Plan Plus,* Second Chamber, session 1989-1990, 21 137, no. 20.

National Institute of Public Health and Environmental Protection, Energy Study Center, Climate and Energy: *The Feasibility of Controlling Carbon Dioxide Emissions.* The Netherlands, 1989.

The Climate Secretariat, Ministry of Housing, Physical Planning and Environment, *The Noordwijk Report.* The Netherlands, 1990.

Ministry of Housing, Physical Planning and Environment, *CFC Action Programme.* The Netherlands, 1990.

The Climate Secretariat, Ministry of Housing, Physical Planning and Environment, *The Netherlands' Policy on Climate Change.* The Netherlands, 1990.

The Netherlands Acidification Abatement Plan, Second Chamber, session 1988-1989, 18 225, no. 31.

Control Strategy for Emissions of Volatile Organic Compounds (Project Hydrocarbons 2000). Ministry of Housing, Physical Planning and Environment, 1989.

Air Pollution Act, Bulletin of Acts, Orders and Decrees 1981, no. 411.

Nuisance Act, Bulletin of Acts, Orders and Decrees 1981, no. 410.

General Environmental Provisions Act 1979, Bulletin of Acts, Orders and Decrees 1979, no. 442.

NEW ZEALAND

1 INTRODUCTION

1.1 Topography, Climate, Population

New Zealand is a Sovereign nation located about 1600 km off the south east coast of Australia. It has a total area of 270 000 sq. km. New Zealand comprises two main islands - North Island and South Island - and a number of smaller ones. It has a fairly mountainous terrain: the Southern Alps extend the entire length of South Island; North Island has several active volcanoes and an area around the centre is noted for its hot springs and geysers.

New Zealand's climate is fairly temperate with average temperatures ranging from 9 degrees C on South Island to 15 degrees C on North Island.

New Zealand has a population of around 3.3 million.

A significant proportion of New Zealand is given over to agriculture. It is also self-sufficient in low sulphur coal and has reserves of natural gas plus considerable access to hydro-electricity and geothermal energy. Due to its major imports of crude oil and petroleum products, New Zealand is a net importer of energy; gasoline prices are typical of many European countries with high excise taxes.

The Government places a high priority on the use of indigenous fuels such as coal, wood, natural gas, hydro and geothermal energy in preference to petroleum based products. There would need to be strong justification on air pollution grounds if coal or wood were to be replaced by oil fuel. Natural gas is not available on South Island.

1.2 Specific National Problems

With an average population density of about 12 persons per sq. km and mountainous terrain (more than 75 per cent of the land mass is over 200 m above sea level), there should be no significant air pollution problems. Good ventilating winds are common and the largest city, Auckland, has a population of less than one million. Consequently, photochemical pollution is also not a real problem.

New Zealand does, however, have a major paper industry as well as steel, aluminium and petrochemicals manufacturing. Also, with large sheep, dairy and timber industries there is plenty of potential for air pollution from rendering works, tanneries, milk and cheese processing and timber mills.

Christchurch, a city of about 250 000 people, is located in an air basin that is subject to a very high proportion of atmospheric temperature inversions. In the winter, wood and coal burning for domestic heating has resulted in heavy air pollution.

2 DEVELOPMENT OF AIR POLLUTION CONTROLS AND LEGISLATION

2.1 Clean Air Philosophy

The concept of "best practicable means" has been used as the basis for air pollution control. This is supplemented by regulations for control of smoke emissions. Ambient air quality is considered acceptable if maximum levels are below World Health Organization goals or other accepted criteria. Where no better data exist or are available, it is common practice to require that the maximum ground level concentrations for any emitted pollutant should not exceed one-thirtieth of the 8-hour occupational health threshold limit value (TLV) or one-fortieth of the TLV for toxic substances.

2.2 Clean Air Legislation

The *Clean Air Act 1972*, and its amendments of 1982 and 1986, contain the principle powers for control of air pollution. They provide wide powers including promulgation of regulations for control of pollution from stationary and mobile sources and for the declaration of clean air zones. The division of responsibilities between national and local authorities is set out in a Schedule to the Act.

2.2.1 Industrial Premises

All industrial plant is subject to the Act; those with a significant potential to pollute are contained in a Schedule to the Act and require a license from the Department of Health.

The British *Memorandum on Chimney Heights* is used to determine stack height for straightforward sites. For large processes and complex locations, height is calculated based on dispersion parameters.

Considerable emphasis is placed on fuel efficiency for industrial fuel-burning equipment and this has a beneficial impact on restricting smoke and soot emissions from industrial sources.

Table 1: Recommended Rates of Emission

Pollutant	*Standard applied to*	*Standard (or guideline)*	*Notes*
Smoke	Stationary sources	20% obscuration	Clean Air Zones
	Stationary sources	40% obscuration	Elsewhere
	Motor vehicles	40% obscuration for 5 seconds	
Solid particles (non toxic)	Small boilers, asphalt plants, older kilns	0.5 g/cu.m	non sensitive areas, or coarse particles
	Cement kilns, processes emitting dust 50% less than 10 micron	0.25 g/cu.m	
	Processes emitting very fine dusts, large combusting sources	0.125 g/cu.m	iron oxide fumes from oxygen lancing
Sulphur dioxide	existing processes	450 μg/cu.m	max glc
	New processes (Guideline)	170 μg/cu.m	max glc
Sulphur trioxide	existing H_2SO_4 manufacture	10 g/cu.m	usual licence
	new plants	0.05 g/cu.m	conditions
Oxides of Nitrogen	gas fired power station		Individual
	coal fired power station	(no set guideline)	Negotiation
Fluorine	existing phosphate rock acidulation Den Chimney	0.1 g/cu.m	0.25 kg/hr mass emission limit may apply in sensitive areas
Lead	Existing plant	0.025 g/cu.m	
	New plant	0.01 g/cu.m	

NOTE: Regulations under the *Clean Air Act* have been issued for smoke control only. "Standards" for all other pollutants represent current "best practicable means" possible, or the result of negotiations between the Air Pollution Control Officer and the industry directly concerned. Therefore these requirements may vary with time, age of plant, technology, availability or locality.

2.2.2 Mobile Sources

New Zealand has about 1.8 million motor vehicles and there are effectively no regulations on exhaust emissions. In 1986 lead alkyl levels in petrol were limited to a maximum of 0.45 g/l by agreement with the industry. Unleaded petrol (91 RON) was introduced in 1987. Use of alternative fuels, such as liquid petroleum gas (LPG) and compressed natural gas (CNG) is encouraged.

Sulphur content of fuel oils is limited by agreement with suppliers to 3.5 per cent maximum for heavy oil, 2.5 per cent for light fuel oil and 0.3 per cent for automotive gas oil.

2.2.3 Domestic and Miscellaneous Sources

Usually, the local or territorial government is responsible for control of air pollution from domestic and smaller industrial and commercial sources. However, in the case of the area of the greater city of Christchurch, the Department of Health has proclaimed it a Clean Air Zone. This includes a restriction to 1.0 per cent maximum sulphur content in coal and the installation of new solid fuel domestic heaters which meet tough design and performance specifications.

The Department aims to encourage the use of "clean" energy sources, such as electricity or LPG and to limit the duration of solid fuel use to the coldest periods of the winter, in an effort to reduce the impact of solid fuel heating in the Christchurch air basin.

3 IMPLEMENTATION AND ENFORCEMENT

Before the passing of the *Clean Air Act 1972*, air pollution control was the responsibility of local government and the national Department of Health through legislation on public health.

As a result of the 1972 Act, direct control of large air pollution producing industries, as well as national policy and coordination of ambient monitoring passed to the Department of Health. Administration within the Department is currently controlled from a head office in Wellington and is implemented through four regional offices in Auckland, Wellington, Christchurch and Dunedin.

Control of non-scheduled sources is through the health departments of local councils and territorial government.

Implementation and enforcement is achieved by one or more of the following means, according to the judgement and experience of the responsible authority:

- negotiate with the operator of the plant to improve the standard of equipment or the level of maintenance and operation to achieve the desired performance;
- for scheduled operations, to attach conditions to the license issued under the *Clean Air Act*;
- issue a notice to install, alter or repair equipment to obtain the necessary level of control;
- prosecute for failure to comply with a regulation or requirement of the Act.

3.1 Monitoring

Ambient air quality monitoring has been carried out on a nationally coordinated basis in conjunction with the control and enforcement programmes emanating from the *Clean Air Act 1972.*

Pollutants are monitored only in areas where ambient levels are likely to be high, since in most areas of New Zealand air quality is very good. For example, fluorides are monitored in the vicinity of the large primary aluminium smelter near Dunedin and lead is measured in the central business district of Auckland. Suspended particulate matter is measured in areas of concern, such as Christchurch.

Suggested air quality guidelines are shown in Table 2; in other cases, WHO air quality goals are used as a guide to acceptable air quality; in those localities where air quality is considered inadequate, programmes are proposed to improve it, e.g. extension of clean air zone.

Table 2: Suggested Air Quality Guidelines

Pollutant	*Limiting factor(s) for determining satisfactory levels*	*Concentration*	*Averaging period*
Sulphur dioxide	Human Health	50 μg/cu.m	3 month average
		125 μg/cu.m	24 hour maximum
Smoke (fine particulates)	Human Health	50 BSSU	3 month average
		125 BSSU	24 hour maximum
Suspended Particulates	Soiling of Certain Materials and Coatings	60 μg/cu.m	7 day maximum
Inorganic Lead	Human Health	1.5 μg/cu.m	3 month average
Carbon Monoxide	Human Health	10 mg/cu.m	8 hour average
		40 mg/cu.m	1 hour maximum
Oxidants (as Ozone)	Human Health	60 μg/cu.m	8 hour average
		120 μg/cu.m	1 hour maximum
Nitrogen Dioxide	Human Health: Precursor for Oxidants	100 μg/cu.m	24 hour average
		200 μg/cu.m	1 hour maximum
Non-methane Hydrocarbons	Precursors for Oxidants	Under consideration	3 hour (6-9 a.m.)
Hydrogen Sulfide	Odour Nuisance: Damage to Certain Materials and Coatings	7μg/cu.m	24 hour average
		70 μg/cu.m	1 hour maximum
Fluorides (as Hydrogen Fluoride)	Vegetable damage	0.5 μg/cu.m	3 month average
		1μg/cu.m	7 day maximum

4 FUTURE DEVELOPMENTS

Prior to the change of government in New Zealand in late 1990, new legislation - *The Resource Management Bill* - had reached its final Parliamentary stages. This Bill is now awaiting the outcome of policy review before being progressed further.

The Resource Management Bill would have repealed the *Clean Air Act* and introduced integrated pollution control. Most of Central Government's responsibilities would have been devolved to regional governments, with central government retaining powers to make regulations relating to, for example, fees for discharge permits, technical standards, etc.

NORWAY

1 INTRODUCTION

1.1 Topography, Climate, Population

Norway is situated between 58 and 70 degrees North, and between 5 degrees West and 31 degrees East. As might be expected, the climate varies considerably. The highest annual mean temperature recorded (1961-90) was at Lindesnes (on the south coast) with +9.4 degrees C; the lowest annual mean temperature was at Siccajavre (inland, Northern Norway) with -4.9 degrees C. The highest annual precipitation recorded was at Brekke (on the west coast) with 5596 mm, and the lowest was at Sjaak (inland Southern Norway) with 191 mm.

Table 1 shows some figures regarding population and land area distribution. To a great extent, people live in narrow bands along the coast and in the valleys, and continuously settled areas of any size are only found in a few places. It should also be borne in mind that a large part of the country - say 60-70 per cent - lies above the tree line. Thus the population density in the settled areas is considerably higher than the mean shown in Table 1. However, these high-lying areas receive ample precipitation owing to prevailing westerly winds, and they are thus the source of Norway's large supply of hydro-electricity, which in turn provides the basis for extensive electrochemical and electrometallurgical industries.

1.2 Specific National Problems

Many electrometallurgical and electrochemical plants - especially the older ones - are situated near hydro-electric power plants at the head of the fjords, surrounded by mountains. Consequently, atmospheric dispersion is poor, especially in winter when temperature inversions of long duration occur. Many towns are in the same locations.

Norway is an important fishing nation. A large part of the catch is processed for fishmeal and fish-oil. This gives rise to odour at some places along the coast.

Forestry provides the raw materials for the pulp and paper industry and the production of chemical pulp is a source of dust, sulphur dioxide and odour.

Norway's rock is mainly acidic with a thin layer of covering soil with a low buffering capacity. Due to the climatic conditions, the air masses that give precipitation, have passed over heavily industrialized areas in Great Britain and Central Europe, picking up sulphur dioxide, nitrogen oxides and other air pollutants. Consequently the precipitation is often rather acidic and also contains other pollutants, such as soot, heavy metals etc.

These facts, coupled with the low buffering capacity of the soil have caused acidification of lakes and water courses in the south western part of the country. An area of more than 18 000 sq. km is devoid of fish, and another 18 000 sq. km has depleted fish stocks. The affected areas are still growing.

It is estimated that about 90 per cent of the sulphur depositions are caused by emissions from other countries.

Lately, increasing attention has been given to the role of nitrogen oxides in the acidification process. When the nitrogen content in the soil exceeds a certain level, acidification occurs. In addition to killing fish, the acid precipitation causes increased corrosion, and also represents a danger to forests. Acid precipitation which is regarded as one of the biggest pollution problems in Norway can, however, only

Table 1: Population and Land Area Distribution

Land area:		
Mainland		323,900 km^2
Svalbard		62,000 km^2
Total		385,900 km^2
Population:		4.2 million
Population density per km^2		13.1
Local administrative units:		
Counties		19
Municipalities		444
Land distribution (mainland):		
Land type	*Area in km^2*	*Percent of land area*
Built-up areas	2,500	1
Arable land	9,000	3
Forestry	64,900	20
Other productive agricultural or forest land	3,500	1
Bogs and wetland areas	30,100	9
Low-production areas	175,500	54
Freshwater areas	16,000	5
Unspecified areas	22,400	7
Total	323,900	100
Coastline:		
Mainland		21,111 km
Islands		31,958 km
Total		53,069 km
Number of islands: 53,789		

be solved by international cooperation. Norway has therefore, played a very active role in various international organizations in order to try to achieve a reduction in acid emissions.

2 DEVELOPMENT OF AIR POLLUTION CONTROLS AND LEGISLATION

2.1 Basic Principles

Air pollution control in the modern sense of the word was established by a number of sections in the *Neighbours Act* of 16 June 1961 No. 5 which came into force on 1 January 1962. The Smoke Control Council, which was established under the Act on the same date, had a central position regarding control of air pollution and was given powers to issue permits to polluting enterprises and set limits on their emissions etc.

Even earlier, however, those close to polluting plants had some protection against nuisances under the old *Neighbours Act* of 27 May 1887. In such cases, they had to bring an action against the plant, which in a few cases were forced to close down.

Originally, the *Neighbours Act* did not apply to plants already operating when the Act was implemented, nor had the authorities powers to issue regulations. By Acts of the Storting (the Norwegian Parliament) of 2 February 1973 and 19 December 1975, the provisions of the Act were extended to cover existing (old) enterprises and the authorities were given powers to issue regulations. Noise was also included, and while it can be regarded as a form of air pollution, it is not mentioned further in the context of this short survey.

By Act No. 64 of 19 June 1970, the authorities were given powers to issue regulations regarding the use of fuel oils restricting the content of sulphur and residues in such oils. Regulations under the Act were issued in 1970 and 1971 for the towns of Oslo and Drammen respectively.

Until 1972, the Smoke Control Council belonged, in administrative terms, to the Ministry of Industry; it was transferred to the Ministry of the Environment following its establishment in 1972. The State Pollution Control Authority (SPCA) was established in 1974, and the secretariat of the Smoke Control Council was incorporated in the new authority.

Following extension of the powers of the authorities to cover old plants, a clean up was implemented. It was carried out, and to all practical purposes completed, during the years 1974-85.

In 1977, the Smoke Control Council issued air quality guidelines for sulphur dioxide, particulates, nitrogen dioxide and fluorides.

These guidelines were revised in 1982 and extended to cover carbon monoxide and photochemical oxidants. In 1990, the State Pollution Control Authority started work on revising the guidelines. Under the Municipal Health Service Act of 19 November 1982, a municipality has powers in certain cases to demand improvements or close down plants if there is a risk that an activity may cause serious health damage in the vicinity. These powers are independent of the powers given to the pollution authorities in the *Pollution Control Act.*

Until 1964, there were no controls on emissions from road vehicles. In that year the Ministry of Transport and Communication issued a set of rules regarding exhaust from diesel powered engines, setting limits on the opacity of the exhaust. Regulations covering vehicles with petrol engines were first made in 1969, when the Health Authorities and the oil companies agreed on a maximum content of lead in petrol from 1 January 1970. This limit has since been reduced by steps to the current limit of 0.15 g lead/l, both for regular and premium petrol. Regulations regarding emissions from road vehicles with petrol engines were implemented for vehicles registered after 1 January 1964.

On 1 October 1983 the *Pollution Control Act* of 13 March 1981 No. 6 came into force, superseding the sections on air pollution in the *Neighbours Act,* and other Acts. The Act is comprehensive and covers air and water pollution, noise and waste. Regarding pollution from transport, the *Pollution Control Act* applies to roads, railways, airports etc; pollution from vehicles and aircraft etc. is controlled by provisions of the *Product Control Act,* the *Road Traffic Act,* the *Seaworthiness Act,* the *Harbour Act* and the *Civil Aviation Act.*

When the *Pollution Control Act* came into force, the Smoke Control Council was replaced by the Pollution Control Council.

On 1 August 1989 a new chapter 8 in the *Pollution Control Act,* (adopted 16 June 1989), concerning compensation for pollution damage, came into force. This introduces strict liability as a principle for all kinds of damages caused by pollution.

Measurements of air quality started in the early sixties. At present sulphur dioxide, particles expressed as soot, lead and nitrogen dioxide are monitored in 25 towns and urban areas.

2.2 Clean Air Philosophy

The *Pollution Control Act* has as its main purpose the protection of the external environment from pollution and to reduce existing pollution. This is to be achieved by ensuring adequate environmental quality, so that pollution (and waste) do not cause damage to health, adversely affect human wellbeing, or damage nature's capacity for production and self-renewal.

The Act also gives guidelines on implementation, which in the main are:

- to prevent the occurrence or increase of pollution and to limit existing pollution, taking into consideration health aspects, welfare, the natural environment, cost and economics;
- cooperation with the authorities who plan use of land to avoid and limit pollution;
- to make use of technology, which, from a total appraisal of present and future use of the environment and of economic consideration, gives the best results;
- to apply the "polluter pays" principle;
- to counteract pollution in the same way, whether damage or nuisance occur inside or outside Norway.

More detailed aspects of Norwegian anti-pollution policies were presented to and discussed in the Storting in White Paper No. 51 (1984-85). The main points in future pollution policies listed here are:

- increased implementation of preventative measures;
- locally adapted plans for improvement of air quality in densely populated or heavily industrialized districts, based on special investigations;
- research regarding health aspects of air pollutants including polychlorinated biphenyls, PAH, chlorinated hydrocarbons, heavy metals, etc;
- research on long range transport of air pollution in connection with acid precipitation;
- international cooperation to increase knowledge of all aspects of pollution.

While these points have a high priority, Norway is also putting much effort nationally into helping restrict and prevent regional and global problems such as climate change and depletion of the ozone layer.

Since control of air pollution began in 1962, all industries and other enterprises that fall within the scope of the different Acts have received their emission permits; regulations regarding the sulphur content of fuel oils have also been implemented.

On the whole emission permits are issued according to a fairly standardized pattern. They are valid for 10 years, but may be modified during this period according to rules laid down in the *Pollution Control Act.*

In new emission permits, the number of pollutants covered is greater than in the old ones, limits are lower, and they are better adapted to local conditions, as the authorities have accumulated knowledge through monitoring and special investigations. Cost benefit analyses are carried out when deemed necessary.

The relative and absolute importance of emissions from road transport has increased as the number of vehicles has risen and emissions from stationary sources have been subjected to control. From 1974 to 1989, UN-ECE standards on exhaust emissions were used, and since then US standards have been implemented for passenger cars. In the first half of the 1990s, US standards will be implemented for medium heavy and heavy duty vehicles.

2.3 Links with Planning and Energy Use Strategies

2.3.1 Land Use Planning

This is the responsibility of the municipalities. In most cases the plans are subject to confirmation by the county governor. To a great extent application of sound planning principles can alleviate the impact on the neighbourhood from polluting enterprises. The possibilities offered by the application of sound planning principles have, however, only been exploited to a very limited extent. In many cases residential areas have been developed in the vicinity of existing polluting enterprises, resulting in complaints. Clearly there is a need to improve planning procedures at the local level.

2.3.2 Energy Use Strategies

The energy balance in Norway is of particular interest owing to the very high percentage of energy consumption met by electricity, of which 99.8 per cent is hydro-electricity. According to energy statistics for 1988, electricity accounted for 49 per cent of final consumption, solid fuels 13 per cent and oil and gas 38 per cent. In the southern and western counties (13 out of 19), use of fuel oils with a sulphur content of more than one per cent is forbidden, unless the sulphur dioxide is absorbed by the product or otherwise bound, so that emissions correspond to a maximum of one per cent sulphur content. Maximum sulphur content is 0.8 per cent for distillates. Special regulations apply for the towns of Oslo and Drammen. Only distillates with maximum 0.8 per cent sulphur may be used. The authorities may grant exceptions.

A paper, discussing energy efficiency and energy research, was presented to the Storting in White Paper No. 61 (1988/1989). The paper discusses measures to encourage energy efficiency and energy research, including:

- electricity pricing policy, with the intent to encourage energy efficiency;
- financial assistance for energy efficiency investments both in industry, and in private and public services;
- how to create a more effective energy market;
- how to reduce the negative consequences of energy use and energy production;
- information and education on the best technology available;
- appropriations for energy saving research and development (R&D);
- better insulation of dwellings;
- appropriations for R&D on exploitation of new energy sources e.g. sea-wave power.

2.4 Economic Basis for Air Pollution Control

As mentioned above, the "polluter pays" principle is strictly adhered to in cases where new plants or extensions to existing plants are involved.

During the 1974-85 clean up period financial assistance was given to old plants where equipment for abating air pollution was installed - old plants being those which were on stream by 1 January 1974. This was done partly to speed up the installation of abatement equipment, and partly because installation of such equipment in old plants is rather costly compared with building new plants. Installation of abatement equipment also interrupts production and causes other inconveniences. In a few cases assistance was also given to new plants replacing old ones. In such cases the assistance given was calculated on the basis of the cost of installing cleaning equipment in the plants which were replaced.

When deciding on emission limits, care is taken to find a good workable solution, taking into account current technology, expected trends, health aspects, costs, neighbourhood, topography, meteorology etc. On the whole, this adds up to a use of "best practicable means". Care is also taken not to issue permits that may cause distortion of trade.

For new plants, emission limits are usually based on the best technology available.

In cases regarding plants in places where atmospheric dispersion is poor, rather strict limits are set.

2.5 Legislation and Instruments

The main Act for pollution control is now the *Pollution Control Act* of 13 March 1981 No. 6 which came into force on 1 October 1983. According to this Act, pollution is defined as:

a) Introduction into air, water or ground of solid matter, fluids of gases;

b) noise and vibration;

c) light and other radiation to the extent determined by the pollution control authorities;

d) temperature modification which causes or may cause damage or disamenity to the environment.

So far, no decision on putting (c) above into force has been taken. Matters concerning radioactive radiation are the responsibility of the Nuclear Energy Safety Authority and the National Institute of Radiation Hygiene.

Other Acts of relevance to pollution control are the *Municipality Health Service Act* (already mentioned) and the *Product Control Act* of 11 June 1979 No. 79. Regulations on the composition of petrol are based on this Act. Further, the *Road Traffic Act*, the *Seaworthiness Act*, the *Harbour Act* and the *Civil Aviation Act* are applicable to pollution from transport.

2.5.1 Industrial Processes

Emissions from industrial plant are controlled mainly by an emission permit for each single plant. Regulations covering a homogeneous group of industries have so far been implemented only for plant producing road surfacing materials.

When an application for an emission permit is received, the authority (SPCA) checks that all relevant information has been given. In cases concerning big plants, this may include a full impact statement. In important cases like this the company usually contacts SPCA before the application is submitted.

The County, the Municipality and the Municipal Health Board are invited to comment on the application. Likewise, a summary is published in the local press, and the application is made available to the public who are invited to comment on it. The applicant is given an opportunity to comment on objections etc. before the permit is issued. The permit is circulated to the above mentioned authorities and organizations, and those who either objected or commented on the application.

There is a right of appeal by the applicant or by other interested parties: the issuing authority (SPCA) may either modify the permit or comment on the appeal and submit it to the Ministry of Environment for the final decision.

In emission permits a maximum production is stated, emissions are controlled by setting limits for concentrations, hourly quantity, per cent of production or combinations of these, as well as stack height, type of fuel and maximum fuel consumption. Monthly and/or yearly means may also be stated.

All common air pollutants such as particles, sulphur dioxide etc. are controlled, as are heavy metals, fluorine, chlorine, hydrogen sulphide, obnoxious smells, hydrocarbons, chlorinated hydrocarbons, polychlorinated biphenyls, polycyclic aromatic hydrocarbons, dioxins etc. and noise as the case may be.

Depending on the type of industry, provisions for disposal of waste may also be stated. Reporting routines are laid down and a control programme must be presented.

As mentioned above, permits are valid for ten years. They may, however, be modified according to rules laid down in the Act. Under the ten-year rule, "2nd generation" permits are at present being issued to all main polluters. Regulations regarding plants producing road surfacing materials are drawn up in the same way.

As part of the control system, all plants are classified into four control classes, ranging from Class 1, which covers the plants with the greatest emission potential, to Class 4 for plants with the smallest emission potential. The type and quality of the recipient is also taken into account when making the classification.

The control system as such consists of two parts. One part, carried out by the plants themselves, consists of sampling, analyzing and reporting to the authorities at intervals laid down in the permit. The other part consists of inspections and thorough controls by inspectors from the relevant authority. Plants in Classes 1, 2 and 3, are inspected every year, every second year and every third year, respectively. Plants is Class 4 are inspected occasionally, mostly in connection with complaints.

Thorough control, which includes emission measurements by the inspectors, is carried out every third and every sixth year for plants in Class 1 and 2, respectively. Plants in Class 3 are subject to thorough control occasionally.

A nationwide monitoring system was established in 1977, and is managed by the National Institute for Air Research. Sulphur dioxide, nitrogen dioxide, soot, lead and polycyclic aromatic hydrocarbons are all monitored.

In a few cases, special monitoring systems have been established. Around aluminium smelters, for example, samples of conifer needles are collected in the spring and autumn. In addition, grass and hay samples are sampled three times during the growing season. Samples are collected at 10-25 sites around each smelter and analyzed for fluorine. Additional samples of bones of slaughtered animals or animal urine may also be analyzed. This system was established in 1965 and gives valuable information on long term trends.

In the Lower Telemark district, where many heavy chemical and other industries are located, a special monitoring network has been established. A special section of SPCA runs the monitoring systems and inspects the plants in close cooperation with the central authority.

2.5.2 Mobile Sources

Until 1964, there were no controls regarding emissions from road vehicles. In that year the Ministry of Transport and Communications issued regulations regarding the opacity of diesel exhaust.

So far as petrol-engined vehicles are concerned, there were no regulations regarding exhaust or petrol composition until 1 January 1970. Under an agreement between the Health Authorities and the oil companies, the lead content in petrol was fixed at a maximum of 0.7 g/l from that date, and reduced to 0.6 g/l from 1 January 1971. By regulation under the *Health Act* the limit on lead in petrol was further reduced to 0.4 g/l from 1 April 1974.

Under the *Product Control Act*, the Ministry of Environment issued regulations concerning the composition of petrol for road vehicles which came into force on 1 September 1980. Under these regulations, the benzene content was limited to 50 ml/l both for regular and premium petrol. The lead content was limited to 0.15 g/l for regular and 0.4 g/l for premium petrol. From 1 September 1983, the lead content of premium petrol was limited to 0.15 g/l.

In 1985 the Ministry of Environment decided that filling stations with more than one pump must offer lead-free petrol after 1 July 1987, and this will apply to all stations as from January 1992.

As mentioned above, UN-ECE standards regarding exhaust from road vehicles were applied, and Norwegian regulations have been modified in step with the UN-ECE standards.

From 1 January 1989, the US-83 vehicle emission standard was made compulsory for petrol-fuelled passenger cars. The emission requirements in the US-83 standard are 2.1 g/km carbon monoxide, 0.25 g/km hydrocarbons and 0.62 g/km nitrogen oxides (city traffic). From 1 October 1990 US-87 standards became compulsory for diesel passenger cars and all other light vehicles with a maximum payload of less than 750 kg. The requirements for carbon monoxide, hydrocarbon and nitrogen oxides emissions are the same as in the US-83 standard, but diesel vehicles have to meet an additional 0.124 g/km particle emission limit.

From 1 October 1991 the US-90 vehicle emission standard for light-duty trucks will be made compulsory for all those with a total weight of less than 3500 kg, and a maximum payload exceeding 760 kg. The emission requirements in the US-90 standard are 6.2 g/km carbon monoxide, 0.5g/km hydrocarbons, 1.1 g/km nitrogen oxides (city traffic) and 0.162 g/km particles.

From 1 January 1994 the US-91 vehicle emission standard for heavy-duty vehicles will become compulsory for all heavy-duty vehicles with a total weight exceeding 3500 kg. The emission requirements in the US-94 standard are 4.9 g/km carbon monoxide, 1.2 g/km hydrocarbons, 7.0 g/km nitrogen oxides and 0.35 g/km particles.

2.5.3 Domestic and Miscellaneous Uses

Current regulations regarding fuel oils were issued by the Ministry of Environment on 11 March 1985 under the *Pollution Control Act.* These state that the maximum sulphur content shall be 2.5 per cent. In the thirteen southern and southwestern counties the maximum sulphur content is one per cent. In the towns of Oslo and Drammen, only distillates with a maximum content of 0.8 per cent sulphur are allowed.

All enterprises having furnaces with a capacity exceeding 150 kg fuel oil per hour must apply for a permit if:

- it was established after 1 January 1986;
- capacity has been increased by more than 20 per cent;
- the type of fuel has been changed from distillate to heavy duty fuel oil;
- the plant has been modified in a way that gives rise to increased pollution.

The SPCA may grant exemptions from the regulations.

The regulations are currently being revised, and the SPCA propose that maximum sulphur content in heavy fuel oil should be one per cent in all parts of the country, and the maximum sulphur content in heavy distillates should be 0.2 per cent.

In permits for the use of heavy fuel oil, emission limits for soot are normally set at 1 g per kg oil, and soot plus particles at 1.5 g per kg oil. The Bacharach smoke scale number must not exceed 3.

There are no regulations covering sulphur content in solid fuels like anthracite, bituminous coal, lignite, coke, or petroleum coke used as raw materials or fuel. In permits, however, the maximum sulphur content has been set at 1.5 per cent for coal used as fuel. So far, no limits have been set on solid fuels used as raw materials.

2.5.4 Nuisance Provisions

The most commonly occurring types of nuisance are dust fall and odour. In principle, these nuisances are controlled by the permits issued by the authorities. As regards dust fall, no standards or guidelines have been implemented. By rule of thumb, dust fall of 5 g/m^3 and 30 days is regarded as satisfactory in housing districts. The soot concentration in air does, however, exceed the guidelines at some monitoring stations. This is mostly ascribed to emissions from road traffic. It should also be mentioned that the use of studded tyres during the winter months causes excessive road wear, and the particles which are rather coarse, are deposited near the roads where they originate. The quantity of such particles is estimated at 300 000 tons a year.

Odour is also in principle controlled by the permit system. This problem is, however, very difficult to solve, and residual obnoxious smells often occur.

3 IMPLEMENTATION AND ENFORCEMENT

Air pollution control is at present mainly based on the *Pollution Control Act* of 13 March 1981 No. 6 which came into force on 1 October 1983. Pursuant to this Act the Pollution Control Authorities are:

- The Ministry of Environment
- The Pollution Control Council
- The State Pollution Control Authority (SPCA)
- County Governors
- Municipalities.

The Ministry has the overall and political responsibility. It sets the targets, defines the policy and decides on the main priorities. It also decides on appeals against decisions made by the subsidiary authorities.

The Pollution Control Council consists of representatives from relevant ministries and organizations. It meets a few times a year, and, under the *Pollution Control Act*, it decides on emission permits in cases where an impact statement has been deemed necessary. The Council also gives its view on cases put before it by the Ministry or by SPCA. The latter acts as the secretariat for the Council. The function of this Council has been evaluated and the Ministry of Environment has proposed to the Storting (Parliament) that the Pollution Control Council be abolished.

SPCA is centrally placed in the system. It has acquired broad technical expertise on all matters concerning pollution control; it oversees monitoring, takes the initiative in carrying out investigations, and administers the necessary projects. It also issues emission permits, and has supervisory responsibilities to ensure that emissions are kept within the set limits. SPCA also draws up proposals for new regulations.

All county governors have a section which deals with all questions connected with the environment. At the moment these sections have no powers to issue permits regarding emissions to air. The county administrations deal primarily with municipal sewage and waste. The transfer of some types of industry to the county governors has been under consideration; food industries, laundries and dry cleaning plants will be transferred by the end of 1991. Further it is expected that stone crushing plants and the regulations regarding plants manufacturing road surfacing materials will be transferred at the beginning of 1992.

The municipalities as such do not handle cases regarding air pollution. They are, however, consulted during the preparatory work on emission permits. As mentioned above, the municipal health boards have independent powers regarding pollution control.

When inspection or reports on an enterprise show non-compliance with the emission permit - for example exceeding the emission limits - the authority sets a deadline within which compliance must be established. This deadline may also be combined with a daily fine, to be paid if the time limit is exceeded. In very serious cases the enterprise may also be prosecuted.

4 EFFECTIVENESS OF CONTROLS

The performance of clean air controls may be evaluated by:

- comparing present emission of pollutants with emission at the time when controls were implemented;
- comparing emission levels at the same place over time;
- ascertaining the degree of compliance with limits in emission permits.

A lack of complete series of data is common to all three models. One reason for this is that nationwide monitoring only started in 1977, whereas controls were implemented in 1962. A few estimates and some curves showing trends are given below.

Figure 1 shows sulphur dioxide and soot levels at a station in downtown Oslo, and Figure 2 shows the mean trend for eight monitoring stations. In the 1970s sulphur dioxide emissions were estimated at about 180 000 tons, in 1986 at 100 000 tons, in 1989 at 65 000 tons and in 1990 at 60 000 tons. Further reductions are being contemplated. These figures do not include emissions from coastal shipping.

Figure 1: Soot and Sulphur Dioxide Levels at St Olav's Place, Oslo

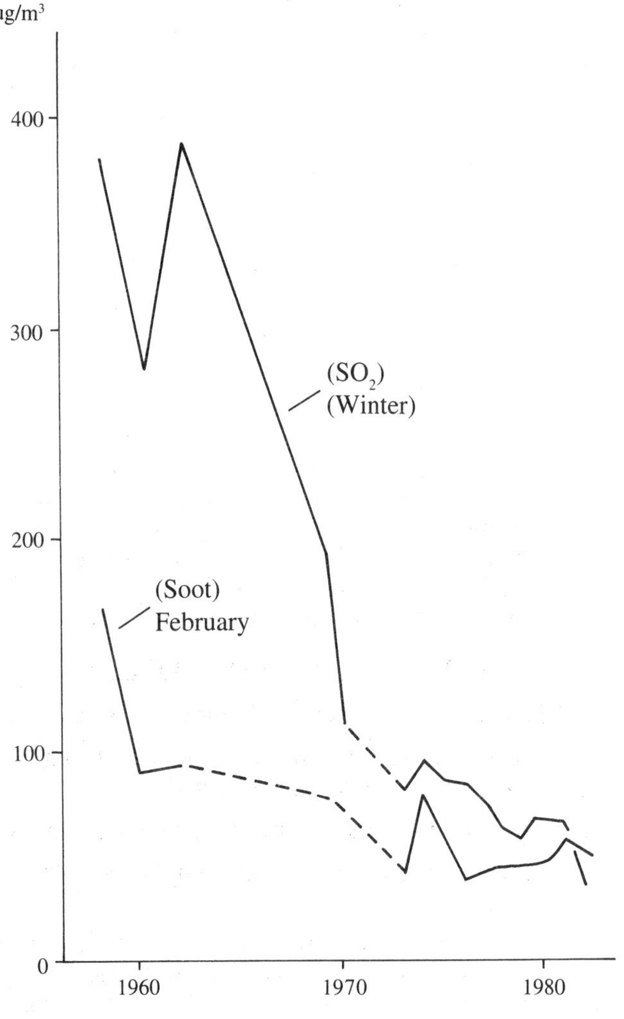

Source: The Norwegian Institute for Air Research (NILU)

Figure 2: Average SO_2 of the Eight Main Towns in Norway

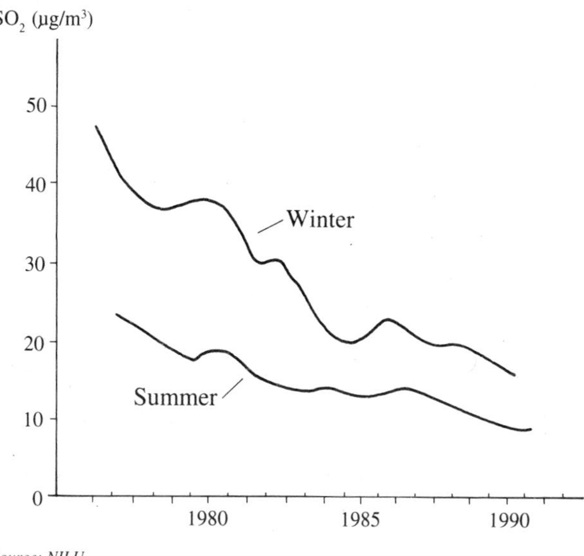

Source: NILU

Figure 3: Average Lead Concentrations of the Eight Main Towns in Norway

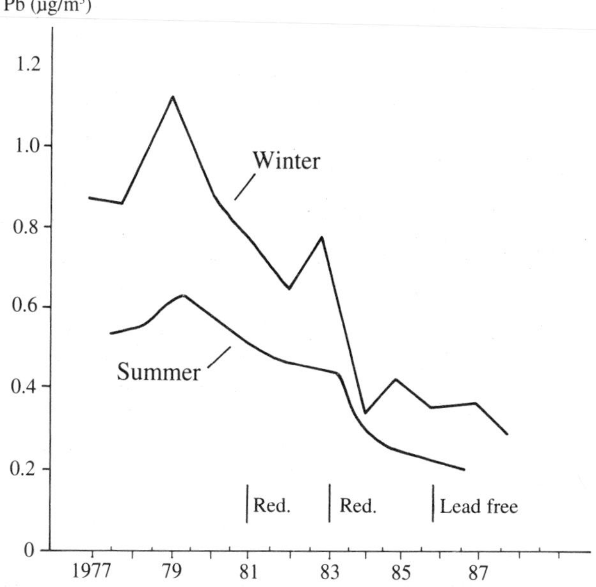

Source: NILU

Figure 3 shows corresponding trends for lead concentrations in ambient air.

In the case of nitrogen oxides, emissions have risen from approximately 180 000 tons in 1973 to 230 000 tons at present. This is due to an increase in transportation. Figure 4 shows the trend in nitrogen dioxide emission levels in six Norwegian towns.

Particles have been reduced by some 250 000-300 000 tons a year. Most of the reductions stem from the production of ferro-alloys and other metallurgical and chemical industries.

Fluorine emissions from aluminium smelters are estimated at 1100-1200 tons in 1962, 900-1000 tons in 1985 and 700 tons in 1990. Production of primary aluminium was 209 000 tons, 760 000 tons and 845 000 tons, respectively.

The degree of compliance with limits in emission permits has to be ascertained mainly by inspections and reports from the enterprises in question. As the number of inspections and reports are of necessity limited, it is only possible to obtain an indication of the level of compliance.

Inspection records etc. for 1985 show that about 12 per cent of the plants inspected had serious violations of emission permits, and about 16 per cent had minor violations. In 1989, the corresponding figures were 11 per cent and 52 per cent, and in 1990 10 per cent and 60 per cent. Eight enterprises were prosecuted in 1989 and ten in 1990. When comparing these figures, it should be borne in mind that the inspection system has been improved between 1985 and 1989. The inspections are more thorough and systematic. It should be noted that the figures above also cover other violations, e.g. limits regarding effluent or waste handling.

5 FUTURE DEVELOPMENTS

With regard to legislation, there are plans to extend the *Pollution Control Act* to cover emissions from railway and road traffic.

In the case of sulphur dioxide, the goal is to achieve a reduction of 50 per cent (compared with 1980) before 1993. A revised sulphur dioxide protocol is now under preparation within the framework of the Convention on Long Range Transboundary Air Pollution. This protocol will be based on the critical load concept. The first draft will be prepared during 1991, with final agreement expected to be reached in 1992.

In the case of nitrogen oxides, the aim is to stabilize emissions at the 1987 level before 1994. In addition, there are plans to reduce emissions by 30 per cent (compared with 1986) before 1998.

Figure 4: Nitrogen Dioxide Emission Levels in Six Norwegian Towns

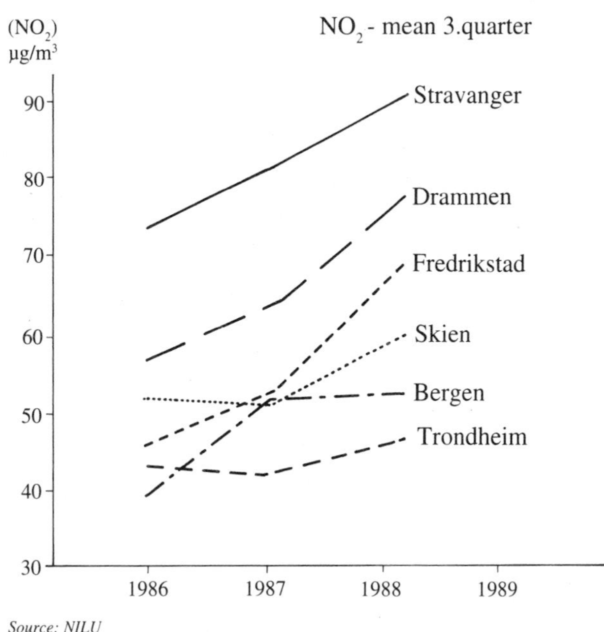

Source: NILU

In the case of chlorofluorocarbons, Norway is aiming at a reduction (compared to 1986) of 50 per cent before 1 January 1991, and a further reduction of at least 90 per cent before 1 January 1995. As regards carbon dioxide, the goal is to stabilize emissions at the 1989 level before 2000.

6 SELECTIVE BIBLIOGRAPHY

Norsk Vannforening (1988). Vann nr. 1. N-1342 Jar, Norway.

Turner D B, (1970). *Workbook of Atmospheric Dispersion.* US Department of Health, Education and Welfare. Cincinatti, Ohio, USA.

Sax N I and Lewis R J, (1989). *Dangerous Properties of Industrial Materials,* Seventh Edition. Van Nastrand Reinholde, New York.

VDI-Komission Reinhaltung der Luft. *VDI-Handbuch Reinhaltung der Luft,* Volume 1-6. Dusseldorf, Germany.

PAKISTAN

1 INTRODUCTION

1.1 Topography, Climate, Population

Pakistan is situated in the north-west of the Indian sub-continent, on the Arabian Sea, and shares borders with India, Afghanistan and Iran. It has a mainly semi-arid climate: winters are cool with slight rain; summers are hot and dry. Pakistan covers an area of about 750 000 sq. km and has a population of about 114 million.

Pakistan is self-sufficient in natural gas and resources of low-sulphur coal and also has considerable access to hydro-electricity and geothermal energy. Due to its major imports of crude oil and petroleum products, Pakistan is a net importer of energy and gasoline, prices are typically different from those of European countries because of heavy excise tax to discourage consumption.

High priority is placed on the use of indigenous fuels such as coal, wood, natural gas, hydro or geothermal energy, in preference to petroleum-based fuels. There are strong reasons, on air pollution grounds, to require the replacement of oil fuel by natural gas. Considerable emphasis is placed on the efficiency of natural gas for industrial fuel-burning equipment and soot emissions from industrial sources.

1.2 Specific National Problems

Pakistan has a number of industries, including pharmaceuticals, paper, steel, aluminium and petrochemicals. Also, because of the large sheep, dairy and timber industries, there are a number of potential sources of air pollution from rendering works, tanneries, milk and cheese processing and timber mills.

In Pakistan, industrial development is seen as all-important and it is very difficult to ensure that industries safely dispose of their toxic wastes. The problem is compounded by the absence of incinerators, landfill sites, and alternative disposal methods for liquid waste which is mainly discharged into the rivers and sea. To give a few examples, one foundry discharges caustic soda, chlorine, hydrochloric and sulphuric acid (which result in acid rain); Ravi Rayon discharges acetic acid, acetaldehyde, ethylalcohol, and suspended solids.

Further downstream on the Sheikhpura Road, the Pakistan paper products factory and, on the Manghopir Road, the Jawedan Cement factory, discharge pulp, suspended particulates, smog and other effluents high in oxygen demand levels.

2 DEVELOPMENT OF AIR POLLUTION CONTROLS AND LEGISLATION

2.1 Clean Air Philosophy

The British pattern of Best Practicable Means (BPM) is used as the basis of air pollution control, supplemented by specific regulations for the control of smoke emissions. Ambient air quality is considered acceptable if maximum levels are below World Health Organization (WHO) goals or other accepted criteria. Where no better data exist or are available, it is common practice to require that maximum Ground Level Concentrations (GLC) for any emitted pollutant should not exceed one-thirtieth of the 8-hour occupational health threshold limit value (TLV) or one-fortieth of the TLV for toxic substances.

A schedule to the *Pakistan Environmental Protection Ordinance,* which came into force in 1983, is used for division of responsibility between national and local authorities, with licensing applied to scheduled premises.

The Pakistan Environmental Protection Agency (PEPA) was established in 1983 and has powers which include the promulgation of regulations for the control of pollution from both stationary and mobile sources, and the declaration of Clean Air Zones. The PEPA defines an "air pollutant" as being any substance that causes alteration in the chemical, physical, biological or radiological integrity of air; soot, smoke particulates, combustion exhaust, exhaust gases, obnoxious gases and radioactive substances are included.

2.2 Industrial Processes

All industrial plant are subject to the *Environmental Protection Ordinance,* but those with significant potential to create air pollution are listed in a schedule to the Act and must hold a license issued by the Department of Health.

The WHO standards on chimney heights are used to determine stack heights for straightforward sites. For large processes and complex locations the heights are calculated on dispersion parameters.

2.3 Mobile Sources

Pakistan has about one million motor vehicles, and effectively no regulations on exhaust emissions. Further work is being carried out before introducing an unleaded regular grade petrol, which would help to reduce lead levels in urban areas in the long term; the use of cars with engines incorporating the technology of natural gas as well as solar energy efficiency is also to be permitted, and the use of alternative fuels such as liquid petroleum gas (LPG) and solar energy is encouraged.

2.4 Domestic and Miscellaneous Sources

Under normal circumstances, the local or territorial government is responsible for the control of air pollution from domestic and smaller industrial and commercial sources. However, in the case of the biggest city of Sind province, Karachi, the Environmental Protection Agency has initiated appropriate action to control the pollution being generated by the National Cement Industries. The Director General of the EPA of Sind has stated that contacts were established with all concerned and arrangements finalized for the installation by 1991 of dust control equipment to be manufactured by the Heavy Mechanical Complex of Taxila.

The national coordinator for the WHO Oral Health Programme for Pakistan has suggested that country level committees be set up to protect the population from industrial and waste pollution. He also felt that the traffic police and city transport department should not allow vehicles emitting large amounts of smoke onto the road.

3 IMPLEMENTATION AND ENFORCEMENT

Before the registration of the Pollution Control Society of Sind, Karachi (PCSS) in 1989, environmental and air pollution control was in the hands of local government and the national Department of Health. With the PCSS, 1989, direct control of large air pollution producing industries as well as national policy and coordination of ambient monitoring was given to the Department of Health to administer. The Society also draws the attention of people towards the control of air pollution from minor sources.

3.1 Enforcement

Administration within the Environmental Protection Council is controlled by a head office in Islamabad, the capital, and is implemented through four provincial offices in Sind, Punjab, Sarhad and Baluchistan.

Enforcement is largely left to the judgement and experience of the responsible authority with the aim of:

- ensuring compliance with the ordinance;
- giving appropriate direction to conserve renewable and expandable resources;
- ensuring that environmental considerations are interwoven into National Development plans and policies;
- ensuring enforcement of the National Environmental Quality Standards;
- directing any Government agency, organization or individual to take the necessary measures to control the pollution being caused by such agency, organization or individual or to refrain from carrying out any particular activity prejudicial to public interest or the purposes of this ordinance.

3.2 Monitoring

Ambient air quality monitoring has been carried out on a nationally coordinated basis in conjunction with the control and enforcement programmes flowing from the PCSS, 1989.

Pollution is monitored only in those areas where ambient levels are likely to be high, as in most of the country air quality is not good. For example, fluorides are monitored in the vicinity of the large primary aluminium smelters, and lead and carbon monoxide are measured in areas of concern such as Hub.

WHO air quality goals are used as a guide to acceptable air quality and, in those localities where air quality is considered inadequate, programmes are proposed to improve it.

4 EFFECTIVENESS OF CONTROLS

Although there are effective laws to control air pollution, unfortunately the methods of implementation are not satisfactory, particularly since the rate of air pollution (especially lead, ozone, carbon monoxide, nitrogen dioxide, sulphur dioxide, particulates, etc.) is increasing with time. For example, in 1983 there were about 0.3 million automobiles and now the figure is over one million and the great majority do not conform to the laws. They constantly emit harmful gases (mostly carbon monoxide) due to defective combustion systems, and also produce much noise pollution; according to an unpublished study, the population is gradually becoming deafer.

None of the factories at Kala Shah Kaku have effective waste treatment plants; raw sewage flows directly from the source into Degh Nullah, a major drainage channel, used for the diversion of river water during the monsoon floods. The farmers on either side of the Nullah used to draw on its waters for irrigating their fields. They are now compelled to draw on other sources, because the water is so contaminated that one can smell it from a distance.

5 BIBLIOGRAPHY

Najam, Adil and Kabraji A M. *The National Conservation Strategy Bulletin*, Vol. 2, Issue 2 (August 1990).

Ibid, Vol. 2, Issue 1, (August 1990).

Acts, Ordinances, President's Orders and Regulations including Martial Law Orders and Regulations, Government of Pakistan, Ministry of Law & Parliamentary Affairs (Law Division), Islamabad (31 December 1983).

PERU

1 INTRODUCTION

Advice on how to avoid pollution in developing countries has come relatively late to Peru. Since the 1920s, Peru has suffered several serious cases of pollution, particularly atmospheric, in various regions of the territory. As this fact may not be widely known, we introduce our presentation with some historical data, indicating the causes of pollution as well as some of the characteristics of this country of "incredible and inexplicable contrasts" (geography, climate, resources, social make-up, etc.) which in turn are reflected in all aspects of its development, including those of the environment.

1.1 Topography, Climate, Population

Peru is situated in the central section of the western coast of the Pacific in the Southern Hemisphere, between latitudes 0 - 18 degrees S and 68 - 81 degrees longitude W of the Greenwich Meridian. It comprises a total area of 1 285 216 sq. km, including the coastal islands and the national area of Lake Titicaca. It is the third largest country in South America.

At present, Peru has an approximate population of 23 million, which gives an apparently sparse density of 18 inhabitants per sq. km. However this is a theoretical figure as the physical conditions of Peru drastically restrict those areas suitable for human habitation, concentrating them in a few cities, especially the capital, Lima. Here there are districts with densities as high as 34 000 per sq. km.

Given its geographical position, Peru should be a tropical country, hot and humid; however it has a very complex climate influenced by many factors, in isolation or combined but principally from its vertical dimension. Peru is a country of geographical compartments, in which the various heights mark differences in relief, climate, soil, vegetation, resources and therefore, the activities and even the attitudes of its population. Such variations — "like crumpled paper", Raimondi, 1890[(1)] - have created four very different natural regions:

- The "200 mile-long territorial sea" with enormous fishery resources, due to the abundance of plankton. It is crossed by a warm water current (17 degrees C average) parallel to the coast

(Peruvian or Humboldt Current), which prevents the normal phenomena of evaporation and rainfall.

- The coast, a narrow desert strip (average 100 km), practically without rainfall (the average over the last 20 years is 40 mm), but very humid (up to 98 per cent). The air, saturated with water vapour, covers the coast with blankets of cloud and rain spray (drizzles) during the long winter (May - October). Normal temperatures on the coast do not exceed 25 degrees C nor go below 7 degrees C. On the other hand, the vertical distribution of this parameter has an abnormal gradient, giving an abundance of isothermic areas because of the almost constant presence of anticlinal movement in the air masses, or anticyclone, of the Pacific.

- The sierra or high lands are wild areas in the central and upper part of the Andes Mountains which cross the country from south-north, rising to 6500 metres above sea level and thus forming the highest tropical mountains in the world. It is a cold and dry region (average 7 degrees C and 40 - 60 per cent humidity) with notable fluctuations in temperature - clear days with "a sun which burns but does not heat" alternating with icy nights, almost always below zero degrees Celsius. Rainfall is seasonal and moderate (averaging at 788 mm in the last 20 years) but interspersed with snow and hail storms. Notable in this region's atmosphere are layers of thermic inversion in the early hours of the morning, disappearing during the sunshine hours. The cold, heavy air on the peaks compresses the hot masses which descend from the sides of the mountains and which reheat, and begin circulating again.

  The Andes are generally inhabited between 2000 and 3500 metres above sea level or more. According to Baumann, Peru has the highest permanent human habitation in the world at 5300 metres above sea level(2). In these areas non-native visitors suffer from serious organic disorders because of the altitude and the rarefied air, generally known as altitude sickness, mountain sickness or "soroche" in the local language. It is also the region which has (in the subsoil) the most notable mineral resources, the exploitation of which is particularly linked with environmental concerns.

- Finally, the fourth region, forest or jungle (60 per cent of the national territory) with luxurious tropical vegetation where the most complex hydrographic systems on the planet can be found. It is a "burning" region (average 27 degrees C) and humid (98 per cent) and the wettest part of the country (4929 mm average in the last 20 years). During various periods in its history, there has been considerable exploration in order to exploit to the full specific resources (latex, timber, medicinal plants, skins). Currently many areas of the region are being exploited for oil and gold. Even so, there are few populated areas and amongst these the majority are inhabited by natives not integrated nationally.

To summarize, with reference to meteorological and climatic conditions, there are eight, possibly twelve, major climatic zones in Peru, in a relatively short horizontal distance of only 200 km[3].

Despite its size and the fact that its natural resources are distributed throughout the country, the most important economic areas have developed on the central coast and have dominated the life of the country since it gained political independence. The capital, Lima, is situated in this area. It is called "A developed capital in an underdeveloped country" to signify its apparent progress and to proclaim a measure of well-being, sought after by its own citizens and immigrants coming en masse from distant rural areas, especially from the high lands. This internal migration and the natural population increase have resulted in a huge rise in Lima's population, which is growing at an annual rate of 5.6 per cent, of which 3.4 is the migratory rate and 2.2 the natural rate. At present, one third of the national population is housed in an area no greater than 0.35 per cent of the country.

Although 70 per cent of industry is located in the area as it has the greatest services infrastructure, it is still impossible to satisfy the needs, even the basic needs, of the immigrant population within the established order. Consequently, a social phenomenon has arisen known as "informality", that is, individual or group activities which are practised for survival. A large part of recent commerce and industry has been marginal, or clandestine, in that they have been developed outside the control of authority. Unstructured or informal work makes the production of average quality goods in improvised workshops and "factories" possible, and there are itinerant businesses on the public streets. While it is true that this generates an economy, at the same time it also creates a spiral of many negative pressures on urban life and its ecology. The city grows at the expense of its hinterland; communities spring up in unsuitable areas with poor housing, encouraged by the politics, poverty and the mild climate. Urban necessities, such as transport, energy, water and sewage services, etc. become major problems which are almost impossible to solve. On the human side, distrust and violence grow and as far as the environment is concerned, the natural countryside is destroyed, and harmful effluents are discharged into the ground, water and air in ever greater quantities.

While most of Peru's environmental problems can be found in Lima, other less populated areas (of less than 100 000 inhabitants) do of course have a great capacity to destroy the environment and must therefore be included in any discussion of pollution in Peru. These cities which include La Oroya, Ilo and Chimbote, have not been developed using any planning procedures or been able to develop naturally over a period of time (Figure 1); instead they grew almost overnight around a basic natural resource which was exploited without any regard for the environment. They have therefore always contributed to pollution, with very serious consequences, as will be shown later.

Figure 1: Main Centres of Air Pollution

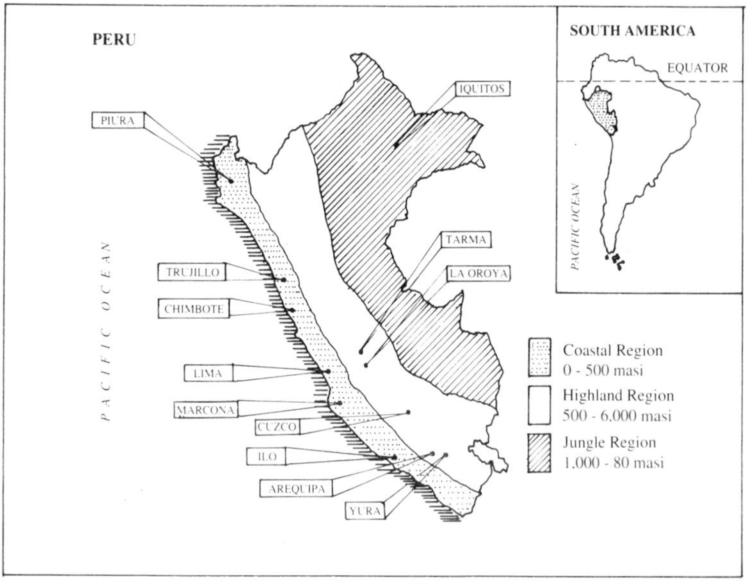

1.2 Early Development

In the 16th century, when the first Europeans arrived in what is today Peru, unusually well developed techniques had already been perfected to transform raw materials (minerals, wood, clay, hides, feathers, wool) into objects of use to man or as religious offerings. This is shown by the small amount of evidence which survived the pillage of the Conquistadors and which continues to amaze the world. Today, Peru is an underdeveloped country, part of the third world where the fight for survival is the greatest concern. Consequently, many of its problems, including pollution, have arisen from poverty, complicated by the difficult geography of the country. The pollution sources, however, are not necessarily indigenous to the developing countries. The destruction of the environment and its consequences is a very complex subject, involving both internal and external factors, of an increasingly serious nature.

Present-day Peru does not have any real industrial tradition of its own, rather it is a producer of different and abundant raw materials, whose prices have almost always been imposed from abroad. For this reason it has been described as a "beggar sitting upon a gold bench".

Until the 1950s, Peru had mainly produced goods related to the crafts. However, it was then realized that it was necessary to supplement the income from natural raw material resources, and so Peru began manufacturing some non-durable goods and products to substitute imports, promoted by legislation.

At the same time, entrepreneurs returned, who in previous years had tried to industrialize the vast hydrobiological resources of the Peruvian sea, with the main aim of manufacturing anchovy meal (Engraulis ringens), greatly desired abroad for its protein content. This industry led to a particularly disagreeable type of pollution (repellant odours) which was of great concern to Lima and its 5.5 million inhabitants. Thus, the term pollution entered the media and the public demanded controls. The matter soon attracted general interest and became a health issue as much for its undeniably spectacular nature as for its effect on the capital. This episode is seen as an initial landmark in spite of the fact that chronologically the problem of atmospheric pollution in Peru began much earlier and also occurred outside Lima in a small town (La Oroya) unknown except to specialists or those directly interested in the matter. Here the problem is linked to the metallurgical mining industry, traditionally the most important industry in the country due to its permanent economic nature, but from an environmental point of view an industry accused of causing many controversial problems.

1.3 Specific National Problems

The causes of the problem in general and atmospheric pollution in particular are numerous, and are to be found throughout all the country regions and the major population centres.

Amongst all the work to be done, the most urgent is to establish a permanent organization dedicated to solving the problems of pollution - a body which is well managed and, above all, protected against changing political interests. At the moment there are several organizations interested in the subject but their work is principally general and theoretical. None of these organizations has a network to control the quality of urban air except an incipient programme run by the Environmental Health Board (DITESA), which, due to recent changes, runs the risk of being withdrawn (see also section 2.1).

Lack of unified legislation is also a problem, as is the shortage of trained staff. More common are the politicians who use environmental issues for self-promotion, than those who work or are prepared to work in the field. Environmentalists recommend that attention to the problem of pollution should be separated from the Ministry of Health, which receives the least help from public administration. Their resources are slim as a typical "non-productive" ministry. Consequently, it is unable to help the research programmes that the problem demands.

The following examples are representative of the overall picture of pollution in Peru.

1.3.1 Fish Meal Factories

Fishing and the processing of fish to produce fish meal and oil marked a period of extraordinary industrial expansion. Initial production of 64 500 metric tons of meal in 1957 increased to two million in 1969 and reached 12.3 million in 1972, making Peru the greatest producer in the world. But along with the benefits it brought disagreeable smells to Lima and other coastal areas. In order to emphasize its economic importance the manufacturers called it "the smell of dollars". The nature and chemical composition of the gaseous effluents coming from these factories are not known in detail, but oxides of carbon, trimethylenes, aldehydes and cetones, hydrogen sulphide, ammonia, organic proteinic particles of various sizes and oily substances were found. This problem has been moderated not so much by effective controls but by the drastic reduction in the raw material, which has almost reached extinction. Currently its exploitation is limited and also, the factories have been moved to smaller inlets on the coast, in other words, decentralized. An exception, however, is the town of Chimbote ("the fishing capital") where the problem still exists together with others, making it worthy of the name it has been given of "the monster", one of the most contaminated areas of the country.

1.3.2 The Metallurgical Mining Industry

Mining is an irreplaceable generator of currency for Peru. It represents 5 - 6 per cent of the gross national product and contributes 45 - 50 per cent currency to the state. The expression "It's worth a Peru" comes basically from this rich resource. However the cost to the environment has been high.

Mining, which was already causing health problems in the 1920s, began with the installation of a metallurgical mining complex in the Central Andes region, 3730 metres high and 180 km south east of Lima, called La Oroya, "The Mining Capital of Peru". It has supplied non-ferrous minerals (copper, lead and zinc) over a large area (800

000 sq. km) since the beginning of the century and was owned by a transnational company, expropriated by the Peruvian government in 1973. The plant at the centre of the complex processes minerals to produce 27 different end products, including refined metals, alloys and chemical products, and is one of the main plants in Latin America. The gaseous residues are channelled through a 183.5 metre high chimney, which given its location above sea level (4066 metres) probably makes it the tallest chimney in the world. Its pollutants - mainly sulphur dioxide, lead and arsenic - have had visible effects on a surrounding area of 4000 hectares of land and 177 000 hectares of natural grass land. The appearance of an illness called "renguera" (literally "lameness"), which deformed the joints in cows and sheep, dramatized the case between 1925 and 1930, since when controls have been implemented. However it is currently recognized that in one way or another it affects some 50 000 inhabitants in the region, particularly children, through environmental lead pollution. Documenting the problem is still to be carried out.

In 1960 a private copper foundry was established, 1200 km from Lima on the south coast, which has a current production capacity of 290 000 metric tons of blistered copper per year based on concentrates which also contain 30 - 35 per cent sulphur. The sulphur resulting from the metallurgical heat processes is converted into residual sulphurous gases resulting in between 530 000 - 580 000 tons per year being vented into the atmosphere through four chimneys, each 108 metres high. This source is situated 17 km to the north of Ilo, a port which had 5000 inhabitants when the foundry was built but now has 80 000.

Between the city and the foundry, 2 km to the north of the former, is a narrow cross valley to the ocean, breaking the monotony and characteristic aridity of the Peruvian coast. For 300 years (the Colonial age) there had been 443 hectares of olive cultivation and other species. However, after only three months operation of the foundry, farmers in the valley were claiming compensation for agricultural damage. Not long afterwards a special committee formed by the government declared that plant toxicity was evident and that the company should pay compensation. This situation has continued and it is calculated that to date some $200 000 per year has been paid for failed harvests, and the controversy continues.

Farmers in another valley, 60 km north of the foundry have likewise claimed compensation 60 to 80 times higher than in the first case, due to the size of this second valley (some 15 times wider than the first) and the main crop (sugar cane). The distance and explanation for the damage ("atmospheric fogginess" or "indirect action") which it is claimed causes lower sugar production, has caused irreconcilable controversies. In 1985 the case was taken to court and has yet to be resolved.

There are many other mining related causes of pollution, including:

- The open pit Marcona magnetite mines held responsible for endangering the world famous Nazca archaeological area;
- A zinc refinery only 22 km north east of Lima has caused controversy because of its proximity to the capital and its potential for pollution;
- The only iron and steel works in Peru operates in Chimbote where a cloud of coloured airborne particles (iron oxides) almost permanently covers part of the city;
- The cement factories linked by our legislation to mining also have their negative influence on the areas of and around Yura, Tarma, Lima and Pacasmayo;
- Oil exploration and exploitation plus the discovery of gold have brought their share of pollution to the forests of the Peruvian Amazon.

1.3.3 Industry in General

The sources of pollution classified under this heading are characterized by their localized effects, due to their small size and the fact that they are isolated from each other. Statistics from 1980, when the country's production plant was better organized than in 1990, show that of the 27 000 industrial centres in and around Lima, only 400 had 100 workers or more. Among those which come near to having the characteristics of medium sized industries are textiles, chemicals, food processing, insecticides, plastic derivatives, and motor parts, etc. The large majority (70 per cent) are in Lima, but other cities such as Arequipa are also areas of relatively important industries (textiles, food packaging, tanning), Trujillo (agro industries, mechanical engineering); Cuzco (fertilizers); all contribute to the pollution load.

On the other hand "small industry" is also very active. For this report the term covers those production centres which are mainly family run, or craft centres of 5 - 20 workers; many operate in urban areas without licenses and in precarious buildings. These small industries, which also cause pollution are continually being reported to the authorities by the affected neighbourhood. For this reason, some are prohibited, for example workshops which recover the lead from batteries. Also included in this category are the numerous bakeries which work at night producing heat and noise in the neighbourhood.

One factor which must be stressed is that the cities are subjected to unplanned development and growth because of demographic pressure. This means that old factories which 15 or 20 years ago were established on the edge of the city are now incorporated into the central urban expansion.

1.3.4 Vehicles

Although in most countries, transport systems can be said to be constantly improving, in Peru, however, there is evidence that the opposite is true: there were more kilometres of usable railway track in the last century than there are now; trams ran in Lima until the 1950s and in Arequipa until the 1970s, and although slow were able to move large numbers of the public and did not pollute the atmosphere. Their withdrawal would not have been so bad except for the fact that there was no programme to replace them, whilst at the same time the cities went through a period of excessive growth. As a result, almost everything about Peru's current transport system, of which 90 per cent belongs to private companies, is improvised, and indeed to call it a "system" is a euphemism: "traffic chaos" is a more correct description.

Approximately one out of every 16 inhabitants owns a vehicle. Sixty per cent of these vehicles have been in service for 20 to 25 years or more. (When describing Lima, one foreign journalist mentioned the year it was founded - 1535 - and said that some taxis had been in service since that date!)

Traffic conditions intensify the pollution potential of vehicles: streets are narrow in the centre of cities; traffic is slow with six to eight stops per kilometre travelled; traffic lights are inefficient, even more so recently because of unforeseen power cuts caused by terrorism. The problems are compounded by other factors such as the quality of fuels, the lack of parking areas, no legislation regarding exhaust fumes from vehicles, and even by the style of driving.

1.3.5 Miscellaneous (National Customs)

Various sources are evident, including a wide variety of non-industrial pollutants generated by individual or group human activities or attitudes, which taken together are important:

- The universal habit of smoking, in particular smoking in enclosed areas, where foul air is forced upon others which is damaging particularly to children, old people and pregnant women;
- Another less international but widespread custom is that of spitting in public places, which is not only unaesthetic but also a risk to collective health. Tuberculosis, carried by sputum, is

currently present in Peru, linked to poverty, hard work, lack of nutritious food and poor toilet facilities;

- Abandoned household rubbish. Urban waste (0.8 kg per person in Lima) is a prime problem still with no solution. This "untreated" rubbish contains a greater proportion of rotting organic material than dry, giving a multiple source of pollution (bad smells, micro-organisms, spread of insects, rodents);
- The disposal of waste, especially garden waste, by burning: in the climatic conditions of the Peruvian coast, waste is transformed into smoke, clouds, flying ash, both annoying and undoubtedly damaging. Such treatment is very common, particularly as part of farming practices on the coast, sierras and forests;
- Business also adds its share to pollution. In the capital and the major cities there are many travelling salesmen in the streets and squares, an activity which is usually linked with various aspects of environmental deterioration.

To summarize, these sources are dynamic, changing in origin, size and risk.

2 DEVELOPMENT OF AIR POLLUTION CONTROLS AND LEGISLATION

2.1 Early Controls

Each major atmospheric pollution episode in Peru has been tackled by a special provision, an "ad hoc" solution, by which time there is so much evidence of the problem that it would be impossible not to take action. The method used is to entrust a specific study to an ad hoc committee. These committees are established by a legal mandate and made up of various ministries, organizations and specialists.

The use of these committees is part of the history of pollution in Peru and began in 1923 with the "Technical Committee on the Fumes of La Oroya", which evaluated "... the visible damage. Areas of influence. The concentration of gases in the atmosphere in places far away from the centre of emission. Toxic elements such as arsenic and lead in the internal organs of animals poisoned by the atmosphere...". The committee continued to operate until the 1930s, and resulted in the installation of control measures (chimneys, electrical precipitators, arsenic collectors) in the metallurgical complex.

In 1960 another famous committee was set up for the Ilo Copper Foundry case. Its mission was to study the phytotoxic action of the waste gases from the foundry on agriculture in the Ilo valley (see section 1.3.2). The magnitude of the problem shown by its findings meant that years later (1967) the committee was enlarged, taking the name of the "High Level Permanent Committee for the Ilo and Tambo Valleys", known as CAN (Law No. 16583), and dealing with the claims from farms in the valley located 60 km north of the Foundry. Later still, it was deemed appropriate to create a sub-committee, permanently based in the Ilo area, and it is still the body responsible for evaluating damage to olive trees.

1961 saw the creation of the "Technical Committee on Fish Meal Plants" to tackle the problem of odour from this industry. It was multi-sectored, with its own budget and power to study and establish the necessary corrective measures. It had notable success. It was in a period of advancement in the knowledge and application of anti-pollution techniques and of specialist education. When this committee had finished its work it was replaced by the "Technical Committee for the Control of Emissions and Harmful Residues", to extend the work carried out and make it "permanent and nationwide". However faced with the absence of concrete objectives it was disbanded but not before providing valuable documentation and legislation in the fight against foul smelling emissions. The decline of the fishing industry has meant that much of that worthwhile experience has been forgotten.

The practice of using committees continues (it is almost a national characteristic of Peruvian administration on any matter). Thus it is that at present Peru has, to name but one, the "Committee for the Ecological Belt of Metropolitan Lima" aiming to reforest the Rimac Valley.

The balance of the work of these committees, made up of specialists rather than politicians, with budgets and other powers, is almost always positive, although their limited duration and application is a disadvantage. This has shown the urgent need to consider setting up an institution dedicated exclusively and permanently to environmental pollution as a whole. Advances have been made but with ups and downs. Its background is to be found in the work of the Occupational Health Institute (ISO), a state body but with technical and administrative autonomy, created in 1947 under an agreement between Peru and North America, the initial aims of which were directed towards mining health and hygiene.

Pollution episodes in the 1960s caused the indispensable intervention of the ISO, which at that time had one of the best infrastructures of laboratories and staff in Latin America with regard to internal industrial pollution. In 1965 it extended its work by creating a Department of Atmospheric Pollution, whose studies and reports are obligatory reference material on the national history on these subjects. With the loss of its budgetary autonomy (1972) and other changes in its structure, the ISO has drastically reduced its impetus in studies of external pollution.

An organization with responsibility for regulating the technical aspects of environmental pollution was subsequently established. The General Board of the Environment (DIGEMA) was formed in 1982, and was succeeded by the Environmental Health Board (DITESA) in 1986. This Board began work on aspects of air, water, soil and food pollution, but was restricted by its budget and the limited amount of specialist staff. The recent change of government (1990) has in turn replaced that Board with another called the General Board of Environmental Health (DIGESA). Formed at the same time as DITESA, the National Board of Protection of the Environment for Health - CONAPMAS - has been operating, and is an advisory body of the Ministry of Health on environmental policy and legislation.

2.2 Clean Air Philosophy

The basis and the reason behind measures for pollution control have been inspired by the Sanitation Code, an old law linked to Public Health. This Code states that "health is not negotiable" and considers that the most important effects of pollution are a negative influence on health (or that health is the priority), setting out to protect human welfare from the outset.

The frequency of problems between mining and agriculture (see section 1.3.2) have in recent years encouraged isolated programmes to demonstrate that "mining does not necessarily have an adverse effect on agriculture or life in general"; this could be a complementary philosophy.

Other principles, as appropriate, are applied such as the "use of the best available measures" or "maximum standards of emission or quality of the environment".

Faced with the lack of a permanent specialized organization, the philosophy, if it can be called that, has been (and still is) that the committees (see section 2.1) use the most practical methods suitable for each case.

2.3 Legislation

A 1977 seminar on legal aspects of controlling the environment in Peru, concluded that the laws "... are scattered, superimpose one upon another and are not applied with decisiveness". The reason for this is that such regulations had to be applied by different sectors of public administration, mainly by the Ministries concerned with production (Industry and Mining) along with local or town government.

This sectoral legislation (some of which has already been abolished) was fundamentally preventative. Thus the *Regulation of the General Law of Industries* (Decree Law No. 18350) established the obligation for newly created industries to include provisions on "... health and environmental pollution regulations...". The *General Mining Regulation* No. 18880, in turn, makes the owners responsible for "... emissions which may cause annoyance to the population or damage to health or to property". The Government is also empowered to clarify conflicts or claims "... deriving from pollution arising from ore treatment plants".

The *Organic Law of Municipalities* No. 23853 gives local government the job of ... regulating and controlling activities related to environmental health. Many other regulations exist but, in reality, Peru is still far from obtaining a rational and coordinated policy towards environmental control. However, from a conceptual, philosophical or doctrinal point of view many advances have been made as a result of Article 123 in the *New Constitution of the Country* (1979) which says: "Everyone has the right to live in a healthy environment, ecologically balanced and suitable for the development of life and preservation of the countryside and nature. Everyone has the duty to conserve that environment. It is the State's obligation to prevent and control environmental pollution".

Under this Constitutional stipulation, public opinion, non-governmental organizations and the government itself considered it to be the time to give the country a structured law to control multiple environmental problems. The task was entrusted to a committee directed by representatives from the National Planning Institute. A first draft was published in 1983 but it caused serious differences between the interested parties, and successive revisions were necessary, with the intervention of organizations such as CONAPMAS. Finally at the beginning of 1990 a "final draft" was delivered to the executive committee, but was not made public.

The new administration which took control in July 1990 issued a decree on 7 September with the official title of *Code for the Environment and Natural Resources* (Decree Law No. 611). Unfortunately much of its content is unconvincing and it has been criticized by all sectors. It has been called a "primitive and draconian" document. Currently under discussion are its improvement, its replacement and even its abolition.

The Code does not refer to atmospheric pollution - or considers it only superficially. For that reason the Peruvian Association Against Air Pollution (APPCCA) has asked the Environmental Protection Board (DITESA) to formulate a "Regulation for the Control of Atmospheric Pollution", proposing permissible standards for the country (see section 3.6).

3 IMPLEMENTATION AND ENFORCEMENT

3.1 Research

As stated earlier, the first studies on atmospheric pollution were undertaken by committees, many of which carried out effective work, establishing the necessary control systems. Three cases which we consider important are the following:

- In the La Oroya metallurgical complex in the 1920s, the study resulted in the establishment of technical systems to reduce pollutants, such as the building of chimneys, installation of Cotrell systems and arsenic "cookers".
- The foul smell issue (at the end of the 1950s) resulted in a very interesting study, laying down not only technical control measures (new transport systems and storage of raw materials, fish treatment, washing and incineration of gases); but also the study of the behaviour of meteorological parameters such as the direction and speed of winds. This work was awarded a prize at international level and its principal authors later made careers as international consultants.
- In the Ilo Foundry case (1960s), the relevant committee (CAN) made a direct study of agricultural damage and acted as an arbitrator in the payment of compensation. This solution to the problem which has been used for nearly 30 years remains unconvincing to environmentalists for whom the important matter is the utilization of gaseous emissions in the manufacture of sulphur derivatives or a change in the processes and operations until less damaging effluents are given off.

3.2 Monitoring

Although restricted, the work of the committees has demonstrated the gravity and constant presence of atmospheric pollution. This knowledge has given an urgent incentive for establishing a programme to monitor air quality. In the 1970s Peru participated with much interest in the programme named Network Panaire, directed by the Panamerican Centre of Sanitation Engineering and Environmental Sciences (CEPIS), an organization with its headquarters in Lima, a subsidiary of the Panamerican Health Organization (OPS). This programme lasted three years (1971-1973) and encompassed practically all Latin America and the Caribbean. It dealt with two kinds of pollutants by manual methods of sampling: particles in suspension (Hi-Vol) and sulphurous gases (acidimetry). Results with regard to Lima and in comparison with other cities in the area were amongst those which showed moderate pollution. However the results for sulphur dioxide gave rise to doubts as to the method used. In fact, the atmosphere in Lima appeared to be alkaline due to the uncontrolled decomposition of organic domestic waste and industrial emissions which also had alkaline reactions (for example fish meal factories). Later tests using other methods of analysis (nephelometry, pararosaniline), confirmed this thinking.

In spite of these difficulties, the Panaire Network is something that the countries of Latin America and the Caribbean, perhaps all the Third World, should continue with to exchange methods, results and solutions.

3.3 Lima Programme - Clean Air

When DITESA was established, one of its immediate objectives was to form a programme to monitor air quality, initially in Lima but with the intention of extending it to other known contaminated areas. Thus the Lima-Clean Air programme was established, the first station being installed in the centre of the city in June 1989. It began by measuring particles in suspension (Hi-Vol), sulphur dioxide (acidimetry) and heavy metals in the particles, this last measurement being without precedent in the country. Frequency of measurement was every six days, along with measurements of material in rainfall (monthly, jar method) sulphatation indices (lead candles), opacity in smoke (Ringelmann), traffic density and meteorological parameters (direction and speed of winds).

Initial results showed serious damage to the environment in Lima - comparing it, for example, with the concentrations of suspended particles found by the Panaire Network, as illustrated in Figure 2. It was hoped that the results might encourage the extension of the programme, with the acquisition of new equipment (those in operation were left over from past studies). However Peru was entering an unhappy stage in its history, with economic difficulties - it is said "the worst of its republican history" - and this of course was reflected in all its activities, particularly those not considered top priority. The Lima-Clean Air programme lost much of its support resulting in the principal staff members leaving the Institution. Decisions are expected from the new administration with regard to this matter.

3.4 Non-Governmental Programmes

In Peru, there have also been programmes carried out by non-governmental agencies which deserve a mention to complete the varied mosaic of concerns and actions brought about by environmental problems:

- The company who own the Ilo foundry and operated it in the 1970s administered an automatic network to determine sulphur dioxide levels by the conductimetric method, material in suspension and meteorological parameters. The results were not published, neither were they placed at the disposal of the authorities;

- The Cajamarquilla Zinc Refinery near Lima also has an integral environmental control programme (monitoring air, water, soil quality, use of industrial liquid residues for forestation). The Refinery belongs to the state but has limited company status with administrative and budgetary autonomy. It was allowed to purchase equipment, form a multi-discipline working group and carry out environmental studies prior to the opening of the plant. The programme has developed since 1981; with regard to air it

Figure 2: Suspended Particulate Matter

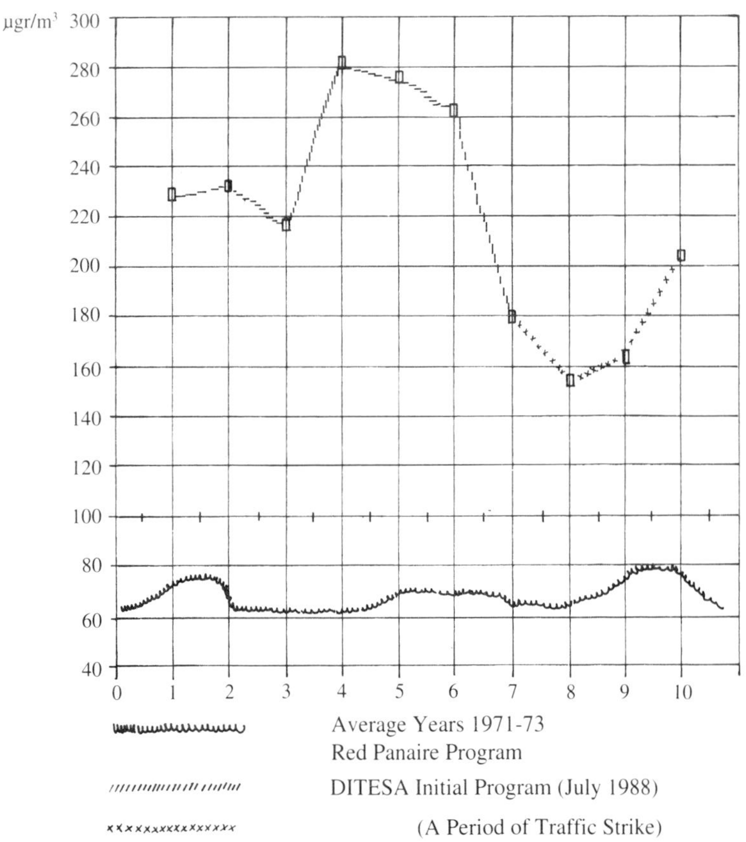

Source: DITESA (1989)

includes measurements of sulphatation indices (lead candles) corrosion indices (steel "medal"), sedimentation materials (jar) and in suspension (Hi-Vol), at 12 stations distributed over 25 sq. km. This permanent monitoring is complemented by periodic measurements for carbon monoxide (Ecolyser), sulphur dioxide (fluorescent UV) and noise (decibel meter). Its principal objective is to prevent conflicts with farmers and cattle breeders in the adjacent valley. This is considered to be a good example although it is not immune to the vagaries of policy and administrative changes.

3.5 Compensation for Pollution

The relevant sections of the Ministry of Health charged with pollution studies (ISO and DITESA) receive applications from private individuals and companies asking them to intervene in the clarification and solution of pollution problems in their neighbourhood. These applications, (averaging about one per week since the 1970s) include very varied cases both in size and significance and involve different pollutants (Figure 3). The results are interesting because without prompting from any agency the concepts of "indoor air pollution" studies or "total exposure assessment" are now considered between us. These new concepts are today much discussed in developed countries as an advanced technique in finding out the real incidence of air pollution on human beings.

Claims are resolved in about 90 per cent of cases when evidence of pollution is established. It is usually possible to do this by applying simple technology (which is also low cost), which was not considered in the first instance through lack of knowledge and not realizing the importance of the problem to the residents. An example of this is the case of a claim from a paint factory which was polluted with products from a neighbouring detergent factory. The problem originated in cyclone saturation, principally at night, a fact which was disregarded by the control staff. The installation of an optic-acoustic alarm solved the problem. In another case of a claim by townspeople, permission was refused for the installation of an iron-manganese foundry in an Andean valley (3000 metres above sea level) outstanding for floriculture. The environment was one consideration, although not the only one.

These actions reassure environmentalists, going some way to balancing their frustrations at the lack of facilities for wider research and give the public some confidence in the authorities, science and technology.

3.6 Quality of Air and Emission Regulations

In the main, US regulations or those recommended by the World

Health Organization are used, and in some cases Russian standards have been used, for example, for hydrogen sulphide.

On finding that the recently promoted *Code for the Environment and Natural Resources* said little regarding atmospheric pollution, the Peruvian Air Pollution Control Association (APPCCA) has proposed, by DITESA, a Control Regulation on Atmospheric Pollution which includes quality regulations. These regulations have been drawn up using specialized literature from the most advanced countries of the third world (India, Korea, Brazil, Mexico) and in some instances observed from national experience.

Figure 3: Complaints for Air Pollution

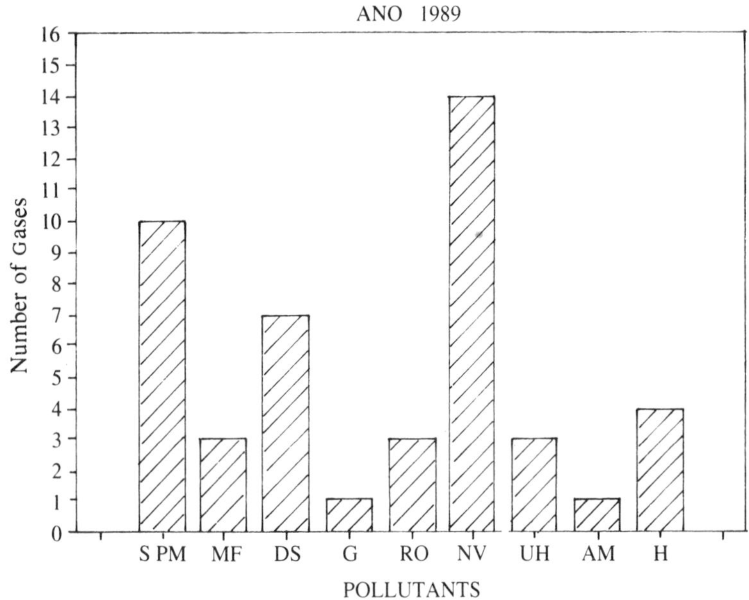

SPM = Suspended Particulate Matter
MF = Metallic Fumes
DS = Dark Smoke
G = Gases (SO_2, CO)
RO = Repulsive Odors
NV = Noise and Vibration
UH = Unburnt Hydrocarbons
AM = Acid Mist
H = Heat

(Note: Pollutants usually come associated one with another.)

Source: DITESA - 1989

Table 1: Air Quality Regulations (All regulations refer to normal conditions: 25°C and 760 mm. Barometric pressure Hg)

Suspended particle material		
0.15 mg/m^3		as annual geometric average
0.35 mg/m^3		maximum daily concentration, not to be exceeded more than once per year.
Method of Reference:		High volume sample
Sulphur oxide		
As SO_2	0.06 ppm	as annual arithmetical average
As SO_2	0.3 ppm	maximum daily concentration, not to be exceeded more than once per year.
Method of Reference:		Conductimetric or nephalometric method.
Photochemical oxidants		
As O_3	0.20 mg/m^3	Average 8 hours
As O_3	0.40 mg/m^3	for 30 minutes, not to be exceeded more than once per year.
Method of Reference:		Oxidant measured by K1 method.
Carbon Monoxide		
CO	20 mg/m^3	Average 8 hours
CO	40 mg/m^3	For 2 hours, should not be exceeded more than once per year.
Method of Reference:		Absorption of undispersed infrared rays.
Nitrogen Dioxide		
As NO_2	0.20 mg/m^3	Average 24 hours
Method of Reference:		Modified from Saltzman.
Arsenic (reference values) (this pollutant is widespread in Peru)		
As As. except arsine	0.006 mg/m^3	Average 24 hours
As As. except arsine	0.030 mg/m^3	For 30 minutes, not to be exceeded more than once per year.
Method of Reference:		Diethyldithiocarbamate.
Lead		
As Pb.	0.015 mg/m^3	Monthly average
As Pb.	0.005 mg/m^3	Yearly average
Method of Reference:		Atomic absorption.
Fumes		
In accordance with the Ringelmann Modified Scale.		
Odour		
Method of Reference:		Surveys or human testers.
Biological Pollutants		
Aerobic Bacteria		Not detectable
Pollen		Not detectable
Mycotic Flora		Not detectable

Noise

Area of Influence	*Permissible Levels of Exposure to Noise (dB A)*	
	Daytime (07.00/22.00 Hr)	*Night-time (22.00/07.00 Hr)*
Residential	60	55
Commercial	70	65
Industrial	80	75

Vibration

Noticeable vibration coming from industrial or commercial establishments or adjacent dwellings is not permitted in residential areas.

3.7 Standards of Emission

These have been used in exceptional cases, the most notable being the Cajamarquilla Refinery. Here the ISO demanded that emissions be kept to no more than 500 ppm of sulphur dioxide.

The above-mentioned Regulation proposed the following with regard to emissions:

> "Industries which generate atmospheric pollutants must instal equipment at points of emission to measure and register gases daily (nitrogen oxides, sulphur oxides and carbon monoxide), and maintain it in working order. At the same time, industries must carry out meteorological measurements (direction and speed of winds, temperature, relative humidity, rainfall and barometric pressure). Using this information the Environmental Authority will establish the maximum emission values applicable in each case."

4 CONCLUSION

This is a final reflection with regard to the causes and processes of atmospheric pollution in countries such as Peru and other latitudes, and will be a point of departure in accepting our most urgent and immediate responsibilities.

Mankind has caused pollution and continues to do so whilst converting raw materials into objects of value and thus win the vital prize of currency to purchase machinery and even food. On the other hand, when these processes reach a certain size, they require capital and more advanced technology from abroad which unfortunately does not necessarily imply environmental care.

Industrial processes are not the only cause of pollution to our environment. Other important sources of pollution are inherent in the use of certain products, e.g. persistent residues, pollution from motor vehicles, and the massive use of agricultural chemicals. These pollutants are made more pervasive through the uncaring attitude of the users, the habits of society, economic incentives, secrecy, the indifference or inability of authority and perhaps, above all, ignorance.

The most essential and greatest task is, therefore, education at all levels - from the home to the highest spheres of government, through formal education centres and massive media coverage. Universities should carry out research in this field, and industry must include environmental considerations in its activities as a normal investment procedure, whether by law or by its own understanding of what is desirable.

It must also be accepted that the fight against pollution linked with poverty has little in common with that other battle - that of searching for a higher standard of living, the commercial application of science and technology and ignominious, antisocial aggressive war industry.

The greenhouse effect, acid rain, damage to the ozone layer and oxygen renewal are currently universal fears. However it should be borne in mind that their greatest causes are found in energy waste, the proliferation of conventional vehicles, space rockets, crude oil transport and exploitation of the sea (as an industrial source and as a rubbish dump). It is from there, then, that such unforeseen problems should be tackled as a matter of principle by the users, to give elemental justice and realism. All have a part to play in tackling the problems facing the world today; actions include:

- Countries which do not manufacture cars, freon, halon, or agricultural chemicals should use substitutes when they are available on the market, although it is also understood that meanwhile everything possible should be done to avoid their indiscriminate use;
- If combustion engines are so damaging and oil reserves become more inaccessible it would seem to be time to launch on the market, with more effort, vehicles with different types of fuel, such as electrical, which have been feasible for many years, and long awaited;
- The Amazon must be protected through getting to know it better and freeing it from myths and exaggerations. It is possible that jungles would be the lungs of the earth, although small ones, because the sea, with all its plankton activity would seem to be the largest supplier of oxygen. As serious, or even more serious than cutting down the Amazon trees is throwing industrial waste, crude oils (accidental damage and cleaning ships), radioactive waste and even atomic bombs into the sea. This last fact implies scorn for others, and indeed for life itself;
- Foreign capital and technology are welcome to the Third World but only if they bring the theory and practice of avoiding environmental pollution;
- Everything possible must be done to banish international trade in rubbish and toxic waste, not only as it causes very real short and long term hazards, but also because it denigrates the human race.

Finally, IUAPPA could perhaps inform Third World political leaders about the existing situation and the importance which should be attached to safeguarding the atmosphere. It should also consider encouraging permanent regional networks to monitor air quality. With these actions work could lead towards the establishment of a world authority to protect the atmosphere as it is one of the few universal resources which is still free, without frontiers and intimately linked to every living thing on the planet. We would then effectively achieve clean air around the world.

5 BIBLIOGRAPHY

Stern A C. *Air Pollution.* Academic Press New York and London - 1962. Volume 2, together with a more recent collection by the same author.

Documentation from the World Health Organization.

REFERENCES

1. Mentioned in *Atlas Historico,* Geografico y de Paisajes Peruanos - National Planning Institute Lima, Peru. Prepared between 1963-70.

2. Baumann F. *Los Andes del Sur del Peru.* Universal Lima Edition, Peru 1984.

3. As 1.

The present report is principally based on:

* Libro TECNOSFERA - *La Atmósfera Contaminada y Sus Relaciones con el Publico* (The Polluted Atmosphere and its Relationship to the Public) M.A. Vizcarra-Andreu, Pacific Press Edition, Lima 1982.
* Documents from the Institute of Occupational Health, (ISO) Lima.
* Documents from the Technical Board of Environmental Health, Lima.
* Air Quality Regulations, proposed by Peruvian Engineer, César Macher B, International Consultant.

SAUDI ARABIA

1 INTRODUCTION

Like all laws in the Kingdom of Saudi Arabia, environmental protection law has its roots in the Glorious Quran and in the Islamic jurisprudence (Shariah). The Islamic juristic rule is "what fulfills and satisfies necessities is itself a necessity". Therefore, air, water and soil are necessities and any attempt at polluting or marring their functions is considered an attempt at hindering God's wisdom and creation. Islam is very keen on the protection of the basic elements of the environment for the benefit of present and future generations. It is equally keen on the protection of human beings and the environment against the harmful impacts of air, water, and soil pollution.

Recognizing the importance of environmental protection, the Kingdom of Saudi Arabia established its environmental protection and enforcement legislation in 1981. This chapter deals with the air pollution part of that legislation.

1.1 Topography, Climate, Population

The Kingdom of Saudi Arabia reaches from below 17 degrees N latitude to above 31 degrees N, and covers some 3 144 000 sq. km. Sandy desert areas predominate in the southern and south eastern Region (Ar-Rub Al-Khali), with a largely arid, high, plateau at 750 metres in the north to 2100 metres in the south and sloping downwards to the east, covering the majority of the country. This plateau is bounded by mountain ranges, with peaks to 3000 metres to the west and south, with narrow coastal belts along the Red Sea and Gulf of Arabian coasts.

While the climate is broadly sub-tropical with a ridge of relatively high pressure being present over central and eastern areas much of the year, with hot, dry summers and cooler, mainly settled and clear winters, there are several significant seasonal features giving rise to much more active conditions in northern, eastern, southern, and coastal areas which are important.

In winter, cyclonic weather systems pass irregularly across the northern part of the Arabian Peninsula, moving primarily from the eastern Mediterranean Sea to the Tigris-Euphrates basin, and the area north of the Arabian Gulf. At times associated troughs with cloud and rain move south and east across Red Sea coasts and inland, reaching Medina and Jeddah regions, and even on rare occasions as far southwards as Gizan.

In summer, as the Intertropical Convergence Zone moves north over the Indian Ocean, and gives rise to the monsoon regime over the Indian Sub-Continent, the effects bring unstable and active conditions into the south west and southern regions, weakening the sub-tropical ridge from the east which covers most of the Kingdom.

During transitional months, weather situations vary considerably as troughs from the north and extensions eastwards from the general low pressure area over Sudan, erode the weak ridge over the kingdom. This can bring unsettled, active weather conditions to all highland and coastal regions.

Winters, from November to February, are cool to warm, and occasionally frost and snow may occur along the highlands. Average daily temperatures for the coolest months are quite comfortable, e.g. Jeddah, 21 - 25 degrees C; Riyadh, 12 - 17 degrees C; and Medina, 16 - 23 degrees C. Summers, from June to August or September, are hot with daytime shade temperatures reaching 40 degrees C almost everywhere (apart from the highlands), and frequently 50 degrees C.

Humidity is generally low, and dry air persists in central and southern regions. In coastal regions, both eastern and western, it can become high for considerable periods of time, with moist air penetration due to varying low pressure weather situations in these areas only changing gradually.

Precipitation is low throughout the Kingdom, but because of its extreme variability mean values of rainfall do not give the normal indication of conditions for most of the time. In the highlands of Asir, more than 250 - 300 mm rain (even up to 600 mm in some places) in a single year has been recorded. In March and April in some years, torrential rainfall has occurred in this region with spasmodic flooding. The summer rainfall, in Asir, associated with the monsoonal conditions to the east and south, mainly coming from the south west and west, supports steppe agriculture.

In ar Rub al Khali as a contrast, a decade may pass without receiving any rain at all. In Jeddah, rainfall generally averages about 55 - 60 mm but in many years has received much less than these figures. In Riyadh and Dharan, the average rainfall is closer to 110 and 90 mm, respectively.

During the winter period, prevailing winds from the north west cover most of the Kingdom. In transitional months, more variability occurs as minor weather systems affect regions differently and often with generally slack pressure fields, local topography or coastal locations are the predominating factors. In the summer season, south east to south west winds affect the southern half of the Kingdom as the north westerly flow decreases over northern areas. Speeds are generally light, with less than 8 kts (4 metres/second), throughout the Kingdom, although fresh to strong winds associated with passing weather systems are irregular events, mainly in winter and transitional periods.

Average cloud cover is usually very small, especially in the summer months when it rarely exceeds more than one-half of the whole sky at any location. Average summer cloud cover is one-eighth or less. Cloud cover for winter and spring months tends to average around one-fourth or less. The highest average, in April, is less than one-half for Dhahran and about one-half for Riyadh. The limited cloud cover contributes to the intense solar radiation or insolation. Thus, more than two-thirds of the available solar radiation penetrates the dry, relatively cloudless atmosphere to heat the land surface significantly.

A feature of the region is blowing dust or sandstorms arising in hot, dry southerly quadrant winds, (Aziabs), which can occur mainly in western and southern regions. These mostly occur in late spring and early summer reaching a peak in June when it is common to have 23 days out of 30 with blowing dust and strong winds usually during the afternoon. These sand or duststorms result from eastward moving low pressure troughs meeting cooler air over the northern and eastern parts of the country.

Any strong wind crossing suitable terrain may give rise to reduced visibility, with the heights to which dust or sand is raised depending upon the local low level atmospheric conditions at the time.

1.2 Specific National Problems

The most important factor governing the air quality of an area is the climate and meteorology of that area. The air pollution potential of an area is directly related to its meteorology. Wind direction determines where pollutants travel and thus what areas are affected. Wind speed controls the relative dilution of pollutants that are mixed with incoming fresh air; temperatures (or atmospheric stability) determine the amount of mixing that occurs in the air.

Because of its climate, the Kingdom of Saudi Arabia is susceptible to several kinds of air pollution. For example, the Kingdom's clear skies and strong solar radiation provide near perfect conditions for the formation of photochemical air pollutants. At night, the same clear skies allow the surface to lose heat rapidly; this leads to very stable atmospheric conditions which greatly limit mixing height and in turn the dilution of pollutants. Frequent low wind speeds also inhibit dilution and allow pollutants to build up. The occasional strong winds raise dust and sand which degrade air quality, and the lack of precipitation means that air contaminants are not washed from the air on a regular basis.

2 DEVELOPMENT OF AIR POLLUTION CONTROLS AND LEGISLATION

2.1 Meteorology and Environmental Protection Administration

During the last fifteen years, the Kingdom of Saudi Arabia has witnessed very rapid development in economic and industrial sectors. The Meteorology and Environmental Protection Administration (MEPA) was established by Royal Decree No. 7/M/8903 in 1401 AH (1981 AD) in order to deal with the anticipated environmental problems resulting from industrialization. In addition to its activities in meteorology, MEPA was charged with the following functions:

- To establish definitive environmental standards and specifications for pollution control and environmental protection, which are to be taken into account by the appropriate authorities when issuing permits for industrial and agricultural projects which may have an environmental impact;
- To conduct environmental surveys to define problems and recommend environmental standards and measures;
- To recommend protection regulations and measures dealing with environmental problems;
- To recommend practical measures necessary to deal with emergency situations affecting the environment;
- To assess existing environmental pollution levels and future variations, such information to be documented for easy retrieval;
- To keep abreast of developments in the field of environmental protection on the regional and international levels.

Under MEPA's Charter, the Environmental Protection General Directorate (EPGD) was established; it is responsible for environmental protection matters such as issuing and implementng standards and evaluation of environmental conditions. Its duties include:

- preparing and recommending environmental quality and source standards and necessary implementation procedures for their application;
- submitting reports on environmental impacts of major projects in the Kingdom;

- providing assistance and technical advice to those engaged in industrial and agricultural activities to enable them to comply with environmental standards;
- submitting reports on the state of the environment and follow up on the application of environmental standards and their effects.

The objectives of the above functions should be appropriate to the Kingdom's development plans and should also lead to the best solutions for selecting sites for new projects and their design and performance to abate environmental damage resulting from industrial and urban activities.

The Charter also established a National Meteorological and Environmental Centre (NMEC) charged with the responsibility of preparing and issuing climatological, environmental and meteorological analyses, forecasts, bulletins and reports in a form conforming with user requirements, including warnings and bulletins on the local, regional and international levels.

2.2 Environmental Protection Standards

In accordance with its Charter, MEPA established an initial set of Standards in 1402 AH (1982 AD). The document includes source and ambient standards designed to protect air and water quality by limiting the emission of pollutants from sources and the concentration of pollutants in air and water. A summary of ambient air quality and source emission standards is given in Tables 1 and 2.

Table 1: MEPA's Ambient Air Quality Standards

Pollutant	*Averaging time*	*ug/m³*	*(ppm)*
Sulphur Dioxide	1 Hour	800	(0.31)a
	24 Hours	400	(0.15)b
	Annual	80	(0.03)
Nitrogen Dioxide	1 Hour	660	(0.35)
	Annual	100	(0.05)
Carbon Monoxide	1 Hour	40000	(35)a
	8 Hours	10000	(9)a
Ozone	1 Hour	290	(0.15)a
Inhalable Particulates	24 Hours	340[b]	—
	Annual	80	—
Hydrogen Sulphide	1 Hour	200	(0.14)[b]
Fluorides	30 Days	1	(0.001)

a = Allowable exceedances : 2 per month
b = Allowable exceedance : 1 per year

Table 2: MEPA's Air Pollution Source Standards

Source	*Pollutant*	*Emission limit*
Petroleum and Petro-Chemical Facilities		
A. Petroleum storage vessels (greater than 1000 bbl capacity)	VOC	a) For liquids with vapour pressure 78-570mm (1.5-11 psi), floating roof with double seal or equivalent. b) For liquids with vapour pressure greater than 570mm (11 psi), vapour recovery or equivalent. c) For crude oil (disregarding vapour pressure), floating roof with seal inspection programme is adequate.
B. FCC unit catalyst regenerators	Particulate CO	1.0 kg/tonne coke burnoff 500 ppm
C. Fuel gas combustion	SO_2	Limit H_2S content of fuel gas to 230 mg/DSCM (0.10 gr/DSCF) or use equivalent SO_2 removal system.
D. Claus sulphur plants	SO_2	At least 95% recovery of total sulfur.
E. Blowdown, purging, draining and waste water separation	VOC	Minimize emissions by enclosure and recycling and/or flaring.
F. Fugitive emissions	VOC	Use good maintenance and inspection procedures as well as monitoring of potential sources.
Fertilizer Plants	NH_3 Particulates	99% controlled by combustion. Best available control technology.
Cement Plants		
A. Kilns	Particulates	0.15 kg/tonne
B. Clinker Coolers	Particulates	0.05 kg/tonne
Aluminium Reduction Plants		
A. Pot-room group	Fluorides	1.25 kg/tonne of aluminium
B. Anode bake plants	Fluorides	0.05 kg/tonne of aluminium
Industrial Boilers and Furnaces (heat input capacity greater than 30 MW)	Particulates SO_2	43 ng/J (0.1 lb/MBTU) 1000 ng/J (2.3 lb/MBTU) (under review)
o Gas-fired	NO_x	87 ng/J (0.2 lb/MBTU)
o Oil-fired	NO_x	130 ng/J (0.3 lb/MBTU)
Iron and Steel Plants (electric arc furnaces)	Particulates	Best available control technology (12 mg/DSCM maximum)
Lime Manufacturing Plants (rotary kilns)	Particulates	0.2 kg/tonne
All Facilities	Visible Emissions	20% maximum opacity except for three minutes during any continous 60-minute period.

The purpose of these Standards is to provide appropriate bases for the evaluation and regulation of industrial and urban activities that currently exist in the Kingdom. In this way, the Standards will ensure that the planning, design, execution and operation of facilities will be developed in a manner which does not adversely affect the health, safety and welfare of the people and which helps to promote their economic and social wellbeing and to protect the Kingdom's environment in general.

This means that all major new facilities, or any major modification to an existing facility, must be designed, operated and maintained so that ambient standards in force at the time of design approval are not violated. The best practical pollution control and waste disposal techniques must be incorporated. Similarly, all major existing facilities must be operated and maintained so that ambient environmental standards are not violated. Additional control equipment must be installed if necessary. Both new and existing facilities must not discharge any toxic substance, whether specifically regulated or not, in quantities harmful to public health.

The Standards apply to all existing and planned facilities, both public and private, including industrial projects, transportation facilities, commercial and agricultural activities, sewage treatment plants, and human settlements within the Kingdom. The Standards permit MEPA to make exceptions by granting variances under special circumstances. However, any exceptions may not result in a violation of environmental quality standards or be detrimental to public health.

2.3 Motor Vehicle Emission Standards

The responsibility for setting and controlling emissions from mobile sources is currently assigned to the Ministry of Transport, which has started a Motor Vehicles Periodic Inspection (MVPI) programme in three major cities: Jeddah, Riyadh and Dammam. Under this programme, every operating vehicle in these cities is required to be inspected annually for emission controls and safety checks. The MVPI programme emission limits which must be met are total hydrocarbons at 250 parts per million per cylinder and carbon monoxide at 6 per cent volumetric for gasoline engines.

3 IMPLEMENTATION AND ENFORCEMENT

3.1 Enforcement

Promulgating standards and publishing procedures, however, do not in themselves ensure that the standards will be implemented. Therefore, MEPA has established a compliance - or inspectorate -

programme within the Environmental Protection General Directorate to support implementation of the Environmental Protection Standards. Compliance efforts include contacts and discussions with various Ministries, governmental organizations, and private sector industries concerning the environmental standards. Extensive efforts have been concentrated on the control of the Kingdom's petroleum, fertilizer, cement, and mineral processing industries.

Industry-wide meetings have been held between MEPA and representatives of these particular industries. The meetings focus on issues such as the industry-specific technical and economic problems associated with compliance with MEPA environmental protection standards and the establishment of mechanisms for implementation of the standards. Discussions are also held with the operators of individual plants in order to resolve particular source specific issues on a case-by-case basis.

Industrial plant overview inspections, engineering evaluations, and computer dispersion modelling are routinely conducted in order to evaluate the environmental impact of sources as well as to determine compliance status. Conclusions and recommendations regarding a plant's environmental situation are formulated in coordination with MEPA's overall strategy for pollution control in the Kingdom.

The Environmental Protection Standards are implemented and enforced by MEPA through a two-stage approach:

- at the time a developer submits to the relevant Ministry an application seeking a license to develop, that Ministry seeks MEPA's views on the adequacy of the proposal. Following negotiations, where necessary, MEPA advises the licensing authority whether, in its view, a development license should be issued or not; and
- following receipt of the development license, and after completing all detailed designs of pollution control systems, the developer must then seek a permit from MEPA for the installation of those control systems.

This approach ensures MEPA's involvement at all relevant stages without in any way usurping the statutory rights of licensing authorities such as the Ministry of Industry and Electricity.

3.2 Monitoring

Basically, MEPA is responsible for enforcing ambient air quality and source emission standards throughout the Kingdom.

To ensure compliance with the ambient air quality standards, MEPA maintains and operates a number of continuous air quality monitoring stations throughout the Kingdom. Also, a mobile ambient air quality laboratory is used to investigate any specific industrial or urban air pollution problems.

MEPA also receives ambient air quality monitoring data from the Royal Commission for Jubail and Yanbu and from ARAMCO. Air quality characteristics monitored at these stations include sulphur dioxiode, nitrogen oxides, carbon monoxide, ozone, hydrocarbons, hydrogen sulphide and suspended particulates. Current data from all stations, except from the Jeddah Industrial City, indicate compliance with MEPA's ambient air quality standards for gaseous pollutants.

At the Jeddah Industrial City Monitoring Station, the hourly concentrations of sulphur dioxide and nitrogen oxides have occasionally exceeded the respective standards with peak readings as high as twice the standard. Poor meteorological conditions for dispersion and emissions from industrial and mobile sources are believed to be the causes. Air quality monitoring data also show that the daily concentrations of suspended particulates have frequently exceeded the standard mainly due to natural dust blowing. A summary of the range of monthly/annual mean concentrations of various air pollutants is shown in Table 3.

Table 3: Annual Mean Concentrations Monitored

Air pollutant	*Range of annual mean concentrations (ppm)*
Sulphur Dioxide	0.001-0.02
Nitrogen Dioxide	0.01-0.02
Carbon Monoxide	0.3-2.6
Ozone	0.01-0.05

MEPA, like any other environmental regulatory agency, initiates its abatement or enforcement activities based on the results from the ambient air quality monitoring stations, source emission surveys, and public complaints.

3.3 The Royal Commission for Jubail and Yanbu

Enforcement activities are very well coordinated with other government departments and are carried out in cooperation with regional and municipal governments, public and private organizations and individuals.

However, in two major industrial cities, Jubail and Yanbu, MEPA has delegated its responsibilities to the Royal Commission for Jubail and Yanbu. The Royal Commission, an agency of the Ministry of

Planning, was established by Royal Decree M/75 in 1395 AH (1975 AD) to implement the basic infrastructure necessary to transform the regions (Jubail and Yanbu) into industrial areas. In its planning, the Kingdom insisted that environmental consequences be given proper consideration and that appropriate safeguards be built into the project to protect the environment. However, MEPA reviews the environmental management practices and compliance records of the Royal Commission on a regular basis. It is worth mentioning here that the Royal Commission, for its excellence in environmental planning and management, received the prestigious UNEP award - the Sasakawa Environmental Prize - in 1988.

4 EFFECTIVENESS OF CONTROLS

4.1 Environmental Protection Coordinating Committee

The Kingdom recognizes that environmental protection activities would not be effective unless they are coordinated with development planning activities and have the cooperation of other governmental agencies. To meet this objective, the Environmental Protection Coordinating Committee (EPCCOM) was established by Royal Decree to coordinate the activities of government bodies involved in environmental protection. The Chairman of EPCCOM is HRH the Second Deputy Prime Minister and Minister for Defence and Aviation and Inspector General. The President of MEPA is Secretary General of EPCCOM and other members are Deputy Ministers or higher, representing: the Ministries of the Interior, Municipal and Rural Affairs, Industry and Electricity, Planning, Health, Petroleum and Mineral Resources, Agriculture and Water, Transport, Commerce (Saudi Organization for Standards), and the King Abdulaziz Centre for Science and Technology.

The resolution of the Committee for Administrative Reform which is approved by the above mentioned Decree defined the following duties and responsibilities for EPCCOM:

- To consider all measures submitted by MEPA in connection with environmental protection and forward them to the Council of Ministers for approval;
- To adopt studies and reports submitted by MEPA;
- To adopt regulations and instructions to be followed by all government organizations in different parts of the Kingdom and submit them for approval by the Council of Ministers;
- To decide measures and instructions applicable only to certain organizations;

- To approve MEPA plans, programmes, and projects for environmental protection;
- To instruct MEPA in connection with the availability of environmental protection studies and information;
- To coordinate environmental activities between concerned organizations within the Kingdom.

Through EPCCOM and the implementation of the Environmental Protection Standards, MEPA has promoted a cleaner environment. The following examples demonstrate the success of the programme.

4.1.1 The Cement Industry

In late 1983, the cement industry signed a memorandum of understanding with MEPA on the extent to which emissions should be controlled and monitored. The Kingdom now has seven cement plants. Some of the older plants were poorly controlled, emitting dust in concentrations of around 200-300 mg/m^3. MEPA introduced standards for the industry which, when met, reduced overall emissions to only 50 mg/m^3. The Yamama plant in Riyadh was retrofitted with bag filters, gas analysers and electrostatic precipitators at a cost of about SR 175 million to achieve compliance with MEPA's standards.

4.1.2 The Rock Crushing and Asphaltic Cement Industry

In 1984, MEPA estimated that there were at least 300 plants mining and crushing gravel for road pavement. Many also produced asphaltic cement and few were adequately controlled. MEPA determined that the technology was available for proper control at a modest cost. The controls imposed by MEPA included installing water sprays on the primary and secondary crushers, watering haul roads and other unpaved areas, and installing water spray and bag filtration units on kilns producing asphalt.

4.1.3 The Phase-Out of Leaded Gasoline

MEPA was well aware of the overseas trend towards lead-free gasoline and the use of catalytic converters to remove pollutants from vehicle exhaust gases. MEPA took the view that, as lead is a known cumulative poison and is no longer a vital constituent of gasoline for modern engines, that it was not a matter of whether lead should be removed but, rather, how and when. MEPA, therefore, undertook a comprehensive study of the environmental and economic ramifications of introducing low-lead and then lead-free gasoline. The government has now adopted a strategy that will, in a few years, result in the in-Kingdom production and use of lead-free gasoline.

4.1.4 The Fertilizer Industry

The Dammam Fertilizer Plant, operated by the Saudi Arabian Fertilizer Company (SAFCO) consists of ammonia, sulphuric acid, urea and melamine production units. This plant was a source of public complaints related to ammonia odours in the past. MEPA's monitoring and enforcement activities from 1985-1989 have resulted in a significant reduction in ammonia and particulate emissions from this plant. This was achieved by the installation of air pollution control systems (incinerator and scrubber) for ammonia and particulate emission sources. Following a request from MEPA, SAFCO was to reduce its ammonia emissions from the processs waste water stream discharged to the evaporation pond before April 1991 by the installation and operation of a steam stripper.

4.1.5 The Programme to Collect and Utilize Flared Gas

This programme was initiated by the Ministry of Petroleum and Mineral Resources (Member of EPCCOM) and completed in 1983. Before that, almost 60 per cent of the total volume of gas produced (5000 MMSCFD) at Saudi Arabian oil fields was disposed by flaring. This was not only a great loss of a non-renewable energy resource, but also a major source of sulphur dioxide emissions into the atmosphere. Currently, less than 1 MMSCFD of produced gas is being flared. Additionally, the availability of natural gas in the eastern Province of the Kingdom has made it possible to switch fuel from oil to gas at the desalination plants in Jubail and Al-Khobar. This fuel-switch has resulted in almost zero sulphur dioxide emissions from these sources.

4.2 International Initiatives

Saudi Arabia is actively involved in the governing bodies of the United Nations Environment Programme (UNEP), the International Union for the Conservation of Nature and Natural Resources (IUCN), the World Meteorological Organization (WMO), and a number of other regional and international organizations such as the the Advisory Committee on Pollution of the Sea (ACOPS).

Senior staff from MEPA, other ministries and universities participate in the various technical commissions and working groups of these organizations. A major initiative in 1988 was the creation by WMO and UNEP of an Intergovernmental Panel on Climate Change (IPCC). Saudi Arabia holds Vice Chairmanship of IPCC and was represented on the working group concerned with future policies to cope with climate change and ozone depletion.

5 FUTURE DEVELOPMENTS

The following legislation, currently under consideration, is expected to further strengthen existing pollution control requirements:

- Development of National Legislation for Protection of the Environment;
- A National Conservation Strategy;
- A National Chemical Safety Programme;
- A National Hazardous Waste Management Programme.

Any future developments at the international level related to global climate change and stratospheric ozone depletion will obviously have some impact on air pollution control requirements in the Kingdom.

6 REFERENCES

The State of the Environment in the Kingdom of Saudi Arabia, Volumes 1 and 2, published by Meterorology and Environmental Protection Administration (MEPA), Jeddah, Saudi Arabia (1989).

Environmental Guidelines, published by MEPA, Jeddah (Document No. 12302A, dated December 1985).

Industry and Environment: The Saudi Arabian Experience; The World Industry Conference on Environmental Management - Versailles, France, 14 - 16 November 1984. A paper presented by Dr. Abdulbar Al-Gain, President of MEPA, Jeddah.

Environmental Protection Standards (General Standards) Document No. 1409-01, published by MEPA, Jeddah, Saudi Arabia (1982).

Siraj, Ahmad A, *Aziab Weather*. Published by General Directorate of Meteorology (now MEPA), Jeddah (1980).

SINGAPORE

1 INTRODUCTION

1.1 Topography, Climate and Population

Singapore has a land area of approximately 620 sq. miles (1605 sq. km) and, with a population of three million, is amongst the most densely populated areas in the world. The Island Republic is situated at the tip of the Malay Peninsula where the land is flat. The climate is warm (26-32 degrees C), humid (80 per cent) and equable. There are two dominant monsoon seasons: the SW monsoon from April to October and the NE monsoon from November to March. The average rainfall is around 2500 mm.

1.2 Specific National Problems

Singapore is a major petroleum refining centre and the chemical and petrochemical industries are growing at a fast pace. With improved standards of living and higher incomes, the number of motor vehicles has increased significantly in recent years. These together with many light industries are potential sources of air pollution. However, the good ventilating wind and high rainfall results in no serious photochemical pollution problem.

1.3 Links with Planning and Energy Use Strategies

Although Singapore is a major oil refining centre, all crude oil is imported. Power generation relies entirely on imported fuel oil. Plans are underway to switch some of these power plants to gas firing facilities. To encourage energy conservation, a heavy excise tax is imposed on gasoline and diesel fuel to discourage consumption. A quota system is imposed on the number of new motor vehicles that can be allowed on the road each year. Those who want to buy a new vehicle are required to bid for allotted licences. In addition, owners of cars more than ten years old must pay added surcharges to keep their vehicles on the road to encourage people to change their cars more often to take advantage of improved technology in emission and noise control.

2 DEVELOPMENT OF AIR POLLUTION CONTROLS AND LEGISLATION

2.1 Basic Principles

Since the intensive effort to promote industrialization which began in the 1960s, there has been a rapid growth in the number and diversity of factories established in Singapore. This growth has continued virtually unabated to the present day.

This has however, brought in its wake several problems, not the least of which is the environmental impact. Recognizing the problem, the Government proceeded to institute environmental pollution control alongside its programme of economic and industrial growth. This was done through the formation of the Anti-Pollution Unit (APU) under the Prime Minister's Office in April 1970 and later by the formation of the Ministry of the Environment (ENV) in September 1972. Since April 1983, the APU has become part of the ENV.

In order to achieve effective control of air pollution in Singapore, the legal liabilities and requirements imposed on industrial polluters has to be clearly stated in legislation. Details of air pollution control legislation are listed in Table 1.

Table 1: Air Pollution Control Legislation

Legislation	*Effective date*
Clean Air Act 1971	2 December 1971
Clean Air (Standards) Regulations 1972	15 January 1972
Clean Air (Prohibition on the Use of Open Fires) 1972	25 January 1973
Clean (Amendment) Act 1975	26 March 1975
Clean Air (Standards) (Amendment) Regulations 1978	1 April 1978
Clean Air Act (Amendment of Schedule) Notification 1978	3 May 1980
Clean Air Act (Amendment of Schedule) Notification 1990	18 January 1990

2.2 Clean Air Philosophy

The purpose of the *Clean Air Act* is to prevent ambient air from reaching a point that it affects human health and the environment. The basic philosophy of air pollution control is the "best practicable means" approach without regard to air quality near the source. To achieve a clean and green environment, air quality objectives are, however, used as an important management tool for planning, organizing and gauging the effectiveness of air pollution control programmes. World Health Organization and US Environmental Protection Agency air quality guidelines are used as guides to acceptable quality.

Industrial and trade premises are divided into two categories - "scheduled premises" and "non-scheduled premises". Issuance of Written Permission to Scheduled Premises is used as a means of controlling operations of these industries. Emission standards are set for stationary and mobile sources. A network of air monitoring stations has been established to gauge air quality changes to aid planning and continuous revision and upgrading of air pollution control measures.

2.3 Legislation and Instruments

The *Clean Air Act 1971* is the main piece of legislation for air pollution control and the regulations detailed in Table 1 are merely to complement it. The *Clean Air Act* empowers Anti-Pollution Unit officers to control air pollution from industrial and trade premises. Under the Act, industrial and trade premises are divided into two categories - scheduled premises and non-scheduled premises. Scheduled premises are those listed in the Schedule to the Act and are deemed to have a greater potential to pollute. All other industrial or trade premises are classified as non-scheduled premises.

The *Clean Air Act* is divided into four parts as follows:

Part I: Definition;
Part II: Provisions affecting scheduled premises;
Part III: Provisions affecting industrial and trade premises (scheduled as well as non-scheduled premises);
Part IV: Miscellaneous provisions.

Part I defines the Act and the various terms used e.g. "authorized officer", "control equipment", "occupier", etc.

Under Part II the occupier of scheduled premises is required to obtain the written permission of the Director of Air Pollution Control before occupying such premises or beginning operations. However, this requirement does not apply to an occupier who began operating before the Act became law. In granting permission, the Director may attach conditions to the written permission. He is empowered by the Act to vary the conditions attached to the written permission at any time. The occupier of any scheduled premises also has to obtain the written permission of the Director before he can do any of the following:

a) alter the method of operation of any trade, industry, process, fuel burning equipment or control equipment or industrial plant within the premises;

b) install, alter or replace any fuel burning equipment or control equipment or industrial plant within the premises;

c) erect or alter the height or dimension of any chimney through which air impurities may be emitted from the premises; and

d) use any other fuel other than the type of fuel specified by the Director.

If there is any change in the ownership of scheduled premises, the new owner is required to inform the Director in writing within 14 days of the takeover. All these provisions are intended to provide the Director with wide-ranging powers to enable him and his authorized officers to exercise effective controls over scheduled premises and thus prevent excessive discharges of pollution.

Part III of the Act lists those provisions which affect all industrial

Table 2: Summary of Emission Standards in the Clean Air (Standards) (Amendment) Regulations 1978

Pollutant	*Standard applicable to*	*Old standard*	*New standard*
Solid particles	Any trade, industry, process, industrial plant or fuel burning equipment (not involving metal heating)	0.4 gm/Nm^3	0.2 gm/Nm^3
Sulphuric acids mist or sulphur trioxide	Any trade, industry or process (other than combustion processes and plants for the manufacture of sulphuric acid)	0.2 gm/Nm^3 as sulphur trioxide	0.1 gm/Nm^3 as sulphur trioxide
Acid gas	Any trade, industry or process in which sulphuric acid is manufactured	6.0 gm/Nm^3 as sulphur trioxide	3.0 gm/Nm^3 as sulphur trioxide
Hydrogen chloride	Any trade, industry or process	0.4 gm/Nm^3 as hydrogen chloride	0.2 gm/Nm^3 as hydrogen chloride
Chlorine	Any trade, industry or process	0.2 gm/Nm^3 as chlorine	0.1 gm/Nm^3 as chlorine
Nitric acid or oxides of nitrogen	Any trade, industry or process in which the manufacture of nitric acid is carried out	4.0 gm/Nm^3 as equivalent of sulphur trioxide	2.0 gm/Nm^3 as nitrogen oxide
Nitric acid or oxides of nitrogen	Any trade, industry or process other than nitric acid plants	2.0 gm/Nm^3 as equivalent of sulphur trioxide	1.0 gm/Nm^3 as nitrogen dioxide
Carbon monoxide	Any trade, industry or process	None	1.0 gm/Nm^3 as carbon monoxide
Antimony and its compound	Any trade, industry or process	0.02 gm/Nm^3 as antimony	0.01 gm/Nm^3 as antimony
Cadmium and its compound	Any trade, industry or process	0.02 gm/Nm^3 as cadmium	0.01 gm/Nm^3 as cadmium
Mercury and its compound	Any trade, industry or process	0.02 gm/Nm^3 as mercury	0.01 gm/Nm^3 as mercury

and trade premises (both scheduled as well as non-scheduled premises). Occupiers of such premises are required to maintain and operate their control equipment in a proper and effective manner. Their process plants are also required to comply with the emission limits for various air pollutants stipulated by the authorities. The best practical means of pollution control must be used.

The *Clean Air (Amendment) Act* was passed in 1975 to amend certain sections of the Act in order to make it more effective. Construction sites were classified as industrial and trade premises so that pollution from them could be controlled. The types of conditions to be attached to written permissions and the requirements specified in notices were spelt out more clearly. A presumptive clause was added to place the onus of proof on the occupier in situations where evidence of non-compliance with an Order was found in the premises. Another important amendment was the granting of jurisdiction to try offenses under the Act in the District Court or Magistrates Court.

The *Clean Air (Standards) Regulations 1972* specify the maximum allowable emission limits for various pollutants such as dark smoke, dust etc. The maximum fine for contravening these regulations is S$5000 or, if the offense is a continuing one, S$200 for each and every day during which the offense continues.

The emission standards were upgraded a few years later with the passing of the *Clean Air (Standards) (Amendment) Regulations* in 1978 because of the increased number of factories that came into operation between 1972 and 1978. Both the old emission standards and the upgraded standards are shown in Tables 2 and 3, respectively.

Table 3: Other Emission Standards in the Clean Air (Standards) Regulations

Pollutant	*Standard applicable to*	*Standard*
Smoke	All stationary fuel-burning sources	Ringelmann No 2 or equivalent opacity. (Not to exceed more than 5 minutes any period of one hour)
Fluorine compounds	Any trade, industry or process in the operation of which fluorine, hydrofluoric acid or any inorganic fluorine compounds are emitted	0.10 gm/Nm^3 as hydro-fluoric acid
Hydrogen sulphide	Any trade, industry or process	5 ppm as hydrogen sulphide gas
Copper and its compounds	Any trade, industry or process	0.02 gm/Nm^3 as copper
Lead and its compounds	Any trade, industry or process	0.02 gm/Nm^3 as lead
Arsenic and its compounds	Any trade, industry or process	0.02 gm/Nm^3 as arsenic

The *Clean Air (Prohibition on the Use of Open Fires) Order 1973* empowers the Director of Air Pollution Control and his authorized officers to deal with the problems of low level smoke and flash emission from open fires. Prior to this Order which came into force on 25 January 1973, it was common practice to dispose of industrial wastes by open burning. With the classification of construction sites as industrial and trade premises in 1975 this Order can also be used to control open fires in such premises.

The *Clean Air Act (Amendment of Schedule) Notification 1980* provides control over premises used for the storage of large quantities of toxic or inflammable chemicals. The written permission of the Director is required before the occupier can use such premises for storage.

The *Clean Air Act (Amendment of Schedule) Notification 1990* provides for control over abrasive blasting works, being works in which equipment or structures are cleaned by abrasive blasting. The written permission of the Director is required before the work can be carried out.

2.4 Mobile Sources

At present, there are about 500 000 motor vehicles in Singapore of which 64 per cent are petrol-driven, 24 per cent diesel vehicles and 12 per cent motorcycles.

Measures to control vehicle exhaust emissions have been in force since the late 1970s. In 1984 Singapore adopted the emission standards stipulated in the United Nations Economic Commission for Europe (UN-ECE) Regulation No R15.03 for registration of petrol-driven vehicles. All petrol-driven vehicles had to comply with the ECE R15.03 emission standards before they could be registered for use in Singapore. In 1986 the standard was upgraded to ECE R15.04 emission standard which imposed a stricter limit on the exhaust emissions.

Diesel vehicles have to pass a smoke emission test before they can be registered for use. Prior to January 1991, the smoke emission limit was 50 Hartridge Smoke Unit (HSU) under no-load free acceleration conditions. With effect from January 1991, the emission standard was upgraded to ECE R24.03 emission standard where tests are to be carried out under full-load conditions. Manufacturers' certification or certification by recognized test laboratories for compliance with the emission standard is required for registration of diesel vehicles.

Motorcycles and scooters at present need only to pass an idling test for carbon monoxide emission before registration. With effect from 1 October 1991, the Government will require new motorcycles and scooters to comply with a stricter emission standard before the vehicles can be registered for use.

As regards fuel controls, the lead level in petrol has been progressively reduced from 0.84 g/l in 1980 to the existing level of 0.15 g/l in 1987. This has effectively reduced the lead level in the air from 0.7 $\mu g/Nm^3$ in 1981 to 0.1 $\mu g/Nm^3$ in 1989. Unleaded petrol has been available at all petrol stations since February 1991. With effect from July 1992, all newly imported petrol driven vehicles will have to run on unleaded petrol. In order to reduce further the emission of carbon monoxide, nitrogen oxides and hydrocarbons, all petrol driven vehicles imported after 1992 will be required to be fitted with a three-way catalytic converter.

3 IMPLEMENTATION AND ENFORCEMENT

Pollution control measures are in general administered by the Ministry of the Environment (ENV). For mobile sources the Ministry of Communication and Information (MCI) is also responsible. The various control measures taken and the roles of these authorities are as follows:

- Setting of exhaust emission standards: ENV & MCI
- Enforcement of exhaust emission standards: MCI
- Maintenance and inspection of vehicles: MCI
- Automotive fuel control: ENV

Planning approval by the Pollution Control Department is needed for all new industrial and trade premises. When plans are approved, conditions are often attached to the licenses issued under the *Clean Air Act.* Operators of plant and equipment are expected to improve the standard or level of maintenance and operation of equipment to achieve the desired performance.

As regards mobile sources, street enforcement against smoky vehicles is carried out by police officers from the Registrar of Vehicles (ROV) and the Traffic Police (TP). ROV operates five vans known as Mobile Smoke Test Units (MSTUs) which are equipped with Hartridge Smoke meters to conduct spot checks on the roads. All in-use vehicles are required to undergo periodic inspection to ensure the vehicles are roadworthy. Exhaust emission tests are also included in the inspection programme.

4 FUTURE DEVELOPMENTS

Air pollution control is constantly evolving. Whenever new pollution problems arise new solutions have to be found which may require a change in existing legislation or even the introduction of new legislation. Hence it will be reasonable to expect that air pollution control legislation will continue to be modified to meet the challenge ahead.

SOUTH AFRICA

1 INTRODUCTION

1.1 Topography, Climate, Population

The Republic of South Africa, with a total area of 1 221 180 sq. km, is divided into four provinces, the Transvaal, Cape (which includes the Transkie and Ciskei), Orange Free State and Natal. Its northern border is formed by the Limpopo River at 22 degrees latitude south. It is a fairly arid country with limited water resources; only areas of Natal and the low-lying areas of the Eastern Transvaal enjoy an average rainfall exceeding 750 mm. This decreases substantially towards the west to about 300 mm in the Northern Cape, while some areas on the West Coast receive less than 100 mm annually.

The main topographical features are the vast high internal plateaux separated from the lowlands and coastal areas by mountain ranges. The most significant of these is the Drakensberg which extends from the North-Eastern Transvaal, near the Tropic of Capricorn, for a distance of about 960 km to end in the Stormberg in the Eastern Cape. Since some 50 per cent of recoverable coal reserves are located in the "highveld" regions of the Eastern Transvaal, which are at an average altitude of some 1500 metres, most generating stations are found there. In addition, the urban and intensive industrial activities in this area produce a large amount of pollution which is injected into an atmosphere with dispersion climatology amongst the most unfavourable in the world. This is characterized by high stability and an anti-cyclonic pressure cell throughout the troposphere.

Conditions are also favourable for the formation of both surface and elevated inversions, chiefly during the winter months. These inversions also occur at coastal areas, namely around Durban and Cape Town. Their impact is twofold, low level emissions are trapped beneath the surface inversions permitting pollutant levels to accumulate. Modern power station emissions on the other hand, released from chimneys of up to 300 metres penetrate and become trapped between the surface and upper inversion levels travelling for long distances, before changing meteorological conditions later in the day allow them to disperse.

The population composition of the Republic consists of approximately 70 per cent Black people, comprising a number of discrete ethnic groups each with their own traditions and social customs. The balance consists of 16 per cent Whites or persons of European descent, 10 per cent people of colour and the balance Asians. The result is that the Republic is a mixture of first world technology and third world customs which creates specific problems regarding the control of air pollutants, it being not feasible to apply first world standards to a third world situation.

1.2 Specific National Problems

The overriding problem that has developed over years is the provision of suitable housing for the majority of the population. This problem became acute with the onset of the Second World War, the large number of factories engaged in the war effort creating an insatiable demand for labour. The result was a flood of people to urban areas seeking work, overtaxing community services, creating uncontrolled squatting, resulting in conditions of squalor. This led to the development of Soweto to the south of Johannesburg and eventually to a number of similar townships to serve industry. Since no electricity was provided at that stage, coal was the most economical method of cooking and space heating, thus creating severe localized air pollution problems.

Attempts to solve this problem over the years resulted in the development of the "smokeless stove" (a stove which reduced the particulates by some 40 per cent) and to investigations into a "low smoke" fuel, but both efforts failed due to cost and maintenance factors. Electrification of Soweto commenced during 1978 and townships built later were provided with electricity, but the traditional preference of the residents for combustion stoves for cooking and space heating remains a social problem. The cost of electricity to the residents has also proved an inhibiting factor and Eskom, the electricity supply authority, has investigated low cost network schemes to overcome this problem.

South Africa has an abundance of coal deposits, mostly of low grade. While this coal can be burnt at pithead power stations, the demand for industrial and export coal of higher quality has resulted in the build up of waste dumps which may contain up to 50 million tons of tailings. Spontaneous combustion under conditions of limited oxygen results in generation of large amounts of hydrogen sulphide, sulphur dioxide and the most dangerous and insidious of all pollutants, carbon monoxide. These gases contribute to the pollutants trapped under the surface inversions, creating unpleasant conditions. It is extremely difficult to extinguish a waste dump, but the increasing environmental awareness of the mining companies has led to a method for tackling this. First of all the existing dump is compacted to reduce air voids and a "skin" of waste material is spread over the dump and itself compacted. Finally a layer of soil is spread over the surface and eventually grassed or covered with impervious material. This method has also been adapted for the construction of new waste dumps. It is an expensive procedure, but has the advantage of maintaining an energy source for possible future use in, for instance, a fluidized bed boiler.

A significant release of atmospheric pollutants occurs in large industrialized areas such as the Eastern Transvaal highveld and Vaal Triangle. This may give rise to regional phenomena such as acid rain with attendant negative effects on the environment in the near to long term.

Photochemical smog from traffic is also becoming a problem, particularly in areas of high population density, high incident solar insulation and adverse meteorological conditions. The extent to which alcohol is being increasingly blended with petrol is likely to increase the incidence of this problem.

The overall control of atmospheric pollution and its impact on health and the environment is made more difficult by the number of individual departments and authorities, each responsible for assessing the impacts of airborne pollutants on health or the environment or to set air quality standards accordingly.

2 DEVELOPMENT OF AIR POLLUTION CONTROLS AND LEGISLATION

South Africa first effectively appeared on the world map in 1652 as a supply station for shipping around the Cape of Good Hope. It remained isolated, to a large extent, from events developing overseas and was not affected by the industrial revolution that led to the promulgation of the *Alkali Works Act 1863* in the UK. This is because the position in South Africa at that time was entirely different. There was no need to industrialize because with its gold and diamonds, South Africa could pay for the importing of everything it needed.

This happy state of affairs terminated with the onset of the Second World War and consequent restrictions on free trade coupled with post war sanctions and boycotts. The need to be self sufficient in manufactured goods triggered off South Africa's own industrial revolution. As early as 1952 Dr E.C. Halliday of the Council for Scientific and Industrial Research (CSIR) drew attention to the developing air pollution problem that would result from this industrialization. It was due to his dedication that the present *Atmospheric Pollution Prevention Act* was developed and enacted into law as Act 45 of 1965. With slight modifications, it remains the same to this day.

It is interesting to note that the same non-governmental personalities who were concerned with the drafting of the Act, also took the initiative in forming the totally independent National Association for Clean Air.

2.1 Clean Air Philosophy

While South Africa has developed a sophisticated first world industralized economy, it also encompasses a large third world component with different aspirations and requirements. Legislation must, therefore, take cognizance of this and be sufficiently flexible to provide for a changing situation. For this reason, it was prudent to adopt as the basis for control the concept of "best practicable means" (BPM) as contained in the UK *Alkali Works Act*, the functional concept being "if you do not have the knowledge or economic means to do a perfect job, do the best you can, but improve as circumstances change".

This principle worked well in the South African definition of BPM as "having regard to local conditions and circumstances, the prevailing extent of technical knowledge and the cost likely to be involved as may be reasonable, practicable and necessary for the protection of any section of the public against the emission of poisonous or noxious gases, dust or any such fumes".

This policy is realistic in that, while new industries may be required to adopt current "state of the art" abatement technology, older installations will be permitted to retain their existing equipment until the end of its economic life, unless the Chief Officer, in terms of part 2 of the Act, requires the abatement plant to be upgraded. There is considerable evidence that this is taking place, particularly in the case of the older power stations where the efficiency of the electrostatic precipitators are being enhanced by using flue gas conditioning and the retrofit with fabric filters.

2.2 Atmospheric Pollution Prevention Act 1965

National enforcement is through the *Atmospheric Pollution Prevention Act*. This Act is divided into five sections and is preceded by a section defining the meaning of key words and phrases, the most relevant being the definition of best practicable means.

Part 1 of the Act provides for the establishment of an Air Pollution Advisory Committee to advise the relevant minister on all matters related to the abatement of air pollution. It also provides for the appointment of a Chief Officer Air Pollution Control (CAPCO) and his staff and defines their powers, duties and responsibilities.

2.2.1 Scheduled Processes

The section controlling emissions from scheduled processes is included in Part 2. Scheduled processes are the main industrial processes such as power stations, metallurgical and chemical processes, cement works and the like. A list of these is contained in the regulations arising from the Act and is updated from time to time. While the Chief Officer is required to consider the locality of the proposed industry as well as its impact and proximity to urban areas, he must also be satisfied that the best practicable means are being applied. This is done in consultation with the industry after detailed investigation of the proposed process, the alternative options for emission abatement and the particular conditions at the location.

By these means presumptive limits are determined in respect of each case. This is interpreted as "if these limits are not exceeded, then it is presumed that best practicable means are being complied with". Presumptive limits are not published. They are determined by the Chief Officer as a guide to his inspectors and they may be obtained for a particular process or emission on request. As an indication as to the methodology adopted:

> "The abatement equipment to be used to control a particular pollutant must be designed with a collecting efficiency high enough to ensure that under normal operating conditions, the ground level concentration of the pollutant will not exceed TLV/ 50 mg/m^3 at any point around the plant. If a pollutant is carcinogenic or accumulative then TVL/100 is used. Also if the pollutant has an odour potential lower than TVL/50 then the odour threshold limit must be used".

The following guidelines apply to the more general pollutants:

Pollutant micrograms/m^3	*1 hour*	*Period 24 hour*	*Year*
Sulphur dioxide	780	265	80
Nitrogen Oxides	1080	540	270
Ozone	240	100	—
Lead		—	2.5
Dust particles	350	150	—
Smoke (S/m^3)		50	30

Guidelines for the pollutant levels in stacks exist for different processes. For example, the concentration of hydrogen chloride, sulphur trioxide and ammonia must not exceed 35 mg/m^3. The general guideline for particulate matter is 120 mg/m^3 unless otherwise stated. For instance the current limit for power stations is 100 mg/m^3.

Provision is also made in the legislation for the Chief Officer to withdraw the registration certificate should the conditions laid down in the certificate not be complied with. There is, however, provision for right of appeal against this action by the Chief Officer as it will in effect shut the installation down.

2.2.2 Control of Smoke and Particulates

The control of smoke and particulates (Part 3 of the Act) emanating from smaller and non-scheduled installations within the area of jurisdiction of a local authority are normally delegated to that local authority. This section of the Act prohibits the operation of any fuel burning device from being operated continuously while emitting smoke darker than permitted by regulation, except during start-up and shut-down. It also provides for the declaration of smoke control zones.

In order to implement the regulations the local authority is empowered to appoint smoke control officers and to make regulations regarding the siting and operation of fuel burning devices. Penalties for contravention are also detailed. Part 4, in a similar manner, provides for the declaration of dust control areas. This enables the Chief Officer to ensure that best practicable means are employed to control the dispersion of dust. This part of the legislation was framed to deal with dust blowing off the gold mine dumps, as well as dust from industrial processes.

The Chamber of Mines has set up a vegetation division to deal with this problem. This organization has succeeded in encouraging vegetation to establish on waste dumps under extremely adverse conditions. The cost of dust control for defunct mines is covered by the State and administered by the Chief Officer, who in the case of dust control is the Government Mining Engineer. Regarding operating mines preparing to close down, the Government Mining Engineer requires sufficient funds to be set aside to prevent pollution of the atmosphere from the abandoned workings.

2.2.3 Mobile Sources

Air pollution from vehicles is covered in the final part of the *Atmospheric Pollution Prevention Act.* Although provision is made for regulations and measurement standards regarding emissions, only smoke from diesel vehicles is subject to control at present. The regulations apply to areas where a local authority has requested the necessary powers. Standards may vary, particularly at high altitudes which adversely affect normally aspirated engines. The owner of a vehicle which does not comply with the smoke limit is served with a notice to repair and bring the vehicle in for retesting. Failure to comply with the notice is a legal offence.

3 IMPLEMENTATION AND ENFORCEMENT

Responsibilities for implementation and national enforcement of air pollution controls have largely been included in the previous section.

3.1 Local and Regional Enforcement

Local enforcement is delegated to municipalities and local authorities. In the smaller towns where combustion sources are limited, control may consist almost entirely in the form of reaction to complaints about excessive smoke.

These minimal emissions have an essentially localized effect with little impact on other communities. The situation is different in the larger cities and municipalities where a large number of small industries and businesses are operating. This requires the services of experienced smoke control officers with extensive knowledge of the combustion process and the factors that give rise to atmospheric pollution. They must also have adequate legal and diplomatic expertise in order to achieve the goals of both clean air and customer satisfaction. In practice, these officials also find themselves having to deal with matters far removed from the *Atmospheric Pollution Prevention Act*, but related to numerous local ordinances. These will include, *inter alia*, the burning of household and garden rubbish, complaints regarding sand blasting and spray painting, quarrying and other dust nuisances, odours from a number of sources and even problems arising from water pollution caused by factory effluent. While scheduled processes fall outside their authority, they are required to cooperate with the inspectors employed by the Chief Officer to administer Part 2 of the Act.

3.2 Monitoring Agencies

Due to the concentration of economic activity in local areas it has not been necessary to establish a national monitoring network. Various local authorities operate their own monitoring facilities and where there is a large concentration of industries, for instance in the Eastern Transvaal Highveld, the Department of National Health and Population Development and large organizations such as Eskom operate joint monitoring networks measuring sulphur dioxide, nitrogen oxides, ozone, particulate matter and meteorological parameters. A total of 71 measuring stations are in operation.

A comprehensive national emission inventory was commenced during 1985 and is now complete. It is being updated regularly and is based on actual emission measurements where available, augmented by published emission factors and material balance design data.

The former Federal Republic of Germany has been actively supporting the CSIR in consolidating and expanding the atmospheric research facilities at Cape Point by contributing sophisticated equipment. The most modern state of the art carbon dioxide and ozone measuring equipment has been provided together with relevant computer software. In view of the possibility that the expanding Antarctic ozone hole may spread over Southern Africa, it is also planned to measure the intensity of ultra-violet light on a continuous basis. Australia and South Africa are the only two countries which carry out continuous atmospheric trace element measurements between 35 and 45 degrees latitude south. These investigations are being supported by the University of Natal which is mounting an active investigation into the extent of and the factors affecting the ozone layer.

3.3 Role of Private Interest Groups

The National Association for Clean Air came into being shortly after the promulgation of the *Atmospheric Pollution Prevention Act 1965.* Its formation was proposed by Mr. John Lewis Easterbrook at the 1967 CSIR conference on Air Pollution at Camps Bay in Cape Town. Mr. Easterbrook became the first Chairman when the Association was founded in 1969 and subsequently its Director during 1972. Under his leadership, negotiations for NACA to become affiliated to the International Union of Air Pollution Prevention Associations succeeded in 1970, with full membership following in 1973. NACA has been represented on the Executive Council since 1977.

The National Association of Clean Air maintains liaison with the control authorities and arranges seminars, workshops, education programmes and symposia attended and addressed by internatonal celebrities. It also advises, provides literature and maintains contact with neighbouring states. The relevant office in Zimbabwe is in fact still a Statutory Member of the Association.

There are also a number of concerned groups that interest themselves in the problems of pollution. The most prominent is Earthlife which is affiliated to Greenpeace as well as to various local groups. The latter are concerned with local problems such as the developing industrialized area around the Richards Bay Harbour. There are also groups concerned about the health effects of pollutant levels around Pretoria/Witwatersrand/Vereeniging as well as to the south of Durban. In Cape Town, Koeberg Alert are concerned with nuclear issues.

4 EFFECTIVENESS OF CONTROLS

Since the inception of the *Atmospheric Pollution Prevention Act,* in excess of 2.5 billion Rand have been spent on air pollution control equipment. Sixty-nine processes have been identified as scheduled processes in terms of Part 2 of the Act (the control of noxious or offensive gases). There are very few remaining scheduled industries without pollution control equipment.

The problems still remaining in the Republic of South Africa are the control of certain gaseous emissions, at present being dealt with by means of a high stack policy, and pollution from non-electrified residential areas, exacerbated by rapid urbanization.

Motor vehicle pollution is not yet controlled as no serious problems are indicated by current monitoring.

5 FUTURE DEVELOPMENTS

5.1 Investigation Regarding a National Environmental Management System

The State has recently requested the President's Council to investigate and make recommendations on a policy for a National Environmental Management System, with particular reference to the ecological, economic, social and legal implications thereof. This investigation stems from the need for a more coordinated and holistic approach towards environmental management in South Africa.

Three committees of the President's Council will attend to the following aspects of the investigation:

- *Committee for Constitutional Affairs:* all legal matters and legislation administered by government departments, provincial administrations and local authorities.
- *Committee for Social Affairs:* all social, demographic and ecological aspects of the investigation.
- *Committee for Economic Affairs:* all economic implications of production methods by mines, industries and power generation, in order to prevent pollution and/or damage to the environment.

Interested parties were invited to submit relevant memoranda to the President's Council. Many institutes and organizations, including the National Association for Clean Air, have already responded to this invitation.

It is expected that the investigation by the President's Council will be completed by the second half of 1991.

5.2 "Clean Air Act"

The *Atmospheric Pollution Prevention Act* was 25 years old in 1990. While it has served South Africa well during this period, it is considered that the time has come to examine whether it continues to meet the requirements of future generations. In order to investigate this, a committee was formed to recommend revisions to the Act, to be known as the "Clean Air Act". The probability that air pollution will in future be combined with other environmental impacts such as water and solid waste pollution was recognized. It was also conceded that a unified system of control from Chief Officer to local authority is desirable.

It was also recognized that the expertise available at local authority level was being under-utilized. An important recommendation is that control of dust from mines and mine dumps be omitted and administered by the Government Mining Engineer in terms of the *Mines and Works Act.* Similarly, the actual physical control and measurement of vehicle emissions should more appropriately be in the hands of traffic control authorities, except that the Minister of Health must be empowered to set standards relating to future gaseous emissions of internal combustion engines.

Standard regulations for smoke, dust, and odours are proposed and the provisions for declaring smoke control areas retained as it is considered that it may not be prudent to apply smoke control restrictions to certain townships at this stage. The proposal to schedule large dusty or odorous industry was considered. It is believed that the establishment of a unified control with the facility to combine with other forms of pollution control, better use of manpower and expertise can be achieved. This would propagate the employment of health inspectors and other disciplines into pollution control, making specialized courses of instruction available to them. This would create a succession of qualified experienced staff.

Cognizance should also be taken of the promulgation of the *Environmental Conservation Act.* This Act established, *inter alia,* a Council for the Environment as advisory body to the Minister of Environmental Affairs.

The Council has given expression to this requirement by issuing a procedure "Integrated Environmental Management" (IEM) as a guideline for incorporating environmental considerations into planning and development activities. The proposed "Clean Air Act", being clearly an environmental activity, has provisions for possible incorporation into IEM procedures. In preparation for this the Council for the Environment, on contract with the Council for Scientific and Industrial Research, is assembling hard data on the status of atmospheric pollution in South Africa and identification of major sources of pollution both from industrial and urban sources.

6 REFERENCES AND SELECTIVE BIBLIOGRAPHY

Atmospheric Pollution Prevention Act No. 45 of 1965.

Deliberations of select committee to recommend modifications of the Act.

Brunke E G and Wells R B. SA Scientists contribute to Research on Climatic change.

Council for the Environment (1989), *Integrated Environmental Management in South Africa.*

Energy Technology ENER M90001, Electrostatic Precipitator Training Course.

South African National Scientific Programme's Report No. 50 (1988), *Atmospheric Pollution and its implications in the Eastern Transvaal Highveld.*

The *Clean Air Journal* (June 1989).

TAIWAN

1 INTRODUCTION

1.1 Topography, Climate, Population

Taiwan is an island separated by the Strait of Taiwan from the Chinese mainland and is about 480 km south-west of Okinawa. To the east and the south are the Pacific Ocean and the Philippines respectively. The island is 377 km long and about 142 km wide. The total area measures 35 966 sq. km of which two-thirds is the mountainous areas in the east. The western part of the island is an open area of rich plains, very densely populated (total population: 20 million). Taiwan has a partly sub-tropical and partly tropical climate with an annual average temperature of 22 degrees Celsius.

Because the Government has concentrated strongly on economic development during the past three decades, Taiwan now enjoys considerable economic prosperity. However, the successful achievements of the past three decades have also brought drastic changes to the environmental ambient quality, and air and water quality in particular are getting worse. In the last ten years therefore, air and water pollution control have been strongly promoted by the Government.

Industrial and traffic sources of fuel consumption in Taiwan have increased by 9 and 21 times respectively in the past 30 years. Thus pollution is becoming a very important socio-economic problem in Taiwan, due to accelerated economic development, the heavy urbanization of the population and increasing volume of traffic.

2 DEVELOPMENT OF AIR POLLUTION CONTROLS AND LEGISLATION

The first air pollution control measure in Taiwan was the regulation on coal burning, passed by the Taipei municipality in 1955. Establishment of the Department of Health, Executive Yuan in 1971 brought improvements to air pollution control, and on 23 May 1975 the *Air Pollution Control Act*, was promulgated. This first step brought together the various regulations enacted by local governments, and was revised on 7 May 1982. On 20 October 1976 the Regulations under the *Air Pollution Control Act* were promulgated and were revised on 5 June 1980 and again on 4 May 1983.

These are therefore the main laws and regulations for implementation of pollution control activities. There are other related regulations, such as the Ambient Air Quality Standards of the Taiwan Area which were established on 1 October 1975 (Table 1). Various emission standards for air pollutants from stationary and mobile sources have also been promulgated by provincial and municipal authorities since 1978.

2.1 Industrial Air Pollution Control

During the past three decades, industrial energy consumption has increased more than 12 times over the 1958 level (1 869 000 kl oil equivalent per year). Before 1982, the sulphur content of fuel oil was 3.5 - 4 per cent. In order to abate sulphur dioxide pollution it was agreed to gradually decrease the sulphur content of fuel oil, with an initial reduction to 2 per cent. Since July 1982 the Taipei and Kaohsiung municipalities, and part of Taipei and Kaohsiung counties have been designated to use low sulphur (2 per cent) content oil. Only stationary sources equipped with flue gas desulphurization installations with proven abatement in the manufacturing process could be granted a waiver.

For the years 1981 to 1984, the annual averages of sulphate in the total suspended particulates in Kaohsiung city were 73.7 $\mu g/Nm^3$, 61.0 $\mu g/Nm^3$, 33.8 $\mu g/Nm^3$ and 16.0 $\mu g/Nm^3$ respectively. Obviously, the results of the low sulphur oil policy are very significant. Since August 1985, Hsinchu city, Hsinchu county and Miaoli county were also supplied with 2 per cent sulphur fuel oil, and from July 1986 the whole area of Taiwan had to use the same. The estimated reduction of sulphur dioxide emissions is 260 000 tons per year. In 1990 the sulphur content of fuel oil was to be reduced to 1.5 per cent, with a further reduction to 1 per cent in 1993.

For particulate emissions, the iron and steel, cement and coke oven industries were selected as the first priority for control targets. Since the beginning of 1987, any plants in these categories assessed as seriously violating the *Air Pollution Control Act*, have been penalised with a daily fine, and ordered to comply with emission standards by a certain date.

The emission standards for stationary sources were promulgated in 1978. During the ten years, the Regulations have been in force, several shortcomings have been discovered, and a major revision is under way to:

a) establish mid-term and long-term emission standards for sulphur dioxides, nitrogen oxides, and particulates;

b) strengthen the control of offensive odours, and adopt olfactometry methods;

c) increase the number of controlled substances, such as asbestos, lead, cadmium and organic solvents;

d) set one-fifteenth of threshold limit values (TLV) as borderline standards for those substances which do not have listed standards;

e) require minimum stack height for dispersion.

The Environmental Protection Administration (EPA) is now drafting and amending the various emission standards, in line with the above-mentioned revisions.

2.2 Traffic Controls

In the past three decades, the fuel consumption for transport has increased about 20 times over the 1958 level (299 000 kl oil equivalent per year). Figure 1 indicates that the percentage of industrial energy consumption had a tendency to decrease, while that of transport increased.

The growth rate of motor vehicles in the Taiwan area is enormous with a total of 8 million automobiles and motorcycles in 1987. The air pollutants related to motor vehicles, such as carbon monoxide and hydrocarbons, had an annual mean concentration in 1987 higher than in 1986.

Controls of air pollutants emitted from motor vehicles were first introduced in 1976. The first pollutant to be controlled was diesel smoke, which could not exceed Ringelmann Chart No. 2 (i.e. 40 per cent obscuration). Exhaust emissions have been periodically inspected for carbon monoxide and hydrocarbons in the Taipei and Kaohsiung municipalities, in Taipei county, and in the cities of Taichung and Keelung since January 1981; roadside inspection of these emissions was started in August 1983 in Taipei and Kaohsiung municipalities. The sulphur content of diesel fuel has been restricted to 0.5 per cent to control sulphur oxide pollution from diesel cars and trucks since September 1983.

Due to the vast number of motorcycles in Taiwan, these too are a significant source of air pollution - a problem which may be unique to Taiwan. According to the idling test, the mean concentrations of carbon monoxide and hydrocarbons from a four-stroke engine motorcycle are similar to that from a passenger car, as indeed are carbon monoxide emissions from a two-stroke engine motorcycle; however, hydrocarbon concentrations from a two-stroke engine motorcycle are 14.6 times more than from a passenger car. Motorcycle emission standards were established and implemented in November 1984. Several measures are used to reduce pollution, e.g.

adoption of new model car certification, motorcycle production quality control, and improved in-use motorcycle maintenance.

At the moment, emission standards for motor vehicles are tested in idling state, but this can control only about 30 per cent of emissions under actual driving conditions. Therefore, the proposed new emission standards for motor vehicles will adopt both the mass emission test and the idling test. New model car certification and production quality control will be tested using a simulated driving cycle to get mass emission (grams per km) of carbon monoxide, hydrocarbons and nitrogen oxides, with effect from July 1990 for gasoline cars, and July 1991 for motorcycles.

Periodic inspection and roadside inspection of in-use vehicles are still being conducted by the idling method. Future vehicle emission control will be through the establishment of a license and lot examination system for new model cars, instead of the existing routine inspection. It is expected that most new model cars will have to be equipped with catalytic converters to meet tougher emission standards by 1990, which will approach the California, USA, emission standards by 1994.

3 IMPLEMENTATION AND ENFORCEMENT

Air pollution control is the responsibility of the Bureau of Environmental Protection (BEP), formerly the Department of Health. The Environmental Protection Administration (EPA) was established on 22 August 1987. The EPA approved the Stationary Emission Standard of Air Pollutant recommended by the Taipei City Government in December 1987.

3.1 Monitoring

The establishment of an ambient air quality monitoring system has been a key factor in establishing air pollution control in Taiwan. Currently there are 169 monitoring stations in the Taiwan area of which 128 are owned by the local governments. Apart from the stations in Taipei City and a few in Kaohsiung City, most are manual particulate pollutants monitoring stations.

Since 1987 the central government BEP has been setting up a nationwide continuous automatic monitoring network which comprises a monitoring centre, 19 automatic whole criteria pollutants monitoring stations and one mobile van. The EPA is planning to increase the number of continuous automatic monitoring stations to 66 in 1993.

The 1987 ambient air quality data show that the air in Taiwan is moderately polluted. According to air quality analyses in recent years, pollution, e.g. particulates emitted from stationary sources, is decreasing, and that caused by pollutants emitted from automobiles, e.g. carbon monoxide, is increasing. Taiwan measures the content of various materials in the air in order to assess the influence of motor traffic and the burning of coal and oil. The measurements of particulate pollution can be divided into several categories: total suspended particulates (TSP, less than 10 μm), dust fall, and coefficient of haze.

Table 2 shows the annual average reading of distributions from the TSP measurements at stations in Taiwan from 1981 to 1987. These show an annual average of over 200 $\mu g/Nm^3$ decrease by year. Compared with the National Ambient Air Quality Standard (NAAQS) of Taiwan, the number of TSP stations with an annual average exceeding the standard also significantly decreased. At the moment 15 per cent of the TSP stations still cannot meet the annual or monthly average standard.

Table 3 shows a general reading of dust fall in Taiwan from 1981 to 1987. Approximately 50-60 per cent of dust fall stations register between 5-10 tons per sq. km per month, however the reduction of dust fall by year is not significant.

Coefficient of Haze (COHS) represents the visual cleanliness of the air and is highly correlated with the pollutants emitted from diesel engines and coal burning. The annual trend of COHS in Taiwan from 1981 to 1987 (Table 4) shows that pollution levels did not improve much between 1981 and 1985, but recently have, with a number of stations registering between 0-1 COHS per 1000 feet. However, due to heavy traffic in Taipei City, two stations still have an annual average greater than 4.1 COHS per 1000 feet. Figure 2 indicates that this can be directly attributed to traffic congestion.

The Pollution Standard Index (PSI) can make people aware of the daily levels of air pollution through accurate, timely, and easily understandable information. At present, PSI reports on five major pollutants - sulphur dioxide, nitrogen dioxide, carbon monoxide, photochemical oxidants, and total suspended particulates. For each air pollutant, the observed concentration is converted into a PSI sub-index on a scale from 0 to 500, and the PSI is reported as the maximum sub-index.

The PSI distribution of 18 EPA monitoring stations in 1989 is shown in Figure 3. Eighty-four per cent of monitoring days have a PSI lower than 100; the categories used are good (0-50) or moderate (51-100). One per cent of monitoring days were categorized as very unhealthy (201-300). The pollutant which has the maximum sub-index of that day is called a critical pollutant. During a certain period the characteristics of one region can be determined from the critical pollutant analysis. For instance, the air pollution problem of Sanchung, Taipei is mainly caused by mobile sources because carbon monoxide showed up most frequently as the critical pollutant. The critical pollutant distribution of the stations with a PSI greater than 100 in 1989 (Figure 4) showed that on 72 per cent of the monitoring days, total suspended particulates were the major cause. Therefore, controlling pollution from this source is the most important target for the EPA in the near future.

4 CONCLUSION

The Government in Taiwan has been taking various actions to abate air pollution which has resulted in gradual improvements in the levels of sulphur dioxide and total suspended particulates. However, the fast growing industrialization and urbanization of Taiwan means that the government must take more responsive and preventative measures to prevent the further deterioration of air quality.

5 SELECTIVE BIBLIOGRAPHY

Chuang C Y, *Air Pollution Control in Taiwan.* The 2nd Joint Conference of Air Pollution Studies in the Asian Area, 1986, Japan Society of Air Pollution.

Chuang C Y, *Industrial Air Pollution Control in Taiwan Area.* The 3rd Joint Conference of Air Pollution Studies in the Asian Area, 1986, Japan Society of Air Pollution.

Ministry of Economic Affairs, *Economic Statistics Annual,* Taiwan Area, 1988.

Energy Committee, Ministry of Economic Affairs, *Taiwan Energy Statistics, 1988.*

Environmental Protection Administration, *Environmental Law and Regulation, 1988.*

Environmental Protection Administration, *Environmental Information, Taiwan, 1989.*

Table 1: Ambient Air Quality Standard in Taiwan Area (Promulgated by Department of Health 1 October 1975. Amended by EPA 12 May 1990)

Suspended particulate TSP (μg/m^3)	Twenty-four hours value Annual geometrical mean value	250 130
Suspended particulate less than or equal to 10 μm of particle diameter (PM10) (μg/m^3)	Daily mean value Annual mathematical mean value	125 65
Sulphur dioxide (ppm)	Hourly mean value Daily mean value Annual mean value	0.25 0.1 0.03
Nitrogen dioxide (ppm)	Hourly mean value Annual mean value	0.25 0.05
Carbon Monoxide (ppm)	Hourly mean value Eight hours' mean value	35 9
Ozone (ppm)	Hourly mean value Eight hours' mean value	0.12 0.06
Lead	Monthly mean value less than 1.0 μg/m^3	

NOTES

1 μm: 10^{-6} meter
2 m^3: Cubic meter
3 μg: Microgram, 10^{-6} gram
4 ppm: Parts per million
5 Hourly mean value: Hourly mathematical mean value of each measured value obtained in an hour.
6 Eight hour's mean value: The mathematical mean value of hourly mean value obtained in eight hours continuous measuring.
7 Daily mean value: The mathematical mean value of each hourly mean value obtained in one day.
8 Twenty-four hours value: The value obtained from analysis of sample by twenty-four hours continuous sampling.
9 Monthly mean value: The mathematical mean value of each daily mean value obtained in a month.
10 Annual mean value: The mathematical mean value of each daily mean value obtained in a year.
11 Annual geometrical mean value: The geometrical mean value of each twenty-four hours value obtained in a year.

Table 2: Distribution of Monitoring Stations in Annual Mean of Total Suspended Particulates, Taiwan Area

Year	*1981*		*1982*		*1983*		*1984*		*1985*		*1986*		*1987*	
Number of Stations percentage (%) *Total suspended particulates (ug/Nm³)*	*number of stations*	*percent-age (%)*	*number of stations*	*percent-age (%)*	*number of stations*	*percent-age (%)*	*number of stations*	*percent-age (%)*	*number of stations*	*percent-age (%)*	*number of stations*	*percent-age (%)*	*number of stations*	*percent-age (%)*
0-100	6	5.0	0 (5)*	4.1	3 (6)*	7.4	20 (21)*	31.8	24 (10)*	29.3	14 (20)*	30.1	12 (25)*	30.6
100-200	69	57.5	65 (10)*	62.0	81 (10)*	74.6	67 (10)*	59.7	66 (10)*	65.5	66 (7)*	64.6	69 (12)*	66.9
200-300	38	31.7	40	33.1	21 (1)*	18.0	11	8.5	6	5.3	6	5.3	2	1.7
300-400	6	5.0	1	0.8	0	0.0	0	0.0	0	0	0	0	1	0.8
400	1	0.8	0	0.0	0	0.0	0	0.0	0	0	0	0	0	0
Total	120	100.0	121	100.0	122	122	129	100.0	116	100	113	100	121	100
Exceeded the ambient air quality standard	77	64.2	67	55.4	54	44.3	27	20.9	25	22	25	22	18	15

Remark 1: ( )* shows the monitoring stations have samples excluding the particulates larger than 10 um.
2: Stations that have data less than 8 months are not included.

Table 3: Distribution of Monitoring Stations in Annual Mean of Dust Fall, Taiwan Area

Year	*1981*		*1982*		*1983*		*1984*		*1985*		*1986*		*1987*	
Number of Stations percentage (%) *Dust Fall (TON/KM2/month)*	*number of stations*	*percent-age (%)*	*number of stations*	*percent-age (%)*	*number of stations*	*percent-age (%)*	*number of stations*	*percent-age (%)*	*number of stations*	*percent-age (%)*	*number of stations*	*percent-age (%)*	*number of stations*	*percent-age (%)*
0-5 (Nil)	5	4.1	19	15.8	6	4.9	7	6.3	13	11.8	8	7.7	7	6.5
5-10 (light)	60	49.6	63	52.5	65	52.8	63	56.2	52	47.3	57	54.8	66	61.7
10-15 (moderate)	37	30.6	23	19.2	36	29.3	29	25.9	35	31.8	25	24.0	22	20.6
15-20 (heavy)	15	12.4	9	7.5	12	9.8	13	11.6	9	8.2	9	8.7	12	11.2
20-(extremely heavy)	4	3.3	6	5.0	4	3.2	0	0.0	1	0.9	6	5.8	0	0.0
Total	121	100.0	120	100.0	123	100.0	112	100.0	110	100	105	100	107	100

Remark 1: Stations that have data less than 8 months are not included.

Table 4: Distribution of Monitoring Stations in Annual Mean of COHs, Taiwan Area

Year	*1981*		*1982*		*1983*		*1984*		*1985*		*1986*		*1987*	
Number of Stations percentage (%) *Concentration (COHs/1000ft)*	*number of stations*	*percent-age (%)*	*number of stations*	*percent-age (%)*	*number of stations*	*percent-age (%)*	*number of stations*	*percent-age (%)*	*number of stations*	*percent-age (%)*	*number of stations*	*percent-age (%)*	*number of stations*	*percent-age (%)*
0-1.0	8	23.5	9	24.3	16	42.1	14	40.0	16	44.4	19	57.6	20	71.4
1.1-2.0	19	55.9	20	54.1	15	39.5	15	42.9	14	38.9	9	27.3	2	7.1
2-1-3.0	2	5.9	3	8.1	3	7.9	2	5.7	2	5.6	2	6.1	3	10.7
3.1-4.0	2	5.9	3	8.1	2	5.3	1	2.9	1	2.8	1	3.0	1	3.6
4.1-	3	8.8	2	5.4	2	5.3	3	8.6	3	8.3	2	6.1	2	7.1
Total	34	100.0	37	100.0	38	100.0	35	100.0	36	100	33	100	28	100

Remark 1: Stations that have data less than 8 months are not included.

Figure 1: Percentage of Energy Consumption for Industry and Transportation in Taiwan

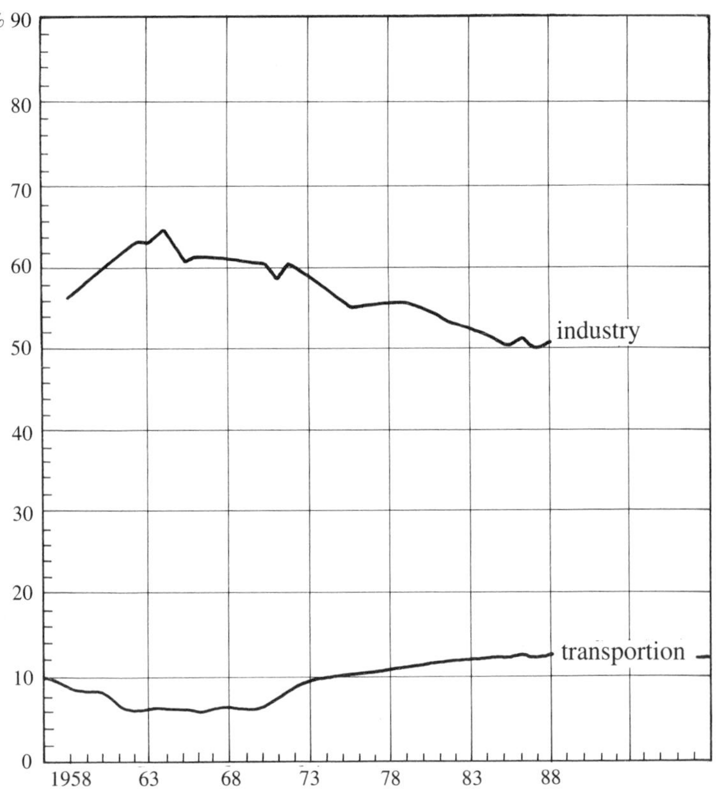

Figure 2: Yearly Variation of COHS in Taipei City

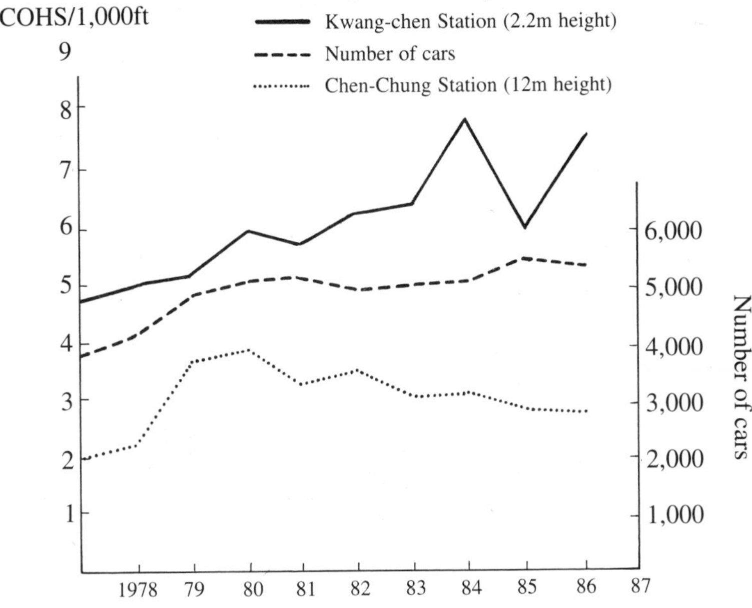

Source: Taipei Municipal Bureau of Environmental Protection

Figure 3: The Distribution in PSI for the Air Quality Data of 18 Monitoring Stations of EPA (1989)

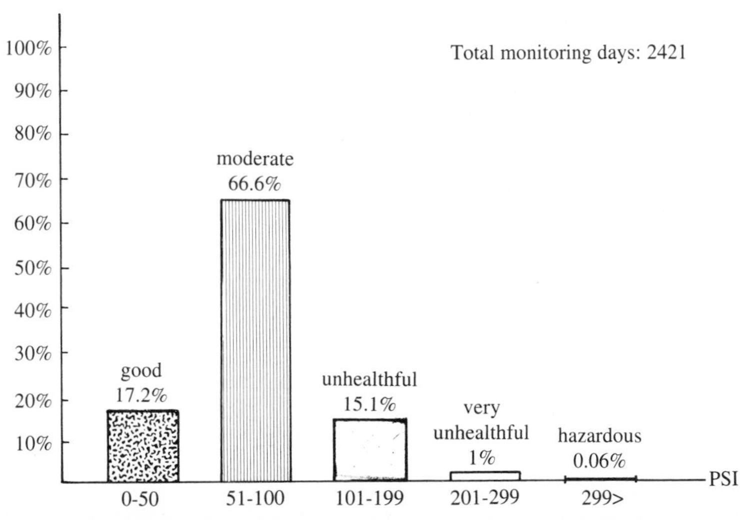

Figure 4: The Distribution in Critical Pollutants for PSI>100 of 18 Monitoring Stations of EPA (1989)

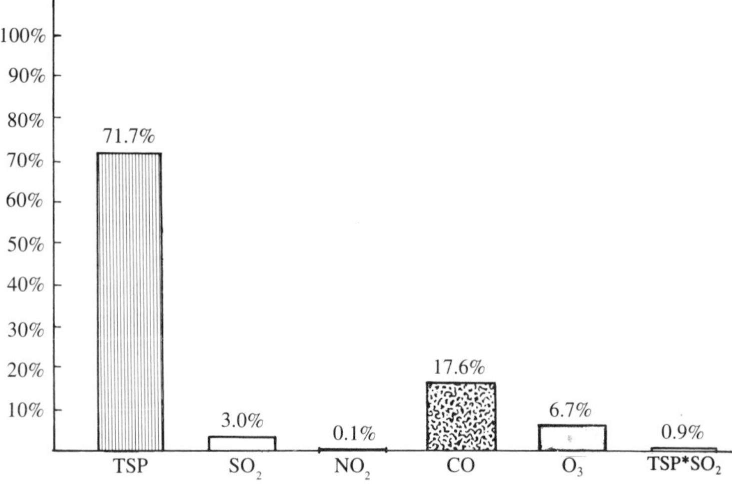

UNITED KINGDOM

1 INTRODUCTION

1.1 Topography, Climate, Population

The United Kingdom, which is one of the twelve members of the European Community, consists of England, Scotland, Wales and Northern Ireland. It is situated between latitudes 50 and 59 degrees N, with coastal borders on the North Sea and to the west on the Atlantic Ocean and, as a result, benefits from the warming currents of the Gulf Stream. It has a total land area of just over 242 495 sq. km and a population of approximately 56 million. The average density of population varies from 66 per sq. km in Scotland to 366 per sq. km in England.

Traditional heavy industry, which was mainly concentrated in the Midlands and north of Britain is generally in decline, and has been replaced by service industries. The agriculture industry is likely to see some changes in the future; cereal farming is mainly concentrated on the east and livestock in the west and north.

The UK climate is generally mild and temperate with a mean annual temperature of between 9 - 11 degrees C. This may fall to -8 degrees C or less in winter in the north and rise to 25 degrees C or more in the summer in the south. The west tends to be wetter and milder than the east.

1.2 Specific National Problems

In most areas of the UK combustion of fuels is still the major source of emissions to the atmosphere. The introduction of domestic and industrial smoke control measures following the *Clean Air Act 1956* and the switch to cleaner and more convenient sources of energy resulted in a decline in coal consumption and subsequent improvement in air quality. Over the whole of the UK emissions of smoke from coal combustion have fallen by over 90 per cent since 1958; in 1989 power stations were estimated to be responsible for 5 per cent of total emissions and road transport for 39 per cent; smoke from diesel engined road vehicles is now estimated to be the biggest source of smoke in urban areas.

In common with other Member States of the European Community, the UK must reduce its emissions of sulphur dioxide to levels specified in the EC Large Combustion Plants Directive (88/609/EEC). The UK must achieve a 20 per cent reduction from the 1980 level by 1993, 40 per cent by 1998 and 60 per cent by 2003. In 1989 - the latest year for which figures are available - total UK emissions of sulphur dioxide fell by 3 per cent to 3.7 million tonnes; power stations were responsible for 71 per cent; emissions from large combustion plant in 1989 were three per cent lower than 1988 at 3.09 tonnes, 20 per cent below 1980 levels.

Emissions of nitrogen oxides are however increasing: the main emission sources in 1989 were road transport and power stations, responsible for 48 per cent and 29 per cent of the total, respectively. Emissions of carbon monoxide are also rising steadily with, once again, road transport being the main source accounting for 88 per cent of the total in 1989. Carbon dioxide emissions are also a cause for concern, with significant emitters being power stations, other industry and road transport. Road transport also accounts for a significant proportion of UK emissions of volatile organic compounds - 37 per cent of the total in 1989; the main sources of emission are processes and solvents.

While acid deposition occurs in the UK, and there are areas where such acidity is only weakly buffered, acidification of the environment has only fairly recently been recognized as a cause for concern. For many years it was known that buildings were corroded by air pollutants in combination with moisture but it was thought that the *Clean Air Acts* had largely arrested the process. However, research has confirmed that decay is continuing at a higher rate in towns and cities than in cleaner, more rural areas. Rainfall acidity is monitored and both forests and rivers in the UK are now being checked regularly for signs of damage due to acid deposition.

As has been shown above, road transport in the UK is now a major source of a number of important air pollutants. Although stricter emission controls are being enforced though the implementation of various EEC Directives (see section 2.5), these only apply to new vehicles and it will be some time before any benefits can be seen. However, any benefits are likely to be small as the Department of Transport is forecasting an increase in traffic of between 83 - 142 per cent by the year 2025. As a result it has been predicted that emissions of nitrogen oxides could be higher than present levels within 25 years, despite the fitting of catalytic converters on all new cars from the end of 1992.

The subject of indoor air pollution and the possible effects on human health of the various chemicals or substances given off by heating appliances, ventilation units, office machinery and even household furnishings is of increasing interest. The fact that many modern buildings are effectively "sealed" and ventilated through air conditioning has given rise to a condition called "sick building syndrome" with research now being carried out into ways of making buildings not only energy efficient but healthier places for employees.

However, with regard to indoor pollution, perhaps the most serious risk is that caused through exposure to high levels of radon gas - an odourless and colourless gas produced from naturally occurring uranium which is present in certain rocks, such as granite and in some building materials. While outside radon disperses in the air so levels are very low, in geologically significant areas, radon seeps into enclosed spaces where it can build up to dangerously high concentrations. Recent estimates in the UK put the number of radon induced deaths from lung cancer at 2500 annually - second only to the number of deaths from smoking induced lung cancer. A recent survey of homes in those areas of Great Britain known to be at risk (much of the south west, smaller areas in the Midlands, and Wales and Scotland) revealed a far higher proportion of homes than previously thought, to have radon levels in excess of the Government's action level of 200 becquerels per cubic metre. Further research is being carried out by the UK National Radiological Protection Board to ascertain the extent of the problem in the UK.

2 DEVELOPMENT OF AIR POLLUTION CONTROLS AND LEGISLATION

2.1 Early Controls

The development of air pollution control legislation in the UK has been a gradual process, most of it stemming from the Industrial Revolution of the late 18th and 19th centuries. There are records of even earlier complaints about air pollution in the 13th century when the use of coal was prohibited in London in 1273 as being prejudicial to health. Complaints continued but were mostly ignored until 1819 when Parliament appointed a committee "to enquire to what extent persons using steam engines and furnaces could erect them in a manner less prejudicial to the public health and comfort".

Still nothing was done and the Industrial Revolution, which was based on coal as the energy source, brought a worsening of urban squalor and appalling air pollution. Around 1860, discharges to the air from an early alkali works ruined the surrounding country, corroding material and tools and destroying vegetation and crops. Air pollution from the works could no longer be ignored. Following overwhelming public complaint and a Parliamentary Enquiry, the first *Alkali, etc. Works Act* was passed in 1863. This did not control smoke emissions, but required that 95 per cent of the offensive emissions should be arrested. The remainder, after adequate dilution, might be allowed to pass to atmosphere.

The second *Alkali Act of 1874* required, for the first time, the application of the Best Practicable Means (BPM) to prevent the escape of noxious or offensive gases. The Act was subsequently extended to all the major industries which pollute the air. The requirement to use the BPM applied whether the escapes arose indirectly from any part of the process or plant, or directly from the exit flues. The words "Best Practicable Means" have often been used to describe the whole approach of UK anti-pollution legislation towards industrial emissions, and indeed towards controlling other types of pollution too. As can be seen from other chapters in this book, the concept has been adapted for use in many other countries. The essential elements of BPM so far as emissions to air were concerned can be defined as follows:

- no emission could be tolerated which constituted a recognised health hazard, either short or long term;
- emissions in terms of both concentration and mass, had to be reduced to the lowest practicable amount taking into account local conditions and circumstances, current state of knowledge on control technology and effects of substance emitted, financial considerations, and the means to be employed;
- having secured the minimum practicable emissions, the height of discharge should be arranged so that the residual emission was rendered harmless and inoffensive by dilution and dispersion.

The implementation of the *1990 Environmental Protection Act* will, however, replace this basic element of UK pollution control with the European Community based concept of Best Available Technology (or Techniques) Not Entailing Excessive Costs (see section 2.3).

The early *Alkali Acts* were eventually consolidated in the *Alkali, etc. Works Regulation Act, 1906.* This linked together a schedule of carefully defined and chosen processes - works - with an equally carefully chosen list of "noxious and offensive gases". The types of works scheduled were those thought most likely to cause pollution problems and included a substantial part of the chemical industry, petroleum refineries, petrochemicals, electricity generation, coal carbonization, iron and steel works, non-ferrous metals, mineral processing works etc.

The *1974 Health and Safety at Work etc. Act* and regulations made under it, e.g. the *Health and Safety (Emissions into the Atmosphere) Regulations 1983*, replaced most of the *Alkali Act.* (The remaining sections of the 1906 Act have finally been repealed by the *Environmental Protection Act 1990*, except in N. Ireland.) A schedule to the 1983 Regulations listed those works which had to be registered with the pollution inspectorate; as an essential prior condition to registration, operators of such works had to satisfy the inspectorate that the works were provided with the BPM for preventing the escape of noxious or offensive substances, and for rendering all such emissions harmless and inoffensive. BPM took into account the cost of pollution abatement and its effects on the viability of the industry.

The legislation was administered in England and Wales by HM Inspectorate of Pollution (or its forerunners), with almost identical legislation in Scotland administered by HM Industrial Pollution Inspectorate.

2.2 Clean Air Acts 1956 and 1968

The *1926 Public Health (Smoke Abatement) Act* had extended the influence of the pollution inspectorate to industrial smoke; however, there were no measures to control the far more widespread problem of smoke from domestic chimneys, although it could be dealt with as a possible nuisance. The atmosphere of Britain's urban areas was characterized by the pervading pall of smoke and sulphur fumes from numerous stacks, chimneys and funnels. The lack of winter sunshine, the frequent dense *pea-soup* fogs, black buildings and even black snow, had become accepted as the price of progress; bronchitis, exacerbated by smoke and sulphur, was a common illness.

However it was not until the great London smog of December 1952, which lasted for five days and caused some 4000 additional deaths, that any real action was taken. The Government appointed a committee to study the problem. The committee's two reports recognized that the constituent parts of the problem were gaseous and particulate emissions, and recommended immediate legislation to reduce smoke, grit and dust. The eventual result was the *1956 Clean Air Act* which was later amended and extended by the 1968 Act.

These Acts are the operative legislation against pollution by smoke, grit and dust from domestic fires and other commercial and industrial processes not covered by the *Alkali Acts.* They also regulate the combustion of solid, liquid and gaseous fuels and control the heights of new industrial chimneys that are not scheduled elsewhere. The legislation also prohibits the emission of "dark" smoke from any chimney or industrial/trade premises and provide for the setting up of "smokeless zones". These Acts have played an important part in enabling the UK to meet EC air quality limits for smoke and sulphur dioxide.

2.3 Environmental Protection Act 1990

The increasing complexity and number of industrial processes led the Government to begin a review of air pollution control in Great Britain (England, Scotland and Wales) in 1986. This review proposed that local authorities should be given similar powers to the pollution inspectorates to control air pollution from a range of industrial processes.

A second review paper, published in 1988, outlined proposals for integrated pollution control (IPC) whereby the pollution inspectorate would control discharges of specified wastes to air, water and land from a range of processes with the potential to cause more serious pollution. Proposals were also made for charging operators for authorizations and providing the public with access to environmental information, including to registers containing full details of authorizations, monitoring data, etc.

The findings of the reviews have resulted in the *Environmental Protection Act 1990* (EPA 1990) which is being implemented in England and Wales from 1991, and in Scotland from 1992. The Act does not apply to N. Ireland, where the *Alkali Act 1906* remains the legislation for controlling industrial emissions. The *Clean Air Acts* also remain in force. The EPA 1990 also reforms UK legislation covering waste on land, updates and consolidates the law on statutory nuisance (except in Scotland), and introduces/amends a number of other provisions relating to general environmental protection. Those aspects of the Act relating to the control of air pollution are summarized below.

2.3.1 Integrated Pollution Control

The *Environmental Protection Act 1990* implements a new system of pollution control - integrated pollution control. This covers all major emissions to air, land and water simultaneously. Those processes with the potential to cause pollution to more than one environmental medium - i.e. to land, air or water - will be required to obtain an authorization from HM Inspectorate of Pollution (HMIP) containing specific conditions which must be met in carrying out the process. Operators of such processes will need to ensure that the best practicable environmental option is secured to minimize pollution to the environment as a whole. The conditions will prevent or minimize the release of the most potentially polluting substances and require all substances that are released to be rendered harmless.

The operator must use the best available techniques not entailing excessive costs to minimise pollution: this replaces the requirement to use the Best Practicable Means and implies both the use of the best means and technology to limit pollution; "available" is defined as being accessible to everyone, although the technology may not be in general use. "Not entailing excessive costs" can have two applications: firstly, if there is one technology which reduces emissions by 90 per cent, and another which reduces emissions by 95 per cent but at four times the cost, it may be a proper judgement to hold that the excessive additional cost is out of proportion to the environmental benefits. On the other hand, however, if the emissions were particularly hazardous, it may be proper to judge that the additional cost was not excessive.

Full implementation of IPC is expected by 1996.

2.3.2 Local Authority Air Pollution Control

As mentioned above, the EPA 1990 also provides new powers for local authorities to control air pollution from a second tier of less polluting processes; these include some 12 000 industrial processes and 15 000 small waste oil burning appliances. All processes to be controlled by local authorities will be brought within the new control regime by Autumn 1993.

The *Environmental Protection (Prescribed Processes and Substances) Regulations 1991* detail those processes to be regulated by HMIP under integrated pollution control and those to be controlled by local authorities for air pollution. A schedule to the Regulations lists the substances to be controlled in relation to air pollution: these are

- oxides of sulphur and other sulphur compounds
- oxides of nitrogen and other nitrogen compounds
- oxides of carbon
- organic compounds and partial oxidation products
- metals, metalloids and their compounds
- asbestos (suspended particulate matter and fibres), glass fibres and mineral fibres
- halogens and their compounds
- phosphorous and its compounds
- particulate matter.

There are separate lists for releases to land and water which, in addition to the above, apply to IPC.

The *Environmental Protection (Applications, Appeals and Registers) Regulations 1991* detail the information to be submitted to the enforcement authority in applying for an authorization. The procedures for applying for an IPC authorization from HMIP or for a local authority air pollution control authorization are broadly similar. In addition to general information about the plant, and description of the process, the application must include the following:

- list of prescribed substances (and non-prescribed substances which might cause harm if released to the environment) to be used in connection with, or resulting from, the process; details of likely quantities and natures of releases should be given assuming the technology and controls have been fitted and are operational;
- description of techniques to be used for preventing or minimizing the release of prescribed substances and rendering harmless any which are released;
- details of any proposed release and an assessment of the environmental consequences;
- monitoring proposals.

The application should be submitted to the enforcement authority, together with the appropriate fee; the purpose of the charge is to recover the relevant costs of carrying out the pollution control functions. The charge covers compliance monitoring and enforcement costs, including sampling and analysis of emissions. There is an application fee to cover the cost of determining applications, and an annual charge payable as soon as the authorization is issued. A reduced fee will be charged for applications for a substantial change to an existing process. Details of the application must be published in an appropriate local newspaper, to give the public the opportunity to comment on the application.

Process Guidance Notes (PG Notes), which are being drawn up within the Department of Environment, will contain advice for local authorities on what constitutes BATNEEC for each category of process; emission limits, monitoring, record keeping, handling arrangements for materials, chimney height standards, together with general requirements for staff training, maintenance and response to abnormal emissions will also be included. The Notes set the standards to be met by new plant, and will include the deadline by which existing processes must upgrade to meet standards for new plant. Guidance Notes covering IPC authorizations are also being drafted.

Authorizations will include specific conditions for the operation of processes to both minimize pollution and ensure that any emissions are rendered harmless. If it is felt necessary, emission standards for specific pollutants can be included. The authorization will also require the operator to use BATNEEC. To ensure that conditions of authorizations are being adhered to, enforcement authorities will need to institute a programme of site inspections and monitoring.

Process operators must inform the enforcement authority if any substantial changes to the process are planned or if it is to be transferred to another person. Where the enforcement authority believes conditions of an authorization are being breached, the following courses of action are available:

- serve a variation notice requiring an operator to change the way in which the process is carried out;
- serve an enforcement notice requiring the operator to remedy the cause of the breach of condition;
- serve a prohibition notice requiring the operator to close down all or part of the process and take the necessary steps to prevent any imminent risk of pollution;
- revoke an authorization.

There is a right of appeal to the Secretary of State against any decision of the enforcement authority.

In general there is a requirement to review authorizations at least every four years, and immediately if complaints are felt to be the result of older standards in operation or if new information about the harmful effects of a pollutant becomes available.

The *Environmental Protection Act* gives the public increased rights of access to information about industrial processes. Under the Act Public Registers are to be established giving full details of applications for authorizations, the authorization itself and any conditions of operation, monitoring data etc. Only information considered to be either of interest to competitors - i.e. commercially confidential - or prejudicial to national security may be omitted from the Register. The public have the right to consult the Register at any reasonable time.

2.4 Air Quality Regulations 1989

These Regulations, made under the *European Communities Act 1972*, came into effect on 31 March 1989 and apply to England, Scotland and Wales. Similar Regulations apply in N. Ireland. They implement EEC Directives setting air quality limit values and guide values for sulphur dioxide and suspended particulates (80/779), a limit value for lead in air (82/884) and air quality standards for nitrogen dioxide (85/203). The Regulations provide for specific areas to be temporarily exempted from complying with the air quality limits for suspended particulates and lead. With respect to the limit values for suspended particulates, a number of districts, mostly in the West Midlands, Yorkshire, North East England, and Glasgow in Scotland have until 1 April 1993 to comply, although programmes for meeting the Directive must be drawn up in advance of this.

The Regulations require that the amounts in the air of suspended particulates and sulphur dioxide (considered both separately and in association), lead, and nitrogen dioxide are measured and (except in the specified areas) reduced below specified limit values. They do not apply to exposure to lead in the air as a result of a person's occupation, nor to nitrogen dioxide in the atmosphere at work or within buildings. The relevant EEC limit values are shown in the table.

Table 1: Air Quality Standards

Sulphur Dioxide and Suspended Particulates: EC Directive 80/779/EEC		
Reference period	*Smoke*	*Sulphur dioxide*
Limit values		
One year (median of daily values)	80 µg/m³	120 µg/m³ if smoke less than 40 µg/m³ 80 µg/m³ if smoke more than 40 µg/m³.
Winter (median of daily values)	130 µg/m³	180 µg/m³ if smoke less than 60 µg/m³ 130 µg/m³ if smoke more than 60 µg/m³.
Year, peak (98 percentile of daily values)	250 µg/m³	350 µg/m³ if smoke less than 150 µg/m³ 250 µg/m³ if smoke more than 150 µg/m³.
Guide values		
24-hour mean		100-150 µg/m³
One year mean		40-60 µg/m³

Nitrogen Dioxide: EC Directive 85/203/EEC		
	Reference period	*Nitrogen dioxide*
Limit value	One year (98 percentile of 1-hour means)	200 µg/m³
Guide value	One year (50 percentile of 1-hour means)	50 µg/m³
	One year (98 percentile of 1-hour means)	135 µg/m³

Limit Value for lead in the Air: EC Directive 82/884/EEC
Limit value: 2 µg/m³ annual mean

2.5 Road Vehicles

Since the 1960s the UN Economic Commission for Europe (which includes both EEC and non-EEC countries) has been responsible for developing model standards on vehicle emission controls which may be adopted by member nations - the UN-ECE has no enforcement powers. In the EEC a number of Directives have been adopted regulating emissions from motor vehicles to standards proposed and agreed by the UN-ECE; more recently however the EEC has taken the initiative and has formulated and adopted strict measures to control emissions of hydrocarbons, nitrogen oxides, carbon monoxide and particulates from individual vehicles. The UK has welcomed the standards (see Table 2) which were agreed at the end of 1990. All new cars registered from 1 January 1993 will have to meet the new standards, with new models required to comply from 31 July 1992.

Table 2: Emission standards for all new cars registered from 1.1.93, and for new models from 1.7.92

	Type approval (i.e. manufacturers' vehicles submitted for certification)	*Conformity of production (all vehicles off production lines)*
Carbon monoxide	2.72 g/km	3.16 g/km
Hydrocarbons and oxides of nitrogen	0.97 g/km	1.13 g/km
Particulates	0.14 g/km	0.18 g/km

In the UK the emission of pollutants - including standards emanating from the EEC - from road vehicles are governed by the *Motor Vehicles (Construction and Use) Regulations* and the *Motor Vehicles (Type Approval) (Great Britain) Regulations* made under the *Road Traffic Acts 1972 and 1974.* The *Transport Act 1982* also specifies requirements for the manufacture of vehicles; Regulations made under the *Control of Pollution Act 1974* impose requirements as to the composition and content of fuel used in motor vehicles.

A further amendment to the *Construction and Use Regulations* is expected to be made in November 1991.This will require emissions of carbon monoxide and hydrocarbons from petrol-engined cars and light goods vehicles to be checked at the vehicle's annual roadworthiness test. The standards are:

- For vehicles first used on or after 1 August 1983, a maximum of 4.5 per cent carbon monoxide in the exhaust gas;
- For vehicles first used between 1 August 1975 and 31 July 1983, a maximum of 6 per cent carbon monoxide in the exhaust gas.
- For vehicles first used on or after 1 August 1975, a maximum of 1200 ppm hydrocarbons in the exhaust gas;
- For all vehicles, a check that there is not excessive smoke from the exhaust.

Since 1985, the lead content of petrol has been set at 0.15 grammes per litre; lead free petrol is widely available throughout the UK and now accounts for 40 per cent of sales.

The prescribed maximum amount of sulphur in gas oil is 0.3 grammes per 100 grammes. This applies to fuel for all diesel engines.

2.6 Smoke Control

As mentioned earlier, both industrial and domestic smoke control are covered by the *Clean Air Acts 1956 and 1968.* Under the Acts dark smoke emissions from industrial or trade premises are prohibited except in special circumstances. New industrial plant must be capable of substantially smokeless operation and there are permitted periods for dark and black smoke emissions from chimneys.

So far as domestic smoke control is concerned, local authorities may make a "smoke control order"; this makes it an offence for an occupier of premises (householder or tenant) to allow smoke emission from a chimney unless the smoke is caused by the use of an "authorized fuel" or an "exempted fireplace". Refuse may not be burnt in an incinerator in a smoke control area, unless smokeless combustion can be achieved or an exemption has been granted.

2.7 Agricultural Pollution

As from the end of 1992, the burning of straw and stubble is to be banned (except in specific circumstances) by regulations made under the *Environmental Protection Act 1990.* Burning is likely to be allowed only for those crop residues not suitable for ploughing in or for other use, or where the land itself is unsuitable for ploughing.

Air pollution and spray drift caused by aerial crop spraying of pesticides is controlled under regulations and a code of practice made under the *Food and Environment Protection Act 1985.* The code details the organizations and individuals to be informed prior to spraying, and gives advice on minimizing spray drift.

2.8 Waste Disposal

In the UK, 90 per cent of all waste is landfilled, with the rest being incinerated. New controls to be introduced under the *Environmental Protection Act 1990* will extend the owner's responsibility for a landfill site until all risk of pollution is past. Incinerators will either be scheduled for local authority air pollution control, or in the case of larger incinerators and those burning or releasing particularly hazardous substances, by HM Inspectorate of Pollution. All incinerators will eventually be required to meet EEC standards.

3 IMPLEMENTATION AND ENFORCEMENT

3.1 Implementation

The completion of the European single market by the end of 1992 as required by the *Single European Act 1986* (which came into force in July 1987), will effectively abolish all barriers to trade between members of the European Community. Such a move obviously requires that the laws and standards of the individual members should also be harmonized. To this end, the influence of EEC Directives on UK legislation can increasingly be seen: for example vehicle emission standards and air quality standards; the EEC Directive on air pollution from large combustion plant, requiring reductions in sulphur dioxide and nitrogen oxides emissions (see section 1.2) is to be implemented through the *Environmental Protection Act* (under the requirements for integrated pollution control).

Increasingly pollution issues - depletion of the ozone layer, global warming, etc. - are being recognized as global problems requiring global solutions. The UK has joined other governments worldwide in ratifying the 1987 Montreal Protocol (which originated from the UN Environment Programme), which limits the production and consumption of those substances (mainly chlorofluorocarbons) known to damage the ozone layer. The UK has also agreed to the further cuts agreed in London in 1990 leading to the elimination of CFCs and halons by 2000. To date the UK has been able to meet its commitment to reduce CFCs through the voluntary actions of industry and consumers.

The UK is also a signatory to the 1979 *Convention on Long Range Transboundary Air Pollution*; this requires a reduction of national sulphur dioxide emissions, or their transboundary fluxes by 30 per cent on 1980 levels to be achieved by 1993.

3.2 Enforcement

So far as enforcement of air pollution control is concerned, central government (usually the Department of Environment) is responsible for the promulgation of the various regulations, with day to day control the responsibility of HM Inspectorate of Pollution, or local authorities as appropriate. The Secretary of the State for the Environment has ultimate responsibility (see also section 2.3).

3.3 Monitoring

Systematic monitoring of air pollution, and in particular of smoke and sulphur dioxide has been carried out in the UK since 1914, culminating in the establishment of the UK Smoke and Sulphur Dioxide Monitoring Network in 1982. This Network comprises some 286 sites monitoring smoke and sulphur dioxide, in compliance with the European Community Directive on air quality limit values and guide values for sulphur dioxide and suspended particulates. The Network is equipped and operated by local authorities, industries and other bodies, and is coordinated by the Department of Trade and Industry's research laboratory, Warren Spring Laboratory, who process and analyze the data on behalf of the Department of the Environment.

In compliance with EC Directives, there are a number of urban and sub-urban sites monitoring ground level concentrations of nitrogen dioxide, as well as a number of sites monitoring concentrations of airborne lead. The Network also monitors levels of ozone, acid deposition, carbon monoxide, atmospheric hydrocarbons, trace gases, and atmospheric chemistry.

Data collected on nitrogen dioxide, ground level ozone and sulphur dioxide are sent by computer to the Meteorological Office which converts the data into air quality bulletins; this information is distributed to the media for publication. Bulletins are also available regionally on an air quality telephone service. Table 3 shows the categories used to classify air quality in the UK. The Department of Health has issued guidance which advises the public on appropriate action during periods of "poor" or "very poor" air quality.

A number of local authorities have set up air pollution monitoring programmes and issue reports and advice to the public via the local media.

Table 3: Department of Environment Air Quality Categories (ppb, one hour mean)

	Nitrogen dioxide	*Sulphur dioxide*	*Ozone*
Very Good	<50	<60	<50
Good	51-100	61-125	51-100
Poor	101-300	126-500	101-200
Very Poor	>300	>500	>200

3.4 Role of Private Interest Groups

There are a large number of private interest groups in the UK, both multi- and single issue groups. Most are registered charities and are non-political, receiving funds from mainly private sources (e.g. individual members, local authorities and indeed industry). Some also receive a grant from Central Government for either a specific research project, or to provide a service to the public.

While most of the private interest groups have no formal (i.e. statutory) role, the Government will often consult established groups in the formulation of legislation, and in the detailed regulations. The influence of private interest groups on environmental initiatives can be said to be quite widespread; the rights of access by the general public to information about industrial processes through the *Environmental Protection Act* is likely to increase that influence owing to the fact that details of polluting emissions will now be easily accessible.

4 EFFECTIVENESS OF CONTROLS

From the preceding sections, it can be seen that the UK has no serious problems of air pollution, and controls are largely concerned with ensuring this situation remains and that any problems of local pollution from individual factories etc. are eliminated. However, the effectiveness of new controls resulting from the *Environmental Protection Act* will depend very much on adequate resources - staff and finances - being made available.

5 FUTURE DEVELOPMENTS

While the problems of local - or national - pollution are now being solved in the UK, there is still much to be done internationally to reach agreement on a framework of controls or agreed actions to deal with the urgent environmental problems facing the world today; pollution from transport, global warming and energy conservation all demand urgent attention.

In September 1990, the Government published a detailed "White Paper" (proposals for future action), outlining its environmental policy and priorities for action both nationally and internationally. The White Paper underlines the importance of international cooperation and pledges the UK's support in working with governments worldwide to find solutions for problems such as global warming, while at the same time achieving sustainable development.

6 SELECTED BIBLIOGRAPHY

Elsom D. *Atmospheric Pollution: Causes, Effects and Control Policies.* Basil Blackwell, 1987.

Environment, Department of. *Digest of Environmental Protection and Water Statistics.* Annual (latest available No. 13, 1990, published 1991).

Haigh N. *EEC Environmental Policy and Britain* (Second Revised Edition). Longman, 1989.

Johnson Stanley P & Corcelle G. *The Pollution Control Policy of the European Communities.* Graham & Trotman, 1989.

National Society for Clean Air (ed Loveday Murley). *Pollution Handbook* (Annual). NSCA.

UNITED STATES OF AMERICA

1 INTRODUCTION

1.1 Topography, Climate, Population

The United States consists of fifty States and three territories. It has a population of about 250 million people. The area of the forty-eight contiguous States within the continental US totals over three million sq. miles (7.7m sq. km). The States of Hawaii, Alaska and the territories add over 600 000 additional sq. miles (1.5m sq. km).

There are great variations across the United States in climate, meteorology, topography, and urbanization. The climate ranges from tropical to arctic. Terrain ranges from desert to mountainous. Population density varies from near zero in portions of some States to thousands of people per sq. mile in cities such as New York, Chicago, and Los Angeles. There are also great variations in technical capability, economic strength, and attitudes toward environmental issues in different regions of the country. These differences have influenced how the United States has defined and sought to solve its air pollution problems.

1.2 Specific National Problems

Despite significant accomplishments achieved by the US clean air program, some major problems are still not resolved. In addition, a number of new problems have been identified over the last decade. Most of these are exacerbated by increased energy demands caused by population and industrial growth.

The reduction of ambient ozone concentrations has proved to be particularly difficult. Even though comprehensive control strategies have been implemented to reduce ozone levels, the standard is still not being met in nearly 100 major urban areas, and one city (Los Angeles) may require up to twenty years to meet it. Many of the cities subjected to high ozone levels also endure unhealthy concentrations of carbon monoxide, particulate matter, and air toxic pollutants. More work is needed to understand the nature of these problems and to develop and implement effective measures to resolve them.

Other major problems include acid deposition, depletion of stratospheric ozone, climate change, indoor air pollution and radon. Some of these are clearly international in scope and can be solved only by many nations working together. US programs to address these problems are described in section 4.

A major challenge is to develop new strategies, such as pollution prevention, to help resolve these problems at the lowest possible cost to the economy.

2 DEVELOPMENT OF AIR POLLUTION CONTROLS AND LEGISLATION

2.1 Early History

Concern with air pollution in the United States began in the last century. The first air pollution laws were passed by cities. Chicago and Cincinnati passed regulations in the 1880s to control smoke emissions. Similar regulations were passed by Pittsburgh and New York in the 1890s. One of the earliest State air pollution laws was passed by Ohio in the 1890s to regulate smoke emissions from steam boilers.

By 1907 there were sufficient municipalities and States regulating smoke emissions to warrant the formation of a Smoke Prevention Association of America. This was the forerunner of the present Air and Waste Management Association, which today numbers over 10 000 members in the United States and Canada, with members drawn from government, industry, education, consulting and environmental groups as well as the general public.

While Americans have long recognized dirty air as undesirable, they paid little attention initially to the risks it presented. Not until the 1940s did it become clear to the general public that air pollution was a serious public health problem. Killer fogs in Donora, Pennsylvania in 1948 and in London in 1952 helped to focus national attention on the potential health hazards of air pollution.

Pressure to enact US Federal legislation on air pollution was initiated in 1950 at the instigation of the California delegation in Congress. A law was passed in 1955 authorizing the Secretary of the Department of Health, Education and Welfare to assist State and local air pollution control agencies by providing research, training and technical assistance.

The necessity for a national approach to address air pollution more effectively resulted in the passage by Congress in 1963 of the first *Clean Air Act.* In 1965 Congress passed the *Motor Vehicle Air Pollution Control Act* which allowed the US Secretary of Health,

Education, and Welfare to set national emission standards for all new motor vehicles sold in the United States beginning with the 1965 model year.

Minor revisions to the *Clean Air Act* occurred in 1966 and 1967. Federal air pollution control legislation was strengthened considerably with the passage of the *Clean Air Act of 1970.* At the same time the US Environmental Protection Agency (EPA) was established as the focal point of the Federal effort on the protection of the environment. The 1970 Act essentially established the overall philosophy and conceptual framework of the US clean air control program until passage of the *Clean Air Act Amendments of 1990.*

2.2 Clean Air Act 1970

The *Clean Air Act 1970* created a partnership between States and the Federal government. It reaffirmed the key role of State and local governments in the regulation of air pollution. It provided for technical and financial support to States, and it expanded Federal activities in research and development. It established a structure whereby air pollution prevention and control was to move forward on three parallel and complementary paths: air quality management, Federal emission limits for stationary sources, and Federal emission limits for mobile sources.

On the first path - air quality management, EPA sets national ambient air quality standards that define good or healthy air. Standards currently are set for six pollutants - ozone, carbon monoxide, particulate matter, sulphur dioxide, nitrogen dioxide, and lead (See Table 1). For areas where ambient air quality violates the national standards for a given pollutant, the States develop implementation plans to attain those ambient air quality standards by certain dates. A State Implementation Plan, or SIP, consists of control strategies - emission limits on existing industrial plants and fuel-burning facilities, for example. The SIP describes how a State will reduce pollution to attain and maintain the ambient standards. SIPs must be approved by EPA. Once approved, they become Federally enforceable.

On the second path, limits are set for both "criteria" and hazardous air pollutants emitted from industrial sources. For "criteria" pollutants, i.e. those for which there is a national ambient air quality standard, New Source Performance Standards (NSPS) are set for new or modified industrial sources. These standards are based on the best demonstrated technology, considering cost.

National Emission Standards For Hazardous Air Pollutants (NESHAP) are set for both new and existing industrial sources. Hazardous pollutants are defined as those that may be reasonably anticipated to result in an increase in mortality or serious illness. Even in small amounts they can be dangerous to public health and frequently are cancer-causing agents. The Act permits only "safe" levels of hazardous air pollutants to be emitted.

On the third path, emission limits are set for new motor vehicles and engines. As with stationary sources, emission limits for mobile sources are set by the Federal government on the basis of technology, although the US Congress has frequently prescribed the specific emission limits. The principal components of the Federal motor vehicle emission control program are pre-production certification, assembly-line testing or selective enforcement auditing, warranty and recall.

The 1970 Act required attainment of all ambient air quality standards by 1975, although EPA could grant extensions to 1977. Also required by the mid-seventies was a 90 per cent reduction in emissions from passenger cars for several pollutants.

Table 1: National Ambient Air Quality Standards

Pollutant	*Primary standards*	*Averaging time*	*Secondary standards*
Carbon Monoxide	9 ppm (10 mg/m^3) 35 ppm (40 mg/m^3)	8-hour[a] 1-hour[a]	None
Lead	1.5 µg/m^3	Quarterly average	Same as primary
Nitrogen Dioxide	0.053 ppm (100 µg/m^3)	Annual (Arithmetic mean)	Same as primary
Particulate Matter (PM-10)	50µg/m^3 150 µg/m^3	Annual (Arithmetic mean)[b] 24-hour	Same as primary
Ozone	0.12 ppm (235 µg/m^3)	1-hour[d]	Same as primary
Sulfur Oxides (SO_2)	0.03 ppm (80 µg/m^3) 0.14 ppm (365 µg/m^3)	Annual (Arithmetic mean) 24-hour[a] 3-hour[a]	— — 0.5 ppm (1300 µg/m^3)

a Not to be exceeded more than once per year.

b The standard is attained when the expected annual arithmetic mean concentration is less than or equal to 50µg/m^3.

c The standard is attained when the expected number of days per calendar year with a 24-hour average concentration above 150 µg/m^3 is equal to or less than 1.

d The standard is attained when the expected number of days per calendar year with maximum hourly average concentrations above 0.12 ppm is equal to or less than 1.

2.3 The Clean Air Act Amendments 1977

The *Clean Air Act* was revised in 1971 and 1974 prior to a major revision in 1977. The 1977 Act extended ambient air quality attainment dates to 1982, with additional time extensions permitted for some pollutants. The Act also included detailed requirements for

State implementation plans if attainment date extensions were granted beyond the 1982 deadline.

A system was established to assure the prevention of significant deterioration of air quality in areas cleaner than the national ambient air quality standards. This was done by limiting the allowable pollution increases to specified air quality increments. In addition, the 1977 Amendments introduced a new national goal - that of protection of visibility in places where visibility values were important, such as national parks and wilderness areas.

The 1977 Amendments created a new time schedule for meeting automobile and truck emission standards. Mandatory automobile inspection and maintenance programs were authorized. Anti-tampering programs were instituted to identify vehicles whose emission control systems were intentionally disabled, and new enforcement and regulatory tools were provided.

2.4 The 1990 Amendments

The most recent Amendments to the *Clean Air Act* were enacted in November 1990. These add important new provisions to the Act and make major changes to some existing provisions. They are expected to set the US clean air agenda for years to come. The 1990 Act is summarized and discussed in section 5.

3 IMPLEMENTATION AND ENFORCEMENT

3.1 Federal/State Responsibilities

EPA is responsible under the *Clean Air Act* for setting national standards and regulations, providing technical expertise and technical and financial support to the States, and enforcing mobile source standards. EPA is also responsible for approval of State programs, program oversight, and for promulgation and enforcement where States fail to do so.

States have primary responsibility for developing, implementing, and enforcing air pollution control programs in response to Federal standards, regulations, and guidelines. Inherent differences between geographic areas of the country require local decision-making and priority-setting by State and local agencies to maximize popular, financial and political support for air control programs that are becoming increasingly demanding and difficult to implement.

3.2 Role of Public and Private Interest Groups

Efforts by environmental organizations and other public and private interest groups often have an important influence on the development, implementation, and timing of State and Federal programs. For example, many State waste reduction programs grew out of the responses to local controversies on the siting of hazardous waste facilities.

Environmental groups active in air pollution control include both long established conservation organizations and younger public interest groups. Among the long established groups are the Sierra Club, the National Audubon Society and the National Wildlife Federation. The environmental groups that have most closely monitored regulations under the *Clean Air Act* are the Natural Resources Defense Council (NRDC) and the Environmental Defense Fund (EDF), two organizations formed in the 1960s largely through grants from the Ford Foundation. Both have combined litigation with lobbying Congress and the EPA and have often been very effective in ensuring that legislation is implemented or, if required, revised.

An important change which has evolved over the past 20 years is the response of American businesses to their environmental responsibilities. Many more corporations today are interested not simply in meeting their legal responsibilities to control pollution before it escapes to the environment, but also in the broad corporate benefits that accompany efforts to reduce pollution at its source. Widespread efforts to redesign manufacturing processes, substitute less harmful production materials, and recycle wastes are beginning to play a major role in protecting the environment. Industry groups also work actively with EPA and other government agencies by providing data and technical assistance pertinent to regulation development and implementation.

Changes in the law and the increased availability of air pollution data have made it possible for interested organizations and individuals to obtain detailed and reliable information about who and what is causing pollution. Future directions will be influenced to an even greater extent than in the past by concerned groups and individual members of the public.

3.3 Environmental Research and Technology

Research and technology are essential to the effective control of air pollution. Extensive national resources are devoted to pollutant identification, the determination of health and ecological effects of pollutants, monitoring and modelling technology, the development of effective control devices, and other technologies related to the mitigation of air pollution.

Many Federal agencies, universities, industry, private non-profit institutions, and consulting firms are engaged in research in these areas. Cooperative research and information exchange programs also have been carried out with a number of other countries. The resulting body of knowledge and expertise is essential to the development, implementation, and enforcement of effective control strategies and regulations.

3.4 Enforcement

The evolution of environmental enforcement over the past two decades demonstrates both the gravity of environmental problems and the Nation's determination to control them. In 1989, record numbers of environmental violations were reported in the United States. The EPA alone took some 4500 enforcement actions in 1989, and EPA-approved State programs reported another 12 800 actions.

Federal and State legislators have empowered environmental enforcers in both the public and private sectors (from the city policeman to the Federal judge and from the individual citizen to large public-interest groups) with an array of tools including high-tech surveillance, environmental audits, contractor debarment, and citizen suits.

Despite the large number of enforcement actions taken by the Federal government, most environmental enforcement is conducted by the States. Facility inspections are the primary tool for monitoring compliance. Surveillance acts as a deterrent, encouraging compliance with the regulations by making non-compliers susceptible to enforcement actions. The overall compliance monitoring program also allows EPA to evaluate the effectiveness of State programs.

4 EFFECTIVENESS OF CONTROLS

4.1 Progress In Reducing Air Pollution Under the Clean Air Act

National ambient air quality standards (NAAQS) have been set for six pollutants - ozone, carbon monoxide, particulate matter, sulphur dioxide, nitrogen dioxide, and lead. In spite of population and industrial growth, emissions of these pollutants have been reduced substantially. Table 2 shows emission reductions over the last decade (1979-88) which range from 8 per cent for nitrogen oxides to 97 per cent for lead. Over this same period, the table shows that average ambient concentrations of all NAAQS pollutants except ozone have been reduced, in some cases sharply.

The reduction of lead in the air is one of the US's most important success stories. Recognizing the health risks posed by lead, EPA in the early 1970s required the lead content of all gasoline to be reduced over time. The lead content of leaded gasoline was reduced in 1985 from an average of 1.0 gram/gallon to 0.5 gram/gallon, and still further in 1986 to 0.1 gram/gallon. Lead emissions from stationary sources have also been substantially reduced.

While the above results are encouraging, there are still formidable challenges ahead to ensure that all the NAAQSs are met in every part of the country. This is especially true for ozone where almost 100 major urban areas did not meet the standard in 1987-89. Carbon monoxide standards are being violated in 41 metropolitan areas, and approximately 30 million people lived in areas where the particulate standard was exceeded in 1988.

The difficulties associated with achieving ambient standards, especially the ozone standard, are recognized in the *1990 Clean Air Act Amendments.* To resolve these problems, new authorities, approaches, and regulatory deadlines have been incorporated in the law with these Amendments (see section 5.3).

Toxic air pollutants are among the most important health-risk problems with which EPA is concerned. Special emission standards are required for pollutants that cause serious or irreversible health effects. These are set under a section of the *Clean Air Act* called National Emissions Standards for Hazardous Air Pollutants, or NESHAP.

Through 1990, EPA has established NESHAP standards for only seven air toxic pollutants: arsenic, asbestos, benzene, beryllium,

Table 2: National Air Quality and Emissions Trends in Criteria Pollutants 1979-1988

Pollutant	*1979*	*1988*	*% Change*
Total Suspended Particulate			
Annual geometric mean (ug/m^3)	63.1	50.5	-20%
TSP Emissions (10^6 metric tons/year)	8.9	6.9	-22%
Sulfur Dioxide			
Annual arithmetic mean (ppm)	.0120	.0084	-30%
SO_x Emissions (10^6 metric tons/year)	24.8	20.7	-17%
Carbon Monoxide			
Annual 2nd Max 8-hr conc. (ppm)	9.07	6.56	-28%
CO Emissions (10^6 metric tons/year)	81.7	61.2	-25%
Nitrogen Dioxide			
Annual arithmetic mean (ppm)	.0258	.0239	- 7%
NO_x Emissions (10^6 metric tons/year)	21.6	19.8	- 8%
Ozone			
Annual 2nd Max 1-hr conc. (ppm)	.1340	.1364	+ 2%
VOC Emissions (10^6 metric tons/year)	22.4	18.6	-17%
Lead			
Annual quarterly max mean (ug/m^3)	.792	.088	-89%
Lead Emissions (10^6 metric tons/year)	108.7	7.6	-97%

mercury, vinyl chloride, and radionuclides. To resolve the problems encountered in implementing the 1970-77 Acts, a technology-based approach for the initial control of toxic pollutants has been incorporated in the *1990 Clean Air Act* (see section 5.3).

4.2 Acid Deposition

Acid deposition occurs in the form of rain, snow, fog, particulates, or gas. Manmade emissions of sulphur dioxide and nitrogen oxides are transformed into acids in the atmosphere, where they may travel for hundreds of miles before falling as acid rain. The political implications of the problem are important because the pollutants may originate in one jurisdiction but affect another.

Extensive research by many organizations in the US and other countries has increased scientific understanding of the causes of acid precipitation and its effects, including the sterilization of lakes and streams, reproductive effects on fish and amphibians, possible forest dieback, and deterioration of manmade structures. These effects have been most obvious in the eastern US and Canada and in Europe.

Under the *Clean Air Act Amendments of 1990* (see section 5.3), power plants must reduce emissions of sulphur dioxide by 10 million tons by the year 2000 and annual emissions are capped at approximately 8.9 million tons. Emissions of nitrogen oxides must also be reduced in accordance with regulations to be issued by EPA.

4.3 Stratospheric Ozone Depletion

Chlorofluorocarbons (CFCs) are compounds that consist of chlorine, fluorine, and carbon. Scientific evidence has increasingly linked higher levels of chlorine and bromine to depletion of the stratospheric ozone layer. If stratospheric ozone depletion occurs, increased levels of harmful ultraviolet radiation will penetrate to the earth's surface, resulting in substantial damage to human health and the environment.

Efforts to restrict the use of CFCs in the United States date back to the 1970s. In response to public concern, manufacturers had begun to shift away from CFCs as aerosol propellants. The *Clean Air Act Amendments of 1977* directed EPA to conduct research, coordinate Federal efforts, and report to Congress in 1978 (and thereafter annually) on actions to protect stratospheric ozone.

In August 1988, EPA issued final regulations pursuant to the *Clean Air Act* to implement the Montreal Protocol on Substances that Deplete the Ozone Layer. The *Clean Air Act Amendments of 1990* (see section 5.3) require new regulations which will assure a complete phase-out of CFCs and halons with interim reductions.

4.4 Global Climate Change

Scientific evidence is overwhelming and not disputed that greenhouse gases such as carbon dioxide and methane have accumulated in the atmosphere as a result of the industrial era and will alter the global climate. Many scientists predict that, within a century, climate change will result in devastating droughts, floods and rising seas.

Scientists believe that existing computer models are somewhat uncertain in their predictions of the timing, magnitude, and region-specific changes that will occur as a result of increases in greenhouse gas concentrations. However, there is an international scientific consensus that, if increases continue as today (business as usual scenario), the expected global mean temperature during the next century will increase between 0.2 and 0.5 degrees C per decade.

The US has established a "no regrets" policy on global warming. This policy basically supports greenhouse gas reduction policies which also provide other environmental and economic benefits. The US believes that there is still too much uncertainty in the General Circulation Models (GCMs) used by scientists to predict a global warming, and that more research is needed to prevent unnecessary economic disruptions.

4.5 Radon

Exposure to indoor radon is one of the most serious environmental health problems facing the American public - second only to smoking as a cause of lung cancer. Radon is a radioactive, colorless, odorless, naturally occurring gas that seeps through the soil and collects in homes. Radon problems have been identified in every State and millions of homes throughout the US have elevated radon levels.

In 1988, EPA and the Surgeon General recommended that all Americans, other than those living above the second floor in apartment buildings, test their homes for radon. EPA has a number of activities under way in cooperation with such national organizations as the American Medical Association and the American Lung Association to motivate the public to reduce radon levels. EPA is continuing to improve the techniques for radon testing, mitigation and prevention, with special emphasis on schools and workplaces. EPA is also promoting the incorporation of radon prevention in building codes and radon inspections at the time houses are financed.

4.6 Indoor Air Pollution

A growing body of scientific evidence indicates that the air within homes and other buildings can be more seriously polluted than the outdoor air in even the largest and most industrialized cities. Other research indicates that people spend approximately 90 per cent of their time indoors. Thus, for many people, the risks to health may be greater due to exposure to air pollution indoors than outdoors.

In addition, people who may be exposed to indoor air pollutants for the longest periods of time are often those most susceptible to the adverse effects in indoor pollution. Such groups include the young, the elderly, and the chronically ill, especially those suffering from respiratory or cardiovascular disease.

In Title IV of the *1986 Superfund Amendments and Reauthorization Act* (SARA), Congress gave EPA a mandate to:

a) establish a federally coordinated indoor air research program;

b) disseminate information on indoor air pollution and mitigation techniques; and

c) assess the appropriate Federal role in solving indoor air pollution problems.

Much of the current emphasis in EPA's indoor air program is on the development and dissemination of guidance documents on specific aspects of indoor air quality for concerned audiences. EPA works cooperatively with other Federal agencies and private sector organizations, where appropriate, to ensure that these guidance documents reflect the best, most current understanding of the nature and potential solutions to indoor air quality problems.

5 FUTURE DEVELOPMENTS

5.1 International Initiatives

Cooperative international programs to assess and respond to problems like stratospheric ozone depletion, global climate change, deforestation, transboundary air pollution, loss of species and habitats, and international transportation of hazardous wastes have expanded dramatically over the last decade. It is now well understood that many hazardous substances cannot be contained by national boundaries or confined to a particular environmental medium.

5.2 Pollution Prevention

EPA established a policy on pollution prevention in January 1989. The *Pollution Prevention Act of 1990* was signed into law in October 1990. The Act requires that EPA develop a comprehensive pollution prevention strategy and implement a number of steps to encourage the development and utilization of pollution prevention techniques.

Several key characteristics of pollution prevention are in sharp contrast to pollution control that has dominated US environmental policy for the past two decades. They include reducing or eliminating pollutants at their source so that waste is not generated, which contrasts with "end-of-pipe," "collect-and-contain," or "release-and-dilute" controls designed to treat or control releases and waste already generated; emphasizing the efficient, and therefore more profitable, use of material and energy resources, as contrasted with the costly treatment of resource wastes that often are byproducts of inefficient use of materials or energy; and the reduction of all pollutants in the environment, rather than simply shifting them from one environmental medium to another, as many pollution control strategies do.

Pollution prevention also stresses applications and strategies at all levels of economic activity, including personal consumption patterns, and relies on information exchange and regulation as well as technological solutions.

5.3 Clean Air Act Amendments 1990

5.3.1 Overview

The *Clean Air Act Amendments 1990* were signed into law on 15 November 1990. This Act contains important revisions and additions designed to curb three major threats to the Nation's environment: acid rain, non-attainment of ambient air quality standards, and toxic air emissions. It adds provisions requiring the phaseout of ozone-depleting chemicals. It encourages market-based principles and includes provisions to encourage energy conservation and to reduce dependency on oil imports.

Major provisions of the 1990 amendments are summarized in the following sections. Where appropriate, a brief discussion of the problems which the new Act is designed to resolve is included.

5.3.2 Attainment and Maintenance of National Ambient Air Quality Standards

As already noted, although the *1977 Clean Air Act* brought about great improvements in air quality, significant urban air pollution problems of ozone (smog), carbon monoxide, and particulate matter persist.

The most widespread and persistent urban pollution problem is ozone, which is caused by the photochemical reaction of emissions of volatile organic compounds (VOCs) and nitrogen oxides. While there are many reasons for continued high levels of ozone pollution, such as growth in the number of stationary sources of hydrocarbons and continued growth in automobile travel, perhaps the most important is that the remaining sources of VOCs are also the most difficult to control. These are small sources - generally those that emit less than

100 tons of hydrocarbons per year. These sources, such as auto body shops and dry cleaners, may individually emit less than 10 tons per year, but collectively emit many hundreds of tons of pollution.

The 1990 Amendments give States more time to meet air quality standards - up to 20 years for ozone in Los Angeles. But it also requires States to make significant progress in reducing emissions. It requires the Federal government to further reduce emissions from cars, trucks, and buses; from consumer products; and from other mobile sources such as ships and barges during loading and unloading of petroleum products. The Federal government must also develop technical guidance that States need to control stationary sources.

The new law clarifies how areas of the country are designated as “attainment” or “non-attainment” and permits the classification of “non-attainment” areas according to the severity of the problem. The worse the air quality in an area, the more controls are required.

5.3.3 Mobile Sources

While motor vehicles built today have far lower pollutant emissions than those built in the 1960s, cars and trucks still account for almost half of the emissions of ozone precursor VOCs and nitrogen oxides, and up to 90 per cent of carbon monoxide emissions in urban areas. The principal reason for this is the rapid growth in the number of vehicles on the highways and the number of miles driven. This growth has offset a large portion of the emissions reductions realized from motor vehicle controls.

Tailpipe emissions of hydrocarbons, carbon monoxide, and nitrogen oxides will be reduced on a phased-in basis beginning in model year 1994. Automobile manufacturers also will be required to reduce vehicle emissions resulting from the evaporation of gasoline during refueling. Fuel quality will also be controlled.

New programs requiring cleaner (so-called “reformulated”) gasoline will be initiated in 1995 for the nine cities with the worst ozone problems, and a clean alternative fuel car pilot program will be established in California. Other States may “opt in” to these programs under certain conditions. Twenty-six of the dirtiest areas of the country will have to adopt a program to limit emissions from centrally-fueled fleets of 10 or more vehicles beginning as early as 1998.

5.3.4 Air Toxics

Air toxic pollutants are those which are hazardous to human health or the environment but not specifically covered under another portion of the *Clean Air Act.* These pollutants typically are carcinogens, mutagens, or reproductive toxins. The *Clean Air Act Amendments of 1977* failed to substantially reduce emissions of air toxics. In fact, only seven air toxic pollutants have been regulated to date.

The new law lists 189 toxic air pollutants whose emissions must be reduced. EPA must, within a year, publish a list of source categories that emit certain levels of these pollutants. The source category list must include major sources emitting 10 tons/year of any one, or 25 tons/year of any combination of these pollutants, and also area sources such as dry cleaners which are generally smaller.

EPA must issue Maximum Achievable Control Technology (MACT) standards for each listed source category according to a prescribed schedule. Standards for forty source categories must be issued within two years, and controls for all sources must be implemented within ten years. Companies will have to comply with the MACT standards within three years after they are issued, but may get time extensions of up to six years under certain conditions where emissions are reduced voluntarily. Eight years after installation of MACT, EPA must examine residual risk levels to determine whether additional controls are necessary.

Standards will also be required to prevent accidental release of toxic chemicals. An independent chemical safety board will be established to investigate major accidents, conduct research, and promulgate regulations for accidental release reporting.

5.3.5 Acid Deposition Control

The new law will result in a permanent 10 million ton reduction from 1980 levels of powerplant emissions of sulphur dioxide. Annual utility sulphur dioxide emissions are capped at approximately 8.9 million tons by the year 2000. The new law also includes specific requirements for reducing nitrogen oxides emissions based on forthcoming EPA regulations.

Affected sources are given allowances based on allowed emission rates and past energy use. An allowance is worth one ton of sulphur dioxide and is fully marketable. Sources must hold allowances equal to their level of emissions or face penalties and a requirement to offset excess tons in future years. Utilities may trade within their systems and buy or sell allowances at special sales and auctions held by EPA.

The program is in two phases. Under Phase I, by 1 January 1 1995, 110 utility boilers must reduce emissions to a level equivalent to 2.5 lbs of SO_2/mm BTU based on their average fuel use in 1985-1987.

Under Phase II, by 1 January 2000, approximately 2000 utility boilers must reduce emissions to a level equivalent to 1.2 lbs (approx. 500 g) of SO_2/mm BTU based on their average fuel use in 1985-

1987. In both phases, affected sources will be required to install systems to continuously monitor emissions.

Other provisions include conditions under which utilities may receive allowances or compliance date extensions. For example, under Phase I, plants that use certain technologies may receive a two-year extension and be eligible for bonus allowances. Plants in certain States also may receive additional allowances.

5.3.6 Permits

A new operating permits program will be established. States must develop and implement the program, and major sources of air pollution must obtain an operating permit. EPA must issue permit program regulations, review each State's proposed program, and oversee the State's efforts to implement any approved program. EPA also must develop and implement a federal permit program when a State fails to adopt or implement its own program.

The program clarifies and makes more enforceable a source's pollution control requirements. All of the source's obligations with respect to its pollutants will be contained in one permit document, and the source is required to file periodic reports identifying the extent to which it has complied with those obligations. Each permit issued to a facility is for a fixed term of up to five years. A new provision authorizes States to collect fees from permitted facilities.

5.3.7 Stratospheric Ozone and Global Climate Protection

The new law requires a complete phase-out of CFCs and halons with interim reductions. It is generally in accord with the existing Montreal Protocol, revised in June 1990.

Under these provisions, EPA must list all regulated substances along with their ozone-depletion potential, atmospheric lifetimes, and global warming potentials. In addition, it must ensure that Class I chemicals be phased out on a schedule (CFCs, halons, carbon tetrachloride by 2000, methyl chloroform by 2002) similar to that specified in the Montreal Protocol, but with more stringent interim reductions. Class II chemicals (HCFCs) will be phased out by 2030.

EPA is required to establish a national recycling and disposal program for Class I substances used in appliances and industrial process refrigeration, effective 1 July 1992. Venting of Class I and Class II substances is illegal after 1 July 1992. Mandatory warning labels will be required on all Class I and Class II containers and products, with potential exemptions based on the availability of substitutes.

EPA must publish a list of safe and unsafe substitutes for Class I and II chemicals and ban the use of unsafe substitutes. Non-essential uses of Class I chemicals must be banned within two years. In 1994 a ban will go into effect for aerosols and non-insulating foams using Class II chemicals, with exemptions for flammability and safety.

5.3.8 Enforcement

A broad array of authorities are incorporated to make the law more readily enforceable. EPA has new authorities to issue administrative penalty orders and field citations. Civil judicial penalties are enhanced, criminal penalties for knowing violations are upgraded from misdemeanors to felonies, and new criminal authorities for knowing and negligent endangerment will be established. Sources must certify their compliance, and EPA has authority to issue administrative subpoenas for compliance data. EPA will be authorized to issue compliance orders with compliance schedules of up to one year.

Citizen suit provisions now allow citizens to seek penalties against violators, with penalties going to a US Treasury fund for use by EPA for compliance and enforcement activities.

6 REFERENCES AND SELECTED BIBLIOGRAPHY

US Environmental Protection Agency. Office of Air and Radiation, (January 1990). *Progress in the Prevention and Control of Air Pollutants in 1988: Report to Congress* (20A-2002).

Council on Environmental Quality. Executive Office of the President, (1990). *Environmental Quality: Twentieth Annual Report.*

Clean Air Act Amendments 1990.

US EPA, Office of Air Quality Planning and Standards. *National Air Quality and Emissions Trends Report, 1988* (EPA-450/4-90-002) Research Triangle Park, NC.

US Environmental Protection Agency. Office of Policy Planning and Evaluation, (August 1988). *Environmental Progress and Challenges: EPA's Update* (EPA-230-07-88-033). Washington, DC: US EPA.

Stern, Arthur C. (Editor). *Air Pollution.* New York: Academic Press, 1968. (Volumes I through IV).

YUGOSLAVIA

1 INTRODUCTION

1.1 Topography, Climate, Population

Yugoslavia lies at the southern end of Europe, on the Adriatic Sea. It has an area of 225 800 sq. km and a population of just over 23 million.

The climate ranges from Mediterranean in the coastal areas to a mountain climate elsewhere.

Industry is directed towards mining, energy resources and transport; the central and south eastern regions are important areas of production for coal, coke, iron ore, steel and crude oil. The natural beauty of Yugoslavia - the sea, mountains and historical monuments - makes tourism a very important part of its economy.

1.2 Specific National Problems

The level of emissions in Yugoslavia is significant despite a relatively low level of industrial development, urbanization and traffic. This pollution results from intensive development, unsatisfactory use of the energy produced, low technical efficiency of installations, their short exploitation time and inefficient use of a vast number of products in Yugoslavia.

There are three levels of air pollution problems in Yugoslavia:

a) *Local*: very polluted air with sulphur dioxide, solid particles and products of incomplete combustion in some urban and industrial areas, as a result of a widespread lack of fuels with low sulphur content and of furnaces adapted for used fuel, as well as outdated technologies; these emissions in certain orographic and meteorological conditions lead to high concentrations of pollutants.

b) *National*: relatively high national emissions of sulphur dioxide from point sources, due to the use of high sulphur content hard and brown coal, and from large thermal power plants due to the use of lignite, as well as from the high sulphur content in some area ores in ferrous and non-ferrous metallurgy.

c) *Global*: climatic change caused by increased emissions of carbon dioxide and highly reactive CFC compounds which have harmful effects on the ozone layer.

Sulphur dioxide is the major air pollutant in Yugoslavia; Table 1 shows the main sources of emissions.

Table 1: Sulphur Dioxide Emissions (000 t per year)

Category of Source	*1980*	*1985*	*1995*
Thermal power plants (TPP)	690	1060	1260
Industry (Use of the energy)	300	180	180
Households, institutions, craft	240	190	133
Traffic	35	30	29
Technology	35	40	48
Total	1300	1500	1650

Compared to other developed west European countries (11 observed), emissions of sulphur dioxide in Yugoslavia, per unit of energy input, are several times higher (Table 2); nitrogen dioxide emissions from thermal power plants and industry, per unit of energy, are however lower.

Table 2: Sulphur Dioxide Emissions per Energy Unit Compared with West European Countries

	1980	*1985*
Thermal power plants	2,19	2,14
Industry	1,83	1,56
Households, institutions, crafts	4,39	3,18
Traffic	1,59	1,19

Air pollution in Yugoslav urban centres was greatest in the period 1965-1970, but has since then decreased. However, in comparison to air quality standards, it is still very high.

Air pollution in many industrial centres has been extremely high for decades, and shows no signs of improving. In contrast to urban centres, industrial centres - apart from pollution from sulphur dioxide and soot - are polluted with specific pollutants (arising from specific industrial processes), especially solid particles with high heavy-metal content.

In the period 1960-1970, the sulphur dioxide emission density in Yugoslavia was low compared with European countries at 3.5 t/km^{2}a; this compares with 15 t/km^{2}a in FR Germany and 25 t/km^2 in Great Britain. In 1980, Yugoslavia was in 15th place in Europe with 5.5 t/km^{2}a, and in 1988 in ninth place with 6.5 t/km^{2}a (whereas FRG has 6.5 t/km^2 and GB 18 t/km^2).

In 1993, with the realization of the Geneva Protocol on the reduction in national sulphur dioxide emissions of at least 30 per cent, and in keeping with energy development trends in Yugoslavia, Yugoslavia would be in 7th place in Europe if certain measures are not undertaken (after GDR, Czechoslovakia, Belgium, Poland, Hungary and Italy) - Figure 1.

As a result of the transboundary transport of sulphur compounds, Yugoslavia has, for the past 100 years, received more sulphur compounds, which were deposited onto the ground, than it emitted into other countries. Today, some 50 per cent of Yugoslav sulphur dioxide emissions are being deposited over the Yugoslav boundaries, but only about the same amount is being deposited in Yugoslavia from other countries.

As regards carbon dioxide, which is now considered a global pollutant, national emissions are not as important as the fact that Yugoslavia is situated in the Mediterranean region, which more than average feels the changes of climate as a result of the increased carbon dioxide emissions on the planet. The decrease in precipitation over the last few years can be regarded as the effect of the climate change, i.e. the imbalance in the production and reproduction of carbon dioxide on the planet.

Figure 1: Comparison of SO_2 Emission Density in Yugoslavia, Other European Countries and the USA

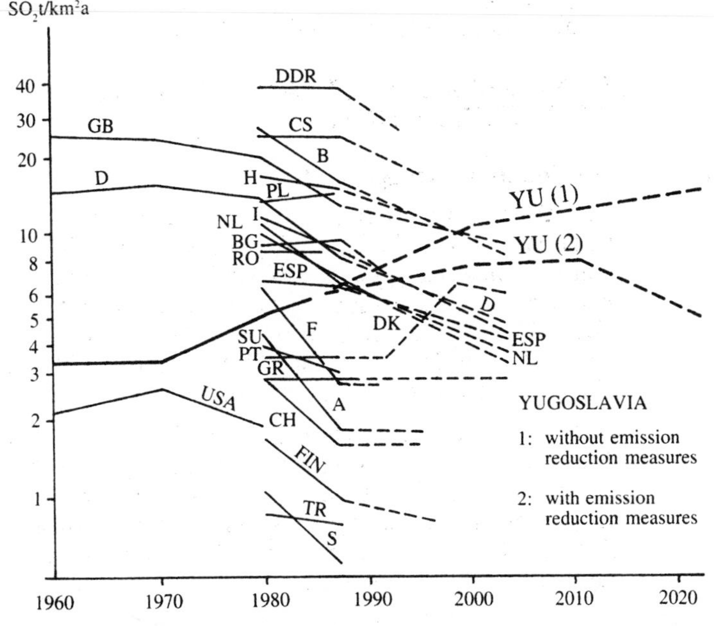

1.3 Sources of Air Pollution

Household fuels have a low heating value - 12-16 MJ/kg - while the fuels for industry and TPP use have an even smaller heating value (less than 10 MJ/kg). The sulphur content in liquid fuels varies from 1-4 per cent (i.e. from 1-4 g/4.2 MJ) and in coal from 0.8 g/4.2 MJ to 17 g/4.2 MJ. These coals have a high ash content, but fortunately many of them have a high content of alkale compounds in ash (Ca/S=1-5).

The main source of air pollution from sulphur dioxide on a national level (large stationary sources), is power production, followed by metallurgy, and then refineries and chemical industry. These emissions are practically in ratio 100:10:1.

Sources of sulphur dioxide emission in Yugoslavia are unevenly distributed, with two areas with especially high sulphur dioxide emission density: the Republic of Slovenia and part of Croatia, and the other is the north-eastern part of Bosnia & Herzegovina and part of Serbia (Figure 2).

With regard to emissions of nitrogen oxides, two-thirds come from traffic, and one-third from stationary sources. In particular, emissions of nitrogen oxides from one thermal power plant (TPP Kakanj), which has a wet bottom boiler are significant.

Lead is also a significant pollutant in Yugoslavia. The permitted lead content in motor fuels is 0.67 g/l; the use of lead-free fuel is very low, although the market is well supplied. Very high lead emissions come from some ferrous and non-ferrous metallurgy facilities.

2 DEVELOPMENT OF AIR POLLUTION CONTROLS AND LEGISLATION

2.1 Air Pollution Management

Until the end of 1989 the protection of the environment in Yugoslavia was under the jurisdiction of Yugoslavia's six republics, but following constitutional changes is now under Federal jurisdiction. The Federal law on air protection has not yet been passed, and the main activity at Federal level is the work of the Commission for Carrying out the Convention on Transboundary Air Pollution which is stationed at the Federal Hydrometeorological Institute.

The permitted sulphur content in liquid fuels is regulated by Yugoslav standard (1-4 per cent depending on oil type), while in some cities, local regulations limit the sulphur content in coals. Emissions of solid particles, as well as of some other pollutants, is limited by republic regulations which, with some delay, follow German TA Luft standards.

There are no regulations limiting sulphur dioxide emissions, although ground level concentrations are limited by "air quality standards" which apply to urban and industrial areas and twice as strict "strict air quality standards" which apply to wider areas and recreational areas. Two parameters are limited - annual average values and 95 percentile.

Figure 2: Areas of High SO_2 Density Emission

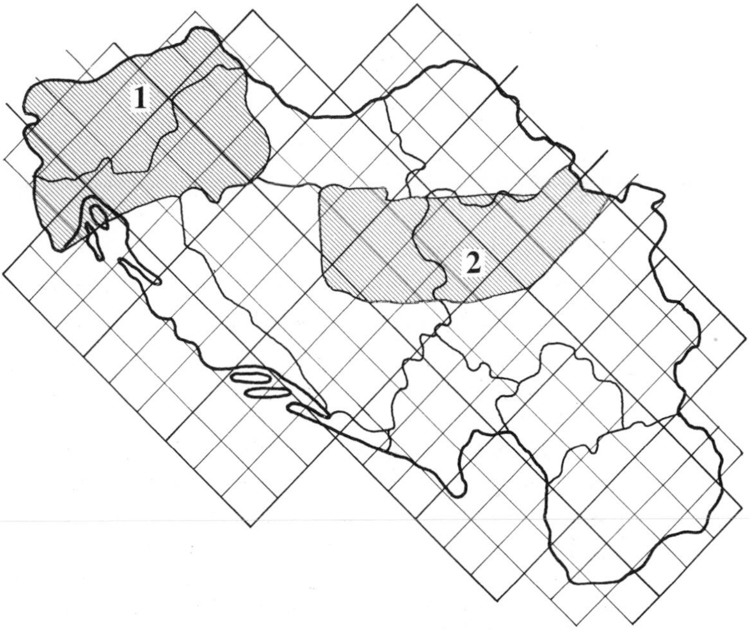

2.2 Approach to Air Pollution Management

Yugoslavia does not have a developed strategy of environmental protection, or of air pollution prevention. Different influences have led to the existence of significantly different, mutually non-consistent solutions. Among them, the emphasis on the principle of best technological means can be seen in the north western parts of the country; and maximum use of atmosphere self-cleaning natural mechanisms in the eastern parts of the country. It would be fair to say, that for Yugoslav practice, the use of both principles is overemphasized.

The author of this paper considers that the Yugoslav air pollution control strategy should be based on three standards:

a) permitted emissions (technological standards);

b) permitted ground level concentrations (ecological standards);

c) permitted depositions of compounds from the atmosphere onto the ground (ecological standards).

Techno-economic possibilities for sulphur dioxide emission control in Yugoslavia are relatively weak. In contrast to solid particles, where the implementation of technological standards would more than satisfy ecological standards, the implementation of eventually set practical technological standards for sulphur dioxide for Yugoslav conditions would not; this is not because they can be satisfied through regulation of stack height, but ecological problems can arise in the phase of atmosphere's self-cleaning which leads to soil pollution from the air through the processes of dry and wet sulphur compounds deposition. That was the reason for the implementation of another ecological standard covering the deposition of sulphur compounds onto the ground.

The following method for regulating sulphur dioxide emission in Yugoslavia is suggested:

- at the local level (small furnaces) only the control of ground level concentrations (principle b above);
- at the regional level (large furnace and large technological plants) by the application of all three principles (a, b, c above); principle c (above) will require stricter emission limits with sources located in regions with high emission density (see Figure 2).

Considering numerical limit values for both emissions and ground level sulphur dioxide concentrations, it is obvious that Yugoslav legislation should adopt European Community standards. However, the main point is the way of understanding the numerical values from EC directives. Emission standards for some pollutants (e.g. soil particles) can be exceeded in Yugoslavia, while for some other pollutants, such as sulphur dioxide, a long term mechanism for achieving the values, maybe even with different timing for different regions of Yugoslavia will have to be made.

A similar strategy should be adopted in the case of air quality standards. Values from EC Directives should in some areas be considered as a long-term goal which to be reached through different measures, and in those regions with clean air they should never be exceeded.

2.3 Local level

For the purpose of satisfying ecological standards at the local level (towns) it is necessary to regulate energy consumption and to control the sulphur content of fuel. In addition to natural gas and electric power, most households use coal with a low heating value and high concentration of ash and frequently sulphur. Yugoslavia will not be able to reach a satisfactory level of air quality in towns if it does not ensure good quality coal with heating value of about ca 30 MJ/kg and sulphur content of under 0.5-1 g/4.2 MJ is available. "Stanari" coal drying and the use of dried coal for low-power boilers and briquets of this coal for household stoves could be of particular benefit. The techno-economical analysis shows the cost effectiveness of investment into the plant for drying and briqueting of "Stanari" coal.

2.4 National level

There are a number of estimates of sulphur dioxide emissions in Yugoslavia. An official evaluation of sulphur dioxide emissions from thermal power plants (TPPs) does not exist. The existing estimate for 1988 is the author's own, amended to correspond with the results of other estimates (Table 3).

The eleven emission sources in Table 3 comprise 50 per cent of Yugoslav sulphur dioxide emissions, and it is considered that these should be made harmless. A change of coal could be considered for one power plant (TPP), while in others flue gas desulphurization in the boiler or at the end of the pipe should be introduced. Taking into account that all these TPPs are already in operation, and that many of them have small power units, 10 or 20 years old, simple (low-investment) methods of flue gas desulphurization will be introduced in most of them.

Table 3: Sulphur Dioxide Emissions from emission sources in 1988.g.

Emission source	*power (MW)*	*SO_2 emission (000 t/a)*	*spec. emission (kg/MWh)*
area of high SO_2 density emission I (see fig. 2)	1115	204	37
TPP Plomin 1	125	42	67
TPP Sostanj	745	92	25
TPP Trbovlje	245	70	56
area of high SO_2 density emission 2 (see fig. 2)	48	743	23
TPP Kakanj I-V	578	90	31
TPP Tuzla I-V	779	70	18
TPP Ugljevik I	300	100	60
TPP NT Obrenovac	2264	170	15
TPP Kolubara	251	23	16
TPP Kostolac A & B	310	70	15
Steelworks Zenica	—	70	—
Mining and Smeltering Cupr. Bot	—	150	—
other areas in Yugoslavia	2288	105	9
Total Point Emission Sources	7885	954	18
Total YUGOSLAVIA	—	1650	

The construction of new thermal power plants is planned for the future. Without sulphur dioxide emission control measures, emissions from these TPPs (potential construction plan) would be as shown in Table 4.

Table 4: Sulphur Dioxide emissions (without the control measures) from TPPs planned for construction

Thermal power plant	*power (MW)*	*SO_2 emission (000 t/a)*	*spec. emission (kg/MWh)*
area of high SO_2 density emission I (see fig. 2)	200	67	67
TPP Plomin II	200	67	67
area of high SO_2 density emission II (see fig. 2)	870	176	40
TPP Ugljevik II	300	100	60
TPP Tuzla VI	300	16	11
TPP Kakanj VI	230	30	26
TPP Kolubara	340	30	18
other areas in Yugoslavia	3000	126	
TPP Kosovo C	2100	31	3
TPP Gacko II	300	31	10
TPP Duvno-Livno	600	90	30
Total	4030	369	16

Without measures for sulphur dioxide emission control it can be seen that with the construction of new TPPs the emission from point sources would grow to 369 000 t/a, i.e. 35.1 per cent. In comparison to emissions from the whole country, the growth of emissions would be 22.4 per cent.

If we take into account the importance of sulphur dioxide emission control, it can be seen that with the construction of new TPPs efficient mechanisms for sulphur dioxide emission control have to be introduced. Efficient mechanisms are those that introduce the measures which will "sufficiently" protect the environment with reasonable costs, and that means low investment technologies for sulphur dioxide and nitrogen oxides emission reduction (non-regenerative) methods, but with higher efficiency in relation to existing plants).

In Yugoslavia, the following measures are needed at a national level:

- development and implementation of boilers with fluidized bed combustion (industrial boilers and low power units in TPPs);
- desulphurization in the boilers through combustion technique and addition of alkaline compounds (existing TPP units);
- desulphurization in the boiler and at the end of the pipe (in the first place with new units of TPPs).

3 IMPLEMENTATION AND ENFORCEMENT

3.1 Air Pollution Management

The Government has established a Federal Secretariat for Development, which includes the Department for Environmental Protection.

The Federal Secretary for Development prepared a proposal for a Yugoslav environmental protection strategy, which will (after adoption) be the basis for branch control strategy and for passing federal laws on environmental protection. Also, working within the framework of the Federal Hydro-meteorological Institute is The Commission for Implementation of the Geneva Convention (Yugoslavia has ratified the Convention, but not all the protocols).

The Yugoslav economy has been open to cooperation both with developed and developing countries. With the reforms in progress in Yugoslavia, international economic cooperation is stimulated through joint ventures of Yugoslav and other countries' economies, in which the investors have free access to their profits. Those developed countries which wish to find a market for their technologies in Yugoslavia can do it best through some kind of cooperation with Yugoslav enterprises.

3.2 Role of Private Interest Groups

It should be noted that the Yugoslav Union of Air Pollution Prevention Associations has been in existence since 1973. The Union publishes a much respected Yugoslav scientific journal, "Zastita atmosfere" (Protection of the Atmosphere), and has organized seven symposia on air pollution control. In 1989 the Union organized the first Yugoslav Congress on Air Quality Control in Yugoslavia.

Because of the lack of Yugoslav laws and standards, the Union has itself published guidelines on emissions, air quality measurement methods, air quality limits and emission limits. To date some thirty guidelines have been published.

MEMBERS OF IUAPPA

ASOCIACIÓN ARGENTINA CONTRA LA CONTAMINACIÓN AMBIENTAL
25 de Mayo 749, 1º Piso
1002 Buenos Aires, Argentina

Tel: (+54-1) 312 1015

CLEAN AIR SOCIETY OF AUSTRALIA AND NEW ZEALAND
PO Box 191
Eastwood
New South Wales 2122, Australia

Tel: (+61-2) 484 3563
Fax: (+61-2) 858 3854

VLAAMSE CHEMISCHE VERENIGING
Krijgslaan 281 S 12
B-9000 Gent, Belgium

Tel: (+32-14) 31 18 01

CANADA: Air and Waste Management Association, USA

CHINESE SOCIETY OF ENVIRONMENTAL SCIENCES
115 Xizhimennei Nanxiaojie
Beijing, China

Tel: (+81-1) 602 1006

FINNISH AIR POLLUTION PREVENTION SOCIETY
Box 335
00131 Helsinki, Finland

Tel: (+358-0) 1991367*
Fax: (+358-0) 1991399*
*Attn: Eija Lumme, Ministry of Environment

ASSOCIATION POUR LA PRÉVENTION DE LA POLLUTION ATMOSPHÉRIQUE
58 rue du Rocher
75008 Paris, France

Tel: (+33-1) 42 93 69 30

KOMMISSION REINHALTUNG DER LUFT IM VDI UND DIN
Postfach 1139
D-4000 Düsseldorf, Germany

Tel: (+49-211) 6214-532
Fax: (+49-211) 6214-575

COMITATO DI STUDIO PER L'INQUINAMENTO ATMOSFERICO
c/o ISMAR
Via Assarotti 15/8
16122 Genova, Italy

Tel: (+39-10) 89 39 22
Fax: (+39-10) 88 77 66

JAPANESE UNION OF AIR POLLUTION PREVENTION ASSOCIATIONS
c/o International Affairs Dept, Industrial Pollution Control Association of Japan
Hirokohji NDK Building, 5th Floor
17-6, Ueno l-chome, Taitoh-ku
Tokyo 110, Japan

Tel: (+81-3) 3832 7084
Fax: (+81-3) 3832 7021

KOREA AIR POLLUTION RESEARCH ASSOCIATION
280-17 Bulkwang-Dong
Eunpyung-Gu
Seoul 122-040, Korea

Tel: (+82-2) 358-1427
Fax: (+82-2) 355-3029

VERENIGING LUCHT (CLAN)
PO Box 186
2600 AD Delft, The Netherlands

Tel: (+31-15) 69 68 77
Fax: (+31-15) 61 31 86

NEW ZEALAND: Clean Air Society of Australia and New Zealand

NORWEGIAN CLEAN AIR ASSOCIATION
Kronprinsensgate 17
N-0251 Oslo 2, Norway

Tel: (+47-2) 838330

ENVIRONMENTAL ENGINEERING SOCIETY OF SINGAPORE (CLEAN AIR SECTION)
Kent Ridge
PO Box 1007, Singapore 9111

NATIONAL ASSOCIATION FOR CLEAN AIR
PO Box 5777
Johannesburg 2000, South Africa

Tel: (+27-11) 728 2418

ENVIRONMENTAL PROTECTION SOCIETY
c/o Institute of Chemistry
Academia Sinica
Taipei, Taiwan 11529

Tel: (+886-2) 738 7730
Fax: (+886-2) 738 1237

NATIONAL SOCIETY FOR CLEAN AIR AND ENVIRONMENTAL PROTECTION
136 North Street
Brighton BN1 1RG, United Kingdom

Tel: (+44 273) 26313
Fax: (+44 273) 735802

AIR AND WASTE MANAGEMENT ASSOCIATION
PO Box 2861
Pittsburgh PA, 15230 USA

Tel: (+1-412) 232-3444
Fax: (+1-412) 232-3450

SAVEZ DRUSTAVA ZA CISTOCU VAZDUHA YUGOSLAVIJE
PO Box 79
71001 Sarajevo, Yugoslavia

Tel: (+38-71) 642 071

CONTRIBUTING ASSOCIATES

ENVIRONMENTAL PROTECTION COUNCIL
PO Box 24395
13104 Safat, Kuwait

Tel: (+965) 2456835
Fax: (+965) 2456836

METEOROLOGY AND ENVIRONMENTAL PROTECTION ADMINISTRATION
PO Box 1358
Jeddah 21431, Saudi Arabia

Tel: (+966-2) 6512312
Fax: (+966-2) 6511124

OBSERVERS

ASSOCIACAO BRASILEIRA DE PREVENCAO A POLUICAO DO AR E DEFESA DO MEIO AMBIENTE
PO Box 64.586
CEP 05497
São Paulo, Brazil

Tel: (+55-11) 259 8253

HELLENIC ASSOCIATION ON ENVIRONMENTAL POLLUTION AND ENVIRONMENTAL PROTECTION
11 Olenou Street (4th Floor)
113 62 Athens, Greece

Tel: (+30-1) 8218954

INDIAN ASSOCIATION FOR AIR POLLUTION CONTROL
School of Environmental Sciences
Jawaharlal Nehru University
New Delhi 110067, India

Tel: (+91-11) 665768

ISRAEL SOCIETY FOR ECOLOGY AND ENVIRONMENTAL QUALITY SCIENCES
The Hebrew University
Environmental Sciences Division
Jerusalem 91104, Israel

Tel: (+972-2) 636841
Fax: (+972-2) 666804

ENVIRONMENTAL PROTECTION SOCIETY OF MALAYSIA
PO Box 382
46740 Petaling Jaya
Selangor, Malaysia

Tel: (+60-3) 7757767
Fax: (+60-3) 7754039

CENTRO DE CIENCIAS DE LA ATMOSFERA
Circuito Exterior Ciudad Universitaria
CP 04510
Mexico 20 DF

Tel: (+52-5) 5 48 97 81

POLLUTION CONTROL SOCIETY OF SIND
IV-D, Ground Floor
Razia Commercial Center
Nazimabad
Karachi — 18, Pakistan

Tel: (+92-21) 624434/628139

ASOCIACIÓN PERUANA CONTRA LA CONTAMINACIÓN ATMOSFÉRICA
Casilla 14.0246
Lima 14, Peru

ASIAN SOCIETY FOR ENVIRONMENTAL PROTECTION
c/o Asian Institute of Technology
PO Box 2754
Bangkok 10501, Thailand

Tel: (+66-2) 529 0100
Fax: (+66-2) 529 0374

USEFUL ADDRESSES

COMMISSION OF THE EUROPEAN COMMUNITIES
DG X1 (Environment and Nuclear Safety)
200 rue de la Loi
B-1049 Bruxelles, Belgium

UNITED NATIONS CONFERENCE ON ENVIRONMENT AND DEVELOPMENT
PO Box 80
CH-1231 Conches, Switzerland

UNITED NATIONS ECONOMIC COMMISSION FOR EUROPE
Palais Des Nations
1211 Geneva 10, Switzerland

UNITED NATIONS ENVIRONMENT PROGRAMME
PO Box 30552
Nairobi, Kenya

WORLD HEALTH ORGANIZATION
1211 Geneva 27, Switzerland

WHO REGIONAL OFFICE FOR EUROPE
Scherfigsvej 8
DK-2100 Copenhagen Ø, Denmark

INDEX

NOTE: This index does not include topics which form the main content of individual chapters, e.g. legislation, including Acts and Regulations, controls on vehicle emissions, monitoring etc. Please refer to the contents list at the front of the book.

(key to countries: Arg — Argentina; Aus — Australia; Belg — Belgium; Br — Brazil; Can — Canada; Fin — Finland; Fr — France; Ger — Germany; Is — Israel; It — Italy; Jap — Japan; Kor — Korea; Kuw — Kuwait; Mal — Malaysia; Mex — Mexico; NL — The Netherlands; NZ — New Zealand; Nor — Norway; Pak — Pakistan; Peru; Sau — Saudi Arabia; SA — South Africa; Sing — Singapore; Tai — Taiwan; UK; US; Yug — Yugoslavia)